THE ROOTS OF EVIL

THE ROOTS
OF
EVIL

A SOCIAL HISTORY OF
CRIME AND PUNISHMENT

Christopher Hibbert

GREENWOOD PRESS, PUBLISHERS
WESTPORT, CONNECTICUT

Library of Congress Cataloging in Publication Data

Hibbert, Christopher, 1924-
    The roots of evil.

    Reprint of the ed. published by Little, Brown,
Boston.
    Bibliography: p.
    Includes index.
    1. Crime and criminals--History. 2. Punish-
ment--History. I. Title.
[HV6021.H5 1978]   364'.9   77-18940
ISBN 0-313-20198-6

© 1963 by Christopher Hibbert

Reprinted with the permission of Little, Brown and Company

Reprinted in 1978 by Greenwood Press, Inc.,
51 Riverside Avenue
Westport, CT. 06880

Printed in the United States of America

10 9 8 7 6 5 4 3 2 1

FOR EDWARD

AUTHOR'S NOTE

A book covering so wide a range of subjects by a writer with expert knowledge of none of them requires, I think, some sort of prefatory explanation, not to say warning.

When I was first asked to write it some years ago, I refused. I knew little of criminology or sociology, less of psychiatry and the criminal law, almost nothing of penal methods. I was, in fact, no more than an amateur historian with an interest in contemporary crime and punishment shared, I suppose, by most of my countrymen. To undertake the amount of research which such a book entailed would not only have interfered with my work for my usual publishers but would, in any case, have taken far more time than I could then afford.

In 1959, however, I changed my mind. There were two reasons for this: I was able in that year to devote all my time to writing and I went inside a prison for the first time, to visit a man I had known in the army who had once been flogged. A few days after my visit, I read in a paper that almost three quarters of those questioned in a public opinion poll had said that they would like to see a return to flogging and an extension in the scope of capital punishment.

I have tried to show in this book by reference to the history of punishments, to the reactions of those who have suffered them or been threatened by them and to the endeavours of those who have concerned themselves with the criminal and the prevention of crime, that Sir Samuel Romilly's belief, which I have chosen as my epigraph, was a well-founded one in 1813, had always been a well-founded one and is a well-founded one now.

In a sense, then, this is a tendentious book, but I hope it is not a prejudiced or misleading one. I have wanted to record facts and events rather than to express opinions. And I have not attempted to draw all the facts and events that I have recorded into the framework of the argument which the book is intended to propound. It is aimed at the general reader. References to sources are given in the text but this is not because I wish to imply that it is a work of scholarship, which of course it is not, but because I think that the general reader should be given the opportunity of referring to those detailed works of scholars and experts on which I have relied, whenever the interpretations and generalisations of the layman seem incomplete or misleading.

I want to thank my brother for helping me with the legal aspects of the book, and Dr. A. J. Salmon for his help with some medical problems. Mr. Hugh J. Klare, Secretary of the Howard League for Penal Reform, has been kind enough to read the proofs. For their help in a variety of ways I want also to thank Mrs. Joan St. George Saunders, of Writers' and Speakers' Research, Miss Frances Ryan, Mrs. A. R. McDougall and my wife.

Most of the books from which I have quoted are by authors long since dead. Of more recent writers I am particularly indebted to Kenneth Allsop, Harry Elmer Barnes, C. R. M. Cuthbert, Charles Duff, J. L. Gillin, T. R. Fyvel, Sheldon and Eleanor Glueck, Max Grünhut, Leslie Hale, Hans von Hentig, D. L. Howard, Howard Jones, James Avery Joyce, Alister Kershaw, Arthur Koestler, Hugh J. Klare, Lord Longford, Hermann Mannheim, Henry D. McKay, Terence Morris, Patrick Pringle, Leon Radzinowicz, Ed Reid, Charles Reith, Henry T. F. Rhodes, C. H. Rolph, Thorsten Sellin, Clifford R. Shaw, E. H. Sutherland, Donald Taft, Frank Tannenbaum, Negley K. Teeters and Lady Wootton.

For permission to reproduce copyright material I am grateful to the authors, editors, agents and publishers of the following books: Kenneth Allsop, *The Bootleggers* (Hutchinson & Co Ltd and Doubleday & Co Inc); Frederick L. Collins, *The FBI in Peace and War* (Putnam's, New York); Harold R. Danforth and James D. Horan, *The D.A.'s Man* (Crown Publishers and Victor Gollancz, Ltd); T. R. Fyvel, *The Insecure Offenders* (Chatto & Windus, published as *Troublemakers* in New York by Schocken); Frank Gibney, *The Operators* (Harper & Bros and Victor Gollancz Ltd); Bernard Glueck, *Studies in Forensic Psychiatry* (William Heinemann Ltd); Sheldon Glueck, *Crime and Justice* (Little, Brown & Co, Boston); Patrick Pringle, (Editor), *The Memoirs of a Bow Street Runner* (Museum Press, Ltd and William Morrow & Co Inc); Alfred Hassler, *Diary of a*

Self-Made Convict (Regnery, Chicago and Victor Gollancz Ltd); Arthur Koestler and C. H. Rolph, *Hanged by the Neck* (Penguin Books, Ltd); Max Lowenthal, *The Federal Bureau of Investigation* (William Sloane); Frank Norman, *Bang to Rights* (Secker & Warburg, Ltd); Sir Leo Page, *The Young Lag* (Faber & Faber, Ltd); Tony Parker and Robert Allerton, *The Courage of his Convictions* (Hutchinson & Co Ltd and W. W. Norton & Co); Leon Radzinowicz, *A History of English Criminal Law* (Stevens & Sons Ltd and Macmillan, New York); Ed Reid, *The Shame of New York* (Random House and Victor Gollancz Ltd); C. H. Rolph, *Personal Identity* (Michael Joseph, Ltd); S. K. Ruck (Editor), *Paterson on Prisons* (Frederick Muller, Ltd); James Spenser, *Limey* (Longmans, Green & Co, Ltd); Don Whitehead, *The FBI Story* (Random House); Peter Wildeblood, *Against the Law* (Weidenfeld & Nicolson); Barbara Wootton, *Social Science and Social Pathology* (Allen & Unwin, Ltd, and Macmillan, New York). The dialogue on page 424 is reproduced with the kind permission of the editor and proprietor of *Twentieth Century*.

C.H.

CONTENTS

PART I
THE GROWTH OF PUNISHMENT
602 - 1750

PART II
THE BEGINNINGS OF REFORM
1750 - 1945

CONTENTS

CONTENTS

PART V

PART VI
THE GREAT MELTING POT

PART VII
PRESENT PROBLEMS

CONTENTS

3 PRISONS 412

'*After a while you forget why you are there, all you know is that you are there and that's all. Maybe one day they will find some thing for all these wasted men to do. What people do not seem to realise is that by sending a man to the nick for a few years they are punishing him for doing wrong: Yes! but they are also doing themselves a great wrong, for as sure as Hells a mouse trap, when that man gets out he will rob someone else.*' FRANK NORMAN, 1958

4 POLICE 424

'*The Cozzpots are not all idiots.*' ROBERT ALLERTON, 1961

5 THE YOUNG OFFENDER 431

"*Juvenile delinquency, particularly in the United States, has come to be considered one of the most urgent social problems of the day, and the epidemic of arrogance and crime seems to be spreading so fast that it obliterates the best efforts society can make to control it—or even to understand it.*' VIRGINIA HELD, 1959

6 THE SEXUAL OFFENDER 442

'*A person who carnally knows in any manner any animal or bird; or carnally knows any male or female person by the anus or by or with the mouth; or voluntarily submits to such carnal knowledge; or attempts sexual intercourse with a dead body is guilty of sodomy and is punishable with imprisonment for not more than twenty years.*' NEW YORK PENAL LAW, SECTION 690, 1950

PART VIII

PROGRESS AND PALINDROME 451

'*It is better to prevent crimes than to punish them.*' CESARE BECCARIA, 1764

REFERENCES

BIBLIOGRAPHY

NOTES

INDEX

'I call upon you to remember that cruel punishments have an inevitable tendency to produce cruelty in the people—'
SIR SAMUEL ROMILLY 1813

Part I

THE GROWTH OF PUNISHMENT

602-1750

CHAPTER ONE

THE AGE OF CHIVALRY

'Kings and knights should govern rightfully, and bind trans-
gressors; and to do so is far better than to fast on Fridays.'
WILLIAM LANGLAND, 1377

'TRAITORS and deserters they hang on trees; the cowardly fighter, the shirker of military service and those who have polluted their bodies by vice, they plunge into a foul swamp with a hurdle put over them.'[1]

The Germans, as described by Tacitus, sixty years after the death of Christ, considered only treachery, desertion, cowardice and sexual perversion to be crimes serious enough to be punished by death. In a society where every fighting man was a valuable asset, execution and mutilation could not reasonably be considered suitable punishments for lesser offences, such as murder or theft; and so, as Tacitus discovered, the German murderer or thief when convicted paid a fine 'in a stated number of oxen or cattle. Half of the fine was paid to the King, half to the person for whom justice was being obtained or to his relatives.'

In England a similar system was developed. The seventh century Kentish laws of King Ethelbert, amongst the earliest documents written in the English language, provided a list of fines for a variety of crimes from murder to fornication. The amount of compensation to be paid in each case was carefully stipulated and carefully graded. While a murderer might have to pay a hundred shillings, the compensation was limited to twenty shillings if the assailant only succeeded in smashing his enemy's chin bone. Every part of the body had its value, from fifty shillings for an eye or a foot to sixpence for a toe-nail. Injuries which interfered with a man's ability to work or fight were compensated at a higher rate than those which disfigured him. The loss of a thumb, for instance, was deemed to be worth twenty shillings and a disabled shoulder thirty shillings, but the loss of an ear was worth only twelve shillings and a front tooth six shillings. To break a man's thigh cost twelve shillings and to cut off his little finger eleven, but to lacerate his ear cost only six. To injure his power of speech cost the same as to break three of his ribs. To pierce his penis cost six shillings' compensation, but to break both his collar bones cost twelve.[2]

These amounts of compensation for injury as assessed by the laws of Ethelbert and other early English kings varied in accordance with the rank of the accused and of his victim. A man who 'lay with a maiden belonging to the King,' for example, had to pay fifty shillings compensation, but if she was 'a grinding slave' the compensation was halved. Compensation for lying with a nobleman's serving maid was assessed still lower at twelve shillings and with a commoner's serving maid at six shillings.[3] If a freeman raped the slave of a commoner he had to pay no more than five shillings' compensation, but if a slave raped this same girl he was castrated.[4] Similarly to break into the house of a rich man was a greater offence than to break into a peasant's cottage.[5] And although fighting in the presence of an archbishop was twenty-five times more expensive than fighting in the house of a commoner,[6] to fight in the house of the King of Wessex could cost a man everything that he possessed.[7]

All these early English codes of law, in which compensation as an enforced alternative to the blood feud plays so important a part, clearly show the influence of the Church whose power had been continually growing ever since Augustine had landed in Thanet in 597 as Pope Gregory's missionary for the conversion of the heathen islanders. Not only was the Church entitled to receive as compensation twelve times the value of goods stolen from a consecrated place, not only was a bishop's compensation sometimes greater than the King's, but large shares of certain payments made by miscreants passed into the hands of the clergy.[8]

The influence of the Church can also be seen in the new offences which were created, in the increasingly severe penalties for fornication and adultery, eating meat during a fast and making offerings to devils, and in the immunity of bishops and priests. A bishop's word, like a king's, although unsupported by oath, was incontrovertible; and a priest could clear himself by taking an oath in his vestments before the altar. A servant who worked 'between sunset on Saturday evening and sunset on Sunday evening, contrary to the Lord's command,' could be fined by his master; and if he 'made a journey of his own on that day' he had either to pay six shillings' compensation or, in the likely event of his being unable to afford this sum, he could have one leg fastened by a ring to a stake round which he was lashed by a three-thonged whip of knotted cords.[9] The amount of compensation for offences committed on Sundays or holy days was double the ordinary rate and by the laws of Alfred a man who stole from a church had to suffer the additional penalty of the loss of a hand.

Punishment by mutilation and death was, in fact, by the middle of the tenth century taking the place of compensation for a growing number of offences. By a law of Canute's a woman was to forfeit 'both nose and ears' for adultery; by the laws of Ethelstan 'witchcraft and sorceries and spells, if death was occasioned by them' and the accused could not deny the charge, were punished by death; and by the laws of Wihtred a freeman caught in the act of stealing could also be put to death if the King did not decide he should be 'sold beyond the sea' or held to ransom. The form the death penalty took was often an aggravated one. A free woman found guilty of theft was either thrown from a cliff or drowned. 'In the case of a male slave, sixty and twenty slaves shall go and stone him. And if any of them fails three times to hit him, he shall himself be scourged three times.' When the slave was dead, each of the slaves who had killed him had to give three pence to his master so that he could buy another one. A female slave guilty of theft was also killed by eighty other slaves, each of whom had to bring three logs to make a fire to burn her on.[10]

Often, it seems, mutilations were intended to be mortal, for the laws of Alfred and Guthrum make specific provision for those who, having had a limb cut off, 'survive the third night'.[11] And the laws of William I, particularly savage when dealing with infractions of forest rights, go so far as to enjoin the punisher not to slay the culprit outright but to hack his body about until he was dead.[12]

Many of the laws invested those who had been wronged with the power to inflict these punishments summarily and personally when proof of guilt had been obtained, and although the step taken by this *infangthief* is a short one it is, nevertheless, as Sir James Stephen said, one more distinct step 'away from private war and blood feuds'.[13]

In the absence of incontrovertible proof, the guilt of the accused was decided by the ordeal. This procedure, not formally abolished in England until 1219, was of very ancient origin but the Church had adopted it, as she had adopted so many other pagan practices, in her efforts to gain influence and power over a highly superstitious people and in her efforts—savage, narrow and selfish though they now seem—to make a barbarous people less brutal. The trial by ordeal took place inside a church although soon after the Norman Conquest this ceremony of 'God's judgment' was removed to specially prepared pits or trenches outside it.[14] Before the ceremony began, a fire was lit in the middle of the church and a deep bowl of water and bandages were brought in by a priest. The spectators, all of whom 'must be fasting and have abstained from their wives during the night', then came in silently and divided themselves into two rows on either side of the church. The priest walked up and down between them, sprinkling them with holy water and giving it to them to sip and the 'Gospels and the symbol of Christ's Cross' for them to kiss. When the water in the bowl was boiling the accused, who for three days had eaten nothing but 'bread and water and salt and herbs' and had attended Mass on each of the three days, approached the fire. The priest bandaged his arm while the spectators prayed that God would 'make clear the whole truth'. At the bottom of the boiling water was a stone. If he was to undergo the 'single' ordeal he had to plunge his hand into the water up to the wrist; if the 'triple' ordeal had been prescribed, he had to put his arm into the bowl so that the water came up to his elbow and then pick out the stone. After three days the bandages were removed. Evidence of scalding was taken to be proof of guilt.[15] As an alternative to the ordeal by water, the accused was sometimes required to walk over red-hot ploughshares without being seared, place his hand in a glove of red-hot iron or to pick up a red-hot iron bar and hold it in his bare hand while he walked three paces. His hand was then sealed by the priest and if after three days a blister the size of half a walnut had appeared, he was declared guilty and might have to suffer mutilation or death. Even if the ordeal pointed to his innocence he was banished if his character was supposed to be bad. The priests themselves, if accused, did not have to undergo these ordeals, but instead were tried by the *corsnaed* which involved eating a piece of consecrated bread and cheese before the altar. God was prayed to send down the angel Gabriel to stop the throat of the priest if he were guilty and so prevent him swallowing the food which would be proof of his crime.

Guilt and innocence could also be decided at this time by compurgation in which a number of compurgators—the actual number required depended upon the rank of the offender and the nature of his offence—swore that they believed in the innocence of the accused. Such oaths, although perjury was common, were taken as proofs of innocence just as the absence of compurgators or an insufficient number of them at the time of trial were taken as proof of guilt. Forms of trial of this sort were common to many primitive societies and in them may be seen some inchoate germs of the jury system which was more fully developed and vastly extended in scope and significance by William the Conqueror and later by Henry II, who encouraged the growth of a Common Law in England long before France and Germany had outgrown their local customs.

Following the Norman Conquest the combat—'private war under regulations'[16]—as ancient in origin as the ordeal, became a recognized method of trial. Trials by battle were more often used to settle civil disputes but a man accused of felony might also establish his innocence by challenging his accuser to a judicial duel which knights fought with swords and lances, commoners with staves made lethal by iron heads.[17] Priests and women and the old and infirm were excused from fighting personally and were allowed to appoint champions to fight on their behalf. In time, as in a court of law, both parties were represented by counsel whose duties, according to a procedure laid down for trials of treason, were to teach them 'all manner of fightings and subtleties of arms that belong to a battle sworn'. Each contestant had to wear shoes made of red leather and red stockings over his greaves 'because his adversary shall not lightly espy his blood; for in all other colours blood will be lightly seen'. It was counsel's duty to engage three priests for the contestants and to see that these priests each sang a Mass on the day of the trial. After the Masses the harness and weapons were blessed by the priests who came up to the barriers of the field of battle.[18]

While primitive trials like this were still held in the fourteenth century, trials by ordeal had by then been abolished and the various courts established over the centuries were administering the law with some regard to the rules of evidence. They were also administering it with increasing, if fluctuating, severity.

The conception of sin, by then fully absorbed into the criminal law, had altered its character. Murder, robbery and rape were no longer regarded as torts which could be settled by compensation, but as sins for which penance was required. Under the influence of the traditions of the rediscovered Roman Law, they had also come to be regarded as crimes against society at large which the King, as leader of that society, was entitled to punish and which he was acquiring the power and means to punish.

New ideas about the virtues and purpose of punishment were gaining ground and while in earlier centuries criminal jurisdiction had been seen largely as a source of revenue, either to the King or, under the feudal system, to the prelates and lords of the manor to whom grants of this jurisdiction had been made in return for other services, now it was more clearly seen as a method of repression, deterrence and retribution. King Alfred had prefaced his laws by extracts from the Book of Exodus but it was not until long after his death that determined attempts were made to put the Mosaic Law of retaliation into general practice by the substitution of physical punishments for many crimes which had previously been expiated by compensation. It was now felt, too, that only by the threat of savage punishments could the people's growing predisposition to crime be checked. Execution or mutilation might, it was hoped, be a better deterrent than the obligation to pay compensation; and if mutilation had already replaced compensation as a punishment for specific crimes, the fact that the number of crimes committed had not decreased was often supposed to be the fault of a too lenient punishment which must accordingly be intensified. Thus it was, for example, that although the laws of Ethelstan had provided that a coiner should have his hand cut off,[19] by the time of Henry I, when this punishment had not deterred others from committing what the more general use of money had made a common offence, coiners could be castrated as well.[20] A century later, coining was still widespread and after an enquiry in Edward I's time 280 Jews were hanged in London for this offence alone.[21]

The idea that criminal jurisdiction should be a source of revenue was not, of course, forgotten by the King once the initiative in criminal matters had been transferred to himself from the kindred of the injured. In the King's courts, fines and forfeiture of goods were still common enough, and outlawry, by which the goods of the outlaw fell to the crown, was a frequent sentence. In 1255 Henry III ordered his justices to recoup the cost of an expedition to Scotland by imposing money penalties during the forthcoming assizes in the north. Of seventy-seven persons presented for murder, all but five were outlawed. In 1279, sixty-eight cases of murder were tried and all but three of those found guilty were outlawed.[22] The Church, too, by establishing the principle of compounding for punishments and penances imposed in her ecclesiastic courts, which considered many matters only remotely concerned with religion, ensured that her rights of jurisdiction were profitable ones.

For those who could not pay or whose goods were worthless there was, nevertheless, scant mercy. She had deserved death, a court decided in the case of a woman found guilty of perjury (a capital offence) during a murder trial, 'but by way of dispensation let her eyes be torn out'.[23] Nor was mercy shown to traitors, whose public punishments were intended to add horror to the sentence of death. 'The award of the court,' the Earl of Carlisle was told in the reign of Edward II, 'is that for your treason you be drawn, and hanged, and beheaded; that your heart, and bowels and entrails, whence came your traitorous thoughts, be torn out and burnt to ashes and that the ashes be scattered to the winds; that your body be cut into four quarters, and that one of them be hanged upon the tower of Carlisle, another upon the tower of Newcastle, a third upon the Bridge of York and the fourth at Shrewsbury; and that your head be set upon London Bridge, for an example to others that they may never presume to be guilty of such treasons as yours against their liege Lord.'[24]

The Church, in her punishment of heretics—as great a threat to her authority as traitors were to the authority of the King—was equally relentless. Lending her approval to the punishment inflicted for treason, for which biblical authority was found, she had already by the twelfth century, before more ferocious punishments were devised, lent her approval to the whipping and branding of heretics. The Paterines, one of whose heresies was a refusal to acknowledge the spiritual necessity of baptism, were seared with hot irons, whipped through the streets and forbidden to seek or accept shelter. As householders were not permitted to offer shelter to anyone displaying the brand of the heretic on his forehead and as it was a severe winter, many Paterines died of cold and starvation. Others joined one or other of the growing number of bands of outlaws which accepted any man prepared to fight with them and any woman prepared to sleep with them.

These gangs of brigands, sometimes led by knights and often employed as mercenaries by powerful barons, frequently remained for years in complete control of towns and of large areas of the countryside, as they had done with even less interference in the time of Stephen when, in the words of the *Peterborough Chronicle,* the dungeons of the barons' castles were full of 'both men and women put in prison for their gold and silver, and tortured with pains unspeakable'. Before the Black Death, Bristol was for some years in the hands of a brigand who had taken military possession of the port, siezed its cargoes and issued proclamations in the royal style.[25] At Yarmouth, three hundred men marched about the country under their own banner like an army of invasion, defying all authority.[26] In Suffolk, a gang of versatile criminals exported stolen wool, imported counterfeit money, forged documents and seals, took people from their homes or from church and held them to ransom and went about the town threatening to bring accusations at the next meeting of the justices unless they were paid not to do so. In 1451 a gang of four hundred armed men rode into Walsingham during the sessions then being held there and secured the acquittal of all their friends.[27]

Bands like these became useful instruments in the forceful settlement of private disputes, in the prosecution of private vendettas and, above all, in the frequent raids upon landed estates. When a 'great multitude of men', including one of his former chaplains, marched in military array upon one of his manors, demolished his fences and gates, broke into his buildings, and carried off three hundred head of cattle and a thousand sheep, the Bishop of Exeter believed at first that a 'foreign enemy had landed' and was collecting supplies for an army.[28] A band of fifty men, including the Abbots of Sherborne and Middleton, who invaded the Countess of Lincoln's estate at Kingston Lacy, not content with killing her game, cut down all her timber and carried it away. An Archbishop of Canterbury, in a similar raid, lost not only his animals and trees but even his corn.[29] Often the people who lived in the manor were themselves attacked; and in a raid upon an estate in Wiltshire, in which the Prior of Bristol took part, all the inmates of the manor house were murdered, the lady of the house was raped and her chaplain was frightened to death.[30]*

The marauding gangs of robbers, which had been part of the hazards of English life for centuries, overran the entire country after the misgovernment of Henry III had provoked Simon de Montfort into leading his followers to civil war. Commissions appointed in 1305 found that these gangs had not only forcibly seized and held landed estates, bought others for paltry sums by threats, 'impeded and corrupted constables, bailiffs and the King's officers', but had invaded manor houses and plundered them from cellar to attic, attacked and maimed jurors and witnesses to prevent them telling the truth at assizes and hired professional assassins for battery, assault and mayhem.[32]

Villages, towns and whole districts were taken over by outlaws until 'robberies, murders, burnings and thefts' were commonplace in the Patent Rolls of the chroniclers. Even the Royal Treasury at Westminster was not safe and when Henry's son and successor, Edward I, was away in the north fighting the Scottish rebels, a gang broke into the Treasury by smashing through a wall of the Abbey and escaped with treasure worth a hundred thousand pounds— more than twice as much as the Kingdom's whole revenue had been thirty years before.[33]

Edward was thirty-five when he was crowned at Westminster in 1274. A tall, good-looking man with a passion for tournaments and dangerous hunting, he had, unlike his father, not only the energy but the capacity to give his dream of a strong yet popular government some promise of reality. Relying on great lawyers, Italian as well as English, to guide him, he began a reorganization and classification of the English legal system which was to earn

---

* It seems that men who had returned from a Crusade were frequently the most ferocious, particularly in the massacres of Jews. At Stamford during the time of the Fair, the threatened Jews took refuge in the castle. The Crusaders, waving banners that they had brought back from the Holy Land, led the attack on those who remained at their mercy. They sacked all the houses in the Jewish quarter and removed the contents without interference or subsequent punishment. The same depredations were reported from Lincoln. The ordinances for their voyage to the Holy Land reveal the kind of brutalities to which the Crusaders may have grown accustomed. A man who killed another on board ship was tied to his victim's corpse and thrown into the sea; if the murder were committed on land he was buried alive with it. If he merely 'wounded to the blood' he was to lose his hand. 'If a thief be convicted of theft, let his head be shaven as though for the ordeal by battle,' the Ordnance continued, 'and let boiling pitch be poured on his head, and, at the first place which the ship may touch, let him be cast forth.'[31]

him the name of 'the English Justinian'. In the first fifteen years of his reign scarcely a year passed without Parliament passing an important Statute until eventually the old feudalism was virtually eliminated from political life and the groundwork of a new land law was built.

Edward realized, however, that the depredations that were beginning to threaten the whole basis of society could not be ended merely by reorganizing the existing legal system and by dismissing incompetent or corrupt sheriffs and other officials whose duty it was to administer justice. And so in 1283 he drafted the Statute of Winchester, the codification of a system of police, which was intended to enforce the observation of the law.

The Statute of Winchester was not a revoluntionary or even a new system of law enforcement but it gave a new importance to traditional methods that were to remain largely unchanged for centuries and were eventually to provide the basis upon which the modern police forces of Britain and the United States are built. Many of these traditional methods were so old that no one knew their origins and some of them had fallen into disuse, but they were now all brought to life again and the people were obliged to make them work.

Since the time of the Saxon Kings, the underlying principle of law enforcement had been one of mutual responsibility. Men had been associated in tithings, originally groups of ten men responsible for each other's good behaviour, and in hundreds which were territorial divisions of ten hides or measures of land sufficient for the support of one family and its dependants. Each hundred had had its own court where justice was administered more in accordance with local customs than with the laws of the kingdom which were difficult if not impossible to enforce.* William the Conqueror had found the hundred a useful instrument. Whenever a member of his Norman garrison was found dead inside its boundaries, for instance, the murderer was presumed, without proof to the contrary, to have been a Saxon; and the hundred had accordingly to assume responsibility for paying the fine for murder.[35] By King Edward's time much of the significance of the hundred had been lost but, theoretically at least, it still held a responsibility for crimes

---

* The Laws of Ethelstan admitted the impossibility of punishing certain offenders who, it was hoped, might be removed to another part of the kingdom, if they were 'so rich' or belonged 'to so powerful a kindred' that they could not be punished.[34]

committed within its boundaries and a responsibility for answering the summons of the King's officers in times of danger. The statute of Winchester attempted to give these and other traditional responsibilities a new force and purpose.

For generations every man had been expected to possess some sort of weapon so that he could obey the summons of the *posse commitatus*, a command entrusted to the sheriff by the King and empowering him to call out every person in the county 'above fifteen years old and under the degree of a peer', not only to 'defend his country against any of the King's enemies' but also to keep the peace and pursue felons.[36] Now, 'to keep the peace' more effectively, and 'to abate the power of felons', the type of weapon each man must have was stipulated. A knight was required to possess a coat of mail and a helmet, a sword, a knife and a horse, and even the poorest man must have a bow and a quiverful of arrows. To ensure that the weapons were kept in good order, royal officers were empowered to visit houses and inspect them.

The mutual responsibility of the hundred for crimes committed within its boundaries was confirmed and extended; and so that no man should 'excuse himself by ignorance', as had been done in the past, the traditional obligations for meeting this responsibility and for following the 'Hue and Cry' were to be made known by proclamations 'in all counties, markets, hundreds, fairs and all other places where great resort of people is'. By regulations defining 'Watch and Ward', the gates of walled towns were to be kept shut during the hours of darkness and no strangers were to be allowed in. Only those whose conduct was guaranteed by a responsible householder could live in a suburb beyond the gates. The responsibility for enforcing these regulations was to be entrusted to a Watch the size of which depended upon the number of inhabitants in the town. Outside in the country, roads were to be 'enlarged so that there be neither dyke, tree nor bush whereby a man may lurk to do hurt' within two hundred feet of either verge, even if this meant that a landowner had to 'minish his park'.[37]

By a special local act passed in the same year as the Statute of Winchester, London was divided into twenty-four wards each of which was to have six watchmen, chosen from all householders in turn, under the orders of an alderman. In addition there was to be a 'marching watch' (the origin of the modern patrol) to give help wherever and whenever it was wanted. As in other towns the gates were to be closed an hour after sunset when the church bells rang the hour of curfew and, thereafter, all taverns were to shut for the night and no one could walk about armed 'unless he be a great man, or other lawful person of good repute, or their certain messengers'. Even in the day-time the gates were to be guarded by 'skilful men and fluent of speech' who could keep out undesirable strangers and foreigners.*

No foreigner, unless he was a freeman of the city, could keep a tavern; and no one at all could keep a fencing-school.[39] In later years new orders were made to restrict the size of carts, to prohibit the use of certain sorts of fuel, to regulate the positions of chains and barriers at the ends of the streets which were intended to impede the flight of burglars, to forbid shops opening on Sunday, to prevent barbers advertising their skill as surgeons by hanging bowls of blood beside their doors, to keep prostitutes outside the city walls in the 'Stews of Southwark' where brothels were tolerated, and to curtail the freedom of the citizens in a variety of other ways all of which the watchmen were obliged to supervise.

By emphasizing the English tradition that every man was a policeman, Edward I was doing no more than confirming the customs of his predecessors but he gave the system more force and effect than it had ever previously known. And during the reign of his lazy and incompetent son, Edward II, the safeguards provided by the Statute of Winchester and similar enactments did much to prevent the state of lawlessness, which the new King's weakness brought about, from degenerating into a chaos as complete as that which followed the Civil War of Henry III's reign.

As Edward II was more interested in enjoying himself than in the welfare of his people, it was left to Edward III to extend the work of his grandfather by enlarging the powers of the justices of the peace at the expense of the sheriffs and by entrusting them with the examination and punishment of criminals, making them magistrates as well as executive officers. The origins of the justice's office can be traced back to the twelfth century but it was not until the fourteenth—and in particular after a statute of 1360[40]—that

---

* Strangers and foreigners had always been suspect and care was taken in the laws of the early English kings to ensure that those who entertained them were made responsible for their behaviour. 'If a man from afar, or a stranger, quits the road,' the seventh century laws of Wihtred provided, 'and neithers shouts nor blows a horn, he shall be assumed to be a thief [and as such] may be either slain or put to ransom.'[38]

he began to assume the importance that he has ever since enjoyed. From being little more than a high-born constable himself he now had the control of constables as assistants in the execution of the law. The constable was the descendant of the Anglo-Saxon tythingman, a man of the people, but the justice of the peace was the descendant of the Knights of Richard I who were enjoined to enforce the observance of the Statutes of the King. Under the feudal system men had been taught to respect the Lord of the Manor as the administrator of the King's justice; now the justice of the peace took the place of the feudal lord and was, like him, a local landowner.[41]

Throughout the Middle Ages his importance grew and the duties that were imposed upon him and upon his constables became more and more extensive. Apart from the enforcement of the law and the administration of justice he was engaged in such diverse pursuits as the supervision of the helpless poor and the regulation of the dinner-hours of labourers. While the justice performed his unpaid duties uncomplainingly, the constable could not afford to do so. Like the watchmen in the town, constables were chosen from all householders in rotation, only 'Religious Persons, Knights, Clerkes and Women' being excepted. And although this system may have been acceptable in a primitive world it was no longer so in the more complex society which was now evolving. The busy merchant could not abandon his business, nor the artisan his tools to perform the duties of constable, still less to drop everything and join in a manhunt every time the 'Hue and Cry' was raised.

So the 'Hue and Cry' gradually fell into disuse and the practice of paying a proxy to perform the duties of a constable came into force.

But if Edward I's success in the permanent establishment of a more efficient form of police by strengthening and extending early traditions was sadly limited, his efforts to reform the administration of justice, despite the immense efforts he made, was even more so. The Statute of Westminster of 1275, although 'a legal code in itself' and the means of correcting many judicial abuses by his officers, had little effect on their subsequent behaviour. New sheriffs and country officials were appointed but within two years they were found to be as corrupt as those they had replaced.[42] A second Statute of Westminster, passed ten years after the first, complained that sheriffs still took innocent men, unlawfully indicted them and imprisoned them in order to 'extract money from them'.[43] Prisoners were tortured in gaol to force them to give evidence against their supposed accomplices and were afterwards left in prison to die. Fifty approvers died in York Castle alone in 1348.[44] Juries were frequently picked by the sheriffs to ensure more convictions and so raise more fines which they themselves pocketed. In the following reign it was reported that a jury which, for once, could not agree on a wanted conviction was ordered to be shut up 'until Monday' without food or drink.[45]

Throughout the next century redress in the courts, whether presided over by sheriff or King's justice, was difficult and sometimes impossible to obtain. Bribery and corruption continued to infect the whole system. The commissions which Edward I was compelled to appoint to enquire into the misdeeds of his legal officers were not the first nor the last of many commissions appointed for this purpose. The Statute of Winchester of 1283 had been preceded and was to be followed by others lamenting the fact that jurors could not be induced to bring in true verdicts against criminals. If juries were not bribed or intimidated they often took the side of the accused as a matter of course, believing that crime was not so reprehensible as the extortion of the judges, who administered justice so obliquely. So long as England's far from impartial justice was in the hands of the rich and the powerful; so long as not only inferior lawyers but a Chief Justice of England could be shown to be in receipt of bribes, as William Thorpe was in 1350; so long as the Chancellor himself could make illegal profits from his high office as William of Wykeham was believed to have done in 1371, the honesty of ordinary men who served on juries was not likely to be assured. Nor were their prejudices against the courts likely to be overcome when so many men, clergy and rich alike, enjoyed special privileges. Benefit of clergy meant originally that an ordained clerk charged with felony could be tried only in the ecclesiastical courts,[46] but it was already changing its nature. It came to be accepted as a plea against capital punishment in any court and the benefit could be claimed not merely by ordained clerks but by anyone accused of crime who could produce evidence that he was an educated man. The ability to read a few lines of a prescribed text, which the prisoner could, in fact, learn by heart with the help of an accommodating gaoler, was often taken as being sufficient evidence of education.

For those who could not otherwise evade the law, the church offered the protection of sanctuary. As it had been considered sacrilege to remove the criminal fugitive from the temples of Egypt and Rome, so it was recognized by Christians that those who sought escape from the law on sacred ground were inviolate. Signposts pointed the way to sanctuaries which had been recognized as early as the seventh century as being not only churches and monasteries but any territory which the Church and the laws that she inspired deemed to be sacred.* A fugitive who sought sanctuary had to confess his crime to a priest, surrender his arms, swear to obey the rules of the religious house which he entered and pay his fee; but he was then safe for forty days. When he delivered himself up to justice, clothed in sackcloth, he was obliged to forfeit all his goods but he was allowed to 'abjure the realm'. Wearing a long white tunic and carrying a cross, he had to walk to the coast. It was usually stipulated that he had to make for Dover and he was given a specific time in which to get there, usually a day for every twenty-five miles or so of his journey, but if there were no ships at Dover ready to sail, the fugitive could walk into the sea up to his neck and that was considered punishment enough.[47]

The likelihood of escaping punishment was also increased by the frequent issue of general pardons to criminals who would enlist in the army for a year's campaigning. The far from universal adoption of surnames ensured that these pardons frequently passed from hand to hand without the possibility of a court being able to determine whether those who held them were entitled to do so.[48]

While punishment for crime remained so uncertain and arbitrary and acquittals could so often be bought or contrived, men continued to settle their own grievances by primitive methods. Some idea of the conditions of the time may be gained from the fact that in 1348 there were eighty-eight known cases of murder in Yorkshire,[49] not the most populous part of England and with a population probably about the same as that of Sheffield today. If murders were committed on this scale now, there could not be less than ten thousand murders a year in England and Wales instead of an average of about a hundred and forty. Most murderers today are imprisoned or commit suicide, but nearly all murderers then were permitted to become

---

* As the centuries passed more and more places were granted the privilege of sanctuary by royal charter. From the sixteenth century onwards, constant and unsuccessful attempts were made to deny their protection to criminals. The Minories, the Mint, Salisbury Court, Whitefriars, Ram Alley and Mitre Court were but a few of those which survived in London until the eighteenth century.

outlaws because this was more profitable for those who convicted them.

Mutilation which the law allowed but which was not often inflicted except upon the very poor, was quite as common a method of private vengeance as murder and as little punished. Guy Mortimer, the rector of the church at Kingston-on-Hull, bearing a grudge against one of his parishioners, William Joyce, for an offence which the courts would not punish, attacked Joyce and with the help of a fellow clergyman and some of his other parishioners cut off his upper lip. Mortimer was eventually fined for what an obliging court decided was a trespass. Not until the fifteenth century was cutting out the tongue of an enemy or putting out his eyes declared to be a felony.[50]

By then the people's exasperation with private justice, with the partiality of the law, with those who so unfeelingly administered it and with those who so easily evaded it, had culminated in a revolt at least one of whose declared objects was the execution of all lawyers. The revolt had been a long time impending. In 1348 and 1349 the Black Death, a terrible sort of bubo-plague which the trade routes had brought westwards from China to Europe, killed about half of the five million inhabitants of the country; and most of those who died were labourers and artisans and the poor clergy who tried to look after them.[51] In the years that followed the Black Death over a third of the arable land in England remained uncultivated; crops rotted in the fields; employers in the towns faced a labour shortage that they had never known before. Workers, who had learned their value, demanded higher wages. Parliament intervened by passing the Statute of Labourers which compelled all unemployed men and women under sixty to accept any work offered to them at the wages current in 1346. Ten years later when the Statute had proved unenforceable, despite the heavy fines imposed upon employers who had paid higher wages than it permitted, Parliament passed another Statute decreeing that any labourer who left his place of work to seek higher wages should be branded with the letter F on his forehead as a sign of falsehood. Other laws were passed to keep the worker in subjection to his master, to preserve the class system, to prevent the social structure from breaking up. It became a crime for a labourer to wear clothes suited only to a higher station in life, for a servant to pay more for his cloth than a prescribed amour.t, for 'common lewd women' to dress like 'good noble dames and damsels' and so make it difficult to discover 'what rank they are'. Eventually on the grounds that 'all the wealth of the Kingdom was in the hands of artisans and labourers,' Parliament levied a tax of one shilling on every individual in the country who was over fifteen.[52]

This was in November 1380. In June the following year the men of Kent, led by Wat Tyler (who had once, so it was said, been a highwayman) and inspired by the 'apocalyptic harangues of the Mad Priest' John Ball, advanced on London. The rebellion spread to other parts of the country and soon became menacing. The more moderate rebels were persuaded to go home with promises that their demands would be conceded and pardons would be granted them. But, as in the Gordon Riots of 1780, there were many who were not to be satisfied with promises. They marched into London, attacked the gaols and released the prisoners, broke into the Tower and, in imitation of public executions, killed the Chancellor, Simon Sudbury who was also Archbishop of Canterbury, and the Treasurer, Sir Robert Hales, and paraded their heads through the streets on pikes.[53]

Further promises were made and more of the rebels went home and the violent ones who stayed to terrorize the city were soon defeated. As soon as order was restored, however, 'every promise made to the peasants in the hour of need was broken and a bloody assize made mock of the pardons granted by the king'.[54]

But although the immediate result of the revolt was a cruel reaction, it was certain now that the movement for emancipation and justice could not be permanently suppressed. Seventy-five years later the Wars of the Roses, that 'bleeding operation performed by the nobility upon their own body', in which the ordinary Englishman was able to remain neutral, weakened the power of the nobles and strengthened the Crown.

In the sixteenth century this new royal authority finally ended the private but infectious wars of barbarous barons and the private and corruptible justice of ambitious nobles, which had formerly made violence and cunning, the tools of the criminal, the accepted manners of a whole society. The criminal was still to retain the attitudes of mind of the past, but his methods were no longer the methods of society and gradually became the methods of an underworld.

CHAPTER TWO

THE AGE OF LEARNING

*'Hangman, I charge you to pay particular attention to this
lady. Scourge her soundly, man; scourge her till her blood
runs down.'*

JUDGE JEFFREYS, 1685

'THERE is no country in the world,' reported the Venetian envoy
after the reign of the Tudors had begun, 'where there are so many
thieves and robbers as in England; in so much that few venture
to go alone in the country excepting in the middle of the day, and
fewer still in the towns at night, and least of all in London.'[1]

Henry VII knew the immensity of the challenge that faced him.
To strengthen a central government and to arm trusted local justices with some of its authority, to establish new prerogative courts
which no man however rich or powerful could overawe, to make
juries more afraid of having to explain their conduct in the Star
Chamber than of bringing in a verdict against an intimidating landowner or criminal, to do these things with the guarded approval
of the new middle classes rising to wealth and influence but without
the backing of a standing army, required all the patience and
shrewdness which the new King possessed.

For some years there was little superficial change. It was still
possible for a cunning lawyer to join forces with an unscrupulous
member of a rich or noble family and for the inhabitants of the
countryside in which they committed their crimes to complain that
'they took sheep, avoided liability to pay fines and to supply men
to the King's army, annexed treasure trove, smuggled wool,
despoiled wrecks, released felons from bribes, poached gulls' eggs,

took bribes for permitting hunting on ground which was not theirs, embezzled clients' money and terrorized complainers into flight.'²

But this sort of behaviour was becoming rarer. The number of crimes committed may not have been appreciably reduced during the first half of the sixteenth century, but far more convictions were obtained and crime was far less flagrant. A specifically criminal class was emerging. Men still raided parks and hunted the King's deer but they did so with their faces blackened or masked or in disguise. As late as the reign of Henry VIII, Lord Dacre of Hurstmonceaux organized a party to hunt on a nearby estate and persuaded all those who joined him to swear to kill anyone who tried to prevent them. They passed three men on their way and although these men did not apparently provoke them, they were all attacked and one of them was killed. The event in itself would not have been exceptional during the previous century, but its sequel certainly would have been: Dacre was executed.

The firm grip in which, by then, Henry VIII held the State was being extended to the Church; and this new revolution of power was to have profound effect on the history of crime in England. Those who had committed crimes against God and against the Church had long been liable to severe punishments but once the King became head of that Church, heresy and treason were confused and these punishments were inflicted with far greater certainty. In the days of Henry IV and Henry V, the Lollards, inspired by Wyclif to question the authority of the Pope and to attack the sale of pardons and Masses for the soul, had indeed been persecuted. Some recanted when threatened with burning and some were burnt. But the deaths do not appear to have been many and Wyclif himself died peacefully in his own country parish at Lutterworth in Leicestershire in 1384.

Compared with heretics on the continent, the English heretic was at that time fortunate. When Philip IV wanted to stamp out the Templars in France torture was used indiscriminately to obtain confessions to crimes which were more often than not imaginary. In England torture was unknown to the Common Law and Pope Clement V wrote to Edward II: 'We hear that you forbid torture as contrary to the laws of your land; but no state can override Canon Law, Our Law; therefore I command you at once to submit these men to torture ... You have already imperilled your soul as a favourer of heretics ... Withdraw your prohibition and we grant you remission of sins.'³

Edward gave way 'through reverence for the Holy See,' and the Inquisition came to England. The evidence was obtained and the men were condemned. But by Continental standards the deaths were few and it was not until religious crimes could be interpreted as political ones that they were punished in England with obvious determination.

To the medieval English mind persecution was nevertheless acceptable because living outside the laws of the Church was no more excusable than living outside the laws of the State. A man was just as much a criminal whether he broke the laws of one or of the other. Most laymen believed this as strongly as the clergymen did; and they continued to believe it long after the Church had begun to lose its hold on a people who were no longer barbarians. The young Henry VIII was as orthodox as his father. He condemned Luther, earned from the Pope the title of 'Defender of the Faith' and encouraged the burning of the Lollards who had once more begun to question the doctrines and practices of the Roman Church. But, as Henry soon came to understand, the Church had lost much of her influence in England. Her refusal to compromise or reform, her insistence on old rights of benefit of clergy and sanctuary, her sale of relics and pardons, her spying interference in the lives of the people to extract fines for sin, her undistributed wealth and the remunerative appointments given to foreign nominees of the Pope, all gave force to a growing tide of anti-clericalism which Henry was able to turn to his own purposes. It was not originally an anti-Catholic revolution. Catholic opponents of it were admittedly executed; and Sir Thomas More, an enemy of religious orders and the popular superstitions they encouraged, was beheaded for disputing Henry's claim to be Supreme Head of the Church and his severed head was fixed on London Bridge. But before this judicial murder had been committed, Protestants, too, had been executed and the clause in the sheriffs' oath requiring them to destroy Lollards was not omitted until 1625. The Act of Supremacy of 1534 was followed in 1539 by the Act of Six Articles which decreed that the death penalty should be inflicted on anyone who denied the doctrine of Transubstantiation or the need for clerical celibacy. It was still possible for a man to be hanged in London for eating meat on a Friday; just as it was possible for a man to be burned—and even for his corpse to be exhumed and burned—for refusing to deny the holiness of relics. For one such man a gallows was prepared in Smithfield.

'on which he was hanged in chains, by the middle and arm-holes, all quick; and under the gallows was made a fire, and he was so consumed and burnt to death. At his coming to the place of execution, there was prepared a great scaffold on which sat the nobles of the realm, and the King's majesty's most honourable Council—only to have granted pardon to that wretched creature, if any spark of repentance would have happened to him. There was also prepared a pulpit where a Right Reverend Father in God, and a renowned and famous Clerk, the Bishop of Worcester, called Hugh Latimer, declared to him his errors; but such was his forwardness that he neither would hear nor speak. And a little before his execution, a huge and great image was brought to the gallows, which image was brought out of Wales, and of the Welshmen much sought and worshipped,' and was burned under him. 'When he saw the fire come and that present death was at hand, he caught hold upon the ladder, which he would not let go, but so impatiently took his death that no man that ever put his trust in God never so unquietly nor so ungodly ended his life.'[4]

Men and women turned into criminals by fanaticism or conscience and punished with ferocity because of their threat to political as well as religious institutions continued to burn at Smithfield for generations. A boy of fifteen was burned for repeating words the meaning of which it is difficult to believe he understood. Catholic priests were hanged in Oxfordshire and Protestant preachers hanged in Devon. The heresy laws put into execution by Mary, in her passionately held belief that she was working for God, kept fires burning for four years and killed at least three hundred men and women who had broken them.

By the time Elizabeth succeeded to the throne and made England Protestant again, 'for the first time in England a sentiment against putting people to death for their religious opinions as distinct from their political acts' had been created in the people.[5] The new Act of Supremacy passed in 1559 abolished the power of the Pope in England; the Act of Uniformity made it illegal to hold any services except those contained in the Prayer Book. Thereafter religious disputes became involved with disputes concerning the succession to the throne and heresy and treason were more confused than ever. Before the execution of Edmund Campion, the Jesuit missionary at Tyburn in 1581, a proclamation that he was being punished for treason and not for religion was read out in the Queen's name. When he said that he would pray for her, he was asked for what Queen he meant to pray. The name of Mary Queen of Scots had often been mentioned at his trial and his indictment accused him of having formed a conspiracy in Rome to murder Elizabeth and of having tried to stir up a rebellion in England in support of a foreign invasion.[6] The tortures to which he was subjected in the Tower failed to elicit a confession to these uncommitted crimes of treason although the very sight of the rack was sufficient to obtain from lesser men admissions to whatever crimes were suggested.

The use of torture, although still not recognized by Common Law, was now often used in criminal trials of this sort after a warrant had been obtained from the Council and may well have been used without a warrant. Its use was not unknown before the Tudor period. Prisoners could legally be tortured by licence of the King at least as early as the reign of Henry II. The rack was in the Tower by the time of Henry VI and by the following century the Scavenger's Daughter—a device which crushed the body until the blood spurted out of the nostrils and the tips of the fingers instead of stretching it 'until the bones and joints were almost plucked asunder'—was also in common and authorized use.

But although the Government felt obliged to resort to torture in the exigencies of the moment, it was recognized, even by those who defended it, as a Continental method of inquiry alien to the English tradition.[7]* The dangers of the times seemed, nevertheless, to justify it in the contemporary mind, just as the continued severity of punishment seemed justified by the numbers of crimes of violence and robberies which were still committed despite the gradual establishment of national order. Many lawyers, indeed, felt that yet severer punishments were essential if men were to have any security against death and ruin. Sir Roger Manwood, the Lord Chief Baron, advocated burning in the face or tongue, punishments 'with all extremity of irons', and public exposure 'with jaws gagged in painful manner' and the pulling out of tongues.[8] The excuse that 'no man in future would have any security against death by such means' was offered in 1531 when, after the household of the Bishop of Rochester was poisoned at his palace in Lambeth Marsh by his cook, poisoning was deemed to be high treason by

---

* The limitations placed upon its use, however, Sir James Stephen thought, might well have been due more to 'the extremely summary character of our early methods of trial, and the excessive severity of the punishments inflicted' than to 'the generalities of Magna Carta or any special humanity of feeling'.[10]

statute,[9] and the offender was to be boiled to death without the 'advantage of his clergy'. Although the Statute was soon repealed the cook was publicly boiled to death in Smithfield, and in the same year a maidservant was boiled to death in the market-place at King's Lynn.[11]

A similar excuse was offered in the next reign when, by the Statute of Vagabonds, a runaway servant was to be branded on the chest with a V and adjudged to be the slave for two years of anyone who cared to buy him. His owner was to 'give him bread, water, or small drink and refuse meat and cause him to work by beating, cheining or otherwise', at any kind of labour 'though never so vile'. If he ran away again and remained away for a fortnight he was to be branded with an S on his forehead and to be adjudged a slave for ever. His owner, if he wished, could put an iron ring round his neck or leg.[12]

The problem of the vagabond had been growing for years as a result of the break-up of the old system of farming and the development of the wool trade which by making sheep raising profitable had put thousands of labourers out of work. The growth of the towns, the increase in population, the spread of commerce, the immediate effects of the dissolution of the monasteries, all tended directly or indirectly to aggravate the problems of vagabondage and of a growing criminal class. The Elizabethan Poor Law eventually helped the weak and the unfortunate, but the distinction between those who could not work and those who would not, was never easy to make and many of those who deserved bread rather than a whipping, suffered with those 'sturdy beggars' who were the Tudor counterpart of the medieval retainers and outlaws. As late as 1572 vagabonds above the age of fourteen could be 'grievously whipped and burned through the gristle of the right ear with a hot iron of the compass of an inch', unless some responsible person could be found to take them into service for a year. If after the age of eighteen a vagabond fell for the second time into 'a roguish life', he was to be hanged unless he obtained suitable employment for two years. A third lapse resulted in hanging without the chance of redemption.[13] As the system of poor relief developed, the severity of these laws relaxed. In 1576 an Act provided for the establishment in every county of 'Houses of Correction', where men and women could be made to work;[14] and in 1597 an 'Act for erecting hospitals and Abiding and Working Houses for the Poor' was passed.[15]

But up to the middle of the sixteenth century many men were mutilated and some were hanged for little worse than idleness. How many criminals were hanged in all during these years cannot be ascertained. The quoted figure of seventy-two thousand as given by Stow for the thirty-seven years of the reign of Henry VIII is ill-founded but there is no doubt that Bishop Rowland Lee, as Lord President of the Council in the Welsh Marshes, 'hanged thieves in hundreds, right and left',[16]—without, on his own admission, making theft any less frequent in the disorderly areas he administered—and in the reign of Elizabeth, Sir Edward Coke protested at the innumerable hangings of 'so many Christian men and women strangled on that cursed tree of the gallows'.[17]

But Coke's was a lonely voice, for the average Englishman of his class believed that, to be effective, punishments must be both frequent and severe. And Coke, himself, like the medieval bishops before him, could find biblical authority for the 'godly butchery' of the punishment inflicted on traitors, even for the dismemberment of their genitals which was sometimes added to the disembowelling and decapitation as an aggravated humiliation. Some of the more painful and degrading parts of the sentence of hanging, drawing and quartering were omitted or commuted in later years but as late as 1817 at a public execution of three peasants convicted of high treason at Derby, decapitation followed hanging.[18] In the sixteenth century, the sentence of the court was normally followed exactly. The man was cut down from the gallows while still alive and often sometimes even survived disembowelment. Collingbourne, who was executed for a libel on Richard III, lived long enough to cry, 'Oh, Jesús, Jesus' as the executioner, having quickly disembowelled him, cut open his chest to take out the heart and hold it up so that the crowd could 'behold the heart of a traitor' before beholding the traitor's severed head.[19] And another man, after watching the quartering of his uncle, cried out 'Oh, Lord! Lord! Have mercy upon me!' as the executioner took out his bowels. Those unable to profit from the spectacle of the execution of these men were reminded of the deserts of treason by the sight of their parboiled quarters, 'set upon sundry gates of the City of London,' and their heads upon London Bridge or Temple Bar. The practice of displaying heads 'for an example to all traitors' was not discontinued until well on into the eighteenth century when passers-by paid sixpence to inspect them through telescopes before they were blown down into the streets on a windy night.[20]

The traditionally ritualistic ceremonial of hanging, drawing and quartering was considered to be an important aspect of the punishment for high treason, as, indeed, of all physical punishments. The ceremonial to be observed during mutilation and branding was carefully stipulated and the complicated procedure to be followed, for example, when a man had his hand cut off for drawing blood during a quarrel at the King's Court was laid down, by an Act passed late in the reign of Henry VIII, with macabre formality. The Sergeant of the Woodyard first brought in a block and cords. The Master Cook then handed the Dressing Knife to the Sergeant of the Larder who held it 'until execution was done'. The Sergeant of the Poultry stood by with a cock whose head was to be cut off on the block and whose body was to be wrapped around the stump of the wrist. Meanwhile the Yeoman of the Scullery stood watching a coal fire on which the Sergeant Farrier heated the searing irons. The Chief Surgeon seared the stump while the Groom of Salcery held vinegar and cold water in case the patient should faint. The Sergeant of the Ewery and the Yeoman of the Chandry attended with basin, cloth and towels for the Surgeon. The Sergeant of the Pantry came with a tray of bread and the Sergeant of the Cellar with a pot of red wine.[21]

The spectacle of these ritualistic executions and mutilations had less effect, however, in serving as object lessons in the wages of crime than in accustoming men to the sight and smells and instruments of human butchery. 'I saw the heads when they were brought up to be boiled,' wrote a seventeenth-century prisoner in Newgate. 'The Hangman fetched them in a dirty dust basket, out of some by-place; and, setting them down among the felons, he and they made sport with them. They took them by the hair, flouting, jeering, and laughing at them; and then, giving them some ill-names, boxed them on the ears and cheeks. Which done, the Hangman put them into his kettle, and parboiled them with Bay-Salt and Cummin-Seed—that to keep them from putrefaction, and this to keep off the fowls from seizing on them.'[22]

A horrifying example was not, though, the only purpose behind the dismemberment and subsequent display of a traitor's body. It was also intended that the victim should be humiliated, for degradation figured largely in all contemporary theories of punishment. That is why hanging, traditionally regarded as degrading, was the usual form the death penalty took for ordinary criminals. Since the time of William the Conqueror, who had the Earl of Huntingdon beheaded in 1076, decapitation had been regarded as a right reserved for the highly born; and burning was regarded as a more suitable death for women. 'For as the decency due to the sex forbids the exposing and publicly mangling of their bodies, their sentence is, to be drawn to the gallows and there to be burnt alive.'[23] But for the common thief and murderer, hanging was not merely a form of death but of debasement.

Public humiliation was a necessary part of all other punishments as well as of hanging, and always had been so. The pillory had been as much a part of the equipment of the feudal castle as the Lord of the Manor's gallows and his drowning pond; and was now in use in every town in the country. Frequently employed to expose dishonest tradesmen to public ridicule, it was also used to punish men and women guilty of rumour-mongering and slander and as a preliminary to other punishments for more serious offences. It was often, in effect, a sentence of death. Far more painful than the stocks which held the culprit only by his ankles, the pillory held him by the neck and by the wrists. His ears were sometimes nailed to the wooden board so that he could not hang his head when the spectators of his misery threw stones or filth at him; and occasionally his feet did not reach the platform so that he was throttled. The treatment of two criminals, James Eagan and James Salmon, who had earned the particular hatred of the mob, was not in the least uncommon: 'Eagan and Salmon were taken to Smithfield amidst a surprising concourse of people, who no sooner saw the offenders exposed in the pillory than they pelted them with stones, brickbats, potatoes, dead dogs and cats and other things ... The blows they received occasioned their heads to swell to an enormous size; and by people hanging to the skirts of their clothes they were nearly strangled. They had been in the pillory about half an hour when a stone struck Eagan on the head, and he immediately expired.'[24] Salmon died in prison soon afterwards.

Men guilty of homosexual offences were often treated in this way. One of two homosexuals pilloried a few years after Salmon and Eagan were killed, 'soon grew black in the face and blood issued from his nostrils, his eyes, and his ears; the mob nevertheless attacked him with great fury'. When the pillory was opened he 'fell down dead on the stand of the instrument. The other man was likewise so maimed and hurt by what was thrown at him that he lay there without hope of recovery.'[25]

Occasionally the court sentenced the prisoner to be punished both before and after being put in the pillory. The Bishop of London described the punishments inflicted in 1630 upon Alexander Leighton, a Doctor of Divinity who had written a 'scandalous book against kings, peers and prelates':

'1.　He was severely whipped before he was put in the pillory.

2.　Being set in the pillory he had one of his ears cut off.

3.　One side of his nose split.

4.　Branded on one cheek with a red hot iron with the letters SS, signifying a stirrer up of sedition, and afterwards carried back again prisoner to the Fleet, to be kept in close custody.

And on that day seven-night, his sores upon his back, ear, nose, and face being not cured, he was whipped again at the pillory in Cheapside, and there had the remainder of the sentence executed upon him, by cutting off the other ear, splitting the other side of the nose, and branding the other cheek.'[26]

Women were far more rarely pilloried than men although Ann Morrow who had been found guilty of disguising herself as a man for the purpose of marrying three different women, was blinded by the stones flung at her by an exceptionally violent crowd; and the procuress, Mother Needham, convicted of keeping 'a common Bawdy House', was pelted in an 'unmerciful manner'.[27] But there were other degrading punishments no less painful to which they were subjected. In Newcastle, 'chiding and scoulding women' were apparently led round the streets on a rope, 'wearing an engine called the branks, which is like a crown, it being of iron, which was musled over the head and face, with a great gag or tongue of iron forced into the mouth which forced the blood out'. Women could also be whipped. An Act of 1530 provided that vagrants of both sexes were to be 'tied to the end of a cart naked, and beaten with whips . . . till the body shall be bloody by reason of such whipping'. By 1597 those to be whipped were obliged no longer to go naked behind the cart but had to be stripped only to the waist. The humiliation might be less but the pain was as great. 'Hangman,' Judge Jeffreys is said to have once commanded, 'I charge you to pay particular attention to this lady. Scourge her soundly, man; scourge her till her blood runs down! It is Christmas, a cold time for madam to strip. See that you warm her shoulders thoroughly.'[28]

The ducking of immoral or nagging women, like the pillorying of men, sometimes resulted in death. And if the woman was being ducked to discover whether or not she was a witch, drowning was frequent. A witch, bound and cross-bound with her right thumb tied to her left toe and her right toe to her left thumb, would float if flung into a pond. If she did float she was pulled out to be punished as a witch; if she did not, her relatives had the comfort perhaps of knowing that, even though dead, she had been proved innocent to their own satisfaction if not always to that of her accusers.

The campaign against witchcraft, fought furiously by Catholics and Protestants alike, spread all over Europe in the sixteenth century until 'witches were burned no longer in ones and twos but in scores and hundreds. A bishop of Geneva is said to have burned five hundred within three months; a bishop of Bamberg six hundred, a bishop of Würzburg nine hundred. Eight hundred were condemned, apparently in one body, by the senate of Savoy.'[29]

Witch-hunts in England were never carried out on this scale, but in the seventeenth century witchcraft, nevertheless, became one of the most common of all crimes. An impetus to the movement for the rooting out of witches came from James I whose *Daemonology* was published before he came to the throne in 1603. James had been moved to write his book by 'the fearful abounding, at this time in this country, of those detestable slaves of the devil—witches and enchanters'. When he came to England, an Act was passed in compliment to him, 'against Conjuration, Witchcraft, and dealing with evil and wicked spirits'. It treated the problem in greater detail than any previous Act and made it a capital offence to 'entertain, employ, feed or reward such a spirit or any part of it—skin or bone—for purposes of enchantment or sorcery' or to practise any witchcraft by which anyone 'should be killed, destroyed, wasted, pined or lamed'.[30]

Although men and women suspected of witchcraft were not subjected to the fearful tortures common on the Continent, the methods adopted for discovering if a person had been seduced by the Devil were agonizing enough. Many women became witches after having fornicated with the devil or having kissed his rectum in which 'lustful women took especial delight'. Coitus was very painful because the devil had an extremely large and hard penis, sometimes shod with iron, at others covered with brittle fish-scales, and his semen was cold as ice. But this did not necessarily mean that the body of a woman who had been entered by him would show that she had been hurt. It was possible for a woman who was proved in court to be a virgin to have 'committed uncleanness' with the Devil as she could have done so without being de-flowered.[31]

In the absence of witnesses who were prepared to swear that they had seen the accused fornicating with the Devil or with an incubus, evidence was accepted from distinguished witch-finders such as Matthew Hopkins who was himself hanged for witchcraft at the height of his career. Hopkins could discover whether or not a woman was possessed by the devil by sticking long pins into her flesh to discover the places rendered insensitive by the Devil's touch. Witches could also be detected by their habit of throwing back their hair, their inability to cry, their practice of walking backwards and intertwining their fingers.[32]

The prevalence and danger of witches was emphasized by Sir Matthew Hale, the Lord Chief Baron, who 'made no doubt at all that there were such creatures'. At a trial in 1665 he sentenced two women to death on the evidence of a woman who said that her children 'coughed extremely and brought up crooked pins' and once a big 'nail with a very broad head' which she produced to-gether with forty pins. A doctor spoke of the 'subtlety of the Devil' while giving his evidence and explained how the working of the humours of the body in relation to this subtlety brought about this 'flux of pins'.[33]

The vomiting of pins was, apparently, a sure sign that the Devil's agency was at work. In 1716 Mary Hicks and her daughter Elizabeth, who was just eleven, were hanged for having, on their own confession, sold their souls to the devil and obliged their neigh-bours to perform this painful miracle.[34] But a man who accused a woman of making him vomit pins and of taking away his appetite was eventually arraigned at Surrey Assizes as a cheat and impostor. This was, however, not before he had succeeded in getting the woman convicted by Sir Thomas Lane, a firm believer in her evil powers. The witch's accuser could only get relief, so he told Sir Thomas, by scratching her. He was told to scratch her to prove his point. He did so and, immediately regaining his appetite, ate a big piece of bread and cheese.[35]

In 1736 the Statutes against witchcraft were repealed but for many years suspicions continued to centre upon any persons whose eccentricities or secretiveness had aroused the hostility of their neighbours; and ducking and measuring a woman's weight against that of a bible were still used to discover witches long after the legal punishments had disappeared. Charges arising out of the drowning of witches were, accordingly, not uncommon in country districts up till the beginning of the nineteenth century.[36]

In the American colonies at the end of the seventeenth century, witchcraft threatened to be an even greater problem than in England. In the spring of 1692 the Massachusetts village of Salem became the centre of one of the most celebrated witch-hunts in history. Here ten girls, between nine and seventeen years old, had met in the evenings of the previous winter at the house of Samuel Parris, the pastor of the village church. Parris's West Indian slave spoke to these girls about magic—in which their parents' conversations had already interested them—and taught them how to read palms. They accused the slave and two old women of being witches. In the subsequent hysteria many more women were accused and eventually hundreds of people were arrested and, largely on the evidence of these bewitched girls, nineteen were condemned to death.

The trials were conducted strictly in accordance with English law and precedent, and the hangings were performed in the English manner. Most methods of punishment in the New World, in fact, were the same as those used in England. The idea that humiliation was an important element in punishment had been recognized by the introduction of the stocks, the pillory, the branding iron and the ducking-stool; and less painful humiliations such as the enforced wearing of a wooden board marked with a red D for those convicted of drunkenness had become part of the Puritan tradition. As in England torture to extort confessions was not generally permitted, except in some trials of witchcraft, but cases have been recorded of men being pressed to death for refusing to plead; and a seventeenth-century Massachusetts code provided the death penalty for idolatry, blasphemy and adultery. In New York and Virginia men were broken on the wheel. This punishment was not, apparently, tolerated in New England but penalties there, particularly for religious offences, were severe enough. A man who denied the existence of God and the Devil had a hole bored in his tongue with a hot iron; and not only blasphemy but even smoking and wearing unseemly clothes were penalized. A Captain Kimble was once put in the stocks for his 'lewd' behaviour in 'publiquely' kissing his wife on their doorstep after his return from a voyage which had lasted three years. It was a Sunday.

The strict regulation of morals by law and custom was as pervasive an influence in life in these colonies as it had been in England during the time of the Commonwealth. Acts were passed in England for the punishment of incontinence, making fornication a crime and adultery a felony. In 1647 an ordinance decreed that all persons who had acted in any playhouse in London were to be punished as rogues;[37] in 1648 men and women who had acted in public could be whipped and those who had watched them act could be fined;[38] in 1654 cock-fighting was prohibited, not because it was cruel but because it was 'commonly accompanied with gaming, drinking and swearing'.[39] Anyone 'profanely or vainly walking' on the Lord's Day was penalized; and stricter rules were made to enforce public worship and to prevent Sunday travelling and trading. A new Act was passed against profane swearing and it became an offence to gamble with cards, and if you were an apprentice or a servant, to remain in a tavern after eight o'clock on a holiday. For six months horse-racing was abolished and it was even considered a crime, in certain circumstances, to play football.

One John Bishop, an apothecary, was charged with having at Maidstone, 'wilfully and in a violent and boisterous manner run to and fro,' and kicked 'up and down in the common highway and street within the said town and county, called the High Street, a certain ball of leather, commonly called a football ...'[40]

Punishment for crimes such as this were unlikely to be severe, but the crime of blasphemy was punished ferociously. James Naylor, who said that he was God, declared that a man might enjoy the pleasures of love with any woman provided she belonged to the same sect. His own sect was mostly composed of women who sat round his chair for hours on end chanting, 'Holy! Holy! To the true God and Great God and Glory to the Almighty!' Naylor was sentenced to be set in the pillory in Palace Yard; to be whipped to the Old Exchange by the hangman; two days later to be pilloried at Old Exchange and to have a hole bored through his tongue; to be branded with a B; to be taken to Bristol to be publicly whipped and to be sent through the town on a horse's bare back with his face to the tail; then to be placed in solitary confinement at Bridewell.[41]

At the Restoration in 1660 many of the laws passed in the Commonwealth against rowdiness, pleasure, blasphemy and vice were repealed; but punishments in general continued to be as savage as they had been for generations. The bodies of Cromwell and other regicides were exhumed and hanged as if to give notice that the return to the House of Stuart meant no relaxation in the severity of the law; and the sentence passed upon Titus Oates for perjury in 1685 was, although extravagant, characteristic of the period. Oates was to be walked round all the courts of Westminster bearing a placard showing the nature of his offence; he was to stand in the pillory at the gate of Westminster Hall for half an hour and on the next day for an hour at the Royal Exchange; and on the third day he was to be whipped from Newgate to Tyburn. On 9 August of every year thereafter he was to stand in the pillory at Westminster Hall Gate, on 10 August every year he was to be pilloried at Charing Cross and on 24 April at Tyburn. It was expected, however, that he would be dead long before this.[42]

Savage as punishments could be in England and in the American colonies, they were, however, mild in comparison with those inflicted on the Continent. In 1666 at Auvergne, 276 criminals were hanged, forty-four were beheaded, thirty-two were broken on the wheel, twenty-eight were sent to the galleys and three were burned.[43] A man who made an attempt on the life of Louis XV had his hand burned off, molten lead and boiling oil was poured into the stump and four horses were set to drag him apart. As the strength of the horses proved inadequate for this task the executioner loosened his joints with a knife.[44] In Germany, men sentenced to death were nipped on their way to the place of execution with red hot pincers which were used to tear out the tongues of blasphemers.[45] Confessions were regularly extracted by means of the *Fass*, a cradle with spikes on the inside of which the prisoner was rocked, the *Kranz*, a headband which was slowly tightened, the *Aufziehen*, a machine that hoisted his weighted body up into the air by a rope tied to his hands which were fastened behind his back, by the thumbscrew, by the rack and by applying lighted candles to his armpits.[46] That these ferocious tortures elicited confessions with equal facility from guilty and innocent alike is not to be doubted. But their efficacy in deterring others from crime may be judged from these typical extracts from the diary of the executioner at Nuremberg whose services were in constant demand. Having committed two murders already, Kloss Renckhart went one night to a mill in the mountains to commit a third with a companion. 'They shot the miller dead, did violence to the miller's wife and the maid, obliged them to fry some eggs in fat and laid these on the dead miller's body, then forced the miller's wife to join in eating them. He kicked the miller's body and said: "Miller, how do you like this morsel?" He also plundered the mill.'[47]

Renckhart was broken on the wheel for these murders, as was Nicklauss Stüller. Stüller, with his companions Phila and Görgla von Sunberg committed eight murders. 'First he shot a horse-soldier; secondly he cut open a pregnant woman alive in which was a dead child; thirdly he again cut open a pregnant woman in whom was a female child; fourthly he once more cut open a pregnant woman in whom were two male children. Görgla von Sunberg said that they had committed a great sin and that he would take the infants to a priest to be baptized, but Phila said he would himself be priest and baptize them, so he took them by the legs and dashed them to the ground. For these deeds, he Stüller, was drawn on a sledge at Bamberg, his body torn thrice with red-hot tongs, and then he was executed on the wheel.'[48]

Legalized torture in England and in the American colonies, however, was by now limited to the *peine forte et dure* which was only inflicted on those who refused to plead. Before 1406 the prisoner who declined to enter a plea was starved to death, but as pressing to death was considered more humane the punishment of *peine forte et dure* was substituted. The sentence was awarded in these words:

'The prisoner shall be remanded to the place from whence he came, and put in some low, dark room, and there laid on his back, without any manner of covering except a cloth round his middle; and one arm shall be drawn to one quarter of the room with a cord, and the other to another and his feet shall be used in the same manner, and as many weights shall be laid on him as he can bear, and more. He shall have three morsels of barley bread a day and he shall have the water next the prison so that it be not current and he shall not eat on the same day that he drinks, nor drink on the same day on which he eats; and he shall so continue till he die.'[49]

Usually the threat of torture (abolished in 1827 when an Act was passed directing courts to enter a plea of 'not guilty' if a prisoner refused to plead) was enough to force a man to change his mind. Sometimes a few minutes of agony achieved the same purpose. Thomas Spiggot, a highwayman, held out for half an hour until the weight of four hundred pounds forced him to give in.[50] Occasionally a man remained obdurate to the end so that his estate might pass to his heirs which would not be the case if he were

hanged. One of those accused of witchcraft in Salem was pressed
to death; and in 1658 Major Strangeways, who was accused of
having shot a man he did not want to marry his sister, was pressed
to death in Newgate. Several of his friends were present and to
hasten his end they jumped on top of the press adding their own
weight to that of the iron and stones, until, after ten minutes of
agony, Strangeways died.[51]

Sometimes an attempt was made to force prisoners to plead by
twisting their thumbs with whipcord.

'If he remains obstinate, he must be pressed,' a judge once told
a prisoner who said he was deaf and could not read.

An officer of the Court bawled in the man's ear, 'The Court says
you must be pressed to death if you won't hear.'

'Ha!' said the prisoner.

'Read the law,' said the judge, 'but let the executioner first tie
his thumbs.'

The executioner tied his thumbs together 'and with the assistance of an officer drew the knot very hard'.

This conversation followed:

Prisoner: 'My dear Lord, I am deaf as the ground.'
Executioner: 'Guilty or Not Guilty?'
Prisoner: 'My sweet, sugar, precious Lord, I am deaf, indeed, and have
    been so these ten years.'
Executioner: 'Guilty or Not Guilty?'
Court: 'Hold him there a little ... Now loose the cord and give him
    a little time to consider of it, but let him know what he must expect
    if he continues obstinate, for the Court will not be trifled with.'[52]

Prisoners condemned to death also commonly had their thumbs
tied together with whipcord in court after sentence had been pronounced upon them. For courts of law, proud as Englishmen were
of them and justifiably proud when comparing their procedure to
that of most courts on the Continent, were also places of punishment. Thumbs were twisted there and brandings were performed
there and as the skin of the prisoner blackened and smoked the
brander turned to the judge to declare, 'A fair mark, my Lord!'[53]

Before 1698 thieves who successfully pleaded benefit of clergy
were branded on the hand; but an Act passed in that year provided
that thereafter they were to be 'burnt in the most visible part of the
left cheek, nearest the nose, which punishment shall be inflicted
in open court, in the presence of the judge'. Eight years later,

however, it was admitted that this had not had 'its desired effect by deterring offenders' for because it prevented them getting honest work, it had made them the 'more desperate'.[54]

The boast that an Englishman was always assumed innocent until proved guilty lost its force when it was so much easier to prove guilt than to assume innocence. The accused had few of the advantages that he has today. If charged with felony he was not permitted, until well on into the nineteenth century, to have a counsel to cross-examine witnesses or to address the jury. The judge had to be relied upon to afford the prisoner his protection but, often enough, the judge considered himself a prosecutor on behalf of the Crown. Up to the reign of James II, judges were appointed to hold office 'during the King's pleasure' and were often instructed how to proceed in the cases of important prisoners. 'Be sure to execute the law to the utmost of its vengeance upon those that are now known (and we have reason to remember them) by the name of Whigs,' Lord Jeffreys advised his successor, 'And you are likewise to remember the Snivelling Trimmers.'[55] Jeffreys, although the most notorious of his brother judges, was by no means unique. Most of them considered it their duty to browbeat everyone in court except the prosecuting counsel; and Jeffreys, after all, was made Lord Chancellor by the King when he returned to London, having sent over three hundred men and women to the gallows during that 'mockery of justice' known as 'the Bloody Assizes' held at Winchester in 1685.

As often as not the only hope for a prisoner lay in what Sir Frank MacKinnon was later to call the 'general conspiracy of benevolence' to mitigate the effects of the system 'by excessive technicalities of procedure'.[56]

It was not unknown, for instance, for a prisoner to be acquitted because of some trifling inaccuracy in the indictment, such as the misspelling of his name. Nor was it unknown for a capital charge to be quashed when a jury committed what Blackstone termed 'pious perjury' and undervalued the articles stolen so that the crime was no longer a capital one.

The system was also mitigated, for those who could afford it, by the wholesale bribery which pervaded it. Perjury was still, despite a special Act[57] passed against it in the sixteenth century, a full-time profession; and perjured evidence could be given for the defence just as well as for the prosecution. 'Straw men,' as they were called from their habit of discreetly advertising themselves by sticking bits of straw into their shoe buckles, walked up and down outside the courts ready to sell their services as witnesses.

Juries, too, could be bought and even when they were not, they frequently gave verdicts which they came to for reasons of sentiment. When William Penn was tried for having taken part in an unlawful assembly, the jury decided that he was guilty, but only of 'speaking in Grace Church Street'. 'I will have a positive verdict or you shall starve for it,' the judge told them. So they decided that Penn was not guilty and were consequently fined for 'going contrary to plain evidence'.[58] According to the *London Evening Post* juries in Middlesex were regularly 'allowed an elegant dinner at Appleby's and five guineas a man, if a verdict be given for the Crown or Government', otherwise they paid their own expenses.[59]

By the beginning of the eighteenth century the corruption in the courts had come to be accepted as a national but inevitable misfortune. In 1725 the trial of the Earl of Macclesfield, the Lord Chancellor, revealed how deep the corruption had gone. Macclesfield's practice of selling the Masterships in Chancery was admitted to be one of the recognized perquisites of his high office. He was not blamed for continuing a custom which extended to many other legal appointments; but he was blamed for charging so much for the Masterships that the newly appointed Masters took to misappropriating the funds lodged in the Chancery Court. It was alleged at his trial that he had, in fact, dipped into these funds himself. He was fined thirty thousand pounds and, although he had recently lost a considerable sum of money in the South Sea speculations, he paid it within a few weeks.

Macclesfield was not so much a worse man than his contemporaries as a more unfortunate one. Ballad writers condemned him for being 'so barefaced a Bungler' rather than for being a rogue.[60]

For it was a time not only of insensibility but of an almost universal greed for quick profits. It was a time, for instance, which accepted without distaste that one of the principal assets of the South Sea Company in 1713 should be the monopoly of the slave trade with Spanish America. Slaves were a commodity, as sugar was.

The apparent success of the South Sea Company inevitably led to 'a mania for speculation'. Hundreds of companies were floated and most of them offered purely imaginary proposals to get money out of the public. 'A wheel for perpetual motion,' 'a design to be hereafter promulgated,' the importation of 'a hitherto unknown breed of gigantic asses from Spain' were all ideas that caught the public imagination and enabled the directors of fraudulent companies to make immense profits. And when the hysteria collapsed and thousands of people were ruined, vengeance was sought and scapegoats were demanded; but few thought to question the values of a society in which the frenzy had arisen.

It was a time, too, in which British pirates who sank Spanish merchantmen and murdered Spanish sailors were national heroes, instruments even of Government policies. When Lord Bellamont was sent to New York as Governor in 1695 'the piracies committed in the West-Indies, which had been greatly encouraged by some of the inhabitants of North America, on account of the advantage that could be gained by the purchase of effects thus fraudulently obtained,' was one of his principal problems. On the advice of a Colonel Levingston, who was living in New York, Lord Bellamont consulted a Scottish sea captain, John Kidd. Captain Kidd also lived in New York where he had become the owner of a small vessel with which he traded among the pirates. It was suggested that a company should be formed to equip an expedition to fight the pirates and that Captain Kidd should command it. A tenth part of the profits was to go to King William III who, with his Lord Chancellor, enthusiastically supported the venture, and the rest was to be divided up amongst the shareholders. Captain Kidd sailed without any conditions being placed upon the way in which he should execute his commission and attacked any merchant ship on the seas which promised being a profitable prize. If he had behaved with more discretion there seems little doubt that the shareholders would not have enquired too closely into his conduct; but his activities as a licensed pirate were so wantonly reckless that he had to be disowned and he was hanged at Execution Dock, East Wapping in 1701.[61]

In previous centuries the condonation of piracy by the Government, by the grants of regular privateering commissions by the Crown, had bestowed not only riches and fame but also a kind of respectability on many criminal adventurers. The Elizabethan buccaneers set the pattern for the Welsh privateer, Henry Morgan who was commissioned by Sir Thomas Modyford, the Governor of Jamaica, to fight the Spaniards in 1668. Although he exceeded the terms of his commission, pillaging the towns of Cuba and killing hundreds of defenceless people, Morgan was entrusted with other expeditions. He was knighted in 1674 and appointed Lieutenant-Governor of Jamaica.

Buccaneers like Morgan, Captain Avery, William Dampier and Edward Teach, the famous 'Blackbeard', all received official or quasi-official support in return for a share in their profits and all of them traded openly with the American colonists. For trading with pirates was considered to be no less pardonable than sharing the profit of wreckers. An unseen and unknown victim was often ignored and rarely pitied, particularly if he were a foreigner.

In some coastal villages, indeed, and more often in villages on the English coast, the victims of the wreckers were not pitied even when they were seen. By an Act of Edward I, no ship could be accounted a wreck if a man, a dog or a cat escaped alive from it. But sailors who tried to swim to safety were left, without help, to drown, and sometimes they were killed if the seas were not too strong to prevent them reaching the shore. For the shares that they might receive in profits from wrecks, Cornish villagers lined the cliff tops on stormy nights to lure ships on to the rocks with false lights. They moved buoys and smashed the lamps in lighthouses, kneeling down to pray, as villagers did on the Atlantic coast of America, that the ships would founder; but not until 1753 were wrecking and plundering made capital offences and then mainly, it seems, because the wreckers had not limited their attentions to foreign ships.[62] Wrecking continued, of course, as smuggling did after an Act[63] had created many more capital offences in connection with it. Neither the wreckers nor the smugglers were outcasts in the communities in which they lived; and attempts to bring them to justice rarely succeeded. When the 'officers of the customs at Eastbourne, Sussex, having intelligence of a gang of smugglers, went with five dragoons mounted to the seaside over against Pevensey' in 1744, a hundred smugglers, supported by villagers, attacked them with pistols and swords and drove them away. The smugglers then loaded their 'run goods on about a hundred horses and made towards London'.[64] In Cheshire a few years later, the captain of a wrecked ship was stripped naked by villagers who cut off his fingers to get his rings. The ear lobes of another sailor were bitten off by a woman who wanted the gold pieces hanging on them.[65]

The men and women of Cheshire and Sussex were by then not the only English people to have become as contemptuous of the law as they were unimpressed by the threat of the hangman's rope.

CHAPTER THREE

THE AGE OF ELEGANCE

'*Executed at Tyburn, July 6, Elizabeth Banks, for stripping a child; Catherine Conway, for forging a seaman's ticket; and Margaret Harvey for robbing her master. They were all drunk.*'

GENTLEMAN'S MAGAZINE, 1750

I LAST week set a man to watch the door of a gin shop on Holborn Hill... Between the hours of seven and ten in the evening there went in and came out 1,411 persons excluding children ... I am shocked at seeing children intoxicated with their fathers and mothers, children of from seven to fourteen years of age.'¹

'In the parish of St Giles there are great numbers of houses set apart for the reception of idle persons and vagabonds who have their lodgings there for twopence. In the above parish and in St George's Bloomsbury, one women alone controls several of these houses, all accommodated with miserable beds from the cellar to the garret for such twopenny lodgers. In these beds, several of which are in the same room, men and women, often strangers to each other lie promiscuously, the price of a double bed being no more than threepence as an encouragement to lie together. But as these places are thus adapted to whoredom, so are they no less provided for drunkenness, gin being sold in them all at a penny a quartern, so that the smallest sum of money serves for intoxication.'²

'Should the drinking this poison be continued in its present height during the next twenty years, there will be by that time few of the common people left to drink it ... gin is the principal sustenance (if it may be so called) of more than a hundred thousand people in the metropolis ... The intoxicating draught itself disqualifies them from any honest means to acquire it, at the same time that it removes sense of fear and shame and emboldens them to commit every wicked and desperate enterprise.'³ 'There is not only no safety of living in this town but scarcely any in the country now; robbery and murder have grown so frequent. Our people have become what they never were before, cruel and inhuman. These accursed spiritous liquors which to the shame of our Government are to be so easily had and in such quantities drunk, have changed the very nature of our people, and will if continued to be drunk, destroy the very race.'⁴

In letters, pamphlets and sermons, in the reports of parliamentary committees and in charges to juries, the evil consequences of the excessive drinking of gin in the first half of the eighteenth century were constantly deplored. The concern was real and justified. In 1721 when the orgy of spirit drinking which was to last for thirty years had just begun, the Westminster justices reported that 'the principal cause of the increase of our poor and of all the vice and debauchery among the inferior sort of people, as well as of the felonies and other disorders committed in and about this town' was the great increase of alehouses and spirit shops. There was no part of the town where the numbers of these places did not 'daily increase, though they were so numerous already that in some of the largest parishes every tenth house at least' sold 'one sort or another of those liquors by retail'.⁵ Four years later, a committee of justices found that the numbers of gin-shops were still increasing and that the known retailers were only a proportion of the total, for there were many others who sold 'privately in garrets, cellars, back rooms and other places . . . All chandlers, many tobacconists, and such who sell fruit or herbs in stalls and wheelbarrows sell geneva, and many inferior tradesmen begin now to keep it in their shops for their customers . . . In the hamlet of Bethnal Green above forty weavers sell it.'⁵

It was sold in workhouses and in prisons, in factories, in brothels and in barbers' shops. By 1743 eight million gallons were drunk a year and every sixth house in the metropolis, whose population seems to have been less than seven hundred thousand⁷ was believed to be a dram shop. The bodies of men, women and children could be seen lying dead drunk where they had fallen, in the middle of the day as well as at night, in many of the streets of the slum quarters of St Giles and Spitalfields. In the gin cellars rows of bodies sat on the straw, propped up against the walls until the effects of the spirits wore off and then they started drinking again. Before the Licensing Act of 1751—forced on an Administration reluctant to act because of its vested interest in the distillation of spirits from English grain—had brought the worst years to an end, cheap spirits were universally blamed not only for the spreading of vice, the abject poverty and the rising death rate but for the many crimes of violence, 'carried to a degree of outrageous passion,' and for the increasing numbers of crimes against property committed by people reduced to desperation by their craving for alcohol.

When in 1734 Judith Dufour, a dipsomaniac 'never in her right mind but always roving,' collected her baby from a workhouse where it had been 'new-clothed', she strangled it and left the naked body in a ditch. She sold the new clothes for 1s. 4d. and spent the money on gin.[8] It was not an exceptional crime. The Sessions Papers for the period are full of such terrible stories of men and women who would do anything to get gin and suffer any punishment rather than live without it. Even when not directly a cause of crime or an aggravation of it, the passion for spirits was indirectly responsible for widespread suffering, degradation and vice. Children were starved by drunken parents and parish nurses, they were sent out to pick pockets, they were forced to become prostitutes and many not more than twelve years old were 'half eaten up with the foul distemper' of venereal disease,[9] they were made to beg and sometimes scarred or crippled so that they might be more successful in exciting pity.

They rarely did excite it. Pity was still a strange and valuable emotion. Unwanted babies were left out in the streets to die or were thrown on to dung heaps or into open drains; the torture of animals was a popular sport. Cat-dropping, bear-baiting and bull-baiting were as universally enjoyed as throwing at cocks, and newspapers every week contained advertisements like this one taken from *The Weekly Journal*:

'At the bear Garden at Hockley-in-the-Hole at the request of several persons of quality on Monday the eleventh of this instant of June, is one of the largest and most mischievous bears that was ever seen in England to be baited to death, with other variety of Bull-baiting and Bear-baiting; as also a Wild Bull to be turned loose in the Game Place, with fireworks all over him. To begin exactly at three o'clock in the afternoon because the sport continues long.'[10]

The baiting of foreigners was no less common a diversion than the

baiting of bulls. The French traveller César de Saussure
described how unpleasant and 'almost dangerous' it was for 'an
honest man, and more particularly for a foreigner, if at all well
dressed, to walk in the streets'. For he was sure of being jeered
at, called a 'French dog' and spattered with mud and 'as likely as
not dead dogs and cats' would be thrown at him. 'If the stranger
were to get angry, his treatment would be all the worse.'[11] If he
assaulted an Englishman himself, he might even be killed like the
Portuguese visitor who after a fight with an English sailor was
'nailed by his ear to a wall. Some time after he broke from there
with the loss of part of it and ran; but the mob was so incensed that
they followed out and wounded him with knives till at last he either
fell or threw himself into a puddle of water where he died.'[12] A
Jew who had also given offence to a sailor was forced to undergo
'the usual discipline of ducking'. He was then chased to his home
in the Jewish quarter of Duke's Place where his pursuers broke
all his windows, smashed the interior and, together with the furniture, threw out into the street 'three children sick of the small-
pox'.[13]

Such wanton cruelties were not, of course, limited to the mob.
The Mohocks, a society whose members were dedicated to the
ambition of 'doing all possible hurt to their fellow creatures', were
mostly gentlemen. They employed their ample leisure in forcing
prostitutes and old women to stand on their heads in tar barrels so
that they could prick their legs with their swords; or in making
them jump up and down to avoid the swinging blades; in disfiguring
their victims by boring out their eyes or flattening their noses;
in waylaying servants and, as in the case of Lady Winchelsea's
maid, beating them and slashing their faces.[14] To work themselves
up to the necessary pitch of enthusiasm for their ferocious games,
they first drank so much that they were quite 'beyond the possibility of attending to any notions of reason or humanity'.[15] Some
of the Mohocks seem also to have been members of the Bold Bucks
who, apparently, had formally to deny the existence of God and
eat every Sunday a dish known as Holy Ghost Pie. The ravages
of the Bold Bucks were more specifically sexual than those of the
Mohocks and consequently, as it was practically impossible to obtain a conviction for rape and as the age of consent was twelve, they
were more openly conducted. An expectation of inviolability was,
indeed, shared by many, if not most young men of this class.
One evening in the 1770's, Richard Savage, who claimed to be a

son of the Countess of Macclesfield, quarrelled with some people playing cards in Robinson's coffee house, lost his temper, and ran one of them through with his sword. He was tried for murder but he was subsequently pardoned. And when a young gentleman named Plunket called at a shop to collect a wig he had ordered he did not hesitate to pick up a razor from the counter and slit the wig-maker's throat from ear to ear, because he would not reduce the price by more than a guinea.

Senseless murders such as this were as common as riots. For violence was still an accepted part of everyday life, and it was not to be expected in an age which set so little store by human dignity that it could be otherwise. Men accustomed to paying twopence to go and laugh and jeer at the lunatics in Bedlam;* to watching women knocking each other about with bare fists in the boxing ring; to throwing bricks at defenceless people in the stocks and pillory; to being given a holiday on the day of a hanging so that they could go to the fair at Tyburn and cheer as men and women slowly died at the end of the rope; to seeing their fellow human beings being whipped and burned and disembowelled and cut into four pieces; to passing the putrescent bodies of highwaymen suspended in iron cages near the scenes of their crimes—men accustomed to a life in which these things were commonplace were not likely to come to the view that brutality was inexcusable. It was not, of course, that the age was any more violent or unfeeling than those which had preceded it, but there were many reasons why it has sometimes seemed so and why it has often been so described. The contrasts between the new elegance and the familiar brutality, the awakening conscience of men who attacked evils which their forebears had not recognized as such or left unquestioned, the growth of population and industry and the means of communication and publicity, the belief that the only answer to the increasing number of criminals was an increasing number of public punishments, all tended to create the impression that Hogarth's contemporaries were somehow more heartless and squalid than Holbein's. But the cruel

* Jeering at lunatics was not, of course, a peculiarly English pastime. At Geneva and in Germany they were given grass to eat to amuse visitors, and in France, they were made to perform grotesque plays. Spectators purposely enraged them to make them more amusing. In America they were, apparently, treated with less inhumanity; but in the first hospital opened for the insane in Virginia in 1773 the emphasis was upon physical subjugation rather than treatment.

diversions of the people in eighteenth-century England were not
new diversions, the savage crimes were not new crimes, the brutal
punishments were not new punishments. A poor man who fell
down in the street was as likely to be left there unaided in 1520 as in
1750, but in 1750 when this happened outside White's coffee
house, Walpole was alive to tell the amusing and well-remembered
story that the customers inside placed bets as to whether the fellow
were dead or not and that a passer-by who suggested that he should
be bled was shouted down as this would interfere with the fairness
of the betting. In 1752 an Act legalized gibbeting[16] but bodies had
been commonly displayed in this way for at least four hundred
years. In 1750 thousands of people came out to watch the hangings at Tyburn but criminals had been publicly hanged there since
the twelfth century and the scenes then could not have been any
less grotesque. If there is no evidence, however, to suggest that
the people's manners and morals were degenerating in the first half
of the eighteenth century and, in fact, much evidence to suggest
that despite the widespread drunkenness, debauchery and violence
the progress towards enlightenment was at last quickening, there
is no denying that the period saw the beginnings of organized
crime, the growth of the first real underworld and the consequent
savage reaction of a frightened society which feared that its very
existence was threatened.

This new development in the history of crime owed much to the
activities of a single, astonishing man.

Jonathan Wild was the son of a poor carpenter and was born
in Wolverhampton in 1683. He was apprenticed when he was
fifteen to a buckle-maker in Birmingham and while still in his
apprenticeship he married and had a son. After about ten years
of buckle-making, however, he became bored with his trade and
his family and set off for London. By means of a peculiar ability
he had for dislocating his hip at will, he gave the impression to
passers-by on the road that he was painfully lame and succeeded
in arousing the pity of a woman who offered him a lift in her carriage. Soon after arriving in London he got badly into debt and
was locked up in the Wood Street Compter, where he met
a prostitute Mary Milliner, whose 'Buttock's twang' (whore's
bully) he became on his release. Within a few years he owned two
brothels and was the principal assistant of Charles Hitchen, the
corrupt and homosexual City Marshal who used his office as a
source of personal profit. Hitchen taught Wild how to make money

out of receiving stolen property and out of the rewards offered for the capture of thieves, but the association was short-lived and soon Wild was in business as a thief-taker and fence himself and his two brothels became receiving houses for stolen goods. The law dealing with the punishment of receivers had recently been made more severe and fences were now making so certain that the profits of their trade justified its risk that thieves were finding it increasingly difficult to sell stolen property for more than a fraction of its true value. Wild, whose ingenuity had already been recognized as being close to genius, conceived a profitable plan for the evasion of the law.

He called a meeting of thieves at one of his brothels and gave them his advice. They were not to bring the things they stole to him any more but to give him a list of them and the name of the person from whom they had been stolen. Wild undertook to go to the owner, say that he was acting for 'an honest broker' who had 'stopped a parcel of goods on suspicion' and that he had authority to return the articles provided that nobody was 'brought into trouble and the broker had something in consideration of his care'.

The scheme was not an original one, having been practised the previous century by Mary Frith, a highwaywoman who had a shop in Fleet Street, but Wild made it work more successfully than it had ever been worked before. The arrangements he proposed usually proved satisfactory both to the thieves who were paid more for their loot than they could get out of the ordinary fences and to the victims of the robbery who were able to take advantage of an offer to recover their property which would otherwise have been irretrievably lost. Wild himself infringed no existing law for, as it appeared, he accepted nothing directly from those who had been robbed but only shared in the legitimate reward paid to the invented broker. His business became so profitable and Wild became so well known that instead of calling on those who had been robbed he opened an office in Cock Alley where the victims of robbery might call on him.

Eventually a Bill,[17] specifically directed against Wild, by which it became a felony to take a reward for restoring stolen goods without prosecuting the thieves who stole them, was brought in by the Solicitor-General. Wild, however, made a few alterations in his technique and carried on as before. He became more and more successful and more and more rich. He bought a country house and he employed a butler and a footman. He had a manager and several clerks. He bought a sloop to take stolen goods to a ware-house he rented in Holland and to bring back contraband. He was soon the acknowledged leader of the criminal class. Those who accepted his leadership profited by his cunning; those who did not were hanged, often on perjured evidence. How far his influence in the underworld extended, it is impossible now to say; but when at last he was brought to trial, the evidence given against him suggested that his power had been immense. He was accused not only of being a receiver but of forming a 'corporation of thieves' and of dividing the whole country into districts and allocating to each its own gang; of training and appointing gangs which specialized in church robbery, picking pockets or the collection of blackmail; of sending other gangs to follow the Court, the law circuits and the various country fairs; of employing several artists and craftsmen to alter and reset stolen jewellery and objects of art.[18] That criminals were organized in this way few people had previously suspected, but that they existed in increasing numbers no one could doubt. Highwaymen infested all the main roads in the country, and in the towns street robbers watched the well-dressed contemplatively from every alley. Walpole's complaint that one was 'forced to travel even at noon as if one was going into battle' was no more than a picturesque exaggeration of an undoubted truth. Men did not wear swords for fashion's sake alone and women who took blunderbusses with them on their way to Court were prepared to use them and sometimes did. Foreign travellers found 'a surprising quantity of robbers ... all very audacious and bold'; and both they and English people took to carrying purses of false money. This, however, did not always save them, for street robbers often 'knocked down people and wounded them before they demanded their money' and were almost as active in daylight as during the night. To be stopped in a chair and robbed in Piccadilly in the middle of the morning, as the Earl of Harborough was, provided a story of only passing interest.

By working in gangs, as Wild insisted they must, criminals achieved an impunity which, in some parts of London, was complete. 'Officers of Justice,' Henry Fielding wrote in 1751, 'have owned to me that they have passed by such criminals with warrants against them without daring to apprehend them; and indeed they could not be blamed for not exposing themselves to sure destruction; for it is a melancholy truth that, at this very day, a rogue no sooner gives the alarm within certain purlieus than twenty or thirty well-armed villains are found ready to come to his assistance.'[19]

Gangs like one known as 'The Thieves' Company' were believed to pay clerks to keep their books and divide their profits, which amounted to about five hundred pounds a year (worth perhaps three thousand pounds today) for each member. Another gang with a hundred members was reported to 'have officers and treasury and have reduced theft and robbery into a regular system'. The 'Resolution Club' imposed on its members rules as strict as those observed by the Mafia. The principal rule was to 'die mute', another insisted 'that whoever resisted or attempted to run away when stopped should be cut down and crippled'. Anyone who prosecuted a member of the Club was to be marked out for particular vengeance.[20]

'London is really dangerous at this time,' William Shenstone told his friend the Rev William Jago in 1744. 'The pickpockets, formerly content with mere filching, make no scruple to knock people down with bludgeons in Fleet Street and the Strand . . . In Covent Garden they come in large bodies armed with *couteaus*, and attack whole parties.'[21] Eight years later Walpole, after having been himself attacked and shot in the face by some highwayman in Hyde Park, thought it was shocking 'what a shambles this country is grown'.[22]

The morning on which Walpole wrote his letter seventeen men were executed at Tyburn. There followed 'not the slightest diminution in crime'.[23] This was by now a tragically familiar sequence of events; but the Englishman's trust in the hangman's rope was not yet questioned. It was, after all, his only defence.

Part II

THE BEGINNINGS OF REFORM

CHAPTER ONE

THE LAW REFORMERS

'We rest our hopes on the hangman; and in this vain and deceitful confidence in the ultimate punishment of crime, forget the very first of our duties—its prevention.'

SIR THOMAS FOWELL BUXTON, MP, 1821

(i)

As Voltaire was not the first to observe, 'a man after he is hanged is good for nothing.'[1]

Even the most obdurate supporters of the 'Bloody Code' could not fail to agree with this view; nor could they deny that of the five discoverable elements in the theory of punishment—deterrence, prevention, expiation, retribution and reform—there was at least one which capital punishment certainly could not contain. But as the reform of the criminal was considered of negligible importance compared with the protection of society, this was not an argument which carried much weight in contemporary discussion.

A distinction is made now between retribution and vengeance and although it is generally recognized as wrong that there should be any degree of revenge in punishment, it is generally recognized as right that punishment should nevertheless contain some sort of retributive or denunciatory element so that there can be a just method of relating the penalty to the offence. But that this retributive element should be taken as far as imposing the penalty of death on the worst offenders, without regard to their motives or personalities, while nowadays considered by thoughtful people to be morally indefensible, was not a matter which gave much trouble to the eighteenth-century conscience.

Even those who then believed that it might be wrong for the State to exact so final a retribution from so many of its criminals, most of whom might not be beyond reform, could at least regard with comfort the fact that the death penalty was unquestionably preventive, for dead men did not escape from prison or return illegally from transportation. They could also console themselves with the reflection that it was, in the very nature of things, bound to be a deterrent to most people. But how effective, in fact, a few men felt constrained to wonder, was it as a deterrent to those whom it was intended to deter.

Cesare Beccaria, writing at a time when the death penalty was still frequently, savagely and publicly inflicted, believed that it was not only an act of ferocity but that as a threat it was neither effective nor necessary. It could only be justified if it could prevent a revolution against a popularly established government or if it was the only way of preventing others from committing crimes. But the State, he argued, had no right to inflict it and, in any event, penal servitude for life would be a more feared and, therefore, more certain deterrent. He agreed with Montesquieu that every punishment which was not soundly based upon absolute necessity was tyrannical and that the more cruel and severe the punishment, the more the minds of men grew 'hardened and calloused'.[2] He wrote these words in 1764. There were at that time few men disposed to agree with him.

Even Montesquieu, who had also insisted that penalties should be moderate, had never suggested that the death penalty should be abolished altogether, for it was the repugnant 'remedy of a sick society'.[3] And of the various new and more enlightened criminal codes which were introduced into eighteenth-century Europe, only two—those of Tuscany and Austria—did, in fact, abolish it. In Prussia, under the influence of Frederick the Great; in Sweden, under the influence of Gustavus III; and in France, after the Revolution, the scope of the death penalty was much reduced by extensive reforms in the criminal law but it still remained in the codes and was still inflicted. Catherine the Great had little success when she attempted in 1767 to curtail its use in Russia.[4] In England the reformers were quite as unsuccessful.

England's was a special case. No influential reformer went as far as to suggest that capital punishment should be done away with entirely. There were far too many earthworks to be destroyed before the citadel itself could be stormed. 'It will scarcely be credited,' wrote a magistrate in 1776, 'that by the laws of England there are above one hundred and sixty different offences which subject the parties who are guilty to the punishment of death.'[5] And the number was constantly growing until by the beginning of the following century, there was 'probably no other country in the world', so it was suggested in a Parliamentary debate, 'in which so many and so great a variety of human actions' were 'punishable with loss of life as in England'.[6] The number of a hundred and sixty capital offences was mentioned in an authoritative work published in the 1760's;[7] but by 1819, according to another authority, sixty-three further offences had been added to the formidable list.[8]

Apart from crimes such as treason, murder, piracy, arson, stealing, rape, sodomy and, in the case of people unable to read and therefore unable to plead benefit of clergy, every sort of theft of money or goods worth more than a shilling—all of which had by then been capital offences for many years—it was now an offence punishable by death to appear armed and disguised in a park 'where any deer have been or shall be usually kept';[9] to cut down a tree 'in any avenue . . . garden, orchard or plantation';[10] to set fire to an out-house;[11] to send a letter demanding money signed with a fictitious name;[12] to impersonate a Chelsea pensioner;[13] to make a false entry in the books of the Bank of England;[14] to strike a Privy Councillor;[15] to damage Westminster Bridge;[16] to refuse to remain in quarantine;[17] and to commit many other acts, more or less reprehensible, some of which had not even been crimes, let alone capital ones, before.

While the numbers of men executed for offences like these bore little relation to the numbers of men liable to execution, hangings were nevertheless common enough. They were not, of course, as common as in former centuries when, although there were fewer capital statutes, the ones that existed were less often evaded. Stow's figure of nearly two thousand executions a year between 1509 and 1547[18] is without doubt extravagant; but certainly in 1598, seventy-four people were sentenced to death in Devonshire alone;[19] and it seems that at the beginning of the following century an average of over seventy executions were being carried out every year in the County of Middlesex which did not, of course, include London where the rate was undoubtedly higher.[20] In fact, the annual number of executions at Tyburn alone has been calculated as being on average 140 in the reign of James I, before dropping to ninety in the reign of Charles I and during the Commonwealth.[21]

But although, after a period of severity in the application of capital statutes in the late seventeenth and early eighteenth centuries, the number of executions did grow less as the nineteenth century approached, there were as many as ninety-seven executions in London and Middlesex in 1785, ninety-two in 1787 and still an average of about one a fortnight in 1799. A veteran Bow Street Runner giving evidence before a Parliamentary Committee said that in the 1780's he had twice seen forty men hanged in a single day.[22] And out of every twenty criminals hanged, so it was estimated, eighteen were less than twenty-one years old.[23]

The offences which resulted in these executions give a clear indication of the intended purpose of the eighteenth-century legislature which, startled by the unrest that the social evils of the Industrial Revolution had brought about, sought to protect property by threatening life. In 1785 (the year of ninety-seven executions in London and Middlesex) only one murderer was hanged. All the other executions (apart from three, the reasons for which are not known) were for crimes against property.[24] As many as seventy-four were for robbery, burglary and housebreaking;[24] and yet robbery, burglary and housebreaking had been increasing for many years, were still increasing and continued to increase.

The reasons for this alarming state of affairs had been examined in 1751 by Henry Fielding, the Bow Street Magistrate, in his important *Inquiry into the Causes of the late Increase of Robbers*. But although Fielding saw the causes of crime in the 'vast torrent of luxury'—with its attendant evils of gin-drinking, gambling, whoring and other amusements more or less expensive—in the inadequacies of poor relief and in the defects of the administration of the criminal law, he did not consider the possibility that the law might have been more effective if it had been less severe. And although a Committee, soon afterwards appointed by the House of Commons, did suggest that the death penalty should be replaced by other punishments for some offences, the steps taken by the Commons to put this suggestion into effect were very limited and, in any event, immediately defeated by the House of Lords. Another committee was set up in 1770 and again some limited mitigation in the severity of the laws was recommended. But the only capital statutes ultimately brought forward for revision were largely obsolete and none of them related to crimes against property; and, even then, the Bill which was drawn up to repeal them was, like earlier measures, defeated in the Upper House.

Despite the caution of the House of Commons, however, and the obduracy of the House of Lords there was a small but a growing number of men in both places who were beginning to doubt the practicability, apart from the humanity, of the existing system. These men, led by such enlightened Members of the Commons as Sir Archibald Macdonald, Sir William Meredith and Sir Charles Bunbury, were not able to prevent altogether the enactment of new capital statutes; but they did succeed, on occasions, in replacing transportation for the death penalty in the Bills which were constantly being brought in for debate. They did succeed also in forcing the House to consider whether, in view of the fact that although 'the gallows groaned' the 'evil continued to increase', the blame might not be laid on 'that extreme severity (which) instead of operating as a preventive to crimes rather tended to influence and promote them, by adding desperation to villainy'.[25] And, although their few supporters in the Lords were unable to influence the decisions which were taken there with such predictable regularity, a man like Lord Holland, speaking with vigour and understanding, could prepare the ground for the more open-minded attitude which was, belatedly, to open the way to progress.

Outside Parliament, too, a feeling of discontent was growing. The national uproar of protest over the execution of a popular preacher, the Rev William Dodd, for a forgery which his champion Dr Johnson thought a crime of 'no very deep dye of turpitude',[26] made it clear that, in particular cases, public opinion was on the side of the reformers.

It was not, however, so much with particular cases, in which the emotions of the people were easily aroused, that the true reformers were concerned, but with the revision of the criminal law generally. They fought to convince their fellow countrymen that the 'Bloody Code' was not only bloody but that it did not work; and in this contention, for the moment, they were disbelieved.

When William Eden, a brilliant young barrister, proposed in his *Principles of Penal Law*, published in 1771, a thorough revision of capital statutes and the continued use of the death penalty only as a 'last melancholy resource',[27] he was angrily answered by those who saw in such pamphlets as *Hanging Not Punishment Enough* a more practical answer to the problems of the day. The author of this pamphlet suggested that for certain criminals breaking on the wheel, whipping to death and hanging alive in chains might prove more effective deterrents than the gallows in the mounting war against the criminal class. Even these methods, however, seemed insufficiently severe to George Ollyffe whose pamphlet, *An Essay Humbly Offer'd, for an Act of Parliament to prevent Capital Crimes* (1731) suggested, amongst other tortures designed to 'produce the keenest Anguish', that a condemned man should not be entirely broken on the wheel but taken off it while still alive and hung on a gibbet where his cries might bring home to other potential criminals the 'most exquisite Agonies' of retribution. Those of Eden's less extreme opponents who could not agree with these pamphleteers, believing that the increase in crime was not due to a lack of more fearful punishments than hanging but to a reluctance to inflict the death penalty in all cases allowed by law, could point with satisfaction to the Rev Martin Madan's severe and influential *Thoughts on Executive Justice* (1785) which advocated the rigorous enforcement, and even extension, of capital statutes. The year after Madan's tract appeared, it was answered by a pamphlet, *Observations on a Late Publication, Intituled, Thoughts on Executive Justice*. This pamphlet was published anonymously. Its author was Samuel Romilly.

Romilly was one of those rare men, combining a passionate humanity with a deep intelligence, who have ennobled the history of the House of Commons. Born in Frith Street, Soho, in 1757, he was the son of a Huguenot immigrant from Montpellier, a watchmaker and jeweller, who had married a fellow Huguenot much richer than himself. Samuel's early education was left largely to a nurse, a religious, gloomy woman who tried to improve the boy's mind by telling him about the sufferings of the martyrs and by reading to him long extracts from the *Newgate Calendar*.[28] He served in his father's shop, by now a rather gloomy young man himself, until a legacy of two thousand pounds from one of his mother's relatives allowed him to be articled to a solicitor and eventually to read for the bar. His great qualities were soon recognized. He was called to the bar in 1783, made a KC in 1800 and, although not then a Member of Parliament, he was offered and accepted the office of Solicitor-General in the Ministry of 'All the Talents' in 1806. He remained in the House of Commons after the fall of the Ministry the following year and in 1808 began the campaign that was to occupy his attention for the rest of his life.

By then his knowledge of the criminal laws both of England and of the Continent was unsurpassed. He had had the opportunity to observe much and he had read much. He had carefully studied the works of John Howard, the great prison reformer. He had read Jeremy Bentham's important and influential treatise on punishments and found it of 'very extraordinary merit'. He admitted a debt to Beccaria, but unlike the Italian philosopher, he thought—as Jeremy Bentham then also did so far as murder was concerned—that the death penalty was a sad necessity. 'One reason why I cannot think that death ought so carefully to be avoided among human punishments is that I do not think death the greatest of evils,' he once wrote to his brother-in-law. 'Beccaria and his disciples confess that it is not, and recommend other punishments as being more severe and effectual, forgetting, undoubtedly, that if human tribunals have a right to inflict a severer punishment than death, they must have a right to inflict death itself.' There was, though, he admitted at the same time, the grave danger of hanging an innocent man 'owing to the errors of human tribunals and the impossibility of having absolute demonstration of the guilt of a criminal', and this struck him 'more forcibly than any argument' he had 'ever before heard on the same side of the question'.[29]

It was not, however, with abstract arguments that Romilly was principally concerned. He strongly disagreed with the Rev Martin Madan's view that capital statutes should be vigorously enforced and with Archdeacon William Paley's contention in *The Principles of Moral and Political Philosophy* that the death penalty, even if only occasionally inflicted, was without question the most effective means of preventing crimes. But Romilly answered them with facts rather than with emotion. He realized, as many of those who have subsequently condemned them outright have failed to realize, that his opponents were not necessarily inhuman. They all believed in the indispensability of the death penalty as a threat to an enormous number of potential wrongdoers, but many of them were well satisfied that the lenience of juries made its infliction comparatively rare and that the criminal deserving mercy could be reprieved by the judge or, in the last resort, pardoned by the King in exercise of his Royal Prerogative of Mercy. And death sentences often were commuted in this way. In the five years 1761-1765, for instance, 567 criminals condemned to death were pardoned, most of them being transported for fourteen years instead.[30] The laws might be severe, Romilly's opponents could argue, but their relentless enforcement was mitigated by such traditional safeguards, and criminal procedure was more liberal in England than anywhere else in Europe.

Aware of the force of arguments like these and the numbers of people who agreed with them, Romilly decided to conduct his campaign with circumspection. He knew that there could be no substantial limitation of capital punishment without extensive reforms, both in the whole field of criminal justice and in social policies, and without adequate alternative punishments; but he believed that by revising or repealing most capital statutes, and thereby relaxing the excessive severity of the law, he would help to reduce crime and create an atmosphere in which more far-reaching reforms might then be possible. His approach might appear unambitious but it was formulated by a man of sound sense who did not make the mistake of underestimating the strength of his opponent's position, who knew that he must not try to achieve too much at once and that even the little that it would be possible in his day to accomplish, could only be achieved by a practical approach and a reasoned questioning of established habits of thought.

And so in 1810, when introducing three Bills to limit capital punishment, he devoted a great deal of his brilliant speech in the House of Commons to a determined refutation of Paley's doctrines, as these had gained great respect amongst the opponents of reform, but at the same time he spoke as a man whose strength of feeling was tempered by the sound common sense of the lawyer. His speech was at once moving and analytical, heart-felt and empirical. As well as a condemnation of a criminal law based on capital punishment as a 'kind of standard of cruelty, to justify harsh and excessive exercise of authority' and consequently as a barrier to social progress, it contained an attack on 'the lottery of justice' which the prevailing practice had become. With many examples and with a firm mastery of the little data which were then available, Romilly showed how the savage severity of the Statutes had resulted in the courts interpreting them in a way which undermined the authority of the law. If punishment were certain, he insisted, they need be less severe.[31]

These were views which did not command much support. Those

who argued against Romilly believed implicitly that the present system based on the death penalty was the only hope of a decent society's survival. They discounted the possibility of an efficient professional police which many of them feared—as indeed Romilly himself feared—would inevitably clash with British concepts of freedom, and they paid little attention to the problem of secondary punishments, although a writer who suggested that capital offenders should be castrated and branded received some support.[32] Led by the judges, by a majority of the bishops, by most of the other Members of the House of Lords and by several influential Members of the House of Commons, Romilly's opponents decided that the only satisfactory path was the one which successive Ministries had chosen to follow. They had allowed Romilly to have his way two years before with the repeal of an Elizabethan Statute which imposed the death penalty for pickpockets. The Statute had after all become almost a dead letter, for most pickpockets were children employed by professional thieves and prosecutions under the Act were accordingly discouraged. But the three Statutes[33] which Romilly now wished to repeal were another matter. They provided for the infliction of capital punishment on shop-lifters who stole things worth five shillings or more, and on thieves who stole things worth two pounds or more from private houses or from ships on navigable rivers. If these Acts were repealed, the death penalty would be removed from most crimes against property. Romilly had started his campaign discreetly but now his purpose of moving against all capital statutes of a like nature 'one by one', as he later put it himself in his memoirs, was revealed. Sir William Grant (Master of the Rolls), George Canning and William Wilberforce supported him; but he had few others on his side. One member said that he would never vote to 'alter the law of England' which preserved property so effectively in this 'rich and flourishing nation'; another member, Mr William Frankland, who, in a later debate, quoted at length the crimes for which the death penalty was decreed in the Book of Deuteronomy, said that capital punishment for stealing five shillings was absolutely necessary as property would not be safe without it. The death sentence frightened malefactors 'like a blunderbuss' did.[34]

Only one of Romilly's three Bills was adopted by the Commons and all of them were vehemently attacked in the Lords.

Both the Lord Chancellor, Lord Eldon, and the Lord Chief

Justice, Lord Ellenborough, basing their arguments on those of Archdeacon Paley, spoke against the Bills with passionate and sincere indignation. Lord Ellenborough's views, in fact, went even beyond those of Paley, for whereas the Archdeacon had argued that it was right that the inoperative statute against pickpockets which Romilly had successfully repealed in 1808, should go, Ellenborough thought its going marked 'a most dangerous innovation'. And when Lord Eldon suggested that, while the death penalty should remain for shop-lifters, the modifying limit should be raised from five to ten shillings, Lord Ellenborough strenuously opposed the compromise.

'I trust your Lordships will pause before you assent to an experiment pregnant with danger to the security of property,' he warned them solemnly, 'and before you repeal a statute which has so long been held necessary for public security. I am convinced, with the rest of the judges, that public expediency requires there should be no remission of the terror denounced against this description of offenders. Such will be the consequence of the repeal of this statute that I am certain depredations to an unlimited extent would immediately be committed . . .

My Lords if we suffer this Bill to pass, we shall not know where we stand; we shall not know whether we are upon our heads or our feet . . .

Repeal this law and see the contrast—no man can trust himself for an hour out of doors without the most alarming apprehensions, that, on his return, every vestige of his property will be swept off by the hardened robber.'[35]

He was, he had said, 'convinced, with the rest of the judges'. And it was probably true that most, and perhaps all, of the judges did agree with him and had their faces set, blank and uniform, against reform. They were not all merciless men. The hanging of a boy aged thirteen in 1801 for breaking into a house and stealing a spoon; of two sisters aged eight and eleven at Lynn in 1808; and of thirteen people hanged in a single assize for being found in the company of gipsies, cannot have been pleasant thoughts for them to contemplate, but the hangings were necessary, they firmly believed, if public order were to be maintained. In 1748 when a boy of ten was sentenced to death, the Chief Justice postponed the execution to consult his fellow judges. They decided, in a characteristic decision, that the law ought to take its course for the example of this boy's punishment might be 'a means of deterring other children from the like offences'. In 1800, when another boy of ten was sentenced to death, the judge who refused to respite the sentence spoke of the 'infinite danger' of it getting about that 'a child might commit such a crime with impunity'.[36] That most of the judges sincerely believed in this 'infinite danger', as so many other people did, cannot be doubted.*

So Romilly's Bills were thrown out. Lord Holland voted for them but he had little support. Lord Ellenborough had not only Lord Eldon and the judges on his side, but the Archbishop of Canterbury and a substantial following of bishops as well. Undeterred, Romilly brought his three Bills in again the following year, together with two others aimed at repealing two recent Statutes which imposed the death penalty for stealing goods worth ten shillings or more from bleaching grounds in England[37] and five shillings or more from bleaching grounds in Ireland.[38] Romilly was able to support his Bills with two significant petitions from the very people for whose benefit the laws had been enacted. The proprietors of the bleaching grounds and the calico printers were petitioning for the repeal of the Acts because their severity had made them ineffective. Their property was not being protected because prosecutions were so rare and convictions rarer.† Even Lord Ellenborough was defeated by this unanswerable refutation of the doctrine of maximum severity and voted for the adoption of Romilly's Bills 'on account of the petitions'.[40] Nine years later it was possible to examine the effect which the abolition of the death penalty for this particular offence had had. 'We have gone on long enough taking it for granted that capital punishment does restrain crime,' one of Romilly's successors, Sir Thomas Fowell Buxton, said in a debate in the House of Commons. 'And the time is now arrived in which we may fairly ask, does it do so?' Fowell Buxton was able to answer his question by telling the house that whereas crime had generally and very noticeably increased in Lancashire since 1811, the number of thefts from bleaching grounds had quite as noticeably fallen.[41]

The abolition of the death penalty for the crime of stealing from

---

* Fifty years later although boys as young as this were no longer hanged they were still cruelly treated. Between 1851 and 1852, fifty-five boys under fourteen were sent to prison for stealing less than 6d. In the same period 136 were imprisoned for stealing less than 2s. 6d.[39]

† The same complaints were made by bankers who twenty years later petitioned for the repeal of Statutes which imposed the death penalty for forgery.

bleaching grounds was the second of Romilly's successes, but he was to have only one other. In 1812 he succeeded in bringing about the repeal of an old Statute[42] which had made it a capital offence for a soldier or sailor to beg without a pass. It was his last success. His Bill to repeal the shop-lifting Act was again defeated in the House of Lords in 1811 as it had been defeated in 1810. He tried for the third time in 1813 and yet once more in 1816 telling the House that even as he spoke a boy of ten convicted of shop-lifting was awaiting execution in Newgate prison. But on both occasions, after it had been adopted by the Commons, his Bill was thrown out by the Lords. He tried for the fifth and last time in 1818 and again it was thrown out and a few months later he died. Bitterly disappointed by this latest defeat and overwhelmed with grief by the death of a wife, whom he had loved devotedly, he killed himself in November 1818 in a sudden access of despair.

Even his opponents lamented his death for the generosity of his nature had been wholly unaffected. When Lord Eldon came into court the next morning 'he was struck by the sight of the vacant place within the Bar which Romilly was accustomed to occupy. His eyes filled with tears. "I cannot stay here," he exclaimed; and rising in great agitation, he broke up his court.'[43]

The greatest and most influential of the reformers had died at a time when he was needed most. The social unrest in the country —particularly in the Midlands and the North where the 'dark Satanic mills' were already painfully changing the whole structure of society—and the end of the Napoleonic wars, which had released nearly four hundred thousand soldiers and sailors into an England unused to peace, had contributed much to a marked increase in crime, particularly in crime against property.

This was no time, the opponents of reform insisted, using a familiar argument, to make any 'dangerous experiments'. Conditions were bad enough as they were; to tamper with the criminal law would only make them worse. The safety of the country had only been preserved during the economic troubles of the 1790's, during the riots that followed the harvest failure of 1811, and during the Corn Law riots in 1815, by the 'terror of death' imposed by such capital Acts as the one passed in 1812—passed despite Lord Byron's passionate protest in the Lords—after rioters in Nottingham had destroyed stocking-frames and other machinery as being the causes of their misery.[44]

But in spite of the widely expressed fears and arguments of

those who agreed with Lord Ellenborough, the feeling in the country was beginning to change. Although Romilly had seen his campaign meet with little but abuse and contradiction in his lifetime, by the time of his death the tide had already begun to turn. It was at first a slow and scarcely perceptible process.

Capital statutes were still being created. In 1817, for instance, the death penalty was re-introduced for the destruction of lace frames and machinery, having been abolished for that crime three years before.[45] But the reformers in the House of Commons were becoming so influential that this sort of legislation would soon become impossible; and they were now supported by a strength of public opinion unknown before. The month after Romilly's death the Corporation of London drafted a petition for the revision of the criminal code. It was followed by several other petitions and resulted in a motion for the appointment by the House of a Committee of Inquiry into the Criminal Laws in 1819.

The debate on the motion was attended by 275 Members, compared with the sixty-seven Members who had attended the debate on Romilly's Bill in 1810,[46] and was remarkable for its sound sense and the obvious desire of all those who took part in it to judge the matter unemotionally upon its merits. Romilly's successors, Sir James Mackintosh and Sir Thomas Fowell Buxton both spoke with power and conviction. It was not the intention of the reformers, Mackintosh told the House, to make a new criminal code or to abolish capital punishment, but to make an attempt to place offences in more reasonable categories and find punishments to suit them. The present system was absurd and discreditable, Fowell Buxton insisted. The chances were five to one against the offender being caught, fifty to one against his being prosecuted, a hundred to one against his being convicted, and a thousand to one against the sentence pronounced by the law ever being carried into effect. He said that there were now 223 different crimes punishable by death, that four of these crimes had been made capital in the reign of the Plantagenets, twenty-seven in the reign of the Tudors, thirty-six in the time of the Stuarts and no less than 156 since.[47]

The motion was carried and the Committee which was accordingly appointed set about its business with great thoroughness. Numerous witnesses were examined and a vast amount of useful evidence was collected from merchants, bankers, shop-keepers and prison chaplains. The views of only one judge were sought because 'judges could not with propriety censure what they might soon be obliged to enforce' and they 'only see the exterior of criminal proceedings after they are brought into a court of justice'.[48]

The inquiry was mainly concerned with larceny in shops and houses and with forgery; and the subsequent recommendations of the Committee on these matters were constructive and valuable. They advised the repeal or amendment of obsolete capital statutes; and the substitution of transportation or imprisonment for the death penalty in most cases.

Although the practical achievements which followed the publication of the Committee's Report were negligible, the long debates of 1820 and 1821 served to keep the reform of the criminal law in the public mind and to prepare the way for the work which Robert Peel began soon after his appointment to the Home Secretaryship in 1821.

Peel's was not an original or creative mind, but it was an alert, sympathetic and receptive one. When Mackintosh and Fowell Buxton passed to him the burden of reform, believing that measures introduced by the Ministry would be more successful because less contentious, they knew they were placing Romilly's hopes and ideas in the hands of a brilliant administrator with the statesman's gift for judging what was practicable and what was not.

He did not go far enough or work fast enough to please the less cautious reformers, but his achievements were nevertheless remarkable. By a series of Acts passed between 1823 and 1827 he abolished capital punishment for larceny in shops, and on board ships on navigable rivers to the value of two pounds or more;[49] he repealed the Waltham Black Act which had created innumerable capital offences;[50] he abolished benefit of clergy[51] and the distinction between petty and grand larceny;[52] he made it possible for courts to abstain from pronouncing the death sentence for all convicted persons except murderers.[53] He reduced over three hundred confused statutes into four intelligible Acts.[54]

Indeed, it was this emphasis on reduction and combination that most displeased his critics. Bentham, who now demanded the abolition of the death penalty even for murder, thought that Peel was 'weak and feeble' and had done 'but little'; the *Morning Herald* said that 'Sir R. Peel's improvements were almost entirely confined to the *consolidation* and *arrangement* of certain criminal statutes, and the pruning away of certain technical incumbrances and impediments to justice. Where there was a mitigation of the severity of the law, it was done with that extreme degree of caution from which little practical benefit followed.[55]

It was certainly true that while abolishing the death penalty for various sorts of forgery he had preserved it for others; while abolishing it for those who stole two pounds from private houses he had retained it for those who stole five pounds[56]—a 'sum', one of his most uncompromising critics said, which fixed *'the price of human life!'*[57] He had consulted the judges on his various Bills, which the reformers had rarely done, and he listened to their cautious advice so that he eventually found himself defending his restraint not only against Mackintosh and Fowell Buxton, but Lord John Russell and Lord Brougham. Peel realized, though, as few of the reformers had done, that reform of the Criminal Law was dependent upon police reform and it was towards the re-organization of the police, 'the obtaining for the metropolis as perfect a system of police as was consistent with the character of a free country,' that he was cautiously but surely moving.[58]

Meanwhile the petitions still came flooding into Parliament. Men complained that the only result of raising the limit from two to five pounds in the case of thefts from private houses was that juries decided £4.19.6. had been stolen instead of £1.19.6.[59] The voices of Bentham, of Wilberforce, of John Bright, of Edward Gibbon Wakefield and of the Quakers became more and more insistent. The Press began to take up their call with less and less equivocation. And then in 1832 the movement to revise Peel's cautious Acts began and slowly gathered momentum.

Men and women were still being hanged for trivial offences and so were children. As late as 1831 a boy of nine was hanged at Chelmsford for setting fire to a house;[60] and two years later another boy of nine was sentenced to death at the Old Bailey for pushing a stick through a cracked shop window and taking two pennyworth of printer's colour.[61] In 1832 the body of a coal miner was hung in chains from a gibbet at Jarrow and the body of a bookbinder, whose execution was witnessed by thirty thousand people, was gibbeted at Leicester.[62]

Such scenes, however, were becoming much rarer now and those who advocated their continuance were becoming rarer too. Gibbeting was abolished in 1834; the pillory was abolished in 1837; and although branding had continued until 1829, for many years before that it had often been done with a cold iron or with a hot iron on a thick piece of ham held in the outstretched hand.[63] In 1831 out of 1,601 persons sentenced to death, only fifty-two were executed[64] and three years later the City of London was obliged to dismiss one of its two salaried executioners for there was so little work for him to do.[65]

Peel continued to insist that the abolition of the death penalty for any other of the diminishing number of offences for which it was retained, would be a 'most dangerous experiment'.[66] But he spoke against the country's feelings. Even in the Lords it was accepted now, as one of its judicial members, Lord Wynford, said in a debate on the abolition of capital punishment for every sort of forgery, that 'the experiment ought, in the present state of public feelings, at least to be tried'.[67]

Seven years later there were only fourteen capital statutes left. And the experiment was proving—as such experiments usually do—not to be dangerous at all.

(ii)

Executions, though, were still carried out in public and the law allowed this until 1868. Many improvements had by then, however, been made in the hangman's methods.

The first of these improvements was demonstrated on 5 May 1760. Shortly after nine o'clock on the morning of that day Earl Ferrers, a homicidal maniac 'dressed in a white suit richly embroidered with silver' left the Tower of London in his own landau drawn by six horses and was taken to Tyburn to be executed. Three months before, conceiving that his honest and hard-working steward, Mr Johnson, 'had combined with the trustees to disappoint him of a contract for coal-mines,' the Earl had ordered him to attend one Friday afternoon at the hall and there had shot him as he knelt before him on the carpet of his room.[1]

While in the Tower, Lord Ferrers had 'exhibited evident proofs of discomposure of mind', but it was not only for the entertainment of seeing a madman taken to the scaffold, nor, as Ferrers himself suggested, 'because they never saw a Lord hanged before'—his petition to be beheaded privately having been rejected—that the crowds of spectators were greater than the sheriff had ever seen.[2] It was known that a new mechanism was to be used and the people were curious to know what it was and if it would work. It did not work. It was a small collapsible platform, about eighteen inches high, supported by beams of wood to which ropes were tied. The intention was that when the condemned man was standing on the top of this platform, with the halter round his neck, the executioner should retire beneath the scaffold and on the word being given by the sheriff should pull the ropes which would drag away the props.[3] Death would thus come more quickly; hanging would be made humane. Unfortunately on this occasion when the signal was given the raised stage dropped a few inches, which was only 'far enough for the toes of the hanging man to touch it, so that Ferrers was slowly strangled'.[4] 'After hanging an hour and five minutes the body was received in a coffin lined with white satin, and conveyed to surgeon's hall, where an incision was made from the neck to the bottom of the breast, and the bowels were taken out, on inspection of which the surgeons declared that they had never beheld greater signs of long life in any subject which had come under their notice.'[5]

But although on its first public appearance the drop was seen to be a failure, its mechanism was afterwards so much improved that by 1783 it was adopted as the general method of execution. In this year also, another reform was instituted. For it had at last been accepted that 'the long parade of criminals from Newgate to Tyburn', far from providing a warning and a deterrent was the excuse for the assembly of the riotous mobs which had, by then, become an established part of the London scene. On the recommendation of the Sheriffs, Sir Bernard Turner and Thomas Skinner, the place of execution was transferred from Tyburn to a 'great area' that had recently 'been opened before Newgate in consequence of the rebuilding of the prison' after the Gordon Riots of 1780. And, in an endeavour to clothe the ceremony in an atmosphere of awful solemnity, the sheriffs also suggested that the scaffold should be draped in black, that the only man permitted to ascend it apart from the criminal and the 'necessary officers of justice' should be the chaplain, and that from the time the condemned man came out of the prison gate until his body was taken down the funeral bell should toll.[6]

The Sheriffs did not for a moment consider that the execution should be performed behind the prison walls. Such a possibility rarely was considered. Even enlightened reformers such as William Eden and Jeremy Bentham believed that the deterrent value of capital punishment would be largely vitiated if executions were not public. Bentham, indeed, advocated an even more awe-inspiring ritual than the Sheriffs, with a black scaffold, the officers of justice dressed in crepe, the executioner masked 'to augment the terror of his appearance', the judges in attendance and 'serious and religious music preparing the hearts of the spectators for the important lesson they were about to receive'.[7] Samuel Johnson, in a celebrated outburst, attacked the new 'fury of innovation'. The old methods, he said, were the best. Why was Tyburn to be swept away? he asked Sir William Scott indignantly. 'Executions are intended to draw spectators. If they do not draw spectators, they don't answer their purpose. The old method was most satisfactory to all parties, the public was gratified by a procession; the criminal was supported by it.'[8] Most people agreed with Boswell in endorsing the Doctor's views.

As it happened there was no cause for their concern. Tyburn Fair was swept away but its spirit remained. 'As many spectators as ever thronged to see the dreadful show, and they were packed into a more limited space, disporting themselves as heretofore by brutal horseplay, coarse jests and frantic yells.'[9] The noise and ribaldry were so great, in fact, that those residents in and about the Old Bailey, who were not fortunate enough to have rooms with windows overlooking the gallows which could be let for the day's performance at high rents, protested strongly against the repeated erection of the scaffold in their neighbourhood. But their protests were ignored and by the beginning of the nineteenth century, as the practice of hanging criminals at the scene of their crimes gradually died out, Newgate became the regular place of execution and the scene of increasingly disorderly outbursts of debauchery and violence. In 1807 when Holloway and Haggerty were executed for the murder of a lavender merchant it was estimated that no less than forty thousand spectators were crammed in the small area round the gallows. Women and children trying to push their way out of the suffocating mass were forced to the ground and trampled to death; and in Green Arbour Lane, when a pieman stooped down to pick up the pies scattered from his basket, several men and a woman with a baby at her breast fell over him and were also crushed to death beneath the feet of the panic-stricken mob. By the time the hanged men had been cut down and the crowds at last dispersed by the City Marshals and their constables, nearly a hundred dead and dying were found lying in the streets.[10]

But the public executions went on; and although stout barriers were put up and placards warned the people to 'beware of entering the crowd!' they had little effect.[11] At Bellingham's execution for the murder of the Prime Minister, Spencer Percival, in 1812; at the forger Fauntleroy's execution in 1824; at the murderer Courvoisier's in 1840; and at the Mannings's in 1849 the crowds were estimated as being even larger than at Holloway's and Haggerty's and quite as impervious to the object lesson in retribution which it was still expected they would be given. When Mr and Mrs George Mannings were hanged on the top of Horsemonger Lane gaol in 1849—the husband's confession: 'He moaned,' (the victim had been shot by Mrs. Mannings, a passionate Belgian woman) 'I never liked him well, and I battered his head with a ripping chisel,' is a classic of its kind—Charles Dickens was present and was, so he told *The Times* the same day, 'astounded and appalled by the wickedness' of the spectacle. 'You have no idea what the hanging of the Mannings really was,' he wrote to a friend. 'The conduct of the people was so indescribably frightful, that I felt for some time afterwards almost as if I were living in a city of devils.'[12] As late as 1864, at the public execution of Franz Müller for the murder of a bank clerk in a railway carriage, *The Times* reported that 'robbery and violence, loud laughing, oaths, fighting, obscene conduct and still more filthy language reigned round the gallows far and near'. The spectators comprised the most 'incorrigible dregs' of London—'sharpers, thieves, gamblers, betting men, the outsiders of the boxing ring . . . the raking of cheap singing halls and billiard rooms'.[13]

Yet in this same year when the whole matter of capital punishment was referred to a Royal Commission, there were still many men distinguished in public life, including several judges, who were not convinced of the undesirability of public executions. They were now, however, in the minority. Twelve years before a Select Committee of the House of Lords had recommended that executions should no longer be in public; now the Royal Commission gave the same advice, drawing attention to a report that out of a total of 167 people under sentence of death in a certain town, 164 of them had witnessed a public execution.[14] This sort of evidence was difficult to ignore, and in the next session of Parliament a private Member's bill, introduced by Mr J. T. Hibbert and providing for the future carrying out of executions within prisons, was accepted by the Government and became law in 1868.[15]*

* Public executions remained legal in France until 1939. During the Paris Exhibition of 1899, the execution of Allorto and Sellier drew more visitors than

By now the apparatus of the drop had been greatly improved. Instead of a collapsible platform, a trap-door, supported by beams and secured by bolts, was fitted into the floor of the scaffold. By means of a lever the bolts were withdrawn, the trap-door fell in and the criminal fell to 'immediate death'.[16] Or so it was supposed. In fact, death was often far from instantaneous. Sometimes, as at Tyburn, the executioner had to pull hard on the hanging man's legs; once or twice the rope broke; often there was a violent struggle. Evidence given before the Commission on Capital Punishment in 1864 revealed that the methods of William Calcraft, the official hangman of the City of London, were 'very rough, much the same as if he had been hanging a dog'.[19] Once, apparently, when executing William Bousfield, a man who had tried to avoid being hanged by throwing himself on the fire in the condemned cell and was consequently so weak that he had to be carried to the scaffold, Calcraft disappeared after having pulled back the bolt. When he was persuaded to return Bousfield, who had managed by means of frantic struggling to regain a foothold on the side of the drop, was still alive. Calcraft pushed him off. Four times Bousfield managed to regain a foothold. Four times Calcraft pushed him off and, eventually, pulled on his legs until he strangled him.[20]

After 1868, when these revolting scenes were no longer public spectacles, they were still enacted often enough behind prison walls. A black flag and a drearily tolling funeral bell were all that the crowds outside saw and heard, but after the first private execution in Newgate most officials would have preferred a return to the older methods. The condemned man broke down at the last minute when the chaplain in a 'voice trembling with emotion' had read the burial service and the execution was not completed 'without some of the officials turning sick'.[21] The responsibility was entirely theirs now. Not only had they to make all the practical arrangements, but they could no longer feel that once the condemned man left the prison for the gallows they had handed him

the Eiffel Tower. Thomas Cook, the travel agent, filled all 280 seats in seven buses which he had hired to transport his customers to the attraction. In 1939 when Weidmann was executed at Versailles all rooms with a view of the guillotine were rented at high prices long before.[17] Public executions were abolished in New York State in 1835. But they were performed in other states until well on into the twentieth century. They were not illegal in Kentucky until 1938; and two years before a man was hanged there before an estimated 20,000 spectators.[18]

over to society and that the mob outside would help in his destruction. They were responsible now, too, for the hangman's bungling and until very recent times he continued frequently to bungle. When Mathew Atkinson, the Durham miner was hanged, the rope broke and it was not until twenty-four minutes later when a new rope had been supplied that, in the words of the official Parliamentary report, 'the second hanging was successful'.[22] Not two but three attempts were made to hang a man named Lee in Exeter Prison and on each occasion the trap failed to open when the hangman pulled the lever. 'Cases also occurred in which the effect of hanging was that the prisoner was decapitated,'[23] as in the case of the hanging of Goodale by James Berry.[24] When Brownless was hanged it was the rope again which was faulty and on this occasion embedded itself into the condemned man's neck. 'The ceremony was very badly bungled,' wrote Charles Duff in his ironic *Handbook on Hanging,* 'And when completed, it presented to the onlooker a spectacle so utterly revolting that all intelligent advocates of the hangman's art trembled for its future.'[25]

In 1886 a committee was appointed to inquire into the way in which executions were carried out, the cause of the recent failures and how these failures might be avoided in future. The present procedure is largely based on the report of this committee which advocated as essential 'a thickish rope, a knot precisely placed under the left ear, and a length of drop adjusted to the weight of the prisoner'.[26]

'The knot,' Mr Albert Pierrepoint, England's most experienced hangman assures us, 'is the secret of it. We have to put it on the left lower jaw, and if we have it on that side, when it falls it finishes under the chin and throws the chin back; but if the knot is on the right-hand side it would finish up behind his neck and throw his neck forward which would be strangulation. He might live on the rope a quarter of an hour then.'[27]

In the days before Mr Pierrepoint was appointed to his post, strangulation was, in fact, the usual result. 'Dislocation of the neck,' a surgeon wrote in the *British Medical Journal,* 'is the ideal to be aimed at, but, out of all my post-mortem findings, that has proved rather an exception, while in the majority of instances, the cause of death was strangulation and asphyxia.'[28]

This, no doubt, accounts for the fact that before the Royal Commission on Capital Punishment 1949-1953 reported the fact, the condemned man was left hanging for an hour. He is now, apparently, always dead within ten seconds of the entry of the hangman into the condemned cell, unless the execution chamber is some distance away. It is usually next door and care must be taken to spare him hearing the sounds of the hangman's rehearsal. He does not, in fact, see the hangman at all until a few moments before his death. This was not so before Mr Pierrepoint's day. One of his predecessors, James Berry, who applied for his post in 1883, recorded in his memoirs that he was always anxious to get the prisoner to confess if he had not done so before the time of the execution. 'I have approached him in the cell,' Berry said, 'in a kindly manner, asking him, as it can make no difference to his fate, to confess the justice of the sentence, in order that I may feel sure that I am not hanging an innocent person. In most cases they have done so, either in the cell, or at the last moment on the scaffold.'[29]

Berry calculated 'for three minutes to be occupied from the time of entering the condemned cell to the finish of life's great tragedy for the doomed man'.[30] He was accompanied in the slow procession to the execution chamber by his assistant, the prison chaplain, nine warders and two wand-bearers.

The procedure laid down for today's hangman is more brusque. He is expected to perform his duty as expeditiously as possible. By the time he enters the condemned cell he knows the prisoner's height and weight and he has had an opportunity of studying his physique unobserved, for there are men the shape of whose necks or jaws will not permit them to be hanged.* He has had a rehearsal in the execution chamber with a bag of sand and has made the necessary adjustments to the chain and the rope.

The prisoner has known the date of his execution for some time. Throughout the time he has been lying under sentence of death he has been in the cell reserved for condemned criminals with his own bath and lavatory and visiting room. He takes exercise alone and is watched continuously by two prison officers working in eight-hour shifts. He is provided with games and books and lives on a hospital diet with special allowances of beer and tobacco and special privileges with regard to letters and visitors. On the morning of his execution, an hour before he is due to hang, the chaplain comes to talk to him. The prisoner sits with his back to the door

---

* In 1949 five men had been reprieved in the last fifteen years on account of some physical deformity. It is illegal in England to execute a man by other means than hanging.[31]

so that he will not see the executioner come in. A few minutes before the time of the hanging the Governor of the prison comes with the medical officer and the High Sheriff or the Under Sheriff to whom this duty is usually delegated. At a signal from the Sheriff, the executioner and his assistant, with the Chief Officer and another prison officer, enter the cell. The executioner pinions the prisoner's arms behind his back and, with the chaplain in front of him and an officer on either side of him, the condemned man is led out to execution. In the execution chamber he is made to stand on a spot marked in white chalk with his feet astride the division of the trap. A white cap is put over his head, the noose around his neck. The assistant executioner ties his legs together and, when everything is ready, the executioner goes down into the pit and pulls the lever which withdraws the bolts. The man falls and his neck is broken.[32]

This is the 'ideal to be aimed at', but it is not always possible to achieve it. The man may struggle or faint and if he faints he has to be carried to the scaffold and held in position by 'an officer on each plank holding him up. There's a rope for the officer to hold on to, and he stands on the plank and holds him up'.[33] Or he may be hanged sitting on a chair. And sometimes the prisoner is sick and often he defecates 'since people usually want to do this when they are frightened, and the huge shock to his nervous system when the rope tightens removes the last vestige of self-control together with the social need for it'.[34] And 'still other things happen which should happen only in nightmare dreams'.[35] Women are now required to wear waterproof underwear.[36]

In Mr Pierrepoint's experience, though, 'untoward incidents' rarely occur. In his evidence before the Royal Commission he said that he had never had to carry anyone to the scaffold. 'I have never done that,' he told the Commission. 'They have just managed to get there.' Once he admitted that a man had rushed at him as soon as he entered his cell, but he was 'not an Englishman. He was a spy and he kicked up rough.' Generally the prisoner was calm and resigned. Women, in particular, were brave. Berry had to drag two women shrieking to the scaffold,[37] but Pierrepoint thinks that 'a woman is braver than a man'. He has seen 'more executions than anyone living' and has 'never seen a man braver than a woman'.[38]*

* Dr Corre's investigations published in *Les Criminels* (1889) bear out this view. Corre investigated the deaths of eighty-eight executed criminals—sixty-

Despite Mr Pierrepoint's restrained and sober evidence before the Royal Commission, however, and despite the fact that he himself didn't 'turn a hair' at an execution, it cannot be supposed that hangings are other than revolting. In other countries and at other times they have been reserved for degraded criminals considered unworthy of any less dishonourable death. Hanging was a rare form of punishment in the ancient world and was regarded in the Roman Empire as unbecoming to a civilized state. Beheading, burning, drowning, crucifixion, impaling, stoning, smothering, boiling, flaying, precipitation from a height, destruction by wild beasts, crushing and cutting apart 'under saws and under harrows of iron and under axes of iron',[39] as employed by David, were all as revolting deaths, and most of them were more painful ones, but few of them were considered so degrading. This feeling persisted. In medieval Europe men were flogged to death, garrotted, buried alive and tied to wheels to be hacked with a sharp-edged bar until at the fortieth stroke life was extinguished by a blow on the breast and above the heart or on the nape of the neck. Heretics and coiners were burned alive together with murderers, robbers, sodomites, adulterous women and wizards suspected of dealing in poisons. Suicides were put in casks and thrown into rivers and matricides were boiled in oil. But only the lowest of men, without friends or money or influence, were hanged and left on the gallows to rot or to be eaten by birds or to be cut up by those who dealt in the magical or prophylactic parts of the human body; and only Jews were hanged on special beams with a cap lined with hot pitch on their heads and a dog beside them to show the world how despicable they were.[40]

Criminals frequently begged to be beheaded rather than die disgraced by being hanged. 'Beheaded as a favour' is a frequent entry in the diary of Hans Schmidt, the Nuremberg executioner, who recorded the case of a man who successfully pleaded to be executed by the sword rather than the rope as otherwise his two daughters might not find husbands.[41] Women were very rarely

---

four men and twenty-four women. Of the men, only eighteen appeared calm and resigned and remorseful, twelve were cynical and theatrical, four 'accepted their fate in a state of extreme nervous excitement accompanied by loquacity,' five seemed indifferent, the remaining twenty-five died in 'abject fear' or after a desperate struggle with the executioner. Of the women only five seemed afraid; one—a poisoner—demonstrated 'a revolting cynicism'; the rest died self-possessed and repentant.

hanged because in an age of chivalry, whatever their crime, their sex must not be dishonoured. By the terms of the Karolina Criminal Code of the Emperor Charles V a woman guilty of infanticide might be buried alive or impaled or 'if water for the purpose was conveniently at hand', she might be drowned; but she could not be hanged. In 1580 women were granted the privilege of decapitation in Germany, but unless the headsman was expert the privilege was one which she might well have wished to forgo. Valentin Deusser, according to a contemporary report, was clearly not an expert. In 1641 he was instructed to behead 'a poor sinner' who was so 'very ill and weak' that she had to be half-carried to the scaffold.

'When she had sat down upon the chair, Master Valentin, the headsman, walked round her like a cat round a hot broth and held the sword a span from her neck and took aim and then struck the blow and missed her neck and struck off a piece of her head as big as a dollar and struck her down from the chair. Then the poor soul got up quicker than she had sat down and this blow did not harm her. Then she began to beg that she should be allowed to go, because she had been so brave; but all in vain; and she had to sit down again. Then the Löwe (assistant) wanted to take the sword and strike with it himself; but this the master would not allow, and himself struck a second blow somewhat stronger, so that she again fell to the ground, and then he cut off her head as she lay upon the scaffold. Whereupon he would soon have been stoned to death if the armed town guard had not rescued him.'[42]

In England, where beheading was unknown to the law, but for peers of the realm traditionally replaced hanging, the ceremony was more often bungled than not.* A characteristic occasion was the execution of the Duke of Monmouth which has been described by Macaulay.

'Here are six guineas for you,' Monmouth said to the executioner. 'Do not hack me as you did my Lord Russell. I have heard that you struck him three or four times.'

Disconcerted by this, the executioner nearly missed the Duke's neck altogether, inflicting only a superficial wound.

---

* The axe was used instead of the sword, although in other countries this was considered a mark of ignominy. In Denmark, for instance, the sword was used for the more privileged criminal who was allowed to have his hands free. The rest were bound, laid face downwards on the scaffold and beheaded with an axe.[43]

'The Duke struggled, rose from the block, and looked reproachfully at the executioner. The head sank down once more. The stroke was repeated again and again, but still the neck was not severed, and the body continued to move. Yells of rage and horror rose from the crowd. Ketch flung down the axe with a curse. "I cannot do it," he said, "my heart fails me." "Take up the axe man," cried the Sheriff. " Fling him over the rail," roared the mob. At length the axe was taken up. Two more blows extinguished the last remains of life; but a knife was used to separate the head from the shoulders. The crowd was wrought to such an ecstacy of rage that the executioner was in danger of being torn to pieces and was conveyed away under a strong guard.'[44]

In France the swordsman was often as clumsy as Jack Ketch with his axe and a bungled execution had the same effect on the crowd. After an execution in 1517 Flurat had to fly for safety to his house which was burned down over his head;[45] and in 1626 the head of the Comte de Chalais was eventually hacked off at the twenty-ninth stroke of the sword.[46]

When there were several heads to sever one after the other, the difficulties naturally increased. 'After each execution, the sword is unfit for another,' warned Charles-Henri Sanson, hereditary Executioner of the High Works, when asked to advise the Jacobins on the problems of dealing with the great numbers of executions which the Revolution entailed. 'It is absolutely essential that the sword, which is liable to chip, should be sharpened and whetted anew if there are several condemned persons to be executed at the same time; it is therefore necessary to have a sufficient number of swords in a state of readiness ... It should further be noted that swords have often broken during such executions.'[47]

But it was not only considerations like these that led Dr Guillotin to suggest to the Constituent Assembly 'a simple mechanism' for decapitation. Another and perhaps even more important reason for his proposal was that a machine, used as a sole means of execution for all Frenchmen, would mean an end to beheading as a privilege confined to aristocrats.

The guillotine certainly seemed not only a faster but also a less humiliating means of death than the hangman's rope. Byron who saw a model despatch three robbers in Rome was deeply impressed by it.

'The ceremony,' he wrote, 'including the *masqued* priests; the half-naked executioner; the bandaged criminals; the black Christ and his banner; the Scaffold; the soldiery; the slow procession, and the quick rattle and heavy fall of the axe; the splash of blood, and the ghastliness of the exposed heads—is altogether more impressive than the vulgar and ungentlemanly "new drop", and dog-like agony of affliction upon the sufferers of the English sentence.'[48]

The guillotine was probably not a French invention. Italy had such a machine in 1266, Germany in 1300; the Irish, too, had an early model.[49] In England the Halifax gibbet law has been traced back to a remote period and by the middle of the sixteenth century a thief found guilty of stealing 'to the sum of thirteen-pence half-penny' was 'forthwith beheaded upon one of the next market-days' by the engine which the people of Halifax had erected for this purpose on Gibbet Hill.[50] In Edinburgh the Scottish Maiden,* introduced into Scotland by the Regent, the Earl of Morton, who had been impressed by the efficacy of the Halifax gibbet which he had seen on a visit to England, was in use by 1581 when one of its earliest victims was Morton himself.[51]

These, though, were isolated machines and although a crude model existed in France at the beginning of the seventeeth century, it was not until Dr Antoine Louis, secretary to the Academy of Surgeons, presented detailed plans for the machine advocated by Dr Guillotin that its use as a national means of execution was accepted. The French imagination was immediately captured. It was reproduced in miniature as a table decoration; its design was incorporated in earrings, brooches, snuff boxes, cups and plates; it was given a profusion of nicknames—*Louisette* and *La Petite Louison* (in honour of the doctor who had designed it), the People's Avenger, the National Razor, the Patriotic Shortener, *La Veuve*, *L'Abbaye de Monte-à-Regret*, *la Butte, la Bascule,* Lady Guillotine, Sainte Guillotine—it became a popular tattoo mark, it became a toy: an expensive toy for '*aristos*' who placed an effigy of Robespierre between its uprights and watched for the blade to fall, the head to be severed and the spurt of red scent from the neck; a cheap toy for children who, as the *conseil général* of Arras discovered, amused themselves by chopping off the heads of mice.[53]

* Its name was, perhaps, derived from the celtic *mod-dun* which originally meant the place where justice was administered. A more popular belief, however, is that it was called 'the maiden' because it remained in Scotland a long time before it was used.[52]

It was immediately recognized as being an undeniably expedit-
ious instrument of death; but did it, those who saw the grimacing
heads in the basket wondered, kill instantaneously? In 1795 this
question was much debated, as when Charlotte Corday's head was
held up that year and slapped by the assistant executioner, men
swore that it not only blushed but showed 'most unequivocal signs
of indignation'.[54] For more than a hundred and fifty years, doctors
in France have been conducting experiments in their efforts to discover the answer to the question.

The debate is not yet ended. Within the last few years Drs
Piedlièvre and Fournier have concluded that 'death is not instantaneous. Every vital element survives decapitation ... (It is) a
savage vivisection followed by a premature burial'.[55] 'Sudden'
death is certainly rarely sudden. When the heart stops beating,
so experiments conducted at Dr Vladimir Aleksandrovich
Negovsky's Resuscitation Laboratory in Moscow suggest, the
brain cut off from its oxygen supply turns to an emergency system
of breaking down sugar for energy by anaerobic glycolysis and this
is effective for five or six minutes. It must be hoped that the brain
in a severed head, as the brain in a man who has been hanged,
although still living is not fully conscious.

But as executions in France have been carried out in the prison
yard since 1939, the number of spectators being limited to nine
officials by Article 26 of the *Code Pénal*, there is no longer an
opportunity of the public to judge for itself like there was in the
days of Charlotte Corday.

At least—although whether this is a comfort or not is arguable
—the condemned man does not know as he does in Britain and
the United States, when he is to die. A little before dawn
two warders in stockinged feet approach his cell. They enter
suddenly, wake him up and tell him his appeal has failed. He is
offered a cigarette, a glass of rum, the consolations of the chaplain;
then he is taken to the records office where the hair is cut from
the back of his neck and the upper part of his shirt is cut away. His
record sheet is produced and he signs it and underneath the
Director of the prison writes, 'handed over to M. the Executioner
for carrying out the sentence'. His ankles and wrists are tied up
(before the film *Nous Sommes Tous des Assassins* was shown he
would have already been kept shackled in leg irons)* and he

* By Article 13 of the French Penal Code of 1810 a parricide was required
to go to the guillotine barefoot, wearing only a shirt, with his head covered by a

hobbles to the prison—it is the Santé Prison as all executions are held there. 'The assistants thrust him sharply against the *bascule*. It tips him into position. The *lunette* closes round his neck. Monsieur de Paris presses the lever. The jaws of the grab open. The knife falls. The head drops into the bucket, the body is tipped sideways into the long coffin-shaped basket. Society can breathe again.'[57]

The guillotine is peculiar to France. The hangman's rope is employed in Turkey and the Irish Republic as well as in Britain. Spain chooses garrotting, Greece the firing squad.[58] In America, custom varies from state to state. New York State was the first to adopt the electric chair and this seemingly clean, painless, quick and egregiously modern device was soon adopted by fourteen other states.

'The culprit is fastened by straps to a firmly-built chair, his head is shaved and upon it is strapped one of the electrodes in a cap fitted with a sponge soaked in salt water so as to make the contact close in order to prevent burning. The other electrode is fastened to the ankle. The current is then turned on at the switch by the executioner, left on for a certain number of seconds, and turned off. After a short interval it is again turned on and then turned off, this process repeated as often as necessary to produce death.[59]

'As the switch is thrown,' a former Warden of Sing Sing wrote, 'there is a sputtering drone, and the body leaps as if to break the strong leather straps that hold it. Sometimes a thin wisp of smoke pushes itself out from under the helmet that holds the head electrode, followed by a faint odour of burning flesh. The hands turn red, then white and the cords of the neck stand out like steel bands.[60]

The length of time before death came, Professor L. G. V. Rota thought, varied 'according to the subject'. Some had a 'greater physiological resistance than others'. But he did not believe that anyone killed by electrocution died instantly, 'no matter how weak the subject' might be.[61]

The realization that it was not, after all, so quick or so painless as its advocates suggested led other states to search for more humane methods. Utah overcame the problem by allowing its con-

black veil. And until 1832 his right hand was to be cut off before his neck. The other provisions were repealed in 1958.[56]

demned criminals to choose between hanging and shooting.* But Nevada in 1921 decided to despatch them by means of hydrocyanic gas; and Major D. A. Turner of the United States Army Medical Corps, who made a thorough investigation of the problem in an attempt to discover the 'quickest and most humane method of putting a human to death', came to the conclusion that there was nothing more efficacious than gas. Three or four attempts had sometimes to be made before a man could be killed in the electric chair; men remained conscious for anything from three to fifteen minutes after the hangman's trap was sprung; death did not always come instantaneously to the man who was shot even after the riddling of his heart; but with gas, Major Turner thought, unconsciousness came immediately and 'death almost so'.[63]

Gas, also, has the advantage that its administrator has a less unpleasant task to perform than the more traditional executioner. Not that the expert executioner seems to find his employment objectionable. Anatole Deibler who did not want to enter the profession that his family had customarily followed for generations was an exception; and even he, after having joined the army where he was received with derision and disgust and having consequently changed his name and tried to settle down in a department store where, on his identity being discovered, he was again tormented, at last decided that he could no longer protest against his fate and joined his father in the service of the guillotine.[64] And although he suffered from haemophobia and on at least one occasion screamed hysterically after an execution that his perfectly clean coat was spattered with blood, he performed his duties thereafter without complaint. By the time he retired he had severed as many heads as all but the most active of his ancestors.

The family tradition has continued to the present day. André Obrecht who was appointed executioner in 1957 has Deibler blood in his veins and is, in addition, 'tortuously related' to the Desfourneaux—executioners before the Revolution—as well as to the Sansons.[65]

The family tradition is almost as strong in England as it is in

* They usually choose shooting.   Since 1912 only one man (executed in 1958) has chosen hanging. When he is to be shot the condemned man is strapped to a chair and a heart-shaped target is pinned on his breast. The firing squad—five volunteers one of whom has a blank cartridge—stand twenty-five feet from him, but the four bullets do not always hit the target. At an execution in 1951 none of them touched the target and the condemned man bled to death.[62]

France. 'It's in the family, really,' says Albert Pierrepoint who succeeded his uncle who had succeeded his father.[66]

In neither country do the rewards of office explain this family loyalty to an esoteric craft. France's executioner receives a monthly income but it is a small one. England's hangman gets ten pounds and expenses for each execution and his assistant gets three guineas.[67] This is much less than his nineteenth-century predecessors received. William Calcraft, who was executioner to the City of London until 1874 had a guinea a week and another guinea for each execution when hangings were much more common. He also got half a crown for each man he flogged and a retaining fee of five guineas for acting as executioner at Horsemonger Lane Gaol. He also hanged men in country prisons for which he got as much as Pierrepoint did a hundred years later.[38] Nor can the family loyalty be explained by any esteem which the executioner enjoys by virtue of his public office. In the past he was detested and was compensated accordingly. Schmidt who began his career as assistant to his father, the Bishop of Bamberg's executioner, received, when he became the 'Mate of Death' at Nuremberg, not only a good salary, a free house and a fee for each execution but fees for each infliction of torture as well. He was given compensation for prisoners who were respited and allowed to make a profit on the rope, wood and brimstone which he used. In addition he was able to increase these perquisites by the sale of human hands and skin to the superstitious. When he retired he felt relieved to have at last become 'a respectable person'.[69]

In pre-Revolutionary France the hereditary Executioner of the High Works was even better rewarded. But with the arrival of the guillotine the art went out of decapitation. There was also no longer any danger that the mob, enraged by an unskilful performance, would attack the executioner; and so the payments gradually diminished. The executioner was, thereafter, regarded not with loathing and awe and occasional admiration but with disdain—and with fascination. The fascination has, of course, increased, with the disappearance of public executions. There is something secret and mysterious about the whole process now; and if the unhealthy attitudes that this secrecy and mystery engenders stood alone as an argument against capital punishment, the argument would be a weighty one.

Did people ask him questions about his duties? Pierrepoint was asked by the Royal Commission on Capital Punishment.

'Yes,' the hangman replied. 'But I refuse to speak about it. It is something I think should be secret to myself. It's sacred to me really.'[70]

These are the words of a devotee or even of a cabbalist. The family tradition, in that sense at least, is explained.

There are, of course, many outsiders anxious to break in. When the last of the Deiblers retired there were numerous applications for the vacant post including three engineers, a solicitor, a former boxer and a former barber, a medical student, two unemployed journalists, a watchmaker and, apparently, a 'deputy foreman of works'.[71] When Berry applied for and obtained the post of hangman in 1883 there were 1,399 other applications.[72] For several years past the Prison Commissioners have received an average of five applications a week.[73] The ambition that prompts these men to apply for so distasteful an appointment, the Royal Commission concluded, 'reveals qualities of a sort that no State would wish to foster in its citizens.'*

Whether many of these applicants possess the qualities necessary in a competent hangman—apart from the apparently not uncommon willingness to become one—is to be doubted. They must be more than mere technicians, Charles Duff has observed, they must be artists. For 'is not a man an artist who can painlessly and without brutality despatch another man? There is a certain delicacy about the operation which needs a steady eye, a swift-working brain, cool and calculating, and a cleverness which is only to be found in the realm of the great arts.'[75]

The hangman must also be unemotional. John Ellis, who resigned in March 1924, tried to commit suicide after his experiences in the cruelly grotesque hanging of Mrs Thompson, and succeeded at a later attempt.[76] In the same year the German executioner, Schweitz, shot himself at Breslau; and his successor, Paul Spaethe, also killed himself having 'prepared the way to depart this life by burning one candle for each head that he had severed during his short term of public office'.[77] In earlier centuries the executioner often had no need of suicide for he was so frequently condemned to death himself. In 1368 the German executioner, Meister Friedrich, was burnt alive for coining; a successor, Meister Hans, was beheaded for treason.[78] Cratwell, the London hangman, was

---

* It is presumably not irrelevant to notice here that an American criminologist is reported to have said that he knew a guard in a Northern penitentiary who had an orgasm while watching an electrocution.[74]

executed for robbing a booth at Bartholomew Fair in 1538; and in later years Derrick, Brandon, Price, Rose, Marvell, Thrift, Turlis and Dennis were all found guilty on capital charges. Marvell, in fact, was actually on his way to Tyburn to hang three other criminals when he was served with a writ. He was told he could carry on with his duties if he promised to obey the summons later. He agreed to carry on but the crowd would not let him. He was attacked and wounded so badly that he lost consciousness.[79]

The ideal executioner is, of course, a man of a different cast. If he has criminal or suicidal tendencies he has overcome or sublimated them. He is usually unimaginative and often pious. It is invidious to despise him or to scoff at him. He is the servant of the State.

CHAPTER TWO

THE POLICE REFORMERS

'My own opinion is that nothing is well done which is not paid for specifically.'

L. B. ALLEN, A MAGISTRATE, 1821

(i)

A FRENCHMAN travelling in England in the early eighteenth century was surprised to discover that there was 'a queer law to encourage counties to get rid of thieves'. If a person 'is robbed of a considerable sum in the daytime and on the high road,' he wrote home to his family, 'and if he declares the theft to the Sheriff of the county before the sun sets, and can prove that the sum has been taken from him in such and such a place, the county in which he has been robbed is obliged to refund him the sum. This happened to a friend of mine, who was robbed of two hundred guineas. Being able to declare the theft, and to prove it before the sun went down, he had no difficulty in recovering the amount from the sheriff of the county of Hertfordshire.'[1]

In some cases, too, a county could be held responsible for the payment of damages to the executors of anyone killed while trying to arrest a criminal. But these attempts to force the people to concern themselves with the repression of crime, and to compel them to remain their own policemen as they had theoretically been for centuries, were losing favour. The principle of mutual liability was being gradually denied by Statutes imposing restrictions and limitations on victims who made claims for damages.[2] And when Edmund Burke brought in a Bill to make local people collectively responsible for the victims of shipwrecking gangs, he had no success; for while his fellow Members agreed that the only way to make the people of the coast behave humanely was to appeal to their selfish interests, they did not agree that collective responsibility was the right means of arousing these interests. They believed in the more positive methods which were by then the established cornerstones of the eighteenth-century system—the stern repression of crime by an increasingly severe criminal law and the offer of rewards to all those who brought criminals to justice. By these two methods, it was hoped, order would be maintained and the establishment of a professional police force might be avoided.

More and more reliance was placed on voluntary associations of armed civilians and the Trained Bands of respectable, trustworthy citizens like John Gilpin, who, always available in times of crisis, had stopped the advance of Charles I at Turnham Green and undertook to protect London against rioters and thieves as well as Jacobites during the rebellion of 1745. Reliance was placed, too, on military guards, on special constables, on squads of additional watchmen raised and paid for by business houses and private residents, and on societies whose members were devoted to the capture and prosecution of felons and other 'lewd and scandalous persons'. These societies, indeed, like the trade guilds of former times, became a sort of voluntary police force employing paid informers and securing numerous convictions. Originally created as societies for the reformation of manners, they had been adopted by the Methodists and were more concerned with morals and religion than with the activities of the professional criminal class. They were particularly interested in the laws against the breaking of the Sabbath which were still numerous. It was forbidden for people on a Sunday to stay away from a place of worship allowed by the Toleration Act without excuse,[3] to play games outside their own parishes,[4] to do 'worldly Labour, Business or Work except Works of Necessity and Charity',[5] to put up for sale 'wares, Fruit and Goods (except Milk and Mackerel) before and after Divine Service',[6] to use a 'Gun or other Engine for destroying Game',[7] to drive cattle or to transport goods in a wagon.[8] It is not, then, surprising to learn that one society alone—the Society for the Suppression of Vice—was able to prosecute over six hundred people during the first two years of its activities for breaking one or other of these laws.[9] Nor is it surprising to learn that this and other societies were viewed with dislike and suspicion not only by those otherwise innocent people who wanted to work or play on Sunday, not only by publicans, prostitutes and brothel-keepers, who were also hunted out by the societies' agents, but also by many people who saw in their activities a threat to freedom and in their emphasis on the blessings of patience, frugality and religion an impediment to political and social reform. Not content that it was an offence for a person having been educated in or 'at any Time having made Profession of, the Christian Religion in this Realm' to deny 'any one of the persons in the Holy Trinity or the Holy Scriptures to be of Divine Authority',[10] not content that swearing and drunkenness were Common Law offences, these societies influenced a movement which strove to make the law even more stringent than it had been during the Commonwealth. They tried, for example, to make it a crime to publish newspapers or play in a band at Windsor on Sunday, to be a prostitute or an adulterer, even to hold a fair. They wanted to tighten the laws against the publication of obscene books and prints; and one of them, the Proclamation Society, persuaded the Attorney-General to institute proceedings against 'Monk' Lewis for writing the macabre book from which he derived his nickname,[11] and succeeded in sending to prison for a year the impoverished publisher of Paine's *Age of Freedom*. But it was not so much the societies' interference with freedom of thought, as their reliance on spies and informers to attack the pleasures of the poor, that eventually caused their decline. One tract published under their auspices went so far as to suggest that men should lay informations against the lower classes but not against their social superiors. Daniel Defoe as early as 1698 condemned the laws which they had inspired as 'Cobweb Laws in which the small Flies are catch'd and the great ones break through;'[12] and more than a century later Sydney Smith was voicing a similar complaint in the *Edinburgh Review* when he said that the 'immediate effect of a voluntary combination for the suppression of vice, is an involuntary combination in favour of the vices to be suppressed'. 'The fear of God,' he thought, could 'never be taught by constables, nor the pleasures of religion be learnt from a common informer.'[13] The Society for the Suppression of Vice ought to denominate itself 'a Society for suppressing the vices of persons whose income does not exceed five hundred pounds per annum'.[14]

These sentiments were repeated in the House of Commons when

a Bill, more commendable than most of those sponsored by the societies, was introduced to prohibit bull-baiting. Canning spoke of the 'unfairness of depriving the poor of their pastimes while the great were left in possession of theirs;' and Windham referred to the 'petty, meddling, legislative spirit' of those who had 'a most vexatious code of laws for the protection of their own amusements'.[15]

While concentrating on the pleasures and vices of the poor, the societies left the problems of the administration of the law and the reform of the police undiscussed; and year by year these problems were growing. The danger came not only from thousands of independent criminals and numerous criminal gangs but from the mob—the 'Fourth Estate' as Henry Fielding had called it, 'that very large and powerful body' which threatened the existence of the other three estates of the realm.

Some attempt to control the activities of the mob in its more dangerous moments had been made in 1714 by the passing of a Riot Act[16] which made it a capital offence for twelve or more people to remain 'riotously and tumultously assembled together' for an hour after being commanded by proclamation in the King's name to disperse. But often, in fact, when any serious riot threatened, no Justice or other authorized officer could be found who was willing to perform what might prove a dangerous duty; and in view of the sort of men whom he had as constables to assist him, this could not always be considered inexcusable.

A series of Acts passed in the early years of the century recognized the need for more peace officers and an improved nightly watch,[17] for the confirmation of the principle that all citizens must assist the authorities in pursuing and arresting criminals,[18] for rates to be levied and money set aside for law enforcement.[19] But no Act could be effective so long as the average magistrate remained a grasping and probably illiterate grocer or chandler or shoemaker whose shop was his court and who made a trade of justice; so long as the average constable remained a man serving by proxy who was paid so little for his service that he soon fell into the habit of taking bribes and collecting protection money; so long as Henry Fielding could truthfully describe the 'watchmen in our metropolis'—like the Bellmen or 'Charlies', who had helped them patrol the streets in Stuart times—as being 'chosen out of those poor old decrepit people who are, from their want of bodily strength, rendered incapable of getting a livelihood by work. These men, armed only with a pole, which some of them are scarcely able to lift, are to secure the persons and houses of his Majesty's subjects from the attacks of gangs of young, bold, stout, desperate and well-armed villains.'[20] And even if not too old, or frightened or lazy to pursue young criminals, watchmen could usually be bribed. John Poulter, a professional criminal who was hanged for robbery in 1753, recorded in the account of his life that he wrote in Ivelchester gaol that once, as he was shopbreaking with his gang, a watchman walked by. One of the gang took him away while the others carried on with their work. This was always 'easily done for a Quart of Drink'.[21]

Yet men preferred to trust their lives and property to such guardians as these, who were, after all, part of the 'ancient institutions established by the wisdom' of their ancestors, and a guarantee, at least, of constitutionality, rather than to establish a professional police. For it was not only from fear of tyranny and love of freedom that the eighteenth-century Englishman refused to countenance such a step, but from fear of change. They felt that their country's escape from what they took to be the prying interference and ruthless oppression of the police of Europe was a constant cause for self-congratulation. The very word police—a French word not used in official English until 1714—was, in its modern sense, unknown. The idea of policemen paid by the Government might be all very well for Frenchmen and other foreigners who had to find a use for their standing armies at times when they were not under danger of attack from across their frontiers—the term *gendarme* was a corruption of the French for men-at-arms—but such an arrangement would not do for the island race of Englishmen. There was, of course, another reason, too, that prejudiced them against a professional police force, and that was its cost. The loss of hundreds of thousands of pounds worth of goods and money stolen each year was more acceptable than the supposedly prohibitive cost of paying enough men to prevent it. What little money was spent by the Government and local authorities was devoted to the payment of rewards as an inducement and encouragement to private enterprise. These rewards, misguidedly offered, often corruptly won and usually accompanied by a free pardon to those in need of one, were the eighteenth century's main answer to the problem of detecting crime.

They had already been given a firm legal basis at the end of the previous century by an Act which offered a reward of forty pounds for the conviction of a highwayman.[22] The recipient of the reward was to receive, in addition, not only a free pardon but the highwayman's horse, weapons and money unless it could be proved that they had been stolen. Once recognized as a practicable device for the apprehension of criminals, the system developed fast until the criminal law became full of 'Parliamentary rewards' for the conviction of a wide variety of criminals and of ways in which pardons could be demanded and obtained. It developed, too, as a system of apprehending criminals for specific crimes. The offer of rewards for the capture of named men or the perpetrators of named crimes had long been practised. After the battle of Worcester in 1651 a reward of a thousand pounds was offered 'for the discovery and apprehending of Charles Stuart and other Traytors his Adherents and Abbettors', and when the Civil War was over similar rewards were offered for the capture of the regicides and for the conviction of Jesuits and seminary priests.[23] But it was not until the following century that the idea took firm hold and rewards were offered regularly both by the Government and by local authorities. By then the offer of a 'Tyburn ticket', exempting the holder from liability for certain parish duties, had also been recognized as an additional incentive by Statute.[24] And as this ticket was transferable and consequently had a cash value, it was a valuable document. In the parish of Covent Garden, where the duties of constable were particularly unwelcome, it could be sold for twenty-five pounds and at an auction in Manchester a 'Tyburn ticket' once fetched as much as three hundred pounds.

The regular practice of the Government in offering rewards was soon followed by insurance companies, businesses and private individuals. In 1716 the directors of the *Hand in Hand Fire Office* and the *Union Office* jointly announced the offer of a reward to 'such who shall discover any wilful and unlawful practices by which any of the late Fires were occasioned'.[25] By 1830 the *County Fire Office* were recommending rewards of as much as five hundred pounds during the Hunger Riots for men who gave evidence which resulted in convictions for arson—'enough to compensate a man for leaving his part of the country, for he could not remain in it with safety after giving evidence'.[26] Manufacturers organized subscription lists and offered rewards for the conviction of men who destroyed their machinery; relatives and neighbours of families who had been robbed made offers of rewards for the conviction of the thieves, often vying with each other for the credit of promising the largest reward; pestered minorities offered rewards for the conviction of their persecutors, like the Dissenters of Birmingham who offered a hundred pounds (without success) for the discovery of the author of various handbills which had maliciously attacked them; while numerous high-minded associations for the prosecution of felons promised rewards to the common informer for conviction of so many sorts of evil-doer that men made handsome incomes by devoting the whole of their time to the 'information trade'.

The common informer, a free-lance policeman, recognized as early as the seventh century by the laws of Wihtred, survived until 1951. Hated and despised for at least five centuries, he had been given extensive powers in the reign of Edward VI by a statute which provided that a man who laid information against a pauper, proved to be 'living idle and loiteringly', was to be given the wretched vagrant as a slave for two years.[27] Although this statute was repealed in 1549, advantage had been taken of it often enough for common informers to be described by Coke as 'viperous vermin' who 'did vex and depauperize the subject . . . for malice or private ends'.[28]

It was not, however, until the eighteenth and early nineteenth centuries that the common informer, used by authority as both a detective and a prosecutor, was able to take advantage of so many statutes making provision for his services, that he could become a rich man. Various offences relating to hackney coaches worth fifty shillings a conviction were, admittedly, not prosecuted with any great profit, but each conviction for illegal hawking and peddling could yield five pounds and a conviction for stealing a dog yielded ten pounds. Commercial frauds were a particularly profitable field, while the successful prosecution of a man who had opened an unlicensed garden for music or dancing within twenty miles of London would bring to the informer the whole of the penalty inflicted which could be a hundred pounds. And as much as £166.13.4. could be earned if the convicted man had offered opportunities for his customers to play an illegal game. A sound knowledge of the law as a whole was not necessary, for most common informers specialized in a particular type of offence or in offences peculiar to specific localities. An informer practising in Oxford, for example, would know that he could make money out of anyone who fraudently claimed exemption from his parish duties, who wrongfully exercised the functions of a proctor, or who failed to obtain the licences which were necessary to practise as an apothecary and to sell wine within the precincts of the University;[29] but he would not need to familiarize himself with the nineteen different offences relating to London hackney coaches.

The opportunities for blackmail were, of course, limitless. An ambitious informer, apparently, once demanded of a rich victualler no less than 'three thousand, six hunder pounds of "lawful money of Great Britain" he having contrary to the statute on sundry occasions, tolerated in his house, room, garden, or other place diverse posture-makings, jigs and violin scrapings'.[30] Few victims were capable of paying such sums, but the Gin Acts forced thousands of otherwise more or less respectable shopkeepers outside the law and provided a reward of five pounds on each conviction. Information was laid against twelve thousand poor people who had been compelled to ignore the regulations requiring them to buy expensive licences in order to stay in business and about three thousand unlicensed dealers, so it was calculated, paid ten pounds each to avoid arrest.[31]

The activities of the detested common informer were directed mainly against the petty law-breaker, but the offers of rewards led to the creation of another species of private policeman who practised as a regular occupation the more dangerous profession of hunting and prosecuting the professional criminal. The man who first demonstrated how profitable this profession could be was Jonathan Wild, whose activities as an underworld leader provided him with exceptional advantages. He was, in fact, as he boasted himself, 'Thief-Taker General of Great Britain and Ireland'. But for Wild, thief-taking was not merely a profitable occupation, it was a means of keeping control of his criminal empire. He was a cruel man, so savage that he could cut off the ear of one of his mistresses during a quarrel to 'mark her for a bitch', so vindictive that he could send a man to the gallows for daring to suggest that he would not let Wild sleep with his wife, but he was cunning and shrewd as well. He knew that by threatening those who tried to cheat him or who refused to work for him with 'the feel of the hangman's hemp', and by proving that it was in his power to make them feel it by regularly sending independent criminals to Tyburn, he could keep his enemies in fear of him and his own men wary of him, while at the same time earning not only a reward for the conviction of those who underestimated his power but also the gratitude of honest people who, from the reports of his activities which he so assiduously supplied to the Press, were led to believe that he was their courageous servant. It was in his power, he once boasted without undue exaggeration, to hang every thief in the metropolis. He had a remarkable memory for a face as well as for a fact and in case this memory should ever fail him he carried a notebook in which were entered details that kept hundreds of thieves in his control. He was careful, too, to maintain a reputation for keeping his word. A criminal promised a safe conduct never had cause to fear a visit to Wild's house whatever the reason for his summons. He could, it was well known in the underworld, secure acquittals as surely as convictions by bribing juries and buying perjured evidence, so that those within the narrow limits of his friendship could feel secure.

How many convictions he secured will never be known. The newspapers of the time were full of stories about his successes which included the arrest of a hundred street robbers in Southwark in a single day. In a petition to the Lord Mayor he said that he was 'very desirous of becoming a freeman of this honourable city' and complacently called attention to the fact that he had sent over sixty criminals to the gallows. Two years later he claimed that he had secured the convictions of 'seventy-two of the worst felons in the metropolis'.[32]

In 1725 Wild was hanged himself for a violation of the Act against receivers which had been named after him.[33] But although his criminal empire split up and fell into less capable hands after his death, the profession of thief-taking, which he had made so profitable, grew and prospered.

A Frenchman who watched Wild's execution thought that it was a mistake to get rid of so successful a policeman. The Government had disposed of a robber but 'he was only one, and by his help several were hanged every year'.[34] The Government agreed that thief-takers were indispensable, and after Wild's death gave them further opportunities by adding to the number of felonies which carried a reward. Already the number of people entitled to share in the reward had been increased, for thief-taking was recognized as being a dangerous profession and it was often impossible to catch a thief single-handed. Rewards were accordingly made available to those who were injured while trying to bring criminals to justice and arrangements were made for shares in rewards to be given to those who helped thief-takers make their arrests. So divided up, in fact, did rewards often become that it was sometimes scarcely worth the trouble of collecting them and frequently the expenses of prosecuting were greater than the profits. The thief-taker soon learned this, and finding it worth his while to prosecute a housebreaker, highwayman or counterfeiter for his share in a reward of forty pounds but not worth the trouble or possible risk to go after an army deserter for one pound or even a cattle thief for ten pounds, he would provoke the man guilty of a lesser crime to commit a greater one so that he could then make more money out of him. Some thief-catchers, indeed, enticed young men from the country to commit crimes and even advised them how to do it and which houses to rob and then arrested them as they came out with the valuables. A few did not even trouble to act as *agents provocateurs* but relied on perjury to obtain convictions.[35]

A case which revealed the corruption that permeated the whole system was tried in 1756.

There were three prisoners in the dock, John Berry, Stephen Macdaniel, and Mary Jones, and they were charged with the 'wilful murder of Joshua Kidden, in maliciously causing him to be unjustly apprehended, falsely accused, tried, convicted, and executed, well knowing him to be innocent of the fact laid to his charge, with an intent to share to themselves the reward'.

They were found guilty and sentenced to death, but they were all immediately respited because there was a doubt that the facts proved against them amounted in law to murder. The Attorney-General, however, declined to argue the question, for what Blackstone called, 'prudential questions'. The Government evidently feared that the incentives of pardons and rewards might lose their efficacy if it were felt that the witness, by giving evidence, might endanger his life. So the three prisoners were discharged.

What had happened was this: One day in December 1753 Joshua Kidden had been in a public house in London where he had had a conversation with a man he had not previously met. He had mentioned to this man that he was out of work and badly needed a job. The stranger asked him to go with him to Tottenham to help a friend of his remove some goods from a house before they were seized for rent. Kidden agreed, but when he arrived in Tottenham the man told him that the goods could not be moved that day and gave him eighteen pence for the time he had wasted. Then the two men set off back to London together.

Travelling on the road that day in a chaise was Mary Jones.

She had been to Edmonton, she said later, to see a man who owed her nineteen pounds and was returning to Drury Lane. A friend drove the chaise and an officer from the Marshalsea prison, who had also gone with her in case she had difficulty in collecting her debt, made his own way home. During the return journey the horse fell because of a worn buckle-strap and she had to get out and walk until the animal, which had kicked up a great deal, calmed down again. She was about to get back into the chaise when two men came up from behind.

'One of them held my arms,' she said at Kidden's trial, 'and taking a great knife out of his pocket said he would stick me and that fellow in the chaise too, if I spoke a word. "You old bitch, if you say a word I'll run you through, and the man too!" '

Having taken her purse the two men ran away. Her companion was lame so he could not do much to help her, but he whipped up the horse and had soon caught up with the robbers. One jumped over the ditch and escaped but the other was caught by the Marshalsea officer who, providentially, happened to have reached that particular spot. Both Mrs Jones and her companion recognized Kidden as the man who had threatened her with the knife.

Kidden protested that he had done nothing of the kind. He said that the man who had taken him to Tottenham had lagged behind him on the road and when he had turned round to find out why he was walking so slowly, he had seen him rob Mrs Jones. 'He then ran after me,' Kidden told the court, 'and said, "Here, I have some money," and would have forced half a crown into my hands, but I refused it. Then he said, "John, don't leave me, I must step into the ditch and ease myself;" and walking gently on, to wait for my companion, up starts a thief-catcher and collars me.'

Kidden's story was not believed and he was convicted. The court ordered that the statutory reward of forty pounds should be divided up between Mrs Jones (fifteen pounds), the Marshalsea officer, Stephen Macdaniel, (twelve pounds) Mrs Jones's companion, John Berry (eight pounds), a constable (five pounds).[36]

Many months later, when the activities of this 'hellish crew', as John Fielding called them, had been exposed by the painstaking efforts of Joseph Cox, a High Constable of Blackheath, the innocence of Kidden—and of many other victims of the 'crew's' perjury—was proved. But by then it was too late. Kidden had been hanged.

Despite the obvious disadvantages of the degrading system of rewards, however, it survived the eighteenth century; for not only was it difficult in the absence of both a public prosecutor and a professional police to find an alternative, but many of those whose opinions on law enforcement were widely respected, supported it in principle. Bentham was one of these, and another was Henry Fielding.

The reputation which this great man and his half-brother John won for themselves as justices was unassailable in their life-time, and remains so still. They made the office of magistrate respected and began a process which resulted in the adoption of what seemed to most of their contemporaries an unthinkable system of police.

When Henry accepted the offer of a magistracy at Bow Street he had no such ideas in mind. He took the appointment because he needed the money. His career as a dramatist had come to an end when, as a consequence of the political lampoons directed against the shameless corruption of the Government in his caustically satirical comedies, the Licensing Act passed into law and the Little Theatre in the Haymarket where his company had performed was obliged to close. His new career as a barrister was not a successful one; and his novels did not sell well enough for him to indulge his many extravagances. He asked a friend who had been at Eton with him to find him a job, and he arrived at Bow Street almost penniless.

His predecessor there, Sir Thomas de Veil, was an extravagant man, too. He was also, in his more limited way, a great one. His methods were crude and his manner was vulgar; he was proud that he made a thousand pounds a year from being a 'trading justice'; he had a huge appetite for women and to the end of his life, after having had four wives and twenty-five children, still kept a 'private closet for the examination of the fair sex' where he 'served himself by means of his office' to a 'great variety of young ladies'.[37] But if he 'had little virtue', as the *Gentleman's Magazine* said of him when he was dead, 'he had less hypocrisy.' He was certainly one of the very few magistrates in London who made any real attempt to enforce the law. Most of the rest, as Burke said, were 'the scum of the earth', only concerned with making money by any means they could.*

---

* One of their most profitable means was to issue warrants against people, usually prostitutes, for imaginary crimes and then to let them out on bail for which the magistrate received 2s.4d. each time. A witness before a Parliamentary

De Veil was the son of a poor clergyman who educated him at home and then apprenticed him to a mercer who went bankrupt. He joined the army as a private, was given a commission in Portugal and in 1729 at the age of forty-five, as a captain on half-pay, was appointed to a magistracy in Leicester Fields. For his services in endeavouring to enforce the Gin Acts and to break up the big criminal gangs he was secretly rewarded by the Government out of the Secret Service Fund and so became the country's first paid magistrate.[38] He deserved the money and his success and he deserved his knighthood for, although his motives were not selfless, he had displayed great courage in his fight against crime with only a few corrupt constables, informers and thief-takers to help him. And when he claimed proudly towards the end of his life that he had been personally responsible for the execution or transportation of 'above nineteen hundred of the greatest male-factors that ever appeared in England', the boast was a well-founded one.[40]

By the time de Veil moved to the house on the Duke of Bedford's estate in Bow Street, Covent Garden, he had become, in effect, London's first police commissioner as well as its first stipendiary magistrate, for his authority extended all over London except the City. Bow Street, thereafter, became the most important magistrate's court in London.

De Veil's career seemed to himself, as well as to the Government, a vindication of the principle that crime was best prevented by an appeal to private interest. Henry Fielding was too much of a realist to discount the effect of this appeal, but he was a more far-sighted man than de Veil, understanding that the prevention of crime was more important than the catching of criminals and that to prevent crime it is important to try and discover what causes it. Fielding had de Veil's courage but he had many other qualities that his predecessor did not possess. He had a remarkable know-ledge of the criminal law and a remarkable capacity for hard work. He was, above all, a man of deep understanding, of determination and of integrity. Although, like de Veil, he received an unofficial allowance from the Government, he refused to make money out of fines or fees levied on the poor and consequently his income was very meagre.[41] He had clear-cut opinions and the ability to express

committee said that by 'taking up a hundred girls, that would make at two shill-ings and four pence, £11 13 4. They sent none to gaol, for the bailing them was so much better.'[39]

them in lucid prose. His *Inquiry into the Causes of the Late Increase of Robbers* published in 1751 contains not only an investigation of the causes of crime, but an indictment of many aspects of the administration of justice. Many of the views expressed seem negative and unoriginal today and some, such as his condonation of the severity of the law, are undoubtedly repressive; but they did not appear so at the time. The tract made a profound impression and much of what was best in it influenced the growing movement for reform. The practical expression of his ideas which were carried out in Bow Street had an even deeper influence.

He arrived at Bow Street in 1748. De Veil had been dead two years and had been succeeded by an inept old man who had allowed the office to decline into its former inefficiency. Of the eighty parish constables of Westminster—most of them proxies—Fielding found that only six had the qualities for which he was looking. But these six, trained by the sensible and trustworthy High Constable of Holborn, Saunders Welch, were fired by Fielding's enthusiasm, and when their year of office expired all of them agreed to stay on, although they could expect no payment other than the ordinary thief-taker's rewards.[42] They became known and ultimately respected as 'Mr Fielding's people' and were the prototypes of the Bow Street Runners.

In handling serious disturbances Fielding had to rely on military troops as his predecessors and successors had to do; but by constant appeals in the Press to the public to report crime to 'Henry Fielding, Esq., at his house in Bow Street', the existence of a small but successful civil organization was made known. After little more than a year the newspapers were able to report that, 'Near forty, highwaymen, street robbers, burglars, rogues, vagabonds, and cheats had been committed within a week by Justice Fielding.'[43] It was, perhaps, a small beginning but each year the efficiency of the force of men at Bow Street grew and each year its numbers increased.

In 1754 Henry Fielding died in Lisbon; but the plan which he had inaugurated was extended by the blind half-brother who had loved him so devotedly and so greatly admired him. The 'Blind Beak' who, it was said, could recognize three thousand thieves by their voices, remained at Bow Street for twenty-six years. When he died most of the plans which he and Henry had drawn up together were developed and shown to be successful. By the 1760's there were always honest orderly men on duty at Bow Street and, between the hours of one o'clock and two and between five o'clock and nine, at least one magistrate. The idea of a preventive police, consisting of regular controls, put into practice as early as 1755, was extended in 1763 when the Horse Patrol began operations to cover all the roads leading into London. A regular Foot Patrol was in existence by 1782.*

The need for an actively co-operative public and a more satisfactory means of tracing criminals, recognized by Henry Fielding's announcements in the Press, was to some extent satisfied by the publication after 1772 of the *Quarterly Pursuit* and the *Weekly or Extraordinary Pursuit*, early forms of police gazettes and John Fielding's 'favourite preventive machine'. In these publications descriptions of wanted criminals were distributed from Bow Street to all 'the Mayors, Chief Magistrates and Acting Magistrates of the United Kingdom'. Early lists contained detailed descriptions of a variety of wanted men such as:

Samuel Broughton, by trade a worsted weaver, about five feet two inches high, brown hair, his right arm is withered and is shorter than the left, generally wears light clothes, charged with felony at Norwich . . . *William Thompson,* by trade a butcher, about five feet five inches high, pale complexion, effeminate voice, light curled hair, flat nose the end of which turns up, charged with felony in Leicestershire . . . *William Rouse,* alias *Riley,* about twenty-two years of age, five feet two or three inches high, fair complexion with a long hook nose, wears his own hair, had on a light coloured fustian frock and waistcoat and leather breeches, broke out of Cambridge gaol, being under sentence for horse-stealing . . .[44] *Benjamin Bird,* a tall thin man, pale complexion, black hair tied, thick lips, the nail of his forefinger of his right hand is remarkably clumsy, comes from Coventry, and is charged with several forgeries, the last at Liverpool . . . *John Godfrey,* pretends to be a clergyman, middle sized, thin visaged, smooth face, ruddy cheeks, his eyes inflamed, a large white wig, bandy-legged charged with fraud at Chichester . . .

---

* The Horse Patrol was reorganized in 1805 and again in 1821 when the London streets were so infested with robbers that the Foot Patrol was obliged to restrict its activities to the Metropolis. The Horse Patrol was consequently reinforced and divided into two branches, the mounted and dismounted, each of four divisions comprising 161 men in all. They were all ex-cavalrymen and they wore a uniform of blue double-breasted coat with gilt buttons, scarlet waistcoat, white leather gloves, and black leather hat. Each carried a pistol, sabre, truncheon and handcuffs. All of them had to be married and they were given a cottage near the road they had to patrol.[46]

Elisha Nash, a husbandman, tall and thin, talks fast, black hair, full teeth, round shouldered, charged with felony in Essex.[45]

It is a tribute to John Fielding's determination that any of the schemes he so persistently recommended came to fruition, for the Government, unwilling to spend any more money than they were obliged to, gave him little encouragement. *The Quarterly Pursuit,* in fact, only came into existence after Fielding had demonstrated the value of circularized descriptions in 1771, when, following the murder of a Mrs Hutchings in King's Road, Chelsea by a gang of Jews, one of the gang turned King's Evidence and described his accomplices. By dispersing their descriptions through the Post Office and the offices of Excise and Customs, Fielding's men were able to arrest four of them almost immediately in Birmingham.

Fielding even had difficulty in getting the Government to reimburse him for his expenses. He had frequently to remind the Home Office that money was due to him and had to account for every penny he spent. In 1756 his annual record of expenditure on his own men and outside informers went into such detail as:

Finding evidence for a murder, 1/3

For an information of counterfeit half-pence, 2/6

For suppressing an illegal music meeting, 4s

For detecting an imposter and suppressing a dance, 8s

For opening a pavement on suspicion of murder, 12s

For dragging the ponds to find the clothes of Cannicot's Wife that was murdered, £2. 2s

For dresses, tickets and other expenses to proper persons for detecting and apprehending nine notorious gamblers at the Ridotto, £8. 2s. 6d.

For sitting up in an hospital with a highwayman that was wounded till fit to be examined, £1. 11s. 6d.

For pursuing Watts, a housebreaker to Bristol, for horse-hire twenty days, £3. 10s.[47]

The more successful Fielding became, the less the Government were prepared to support him. As soon as crime seemed less prevalent, his allowances were reduced. Thus, having allowed what they considered a generous sum for the destruction of street-robber gangs, which had more or less been broken up by the middle of the 1750's, the Government decided that the police funds could thereafter be cut down. Then, after the Horse Patrol, established in 1763, had kept the roads relatively clear of highwaymen for some months, the fund which had been made available to Fielding for this purpose by the Chancellor of the Exchequer was discontinued.[48] And yet all the allowances which were paid to Fielding as the 'first magistrate for Westminster', were insignificant compared to the sums which were still paid out annually by the Government in rewards. By 1786 the total of these had risen to £10,840 and by 1787 to £15,060. After falling in the intervening years, the figure rose to £18,000 in 1815.[49] The share which the Bow Street Runners had of these rewards, according to their own evidence before a Committee on the State of the Police of the Metropolis, was negligible. By the time the money had been divided up amongst all those who had a claim upon it, John Vickery, one of Bow Street's most successful Runners, said there was not enough left for either himself or any of his colleagues to make more than forty pounds a year.[50] Men as well-known as Vickery, of course, made good incomes by accepting private commissions; and some of them were worth the large sums paid to them, although there were others who brought the Bow Street Runner into disrepute and evoked memories of the McDaniel and Berry scandal which had almost destroyed John Fielding's little force in its early stages and caused him to publish a denial in the *Public Advertiser* that his own 'honest and faithful men' had any connection with 'wretches' who 'by assuming the character of thief-takers' had brought that very 'laudable employment' into disgrace.

So long as Fielding was alive the claims he made for his men were more or less justified. But after his death the reputation of the Bow Street Runner as an impartial servant of the law began to decline. The famous Runners, like Townsend, Sayer, Vickery and Ruthven, became little more than private detectives. James Townsend, an amusing man with the tastes of a dandy, was often employed by the Court and was on friendly terms with both George III and the Regent. George Ruthven spent a great part of his time travelling in Russia and Germany in the service of the Empress and of the Prussian Government. 'We attend the nobility and gentry,' John Sayer said, 'and if any accident might happen to them, we might get five or six guineas.'[51] Others were paid by the proprietors of theatres or banks and all of them, it seems, considered themselves quite independent. When John Vickery learned that there was to be a robbery at a post office he did not give the information to a magistrate but went direct to the solicitor to the Post Office and made sure that he was paid for it.

John Sayer, on his own initiative, carried on negotiations between the bank robber, James MacKoull and the Paisley Bank in Glasgow for the return of about twenty thousand pounds that MacKoull had stolen on the understanding that proceedings against MacKoull should be dropped. Sayer left thirty thousand pounds when he died and at least some of the money was in notes stolen from the Paisley Bank. Townsend left twenty thousand pounds and Ruthven died in receipt of pensions from Russia and Prussia as well as from the British Government.[52]

But although the Bow Street Runner was the most celebrated result of a system based on personal incentives, all constables were open to private hire. Being unwilling and unpaid delegates of the parish or corrupt proxies, 'necessarily degenerate,'[53] or even men who 'from age and imbecility (were) not equal to any service',[54] they were, with few exceptions, as likely to encourage crime as to prevent it. They did not consider themselves liable, 'to interfere in any criminal case, unless expressly called upon to do so.'[55] They were encouraged to do their duty partly by the thief-takers' rewards which they, of course, like all other citizens could win or share, and partly by being allowed fees for a great variety of jobs which they might otherwise attempt to avoid. These included attending petty sessions, billeting soldiers, going on a night search, making sure that shops and public houses were shut during Sunday services, patrolling fairs and making lists of jurors.[56] They were rewarded, too, by being given a share of fines imposed by magistrates who, so one of them once said, sometimes ordered a fine to be paid rather than condemn a criminal to some other form of punishment, which would leave the constable with 'nothing for his pains'.[57] A Hornsey constable got ten shillings for every vagrant he brought before the local magistrate, the Rev Henry Owen, who admitted having sentenced 'about five hundred' of them, sometimes on the constable's evidence alone.[58] It was, after all, quite wrong, another magistrate considered, that a constable should be 'compelled day after day and night after night to go in search of some atrocious ruffian' without specific reward and merely because it was his duty.[59]

These views might have been more acceptable if, in fact, constables had gone out night after night in search of atrocious ruffians. But for the most part they could not be induced to do so, often coming to terms with informers and thief-catchers so as to avoid competition for the rewards and even refusing to arrest criminals in districts where the allowances for doing so were too low. They sometimes even declined to bring in offenders against one law in case by doing so they reduced the numbers of offenders against another and more profitable one. It was, for example, more profitable to leave coiners alone so that the supply of rewards for bringing in utterers did not dry up. Constables in many districts, indeed, contributed more to the crime rate than the criminals themselves. They could be fined for neglect of their duty, but there was no satisfactory way of proving that they were neglectful.

Many of them went into business as coal or tobacco merchants or into any trade which supplied not only publicans who could be threatened with the loss of their licences but also the owners of disorderly houses and gambling dens who could be threatened with a closing order. And the number of such places was immense. A return for three parishes, with less than sixty thousand inhabitants in all, revealed that in 1817 there were 360 brothels of one sort or another in the area, employing two thousand prostitutes.[60] Apart from the profits to be made out of supplying these houses with the goods of their particular trades, constables grew rich on 'hush' money which for some of the more successful proprietors meant as much as a thousand pounds a year.[61] Even if a constable was not an active profiteer in vice, by being in trade he made it difficult for himself to act impartially; and one constable complained to a Parliamentary committee that his business had suffered a loss of two hundred pounds a year because he had offended his customers during the Corn Law riots merely by doing his duty.[62]

If the average constable was becoming increasingly corrupt, the watchmen were no less lazy and decrepit than they had been a hundred years before, and newspapers were repeatedly making jokes at their expense. 'It is said,' the *Morning Herald* told its readers, 'that a man who presented himself for the office of watchman to a parish at the West End of the Town very much infected by depredators, was lately turned away with this reprimand—"I am astonished at the impudence of such a great strong sturdy fellow as you are, being so idle as to apply for a watchman's situation, when you are capable of labour".'[63] In another paper a derisive advertiser called for:

'A hundred thousand men for the London Watchmen's Company. None need apply for this lucrative situation that have not attained the age of sixty, seventy, eighty or ninety years, blind with one eye and seeing very little with the other; crippled with one or both legs; deaf as a post ... and such that will neither hear nor see what belongs to their duty, or what does not, unless well palmed or garnished for the same.'[64]

Prostitutes were their most common garnisher, paying them 'gin money' for a licence to parade unmolested up and down particular beats.[65] When not asleep in their watch-boxes, as these watchmen so frequently were, they would pass their spells of duty sitting in public houses or brothels or even in flash houses.

No one knew how many flash houses there were, for the police were unwilling to admit the existence of more than they could plead the necessity for as means of communication with the underworld; but they could be found all over London. Some of the more notorious were the *Jane Shore* (the landlord here was a parish officer who hung his staff above the bar), the *Adam and Eve* in Shoreditch, the *Angel and Crown* in Whitechapel, the *Falcon* near Soho Square, the *Wheatsheaf* in Drury Lane, *The Rose* in Monmouth Street, the *Cock* in Bishopsgate, the *Jew's Harp* near Regent's Park, *Jesse's* beyond Clement's Inn, the *Brown Bear* in Bow Street and the *Black Hell* in Winfell Street. Besides providing food and drink and an escape at the back or through the roof, these flash houses let out 'beds and private rooms either for the night or otherwise' for 'gambling and debauchery'. Some were patronized largely by coiners, some by 'petty thieves', others by criminals 'of the higher scale', but nearly all of them were remarkable for the numbers of young boys and girls that frequented them.[66] Indeed, at several houses in St Giles's there were never any customers but boys and girls and at one of them four hundred beds were made up for them every night.[67] At the *Bull's Head* in Vere Street the boys were rarely more than eighteen years old and often only twelve and some of the girls were no more than eight. There was dancing here twice a week and beds were provided for 'the occasional retirement of the boys and girls but not to sleep all night'. Several of the girls between eight and ten were prostitutes under the protection of boys of 'nearly a correspondent age'.[68]

But they were not only places of entertainment, they were also hiding places for men and for booty and the known haunts of fences. Crimes were planned in them and thieves started out on their excursions from them and returned to them to share their plunder. They were clubs for criminals and schools of crime.

Constables, like watchmen, were frequent customers, joining in the gambling and being plied with drink until they were 'dead drunk at the expense of the boys and girls' and 'the business of the house' could go on 'without any molestation'.[69] The constables, when questioned by a conscientious magistrate, would excuse their visits as necessary in order 'to obtain information'. And on occasions—although they were comparatively rare occasions—the excuse was justified and information was obtained and used. A magistrate 'felt bound to tell' a Parliamentary committee in 1816 that 'many of the most notorious thieves' would have escaped had it not been for these 'particular places of rendez-vous' which afforded the means of getting them into his power.[70]

But in the same year in which that Parliamentary committee was appointed, the trial of various police officers showed how many of them were concerned to keep these places—and indeed all facilities and agencies for crime—open for quite different reasons. At this trial the activities of the policeman as the instigator of crime was again revealed. George Vaughan of the Bow Street Patrol and Robert Mackay of the City Patrol, together with other police officers, had apparently been working for months in conjunction with professional burglars and as *agents provocateurs*. One incident suggests the ruthlessness of their methods. An accomplice, named Barry, went up to a ragged Irish labourer in Cheapside market.

' "My master," said Barry, "has plenty of employment for some smart fellows; but it is very *hard* work."

"Oh!" answered the poor man, "I want bread and do not mind how hard the work."

"Oh! But there is some hazard in it!"

"Why," continued the poor fellow, "So has every kind of work; mounting a ladder five stories high with a heavy load of mortar . . . is attended with great hazard; but an Irish labourer does not care much for danger."

"I know that," said Barry. "But this is work of a very peculiar kind, and I know that no man is bound to stay at work he does not like . . . My master would not hire anyone, but such as will take a solemn oath that if he leaves the work he will never speak about it." '

This young Irishman together with three others who joined him, agreed to take the oath and so all four of them were taken to a room where some metal, a file, a pair of scissors and other tools were laid out on a table. Realizing now what it was they were required to do, they decided to leave the house under the pretence of going out for their dinner. But in the hall Barry stopped them and told them that they need not go out, as dinner had been ordered for them. Soon afterwards the police officers came into the house and arrested them for coining. At their trial they felt bound by the oath which they had taken, and refused to reveal the plot and so were found guilty and sentenced to death.

It was only through a revealing remark made during the trial and followed up by the Lord Mayor, Sir Mathew Wood, whose suspicions had been aroused by it, that the true facts came to light. Fortunately by then a priest had told the four young Irishmen that they need not consider themselves bound by an oath which had been administered unlawfully. They were pardoned and discharged and settled down on a farm in Ireland bought for them out of money collected on their behalf by the Lord Mayor.[71]

It was, of course, inevitable that a system of law enforcement based largely on appeals to personal interest should have led to so much corruption. Despite the obvious incapacity of the system to check the growth of crime, however, the movement for police reform developed pitifully slowly and with many setbacks. Henry Fielding's ideas influenced the Committe of Enquiry appointed by the House of Commons in 1750 and John Fielding's work influenced the Committees of 1770 and 1772 but none of these committees did more than suggest minor improvements. Some of their suggestions passed into law, but little of this legislation was of even temporary value. Acts passed in 1751 and 1753 regulated the licensing of public houses, but magistrates connived at their evasion and twenty years later the 'liquid fire by which men drink their hell beforehand' was being sold as before.[72] An Act passed in 1752 empowered judges to reimburse private prosecutors for their expense in taking criminals to court, but the office of public prosecutor was not instituted for many years and in the meantime private people continued to be reluctant to go to the trouble and expense of prosecuting.* An Act of 1756 allowed the

---

* This problem was still not solved in 1818 when the Hon. Henry Grey Bennet, the Radical M.P. for Shrewsbury, brought in his Bill to abolish Parliamentary rewards and to give new powers to the courts to compensate prosecutors and witness for their trouble and loss of time. Bennet had been chairman of the Select Committee on the State of the Police of the Metropolis which had sugges-

constable of Westminster to pursue criminals across parochial limits but only a few constables were prepared to pursue criminals even within their own parishes. An Act of 1774 carefully prescribed the duties of watchmen, regulated the length of their beats and specified their rattles and staffs, but the watchmen themselves remained the ineffective 'perambulating Horologists' and 'Hour-bawlers' which they had always been.[73] Several Acts were passed in attempts to limit the amusements and regulate the morals of the people, but the people's appetite was merely whetted. The traditional framework was left unquestioned.

And then, in the stifling hot June of 1780, London fell for four wild days into the hands of a desperate mob and the imperative need for a new system of professional police was unmistakably clear.

The riots began on 2 June when the Protestant Association led by Lord George Gordon, a lank, embittered demagogue of striking gifts and astonishing eccentricity, delivered to Parliament a petition demanding the repeal of a recently passed Act granting some minor relief to Roman Catholics. By nightfall the town was in uproar. Chapels, prisons and hundreds of houses were burned to the ground within the next few days; escaped convicts, drunken toughs and gangs of apprentices and prostitutes terrified and molested the inhabitants. At least seven hundred people lost their lives.[76]

'Such a time of terror,' Dr Johnson told Mrs Thrale, 'you have been fortunate in not seeing.' And in this time of terror, while the flames from Langdale's distillery made the sky 'look like blood' and the screams of rioters filled the air, 'a watchman with his lantern in his hand,' passed by the wall of St Andrew's church-yard, 'calling the hour as if in time of profound tranquillity'.[77]

It was not only the watchmen who were useless. Everywhere that constables or magistrates were wanted they were not to be found, or being found were not to be persuaded to use their authority. All except a very few hid themselves away until the trouble was over and some City aldermen, who hoped to profit from

ted that apart from relaxing the severity of the law the only way to bring more criminals to justice was to make it a less expensive business for the private prosecutor and his witnesses. His Bill eventually became law after some amendments.[74] But pleas for a Public Prosecutor, backed by Jeremy Bentham and Patrick Colquhoun, were ignored. It was not, in fact, until 1879 that a Public Prosecutor was appointed.[75]

the Government's danger, actually professed themselves on the side of the rioters. The constables in Alderman Bull's Ward continued to wear blue cockades, the symbols of the Protestant Association, long after this organization had dissociated itself from the riots; and the Lord Mayor, a former brothel owner, unconcernedly told Lord Beauchamp, as the houses of Irish labourers in Moorfields blazed around them, 'The whole mischief seems to be that the mob got hold of some people and some furniture they do not like and what is the harm in that?'[78]

Even when troops were called out, magistrates could never be found to give them any orders, let alone to read the Riot Act. It was not until the King threatened to head the Guards himself if the military authorities were not given the powers which the 'great supineness of the civil magistrates' denied them, that order was restored by a decision of the Privy Council permitting military officers to open fire on a lawless mob without waiting for a magistrate's orders.[79]

The decision, as Horace Walpole predicted, although accepted at the time, raised a storm of protest when the Riots were over. During a debate in the House of Lords, the Duke of Manchester strongly attacked the Government for authorizing the military to open fire on civilians and a suggestion made in a previous debate by Lord Shelburne, while the rioters were shouting in the streets outside the House, that the alternative to martial law was a more efficient police, based perhaps on the better aspects of the French police, was almost universally condemned.

'It must be evident,' Lord Shelburne thought, 'that the Police of Westminster is an imperfect, inadequate, and wretched system. The commission of the peace is filled by men, base to the last degree, and capable of every mean act derogatory and opposite to the justice of the laws which their office obliges them to administer with truth, equity and wisdom. The miserableness of the Westminster Police is so obvious that the example of yesterday points it out as the fit object of reformation and shows most forcibly that it ought to be entirely new modelled and this immediately ... Recollect what the Police of France is. Examine its good but do not be blind to its evil.'[80]

There was no doubt that this advocacy of a professional police on the Continental model deeply shocked most Members in both Houses, and when the danger was past it was not seriously debated again for many years. The Gordon Riots had made them aware of the problems presented by so large and so unruly an under-world, growing year by year and scarcely submerged beneath the level of decent life; but the Government looked back to the old methods for a solution rather than forward to new ones.

The associations of armed civilians, such as the London Military Association, which had done so much to help to restore order during the riots, seemed to provide one solution. Jonas Hanway, the philanthropist, whose book *The Citizens' Monitor* appeared a few months after the riots, was one of the associations' most influential advocates. He recommended 'a plan of police', comprising volunteer bodies each of twenty-three men from the 'opulent part of the community in each parish'.[81] The idea found some support, particularly in the City where the aldermen saw in it a chance to create a sort of City army under their command;[82] but although the London Military Association, which was merged with the Honourable Artillery Company in 1781, did on at least one occasion go out 'on a spirited search' after some violent criminals in Islington,[83] the Government saw to it that the dangerous experiment of an armed amateur police outside its control was not carried into general practice.

Similar suggestions that reliance should be placed on the old institution of the *posse commitatus* by which the sheriff could call to arms everyone over fifteen and 'under the degree of a peer' for the purpose of 'keeping the peace and pursuing felons', or on a transformed militia, were put forward, and largely ignored. The Government fell back into complacency and appeared willing to subscribe to the Solicitor-General's comfortable opinion that the Gordon Riots had been 'a single instance of a defect in the civil power which, in all probability, would never again occur'.[84]

There were, however, a few men in the Government who were not prepared to let the problem slide. The Earl of Shelburne was Prime Minister between 1782 and 1783 and was succeeded by the younger Pitt in 1784. Both these men were known to have strong ideas on police reform, and in 1785 Pitt's Solicitor-General, Sir Archibald Macdonald, introduced the London and Westminster Police Bill.

The Bill was a remarkable attempt to incorporate all the important and practicable proposals that had been made since Henry Fielding went to Bow Street. It provided for the unification of the Cities of London and Westminster and the Borough of Southwark into one 'District of the Metropolis' which was to be divided

into nine Divisions. Three Commissioners were to be appointed
with wide powers to enlist constables and to 'organize a Public
Office in each Division and to select a suitable Justice of the Peace
to act there'. Commissioners and Justices were both to be paid
salaries.[85]

The Bill raised passionate opposition, particularly in the City
where as a Member of the House of Commons said, 'if a torch had
been applied to the buildings there it could not have created greater
alarm'.[86] Another City Member, Alderman Townshend, said he
was not being 'bloody-minded' but the Bill, which intended to take
away from the City its traditional independence and liberties, was
'derogatory to the dignity and destructive to the authority of the
Aldermen'.[87]

Pitt, relying so heavily for support upon business interests in
the City, felt obliged to give way and the Bill was abandoned. Not
for over thirty years did a comparable measure emerge.

In 1792, however, an Act was passed in the face of renewed
opposition, creating seven new Public Offices, soon to be known as
Police Offices, each of which was to have three paid Justices of
the Peace.[88] Three more Police Offices were created for the new
River Police in 1800[89] so that by then, counting the one at Bow
Street, the Metropolis had nine Police Offices with twenty-seven
magistrates receiving salaries of not more than four hundred
pounds a year. The magistrates were authorized to employ six
constables at each office and to pay them twelve shillings a week
for their services.

There were numerous applications for the various appointments
to the magistrature—one from a man whose reason for applying
was that he wanted an opportunity of giving his daughters
'advantages which they could not have in the country', another
from a man who said that to deal with the villains of the criminal
class and their attorneys, a candidate needed 'the Eyes of Argus
with the patience and strength and fortitude of Hercules' and, as
it so happened, he possessed all these qualities.[90] The men eventually selected, however, were for the most part intelligent and conscientious. But the fundamental problems remained.

There was still the same muddle of independent police
authorities, directed, it was estimated in 1797, by 'above seventy
different Trusts; regulated by perhaps double that number of local
Acts'.[91] Each parish jealously guarded its own privileges and
boundaries, and its watchmen could rarely be persuaded to offer

any help outside it, preferring to 'stand and look on' if anything happened or to pretend not to notice it.[92] In any case, most of the night watches came off duty several hours before the day watches came on, so there was plenty of time for criminals to do their work in unwatched streets; and if one parish did happen to have a reliable watch, its neighbours suffered accordingly. A witness before a Parliamentary committee gave evidence of this. Was there any district near his, he was asked, in which 'depredations or crimes [had] increased lately?'

'Very much in the Hendon and Mill Hill Road,'
'Towards Edgware and Harrow?'
'Yes.'
'That is where you have driven them?'
'Yes.'[93]

The rivalries between parishes extended to the magistrates at the new Police Offices, one of whom was asked by a member of another committee if there was any correspondence between the various Offices. 'Certainly not,' he replied. 'Different Police Offices keep information to themselves, and do not wish to communicate it to others, that they may have the credit and advantage of detecting offenders.'[94]

Some areas were outside the known responsibility of any authority. The Royal Parks, for instance, were so rarely patrolled that householders in the vicinity were frequently obliged to petition for protection from the 'many, daring, alarming and repeated attacks' which were made upon their houses from Hyde Park. One man complained that the scenes had become 'so disgusting to common Decency' that he had had to forbid 'his wife and friends to go to the back windows'.[95]

But although the Act of 1792 had little immediate effect on the spread of crime, it had an indirect and profound effect on the reform of the police, for one of the new magistrates appointed under it was Patrick Colquhoun.

Colquhoun had been a highly successful businessman in Glasgow when he had been elected Lord Provost at the age of thirty-seven. He came to London with his family in 1789, a respected man with an immense variety of ideas on social reform, and he saw in the Act of 1792 an opportunity to put these ideas into practice. He was an inflexible enemy of the popular agitator and had no patience with those middle-class radicals who praised the principles of the French Revolution, but did nothing to alleviate the misery of the poor and unfortunate at home. During the Hunger Riots of the 1790's he helped to organize the soup-kitchens for the starving poor which the Quakers, in default of Government action, had paid for; and throughout his life he showed himself to be a man whose good feelings could not find satisfaction in mere sympathy. As a philanthropist he was not without pride, perhaps, and not without a certain prudery but entirely without condescension. In numerous pamphlets he attacked the severity of the law, the abuses of the system of granting pardons, imprisonment in hulks, and the absence of any reformatory tendencies in a prison system which disgorged hundreds of not only unreformed but brutalized convicts back into society each year. He urged the appointment of a public prosecutor and the establishment of a comprehensive register of criminals and a department for receiving information about them. He attacked, like Fielding, the profligacy and extravagance of the time and believed that the prevention of indigence was closely related to the prevention of crime. 'The morals and habits of the lower ranks in Society,' he decided, were 'growing progressively worse and worse'; but these evil propensities were 'no longer to be restrained by the force of religion or the influence of moral principle'. Something more practical was urgently required. In his most celebrated work, *A Treatise on the Police of the Metropolis* (1795) he defined what the main agency in the war against this increasing crime must be—a police force divorced from the judiciary and concerned not with punishment, but with 'the Prevention and Detection of Crimes'.[96]

By reference to a mass of illuminating if somewhat haphazardly prepared and unscientifically treated statistics, he showed how urgent was the problem with which society was confronted. Two million pounds, he maintained, were lost through theft every year; 115,000 people in London (including fifty thousand prostitutes) supported themseves by 'pursuits either criminal, illegal or immoral'; three million pounds were spent each year by 'labouring people' on drink in 5,204 licensed houses; seven and a quarter million pounds were spent annually by eight thousand gamblers in forty-three gaming houses; three thousand shops dealt in stolen goods and some fences were worth thirty thousand pounds; professional thieves were so numerous that it was 'much to be feared that no existing power will be able to keep them within bounds' unless the Police of the Metropolis was 'not greatly improved and better adapted to the present state of Society, by the Introduction of more energy, and a greater degree of system in its administration'.[97]

Colquhoun's plans provided for a police which would not only be responsible for the maintenance of order and the prevention and detection of crime but for the correction of manners and morals as well. He suggested a system of inspection of public houses and other places of amusement and the strict supervision of various people such as prostitutes, gipsies, servants, retail dairymen who might sell polluted or watered milk and ballad singers who might sing obscene or subversive songs. This aspect of his plan naturally aroused the protests of those who thought that repressive measures like these endangered the freedom of the subject and that, in any case, the morals of the lower classes could only be improved by social, economic and political reforms. 'The Police of the Metropolis,' one of Colquhoun's critics wrote, was 'already curious, insulting and oppressive enough without employing new ferrets to scrab the remaining pleasures out of their skulking holes'.[98] But the deepest resentment came from those who saw in his praise of the French police a new threat to liberty, and it was certainly unfortunate that his one example of their efficiency seemed to imply a condonation of their inquisitional methods.

He held up for their approval the exploits of de Sartine, perhaps the most notorious of the Pre-Revolutionary *lieutenants-généraux de police*, and he gave an instance of his efficiency by recounting his part in the capture of a criminal wanted by the Viennese police. This criminal had escaped from Vienna to Paris where the Austrian Ambassador approached de Sartine, then chief of the Paris police, and asked him to hand him over to the Austrian authorities. De Sartine said that he would have been glad to help but that the man had now gone back to Vienna. The Ambassador doubted that de Sartine was right as the information he had received from Vienna was categoric. 'Do me the honour, Sir,' de Sartine replied, 'to inform the Emperor, your Master, that the person he looks for left Paris on the tenth of the last month; and is now lodged in a back room looking into the garden on the third storey of a house, number ninety-three in ———— Street, in his own capital of Vienna.'[99]

To the eighteenth-century Englishman this sort of efficient watchfulness was not admirable but hateful; and when Colquhoun condemned the 'pride and ill-grounded jealousy' of the City which had brought Pitt's Bill of 1785 to disaster, he earned new enemies and fresh abuse for projecting an 'Engine of Power and Authority, so enormous and extensive as to threaten a species of despotism and inquisition hitherto without a parallel in this country'.[100] Men were reminded once again of 1655 when Cromwell, unable to restore order without resort to his army, had divided England and Wales up into twelve police districts each under command of a Major-General with wide judicial powers and with the authority to use spies and a special force of militia to compel obedience and hunt down the unruly and the vicious. This taste of a police state on the continental model had been remembered for generations and was frequently used as an argument against a professional police by all those who wished to avoid one.

And so, despite Pitt's sympathy, nothing came of Colquhoun's plans for the moment. Two years after the publication of his *Treatise*, however, he was asked by the West India Merchants to suggest a plan for the prevention of thefts from the ships and docks in the Port of London which then amounted, the Merchants believed, to 'nearly three hundred thousand pounds'. Colquhoun set to work with characteristic industry and in a subsequent report suggested that not three hundred thousand but over half a million pounds were stolen each year, mostly by port workers and sailors, watchmen and customs officers.[101] Large professional gangs of river pirates, Colquhoun also found, were bribing customs officers with money provided by receivers and were boarding ships at night carrying special tools, to open and re-seal casks, and black bags, also provided by receivers, designed to hold a hundred pounds of sugar. For granting 'a licence to plunder' sugar, coffee, rum and ginger to these 'depraved nautical vagabonds', ships' mates and excise officers were getting as much as thirty guineas a night. During the day mudlarks prowled about in the mud under the ships waiting for the lumpers to throw down bits of the cargo which they were unloading; and rat-catchers used the opportunities afforded by their trade to pilfer from ships which were infested by vermin and to push rats through the port-holes of other ships in which their services had not until then been required.

The West India Merchants, whose losses amounted to nearly half the total in the Port of London, together with the Commissioners of Excise, had tried for years without success to stamp out the crime in the docks. In 1711 constables had been appointed and paid ten shillings a week and five shillings for each conviction, but they had merely become connivers, and towards the end of the century pilfering and smuggling by armed gangs had become so extensive that the help of troops had to be demanded from the Government.

On Colquhoun's recommendations a Marine Police was established in 1798. It was an ambitious Establishment with more regular men than all the Metropolitan Police Offices put together. These men, instilled with a sense of discipline and of the importance of their profession as officers of a preventive police, were led by Captain John Harriott, the tough magistrate of a new River Police Office opened at Wapping Stairs. And they were immediately successful. The West India Merchants, who had borne nearly the whole of the expense of the new Establishment, could feel that it was money well spent. By June 1799 they were able to claim that in the preceding year the only ships to be extensively plundered in the river were those which were not under their protection. The following month the new West India Dock[102] made the supervision of loading and unloading much easier, and in 1800 the Government, ready to adopt an organization once it had been proved successful by private enterprise, transformed the Establishment into an official Thames River Police[103] which remained independent until its absorption in the Metropolitan Police in 1839.

The triumphant example of the Marine Police was not, however, followed by the establishment of any comparable force; and during the next few years, a period of prosperity and an improvement in social conditions allowed men to hope that a professional police force for the metropolis as a whole would not, after all, be required. But when the blockade enforced by Napoleon in the renewed war with France resulted in the Government's attempt to make all neutral traffic pass through British ports, the economic effects of this action were disastrous. Neutral traffic virtually meant American traffic and the United States refused to accept so one-sided a solution. Trade with Europe came to an end, and by 1811 many factories had closed, bands of unemployed came out into the streets and the failure of the harvest brought starvation and misery to thousands.

In December of this terrible year, the fear caused by the hungry, machine-breaking rioters of the Midlands was increased, unreasonably but nevertheless appreciably, by the ferocious murder of two families in London. These murders, Southey told de Quincey, were 'amongst the few domestic events which, by the depth and expansion of horror attending them, had risen to the dignity of a *national* interest'. De Quincey, himself, thought them 'the most superb of the century by many degrees' marking the *début* of an 'artist; at least, for anything the public knew . . . a great exterminating *chef-d'œuvre*.'[104]

De Quincey's artist had made his *début* on Saturday night 7 December 1811 at 29 Ratcliffe Highway, the shop of Mr Marr, a draper, who lived there with his wife and child, shop-boy and maid. At about midnight, Mr Marr, with the help of the shop-boy began to put away the rolls of cloth that he had been offering for sale during the day; but before locking up his shop for the night he sent out his maid for a bowl of oysters for supper. When the maid came back she found the door, which she had left open, locked; so she rang the bell. There was no reply. She went to find a watchman who, an hour later, was still ringing the bell and knocking on the door. Then a neighbour saw that the back door was open and, jumping over the fence, he entered the house through the yard. Inside the shop, Mr Marr and the shop-boy, covered in blood which was also spattered over the floor and window, lay battered to death. Upstairs Mrs Marr and her child were also dead. A ripping chisel and a maul were found lying on the floor of the shop.[105]

A few days later an almost naked man, clambering out of a second-floor window of the King's Arms, a public house nearby, shouted in terror to the people below, 'They are murdering the people in the house!' A constable and several neighbours broke into the house and found the publican, Mr Williamson, his wife and maid all lying soaked in blood. Each of them had a fractured skull and a deeply cut throat.[106]

According to a contemporary newspaper, 'all Wapping was immediately in an uproar. The drums of the volunteers beat to arms, the fire-bells were rung, and every person flew in consternation to the spot. The police searched every house around and every boat in the River, while every cart, waggon and carriage was stopped.' Magistrates and police officers were 'assailed with enquiries' about the progress of their investigations; rewards were offered by the Government, the parish and the Thames Police Office; Bow Street Runners and the Bow Street Patrol lent a hand in the investigations; numerous men were examined and several, including a neighbour of the Williamsons and a brother of Mr Marr, were arrested. At one moment the murders were said to be the work of Portuguese sailors, at another of Irishmen, at another of a man who had hanged himself in Hertford gaol. But the real 'inhuman Murderer' was not found.[107]

The fear of 'further Horrid Depredations' spread far beyond Wapping. The Home Secretary was told that a 'general alarm' had been caused 'not only throughout the City but throughout the Country'; and in Parliament Sir Samuel Romilly attacked the authorities for giving way to the general panic by apprehending 'no less than forty or fifty persons on bare suspicion'. Sheridan accused the Shadwell magistrates of intensifying the suspicions of ignorant people that the murders were a Popish plot.[108]

At last through the maul which had been found in Mr Marr's shop, John Williams, a lodger at the Pear Tree public-house in Wapping, was arrested. Before he could be committed for trial he hanged himself in his cell at the House of Correction in Cold Bath Fields, but there was little doubt that he was guilty of all seven murders.

He was responsible for much else besides. 'Never before,' as Dr Leon Radzinowicz has said, 'not even after the Gordon Riots which brought the capital so close to utter destruction, and gave so striking an illustration of the failings of the justices and parish constables, did the public express so vigorous and persistent a condemnation of the traditional machinery for keeping the peace.'[109]

All the watchmen in Shadwell were discharged and new patrols were formed of men armed with cutlasses and pistols. In addition the river police were ordered to patrol the streets over the holidays; and new voluntary associations of 'gentlemen and respectable inhabitants' were formed for police duties. 'Either respectable householders must determine to be their own guardians,' said *The Morning Post*, 'or we must have a regularly enlisted armed police under the orders of proper officers.'[110]

Suggestions as to how this police force should be organized and armed and how citizens could best protect themselves came into the Home Office by every mail and included a proposal— amongst others no less eccentric—that every house should contain 'a Hanger, Javelin or Pike' together with a wicker-basket shield to ward off a blow while one or other of these weapons was being brought into action.[111] A pamphleteer, whose proposals were published the following year, had other ideas. He advocated a system of alarm based on what he termed the 'Glazier's Tocsin'. Believing that alarm bells were cowardly, he suggested that 'in case of attack really happening', the threatened householder should 'flee to the window and *dash out* a pane or two *with force* . . . This would be a *TOCSIN, ready in every chamber*.' If persons could not reach the window they were advised to 'throw something through the panes, a shoe, or anything near them'. This ingenious writer had ideas, too, for watchmen. They should all be 'furnished with a stick of two or three yards long, and at the end should be an iron talon or hook, which being struck at the drapery of the fugitive, would stop his course sooner and better than grappling with the hands. Let not this important suggestion be overlooked. It will have good in two ways; it will not only strike into coats, but possibly also into the skin, and so far may *strike terror* into the wicked.'[112]

Most suggestions, however, were more conventional. But few of them so much as hinted at a sympathy with Colquhoun's hopes for a fundamental alteration in the national attitudes towards the police idea.

Certainly the Government seemed unwilling to embark on any far-reaching reforms and the Opposition showed no signs of prompting them. At the beginning of 1812 a Parliamentary Committee to investigate the state of the police was set up, but its report issued at the end of March was a humdrum document and a Bill, based mainly on its recommendations and debated in July, was ultimately abandoned.

And so the panic engendered by the Ratcliffe murders relapsed once more into complacency. 'They have an admirable police at Paris,' wrote John William Ward expressing a general opinion, 'but they pay for it dear enough. I had rather half a dozen people's throats should be cut in Ratcliffe Highway every three or four years than be subject to domiciliary visits, spies and all the rest of Fouché's contrivances.'[113] It was a far from uncommon sentiment.

Certainly it was to take more than a few murders, however ferocious, to convert men like these to a belief in the necessity for a professional police force. And after the creation of the River Police, over a quarter of a century was to pass before its example was followed—a quarter of a century of undiminished crime, of reckless industrialization and of economic crises which brought the country almost to the edge of revolution.

The Luddite riots of 1811 were followed by the Corn Law riots of 1815, the Spa Fields riots of 1816, the riots of 'The Blanketeers' in Lancashire in 1817 and the 'Peterloo' riots in St Peter's Fields, Manchester in 1819; and in all of them regular troops or Yeomanry Cavalry had to be used to disperse the crowds. There were many casualties and a fierce resentment, particularly when Lord Sidmouth, the Home Secretary, a strong supporter of the use of Yeomanry, created several new squadrons of them in the northern towns. In the riots which spread all over the country in 1816, troops of Yeomanry were on many occasions attacked by the mobs which they had been called out to disperse. In Devon and Cornwall they had to be rescued by Dragoons; at Norwich they were attacked with stones and fire-balls; in Essex they were thrown back by rioters who took shelter behind tombstones in a churchyard and pelted them with bits of rock.[114] In Glasgow, Dragoons and Highlanders were stoned for hours until they had to be withdrawn and replaced by special constables who 'appeared to be a more effectual means of suppressing the riot than the soldiers ... The circumstances of their knowing many of the crowd personally must have had much influence in keeping order.'[115] At 'Peterloo' both Hussars and Manchester Yeomanry, their ranks 'filled chiefly by wealthy master manufacturers and without the knowledge possessed by a (strictly speaking) military body,'[116] were used against a largely peaceful crowd, including many women and children, several of whom were killed or wounded.

By the autumn of 1819 Lord Sidmouth was seriously worried by 'the clouds in the North' which he thought must soon burst; and he wrote to the Lord Chancellor, Lord Eldon, who was still pressing for laws of greater and greater severity, to tell him that he wished he could persuade himself of the 'sufficiency of the means, either in law or force', to curb the spirit of revolt and 'crush its impending and too probable effects'.[117]

The forces of law were weakened, in Eldon's opinion, by the courts sentencing batches of rioters to death and then reprieving most of them; and, in Sidmouth's opinion, by an insufficiency of troops. But neither man, apparently, considered the possibility of a professional police and continued to rely on 'the formation of corps of yeomanry'.[118] They did have, it must be said, reason for rejecting the idea of police, for in the previous year the *Third Report* of a new *Committee of Inquiry into The State of the Police of the Metropolis* had been published. The members of the Committee which had been appointed in 1816, collected a mass of evidence after interviewing numerous witnesses; but although their subsequent reports confirmed the utter incapacity of the existing system, they concluded that the prevention of crime 'is a subject of great difficulty. It is no doubt true that to prevent crime is better than to punish it; and though your Committee could imagine a system of police that might arrive at the object sought for, yet, in a free country, or even in one where any unrestrained intercourse of society is permitted, such a system would of necessity be odious and repulsive, and one which no Government would be able to carry into execution'.[119]

The problem was, accordingly, returned to Lord Sidmouth unsolved. In 1820, however, Government spies discovered a conspiracy of such bizarre and monstrous eccentricity that the question of police and the rankling memories of 'Peterloo' were temporarily forgotten. 'Every argument for moderate measures,' as Walpole said, 'was hushed amidst the universal indignation of the country;' and the Ministers of the Government could relax in the warmth of an astutely fostered sympathy as they encouraged the conspiracy by means of *agents provocateurs* and at the same time pointed to the evident necessity of the six Acts which they had recently passed limiting the freedom of the people.

The Cato Street Conspiracy, as it was afterwards called, was born in the disordered brain of a fanatical idealist, Arthur Thistlewood, a former estate agent and soldier from Lincolnshire who had been arrested after the trial of the Spa Fields rioters under the provisions of the Habeas Corpus Suspension Act which allowed the Government to arrest and imprison for indeterminate periods any suspicious character. When he was released, Thistlewood challenged Lord Sidmouth to a duel and was accordingly imprisoned for a year. He came out of prison with a passionate hatred of authority and he collected around him a gang of terrorists, anarchists and criminals who, he hoped, would help him destroy the institutions of the country. Some of these terrorists, though, were more interested in making money than beginning a revolution and one, a man named Edwards, a Government spy, promised to sell to Sir Herbert Taylor, an officer of the Royal Household at Windsor Castle, information about Thistlewood's plans.

Thistlewood, it transpired, had decided to murder the entire Cabinet, attack the 'old man and the old woman'—the Mansion House and the Bank of England—set fire to London and establish a 'Provisional Government' with himself as dictator. This was an ambitious scheme for a band of thirty odd men, but the murder of the Cabinet Ministers which was to inaugurate it seemed a possibility when it became known that one of them, Lord Harrowby, was to entertain his colleagues to dinner in his house in Grosvenor Square on 23 February 18ᴌ0.

Thistlewood decided that he and the main body of his supporters would wait at their headquarters in a ruined stable in Cato Street, Edgware Road, while a secondary party dealt with the Ministers in Grosvenor Square. One of his party was to call at the house, pretending that he had a parcel to deliver, and when the footman opened the door, all the others were to rush in with knives, pistols and hand-grenades. The Ministers were to be slaughtered in the dining-room and the heads of Lord Sidmouth and of Lord Castlereagh, a strong supporter of the Home Secretary's methods, were to be carried off in a bag.

The arrangements, confided to Sir Herbert Taylor by Edwards and to Lord Harrowby himself by another member of the gang, were forestalled by the simple device of postponing the Ministers' dinner. While the would-be assassins waited in Grosvenor Square for their victims to arrive, a squad of Bow Street Runners and a detachment of guards were sent to Cato Street to arrest the other conspirators.

The Guards entered the street at the wrong end and the Bow Street Runners rushed up a ladder to the loft above the stable on their own. The conspirators were discovered cleaning their pistols by candle-light and after a fierce fight, in which Thistlewood killed a Runner with his sword, nine of them were arrested. Thistlewood and fourteen others managed to escape but most of them were subsequently captured and Thistlewood himself was found next day in bed in a house in Moorfields with his pockets full of cartridges.

Six weeks later he was put on trial with eleven of his supporters. Edwards, the informer, had gone abroad to enjoy, so it was said, an ample Government pension; but another conspirator turned King's Evidence and ensured the conviction of the remainder, five of whom were condemned to death. Thistlewood's defence consisted mainly of abuse of Lord Sidmouth whom he continued to condemn on the scaffold where, to emphasize his scorn of this particular national institution, he sucked an orange.

All the conspirators, except Davidson, seemed quite indifferent to their fate and one of them, Ings, who joined Thistlewood in sucking oranges, seemed hysterically cheerful. 'Come, old cock-of-wax,' he said to Davidson. 'It will soon be over.' He nodded to a friend in the crowd, sang snatches of songs about death or liberty, asked the executioner to 'do it tidy' and 'pull it tight', smiled at the sight of the row of coffins lined beneath the gallows, and gave three cheers for the spectators.

When the five bodies had been hanging for half an hour, a man in a mask came forward to cut their heads off, to remind the crowd that they were traitors. At the sight of the first head the spectators gasped in horror. At the sight of the fifth—as Romilly might well have predicted—they laughed.[120]

The Ministers, whose popularity had risen on the wave of sympathy created by the conspirators' outrageous intentions, attended a service to give thanks for their escape, but by June they were in trouble again and were obliged once more to consider the recurrent problem of police. In that month George IV's foolish and ill-used wife Caroline returned to England and was the cause of fresh riots in which the houses of several Ministers, including Lord Sidmouth's, were attacked by the mob. The Guards were called out, but this time the appeal to force had a fearful consequence. One battalion of the 3rd Guards mutinied. It was not a serious mutiny and was confined to a few men, but it had a fateful significance. At first this significance was not appreciated. There was one man in the Cabinet, though, who saw clearly what the mutiny meant. He was the Duke of Wellington and he wrote immediately to the Earl of Liverpool, the Prime Minister. 'In my opinion,' he told Lord Liverpool, 'The Government ought, without the loss of a moment's time, to adopt measures to form either a police in London or military corps, which should be of a different description from the regular military force, or both.'[121]

The warning from this great man was not lost upon Lord Liverpool who, when Lord Sidmouth was, in January 1822, at last persuaded to retire, appointed Robert Peel to the Home Office in his place. Peel's views on the need for reform in the criminal law and for a centrally controlled police force were well known. He had been in office only two months when he moved for the appointment of yet another committee to report on the police of the metropolis. The Committee was appointed but its Report, hastily given three months later, showed how much work Peel and his supporters had yet to do. It was difficult, the Report concluded, repeating a traditional formula, 'to reconcile an effective system of police with that perfect freedom of action and exemption from interference which are the great privileges and blessing of society in this country'. The committee had, therefore, decided that the 'forfeiture or curtailment of such advantages would be too great a sacrifice for improvements in police'.[122]

Peel shrewdly changed his tack. For the moment he left the matter of police reform to concentrate on the reform of the criminal law. And in 1828 when his great work of consolidation was almost completed, he moved for another committee. This time the ground had been most carefully prepared. The Committee gave the Report that Peel wanted and in the following year he was able to introduce his *'Bill for Improving the Police in and near the Metropolis'*.

The Bill owed much to the work of the pioneers of police reform in the previous century, to the Fieldings and to Colquhoun and, less directly to Bentham and Edwin Chadwick; but it owed something, too, to Peel's own experiences as Chief Secretary of Ireland where Pitt's abortive Westminster Police Bill of 1785 had become, with some modifications, the Dublin Police Act of 1786.[123] When introducing his new Bill, which became law in 1829, Peel did not refer to his predecessors but was content to recall the numerous police committees since 1770, their revelations of defects and the absence of any consequent reforms. He said that while the population had increased by fifteen and a half per cent between 1821-1828, crime had increased by over forty per cent. Something must clearly be done 'but he did not intend to proceed at first on too extensive a scale but would endeavour in this, as on other occasions, to effect a gradual reformation'.[124]

This promise of caution and restraint, emphasized by the Duke of Wellington who introduced the Bill in the Lords, set many uncertain minds at rest. The Bill passed both Houses without serious opposition and became law in 1829.[125]

It provided for a new Police Office in Westminster with a new force of paid constables commanded by two Justices, later called Commissioners, who had administrative but not judicial duties. It defined a new Metropolitan Police District which comprised Westminster and various parishes in Middlesex, Surrey and Kent. The City, in view of the history of the 1785 Bill and in view, also, of the City Police's recent improvements, was excluded.

The first two Commissioners appointed were men of remarkable gifts. The younger was Richard Mayne, a clever barrister who was making a reputation on the Northern Circuit; the other was

Colonel Charles Rowan, who had, in Peel's own words, brought his regiment, the 52nd, 'to the highest state of discipline'.[126]

The office with which the Metropolitan Police Act provided them was at 4 Whitehall Place, the back of which opened on to a courtyard known as Scotland Yard. When the two Commissioners moved there in 1829 a new era in the history of police had begun.

(ii)

The speed with which the new police was established was astonishing. Rowan and Mayne first met on 6 July 1829 when Peel asked them to prepare a 'detailed plan for organizing the Police'. A fortnight later the plan had been drawn up and approved.[1] In less than three months, the Duke of Wellington was able to write to Peel to congratulate him 'on the entire success of the Police in London'.[2]

Although the Metropolitan Police District, as originally defined by the Bill, was limited in area, by 30 July practically the whole of London had been divided into police divisions, sections and beats. Rowan, who had been trained and influenced by Sir John Moore, perhaps the greatest training officer the British Army has ever had, adapted the organization of the military regiment to the civilian police. Company commanders became superintendents, subalterns became inspectors, and privates became constables. It had at first been intended that the uniform should be red and gold,[3] but as this might have taken the military tradition too far, blue was chosen instead. The men wore top hats and tail-coats and on the collar of their jackets the number and letter of their division. Their only weapon was a short wooden baton.

They were very poorly paid and the Commissioners' difficulties in finding suitable men are emphasized by the numbers of dismissals—nearly five thousand—between 1830 and 1838. In these years there were also more than six thousand resignations, most of them 'not being altogether voluntary'.[4] Superintendents received two hundred pounds a year, inspectors a hundred pounds a year, sergeants twenty-two shillings and sixpence a week and constables (after two shillings had been deducted for their uniform) nineteen shillings a week. 'Your policemen are not paid sufficiently,' Croker told Peel. 'Three shillings a day for men capable of even *reading*, to say nothing of *understanding* and *executing* the printed instructions seem wholly inadequate. Every artisan has five shillings a day and can you have higher and more laborious duties done for (considering the deductions) about one-half the rate of a common workman's wages?'[5] Peel did not agree and the pay of policemen remained disgracefully low throughout the nineteenth century, in the early years of which policemen habitually asked householders on their beats for a Christmas box.[6]

The meagre rewards of their difficult profession was but one of the problems that the new police had to face. They were almost universally resented. Tories associated them with Peel, now an 'upstart' and renegade for his unexpected support of Catholic Emancipation, and both they and the Whigs hated having to pay the Police Rate.* Radicals of all sorts saw in the police an instrument of possible tyranny, and extreme Radicals feared that their revolutionary hopes, which had seemed near to realization in the 1820's, would not now be fulfilled. 'Liberty or Death! Britons!! And Honest Men!!!' was the heading of a handbill which was circulated in thousands during the Reform Riots of November 1830: 'We assure you from ocular demonstration that six thousand cutlasses have been removed from the Tower for the use of Peel's Bloody Gang . . . These damned Police are now to be armed. Will you put up with this?'[7]

Several newspapers which clearly believed that the people ought not to put up with the police, armed or not, published the wildest rumours—Sir Robert Peel was going to use the police to put Wellington on the throne, the Cromwellian experiment of military tyranny was to be repeated, the introduction of a secret political inquisition was imminent.[8]

The aristocracy, although willing to accept the protection of the new police, also attacked it because the Commissioners, refusing to obey the traditions of eighteenth-century patronage, ensured that the force did not provide employment for the numerous nominees whose characters were recklessly guaranteed by their patrons. The magistrates, for reasons of jealousy, were even more condemnatory and openly showed their sympathy for those arrested for assaulting the police. The ringleader of a mob who threw a constable on to spiked railings was fined a pound; twelve men were merely bound over to keep the peace after being found guilty of attacking and almost killing one policeman, severely

* In previous years the poorest and most decrepit men in some parishes had been chosen to be constables so as to make savings in the Poor Rate.

wounding three others and incapacitating eight more.[9] Bankers and merchants disliked the idea of the new force because they feared that they might not now be able to come to terms with thieves for the return of stolen property. Criminals, of course, disliked the idea and did all they could to encourage opposition. And even those with no personal motives for resentment still believed that a professional police was incompatible with British liberty.

But liberty did not consist, as Peel wrote to Wellington, 'in having your house robbed by organized gangs of thieves, and in leaving the principal streets of London in the nightly possession of drunken women and vagabonds'.[10] And soon no one could doubt that houses were less frequently robbed and the streets were quieter at night; nor could anyone deny that the police had shown an unexpected ability to control mobs in London without the help of troops and even to prevent mobs assembling.

In 1833 the tide of resentment began to turn. In May of that year Lord Melbourne, the new Home Secretary, refused the National Political Union permission to hold a public meeting in Cold Bath Fields and instructed Colonel Rowan to arrest any ringleaders who disobeyed this order. The order was disobeyed and Colonel Rowan was ready with nearly five hundred policemen to carry out his instructions. Rowan told them to be 'cool and temperate'; and in general they were.

The mob threw stones at the advancing constables who charged with their truncheons. Three policemen were stabbed and one of them was killed. But although the remainder dispersed the crowds energetically and chased them needlessly far from the scene of the meeting, when all was over there were no serious injuries to anyone who was not a policeman. Of course, the usual charges were made—the police had been drunk, women and children had been knocked about brutally, men had been struck as they lay defenceless on the ground. At the inquest on the killed constable the jury brought in a verdict of 'justifiable homicide'; and the Government then attempted to shuffle their responsibility on to Colonel Rowan. Even the most violent radicals who had been in the crowd at Cold Bath Fields acknowledged that both the jury's verdict and the Government's subsequent behaviour were grossly unfair. A reaction in favour of the police set in. Former uncompromising critics of the new system found good things to say of it; parishes outside the Metropolitan District asked to be taken into it; and soon provincial towns were asking for police officers trained in London to come to their help.[11]

For in the provinces crime was increasing fast and the violent riots, such as one in which the centre of Bristol was burned, demonstrated the urgent need for the reform of local police forces. Criminals driven out of London by the new Metropolitan Police were operating in the large provincial towns where the old parochial system still prevailed. The proportion of known bad characters to the general population had risen, so it was calculated in 1837, to one in forty-five in Liverpool, to one in thirty-one in Bristol and as high as one in twenty-seven in Newcastle-on-Tyne.[12] And the population of all these and other industrial towns in the Midlands and the North was growing rapidly. The population of Birmingham, for example, which was 150,000 in 1832 had almost doubled in twenty years.

In 1839, in an effort to find a national answer to the problem, a Royal Commission was appointed to enquire into the best means of establishing an efficient constabulary force in the counties of England and Wales. Soon after publication of the Commission's Report, which revealed an appalling amount of crime and a disastrously inadequate means of repressing it, an Act was passed permitting counties to raise and equip paid police forces.[13] The objections raised to taking advantage of this 'Permissive Act' were similar to those raised to the Metropolitan Police Act, but those counties which did take advantage of it soon had cause for self-congratulation. Cheshire had already had a paid constabulary for ten years but it was so ill-run that it was scarcely more efficient than the parochial system which it had replaced. Essex, however, which was the first county to make use of the 'Permissive Act', appointed a retired naval officer of remarkable talents to be its Chief Constable and the results were immediate. Soon the adjoining counties of Suffolk, Hertfordshire and Cambridgeshire felt obliged to follow Essex's example. Other counties tardily and sometimes unwillingly did the same. But by May 1853, there were still twenty-two counties completely without a paid police force. Of these, some continued to rely solely on the old, outmoded parochial system; while others vainly attempted to modernize it by employing trained Superintending Constables to look after their amateur force.[14] But in both cases the results were disastrous, particularly for the poor who could not afford the payments the local constables still demanded. The following bill[15] was one presented to a

poor man who lived in Devizes and in 1853 chased a thief who had
stolen his boots. He caught the thief in Somerset and handed him
over to a constable who brought him back to Wiltshire. Having
paid the bill he was poorer by many times the value of his boots.

	£	s.	d.
To apprehending prisoner		2	6
To maintaining prisoner (2 days)		3	0
To guard watching (one night)		2	6
Conveyance of prisoner at 9d a mile and allowance to constable at 8d a mile	2	15	5
3 days' loss of time		15	0
Hire of conveyance, coach and other fares	1	1	2
	4	19	7

The man might have been considered lucky for finding a constable
willing to help him at all, for many could not. A Bedfordshire
constable once pleaded that he was not allowed to arrest the murderers of a local farmer without a warrant, although the murder
had been committed in daylight and there were many witnesses,
and in another county a constable apologized for not being able
to come out to quell a riot but he 'sent his staff by bearer'.[16] Men
understandably felt that they must continue to protect their houses
from burglars with spring guns and man traps, although these
had been declared illegal in 1827[17] and in Cambridgeshire they
chased thieves with bloodhounds.[18]

So unsatisfactory a state of affairs could clearly not continue,
and in 1856 another Police Act was passed making it obligatory
for all counties to raise and maintain a constabulary.[19] At last,
over a hundred years after Henry Fielding had taken up his
appointment in Bow Street, all England had a paid police force.

The advantages of it, as a means of preventing crime, were
impossible to deny. In the ten years between 1811 and 1821, during
which the average increase of population was about nineteen per
cent, the average increase of commitments was forty-eight per cent;
but in the ten years between 1851 and 1861 when the population
of England and Wales increased from 17,927,609 to 20,066,224,
the number of commitments fell from 156 for every hundred thousand of the population to ninety-one.[20]

By then the British police, helped by the 'almost fanatical devotion' of Charles Dickens,[21] were already earning the admiration

and envy of the world. Speaking to Eckermann about the 'blessings of personal freedom' in England, Goethe had said some years before that he only had to look out of the window in Weimar to see how different things were in Germany.

'Recently,' Goethe said, 'When the snow was on the ground, my neighbours' children wanted to try out their sledges in the street. Whereupon a policeman instantly appeared, and I saw the poor little creatures running away as fast as they could. Now the spring sun tempts them, and they and their companions would like to have a game out of doors, but I can see that they are always half afraid, as though they were not quite sure of themselves and feared the approach of some big bogeyman of the police. A boy cannot crack his whip or sing or shout but some policeman will appear at once to forbid it.'[22]

Goethe was right. The constantly repeated determination that the British 'Peeler' should never become a 'bogeyman' or a 'mercenary in the hands of the Government' had had its effect. He was, and has remained, immune from political manipulation and bound, as any other citizen, by the laws of his country.

CHAPTER THREE

THE PRISON REFORMERS

'The mood and temper of the public with regard to the treatment of crime and criminals is one of the most unfailing tests of the civilisation of any country.'
WINSTON CHURCHILL, 1910

(i)

IN 1773 John Howard, a land owner in Bedfordshire, was appointed to the office of High Sheriff of the county. He was a small, thin man whose sad and sallow face was enlivened by bright eyes and a warm and gentle smile. He was forty-seven and apart from long periods spent in foreign travel he had devoted his life to his estate at Cardington, to philanthropic work in the district and to meteorological observations. He had been married twice, firstly to a widow of more than twice his age who had nursed him through a dangerous illness and after her death to a younger woman who had also died some few years later. Deeply religious, self-consciously obstinate and painstakingly thorough in everything he did, he took up his duties as High Sheriff with a strong sense of social responsibility.[1]

One of these duties was to accompany the judge at the Assizes, but although his predecessors had largely contented themselves with the formality of the obligation, Howard felt compelled not merely to watch the operations of the court but to visit the gaol from which the prisoners came and back to which they were sent. The condition of the place horrified him and he was particularly concerned to discover that the gaoler and turnkeys received no

131

salaries but got what they could out of the prisoners by levying fees, and that even when prisoners were acquitted by the court, they were not released until they had paid for their freedom. Immediately he demanded that the county should pay a salary to its gaol officials so that these unjust fees might be abolished; but the justices refused to burden the county with the charge unless some precedent could be found. Howard left Bedford to find one. He did not succeed; but the cruelty, injustice and squalor he discovered in his search confirmed him in his determination to spend the rest of his life in the cause of prison reform. 'I could not enjoy my ease and leisure,' he confessed later, 'in the neglect of any opportunity, afforded me by Providence, of attempting the relief of the miserable.'[2]

The appalling conditions in English prisons had remained virtually unchanged for centuries, despite the recent activities of the Society for Promoting Christian Knowledge, a growing Parliamentary movement for their reform and the accurate descriptions of their horrors given by such writers as Henry Fielding. They were not, and never had been, prisons in the modern sense, but places where people could be held while awaiting trial or physical punishment and where debtors, who formed most of the prison population in the eighteenth century, could be held until their creditors were satisfied. Even the Houses of Correction which had been established in 1576 on the model of Bridewell, a house given by Edward VI where work could be provided for vagrants and the unemployed in uncomfortably severe conditions, had by Howard's time become indistinguishable from the ordinary gaols. Imprisonment as a form of punishment for various crimes had, indeed, been known since the time of Ethelstan but so long as death, mutilation, banishment and the infliction of physical suffering or public indignity were the principal methods of dealing with offenders, prisons remained for the most part places of confinement rather than of punishment.* They were, of course, as Howard discovered, places of punishment as well; but this was, theoretically,

---

* As early as the fifteenth century the law had allowed imprisonment as an alternative to a fine in certain cases. For example, the penalty for inflicting a wound with a sword in the City of London was a fine of twenty shillings or forty days' imprisonment. Sentences of imprisonment seem, however, to have been very rarely awarded. In many country districts there were, in any event, no prisons where they could be served. Men sometimes had to be hired so that prisoners awaiting trial could be handcuffed to them. There were 'cages in several parishes but never used, being unsafe'.[3]

incidental to their main purpose. The prisoners were punished not so much to make them better men but because the threat and example of punishment helped those who owned or ran the prisons to make money out of them.

Almost half the local prisons in the country were privately owned. The Duke of Leeds owned Halifax Prison; Lord Derby owned Macclesfield Prison; the Bishop of Durham owned the County Gaol at Durham; the Duke of Portland owned Chesterfield gaol which he hired out for eighteen guineas a year; in Mr J. R. Walter's prison at Exeter there was 'no chimney, no water, no court, no sewer'; in the Bishop of Ely's prison men were chained down to the floor on their backs with spiked collars round their necks and heavy iron bars over their legs unless they were able to pay for their removal.

Payment for 'easement of irons' was, in fact, common to many gaols and this was only the first of the fees which the new prisoner was expected to pay. He had not only to pay to avoid being tortured, he often had to pay even to exist, for in many gaols prisoners were given nothing to eat and charitable contributions of food, confiscated in the markets as unfit for human consumption or of light weight, soon fell into the hands of the prison bullies. At Exeter the debtors' ward was called the 'shew' because the inmates begged for food by letting down a shoe from the window; other prisoners were marched through the streets of the town to beg. In some prisons even when food was provided, it did not amount to much more than a bowl of 'bread boiled in mere water'. In 1729 a Parliamentary Committee found that more than 350 prisoners were dying of starvation in Marshalsea prison and that in only three months of a previous year the death toll had reached three hundred. The sight of men and women in many other prisons fighting with rats in damp cellars for the scraps of food 'thrown to them through a trap-door' was not uncommon. A man took his dog into Knaresborough gaol with him 'to defend him from vermin, but the dog was soon destroyed and the prisoner's face much disfigured by them'.[4] These terrifying cellars were 'often damp and noisome, half a foot deep in water, or with an open sewer running through the centre of the floor. They had no chimneys, no fireplace, no barrack beds; the wretched inmates huddled together for warmth upon heaps of filthy rags and bundles of rotten straw reeking with foul exhalations and fetid with all manner of indescribable nastiness.'[5]

Frequently the daily ration of water allowed was not enough for washing and in one prison, Howard found, that even this had to be bought. With insufficient water and ventilation, with vermin and insects crawling everywhere, without proper food or light or sanitation, shivering half naked in the winter and suffocating in the summer heat, most prisoners lived out the days and nights in unutterable misery. Others who could afford it got drunk and stayed drunk, oblivious to the stumbling lunatics, to women giving birth to babies who were left to die on the piles of filthy straw, to rats burrowing in the dirt and excrement, to fellow prisoners suffering from gaol fever, that virulent form of typhus which killed a high proportion of prisoners every year.

Immense quantities of spirits were consumed in all but the smallest prisons, for the keepers, although prohibited by statute in 1751 from doing so, derived part of their large profits from the sale of alcohol.[6] '120 gallons of gin were sold every week' in the King's Bench Prison 'besides other spirits in proportion'.[7] A seventeenth-century governor of Newgate, the oldest of the London prisons, paid a magistrate forty pounds a year 'on condition of sending all his prisoners there'; but a hundred years later there was no need to do so, for the prison had as many inmates as it could contain and the tap-rooms and bars were constantly full. One eighteenth-century governor, indeed, paid a thousand pounds for his place and considered that, even without his profit on drink, he had 'got a bargain'. During three or four months of one year, when his prison was full of wealthy Jacobite prisoners, he made between three thousand and four thousand pounds 'besides valuable presents given in private'.

In return for this sort of disbursement rich prisoners were allowed to live a life of comparative ease in Newgate. Although it was illegal to charge prisoners more than 2s. 6d. a week rent for any particular accommodation, the governor of Newgate charged twenty guineas for the right to live in the less uncomfortable wing of his prison which, in order theoretically to comply with the law, was deemed to form part of his own house. Once admitted to these quarters the prisoner was charged eleven shillings a week rent, although he rarely had a room or even a bed to himself. His life, however, was comfortable enough. He could have as many visitors as he liked, provided they all paid their three shillings entrance fee and he could order what food and drink he wanted. His wife or mistress could live with him and he could send for his servants.

Major Bernardi, a political prisoner who died in Newgate in 1736 at the age of eighty-two had married twice during the forty years that he had waited for a trial that was never held and, by his second wife, had had ten children all born in the prison.[8] Lord George Gordon who died there in 1793 spent his years of imprisonment in placid contentment. He carried on an enormous correspondence with friends and acquaintances all over the world, particularly in America. He had all the books and newspapers he wanted; he was attended by two little maidservants; he rarely entertained less than eight guests for dinner. On occasions he would give a party in his cell and there would be dancing to the music of a band lent by the Duke of York. On Saturdays Lord George, who had become a devout convert to the Jewish faith, turned his room into a synagogue and with the help of various Polish Jews held a public service.[9] But although he lived in the most healthy part of the prison, it was impossible even for him to escape the dreaded disease of gaol fever which killed so many of his fellow prisoners in the autumn epidemic of 1793.*

Outbreaks of gaol fever were, by then, becoming rarer but in earlier years they had been a serious threat to the general community. Prisoners brought into court, workmen engaged in repairs, visitors to the prisons and particularly prostitutes who earned their living within the walls while free to move outside them, men released with the virus in their saturated clothes if not in their bodies, were all carriers of the disease. Five hundred people died at Oxford during the Black Assize of 1577; almost as many died at Exeter in 1586; in 1730 'some hundreds' died during the Lent Assizes in Taunton; and in 1750 the Lord Mayor of London and two Judges were among the many victims.[11] There were regular epidemics in the army and in the fleet. 'The first English fleet sent to America lost above two thousand men . . . the seeds of infection were carried from the guard-ships into the squadrons; and the mortality thence occasioned was greater than by all other diseases or means of death put together.'[12] In the enclosed area of a prison, a serious epidemic might halve its population within a few weeks. According to Howard more people died of gaol fever in 1773-1774 than were executed.

* Gaol fever is described as 'a contagious, putrid, and very pestilential fever, attended with tremblings, twitchings, restlessness, delirium with, in some instance, early phrenzy and lethargy; while the victims break out often into livid pustules and purple spots'.[10]

Apart from the danger to health that incarceration in a prison entailed, the danger to a young prisoner's character was quite as great. For prisons were not only prototypes of hell, as Fielding described them, they were not only the most expensive places on earth to live in, they were also 'schools of crime and of profligacy'.

Every prisoner, as soon as he entered one of them, was set upon for what was known as 'garnish' or 'chummage' which entailed emptying the pockets and buying drinks for all the other inhabitants of the ward into which he was put. Thomas Fowell Buxton in his *Inquiry into the System of Prison Discipline* described the case of a young lawyer who after being forced to pay 'chummage' in Newgate was then invited to join in the drinking himself. He refused and was accordingly brought before a prisoners' court over which the oldest and most skilful thief presided, wearing a towel tied into knots in imitation of a judge's wig. Acquittal could only be obtained by means of bribes to the judge and jury and as he could not pay these, the guilty man was condemned to the pillory, that is to say his head was forced through the legs of a chair to which his arms were painfully tied. The lawyer was frequently tried and punished by this 'kangaroo court' for a variety of invented offences such as 'touching objects which should not be touched', and 'coughing maliciously to the disturbance of his companions' until, fearing for his life, he gave in and consented to drink with them. 'By insensible degrees,' Fowell Buxton said, 'he began to lose his repugnance to their society, caught their flash terms and sang their songs, was admitted to their revels and acquired, in place of habits of perfect sobriety, a taste for spirits'.

His wife visited him and was heartbroken. He had slept for the first fortnight in the same bed as a highwayman and a murderer and now with 'female associates of the most abandoned description'. She could not face being in the same room as his companions and asked him to come to the bars so that she could talk to him from the passage. Once he was too ill to come to her and she was forced to go inside and found him, so she said, 'pale as death, very ill and in dreadfully dirty state, the wretches making game of him and enjoying my distress'. He had been up the whole night and owed the others five shillings which she was obliged to pay on his behalf 'otherwise he would have been stripped of his clothes'.[13]

Some wives could not enter the prison without being made sick by the smell of it even when they held a handkerchief soaked in vinegar to their nostrils, and others stayed away because they could not bear being searched by the vulgar woman in the lodge who affected to believe that all female visitors were prostitutes or criminals going in to plot a new crime with their temporarily disabled confederates. Many visitors were, indeed, criminals and used the prison not only as a meeting place, brothel and tavern but as a printing shop for forged notes, a mint for counterfeit coin and even a hiding place for stolen goods.[14]

Early attempts to reform this and other equally grotesque institutions had not been successful. The Society for the Promotion of Christian Knowledge made an investigation into London prisons in 1702 but its extensive proposals were never published.[15] A Committee was appointed in 1729, under the chairmanship of General James Oglethorpe, the nobly philanthropic friend of Johnson and Burke, and was instructed 'to enquire into the State of Gaols in this Kingdom'. The members of the Committee subsequently reported that the more they 'proceeded in their enquiries the more dismal and shocking was the scene of cruelty, barbarity and extortion which they disclosed'.[16]

Hogarth's painting of a meeting of this Committee shows the instruments of torture which were part of the equipment of the officials of the Fleet prison. In the foreground a man in rags demonstrates how prisoners were tortured by having their hands and necks fastened together by metal clasps. Thomas Bambridge, the Warden, described by Walpole, to whom Hogarth gave his oil sketch for the picture, as an 'inhuman gaoler', appears at the head of the table near John Huggins a previous warden who had purchased the office from the Earl of Clarendon for five thousand pounds.[17] The treatment in the Fleet of a prisoner named Arne was cited by the Committee as a characteristic example of the barbarous manner in which prisoners there were treated.

Arne's clothes were stripped off him on his arrival as a punishment for being unable to pay 'chummage' and he was thrown naked into a dark, unventilated, foul-smelling dungeon above the prison sewer where he remained for some days. Food was occasionally thrown to him and a fellow prisoner, pitying his poor shivering body, somehow managed to get him a mattress. One day noticing that the door of his dungeon had been left open, he escaped and ran into a room next to the chapel, the feathers from the mattress sticking to his skin and giving him the appearance, so it was said, of a 'fantastic and repulsive bird'. He was ordered back to his dungeon and the Warden, 'having no compassion on him caused the door to be close locked'.[18]

Bambridge, the Committee decided, had not only permitted many debtors to pay for their escape but had been guilty of the 'most notorious breaches of his trust, great extortions and the highest crimes'. He was subsequently brought to trial but was twice acquitted by juries who may have been paid for their verdict. His predecessor, Huggins, after having treated the Committee members with the same scant respect as Bambridge, was censured by them in similar terms. He was imprisoned in Newgate for a time but 'afterwards lived in credit to the age of ninety'.[19]

The sad and inescapable fact was that prison reform was not of much concern to a largely complacent and uninterested public. The report of the Committee of 1729, like that of another committee appointed in 1753, had little effect. Measures of reform were proposed; a few, such as the provision of debtors with fourpence a day for their maintenance, were adopted and passed into law; nearly all were evaded or ignored. After John Howard, whose standing as a prison expert was already recognized by 1774, had given evidence to yet another Committee of the House of Commons appointed in that year, Alexander Popham, the member for Taunton, introduced two Bills—one to abolish the fees that a prisoner had customarily to pay after his acquittal before he could be discharged; the other to lessen the danger of gaol fever by providing for the whitewashing of prison interiors. But, as Howard subsequently discovered years later, 'it was only in fifteen out of a hundred and fifty prisons that the law had been strictly obeyed'.[20]

The effect of the publication in 1777 of Howard's important and exhaustive work, *The State of the Prisons in England and Wales*, was less disappointing. This great book, written after extensive tours in France, the Low Countries, Germany and Switzerland, as well as in his own country, not only described in graphic detail what the author had seen but made many valuable suggestions for reform. It proposed, amongst other things, the classification of prisoners according to their offences; their employment in useful labour; the appointment of honest and humane gaolers, and conscientious chaplains and medical officers; the closing down of prison bars; the provision of infirmaries and chapels, of baths and ventilators, of proper clothes and sanitation; a daily allowance of wholesome food; and the appointment of inspectors to make sure these improvements were insisted upon.

He wanted prisons 'to have so many small rooms or cabins . . . that each criminal may sleep alone. If it is difficult to prevent their being together in the day-time, they should by all means be separated at night . . . Women should be quite separate from men and young criminals from old and hardened offenders . . . Prisoners should not remain in the day-time in the rooms in which they sleep; they should have a common ward, day-room or kitchen.'[21]

Howard's proposals that prisoners should be set to work in the day-time and separately confined at night, caught the imagination and approval of two lawyers of great influence, Sir William Eden (afterwards the first Baron Auckland) and Sir William Blackstone, whose monumental *Commentaries on the Laws of England* had recently been published. Eden and Blackstone envisaged the building of several new prisons where tasks 'of the hardest and most servile kind, for which drudgery is chiefly required' should be performed by convicts who were otherwise to remain in solitary confinement.[22]

It was, however, not entirely a reformatory spirit that led Parliament to give these proposals effect by the Penitentiary Houses Act of 1779, for by then some new means of dealing with an increasing criminal population had become essential. Four years before, on 19 April 1775, the first shots of the American Revolution had been fired at Lexington and the Government had soon been obliged to face the fact that the transatlantic colonies could no longer be considered a convenient dumping-ground for unwanted men.

(ii)

The systematic transportation of criminals to the American colonies had been initiated by Act of Parliament in 1717.[1] For some years before that the sale of criminals to planters in America and in the West Indies had been carried on, although transportation had never been recognized as a punishment by the Common Law.[2] Advantage had been taken of some of the clauses of Elizabeth's Vagrancy Act,[3] which empowered justices to banish offenders overseas, and by a decree of James I, a hundred 'dissolute' men had been transported to Virginia. Cromwell made use of the practice which was afterwards established in Statute law[4] as being applicable to all classes of offenders who were under sentence of death. But it was not until the 1717 Act was passed that regular transportation became part of the penal system. By this Act prisoners were made over by order of the Court to private contractors who sold them (or, to be legally precise, who sold their service) in the New World. They took their place beside the negro slaves from West Africa and it was hoped that 'by their labour and industry' they 'might be the means of improving and making the colonies and plantations more useful' to the home country.[5]

On some plantations the conditions in which they worked and the cruelty with which they were treated were appalling, but on others the hard and healthy work, the strict supervision, the new surroundings 'combined to effect a reformation in the case of even some of those who had before been the most abandoned criminals'.[6] In Maryland transported criminals were so much in demand that contracts were made to convey them across the Atlantic without expense to the Government; and some of them in time became farmers and planters, buying criminals in the ports of disembarkation as they had once been bought themselves. This absorption of transported men into the general population was well advanced by the time the Revolutionary War suddenly forced the British Government to look for other means of disposing of those criminals who were allowed to escape hanging.

For ten years no alternative method could be found. William Eden suggested that criminals might be exchanged for Christian prisoners taken by the Mohammedan pirates of the North African coast; but a more practical and immediate solution was the use of the ships that had formerly taken their human cargoes across the Atlantic as floating prisons moored in the estuaries of rivers.

And then in 1786 it was accepted that the new continent discovered on the other side of the world some years before by Captain Cook might provide the answer that had so long been sought. Captain Cook had recorded in his journal that the great quantity of plants which had been collected when his ship laid at anchor off the coast of what he called New South Wales, had induced him to give this part of it the name of Botany Bay. Its 'series of beautiful meadows abounding in the richest pastures and only inhabited by a few savages', so it was suggested in an official letter addressed to the Lords Commissioners of the Treasury, would prove 'an admirable destination for the savages at present a heavy charge upon their Lordships at home'.[7]

In the spring of 1787 a Governor, Lieutenant-Governor, Commissary and Chaplain were appointed, and a fleet of six convict ships, containing 558 men and 192 women, set sail from Spithead to establish the new penal settlement in Australia. In January 1788 the fleet arrived in Botany Bay and found it, far from being the fertile, pleasant land they had expected, a barren area of swamp and sand. Captain Arthur Phillip, the Governor, took his apprehensive charges on to an inlet which Cook had named Port Jackson and here he disembarked them. There were far fewer of them now than there had been when the convoy had left England. Over forty had died on the long journey; others had managed to escape; and two women had gone off in a French discovery ship. Those that remained had not been selected with any regard to their capacity for building a settlement or for farming the land they were expected to clear. Many of them had scurvy or syphilis or dysentery and there were no medical supplies. There were not enough guards and these were obliged to spend more time in fighting off the constant attacks of natives, provoked into hostility, than in getting the sick and unruly convicts to work.

Soon the food began to run out and the stores were further diminished by raids upon them by the uncontrollable convicts. Captain Phillip felt compelled to hang seventeen men for this offence; others were banished from the colony or whipped. But still the thefts went on. What little wheat grew and ripened was pilfered by the hungry men.[8]

'In the whole world there is not a worse country than we have seen,' Captain Phillip complained in desperation. 'Almost all the seeds we have put in the ground have rotted ... I think it will be cheaper to feed convicts on turtles and venison at the London Tower than to be at the expense of sending men here ... If the Secretary of State sends out more convicts I shall not scruple to say that he will bring misery on all that are sent.'[9]

The transportations nevertheless went on. Men came out of the ships, some of them still chained together, the Governor reported, 'so emaciated, so worn away by long confinement or from want of food' that many of them died immediately on landing. 'Of the 939 males sent out by the last ships,' one of his surgeons reported in 1790, '261 died on board and fifty have died since landing.'[10]

The transport contractors were paid by the numbers of convicts they took on board and not by the numbers they landed. 'The more, therefore, that died, and the sooner, the less food was consumed, and the greater the profit ... The rations were so much reduced ... that many convicts were actually starved to death.'[11]

Mutiny on board the transports was not infrequent and Captain Hogan of H.M.S. *Marquess of Cornwallis,* en route for New South Wales in 1796, reported a mutiny of men who tried to take over the ship and take her to America. 'At eleven o'clock,' Captain Hogan wrote, 'we commenced flogging these villains and continued engaged on that disagreeable service till forty-two men and eight women received their punishment ... On the 22nd at 9 p.m. I heard dreadful cries in the prison and found those who had not been punished were murdering those that gave any information. To rescue these from the vengeance of the others I was obliged to fire amongst them with blunderbusses and pistols.'[12]

As soon as the transports laid anchor in the cove, the officers first, the non-commissioned officers next and finally the men of the garrison came on board to 'select such females as are most agreeable to their persons'. Then the rest of the convicts came ashore to begin their seven or fourteen years of work in the squalid conditions which were ruinous 'both to their health and to their morals'. The 'whole community might be classed into those who sold spirits and those who drank them ... there was neither marrying nor giving in marriage ... two thirds of the births were illegitimate. Bands of robbers ... infested the country, levying black-mail' and committing 'the most fearful atrocities'.[13]

The Governor insisted that the colony would continue to develop with the same pitiable and depressing slowness unless the Government encouraged honest, healthy, and capable emigrants to come out by paying their fares for them. After 1796 a few subsidized settlers did emigrate but most of them were described as 'not very superior' to the convicts; and their numbers were swamped by the floods of criminals who were still pouring in.

By 1810, according to a House of Commons Committee appointed to report on the affairs of New South Wales, the population of the colony, apart from the 1,100 troops, was just over ten thousand and 'the great majority' were convicts. The method of assigning these convicts amongst the settlers had not worked well. Although the settlers were required to provide nothing but food and shelter for prisoners assigned to them as farm workers or servants, less than an eighth of the convicts were employed in this way and women, if accepted by settlers at all, were 'received rather as prostitutes than as servants'. The rest of the convicts, apart from a few who had 'been in a higher station in life' or who were 'unused to active employment' and were consequently given tickets of leave and exempted from compulsory labour, were employed in gangs in the Government service. Convicts employed in these chain gangs worked at least ten and usually twelve hours a day. At night they were shut up in wooden shanties, still wearing their heavy iron fetters, and were often so cramped that there was not enough room for them all to lie down on the floor at the same time.[14]

After 1809 when General Macquarie came out as the new Governor, these gangs were at least employed to some good and lasting purpose. Roads and harbours were built, shanty camps were turned into solid towns, Sydney—the tumbledown jumble of huts and cabins named after the Secretary of State for the Colonies —was pulled to the ground and rebuilt. But although Macquarie kept the gangs busy in construction work on an imposing scale, he neglected agricultural development which was at that time far more important. He hoped that grants of land to convicts when their years of enforced labour had expired would make them good and ambitious citizens; but he was to be disappointed. The convicts preferred to sell their newly-acquired land and go back to the towns they had helped to build so that they could spend their money on women and drink, or to go home to England. His hope that if convicts were given posts of responsibility when they were freed, they would become reliable, was also to be unrealized. Few convicts, after the treatment they had received, proved worthy of the opportunities granted them and the fact that they were given these opportunities at all discouraged the emigration of free settlers which did not begin on a satisfactory scale until Sir Thomas Brisbane succeeded Macquarie in 1821.

Meanwhile, although the colony was slowly prospering, the convicts in Government service were still treated with cruel severity. They were 'fed with the coarsest food', the *Sydney Gazette* reported in 1820, 'governed with the most rigid discipline, subjected to the stern and frequently capricious and tyrannical will of an overseer,' who was often a convict himself.

The well-being of those assigned to private masters depended, of course, entirely on the type of settler who employed them. A few were treated well; but others, allocated to severe or sadistic settlers by the Assignments Board, which before 1836 was not required to make any inquiry about the conditions in which convicts would serve their period of slavery, were cruelly misused. 'I have seen men for mere venial offences scourged until the blood has dripped into their shoes,' a witness told a Parliamentary committee. 'And I have seen the flesh tainted and smelling on a living human body from the effects of severe flagellation. After being flogged he must go again instantly to the fields . . . There is no compassion.'[15] Even when he was better treated, after reforms in the methods of assignment had been instituted by Sir Ralph Darling and his successor as Governor, Sir Richard Bourke, the convict was not likely to be happy. 'I believe the years of assignment are passed away with discontent and unhappiness,' wrote Charles Darwin after visiting the colony in the 1830's in the survey ship *Beagle*. 'The convicts know no pleasure beyond sensuality and in this they are not satisfied.'[16]

By this time the end of transportation was already in sight. Grants of land of up to two thousand acres, offered to any settlers willing to employ twenty prisoners, had enormously increased the demand for convict labour, but there was a growing feeling in the colony that the demand should not be satisfied. A better sort of settler was now arriving. He resented the influence that rich and disreputable ex-convicts, who had been able to rise to positions of power, were able to exercise over his life. He was disheartened by the excessive crime rate; by the numbers of escaped convicts who became bushrangers and by the hundreds of ticket-of-leave men who lived as squatters on the outskirts of towns and acted as fences for the robbers inside them; by the knowledge that there were more convictions for highway robbery every year than there were for all robberies put together in England. He was disgusted by the amount of drunkenness and the number of brothels in Sydney. And he was outraged by the conduct of some of the employers of convict labour who not only ill-treated their slaves but actually encouraged them to go out in gangs to rob and plunder the neighbourhood. Gradually the influence of the new settlers, who wanted New South Wales to become a decent and respectable colony and who saw an end to transportation as the only means of achieving this aim, became irresistible. 'What would you say,' Benjamin Franklin had protested when transportation to the American colonies was at its height, 'if we were to transport our rattlesnakes to England?'[17] Now similar protests came from Australia.

In England, too, transportation was condemned, but for different reasons. It was attacked as a wastage of man-power. If roads and harbours could be constructed by convicts in New South Wales, it was argued, why could they not be built by convicts at home? Also was transportation really a punishment at all? Sydney Smith, for one, certainly did not think it was.

'A sentence of transportation to Botany Bay translated into common sense is this,' he told the Home Secretary; "Because you have committed this offence, the sentence of the court is that you shall no longer be burdened with the support of your wife and family. You shall be immediately removed from a very bad climate and a country overburdened with people to one of the finest regions of the earth where demand for human labour is every hour increasing and where it is highly probable you may ultimately regain your character and improve your future." '[18]

That some men had improved their future could not be denied. There was one well-authenticated story of a man who had been sentenced to transportation paying his wife's fare to Australia where she arranged for him to be assigned to her as a servant. Thereafter they lived happily in Sydney on the proceeds of their crimes. Many other men, it was suggested, had committed crimes for the sole purpose of earning a free passage there. But there was another reason, too, apart from wastage of man-power and its lack of deterrent value which lent weight to the arguments of those in England who wished to end transportation; and that was that it had proved to be in no sense reformative. Punishment, Dr Whateley insisted, should be corrective, 'or at least not corrupting,' but transportation was corrupting and was, in fact, 'open to more objections' than any punishment which had been proposed or even could be 'conceived as a substitute' to the death penalty.[19] And Jeremy Bentham, in large measure, agreed with him.

These objections, together with those of the protesting settlers in New South Wales which were arriving with increasing force at the Colonial Office, were considered in 1837 by a Select Committee which proposed that transportation to Australia should be discontinued as soon as possible and that confinement with hard labour at home or abroad should be substituted.

This was a policy which it was impossible to carry out immediately, for there were at that time far too few prisons where convicts who would otherwise have been transported could be confined and the hulks were already hideously overcrowded. It was, therefore, decided that although transportation to New South Wales would be abandoned, the islands to the south and east of it would continue to receive prisoners from England.

The largest of these islands, Tasmania (or Van Diemen's Land as it was then called) was already in use as a penal settlement and life here was as terrible as it had ever been in the early days of transportation on the mainland. In 1835 a quarter of the male convicts and a fifth of the women were undergoing punishments for crimes committed since they had been sent there; and the punishments were peculiarly savage. Prisoners sometimes in chains and often naked were taken out to spend the night on rocks in the bay; they were flogged with special cats-o'-nine-tails which had nine knots in each tail. A man who had walked across the punishment ground of a convict station on his way to give evidence in court described in a scarifying book how he saw the blood from the back of a man who had been flogged running down his legs and

'squashing out of his shoes at every step he took. A dog was licking the blood off the triangles, and the ants were carrying away great pieces of human flesh that the lash had scattered about the ground ... The scourger's feet had worn a deep hole in the ground by the violence with which he whirled himself round on it ... The infliction was one hundred lashes at about half-minute time, so as to extend the punishment through nearly an hour ... they had a pair of scourgers who gave each other spell and spell about and they were bespattered with blood like a couple of butchers.'[20]

Some convicts committed serious crimes so that they might be executed; sometimes three men drew lots to decide who should be murderer, who victim and who witness; others went off to almost certain death in the wilderness rather than go on living in the fearful camps.

One of these men was Alexander Pierce whose experiences, horrifying as they are, were not exceptional. Pierce and some other men who were working in a gang on one of the islands in the bay decided to steal a boat and make their escape to the mainland. Their theft was discovered and they made for the barren hills where after a time they became obsessed by thoughts of food. One of them said he was so hungry he 'could eat a man'. The like had been done before, he said, and it 'tasted much like pork'. That night, another member of the gang, who had once acted as a flogger at the convict station, had his throat cut. Some of his companions bled him, cut off his head and eviscerated the trunk. Then they fried his heart and ate it. Four days later another man was killed; and while eating parts of his heart and liver yet another man was struck down from behind by one of his fellow cannibals. Only

Pierce and two others were left now, and these three men went on alone. One of them lagged behind the others and fell down exhausted. The leading man, Greenhill, went back and finding him asleep killed him with an axe. Greenhill strapped the axe to his body so that Pierce should not take it from him and rejoined his now only remaining companion. That night after Greenhill had gone to sleep with the axe still strapped to his body, Pierce, so he later confessed, began to fear he would be killed in the morning. So he got up and killed Greenhill instead. He cut off an arm and part of a thigh and went on by himself. In the morning he wandered into a flock of sheep and killing a lamb, he ate it raw. Soon after this he was recaptured. But he escaped again the following year with a man named Cox whose mangled body was found some days later. When Pierce was recaptured for the second time he was still carrying the bread and pork and the fish with which he had escaped. He had killed Cox, he said, because food from the human body, particularly the thick part of the arm, was 'by far preferable'.[21]

Stories like this, illustrative of the degradation to which men subjected to years of punishment in the worst penal settlements could sink, had their effect on the recommendations of the Committee of 1837 and the subsequent administration of the island prisons. By 1840 transported convicts were allowed to work their way up through various grades of a 'probation' system from detention on Norfolk Island and gang labour, through a stage in which the well-behaved convict could get a paid job while holding a probation pass, to a final stage—before being pardoned—in which he held a ticket of leave.[22]

This system was extended in scope by Alexander Maconochie, Superintendent of Norfolk Island, where all the worst of transported criminals were sent. Maconochie, a Scottish retired naval captain who had been the first Professor of Geography in University College, London, had gone out to Tasmania in 1837 as secretary to the Lieutenant-Governor. He had taken no part in the controversy about transportation while in England, but once in Tasmania, investigations he carried out on behalf of the Society for the Improvement of Prison Discipline convinced him that the system was iniquitous.[23] 'The proper object of prison discipline,' he wrote later, 'is to prepare men for discharge.'[24] No attempt to reform them was being made in Tasmania, where he believed the brutal punishments not only debased the convicts as Alexander

Pierce had been debased, but also those who inflicted the punishments and authorized their infliction. He did not advocate lenity to criminals which 'when injudiciously extended, injures rather than benefits them'. But severity should be made 'parental, not vindictive'. There was 'no lesson more important in social science', he thought, 'than that the common interest is the interest of each and all, not of any section merely; that when beyond all question individuals are sacrificed, the public also indirectly suffer'.[25]

On Norfolk Island, the largest of a group of islands in the Pacific about nine hundred miles north-east of Sydney, Maconochie was given an opportunity to put his theories to the test. It was quite unsuitable for the experiment, being inhabited for the most part by supposedly irreclaimable men who had been reconvicted for the second or third time after their original terms of punishment had expired. There were, in Maconochie's own words, 'two thousand men cooped up in a nutshell. Two-thirds were the refuse of both penal colonies.'[26] But he accepted the appointment of Superintendent and set to work. He found the island a 'turbulent, brutal hell' and left what he claimed without undue exaggeration, had become 'a peaceful well-ordered community'.[27]

His system was a simple one. Instead of a sentence to be determined by the expiration of time, he instituted one to be lessened by hard work. The convicts were told to 'earn their freedom by the sweat of their brows'.[28] Marks were given as wages and deducted as punishment. A good day's labour at piecework rates earned the convicts ten marks each, although more could be earned by extra work. To teach them self-denial and self-reliance they had to buy their own food which varied in price, the simplest meals costing three marks, the best meals five marks. And for every ten marks a man saved, he shortened his sentence by a day. Sentences were divided into three periods; the first period was one of stringent discipline; the second one of association, in which men formed themselves into groups of six and by being paid or fined as a group became interested in each other's work and behaviour; the third period was one of conditional freedom.

Maconochie was a good and brave man although perhaps a somewhat puritanical one. He walked unarmed amongst his convicts with his wife and children; he took down the protective bars from the Superintendent's house; he also took down the gallows. The lash and irons which his predecessor had found constantly necessary, he hardly ever used. He built two churches and re-established schools; he held his court in public and made the convicts 'stand up like men' when talking to his officers instead of bowing their heads as they had formerly been obliged to do; he allowed privileged prisoners to wear ordinary clothes and to grow and smoke tobacco 'not to encourage its consumption, but to legalize an indulgence which it is impossible to prevent'. His success was remarkable. Of 1,450 prisoners discharged during the four years he lived on Norfolk Island only three per cent were known to have been reconvicted.[29]

The idea that imprisonment was a punishment in itself, however, and that additional penalties, punishments and humiliations should not be heaped upon the convicted prisoner while undergoing it, was one which few other men then shared. Maconochie was severely criticized. When the news reached London that on the occasion of the Queen's birthday he had allowed his convicts to have a holiday, play games, act in a play and drink Her Majesty's health, 'the decision to recall him,' in the words of his biographer, 'waited only on the choice of a successor'.

Maconochie went home in 1844. The work that he had so promisingly begun was abandoned by his successors who brought back the gallows and the lash. In a revolt two years later, four of the staff were murdered and afterwards twelve prisoners were hanged. For the next ten years, until it was abandoned as a penal colony in 1856, Norfolk Island became once more the 'brutal hell' that Maconochie had discovered. Gags, bridles and headstalls were used and an instrument of torture known as the stretcher, an iron frame on which a man was extended with his head hanging down backwards without support so that twelve hours spent on it could—and on at least one occasion did—result in death. Chained prisoners were strung up to the ceiling of their huts by one hand, and sent to work, with lacerated, foul-smelling, putrescent backs, in the Cayenne pepper mill where the stinging dust maddened them.[30]

At Port Arthur years of such treatment had turned a convict who had been transported at the age of thirteen for stealing a hare into 'a grizzled, gaunt and half-naked old man coiled up in a corner'.

'The peculiar wild-beast smell which belongs to some forms of furious madness exhaled from his cell' (a man who visited him in 1870 said). 'The gibbering animal within turned and his malignant eyes met mine.

"Take care," said the gaoler, "he has a habit of sticking his finger through the peep-hole to try and poke someone's eyes out." I drew back, and a nail-bitten hairy finger like the toe of an ape was thrust with rapid and simian neatness through the aperture. "This is how he amuses himself," said the good warder, forcing to the iron slot. "He'd best be dead, I'm thinking." [31]

By this time the whole system of transportation had collapsed. Tasmania, 'swamped with the criminal classes' from England, was being deserted by its free colonists. Thousands of prisoners with probation passes, tickets-of-leave or pardons were looking for work and there was no work for them to do. The colonial government was going bankrupt. In 1852 it refused to accept any more convicts. The Colonial Office in London began a desperate search for a new dumping ground. Northern Australia, New Guinea, the Falkland Islands, and Labrador were all considered and for various reasons found unsuitable. Bermuda and Gibraltar had already taken as many convicts as they reasonably could. A request to the Executive Council of Queensland was immediately answered by an inquiry as to whether there was not some part of Britain which might prove a good settlement for Queensland's criminals. For a time Western Australia supplied settlements for transported convicts but by now another stage in penal history had begun. The convict ship that left for Western Australia in 1867 was the last to sail from England.

(iii)

The passing of the Penitentiary Houses Act in 1779, like so many earlier attempts to reform the English prison system, had had little immediate effect. There had been an argument over the site for the first of the proposed new penitentiaries and the obstinate and intractable John Howard, whose great gifts did not include an ability to work with his fellow men, resigned as one of the three supervisors created by the Act, and the whole scheme had lapsed.

The temporary measure—continued, in fact, until well on into the 1850's—of imprisoning men, who would formerly have been sentenced to transportation, in the hulks of the suddenly idle convict ships, interfered with the schemes of the reformers in the House of Commons as did the discovery of Australia, which made a return to transportation on a large scale possible again. They con-

tinued to do their best to arouse the enthusiasm of their countrymen for the improvement of prison conditions, but they had little
success. Some local acts were passed, permitting the erection of
prisons on the new cellular model and a model prison was, in fact,
built at Gloucester in 1791. But, despite the passage of a
General Prisons Act in the same year, the establishment of a
national penitentiary scheme remained a chimera. Such a scheme,
its critics continued to maintain would, apart from any other draw-
backs, be quite outrageously expensive. And it was largely because
it appeared so economical that Jeremy Bentham's proposals set out
in *The Panopticon, or Prison Discipline* appealed to the Government. The idea of the Panopticon was originally not Jeremy's
but that of his remarkable brother Brigadier-General Sir Samuel
Bentham who had adopted both his rank and his knighthood as
being the rough equivalent of honours conferred upon him in
Russia where he had become recognized as an authority on naval
gunnery and dockyards. He had shown his scheme for the supervision of dockyard labour to his brother who saw how it might be
adapted to the supervision of prisoners.

Jeremy Bentham's Panopticon was to be a circular building, 'an
iron cage glazed,' as he described it, 'a glass lantern about the size
of Ranelagh. The prisoners in the cells occupying the circumfer-
ence; the officers, Governor (Chaplain, Surgeon, etc.) the centre'.
The officers, concealed by 'blinds and other contrivances', would
give to the prisoners a feeling that they were being watched by 'a
sort of invisible omnipresence' and would be able to review the
whole circle of cells from their vantage-ground.[1]

The prisoners would be taught to 'love labour' by being set to
useful work and by being allowed to share in their produce. But
although the scheme contained many sound ideas, some of which
were ultimately adopted, Bentham's proposition that he could
complete the building for only nineteen thousand pounds, and thereafter maintain each man for a Treasury grant of twelve pounds
a year was recklessly hopeful. The Government, however, were
prepared to believe him and entered into a contract by which he
was paid two thousand pounds on signature so that he could place
an order for a cast-iron frame-work. Enthusiastic and impatient,
Bentham went ahead with his project, talking to architects, looking
for a suitable site and buying materials, until he was many thousands of pounds out of pocket without anything very much to
show either for his efforts or for his money. Ministers with the

Napoleonic War on their minds were content to leave the matter in abeyance, particularly as the King was strongly opposed to the whole idea, and it was not until 1810 that a definite decision was taken to relieve Bentham of his personal responsibility and put the matter in the hands of a Government contractor. Three years later Bentham was paid twenty-three thousand pounds compensation for his loss and the construction of the long-awaited penitentiary at Millbank was at last under way.

It was, however, to be several years before the vast structure was finally completed (at the cost of over half a million pounds) and in the meantime, as indeed after its completion, prison conditions continued to show few signs of improvement. As late as 1823 some prisoners were still chained to the floor; and in one county, at least, 'there were but two gaol deliveries for the year,' so a prisoner could be chained down like this 'from six to eight months and then acquitted as innocent'.[2] Nor was there much attempt at classification in many prisons. In Newgate, as Edward Gibbon Wakefield, who was imprisoned there in 1827, discovered, there was scarcely any.[3] A Select Committee had reported some years before that boys were mixed 'indiscriminately together from the ages of eight to sixteen or eighteen, exhibiting a great variety of character and differing in degrees of guilt, the tried and the untried, and the first offender with the hardened convicts'. None but those who had witnessed such painful exhibitions could be aware of the pleasure which the older thieves took in corrupting those who had 'just entered vicious courses'.[4] Twenty years after this Report was published, although the classification of prisoners was by then required by Act of Parliament, 'the greatest contempt was shown for the law'. Two Inspectors of Prisons, appointed in 1835, found that in Newgate men convicted of homosexual offences were shut up in the same wards as young boys awaiting trial and slept on the same rope mats with them; minor offenders were put with hardened criminals awaiting transportation; lunatics with those who were obviously pretending to be mad. The ward which a newcomer entered was settled by prisoners, known as wardsmen, to whom the Governor assigned this duty and to whom bribes were openly paid. Most of the prisoners were in rags; food was served out by the wardsmen who made as much money out of their office as they could.[5]

'The days were passed in idleness, debauchery, riotous quarrelling, immoral conversation, gambling, instruction in all nefarious processes, lively discourse upon past criminal exploits, elaborate discussion of others to be perpetrated after release. No provision whatever was made for the employment of prisoners. There was no school for adults; only the boys were taught anything, and their instructor, with his assistant, were convicted prisoners ... Drink, in more or less unlimited quantities was still to be had ... Women saw men if they merely pretended to be wives; even boys were visited by their sweethearts ... Perhaps the worst feature of the visiting system was the permission accorded to male prisoners to have access to the female side.'[6]

On the female side, in contrast, 'more system and a greater semblance of decorum was maintained'. And this was almost entirely due to the efforts of a single, remarkable woman. Elizabeth Fry had visited Newgate for the first time on an icy January morning, more than thirty years before this report of the Prison Inspectors was written. She saw starving women, many of them drunk, lying on the stone floors without bedding. 'The women, seeing visitors, pressed to the bars, stretching out greedy hands, whining, begging for pence to spend in drink at the tap of the prison. Those in front were fought with by those behind; hands snatched them back by the hair, pinched them, punched them in the ribs with fists and elbows.'[7]

Elizabeth Fry had been persuaded to make her visit to Newgate by the American Quaker, Stephen Grellet, who told her that conditions there were far worse than anything he had seen during his Continental travels. Mrs Fry, herself born a Quaker and married to one, for whom she was eventually to bear eleven children, was already well known for her philanthropic work; and she immediately agreed to extend it in the way that Grellet suggested. Her success was astonishing and deeply moving. Having so large a family it was impossible for her at first to devote much of her time to the prisoners, but at Christmas 1816 she started with her friends the selfless work for which she is so deservedly admired. She organized regular visits, she started a school for the prison children, she gave the women clothes and food and work. She demanded nothing in return but 'a voluntary subordination to the rule of sobriety, cleanliness and decent conversation'.

To the surprise of the prison authorities she had her reward. So sincerely sympathetic, so spontaneously tender, so understanding, and with a Christian outlook so refreshingly and com-

pletely without humbug and hypocrisy, she was accepted by most
of these poor women, reduced as previously they had been by
cruelty and neglect 'to the level of wild beasts', as a woman they
could both respect and love.

It was a triumphant achievement but the example she set was
followed by only a very few others. She was admired rather than
imitated. Her tours of provincial and foreign prisons and of the
hulks, her useful and heartfelt evidence before a Committee of the
House of Commons, her belief that it was society's duty to try
and reform prisoners and not to starve and degrade them, were
all looked upon by the general public as indications of a soft heart
rather than of a practical mind. The travels of Howard's successor,
James Neild, whose book *The State of Prisons in England, Scotland and Wales* had been published in 1812; the work of Sarah
Martin, who had devoted her life to the prisoners of Yarmouth
Gaol; the work of Elizabeth Fry's brother-in-law, Samuel Hoare,
and of her other brother-in-law, Thomas Fowell Buxton who had
founded the Society for the Reformation of Prison Discipline in
1816, all alike were accorded scant respect by a people whose
sympathies lay more with the Rev Sydney Smith who voiced his
opinions unequivocally in the *Edinburgh Review*. 'Mrs Fry is an
amiable excellent woman,' Sydney Smith thought, 'and ten thousand times better than the infamous neglect that preceded her;
but hers is not the method to stop crimes. In prisons which are
really meant to keep the multitude in order, and to be a terror
to evil-doers, there must be no sharing of profits—no visiting of
friends—no education but religious education—no freedom of diet,
no weavers' looms or carpenters' benches. There must be a great
deal of solitude; coarse food; a dress of shame; hard incessant,
irksome, eternal labour; a planned and regulated and unrelenting
exclusion of happiness and comfort.'[8]

The immense penitentiary at Millbank had been completed in
1821, some months before these words were written, and it seemed
to Sydney Smith and those who thought as he did a very dangerous
enterprise. It was possible, one of its critics admitted, that 'this
nursing and petting of felons' might reform a few 'but for his own
part' he would 'rather take a culprit for a servant after six months'
real hard labour prison discipline' than after three years in the
new penitentiary.[9]

The inmates of Millbank were hardly likely to agree that they
were being nursed and petted. Architecturally the prison owed

something to the influence of Bentham's Panopticon, being built
in the shape of a six-pointed star, and in its organization and
management it owed something to the ideas of John Howard, Fowell
Buxton, and Elizabeth Fry. But it seemed to those who entered
its coldly echoing halls like an immense and nameless tomb. It
sprawled over seven acres and one warder after years of service
there had still not learned his way about it. 'He carried with him
a piece of chalk, with which he "blazed" his path as the American
backwoodsman does the forest trees. Angles every twenty yards,
winding staircases, dark passages, innumerable doors and gates'
bewildered him as much as they did every newcomer.[10]

The convicts occupied separate cells where they worked alone
for the first half of their sentences; during the second half they were
allowed to work in association with others. But it was difficult to
find work for them to do; and eventually the only activity carried
on in the penitentiary was weaving and this could be as monotonous and boring as prison life itself. There were few physical
punishments; the Governor was more kindly than most and seemed
sincerely to regret the occasional floggings of recalcitrant convicts;
the food was stodgy but adequate. Many of the prisoners, however,
particularly the female prisoners, found it impossible to live the
quiet, ordered, phlegmatic, lonely life that their Evangelical supervisors expected of them. There was a serious riot and the
Governor was compelled to call in the Bow Street Runners to
restore order. Five years later there was an epidemic of scurvy,
dysentery and cholera in which more than half the prisoners fell
ill and thirty of them died. A special Act of Parliament had to be
passed to permit the removal of the survivors. All the women were
eventually pardoned as this was felt to be the only way of restoring
their health, and the men were distributed between various hulks.
When the prison was re-opened after being fumigated, the diet was
made more healthy and palatable, the ventilation was improved,
some games were allowed, candles were put in the cells, a few
limited educational facilities were provided and prisoners were
classified in three groups. Millbank became a promising prison
again. But it remained, in fact, an unutterably dreary one.

However much the dullness of existence there tended to destroy
the mind and spirit, though, this tendency was to be emphasized
by a new system of prison discipline which, however creditable
the intentions of its advocates, was almost as cruel as the physical
deprivations and tortures of the previous century.

Howard's suggestion that prisoners should be separated at night and, if it were 'difficult to prevent their being together', work in association by day, had been questioned by, amongst others, that prolific pamphleteer, Jonas Hanway, who believed that it was essential that they be separated all the time. This was clearly impossible so long as the old prisons were still in use, but now that new ones were being built, it seemed to some reformers that the experiment should be made.

In the United States, it was pointed out, this system was already in operation in Pennsylvania where penal reform had long been considered a matter of importance by the legislature. In 1682 William Penn had made his 'Holy Experiment' and founded the Province of Pennsylvania and a new 'Great Law' had been enacted. It was almost as theocratic as the Puritan conception of English seventeenth-century law which had made 'denying the true God' a capital offence with sodomy, buggery, adultery and the smiting by children of their parents. But although swearing and drunkenness ranked as equal crimes with murder, corporal punishment was replaced by imprisonment in work-houses which were to be 'free as to fees, food and lodging';[11] and by an amendment of 1683 only murder was a capital offence. On Penn's death the Assembly was persuaded by the Governor to re-introduce English criminal law; but by 1786, ten years after the Declaration of Independence, the death penalty was reserved for treason, murder, rape and arson, all other serious crimes being punished by whipping, imprisonment or hard labour performed by chain gangs in public.

In 1790 the legislature had created what afterwards became famous as the Pennsylvania prison system by providing that a new block of cells should be built within the grounds of the Walnut Street Prison in Philadelphia. The convicts imprisoned there were placed in solitary confinement and given no work. In every cell, according to a contemporary account, there was 'one small window, placed high up and out of reach; the window well secured by a double iron grating, so that, provided an effort to get to it was successful, the person could perceive neither heaven nor earth, on account of the thickness of the wall. The criminal, while confined here, is permitted no convenience of bench, table or even bed, or anything else but what is barely necessary to support life.'[12]

There were only twenty-four cells in the new block, however, and the majority of the prisoners were still kept in the old part of the prison where, although some attempt was made to classify them and silence was enforced at work and meals, separate confinement was impossible. As the years passed the prison became more and more crowded, discipline relaxed, the Quakers were replaced on the board of management by political appointees and the conditions were eventually compared with those of the old High Street Gaol of colonial times and even with conditions in Connecticut, where abandoned mines were used as prisons, and with those in Maine, where convicts were kept in deep pits which could only be entered by ladders.[13] Other prisons modelled on the new Walnut Street block were built in New York and at Charlestown in Massachusetts, but in these as well overcrowding and mismanagement soon resulted in conditions even worse than those in Philadelphia and led ultimately to an abandonment of separate confinement.

In the face of these setbacks and disappointments the Pennsylvania Prison Society and the Philadelphia Society for Alleviating the Miseries of Public Prisons, both inspired by the Quakers, demanded that the separate system should be given a new chance. And eventually it was. Two new state prisons were built in Pennsylvania and in both of them all the prisoners were separately confined. The Western Penitentiary was built at Pittsburgh in 1818 on the pattern of Bentham's Panopticon and the Eastern Penitentiary was built at Cherry Hill in 1829 to the design of John Haviland whose plan of several wings radiating from the centre had already been used in the construction of Ipswich Prison in England.[14] Once in his cell a prisoner might remain alone in it for years, taking his exercise by himself in a little yard adjoining it, working at some lonely task if suitable work could be found for him, reading the Bible—in most cells the only book allowed—if no work could be found, meditating—so it was hoped—on his sins, not even being allowed out of his cell for divine service but having to listen to the voice of the chaplain who preached concealed behind a black curtain. One predictable result of this régime was that 'a number of convicts became insane.'[15] Dickens after a visit to the Eastern Penitentiary in 1842 decided that 'very few men were capable of estimating the immense amount of torture and agony which this dreadful punishment, prolonged for years, inflicts upon the prisoner' and believed that the 'slow and daily tampering with the mysteries of the brain' was 'immeasurably worse than any torture of the body'.[16]

'Over the head and face of every prisoner who comes into this melancholy house,' Dickens wrote, 'a black hood is drawn; and in this dark shroud, an emblem of the curtain dropped between him and the living world, he is led to the cell from which he never again comes forth, until his whole term of imprisonment has expired. He never hears of wife or children; home or friends; the life or death of a single creature. He sees the prison-officers but with that exception he never looks upon a human countenance or hears a human voice. He is a man buried alive; to be dug out in the slow round of years; and in the meantime dead to everything but torturing anxieties and horrible despair.'[17]

Some of the new cell blocks at Auburn Prison in the State of New York, built at about the same time as the Pennsylvanian penitentiaries, also contained criminals meditating alone by day and by night, and here without even the consolation of work. But in other blocks at Auburn prisoners were kept alone in their cells during the night but were allowed to work together in the day-time, provided they observed the strictest silence.

'In their solitary cells,' the Boston Prison Discipline Society reported, 'they spend the night with no other book than the Bible, and at sunrise they proceed in military order, under the eye of the turnkey, in solid columns, with the lock march to the workshops, thence in the same order at the hour of breakfast, to the common hall, where they partake of their wholesome and frugal meal in silence. Not even a whisper might be heard through the whole apartment.

Convicts are seated in single file, at narrow tables with their backs towards the centre, so that there can be no interchange of signs.'[18]

The silent system at Auburn was maintained by the fear of the lash. Men and women were flogged for offences no more serious than looking up when they should have had their eyes fixed on their work.[19] Captain Elam Lynds, the Warden, a relentless martinet, did not believe in the possibilities of reform and aimed only at producing obedient prisoners and keeping them securely incarcerated. With the help of John Gray, he invented the inside cell, a sort of cage in a large room of similar cages with no access to the outer wall, an invention which was to have a profound influence on subsequent prison architecture in America.

That he did produce obedient prisoners, no visitor could deny. The rows of silent men marching from their cells to the workshop or the dining-hall with their heads cast down submissively, was a sight which impressed many official observers. One of these, the Rev Louis Dwight, Secretary of the Boston Prison Discipline Society, advocated the Auburn method during his extensive travels with unqualified enthusiasm. Other states began to adopt the system; while some, believing that the training of good citizens was more important than the production of obedient prisoners, tried more liberal experiments. In Georgia as early as 1832 a system of rewards as well as of punishments was instituted; in Kentucky prisoners were credited for the work they did and debited for their maintenance; in Tennessee by 1833 sentences were being commuted as a reward for good behaviour; well-behaved prisoners in Vermont were allowed tobacco, letters and visitors; in Massachusetts education other than religious instruction was permitted; at the new Connecticut State Prison at Weatherfield the first honour system in United States prisons was inaugurated by the strict but humane Moses Pilsbury.

It was, however, the separate system of Pennsylvania and the silent system of Auburn which had the greatest influence on English observers. One of these was William Crawford who had recently been created an Inspector of English Prisons, a new office created by an Act of 1835.[20] Crawford, in company with several other European observers, visited America in 1836 and on his return drew up an enthusiastic report which caught the interest of the Home Secretary, Lord John Russell.

In 1842 a large new penitentiary was completed at Pentonville and by 1848 no less than fifty-four other prisons had been built on the same plan, having rows of single cells arranged in tiers and in separate blocks radiating from a central hub like the spokes of a wheel. Apart from Wormwood Scrubs which was built in 1874 and Dartmoor, begun in 1806 for French prisoners-of-war but made into a convict prison in 1850, practically all the large English prisons were, in fact, built in the 1840's, many of them, like Reading Prison, which itself was considered the finest building in Berkshire after Windsor Castle, combining 'with the castellated . . . a collegiate appearance'.[21]

Pentonville, a characteristic example, had 520 cells with little windows on their outside walls and doors leading to the narrow landings in the galleries. Each cell was thirteen feet long, seven feet broad and nine feet high and had a shaded gas-burner, a stool, a table and a hammock with mattress and blankets.

'It is admirably ventilated,' an admiring visitor wrote, 'on the newest
scientific principle, and by means of warm air it is kept at an even and
agreeable temperature. It has even the luxuries of a water-closet, and of
an unlimited supply of warm and cold water. The bedding is clean and
good; the food is also good and plentiful in supply. There is a
bell-handle, too.'[22]

But although the prison was comfortable enough, and no doubt
more pleasant than it is today now that—because they were always
getting blocked and because the pipes served as a means of communication—'the luxuries of a water-closet' have been replaced
by communal, evil-smelling 'recesses', the life of a prisoner there
was so appallingly monotonous and dreary that in time the men
took on that look that Dickens had noticed in Philadelphia—'something of that strained attention which we see upon the faces of the
blind and deaf, mingled with a kind of horror, as though they had
all been secretly terrified'.[23]

During the first eight years of Pentonville's existence, there
were apparently 'upwards of ten times more lunatics than should
be according to the normal rate'.[24] And in later years there were
twenty times more cases of mental disease than in any other prison
in the country.[25] An official report admitted that 'for every sixty
thousand persons confined in Pentonville there were 220 cases of
insanity, 210 cases of delusions, and forty suicides'.[26]

As at Auburn, there was perfect order and perfect silence as
the men tramped from their lonely cells wearing masks of brown
cloth so that none should recognize them, 'the eyes alone appear-
ing through the two holes cut in the front, and seeming almost
like phosphoric lights shining through the sockets of a skull'.[27]

On reception all the new prisoners were perfunctorily inspected
by the medical officer, then lectured by the Governor about the
rules and punishments, then preached at by the chaplain, then
stripped and made to stand before an officer 'in a perfect state of
nudity while he examined with disgusting particularity every part
of their persons'. The officers barked their orders and left no doubt
in the minds of the convicts that prison was a place of punishment
and repression.[28]

Breakfast consisted of ten ounces of bread and three-quarters
of a pint of cocoa; dinner was half a pint of soup (or four ounces
of meat) five ounces of bread and one pound of potatoes; the last
meal of the day was a pint of gruel and five ounces of bread.

Work began at six o'clock in the morning and continued until seven at night with breaks for meals, exercise, and the daily service in the chapel where each prisoner had his own pigeon-hole of a pew so that although his head was visible to the warders on duty, he was hidden from the view of his neighbours. Punishments, mostly for attempts to communicate with other prisoners were common. The refractory cells were completely dark without a single 'luminous chink or crack' and prisoners could be confined here for three weeks on end. The most dreaded punishment, though, was to be denied the privilege of work.

In many prisons the provision of useful work was impossible or disregarded and recourse was had to other means of keeping prisoners occupied. Sir Robert Peel's Act of 1823 had insisted on the observance of a 'reformatory regime' in prisons, and had obliged prison authorities to inform the Justices of every infliction of 'tyrannical punishments'. But it was many years before the performance of arduous yet completely useless tasks was completely abandoned. Just as classification of prisoners and their subsequent confinement in different blocks, as at Maidstone, had been advocated on the grounds of economy by those who were horrified by the cost of cellular prisons, so the treadwheel and the crank had been advocated as punishments that would be easy to apply and as means of occupation that would not threaten the livelihood of honest men. They were still, in fact, advocated in the 1860's by those who believed that prison labour should be pointless so that it should be degrading, exhausting so that it should be deterrent. Pointless, degrading and above all exhausting, the treadwheel and the crank certainly were. The treadwheel, a big iron frame of steps around a revolving cylinder, could be fitted to a mill or used for pumping water; and the crank, a wheel like the paddle wheel of a steamer fitted into a box of gravel which the prisoner had to turn by means of a handle, could also be used for productive purposes. But it was rarely that either of them was. Prisoners, male and female, trudging up the steps in their own separate compartments on the wheel might work as they did at Cold Bath Fields Prison for six hours a day and achieve nothing except the climbing of 8,640 feet; and others, turning the crank, worked for the same length of time to do nothing but break the resistance of the gravel in the box and turn the handle through ten thousand revolutions. This sort of useless and fatiguing activity was, as Dostoevsky discovered while 'buried alive' in a Siberian prison, not only a degradation but a provocation, an embittering 'torture and most cruel revenge'.[29]

The dangers of this embitterment, caused not only by the tread-mill and the crank and the picking to pieces of old rope long after the use of iron in the building of ships had made oakum largely unsaleable, but also by the whole repressive, punitive system, were little understood, or if understood, disregarded. Sir Robert Peel recognized, for instance, that solitary confinement varied in its severity 'according to the disposition of the culprit' but he, like so many of his countrymen, also believed that prisoners lived 'too comfortably for penance'.[30] So did Dr Richard Whateley, Archbishop of Dublin, whose views on punishment were much respected. Whateley attacked transportation, which he believed was inclined to favour the criminal rather than punish him, and warned against making prisons so much resemble abodes of 'comparative comfort and ease, as to forfeit all right to the name and even to tempt men to commit crimes for the sake of obtaining in them a refuge from distress'.[31]

Views such as these found wide support. It was only when some prison scandal caught the attention of the Press that public concern over the treatment of prisoners was aroused. Peel's consolidating Act of 1824[32] establishing the principle of classification of prisoners, the Act of 1835[33] creating Inspectors of Prisons, the first Penal Servitude Act of 1853[34] substituting periods of hard labour for certain sentences which would formerly have been for periods of transportation, all passed without much notice. In 1854, however, the report of a Royal Commission appointed to enquire into the allegations of cruelty at Birmingham Prison caused country-wide concern.

Between 1849 and 1851 the Governor of Birmingham Prison was Captain Alexander Maconochie, the former Superintendent of Norfolk Island. Maconochie believed that the silent system of Pentonville was ruinous of a man's body and mind and had put into operation the marks system that he had developed in Australasia. Although he had done so with the approval of the Birmingham Justices, the apparent decline in the rigidity of the discipline in the prison which they subsequently noticed was not to their liking. The Assistant Governor, Lieutenant Austin, was instructed to take over certain of Maconochie's duties and thereafter exercised over the prisoners a cruel tyranny. Maconochie protested. Austin offered to resign. The Justices refused to accept his resignation and asked the Governor himself to go.

What happened when Austin was left to himself was hinted at during the inquest on a fifteen-year-old boy who had hanged himself to escape further torture and was later described in the Royal Commission's report and in Charles Reade's novel *It's Never Too Late to Mend*. Prisoners, including boys, were savagely and continually whipped; a special type of crank, invented in Leicester Prison, made the ten thousand daily revolutions a trial of agonizing difficulty, and failure to complete the required number was punished by a night in the crank cell without food; a strait-jacket was frequently in use and, in the Royal Commission's far from emotional report, was described as an 'engine of positive torture'.[35] At Leicester Prison, the Royal Commission found, no convict could eat, except on Sundays, until he had completed his requisite number of revolutions; 1,800 revolutions were necessary before he could have breakfast of watery cocoa and dry bread; 4,500 before the midday meal; and 5,400 before supper. A further 2,700 turns had to be done afterwards if they had not been done before. One man the Commission believed had only had nine meals in three weeks of working days.[36]

The revelation that such cruelties could be perpetrated in prisons supposedly under the care of the local and unpaid visiting Magistrates led to a growing demand that all prisons should be placed under national control. It was to be some years before this idea was reached but in 1865 a new Prison Act[37] took away many of the powers formerly exercised by local authorities and in 1877 a further Act[38] swept away the rest of their powers and provided for the appointment of not more than five prison commissioners who were to be responsible to the Home Secretary.

Apart from its progressive step in the direction of national control, the 1865 Act was, however, a distressingly unimaginative measure, reflecting a general return to the view that 'prisons should deter through severity instead of making futile attempts to alter prisoners' character'.[39] It confirmed the hold that the silent system had already obtained by providing that 'prisoners shall be prevented from having any communication with each other, either by every prisoner being kept in a separate cell by day and by night except when he is at chapel or taking exercise, or by every prisoner being confined by night in his cell and being subjected to such superintendence during the day as will prevent his communicating with any other prisoner'.[40] 'Hard bodily labour' by treadwheel, shot-drill, crank and capstan was approved; the use of chains and irons was authorized as were punishments of a month in a refractory cell, close confinements for three days and nights on bread and water at the discretion of the Governor, and flogging.

The harsh régime approved in 1865 was continued after 1877 by the new Prison Commissioners under the chairmanship of Lieutenant-Colonel Edmund Du Cane a highly talented but unimaginative organizer who 'prided himself on achieving an aim which is the very reverse of that sought in any modern penal institution: the treatment of all offenders exactly alike'. The English prison system under his control became 'a massive machine for the promotion of misery'.[41] Conditions in some prisons were almost as bad as they had been at the beginning of the century. At Chatham, according to a Royal Commission which made its report in 1879, prisoners severely mutilated themselves and threw themselves beneath the wheels of the railway wagons in the dock basins in their efforts to escape from the fearful place. If they did not die they were flogged. 'There was no reason,' the Governor said, 'why they should not be flogged, because they had only mutilated an arm or a leg.'[42]

Because they were so badly fed, the convicts at Chatham were driven to eating live worms and frogs and rubbish[43] and at Portland, Dartmoor and other prisons they melted candles in their gruel to make it more satisfying.[44]

The Progressive Stage System, introduced by the Penal Servitude Act of 1853, like Maconochie's marks system, allowed a prisoner to work his way up from 'Hard labour of the First Class', involving at least six hours on the treadwheel or crank, to a fourth stage in which he might write and receive a limited number of letters and have a limited number of visitors. And the Star Class system introduced as a consequence of the report of the Royal Commission of 1878, segregated first offenders from the others. But otherwise, apart from improvements in sanitary conditions and a reduction in overcrowding until practically every prisoner had a separate cell, there was little in the national prison system of which the Commissioners could justifiably feel proud. The encouraging industries, which some prisons had built up, were abolished; cells were made as cheerless and comfortless as possible; the daily grind of a lonely life was as dreary as it had ever been. Prisoners came out into the world numbed and stupid, sometimes insane, often unemployable, nearly always bitter and resentful, with an average (at least for the three years preceding 1878) of seven-pence in their pockets,[45] ready to commit more crimes, undeterred and unreformed. It was, in fact, 'the moral condition in which a large number of prisoners leave prison and the serious number of recommittals' which led a Departmental Committee of Inquiry into Prisons, which had been appointed soon after Oscar Wilde's *Ballad of Reading Gaol* had so stirred public opinion, to report that there was 'ample cause for a searching enquiry into the main features of prison life'.[46]

The Committee under the chairmanship of Herbert Gladstone made this searching inquiry and came to the firm conclusion that the prison system was failing in its purpose. 'Prison discipline should be more effectually designed to maintain, stimulate or awaken the higher susceptibilities of prisoners, to develop their moral instincts, to train them in orderly and industrious habits, and wherever possible, to turn them out of prison better men and women physically and morally than when they came in.'[47]

This was clearly not being done. The Committee recommended that better progress might be made if useless labour was abolished; if cellular confinement was limited to short periods; if the excessive severity of Du Cane's régime were to be relaxed. The Government agreed. Du Cane was about to retire and he was replaced by his intelligent and more liberal deputy, Evelyn Ruggles-Brise, to whom Du Cane had not spoken for some years because the younger man had diffidently expressed disapproval of some minor point of policy. And so, at last, began a new and seem-ingly hopeful era in the history of English prisons. In 1898 a new Act[48] was passed incorporating most of the Committee's recom-mendations. Corporal punishments were limited, remission of sen-tences conditional upon good behaviour was introduced, 'Hard Labour of the First Class' was abolished, the system of enabling the sentencing court to decide in which of three divisions the prisoner should serve his sentence was established, and greater elasticity was provided by enabling the details of routine to be fixed by rules made with the authority of the Home Secretary but without the necessity of recourse to legislation. In the following years a whole series of Acts was passed and a constant succession of standing orders was made and amended extending the scope of punishment and limiting its abuses.

The difficulties of translating legislation into profitable practice were, however, still almost as great as they had been before the prisons were nationalized. Prisoners might be placed in separate divisions but they still 'all went through the same mill of grinding monotony, loneliness, silence and futility'.[49] A visitor to Dartmoor in 1906 was deeply shocked by the conditions he found there.

'As I walked along the endless landings and corridors in the great cellular blocks,' he wrote, 'I saw something of the 1,500 men who were then immured in Dartmoor. Their drab uniforms were plastered with broad arrows, their heads were closely shaven . . . Not even a safety razor was allowed, so that in addition to the stubble on their heads, their faces were covered with a sort of dirty moss, representing the growth of hair that a pair of clippers could not remove . . . As they saw us coming each man turned to the nearest wall and put his face closely against it, remaining in this servile position until we had passed him. This was a strictly ordered procedure, to avoid assault or familiarity, the two great offences in prison conduct.'[50]

The Gladstone Committee had warned of the effect on a man's subsequent behaviour of cellular confinement; but the effect of contamination in a prison like this might be equally disastrous. 'Any man who came from a decent house outside was appalled to discover that men could fall to such depths of moral beastliness, and the average man was inextricably dragged down by the conduct and example of the men around him, whose company he could not escape. Within a year, he was almost unrecognizable in speech and habit and point of view.'[51]

It was in the knowledge that young men sentenced to prison were almost invariably corrupted in this way, that led Evelyn Ruggles-Brise to visit the United States where the growing system of state Reformatories deeply impressed him. In England little had yet been done to establish efficient prisons specifically for young offenders. The Parkhurst Act of 1838[52] had provided a severely repressive prison in the Isle of Wight for young criminals under eighteen, but it was only intended to prepare them for life after deportation to Australia. The Schools Act of 1854[53] while empowering magistrates to order grants for reformatories—as Mary Carpenter, leader of the reformatory school movement, had long demanded—had had little to say as to how they should be run and boys sent to them were to spend a fortnight in prison first. Another Reformatory Schools Act[54] which became law in 1866 also insisted on an initial period of imprisonment. This was altered by an Act of 1893[55] and the position was again modified in 1899.[56] But while new laws were being passed about who might go to reformatories and industrial schools, regulations concerning their running were comparatively rare and punishments in them remained extremely severe. The Rev Sydney Turner, in charge of the Redhill Reformatory which was under the auspices of the Philanthropic Society, believed in severely punishing boys by putting them alone for 'a few days' in unheated cells on a bread and water diet and by whipping them 'with as much solemnity and form as possible'.[57]

It was not until Ruggles-Brise returned from America that any real advance in the treatment of young offenders was made. Soon after he came back a building in the village of Borstal, Kent was taken over as an institution where boys who might otherwise be sent to prison could be trained 'mentally, morally and physically' by an experienced staff. Within four years the experiment seemed so promising that the Prison Commissioners asked the Home Secretary for legislation to establish the Borstal system as an official one, and to permit the courts to sentence girls and boys between sixteen and twenty-one to reformatories for periods of up to three years. The request was granted in the Prevention of Crimes Act 1908.[58]

With the help and encouragement of Sir Alexander Paterson, the most understanding and far-sighted of Prison Commissioners, the Borstal system grew and prospered. In 1930, in official recognition of Paterson's belief that 'you cannot train men for freedom in a condition of captivity',[59] a Borstal without walls or wire, largely built by the boys themselves, was opened at Lowdham Grange, near Nottingham. Four years later the first 'open prison' in England was started at New Hall Camp, near Wakefield. At last, after so many years, steps were being taken to prevent crime by the reformation of the criminal rather than by his degradation in humiliating punishments. The 'open prison' system, successful from the beginning, was quickly extended and the Borstal system came to be 'generally regarded as the principal asset of the administration of criminal law in England'.[60]

But although the former insistence on obedience and conformity was now being replaced by fresh attempts to help a boy lead a more satisfactory life after his discharge, the difficulties of finding the right type of men to enter the prison service and put these excellent theories into practice were as great as ever. During the early years of their existence there were Borstals which, far from reforming the young offender, seemed actively to encourage his criminal instincts. 'I learnt more about thieving from the chaps there than anywhere else I have ever been,' a confirmed criminal told a magistrate when describing his Borstal training. 'I got taught nothing in the way of a trade either. There were two trades taught, but I never got a chance to learn one. All I did was a sort of handyman's job—sweeping up and that.'[61] 'The reason I hated the place was because there were a lot of chaps there much bigger than me, and they bullied me,' another former Borstal boy said. 'There was a lot of sexual stuff went on in that place . . . if you refused you got beaten up.'[62]

The recollections of embittered criminals are naturally suspect but there is far too much corroboratory evidence for it to be possible that the experiences of these boys were either invented or exceptional. Nor is it possible to believe that even the most scarifying books about prison life which were published in the 1930's and 1940's did not have a foundation of terrible truth.

Sir Alexander Paterson, during the years in which he served the Prison Commission, continued the work, which men like John Howard had begun in the eighteenth century, to turn prisons into something more than squalid places of confinement. Hard as he worked and much as he achieved, the fundamental problem remained unsolved at his death in 1947.

(iv)

The history of American prisons throughout this period is even more distressing. By the end of the Second World War conditions in many American gaols had improved little in more than a hundred years. Although the crank and the treadwheel had never been used, punishments during the whole of that century had often been ferocious. In 1835 a Committee reported that prisoners had been kept in darkened cells on bread and water for as long as forty-two days and had been brought out delirious; they had been ducked in ice-cold water; they had been deprived of food for three days on end or of their main meal in the day for three weeks; with their arms and legs strapped and wearing handcuffs they had been placed in the 'mad chair', a box made of planks in which it was impossible to move; strait-jackets had been laced so tightly that when released the men's necks were black with congealed blood;

gags of wire and chain had cut men's mouths and tongues open; their hands in leather gloves had been drawn so tightly up behind their backs to chains round their necks that some prisoners had been strangled.[1] Seventy years later at a penitentiary in the Middle West, 'punishments were varied and frequent but the most common was by paddle, a scientific instrument carefully designed, it seems, to inflict a maximum of suffering without infringing upon the humane law of the State'.[2] The law expressly forbade 'showering with cold water' and 'whipping with the lash on the bare body', but by the use of the 'paddle', a sort of leather tennis racket, a man could be punished with equal severity and a sheet placed over his naked back conformed with the law and lessened the likelihood of incriminating marks. In a book published in 1912 a former prisoner described the strait-jacket used in San Quentin: 'a piece of canvas about four and a half feet long, cut to fit about the human body. When spread out on the floor it has the same shape as the top of a coffin, broad near the end for the shoulders and tapering either way. Big brass eyelets run down the sides. It is manufactured in various sizes, and is designed solely as an instrument of torture. I know many cases,' this prisoner said, 'when a man was "cinched" up for a week and in one instance for ten days.'[3]

When one man was paralysed by such treatment and another man died, the State legislature decided not that the strait-jacket should be abolished as a form of punishment but that its use should be more carefully regulated. Accordingly, the State Board of Prison Directors adopted a resolution forbidding the lacing up of prisoners in strait-jackets for more than six consecutive hours. After this resolution became operative, the strait-jacket was applied for six hours, then the prisoner was 'permitted the freedom of the cell for six hours' before being tied up again.[4]

As late as 1928 visitors to one gaol found barefoot boy prisoners with swathes in the shape of a cross cut through their hair for easy identification.

In each corner of the punishment room was 'an iron pipe attached to the floor and ceiling. These boys were handcuffed to the pipes and were kept thus manacled night and day. The boys have two blankets but have to sleep on the concrete floor. The jailers said that the boys were usually handcuffed here for ten days. One case, however, was reported by a former employee in which two boys had been handcuffed to the pipes for three weeks for the offences of homosexuality and running away.'[5]

Other violent punishments in common use were beating on the bare feet and on all parts of the naked body, beating on the hands after ice had been held in them and the enforced chewing of soap.[6] At least as late as 1938 in some prisons convicts were kept on bread and water for fourteen days on end, eight prisons still regularly used the strap, in eight others prisoners were still handcuffed to their cell doors and in at least one the strait-jacket remained in use as a form of punishment rather than of restraint. The guards in Wyoming State Penitentiary still continued 'shackling a man to a post and turning a stream of cold water on him'.[7] 'Treated like a beast I am going to act like a beast,' a convict, repeatedly subjected to such degrading treatment, said afterwards, 'Can society expect me to reform? In the first place I could not reform if I did try. I was told right in my face when I came out they will send me right back . . . I don't care anymore.'[8]

The sense of injustice and resentment was increased by there being 'no conceivable relation between the seriousness of the offence and the severity of the punishment' in prison. Murder, assault, theft and sodomy were in 1920, at least, all 'included in the same list with talking, looking in the wrong direction . . . absence of button from clothing etc. without corresponding variation in the punishment inflicted.'[9]

Indeed, the list of rules in many prisons contained—and indeed in some cases still do contain—so many and such bizarre offences that the best-behaved prisoners could scarcely avoid breaking them. The Iowa State Penitentiary had over a hundred rules which took up twenty-eight printed pages of the rule book. Behaviour during the silent meal, even after the Second World War, was regulated by Rule 51 which read: 'If you want bread, hold up your right hand; coffee or water, hold up your cup; meat, hold up your fork; soup, hold up your spoon; vegetables, hold up your knife; if you want to speak to an officer about food or service, hold up your left hand.' Among the sixty-nine offences covered by the *Manual of the Massachusetts Reformatory for the Use of Prisoners* were eating before the signal, wasting food, being profane, being dilatory, being inattentive in chapel, being inattentive in line, staring at visitors, 'laughing and fooling,' 'gaping about' and the ill-defined offence of 'crookedness'. To these and other offences, one institution added that of 'acting queer in room'.[10]

The offence of talking at various times and in various places was a common one in most prisons, but it was not, nor ever had been, possible to prevent prisoners communicating with each other. In the prison at Cold Bath Fields in England 'where', as an official report put it, 'the silent system is believed to be brought to the highest degree of perfection, there were in the year 1836 no less than 5,138 punishments for talking and swearing'.[11] Nor was it necessary to talk. Signs and gestures, symbols scratched on white-washed walls and dirty window panes, patterns of foot marks in the earth of exercise yards all had their peculiar significance. Even in the most silent and apparently well-disciplined prisons, conversations were being continually carried on and messages passed from man to man.

'The walls of a prison under the very eyes of the guard offer a world of information and are marvellous instruments of correspondence,' Gautier discovered. 'There is first the little cord, stretched by the weight of a ball made of bread crumbs, and so thrown from one window to another, while one holds on to the bars of the window. There are books in the library which circulate covered with cryptograms. Then the pipes for water and hot air make excellent speaking tubes. Another dodge, which needs persons with some instruction, is that of knocking on the wall. It is not necessary that the persons communicating by this method should be in contiguous cells. I once got valuable news in this way from a comrade forty or fifty metres off.'*[12]

In only a very few prisons and gaols in the United States, however, had any pretence of segregation ever been possible and it became increasingly difficult to enforce the rule of silence. As the general population grew, the prison population grew too; and the buildings were hopelessly ill-equipped to deal with the newcomers. When an official observer found between eight and ten negro men, one negro girl and one white woman in a single room in South Carolina in 1919[13] he was witnessing no more than an exaggerated example of a general problem. Ten years later few prisons were making any attempt to segregate the mentally defective, and some did not institute examinations for venereal disease until 1928 although when examinations had begun in federal prisons two years earlier, twenty per cent of prisoners were found to be infected.[14]

In the Cook County Jail in Chicago in 1920 'cells originally intended for single occupants' were filled with 'two, three, four or sometimes five men'.

* The most usual wall-knocking code is that used by Rubashov in Arthur Koestler's *Darkness at Noon*.

'Prisoners are in these cells twenty hours out of every day,' it was reported. 'Their food is pushed to them in pans through the bars of their door; they eat it crouched on the sides of their bunks or sitting on the floor. Particles of food left behind attract vermin, the food is of poor quality . . . For two hours each morning and again in the afternoon the men are herded into dimly lighted, inside recreation rooms, or "bull pens". Here there is nothing to do but stand around, sit on the floor or form in groups and walk slowly about a small space. The congestion is so great that it is almost impossible to move without brushing your neighbour. At one end of each of these "bull pens" is an open drain in the floor used as an urinal.'[15]

In 1924 three quarters of the gaols in Georgia did not isolate prisoners suffering from contagious diseases; in seventy-seven per cent of the gaols there were no towels; in seventy-four per cent there was no running water; and in half the blankets were never washed.[16]

During the 1930's the position deteriorated still further all over America. Between 1923 and 1940 the yearly average prison population of the 150 state and federal institutions rose from 84,761 to 191,776.[17] In 1933 there were 693,988 commitments to these various institutions nearly all of which were overcrowded and out of date. Joliet, the Northern Illinois Penitentiary, was over seventy years old and had repeatedly been condemned as unfit by various prison commissions.[18] The cells at Sing Sing, some parts of which dated from 1825, were only 3ft 3in wide by 7ft long by 6ft 7in high and there was no internal plumbing. In fact in twenty-one per cent of men's prisons in the United States in 1933 buckets were standard equipment in all cells. The whole system, the Wickersham Report concluded, was 'antiquated, unintelligent and frequently cruel and inhuman'. And George W. Kirchwey, a warden of Sing Sing, believed this verdict 'erred by moderation'.[19]

Men were locked up for most of the day in their cells, not only because overcrowding made it essential but also because there was so little work for them to do. In the previous century, after experimentation with solitary work in cells, many prisons had been turned into factories and some of them had been moderately successful ones. The Connecticut Penitentiary, for example, between 1833 and 1850 earned a profit of over ninety thousand dollars.[20] A few prisons adopted the Graded System, originally devised by Sir Joshua Webb and developed in Ireland by Sir Robert Crofton, and by this men who had passed their way through the first grade of solitary confinement were allowed to work their way up through various higher grades of collective labour, each more privileged than the last. Various systems were also devised by which prison labour could be hired out to contractors; but the abuses to which this led, the activities of reformers who publicized the horrors of chain-gang labour particularly in the swampy plantations of the South and in lumber camps guarded by bloodhounds, and, above all, the objections of labour unions to the unfair competition of convicts, led to the development of other systems in which the state as entrepreneur, customer or employer took more responsibility in the organization of prison labour. None of the new systems, however, was found to be ideal and the continued opposition of the unions to the more promising ones successfully limited their scope. And so the little and usually boring and repetitive work which he was allowed to do, apart from being in no sense rehabilitative, came to be regarded by the prisoner neither as a means to an end, nor emphatically 'as a craft, but as a prescribed task to be fulfilled as part of the punishment of imprisonment'.[21]

Rehabilitation in these years could not, of course, be a matter of primary concern to the prison authorities. The important and successful experiments in self-government by the prisoners, made in Auburn, Sing Sing and the Portsmouth Naval Prison under the influence of Thomas Osborne, who had served as a voluntary prisoner himself before becoming a warden, were not widely imitated. Osborne was, after all, an exceptional man. Most wardens in his day were political appointees more anxious to take what opportunities they could of making money out of their charges— by such devices as feeding them for fifty cents each a day when they received seventy cents[22]—than to rehabilitate them.

It was often, indeed, difficult enough to make any attempt at social education, for the state authorities were more likely than not to consider that a warden's first duty was to make his prison pay; and if it was impossible to turn the prison into a reasonably profitable factory, as only a very few wardens were able to do, it was usually cheaper and easier to keep the prisoners idle than to put them to some profitless task. In many prisons, in fact, the large numbers of convicts and the small, ill-paid, corrupt and inefficient staff made the supervision of work out of the question. Even when work, other than work connected with the day to day cleaning and running of the institution itself, was a part of the prison routine, it was often easy enough to pay for its avoidance. A prisoner in San Quentin in the late 1920's gave on his release an account of life there which, subsequently corroborated, is certainly characteristic of other American prisons at this time. The prisoners who had no money or influence did the work, the rich lived much as they wanted to. In the jute mill where 'the noise was deafening and the air was full of jute dust and the smell of oil and sweat' men paid a tough Mexican criminal, who controlled the labour there, to do less work a day than the regulations prescribed. The balance was made up by prisoners who could not afford the price demanded. Even the armed guards were 'scared of this Mexican and his gang. They didn't like to feel that they might be picked up some fine day with a ten inch knife stuck in their ribs. Naturally they saw that they got their rake-off from Marino's racket, but, apart from that, they left him alone.'[23]

The prison aristocracy never went near the jute mill at all. One rich gangster 'spent all his time loafing around with his pals, watching the ball games, playing cards in the offices of the "con bosses" of the various shops, smoking and drinking as much whisky as he wanted, the latter smuggled into the jail at fancy prices ... Nominally he was attached to the prison library and, just occasionally, he would stroll in there for a read and a snooze ... The ordinary guards not only did not interfere with him: they treated him with deference.'[24]

Apart from being able to live a life of comparative ease in prisons such as this, drinking, smoking, buying the bodies of young prisoners and even apparently of women brought in and out by the guards,* rich and influential criminals could continue to exercise their power over warders whose positions rested upon political favours. Dr Louis Berg a former doctor at Blackwell's Island Penitentiary has described how he saw 'Warden McCann spend a half-hour on one of his busy days getting a lot of lemons' for one of the convicts, Joe Rao, a powerful gangster. 'I have been in Warden McCann's office when Joe Rao came in,' Dr Berg said, 'and I have seen the Warden hand Rao a list containing the marks given to prisoners by the parole board and ask Rao if they were

* 'In badly managed prisons, particularly in some of the large city jails,' wrote J. F. Fishman in 1934, 'when guards are selected because of political influence, the practice of permitting prisoners who pay to have sex relations with their wives or former friends is allowed to flourish untroubled by the officials.'[25]

satisfactory.'[26] In another prison the gambler Frank Erickson was said to have had as many visitors as all the other 2,400 prisoners put together.

Possibilities of reforming young prisoners at this time could scarcely be said to exist; and, indeed, in most prisons in the country never had existed. Before the First World War half the population of the gaols of Virginia had already served a previous term and Virginia's record was better than many others.[27] Some of the women in San Francisco gaol had been committed over fifty times before. One set of statistics showed that forty-six per cent of prisoners in another city had had three or more previous convictions.[28]

'I was sent to a juvenile institution at the age of eleven and returned at about fifteen as a good pickpocket' confessed a young criminal whose career was typical of thousands of others. 'I went to a reformatory at seventeen as a pickpocket and returned as a burglar ... As a burglar I went to a state institution where I acquired all the professional characteristics of the criminal and have since committed all the crimes, I suppose, which most criminals commit and expect to end my life as a criminal.'[29]

'I met crooks of every creed and color,' another criminal remembered. 'They were there for every crime ... It was a novelty to learn that there were so many crimes and ways of stealing that I had never heard about. I was green at first ... but I was well on the way to crookdom at the end of my second month in the place.'[30]

The reformatories, despite their objects, were no more reformatory than the prisons. The movement had begun in a mood of great hope and enthusiasm. Much more than any European country, the United States had been 'prepared to accept and develop the new ideas of individualization of treatment and a progressive form of prison discipline'.[31] The end of the Civil War had begun a new period of attempts at imaginative prison reform. The first National Prison Congress met at Cincinatti in 1870 and as a consequence of this, after years of preparation, the New York State Reformatory was opened at Elmira and the problem of juvenile offenders seemed to be nearer its solution at last.

Elmira, a state prison for first offenders between the ages of sixteen and thirty, was placed under the direction of Z. R. Brockway a dedicated prison officer of experience and originality whose address at Cincinatti in 1870 had 'anticipated the programme of modern penology'.[32] During the first few days the men were shut up alone to think, then they were taught a trade and while working their way up through the various grades into which promotion was possible, great emphasis was laid upon physical fitness, therapeutic exercises and education. Brockway's system was admired and copied. Professor Lombroso, perhaps the most celebrated criminologist of his time, thought that 'together with the agricultural colony system' it was the 'best possible substitute for the prison.' But he had to admit that its record of success was not very encouraging.[33]

By 1900 there were sixty-five reformatories in the United States with over nineteen thousand inmates; but many, perhaps most, of them were as ill-managed, as overcrowded and degrading as the prisons. And during the ensuing years they continued to deteriorate. They began more and more to resemble prisons and, although intended principally for first offenders, they contained many men who were not. A study made in 1917 revealed, in fact, that over seventy per cent of their inmates had served between one and ten previous sentences.[34] Another study published in 1930 revealed that out of five hundred ex-prisoners of the Massachusetts Reformatory no less than eighty per cent continued their criminal behaviour during a five-year test period following the end of their parole terms.[35] George W. Kirchway, Warden of Sing Sing, said that between two-thirds and three-quarters of his charges had been in juvenile institutions and that 'without exception' they attributed their criminal careers to the lives they had led there. He had become 'absolutely disillusioned, if not absolutely hopeless, with regard to the possibility of bettering a child through commitment to any institution whatever'.[36]

The daily routine was unvaried and tediously arid.

'Awakened at 6.30,' runs a 1932 report on a New York reformatory, 'the boys are taken to the washrooms for the only wash of the day. There are no toilets or washing facilities in the cells. Setting up exercises at 7.30 are followed by breakfast at 8. At 8.25 the boys are marched out in gangs for their day of hard labor . . . At 11.30 they are marched back for lunch; at 12.20 they return to the work gangs. At 3.45 they return to the yard and almost immediately have their evening meal . . . They are locked in their cells from 4.15 p.m. to 6.30 a.m., more than fourteen hours a day.'[37]

The routine in a girl's reformatory was no less stringent. In the average institution in the 1920's the girls got up at 5.30 and began scrubbing the floors or went to work in the laundry or the bakery. Breakfast was at 6.30 and was eaten in silence. School classes began at seven o'clock and continued till the midday meal. After supper at five o'clock the girls were locked in their rooms for the night. Chapel services and an occasional riot were the only breaks in the monotony. In many institutions flogging, particularly for homosexual offences, was a regular punishment; in others, girls were given medicine to make them sick or were tied up and douched with cold water from hose-pipes.*[38] The proportion of girls who were reconvicted after discharge from such places as these was extremely high;[39] although rather less so than the proportion of those discharged from boys' reformatories.

'There was lots of sex perversions in the form of masturbation and sodomy,' a former inmate of one of these reported. 'The bullies would take the younger boys and force them to have relations. Some of the boys caught venereal diseases . . . I knew little boys who had sex relations with four or five older boys every night. It was easy in the dormitory to slip into another boy's bunk.'[40]

The guards at the House of Refuge on New York's Randall's Island openly encouraged the 'rampant sex perversion', according to a man who had formerly been an officer there. Soon after his arrival when he was walking down a corridor with one of the guards he saw 'a burly tough of about eighteen or nineteen half dragging a young boy' towards the boiler room steps. The youth smiled at the guard 'who just chuckled and waved'.

'That's Rocky,' the guard said, 'the leader of one of the toughest gangs in here. He's got a new "girl". His "wife" went home last week.'

On his first night on duty in the dormitory, the young officer, sitting at his desk on a raised platform, heard terrified screams coming from one of the hundred and fifty beds. He jumped down and from under one of them he dragged a sobbing fifteen-year-old boy whose face had been lacerated and whose jaw had been broken by a firehose nozzle passed from bed to bed in the silent darkness of the dormitory. The boy, who had to have seventy-five stitches in his face, would not say anything, nor would the other occupants

---

* In England at the female Borstal at Aylesbury nearly every other girl was punished in 1921. One in every eight of them was put in irons, as compared with one in every 226 Borstal boys. Girls at Aylesbury, in fact, 'were put in irons more often than all other prisoners women and men, put together.'[41] Straitjackets and handcuffs are still in use in women's prisons.

of the dormitory. When the officer suggested the Superintendent should be woken up and told what had happened, a guard advised him to save his breath. The advice seemed justified for on another occasion after the officer reported angrily that a boy's liver had been punctured by a table knife, the blade of which had been worn down to the sharpness of a razor, the Superintendent said coldly that he would 'look into it'.

'I found some of the guards brutal, illiterate and almost totally contemptible,' the officer said. 'They sold everything from food to cigars. The brutality was incredible. I once saw a guard club a young boy, scarcely more than a child, into unconsciousness.' The brutality was reported to the Superintendent who 'noted' it. One boy threw himself into the river; another died because a guard said he didn't need a doctor but a 'kick up the arse'.

The officer's hopes that Randall's Island was a uniquely appalling reformatory were dispelled when he was transferred to another in Queens. 'I saw boys, mere babies,' he reported, 'beaten black and blue with hoses, sticks, fists and heavy shoes. Boys, black and white, were forced to fight each other with stones and fists—no holds barred—for the enjoyment of brutal house-fathers. Mass punishment was approved; a boy would be turned over to five or six other boys and the house-father would sit by, encouraging the boys to "muss him up". Older boys were ordered to string up smaller boys and whip them with hoses.'[42]

Although stories of the institution's reformatory methods were related to its governors, no action was taken until a series of articles in the New York *World-Telegram* brought about a grand jury investigation in August 1934. Ten years later the *New York Star* exposed the conditions in some other distressingly similar juvenile institutions. At one of these, the Boys Industrial School at Lancaster, Ohio, 'they believed in strict discipline,' a criminal who had been sent there at the age of eleven reported, 'choosing inmates as monitors to help the officials enforce it. These monitors were always the biggest and toughest boys in the school, and nothing made them happier than beating up the smaller boys.'

'We did everything military fashion. When we moved from one place to another it had to be in lock step, with severe punishment for getting out of step. Standing was at attention always. Even in bed the boys had to keep in one certain position, facing the guard and with both arms outside the cover no matter what the temperature. All actions such as dressing, making bed, marching to meals, and so on had to be done by count. We even prayed by count before going to bed, lowering our heads at "one" and raising them again at "two". I used to whisper, "Oh, God, if you believe in this you're not my God. If you are God why don't you stop all this?" '

Punishment for minor offences, such as dropping a shoe when ordered to put it on at the count of 'Four!', involved standing to attention all day except when working or at meals; greater offences were punished by being beaten with a wooden paddle 'on the buttocks, the back of the legs, back and shoulders, each blow leaving a red mark that later turned black. On several occasions boys were struck on the face because the paddle hurt them so terribly they had to turn round.'[43]

This school, like the one in Queens and the reformatory on Randall's Island were, no doubt, exceptional; but even when allowances had been made for the embittered and exaggerated memories of former inmates and the tendency of the Press to make its disclosures as sensational as possible, there remained enough incontrovertible evidence from both personal and official reports to justify the belief that American reformatories, with very few exceptions, were, in fact, (at least up to the beginning of the Second World War) the schools of crime which those who had been in them protested they were.

It was also difficult to avoid holding the same sad belief about American prisons. In the middle of the 1930's it was still possible for Sheldon Glueck passionately to indict the whole system in one of those frequent outbursts of pitiless self-criticism, which, so valuable an attribute of the American character, might well be imitated in other countries where self-complacency hides similar faults. Many prisons, Glueck wrote, even then indiscriminately contained men and women, juveniles and adults, the sick and the healthy, the sane and the insane.

'Sanitary conditions are little short of atrocious, disease is common, food is unwholesome, prisoners are crowded into cells and, worst of all, they rot in idleness and moral contagion. No words of condemnation are strong enough . . . Implicated in the lowest politics, having no system of industries, possessing no programme of education or constructive recreation, trafficking in drugs and immoral practises, staffed by incompetents who are sometimes not distinguishable from the prisoners themselves, many of these institutions are a reeking tribute to justice.'[44]

Ten years later many of the worst aspects of the system which Glueck condemned still existed. Most prisons were cleaner, the food was better, there was a great deal less brutality (although as late as 1957 men in some Southern prisons were still savagely mutilating themselves as a result of unendurable treatment), there was a great deal more effort made to fill the prisoners' time with educative, reformative or creative pursuits, but the ideal of returning to society a man who could lead a better life than he had formerly done, was as far off as ever. A man sentenced in 1944 to the Northeastern Penitentiary at Lewisburg, one of the show-places of the American prison system, found that despite outward improvements even one of the best of prisons was in no sense a means of reform or rehabilitation. The uniform of prison stripes had long been replaced by not uncomfortable blue denim; the prison library was 'excellent, far superior to many a public library'; every month he was allowed to spend up to ten dollars on fruit and sweets and could go to buy things like these once a week; there were fairly frequent film shows; there were handball and horse-shoe courts, a running-track and a baseball diamond; and the cell which he was given, having applied for a transfer from a dormitory, except for the barred window and locked door, was 'not greatly un-like a typical Y.M.C.A. room'.[45] But the dreadful, timeless, unchanging, regimented monotony of prison life and the tensions that grow out of it, the attempted 'rapes' in the latrines and the fights over 'girls', the commonplace sights of men 'masturbating into the urinals', the rich criminal with his servile friends and his uninspected locker full of cigarettes, the meandering and endless conversations limited to food, crime and sex, the deprivation of individuality and the imposition of feelings of humiliation and degradation by the system and those whose livelihood depends upon it, all the hidden and dangerous undercurrents of an un-natural life that the visitor does not normally see, combined then, as before and often as now, to make prisons instruments not of reform nor of rehabilitation but merely of retaliatory punish-ment, and with few of the benefits to society which punishment may be expected to bestow.

When the Second World War ended men had been trying to find solutions to the problems of imprisonment for almost two centuries. They had experimented with different systems and one after another the experiments had failed. No system—and least of all, so it seemed, the severest system—helped men to stay out of prisons once they had served a sentence in one. The history of prison reform was a long and sad one, not so much because the reformers had never found the right answers but because, so it now seemed, there were no right answers to be found.

Part III

CRIMINAL MAN

CHAPTER ONE

L'UOMO DELINQUENTE

'The atavism of the criminal when he lacks absolutely every trace of shame and pity, may go back beyond the savage even to the brutes themselves.'

CESARE LOMBROSO, 1899

(i)

IN 1864 a twenty-nine year old Jewish doctor in the Italian army beguiled his 'ample leisure', as he himself put it, 'with a series of studies of the Italian soldier. From the very beginning I was struck by a characteristic that distinguished the honest soldier from his vicious comrade: the extent to which the latter was tattooed and the indecency of the designs that covered his body.'[1]

The doctor's name was Cesare Lombroso. A highly gifted young man with a hunger for learning and an insatiable curiosity, he had taken degrees at the Universities of Pavia and Genoa and had studied psychology in Vienna. Deeply interested in the works of the French positivists, the German materialists and the English evolutionists he had already rejected the free-will philosophy then fashionable in Italian academic circles[2] and had thus taken the first step towards the development of a highly controversial theory which was to have profound influence throughout the world.

For some time he had been absorbed in the study of pellagra, a disease marked by the eruption of painful red or livid spots on the skin followed by gradual mummification. The disease had been endemic in Lombardy since the seventeenth century and Lombroso suggested that it was caused by a poison contained in mouldy maize.

It was, however, the effect of the disease on the mental capacities of its victims, whom it reduced to melancholia, often to imbecility and sometimes to forms of homicidal mania, that particularly interested him and resulted in his study of brain pathology. While stationed in Pavia, he obtained permission to examine the patients in a mental hospital; and eventually, after his service in the army was completed, he was placed in charge of the insane at hospitals in Pesaro and Reggio Emilia.

It was at this time that he began to compare the criminal with the insane and to make an attempt to resolve the 'problem of the nature of the criminal'. The answer, so he says, came to him as a sudden revelation while he was performing a post-mortem on the brigand Vilella.

'I had made the acquaintance of the famous brigand,' he wrote many years later. 'The man possessed such extraordinary agility that he had been known to scale steep mountain heights bearing a sheep on his shoulders. His cynical effrontery was such that he openly boasted of his crimes. On his death one cold grey November morning, I was deputed to make the post-mortem, and on laying open the skull I found on the occipital part, exactly on the spot where a spine is found in the normal skull, a distinct depression which I named *median occupital fossa,* because of its situation precisely in the middle of the occiput as in inferior animals, especially rodents. This depression, as in the case of animals, was correlated with the hypertrophy of the *vermis,* known in birds as the middle cerebellum.

This was not merely an idea, but a revelation. At the sight of that skull, I seemed to see all of a sudden, lighted up as a vast plain under a flaming sky, the problem of the nature of the criminal—an atavistic being who reproduces in his person the ferocious instincts of primitive humanity and the inferior animals. Thus were explained anatomically the enormous jaws, high cheek bones, prominent superciliary arches, solitary lines in the palms, extreme size of the orbits, handle-shaped or sessile ears found in criminals, savages and apes, insensibility to pain, extremely acute sight, tattooing, excessive idleness, love of orgies, and the irresistible craving for evil for its own sake, the desire not only to extinguish life in the victim, but to mutilate the corpse, tear its flesh and drink its blood.'[3]

For many years after this 'revelation', Lombroso devoted himself to the explanation and amplification of his theory. Influenced by the works of Auguste Comte, who had related so many mental conditions to biological causes, by Rudolf Virchow's studies in cellular pathology, by B. A. Morel, the French alienist, whose *Treatise on Degeneracy* had been published in 1857, by Darwin's *Origin of Species* published in 1859 and by many earlier writers who had attempted to show the relationship between the physical characteristics of the criminal and his behaviour, Lombroso produced a mass of evidence, based on a close examination of great numbers of criminals, to support his theory that the criminal can be distinguished from the non-criminal by a variety of physical anomalies which are of atavistic or degenerative origin.

The first edition of his best known work, *L'Uomo Delinquente,* was published in 1876 the year that he joined the staff of the University of Turin where he was later to become professor of criminal anthropology. And it was in a prison at Turin that he had minutely examined many of the prisoners whose physical peculiarities lent his theory so much weight and his work so much interest.

Criminals had never before been examined with such thoroughness and care. It had, of course, already been suggested that personality had a physical basis and that outward forms often gave indications of inward character. In the most remote periods it had been accepted that physical handicaps and disfigurements were punishments inflicted on men by gods, just as it had been noticed that men of evil disposition could frequently be recognized by organic peculiarities; for physiognomy is an antique art. A Greek physiognomist told Socrates that he had the face of a brutal, sensuous man inclined to drunkenness, and Socrates replied that, although he had managed to overcome it, that indeed was his natural character. Polemon claimed that criminals could be recognized by their pallid complexions, long hair, large ears and small eyes. At other times and in other countries people with red hair have been distrusted. On the Greek and Roman stages, some sort of inferiority was indicated by an actor wearing a red wig. Judas Iscariot has often been depicted with a red beard. Those with indications of hermaphroditism or pronounced strabismus have also been distrusted in the past, as have cripples and hunchbacks. Some medieval laws went so far as to enact that when two people were under suspicion for the same crime, the uglier or more deformed of the two was to be considered the more likely to be guilty of it.

In the early seventeenth century, the Neapolitan, Della Porta, intrigued by the ideas of Aristotle and Galen on the subject, attempted to show that man's nature was bound up with his body and that crime was the consequence of various abnormal physical conditions. In the following century Franz Joseph Gall, who has been described as the founder of the science of criminal anthropology, made a particular study of the brain and the effects of its irregular growth on the skull, and in a work published as early as 1810 he wrote, 'There can be no question of culpability or of justice in the severe sense; the question is of the necessity of society preventing crime. The measure of culpability, and the measure of punishment cannot be determined by a study of the illegal act, but only by a study of the individual committing it.'[4]

The study of the skull seemed, indeed, a promising field of inquiry. In 1841, Lauvergne, the chief medical officer at the hospital for convicts at Toulon, published a study of the nature of the convict, *Les Forçats*, in which stress was laid on the importance of phrenology. Paul Broca, the neurologist, who founded the *Société d'antropologie de Paris* in 1859, confirmed that the skulls and brains of criminals possessed unmistakable peculiarities. '*The Moral Imbecility of Habitual Criminals as Exemplified by Cranial Measurements*' was the title of a paper read to the British Association a few years before Lombroso's book was published. The writer of this paper had measured 464 heads and found, so he claimed, that habitual thieves presented well-marked signs of retarded cranial development.

Lombroso felt confident that these studies were of vital importance and that anomalies in the shape of the skull were at least one physical indication of criminal tendencies. 'Cranial abnormalities,' he wrote, 'are found occasionally in ordinary persons; very rarely are they found combined in normal persons to the extent that they are found amongst instinctive criminals.'

But it was not only the skull that Lombroso examined. He, and the many scholars subsequently infected by the growing enthusiasm for criminal anthropology inside and outside Italy, examined every part of their specimens' bodies, their capacities both intellectual and physical, their antecedents and ways of life, their speech, their powers of memory, their handwriting, their clothing, their tattoo marks, their urine and their faeces. They used plethysmographs and hydrosphygmographs, volumetric gloves and anthropometers, tachyanthropometers, craniographs, pelvimeters and dynanometers. They tested their sensitivity to pain with algometers, their sensitivity to heat with thermo-esthesiometers, to smell with somometers and to touch with esthesiometers.

They tested their hearing, their vision, their sense of taste, their reaction to metals, their judgment of colour and of weight. And they produced numerous and remarkable statistics.

It appeared that for the most part convicts were, in fact, physically abnormal. Beginning with their heads, their hair was unusually abundant (although their beards were often scanty) and in contrast with the insane, baldness was rare. In one selection of prisoners eleven per cent were found to have continuous eyebrows. Sexual offenders were particularly hairy.

Criminal jaws were heavier than the normal jaw and progenism (the lower teeth closing over the upper) was common. Also common were large, drooping and projecting ears, and Ottolenghi, after examining over a thousand of them, discovered that their owners possessed an extraordinary power of moving them. Ottolenghi also discovered that criminals were uncommonly wrinkled (a peculiarity also noticed by the German, Fuchsius, in the early seventeenth century who associated it with what was now called degenerescence occurring in those born of enfeebled parents.) When Ottolenghi turned his attention to their noses he found that they were generally straight but had a tendency to deviate to one side. In examining criminal women, Salsotto found that a surprising number of them were particularly hairy between the pubes and the umbilicus and around the anus and that down on the face was common amongst women found guilty of infanticide. The hair of criminal women in general was found to go grey at an early age, but this was not so with the men. Criminal women lived longer than men and had greater powers of resistance to misfortune and grief. They were also, although fewer in number than the men, often much more ferocious. Beautiful criminals of either sex were extremely rare and most of their faces were characterized by a curious fixed look. The feline and sometimes ferocious look of male murderers alternated with a gentle, almost feminine gaze; and this combination of expressions was often found to have a strong sexual fascination for women. 'Habitual homicides,' Lombroso thought, 'have cold, glassy eyes, immobile and sometimes sanguine and inflamed; the nose, always large, is frequently aquiline or rather, hooked; the jaws are strong, the cheek bones large, the hair curly, dark and abundant; the beard is frequently thin, the canine teeth well developed and the lips delicate; they suffer often from nystagmus and unilateral facial contractions, with a baring of the teeth and contraction of the jaws.'[5]

Most criminals although agile and often physically vigorous were muscularly weak. They were inclined to have sunken or pigeon breasts and tuberculosis. Atavistic anomalies were particularly noticeable in the vertebrae and ribs, as well as in the skull and jaw, and in the length of the arms, the flatness of the feet and the prehensility of the toes. Gynecomasty was common and its high rate of incidence among young criminals was later confirmed by Dr Hamilton Wey of the Elmira Reformatory in the United States who found that it ranged 'from a rounded development of the bust and prominent nipples, surrounded by a deeply pigmented areola, to well-defined mammary glands that have periodic seasons of congestion and attempts at functional activity.'* Arrested development of the sexual organs and congenital phimosis were also common; while moral imbeciles were often prone to hypospadias (congenital malformation of the glans penis) and either exaggerated or retarded development of the sexual organs. In criminal women, also, pathological conditions of the sexual organs were common and menstruation was frequently irregular or suppressed. Pasini discovered that women tended to blush when questioned about their menstrual periods although they did not often blush when asked about their crimes. Murderers blushed much more readily than thieves. Criminal women in general were peculiarly sensitive to the weather and time of year and quarrelled frequently during the spring. They showed an abnormal fear of pain to which, however, they were peculiarly insensitive.

Men, also, were insensitive to pain. One man, a moral imbecile and a murderer, whose father and grandfather had also been murderers was, Lombroso found, almost completely lacking in the capacity to feel pain. A doctor at Santo Stefano said that the

---

* In America, where a tendency to over-compensation is so frequently remarked, the effeminacy of many of the country's most violent criminals has assumed a particular significance. 'The most notorious mass murderer', one of San Quentin's medical officers ever knew, 'was close to being a hermaphrodite and swayed between the mental processes of male and female.'[6] The sex of another prisoner was so indeterminate that the staff were unsure whether to send him into the 'men's ward or in with the women.'[7] 'Pretty Boy' Floyd and 'Baby Face' Nelson are only two of those hundreds of American gangsters who could have passed for women. 'Frankie Cole was about twenty-three and didn't need to shave more than once a week; when his beard was three days old it looked like fluff on a rabbit's tail. Give him a white smock and he would have made a pretty choir-boy; get him light with a shot of morphine and he became a smooth and deadly ruffian, who would shoot with a smile on his baby lips.'[8]

majority of his 'instinctive criminals' were similarly fortunate. 'I have extirpated tumours of considerable size,' he wrote, 'without causing pain.' And his patients recovered from their wounds with the rapidity of the lower animals. They were often unconscious of severe illnesses although quick to complain of minor ailments such as common colds. The insensitivity of the criminal to feel pain seemed to be confirmed by the numbers of convicts who inflicted severe wounds on themselves for supposedly trifling reasons. In one prison in a single year, seventeen prisoners wounded themselves with such severity that they had to submit to amputation. Lauvergne recorded the case of a convict who smiled with pleasure when he saw his skin burning and heard it crackle after moxas had been applied to it. Powdered glass was sometimes swallowed to bring on blood spitting and one prisoner, not known to be insane, sewed his lips and eyelids together.

Other noticeable peculiarities amongst several of the many groups of criminals examined were the high incidence of left-handedness, of stammering, and of muscular incoordinations such as an inability to contain urine, the absence or exaggeration of tendon reflexes, pronounced addiction to tobacco, good eyesight but poor hearing, and obtuse senses of smell and taste. The handwriting of violent criminals was clumsy but energetic with dashing cross strokes, that of swindlers uniform but difficult to read. Monomaniacs interspersed their writing with symbols and illustrations; megalomaniacs used many exclamation marks and capital letters and wrote very closely in imitation of print. The tattoo marks which seemed to Lombroso of such peculiar significance were often obscene and the penis was a not uncommon *motif*. The genital organs were frequently decorated and prostitutes sometimes had the initials of their female lovers tattooed in their arm pits. Homosexuals decorated their thighs with representations of wild pansies. The hands were sometimes marked and even the face; one man was found with a dagger tattooed on his forehead and above it the legend: *Death to the middle classes*. Criminal women, unless they were also prostitutes, were hardly ever tattooed but occasionally a woman's face was branded. Branded women were usually the mistresses of *Camorristi* who marked their women in this way not in revenge but as a sign of proprietorship.[9]

Lombroso's *L'Uomo Delinquente* which did so much to promote this minute study of the criminal was originally published as a short book of no more than 252 pages. Its emphasis on the atavistic origin of crime, which Lombroso even discovered in the activities of plants and animals as well as of primitive savages, was largely responsible for the attacks that were later made upon his theories by those who did not study his later works in which these theories were extensively qualified. The immediate reaction of his critics was, however, understandable; for the importance given in the first edition of his book to craniology and anthropometry seemed supreme. Psychology was virtually ignored and all criminals—or rather all convicts for the criminal lucky or intelligent enough to escape prison could not be examined—apparently belonged to a single class. No one denied that physical characteristics might affect a man's conduct by making it difficult for him to earn an honest living or by making it impossible for him to escape the scorn or dislike of his fellows and thus forcing upon him feelings of inadequacy or inferiority. In San Quentin prison, for example, as many as twelve per cent of the men have been found to be crippled compared with a national average of less than two per cent.[10] But to suggest that a man became a criminal because ontologically he belonged to an earlier stage of evolution seemed absurdly far-fetched.

It seemed absurd, too, that Lombroso should take such pride in his ability to recognize a criminal by his appearance or even by some part of it. 'I do not need to see the whole of a criminal's face to recognize him as such,' Vidocq, the French detective had once said, 'it is enough for me to catch his eye.'[11] And Lombroso made claims almost as extravagant. His identifications, were, of course, far from infallible, sometimes being proved to be wrong in embarrassing circumstances, and even when he was right there seemed little enough to justify his satisfaction. He was fond of telling the story that he had once examined a respectable coachman accused of raping and murdering a little girl of six in Turin and had afterwards declared that the coachman was 'incapable of committing the crime'. The real culprit was discovered some time later to be 'an imbecile—afflicted with goitre, stammering, strabismus, hydrocephaly, trochocephaly and plagiocephaly, with arms of disproportionate length, the son and grandson of drunkards.'[12]

His satisfaction in picking out the man who had raped a girl of three and a half and infected her with a venereal disease seemed no less bathetic. There were six suspects. 'I picked out one among them immediately,' he wrote. 'He had obscene tattooing on his arm, a sinister appearance, irregularities of the field of vision, and also traces of a recent attack of syphilis.'[13]

But if Lombroso's pride in identifying such unprepossessing types seemed absurd, it could not be denied that men displaying these characteristics were, in fact, often criminals. What seemed to Lombroso's critics a more telling argument against his theories was that there were many men who presented the same anomalies as the 'born criminal' who lived honest lives, and that many men who did not present these anomalies behaved like 'born criminals'. Also what seemed a sinister appearance to one observer might not seem so to another. The murderer Menesclou, for instance, was described by a man who saw him at his trial as 'a sort of abortion, bent and wrinkled, with earthy complexion, shifty eyes, a face gnawed by scrofula, of a cunning dissipated and cruel aspect. The forehead is low, the beard sparse and slovenly; the hair is black and thrown backwards and reaches almost to the shoulders. It is an absolutely repulsive head.' But to the prison chaplain he looked 'like a page in a good house'. He had 'a sympathetic and prepossessing countenance, the air of a young man who had been well brought up, a gentle, honest, naive face'.[14]

A former prison medical officer once told the story of his conversation with a woman on his way by train to San Quentin. 'I learned a matron was on board with a new woman prisoner,' he said. 'I introduced myself and we spent the trip in delightful conversation. I had never met a matron more refined and well-spoken. Talking with her I covertly studied the prisoner. She was low-browed, loud voiced and glowering. I . . . decided she might be capable of anything.' She, in fact, was the matron, while the woman he had so much admired was the prisoner.[15]

It was not only Lombroso's theories which were attacked but the methods he used to establish them. He had no real basis for a comparison with honest people of the same economic and social class and of the same level of intelligence. Gabriel Tarde, the great French magistrate who believed that the origins of crime were mainly social, denied the existence of Lombroso's atavistic type, the born or instinctive criminal, and strongly criticized the Lombrosians' methods of examining countless criminals in their efforts to invent him. 'If one examined hundreds of thousands of judges, lawyers, labourers, musicians, taken at random and in various countries, noticing their different characteristics, craniometric, algometric, sphygmographic, graphologic, photographic, etc., as

Lombroso has examined hundreds and thousands of criminals, it is extremely probable that we should ascertain facts not less surprising; thus, for instance we might succeed in finding *instinctive lawyers*.'[16]

Furthermore, it was maintained, Lombroso was far too ready to interpret facts from meagre data, to jump to conclusions from ill-defined measurements with impatient recklessness. The criticisms were not unjustified but in his defence it must be said that he was imaginative, intuitive, ready to have his theories tested impartially and, above all, prepared to qualify them in the light of new or overlooked facts.

The most gifted of those who helped Lombroso in this work of qualification and amendment was a young man, Enrico Ferri, twenty years his junior. While deeply influenced by Lombroso, whose atavistic *uomo delinquente* he included as 'the born criminal' in his classification of criminal types, he was nevertheless able to extend the range of his master's thought and bring him to a keener awareness of sociological concepts. Some years after Ferri arrived in Turin, a fourth and longer edition of *L'Uomo Delinquente* had been published. The broadening of Lombroso's theories was apparent. The existence of other types of criminal and other causes of criminality were emphasized. Degeneration assumed a new importance and the epileptic criminal and the insane criminal were seen as separate types.*

* These types had been more completely broken down by Enrico Ferri in the first volume of Lombroso's periodical *Archivio di psichiatra* and later in *Sociologia Criminale*. Apart from born or instinctive criminals with little resistance to temptation and a natural propensity to crime caused by alcoholic, insane, syphilitic or criminal forebears, apart also from insane criminals and epileptics, Ferri classified the rest as criminals through passion or emotion, who usually had good but excitable characters; habitual criminals, who were the products of particular social environments or the prison system; and occasional criminals who formed the majority of lawbreakers and whose psychological traits did not differ greatly from those of the social class from which they came. 'Thus then,' he wrote, 'the entire body of criminals may be classed in five categories, which as early as 1880 I described as criminal madmen, born criminals, criminals by contracted habits, occasional criminals and criminals of passion.' In the fifth edition of *Sociologia Criminale*, Ferri added a sixth category—'involuntary criminals.'[17] Raffaele Garofalo, Ferri's contemporary, the practical Neapolitan magistrate, differed from him in his classifications of criminals. Crimes, Garofalo wrote in his *Criminologia*, were simply those actions which were against the sentiments of pity and probity although he later added acts which were 'injurious to society'.[18] And he denied that those who committed them could be classified as Ferri suggested.

The born criminal, however remained—and was always to remain—rooted in Lombroso's theories. And it is for this reason that his name is so widely remembered and so frequently denigrated even now.

Occasionally new theories as to the physical basis of criminality erupt, particularly in Italy where Lombrosianism is still an active force. And the theories were given new weight when Ernst Kretschemer's *Physique and Character* was published in the early 1920's and prompted fresh study in an almost abandoned field. In 1928 a book came out in America,[19] which attempted to show that criminal actions were 'in reality actions caused by the disturbed internal chemistry of the body' and that 'the vast majority of all criminals' were the 'products of bodily disorders, that most crimes come about through disturbances of the ductless glands in the criminal or through mental defects caused by endocrine troubles in the criminal's mother'.[20] This book was followed in 1939 by E. A. Hooton's unconvincing *The American Criminal* in which criminals were supposed to be the result of environment operating upon inferior biological organisms; and in 1949 by William H. Sheldon's *Varieties of Delinquent Youth* in which related theories are put forward with rather more satisfying evidence. And although the original Lombrosian proposition of the born criminal has become, in fact, a 'criminological myth',[21] it is generally accepted that the essence of Lombroso's theories may still offer a promising field of inquiry, and that the influence of biological factors such as the endocrine or ductless glands on human conduct may be much greater than is usually supposed.

The real importance of Lombroso, though, lies outside his most celebrated theory. 'Whether or not Lombroso was right or wrong,' as Dr Thorsten Sellin has justly said, 'is perhaps in the last analysis not so important as the unquestionable fact that his ideas proved so challenging that they gave an unprecedented impetus to the study of the offender. Any scholar who succeeds in driving hundreds of fellow students to search for the truth, and whose ideas after half a century possess vitality, merits an honourable place in the history of thought.'[22] For the essential end of the Italian or Positive school was a humane one. Lombroso was bitterly criticized for having challenged the concept of free will by suggesting that the criminal might not be a good man gone wrong, but a man incapable of going right. It was a challenge to the authority of religion and the law; but it was a challenge as well to accepted ideas of punishment. The

French jurist Raymond Saleilles, in his plea for what he termed 'the individualization of punishment', recognized this. We should be grateful to the Italian School, he thought, for having called attention to the need for 'the adaption of the punishment to the psychological character of the criminal'.[23]

The Classical School, whose concepts the Italian School questioned, had been founded by Bentham and Beccaria in an attempt to reform the harsh legal system of the eighteenth century. The savagery of the European codes and the arbitrary and corrupt practices of their administrators, the use of torture to elicit confessions, the secret accusations, the unlimited discretion of the judges in the infliction of cruel punishments, the utter absence of equality before the law as a principle of justice, had made it necessary for the Classical School to insist upon a definition of crime within the strict limits of the law. Both Bentham and Beccaria had accordingly been more concerned with crime than with the criminal. Their principle of 'equal punishment for the same crime' had been adopted in the French Code of 1791 and its disadvantages had been there apparent. Men were reduced to objects; the first offender was treated in the same way as the old lag; the reform of the criminal became impossible. The Italian School, in an age when the uselessness of savage punishments arbitrarily administered had been generally admitted, believed that a concept of natural crime should be substituted for the strict legal definition of crime, that explanations of criminal acts should be sought for in the study of human behaviour. Lombroso, Ferri and Garofalo had accordingly concerned themselves with the individual offender. 'Crime,' Ferri wrote, 'must be studied in the offender.'[24] 'Crime is like sickness,' he wrote elsewhere, 'the remedy should be fitted to the disease. It is the task of the criminal anthropologist to determine in what measure it should be applied. What should we say if a physician who, stopping at the door of a hospital ward, said to the patients brought to him, "Pneumonia? Syrup of rhubarb for fifteen days. Typhus? Syrup of rhubarb for a month." And then at the end of the time send them out of doors cured or not?'[25]

(ii)

The challenge of the Italian School to existing theories of punishment was a natural consequence of Lombroso's emphasis on physical characteristics. The challenge became even more forceful when the emphasis was placed upon the mentality of the criminal rather than upon his physique.

The main reason for the new emphasis in England and the United States was the publication in 1913 of *The English Convict* by Charles Buckman Goring. Gabriel Tarde's *La Criminalité Comparée* had systematically contradicted most of Lombroso's theories but Tarde's views were not widely disseminated outside France and it was only after Dr Goring's book was published that the intellect of the criminal was accepted as being a more promising field for study than his body.

Tarde, like two other French writers Lacassagne and Durkheim, had stressed the importance of social factors in the causation of crime; but to Goring a far more important factor was defective intelligence. Goring, a prison medical officer, had examined three thousand English convicts during the twelve years before his book was published and had come to the conclusion that there were no specific stigmata characterizing the criminal.[1]

The convicts he had examined, except those convicted of fraud, were smaller and lighter than the general population. Violent criminals were stronger and generally more healthy than honest people, while burglars and thieves—the great majority of the criminal population—were more puny; but criminals, as a whole, did not display the identifiable marks which Lombroso claimed to have discovered, nor was disease, as Lombroso had suggested, a factor in criminality if nervous and venereal diseases were to be excepted.* Criminals were, however, Goring insisted, different from the general population with regard to their intelligence. 'The one vital mental constitutional factor in the etioloy of crime,' he thought, 'is defective intelligence.'[3] And the more often a

---

* This seems also to have been generally true of American convicts, although in the ten years before Goring's book was published over half the deaths in Wisconsin State Prison were due to pulmonary and cardiac diseases and a third of the prisoners suffered from defective sight.[2]

man was convicted, the less intelligent he was likely to be.*

Some sorts of crime were, of course, more likely to be committed by mental defectives than others; and to illustrate this point Goring produced a table which showed that the number of mental defectives convicted of malicious damage to property was as high as forty per cent. Nearly thirteen per cent of sexual offenders were mentally defective, more than ten per cent of burglars and thieves, six per cent of those guilty of crimes of violence against the person and about two and a half per cent of forgers. At least ten per cent of all criminals, he believed, were feeble-minded.[4] And this figure of ten per cent was also given by Basil Thomson as the proportion of feeble-minded men he believed he had amongst his convicts at Dartmoor when he was Governor there in the 1920's.[5] Gustav Aschaffenburg, writing some years before in Germany, said that, 'the fact that the intellectual capacity of the criminal is far below the average has already been the subject of detailed discussion. The experience of teachers and overseers in penal institutions fully confirms it.'[6] The chaplain at Wormwood Scrubs found that only nine out of eighty-four prisoners could without elaborate finger reckoning multiply nine by seven and only one woman in twenty could work out the cost of five eggs at three halfpence each.[7]

In the United States at this time much higher figures were given than in England; and in one study published in 1914 it was estimated that between a quarter and a half of all convicts in American prisons could be classified as mentally defective.[8] Another report published six years later suggested that whereas two per cent of the ordinary population could be classified as mental defectives, twelve per cent of convicts in Wisconsin were feeble-minded and over half of them showed abnormal personalities.[12] In 1920 over thirty-three per cent of the men in a Massachusetts reformatory were estimated as being of subnormal intelligence; and in 1922 as many as sixty-four per cent of the men at Elmira.[13] A study of girls at a reformatory in Illinois suggested that only twenty-two out of

* American surveys on this particular point have been contradictory. Some support Goring's contention, others tend to show that first offenders in the United States are less intelligent than recidivists.[9] In New York, ninety per cent of those arrested four or more times have been shown to be intellectually abnormal; and a study of male convicts in the Illinois Penitentiary at Joliet suggested that 'recidivism increases as the average mentality lowers'.[10] But more recent studies indicate that neither the first offender nor the recidivist are to any appreciable degree different in intellectual capacity either from each other or, indeed, from the ordinary citizen.[11]

432 were of average intelligence.[14] Again the degree of mental defectiveness naturally depended upon the crime for which the convict had been sentenced. Forty-one per cent of the men in the Illinois State Penitentiary in 1939-1940, who had been convicted of fraud or embezzlement, were of 'superior or very superior intelligence'.[15]

The difficulty was, of course, to determine what precisely was meant by feeble-mindedness. In a survey of 2,058 convicts in Sing Sing it was found, for instance, that the average mental age was that of a thirteen-year-old-boy, but when selections of American soldiers were given similar tests it was found that their average mental age was only just over thirteen-and-a-half.[16] The difficulty was also to find means of testing not only the intelligence but the temperament and emotional organization of the criminal as well. For criminality was often due to a lack of co-ordination between a man's intellectual qualities and his emotions rather than to any identifiable lack of mental ability as such. The intellectual equipment of prisoners, as Max Grünhut has recently written, differs less from that of the average honest citizen than was originally supposed;[17] but that quite a high proportion of them—East and de Hubert have estimated the proportion as being twenty per cent —are 'abnormal in the sense that their behaviour and reactions do not correspond to those of ordinary men', seems unquestionable, although whether this proportion is greater than would be found among the general population may again be doubted.[18] It can at least not be doubted that while there are many criminals who are mentally defective there are others of exceptional intelligence, and this was a fact which Lombroso found of peculiar interest. Long before he wrote *L'Uomo Delinquente*, he had become interested in the relationship between genius and insanity and when he began to emphasize factors other than physical stigmata in the make-up of the born criminal, a lack of moral sense and of any feelings of repentance and remorse were not the least important of these factors. He began to believe that the relationship between genius and insanity was reflected in the relationship between the moral imbecile and the criminal and that the 'uniting bond' which connected them was epilepsy.* All born criminals, he believed, were epileptics, although not all epileptics were born criminals. Not all

---

* It should be said that epilepsy was much more common in Italy than it was in England and America and that it was more broadly defined there.

geniuses were epileptics, either; but he cited many great men from Julius Caesar to St Paul and Mahomet, from Peter the Great to Richelieu and Napoleon, from Petrarch to Flaubert, de Musset and Dostoevsky who suffered from seizures which were symptomatic of epilepsy. 'When a genius attains to the fulness of his development and consequently to the widest possible deviation from the normal,' he believed, 'he is more or less in that condition of unconsciousness which characterizes psychic epilepsy.'[19]

While Lombroso's identification of the born criminal with the epileptic was strongly contested, it could not be denied that there was a strong pathological likeness between the two and that the mental peculiarities of epileptics—their inconsistencies, emotionalism and impulsiveness—were like those of moral imbeciles. A more recent study of juvenile delinquency in Chicago revealed that of a thousand young criminals examined, seventy were known to be epileptics as compared with a national average of only two to every thousand.[20]* The problem, of course, raised again the question of moral responsibility. For an epileptic is often unaware of what he has done during a seizure. He may commit crimes of savage violence and then completely forget them. An epileptic who had an attack during the night in a state hospital in Iowa escaped from his room, walked several miles through the snow until he came to a farmhouse where a man, his wife and several children were asleep. He massacred the entire family with an axe he had

---

* Some of these young delinquents may, of course, have taken to crime because of the social and economic difficulties which the epileptic has to face. In the belief that epilepsy is inherited, ten states in the U.S. prohibit epileptics from marrying, eighteen allow them to be sterilized, in all of them obtaining work is often difficult. Indeed, any defect which leads to real or imagined social incapacity may lead in turn to juvenile delinquency. A study of the effect of abnormal physical development upon juvenile delinquency made in 1915 by Dr William Healy showed that young offenders were often either physically retarded or overgrown.[21] A later study of two thousand young recidivists in Chicago revealed that nearly three-quarters of them were over-developed physically.[22] The resultant restlessness and lack of balance had led to crime in the boys and sexual delinquency in the girls. Whether or not juvenile delinquents had any physical peculiarities, William Healy and Augusta Bronner decided that they were almost always emotionally maladjusted. In one of their studies they showed that ninety one per cent of the young delinquents whose cases they examined were under some sort of emotional stress. It is important to notice, though, that thirteen per cent of their brothers and sisters were under similar emotional stress and had not committed crimes,[23] so that while disturbances of this sort may be causes of crime they are not necessarily excuses for crime.

picked up and was found the next morning fast asleep in a hay-stack, apparently unaware of what he had done and astonished at the sight of the axe.[24] The Rev Clarence Richeson, an American Baptist minister, was another epileptic murderer. One of his choir girls said she was pregnant and he told her to get into a bath and swallow a capsule which would bring on an abortion. The capsule he gave her contained potassium cyanide. At his trial he wanted to plead guilty and appeared utterly confused. He had repeated epileptic seizures in prison and during one attack he emasculated himself with the jagged lid of a tin can. After his plea for mercy had failed, he had a further attack and lay rigid and unconscious for fourteen hours. When he had recovered he was 'dragged out like a sack of meal and thrown into the electric chair'.[25]

Epilepsy is an ancient disease and was formerly considered a holy disease. It has a long, well-documented history because no other form of neuropathy has such unmistakable physical symptoms. But there are, of course, many other forms of nervous disorder which are less readily identifiable and often impossible to diagnose; and ever since insanity has been accepted as a defence in criminal proceedings, there has been the problem of deciding the degree of mental illness which should be accepted as entitling the criminal to special treatment by virtue of his irresponsibility.

In the criminal law of the Middle Ages very little notice was taken of the insane, and insanity could not usually be pleaded in extenuation of a criminal act except in the case of wild lunatics *demens et furiosus non per feloniam*. Even raving lunatics were sometimes hanged and were, in any case, often treated as criminals whether they had committed an offence or not. They were frequently flogged, as criminals were, to drive the devils out of them. 'In case a man be a lunatic,' one ancient prescription runs, 'take skin of a mereswine or porpoise, work it into a whip, swinge the man well therewith soon he will be well.'[26] At one monastery the lunatics were apparently given ten lashes every day by the monks in charge of them.[27] Animals, too, were punished; and for this there was biblical authority.[28] A sow, mutilated and dressed in human clothing, was hanged at Falaise in 1386 for biting a child, and three years later a horse was hanged for killing a man at Dijon. In 1454 the Bishop of Lausanne initiated legal proceedings against the leeches which had infected the water at Berne. And in 1474 a cock was burned for having committed a crime against nature and laid an egg.[29] Animals were often considered responsible for the sexual offences committed upon them by human beings and were even tortured to elicit groans which were accepted as confessions.[30] When George Schörpff of Ermb was 'found guilty of beastliness with four cows, two calves and a sheep' he was beheaded and 'afterwards burned together with a cow'.[31] Even inanimate objects which had caused death could be punished and, until the law of *deodand* was abolished in 1846 after a train which had killed four people was declared to be *deodand*, things like this could be 'given to God', that is to say handed over to the King to be sold so that the money could be used 'in works of charity for the appeasement of God's wrath'.[32] They were sometimes flogged; and as late as 1685 a bell was whipped 'to punish it for having assisted Heretics'.[33]

So far as human beings are concerned, it was not until the seventeenth century that the first legal decisions that have any relevance to the modern attitude towards responsibility were taken in Europe. Sir Matthew Hale, who was Lord Chief Justice between 1671 and 1676, decided that any person who suffered from distempers but still had the faculties of a fourteen-year-old boy could be found guilty of treason or felony. And early in the next century when Edward Arnold was tried for shooting the Earl of Onslow who, he imagined, was besieging him with devils and demons and other horrible creatures which appeared in his bedroom at night, it was laid down that insanity was no defence unless it could be shown that the defendant was 'totally deprived of his understanding and memory' and knew what he was doing 'no more than an infant, than a brute or wild beast'.

This attitude was somewhat softened in 1760 when Earl Ferrers was tried for shooting his steward. On this occasion the House of Lords ruled that the only permissible defence was a total and permanent absence of reason or a total and temporary absence of it at the moment of committing the crime. But Ferrers, who seems to have been suffering from homicidal mania, was nevertheless hanged. Forty years later, however, at the trial of Hadfield, a madman who believed that God was commanding him to kill the King and who attempted to obey these instructions one evening at the Drury Lane Theatre, Lord Chief Justice Kenyon said that the question to be decided was whether 'at the very time the act was committed the man's mind was sane'. The jury decided that Hadfield's mind was not sane and he was not hanged.

This was a somewhat arbitrary decision for no one was clear

what insanity, in a legal sense, actually meant. And it was not until 1812, at the trial of Bellingham, that Sir James Mansfield made some attempt to define it. To be sane, Mansfield said, a man must be able at the time of his crime to distinguish between right and wrong, good and evil. It was felt that Bellingham could do this and he was executed. Mansfield's statement of the law was bitterly attacked both in England and in the United States where English precedents had been closely followed. Many madmen, it was argued, could make these distinctions perfectly well in general cases but yet had no sense of guilt or of conscience about their particular crimes.[34]

In 1843 the whole question was settled as well as seemed possible by the McNaghten Rules. Daniel McNaghten had attempted to kill the secretary of Sir Robert Peel and was acquitted when Lord Chief Justice Tindal told the jury that the question was whether or not McNaghten was capable of distinguishing between right and wrong 'with respect to the act with which he stands charged'. This view of the law was as severely criticized as Sir James Mansfield's and the judges were asked to answer various questions put to them by the House of Lords. The main rule is that every man is to be presumed sane until the contrary is proved. To establish a defence on the grounds of insanity it must be clearly proved that, 'at the time of committing of the act, the party accused was labouring under such a defect of reason, from disease of the mind, as not to know the nature or quality of the act he was doing, or if he did know it, that he did not know he was doing wrong'.

The influence of the McNaghten Rules was lasting and profound. They were admitted to be less than ideal; but so long as society failed to invent 'an instrument for diving into a man's mind and determining the exact capacity for self-direction and self-control',[35] they were considered to be the best rules that could be devised. In England they still apply, although their application, so far as murder is concerned, was modified by the Homicide Act of 1957 which introduced the defence of 'diminished responsibility'. Their revision has frequently been advocated and the Royal Commission on Capital Punishment 1949-1953 suggested that they were so defective they ought to be changed; but it has long been felt that whatever their defects, their 'great advantage', as Sir Harold Scott, a former Commissioner of the Police of the Metropolis, has said, 'is that they are simple and easy for a jury to understand'.[36] Henry Maudsley, in the nineteenth century expressed a contrary

view. 'Why maintain a test,' he asked, 'which is so hard to understand, so false in science and so uncertain in application, so often
interpreted by different judges in different ways?' He illustrated
the difficulty of interpreting the rules satisfactorily by quoting the
case of an eighteen-year-old boy who had murdered someone because he wanted to be hanged. This argued his counsel, clearly
showed that the boy was insane. On the contrary, said the counsel
for the prosecution, as he had murdered in order to be hanged, he
knew the consequence of his act and was, therefore, criminally
responsible.[37]*

In the United States, the McNaghten Rules have also been
widely accepted as being the best formula that can be found. They
still apply in twenty-nine states. Seventeen states, however, allow
a defence of 'irresistible impulse', or an 'inability to control' an
impulse, by which a man may plead that even if he understands
the difference between right and wrong, he may yet have been
incapable of preventing himself from doing what is legally wrong.
The task of proving this irresponsibility does not, as in England,
always lie with the defence but it is the prosecution who 'must
prove beyond a reasonable doubt that the accused was mentally
capable of the criminal intent'.[39] The acceptance of the idea that
an irresistible impulse qualifies a man's guilt owes much to Dr
Isaac Ray's great book *The Medical Jurisprudence of Insanity*
first published in Boston in 1838 by Charles C. Little and James
Brown whose firm was later to bring out so many important
criminological works. 'In medical science,' Ray wrote, 'it is dangerous to reason against facts. Now we have an immense mass of
cases related by men of unquestionable competence and veracity,
where people are *irresistibly* impelled to the commission of criminal
acts while fully conscious of their nature and consequences . . .
They are not fictions invented by medical men for the purpose of
puzzling juries and defeating the ends of justice, but plain, un-
varnished facts.'[40] The theory of the 'irresistible impulse' did not,
at first, carry much weight with lawyers, but there was one who

---

* The Home Secretary has a statutory duty to order a special medical examination if he thinks that an insane man has been condemned to death.   Nowadays
these examinations are ordered much more often than in the past.   Between
1940 and 1949 eighty-six condemned men (out of a total number of 262) were
examined by a panel of doctors and about half of them were certified insane or
had their sentences commuted to imprisonment.   Between 1900 and 1909 only
about one in every eight condemned men was examined.[38]

felt convinced that Ray was right. He was Judge Charles Doe of the New Hampshire Supreme Court and by 1870 the New Hampshire Rule, based on this theory, was in existence. The conception of irresistibility was taken a step further in 1954 when a judge of the Court of Appeals of the District of Columbia laid down a new rule, afterwards known as the Durham Rule, which provided that the accused was 'not criminally responsible if his unlawful act was the product of a mental disease or mental defect'. This Rule, adopted in 1961 by the State of Maine, has the advantage that the jury do not—as under the McNaghten Rules they do—have the difficult, if not impossible duty of deciding whether the accused was capable of considering his predicament. Mental diseases and mental defects are accepted by the Durham Rule as being matters of fact on which expert evidence can be given. Whether the evidence will be accepted, however, is another matter. In Washington, since the new Rule was introduced, three quarters of the pleas of mental illness have failed.[41] The remark of a judge at the Old Bailey, when delivering sentence on a man whom an expert witness had declared to be schizophrenic, is a celebrated example of this general scepticism which is as common in England as in America. 'If I accept this evidence at its face value,' the judge declared, 'you are really two men and only one of you is really guilty of this offence. Well I'm afraid both of you must go to prison.'[42]

The suspicion that insanity can be convincingly feigned is of course, very strong and is not always unjustified.

'Once I came up to the sessions for stealing twenty-three pounds at an inn I was staying at,' a young habitual thief told a barrister. 'I was beginning to get wide awake about that time. What's more, I had heard they were pretty hot at that court. I didn't want to get a long stretch so I pretended to be a bit balmy to the prison doctor while I was on remand. A chap told me what to do, but as a matter of fact I didn't have to do much. I just acted dumb, and kept saying all the time that I didn't know why I did things. It worked like a charm and the doctor came to court and gave evidence that I was some sort of mental. All they did was to send me to a mental institution in Somerset, where I stayed seven months. That was a sight better than a three year stretch which I had thought I might get.'[43]

The Borstal 'was a rotten place,' another young thief said. 'There were a few decent chaps there who wanted to learn trades and to pull them-

selves together. But there were very few of them, and the place was run
by gangs and mobs. I got sick of having my meal with chaps whose only
conversation was bashing, and picking locks and dirt. If you get looked
on by these chaps as pi or soft, they gave you hell. I wasn't brave
enough to stand up to those chaps. I was frightened of them, and all I
wanted was to get away. I decided to work my ticket. There was a chap
there in the hospital. I was told he was going to be sent away as he was
balmy. So I decided to pretend to be insane, too. I studied all his antics
and added some more of my own. He got sent to Feltham, and some
time later I was sent there, too. I found it was quite easy to fool the
doctor, and I was afraid of being punished if I was found out to have
pretended to be mad, so I went on doing it. Then I was certified as a
lunatic and sent to an asylum.'[11]

'The doctors did it all for me,' yet another young criminal said, 'Someone or other told me what to do so as to swinging it that you were a bit
balmy. Really I didn't have to do much.[45]

The malingerer may be, and often is, suffering from an actual
psychosis, the American psychiatrist Dr Bernard Glueck thinks,
and cases of 'pure malingering in individuals absolutely normal
mentally, are becoming rarer every day in psychiatric
experience'.[46] Certainly many men go to such extreme and
motiveless lengths to feign a particular type of insanity that they
can reasonably be assumed to be suffering from some sort of mental
disorder. Ferrero quotes the case of a man who had several times
been convicted of theft, displaying extraordinarily varied signs
of mental alienation after six months' imprisonment. He lost his
powers of speech, tore his clothes, did not appear to feel pain
when a needle was stuck deep into his neck, put ice between his
clothes and his skin, decorated himself with ribbons, made holes
in his flesh with a needle and stuck hairs into them, snatched at
any bright object, ate mice, spiders, nails and sputum, became
addicted to coprophagy and masturbated in public. His look of
vacant apathy was replaced by one of vivacity, however, when
he thought he was not being watched; and he frequently stole away
to vomit unseen. In the barber shop, where he was put to work,
he gave no trouble and seemed to enjoy helping the barber, until a
doctor appeared when he slapped shaving soap all over the nearest
face.[47]

The difficulties of diagnosing a mental disorder when less
strenuous efforts are made to display it was demonstrated during

the trial of Gunther Fritz Podola at the Old Bailey in 1959. Podola had shot and killed a London policeman in July and three days later was arrested in a room in West Kensington. Police officers half carried him out into the street with his head in a sack. Allegations of police brutality were made in the newspapers and these increased when Podola appeared in court with the still remaining traces of a black eye. A detective said that he had had to charge Podola's door with all his strength and that he had crashed into the room falling 'full length on top of him'.

His counsel pleaded that 'a very, very severe fright' had caused Podola to lose his memory. He had completely forgotten the crime with which he was charged. A neurologist testified that only a genuine case of hysterical amnesia or a man with a specialist's knowledge of uncommon symptoms would behave as Podola was behaving. The senior medical officer at Brixton Prison, however, said that Podola's amnesia was 'definitely not genuine'. The jury agreed with this view and Podola was hanged.[48]

The reluctance of juries to accept the evidence of neurologists and psychiatrists is often understandable, for the apparently outlandish and irrelevant diagnoses given by some of these witnesses seems on occasions an affront to intelligence and common sense. That psychology is of immense importance no sensible juror would deny, nor should it be denied that a psychologist who has devoted a lifetime's study to the infinitely complicated operations of the human mind is likely to know more about them than, say, a fishmonger. But juries cannot be blamed for wondering whether they ought to accept as facts what can often be no more than opinions, however didactically and with whatever confidence they are expressed. Psychology, Sir Leo Page has said, 'is a good servant but a bad master';[49] and quoted examples of the 'phantasies' of those whom he believed to have become its slaves.

'My first example,' he wrote, 'is taken from a textbook of which the author is a superintendent physician of a mental hospital and a qualified psychiatrist. He raises for discussion what he himself describes as an interesting and rather perplexing problem—the question why a prostitute should steal money from her clients ... According to the author, a prostitute is by the nature of her occupation a robber of men's strength. She steals their virility. Unconsciously, therefore, she seeks continuously to carry out this robbery of men, though in another form ... The author gravely gives the name of "castration complex" to this type of larceny.'

Sir Leo had another theory. He hoped he would not appear arrogant when he said that however baffling the enigma had been to the doctor, it did not perplex him at all. 'A prostitute takes money from the pocket of her client because she likes money.'[50]

He quoted other examples. One was of a boy who telephoned from public call boxes and asked the girl at the exchange indecent questions about her body. The boy's parents, the psychiatric report informed the justices, had not given him proper sex instruction, so that he was 'ignorant of the anatomical differences between the sexes and was thus driven to discover the secret for himself by the unfortunate expedient of asking a woman on the telephone'.[51] Another example was of a young man who pleaded guilty to a charge of indecent assault on a young woman. A psychiatrist called for the defence 'gave evidence to the effect that the prisoner suffered from defective eyesight and that this handicap was the cause of certain emotional disturbances which were the real cause of the man's behaviour, with the result that the witness was prepared to advise the court that what the prisoner really needed was not punishment but a new pair of spectacles'.[52]

Despite his derision, Sir Leo Page was not blind to the fact that 'there are psychiatrists who are wise and helpful, experienced and level-headed, who lose not the smallest fraction of their common sense because of the additional knowledge which their special science gives them'.[53] His suspicion, however, that wise psychiatrists were outnumbered by those who could not 'think normally and practically', who showed 'not appreciation but a sort of adolescent intolerance and dogmatic contempt of the experience of practical men', was surely unjustified. And even in the extreme examples which he quoted, there is perhaps more sense in the psychiatrists' diagnosis than he was prepared to recognize. But Sir Leo wrote as a barrister and a magistrate of great intelligence and experience and it is not surprising that less judicious men than he should be misled by the incompetent psychiatrist into supposing that psychiatry is a sort of whimsical mare's nest. For this reason alone there seems good reason for supporting the more general adoption of the Briggs Law of Massachusetts which takes the psychiatrist out of the court room and orders the Department of Mental Diseases to examine the defendant and submit a complete report on him prior to the trial. Apart from the suspicion that mental disorders may be invented or exaggerated to fit defences allowed by the law, there are still men who believe that mad criminals should be allowed no special defence and that, as has often been proposed from the times of Seneca and Galen, to those of Diderot and G. B. Shaw, they should be done away with whenever possible in the interests of 'social hygiene'. The former Lord Chief Justice, Lord Goddard, when asked about the verdict upon the murderer Ley, who had been found insane, and who, Goddard agreed, was insane, said that he would have 'thought it very proper that he should have been hanged'.[54] Many legal authorities have agreed with him. Sir James Stephen could not 'quite see why a person, who suddenly becomes bad by reason of a disease should be in a better position than he who is bad by birth, education or natural character'. He believed that it should be possible to put both to death.[55]

Similar sentiments were expressed during the trial of Marie Schneider, a twelve-year-old schoolgirl, at the Berlin Criminal Court in 1886. Marie Schneider had gone on an errand for her mother and had met a little girl of three-and-a-half who was wearing earrings. Marie thought if she could get hold of these earrings she would be able to buy herself some sugar buns. She saw a landing window open on the second floor of an apartment house and took the girl up to it. She put her out on the ledge, tore the rings from her ears and threw her out into the street. She spoke to the President of the Court lucidly and without emotion. This is the essence of her answers to his questions:

'I was born on 1st May 1874 in Berlin. My father died long ago. I do not know when. I never knew him. My mother is still living. She is a machinist. I also have a younger brother. My sister died a year ago. I did not much like her, because she was better than I and my mother treated her better. My mother has several times whipped me for naughtiness and it is right that I should take away the stick with which she beat me and beat her. I have gone to school since I was six years old. I have been in the third class for two years. I stayed there because I was lazy. Sometime ago, while playing in the yard, I came behind a child, held his eyes and asked him who I was. I pressed my thumb deep in his eye, so that he cried out. I knew that I hurt him and I did not let go until I was made to. It did not give me special pleasure, but I did not feel sorry. When I was a little child I stuck forks in the eyes of rabbits and afterwards slit open their bellies . . . I knew that Conrad murdered his wife and children and that his head was cut off. I am very fond of sweets and have several times tried to get money to buy myself sweets.

I told people that the money was for someone else who had no small change. I knew that was deceit. I know as well what stealing is. Anyone who kills is a murderer. I am a murderess. Murder is punished with death. The murderer is executed. His head is cut off. My head will not be cut off because I am too young. I did not think about Grete's parents being sorry about her being murdered. It did not hurt me. I was not sorry. I was not sorry all the time I was in prison. I am not sorry now. I was taken in a cab to the mortuary. I ate a piece of bread they gave me. I was hungry. I saw Grete's body undressed on a bed. I did not feel any regret and I was not sorry. They put me with four women and I told them the story. I laughed while I was telling it because they asked me such funny questions. I wrote to my mother in prison. I asked her to send me some money to buy some dripping for we had dry bread.'

At the mention of the dry bread, she showed emotion for the first time during the whole of the long examination. Her eyes filled with tears. She was sentenced to eight years' imprisonment.[56]

Demands that women like this and men like Ley should be put out of the way as they can never be cured and, if kept in institutions, are an unnecessary burden to the state are still made and, no doubt, receive wider support than public expressions of agreement with them suggest. It is, however, becoming more generally admitted now that such solutions are impracticable and immoral and that attempts must continually be made to find means of curing the insane criminal and, if his cure is impossible, of caring for him. But only recently have any serious attempts been made to achieve these aims. When Broadmoor was established in England in 1863 there was no other asylum in Europe specifically devoted to the care of insane criminals, and it was many years before this situation altered. Not, indeed, for a hundred years was England to have a psychiatric prison for those criminals who are now called psychopaths, and in America there is little to compare with the California Medical Facility in Vacaville.

Psychopaths—a loosely defined term to denote those whom past generations would have termed morally insane or morally imbecile —who form a significant part of the prison population of any country, are not considered insane by the law. They cannot be accurately defined; but their reckless, purposeless and erratic behaviour, their callous indifference to the suffering of others, their chronic, sometimes compulsive lying, their powerful—and perhaps irresistible—impulses clamouring for constant satisfaction, are symptoms of their disorder. They are not all aggressive, but those who are have an obsessional sense of being persecuted and a consequent desire for revenge. They are not all criminals, either, and as Brian Inglis has shown,[57] 'are not necessarily more prone to violence than anybody else,' although their treatment sometimes makes them so. It is as yet usually impossible to treat them or cure them and, in any event, to keep them in ordinary mental hospitals hampers the treatment of the other patients. 'They fail to appreciate reality,' Sir David Henderson, the psychiatrist, told the Royal Commission on Capital Punishment 1949-1953, giving what is perhaps as good a description of them as is possible in a few words. 'They are fickle, changeable, lack persistence of effort and are unable to profit by experience or punishment. They are dangerous when frustrated. They are devoid of affection, are cold, heartless, callous, cynical, and show a lack of judgment and foresight which is almost beyond belief. They may be adult in years but emotionally they remain as dangerous children whose conduct may revert to a primitive, sub-human level. Neville Heath and John George Haigh are extreme examples.'[58]

Neville Heath was a good-looking man, strong, healthy, charming, self-confident and intelligent, the antithesis apparently of Lombroso's born criminal. He was born at Ilford in 1917 and on leaving school joined the Army. He was later commissioned in the R.A.F. Dismissed from the service in 1937, he was soon afterwards convicted of fraud and false pretences which included posing as Lord Dudley to whom he bore some resemblance. He was sent to Borstal but at the outbreak of war he was released, joined the army again, and again was commissioned. Cashiered while serving in the Middle East he joined the South African Air Force under another name, was given his third commission and in 1945 was court-martialled and dismissed for the last time.

Soon after his return to England he was convicted of unlawfully wearing military uniform and various decorations to which he was not entitled. In June 1946 he booked a room at a London hotel, signing the register with his own name to which he added the rank of Group Captain. On the morning of 21 June a chambermaid went into his room and was terrified when she saw on the bed the body of a woman whose ankles were tied together with a handkerchief. The body had been ferociously whipped and bore the marks of teeth. The nipples had been practically bitten off and something —perhaps the handle of the whip—had been thrust up the vagina.

The following day Heath wrote to the police telling them that he had given the key of his bedroom to the dead woman as she wanted another man to visit her there. When he had returned to the hotel he had found the body. He gave no address in his letter, but on 5th July he telephoned the Bournemouth police and told them that he had dined two days before with a Miss Doreen Marshall who had not been seen since. He went to the police station and identified a photograph of the girl whom, he said, he had left near the pier at half past twelve. He was calling himself Group Captain Rupert Brooke by this time, but a detective noticed his resemblance to Heath, whose description had been circulated in the *Police Gazette* and he was detained. In the pocket of his coat was found a railway cloakroom ticket and when this was presented at Bournemouth West Station a suitcase was handed over. The case contained a pearl, a blood-stained blue woollen scarf and a heavy riding crop. The blood on the scarf was of the same group as that of the woman who had been murdered in London and the pattern of the thong of the whip matched the scars on her body; the pearl had belonged to Doreen Marshall whose body was discovered on 8th July under a rhododendron bush in Branksome Chine. Apart from one shoe the body was naked, it had been mutilated, both nipples had been bitten off and the throat was cut.

Dr W. H. de B. Hubert, an eminent specialist in psychiatry, said at Heath's trial that he was morally insane. Dr Grierson, Senior Medical Officer at Brixton Prison, however, thought that although perverted and sadistic he knew what he was doing and that what he was doing was wrong. The jury accepted this view and Heath was convicted and hanged.[59]

The same plea of insanity was made by an expert witness, Dr Henry Yellowlees, at the trial of John George Haigh three years later. Haigh, Yellowlees said, was a classic case of paranoia who felt that the influence of a mystic force drove him to drink the blood of his victims and his own urine.

Haigh, like Heath, came from a middle-class family and had a criminal record. He was brought up strictly by very religious parents. He had been convicted of forgery and fraud in 1934 and again in 1937. In 1949 he was staying at the Onslow Court Hotel, South Kensington, where two elderly ladies, Mrs Durand-Deacon and Mrs Lane, were also guests. On 18 February Mrs Durand-Deacon told Mrs Lane that she was going with Mr Haigh down to

Sussex where he experimented 'on different things'. He was interested in an idea she had for a new type of artificial finger-nail and had suggested that it might be possible to manufacture a prototype at his factory in Crawley.

Mrs Durand-Deacon did not return to her hotel and the following day Haigh said to Mrs Lane, 'I was to have picked her up at the Army and Navy Stores. I waited for her until 3.35.'

Mrs Lane said she would go to the police. Haigh said that he would go with her and at the station he asked especially that his name should be taken. Haigh's past criminal record aroused the suspicion of the police who searched his premises at Crawley and found, amongst other incriminating articles and papers, a receipt from a firm of cleaners between the pages of a ration book. The receipt was for a coat which had belonged to Mrs Durand-Deacon. At an interview at Chelsea Police Station on the evening of 26 February, Haigh asked calmly, 'Tell me frankly, what are the chances of anyone being released from Broadmoor?'

The inspector said he did not intend to discuss the matter, and then Haigh said, 'If I told you the truth, you wouldn't believe me. It sounds too fantastic for belief.'

The inspector warned him that anything he said would be taken down and might be used in evidence.

'I understand all that,' said Haigh impatiently. 'Mrs Durand-Deacon no longer exists. I've destroyed her with acid. You'll find the sludge that remains at Leopold Road.'

Haigh went on to say that he had shot Mrs Durand-Deacon in the back of the head. Then he made an incision in her throat with a pen knife and collected and drank a glass of her blood. After he had put her body in the tank he went out for tea at a restaurant in Crawley.* Later he took her coat to the cleaners and sold some of her jewellery.

* However insensitive this behaviour appears, it cannot be matched by that of a murderer in Northampton who, having killed his mistress with a shoe-maker's rasp while in bed with her, got up, cooked himself a rasher of bacon and then went back to bed with the corpse to 'get a bit of sleep'. He left the house when he awoke and on his return found the dead woman's brothers charging sixpence each to people who were queuing up to witness his handiwork. The Governor of Northampton Prison described him as a 'polite and very gently spoken man of about forty'. He gave no trouble and was profuse in his thanks for all that was done for him. Ten minutes before his execution, the date of which coincided with a visit to Northampton by one of the Royal Princesses, the Governor went into the condemned cell to ask him how he was feeling. 'He said that he felt very

Haigh confessed to the murder of five other people whose bodies he had also destroyed by acid and seemed to suppose that he could not be convicted because there were no bodies to show that murder had been done. In the sludge at Leopold Road, however, some false teeth were found and a dentist identified these as having been supplied to Mrs Durand-Deacon.*

The contention by the defence's psychiatrist that Haigh did not know that he was doing wrong when he killed Mrs Durand-Deacon was rejected by the jury who reached their verdict of guilty within a quarter of an hour.[60]

Both Haigh and Heath are, as Sir David Henderson said, extreme examples of the psychopathic personality. Neither of them had been able to profit by experience; they had, although not unintelligent, failed to appreciate reality and they had both showed 'a lack of judgment and foresight almost beyond belief'. It seemed in both cases that they had so assured a confidence in their abilities that they felt there was no reason to avoid courting attention by the police, that this might even be pleasurably exciting.

These characteristics of the psychopath were all shared by Miles Giffard, a schizophrenic who murdered his parents at their home in Cornwall in the summer of 1952. Between the ages of two and four, Giffard had had a nurse who beat him and kept him locked up in dark cupboards for long periods. The family's doctor advised the dismissal of this nurse but the parents ignored the advice and allowed her to remain in charge of the boy until she decided to leave of her own accord. She was then replaced by an affectionate sixteen-year-old girl who stayed five years and of whom Giffard

well indeed and he wanted to thank everybody for their kindness. "It's terrible weather, though, sir," he added unexpectedly.' When the Governor looked surprised that he should be concerned about the weather a few minutes before he was due to be hanged, he went on,' "Oh, I wasn't thinking of myself, sir. I was thinking of the Princess." '[61]

* The presence of a body is not, of course, necessary to a murder charge. In 1948 James Camb, a deck steward employed by the Union Castle Line, was convicted of the murder of a young woman passenger whom he had pushed out of the porthole of her cabin into a shark-infested sea about ninety miles from the African coast. The prosecution maintained that he had strangled her. He said that she had suddenly clutched at him and foamed at the mouth while he was, with her consent, having sexual intercourse with her and that he had panicked and pushed her body, naked save for a dressing gown, into the sea. He could not explain, however, why a pair of the girl's black pyjamas were missing or why two bells, one for the steward and another for a stewardess, were rung while he was in the cabin with her.

became extremely fond. She said afterwards that the boy had fearful nightmares in which he screamed piteously. She always had great difficulty in bringing him back to consciousness and reality. At the age of fifteen he was sent to a psychiatrist who thought that he was twelve and who, according to the boy's uncle, General Sir George Giffard, 'warned his parents then of the possibility of mental breakdown in the future'.[62]

The revealing confession he made at Scotland Yard shows how dream-like is the world which this sort of mind inhabits.

'I want to be frank,' he said. 'I want to tell you the whole story ... Up to twelve months ago I was studying; firstly for the law as a solicitor, and latterly as an estate agent. My father made me an allowance of five pounds a month. I couldn't settle down to my studies. I gave up working last November and then I got a legacy of £750. I had spent the money by about March. I scrounged around a bit and did some work—about eight weeks. I was selling ice-cream for Walls. I left them and some time in June I went home and broke into my father's house. Then I came to London and spent the money ... Then I went home. I straightened it out with my father. I stayed home until the middle of August, and then I came to London. I lived in Chelsea and took a furnished room. I began to visit the White Hart in King's Road, Chelsea. I met a Chelsea pensioner who frequented that public house. About a month ago—no, six weeks ago—he introduced me to a young lady and her mother, with whom I became great friends. I became a frequent visitor at their house, where I was made very welcome.

'I had been living from hand to mouth. I had odd bits of money from various people, and there are some cheques which were "R.D." I'd been drinking very heavily, and about a month ago the girl began charging me about my untidy appearance. I told her my parents had arranged to send my clothing up, but this was a lie just to stall her off. I was tight for money at this time and had no means of tidying myself up; so about a fortnight ago I said I would go home and get my clothing myself. That is what I told her, but in fact I wanted to go home to try and get some money from my father ... I went, arriving on November 2nd. (I actually did hitch-hike). I phoned her practically every day ... I telephoned her twice on Friday 7th November, the first time at half past five. I told her I was coming up to do some business for my father. This wasn't true. I promised to phone her again at half past eight to confirm whether in fact I was coming; and I told her if I did come, my father had promised to let me use his car—it is a Triumph, the number is ERL 1.

'At the time of my first call my father and mother were both out. They came back almost together in separate cars at about 7.30 p.m. My father was doing something to my mother's car. Both cars were in the garage. God knows for what reason, I hit them over the head with a piece of iron pipe. I hit him first and he slumped to the ground unconscious. Mother had gone into the house. I went into the house after her. I found her in the kitchen; I hit her from behind. Everything went peculiar— I got into a panic.

'Shortly after this I made a second phone call to the girl in London— this was about 8.15—and told her I was definitely coming to London with my father's car. I asked her if I could come around to her house in the morning for a wash and shave.

'I went out with the intention of getting the car and found my father coming round. I hit him again, several times. Then I got the car out and went in to get some clothes. My mother was coming round, then. So I hit her again. She was bleeding very heavily. They both were by this time. I didn't know what to do. There was blood everywhere. I got the wheelbarrow; put my mother in it, took her out to the Point and pushed her over. I then went back and did the same with my father's body. I pushed the wheelbarrow over that time. Then I went back to the house and washed the place out. I went to my mother's room and took some pieces of jewellery. And I took some money from my father's coat pocket. I packed a change of clothing; my own clothes were very bloodstained. I then drove the car out and drove to London . . . I picked up two hitch-hikers somewhere near Ilchester.'

When he arrived in London he went to sleep in the car and then he went to his girl friend's house and arranged to meet her and her mother in Leicester Square at two o'clock in the afternoon to go and see Charlie Chaplin in 'Limelight'. After leaving the cinema, the mother went home and Giffard and the girl went to a public house and had a meal. There was still blood on his cuffs and sleeves and tie. At the Star in Chesham Mews he told her what he had done. 'That's the whole truthful story,' he said. 'I can only say I have had a brainstorm. I can't account for my actions, I'd drunk about half a bottle of whisky on the Friday afternoon before all this happened. It just seemed to me that nothing mattered so long as I got back to London.'[63]

His extraordinary telephone call to his girl friend while his father lay dying in the garage and his mother was dying in the kitchen, can be compared to Haigh's going out for a cup of tea while Mrs Durand-Deacon's body was dissolving in the bath. The little care that either of them took to avoid discovery is as remarkable as Heath's blind confidence. 'Anything can happen,' Giffard wrote to his girl friend from prison. 'After all, if everything is all right we can still take up where we left off.'

Giffard, like Heath and Haigh before him, was hanged because his behaviour at the time of his crime was not considered to be that of an insane person within the limits defined by the McNaghten Rules. If a defence of 'diminished responsibility' introduced by the 1957 Homicide Act had been available to him it might have succeeded, although juries are still as reluctant to accept the medical evidence of the defence in criminal trials as they were before the Act was passed and seem often to prefer the rebuttal evidence of the prosecution. The burden of proving 'diminished responsibility' lies on the defence and it is a heavy one. This is one of the reasons why the defence did not reveal the evidence it possessed concerning the mental condition of James Hanratty during his trial in 1962.[64]

James Hanratty was a professional but not particularly successful criminal who was found guilty and hanged for the murder of a man whom he had forced to give him a lift in his car. Having shot the driver, Hanratty raped the driver's girl friend and then tried to kill her too. He could neither read nor write and had been diagnosed ten years before as a mental defective. So long as Hanratty, whose talents as a criminal were unworthy of the high opinion he had of them, continued to deny the crime, a plea of 'diminished responsibility' was clearly impossible; but there is no doubt that the defence counsel could not feel confident, in the light of previous experience, that such a plea would have succeeded even if it had been made.

For it is not enough to prove that a man is mentally defective, the court requires evidence that his defect constitutes 'such abnormality of mind as substantially impaired his mental responsibility'. And even in the United States Court of Appeals in the District of Columbia, where the Durham Rule applies to all criminals and not only to murderers, it has been held that 'unexplained medical labels—schizophrenia, paranoia, psychosis, neurosis, psychopathy—are not enough'. The development of the disease must be explained and its effect on the accused's behaviour; and this, as Dr Manfred S. Guttmacher, the distinguished forensic psychiatrist, has observed, 'is a challenge which few psychiatrists are equipped to meet'.[65]

'She would have to be insane, to have done it,' said Frank Duncan, a lawyer from Santa Barbara, when told that his mother had hired two men to kill his wife of whom she was hysterically jealous.* A similar comment was made by his employer when Harvey Glatman was found guilty in San Diego in 1958 of strangling three women after having taken photographs of them in their underclothes. And it is, in fact, an opinion which most people share when presented with the facts of almost any murder done neither for profit nor in sudden anger. It has, indeed, often been suggested that all criminals, and not just most murderers, are in some degree insane. Jeremy Bentham thought that, 'delinquents, especially of the more criminal descriptions, may be considered as a particular class of human beings ... they may be considered as persons of unsound mind, but in whom the complaint has not swelled to so high a pitch as to rank them with idiots or lunatics'.[66]

Bentham died before the conception of the moral imbecile was much propounded, except by Philippe Pinel and by Grohmann. But a few years after Bentham's death, Prichard's *Treatise on Insanity* formulated a doctrine of moral insanity and by the time Despine's *Psychologie Naturelle* appeared in 1868 and expressed the view that, although the criminal might not be insane in the legal sense he could still be 'morally mad', the problem of the moral imbecile had been carefully studied both in Europe and in the United States by Mayo and Isaac Ray amongst many others. It was left, however, to Henry Maudsley whose celebrated book, *Responsibility in Mental Disease* was published in 1874, to propound the belief that criminals go 'criminal, as the insane go mad, because they cannot help it'.[67] The causes of this irresistible impulse to criminality were, as Maudsley tried to make clear, numerous and varied but the result, he insisted, was the same: the criminal could not help it. He was not even, if a genuine criminal, 'thoroughly conscious of his crime'.[68] To punish such an offender was pointless. But Maudsley was pessimistic about the prospect of treating him.

The problem remains. When Dr Benjamin Karpman, at the

---

* Mrs. Duncan (who, it transpired, had been married at least eleven times) and both her accomplices (dim-witted, part-Mexican labourers) were executed at San Quentin on the same day in August 1962.

1960 convention of the American Psychiatric Association, sug-
suggested, as Harry Elmer Barnes and Negley K. Teeters had also
rather more tentatively suggested in their *New Horizons in
Criminology*, that as 'you can't have mental illness and criminal
responsibility in the same person at the same time', in fifty years
prisons in the United States would be replaced by psychiatric
treatment centres for lawbreakers, the prophecy was derided.[69]
And so long as mental illness is so variously defined and so little
understood the derision is understandable. Whether or not Dr
David Stafford-Clark is right in defining 'medical crime' as 'crime
in which the individual capacity of the criminal to refrain from
committing the act is effectively diminished by factors both recognizable and, at some stage, treatable by medical means', his suggestion that 'it does not and cannot overthrow or exclude the
concept of normal responsibility in the majority of people, as
distinct from those who are clinically clearly not responsible' would
presumably go unquestioned by most psychiatrists as by nearly all
laymen.

But many, if not most violent criminals, it has often been proposed, are to some degree psychopaths and therefore untreatable.
In the large Bellevue psychiatric hospital in Manhattan, of fifty
thousand such criminals examined over a period of twenty-five
years, only five per cent were found to be suffering from a mental
disease which might profit from treatment. Nearly all the rest were
considered to be psychopaths and being, for the most part, beyond
the reach of psychiatry, they were returned to prison. In England,
until more psychiatric prisons are available, most psychopaths will
also continue to be sent to prison. The Mental Health Act of 1959
allows hospital orders to be made instead of sentences of imprisonment, but as Lady Wootton said at the 1962 conference of the
National Association for Mental Health, little use is made of the
Act's provisions. Between the time it came into force on
1 November 1960 and 30 September 1961 there were 10,099
convictions for crimes of violence, but only in ninety-seven cases
were hospital orders made.[70]

The reluctance to admit that a man not obviously insane who
is convicted of a violent crime may belong in a hospital ward
rather than in a prison cell is understandable. It is to be expected,
too, that until a closer association is conclusively shown to exist
between such crimes (including aggressive sexual offences) and
mental illness and until some greater hope is offered that those who

commit these crimes, if they are, in fact, mentally ill, can be cured, courts will go on sending psychopaths to prison as a punishment rather than to the psychiatrist for cure.* But at least there is now little chance of a clearly deranged person being executed for murder as the toxicomaniac Anna Maria Schonleben was in 1881.

This curious woman, the well educated, rather plain daughter of a Nuremberg innkeeper, married a lawyer who drank himself to death. For some years afterwards she wandered about Germany taking various jobs as a confectioner, doll-maker, needlewoman, housekeeper, cook and nursemaid. She twice attempted suicide and may for a time have been a prostitute. She started a girls' school in Neumarkt but after a scandal in which accusations of Lesbianism were made she went to Munich and later to Bayreuth to become housekeeper to a judge who was separated from his wife. She brought about a reconciliation but soon after her return the wife died in agony. Maria Schonleben was seen later in her bedroom clutching a paper packet to her breast and shivering with pleasure.

Her next employer, also a judge, died with symptoms of arsenical poisoning and the wife of the one after that, yet another judge, was also poisoned. Guests and servants in both houses were frequently dosed with arsenic and tartar emetic, but it was not until she had been dismissed by the third judge, after his whole family had been taken seriously ill, that Maria Schonleben was arrested. Immense quantities of arsenic were found in the salt at the house where she had worked and amongst her clothes. She 'trembled with pleasure', so it was said in evidence, when the arsenic was found, 'and gazed upon the white powder with eyes beaming with rapture.' She confessed that it was a good thing for mankind when she was condemned to death, as she had 'lived for poison alone'.[72]

Most mentally abnormal criminals do not, of course, offer such clear indications of the causes of their behaviour. Richard Dowling, a young American thief, is a more characteristic example of those who commit crimes compulsively. Dowling, the oldest of six children in a good family, had made friends with various young

---

* Although many doctors still believe all psychopaths to be untreatable, some successes have been reported, most of them from the United States where the criminal wings of a few mental hospitals are well equipped to deal with this type of patient. 'Certainly, one may think,' as Giles Playfair and Derrick Sington wrote in a recent article, 'that to dismiss someone as a psychopath and therefore by definition incurable is hardly more humane and civilised than to pronounce him a 'monster' and therefore irredeemably bad.'[71]

criminals and became a thief himself at the age of six. He spent much of his youth in various institutions where he behaved well. He was polite, willing, of normal intelligence, likeable and by no means lazy. An examiner described him as being 'spontaneous, sincere, and genuine'. As soon as he was released he returned on each occasion to his criminal life. According to his own admission, he never thought of stealing beforehand. He saw something he wanted and 'grabbed it'. He 'volunteered the information that he supposed his conduct was due "to what you'd call an impulse" '.[73]

A more certainly identifiable case of kleptomania is that of another American boy, a Negro, the son of a minister who gave a quarter of his earnings to charity. The boy was intelligent and had studied at Harvard.

'I begin to feel giddy and restless,' he said, describing the symptoms of his attacks. 'I feel as if I have to do something. This feeling becomes gradually more marked until I feel compelled to enter a house and steal. While stealing I become quite excited, involuntarily begin to pant, perspire and breathe rapidly as if I had run a race; this increases in intensity and then I feel as if I have to go to the closet and empty my bowels. After its all over I feel exhausted and relieved.'

The boy's only ambition was to be a detective and sometimes he would track people and from this activity he derived the same sort of excitement, although less intense, as from stealing. He compared the feelings of relief and satisfaction he had after stealing to those enjoyed after copulation.[74] 'It is in our very blood,' a thief once told Lombroso, 'it may be only a pin, but I cannot help taking it, although I am quite ready to give it back.'[75] A pickpocket confessed that he could not go to sleep unless he had stolen something before he went to bed.[76] 'Stealing is a passion that burns like love,' another thief said. 'and when I feel the blood seething in my brain and fingers, I think I should be capable of robbing myself, if that were possible.'[77]

Joly in Le Crime, described how a taste for the pleasures of stealing can be gradually acquired:

'This is the beginning. From a gallery one sees a woman—rich or well-to-do—who buys a certain number of objects and pays for them; but without asking for permission she takes some little, almost insignificant object—a little ribbon to fasten a parcel, a more commodious paper bag. No one will say that she is stealing; no one will think of speaking to her or disturbing her. But she is observed, and even watched, for one expects to see her again some time after, taking, as she walks along, a flower worth twenty-five centimes. A little later she will appropriate an article of greater value, and henceforth she will take for the pleasure of taking.'

The sexual root of kleptomania and its guide to an understanding of other peculiarities of behaviour seemed a hopeful field of study to many of the greatest of the early psychologists, psycho-analysts and psychotherapists. Jung and Krafft-Ebing paid particular attention to it, as did Adler whose theory of the 'inferiority complex' has been used to explain much criminal behaviour, and as did Freud whose uncovering of the repressions of the 'unconscious' has also influenced much subsequent inquiry. Stekel after a prolonged study came to the conclusion not only that kleptomania was the result of ungratified sexual instincts but that it was an open question whether any impulsive acts at all were 'other than sexual'.[78]

Kleptomania was, he discovered, a nervous disorder that affected women more than men. The men who suffered from it were usually homosexual. Another scholar maintained that practically all shoplifters whom he had examined were 'at the time of their offence in or near their period of menstruation'.[79] Dr Schlapp quoted the case of a school teacher of fifty-two who had for years been subject to mild eccentricities of behaviour during her menstrual periods. She was, however, scrupulously honest and had an 'almost exaggerated sense of duty and devotion'. Shortly before the onset of her menopause, she had become conscious of homosexual tendencies and had had a brief affair with another woman. These tendencies subsided and were superseded by intense periodic nervousness. After the death of two near relatives she moved out of the small town where she lived to New York. One day she went to a shop to buy some stockings. She paused on her way to the stocking counter to look at some suitcases. 'A feeling of vagueness and uneasiness came over her. As she examined one of the bags she was seized with sudden trembling. Her knees sagged under her, her heart pounded and the perspiration stood out on her wrists and temples. She saw and heard indistinctly and seemed surrounded by a mist. Unable to resist the impulse that swept over her, she took the large, obvious, quite unconcealable bag.'[80] She had no need of it and had money in her purse with which to pay for it.

Stekel's contention that not only kleptomania, but all impulsive acts might be sexual in origin did not, of course, answer the wider problems of the creation of the criminal mind. And to many of Stekel's contemporaries, heredity seemed at least one simple and satisfactory way of explaining the professional criminal as well as the compulsive one.

Lombroso's early emphasis on atavism had naturally led him to believe that heredity was the 'principal organic cause of criminal tendencies',[81] (although many of the characteristics which he calls atavistic are not hereditary but are due to arrested development either before or after birth). The taint, Lombroso thought, might come from parents who were alcoholics or who were diseased or insane, or from a degenerate family; and in either case the effects were catastrophic.

It is true, of course, that criminal parents tend to produce criminal children but this may well be due to causes other than heredity. One woman member of the French criminal family Cornu, for example, was peculiarly ferocious but this was attributed to the fact that as a little girl she had been compelled to carry the head of one of the family's victims in her pinafore pocket for two miles to cure her of her disinclination to be wicked.[82] The inheritability of mental disorders is, nevertheless, unquestioned, as the history of the descendants of Martin Kallikak, a soldier in the Revolutionary War, amply demonstrated. Kallikak had a baby by a feeble-minded girl during the war, and after the war he had legitimate children by a Quaker girl from an honest and intelligent family. 496 descendants of the Quaker girl were traced; there were no criminals amongst them and all but one of them were mentally normal. 480 descendants of the feeble-minded girl were traced; only forty-six of them were normal.[83] This does not, of course, prove that all these feeble-minded descendants inherited their defects in the Mendelian manner; and, indeed recent researches have suggested that almost as much mental deficiency is acquired as inherited.[84]

The history of another American family, the Jukes, seemed to suggest that not only the mental abnormality that might lead to criminality could be inherited but criminality itself. The originator of this remarkable clan was born in New York in the early eighteenth century, the descendant of Dutch settlers. He worked by fits and starts, drinking hard and whoring as often as he could afford to. He left behind him a large and mostly illegitimate family. Two of his sons married two of his five illegitimate daughters and over seven hundred descendants of these five daughters were traced. The vast proportion of them were criminals or prostitutes. Less than twenty of the men were skilled workmen and of these more than half learned their trades in prison.[85]

When the history of the Jukes family was published in 1877, it was widely supposed that the inheritability of a natural predisposition to crime had been proved. Lombroso's early work had just appeared and was soon to exercise its deep influence. The theory of atavism supported theories of heredity. The subsequent work of Goring in England and Healy in America led to a more detailed study of the criminal's mind at the expense of his body; but the individual criminal rather than crime in general remained the principal field of criminological inquiry, and Goring himself believed that criminal tendencies were hereditary. The problems of heredity continued, therefore, to exercise their traditional fascination and numerous studies were accordingly made of criminal twins in the hope that here illuminating answers would be found. In one of these studies thirty twins with at least one criminal brother or sister were examined and it was discovered that whereas in only twelve per cent of the cases of ordinary twins were both of them criminal, with identical or one-egg twins the proportion rose to seventy-seven per cent.[86] A later study suggested that these figures might be exceptional; but, in any case, to accept the fact that twins are more likely to follow each other into crime than brothers and sisters of different ages and that with identical twins the likelihood is even far greater, is not necessarily to believe that twins have inherited similar characteristics and criminal predispositions. For it may well be that their behaviour can be attributed to a close companionship and identity of feeling—closer perhaps with one-egg twins than with the others—which has led them into similar problems and similar environments.

While these studies were being made it had become generally admitted, in fact, that often what seemed an inherited trait was more likely to be a characteristic imposed upon a man by his environment. This was, of course, no new conception, but it seemed, as the twentieth century progressed, to be an increasingly important one. No permanently satisfying answers to the problem of crime had been elicited from the study of the criminal; so now it was hoped that these answers might emerge if men gave their attention once more to the conditions in which he lived and to his relationship with his environment.

CHAPTER TWO

CAUSES AND CURES

'Criminality proceeds from the very nature of humanity itself.'

ADOLPH PRINS, 1886

(i)

'THE social environment is the cultivation medium of criminality,' wrote one of Lombroso's French critics, Lacassagne. 'The criminal is the microbe, an element which only becomes important when it finds the medium which causes it to foment. Every society has the criminals which it deserves.'[1]

The criticism of writers such as Lacassagne, as well as the encouragement of friends like Ferri and the views of the Belgian mathematician Adolph Quetelet, one of the promoters of the growing enthusiasm for statistics, and of the French lawyer A. M. Guerry, induced Lombroso to turn his attention from biological factors to social factors. His last important work *Crime: Its Causes and Remedies* appeared in 1899. Like his other books it is full of curious information. Its main thesis is that there is a mutual interactive relationship between heredity and environment, that social conditions may be responsible for biological abnormalities which can be inherited and can therefore, in time, affect the social conditions that produced them. But although the emphasis is still biological, the book's content is not unduly tendentious. He discussed, as he had done less minutely in earlier works, the existence of all sorts of environmental conditions and external influences that might affect criminality, from poverty to religion, from diet to the

225

density of the population, from climate to geology, from education to illegitimacy. He was able to draw on a mass of studies undertaken by previous students in Italy, France, England, the United States and elsewhere so that the book gives a fair summary of contemporary knowledge and opinion. It was not a seminal book like *L'Uomo Delinquente* but it was, and remains, a fascinating catalogue. It was followed by the works of a new generation of criminologists who emphasized, in a way that Lombroso had not done, the importance of studying crime as the 'social fact' that Ferri termed it. Gustav Aschaffenburg's important book *Crime and its Repression* appeared in German in 1903 and stressed with vigour and conviction the sociological aspects of crime; Aschaffenburg's near contemporary, Emile Durkheim, was working at the same time in France to show that it was necessary to look at the very nature of society, at the lack of social standards and controls for an explanation of the causes of crime; and in Holland, Willem Adriaan Bonger was beginning work on his Marxist *Criminality and Economic Conditions* which was published in 1905 and was the first of Bonger's many works to demonstrate the importance of social conflict and economic conditions as influences on criminality. Ferri himself published an enlarged and revised version of his *Sociologia Criminale* in two volumes in 1929-1930.

These writers, and others like them, approached the problem from different points of view and often their views were narrow and restricted, limited to single or related causes which were in fact little more than probable influences but which seemed to those who expounded and exaggerated them an explanation of the whole complex of crime. And yet for all of them, whatever their individual interpretation, the verifiable facts remained the same. It was, for instance, a fact, that in almost all parts of Italy there were, as Lombroso said, 'villages renowned for having furnished an unbroken series of special delinquents;'[2] but the deductions that could be made from this fact were innumerable. It was also a fact, as Ferri showed from his study of French criminal statistics from 1825-1878, that there was a very close parallel between hot weather and criminality,[3] just as there was, for different reasons and to a less noticeable degree, a parallel between poverty and criminality. But again the causes which could be ascribed to these facts were not single ones. Rape and indecent assault were more common in the spring and summer than in the winter; but how much was this due to the effect of heat on the sexual instincts of men, to the possible vestiges of man's sexual periodicity, to the fact that more alcohol was drunk in hot weather and to the fact that in summer the opportunities of raping a woman—usually an out-of-doors practice—were greater than in winter? Murder also was more common in hot weather than in cold, in the south of Italy than in the north, amongst the children of foreign-born inhabitants of the United States than amongst the children of those born there. But the emotions aroused by heat, the differences in manners and morals and racial characteristics between the southern Italian and the northerner, and the conditions in which foreign-born Americans usually lived, were only the more obvious of the many identifiable reasons for these phenomena. But although the facts and statistics presented by the sociological investigation of crime were usually so contradictory and so difficult to interpret, they did, nevertheless, open up new and varied fields for speculation and inquiry.

The investigation of the relationship between poverty and crime, for example, did not reveal so close a connection between economics and crime as Bonger, in his determination to show that every crime led to the hell of capitalism, supposed; but it did reveal much that was both useful and stimulating and the undoubted fact that, whatever the reasons might be, criminals were nearly always poor and often unemployed.

When food was cheap, crimes against property, with the exception of arson, decreased while those against the person, particularly rape, increased. Famine and great cold diminished to a marked degree all crimes against the person, especially murder, and yet hunger seldom led to theft, although it was 'notorious that in years of dear provisions, or severe winters, a large number of thefts and petty offences' were committed 'for the sole object of securing maintenance within the prison walls'.[4] On the rare occasions when provisions were stolen, the women usually took 'bonbons and chocolate, the grown men liquors'.[5]

The investigations which resulted in these and other deductions were, of course, severely limited in scope and did not always confirm the deductions made by other investigators of the same problem. Lady Wootton in an important and salutary book has shown how misleading and contradictory are the published conclusions of even the more modern researches of this sort. All of the many attempts made in the 1930's, for instance, to get at the facts of problem families failed, so she says, 'to distinguish between personal inadequacy and simple economic misfortune'.[6] And now, apparently, although many of the earlier mistakes are not repeated, investigators are still prejudiced by their own interests, concerns and predispositions.[7] If, however, 'not very much of practical value' has yet emerged from their efforts, as it did not emerge from the earlier and even more confusing statistics of the Lombrosians and neo-Lombrosians, it is obviously of some use to know that a detailed study made of twenty families in a London borough in the 1950's revealed that the only common characteristic was poverty, all but two families sharing an inability to manage money and nearly all of them having very small incomes. It is also, perhaps, significant that a 'tendency to drink' was not listed as a problem in a single case.

② Yet alcohol was formerly found by some students of the subject to be a very common cause of crime 'first, because many commit crimes in order to obtain drink; further, because men sometimes seek in drink the courage necessary to commit crimes, or an excuse for their misdeeds; again, because it is by the aid of drink that young men are drawn into crime and because the drink shop is the place for the meeting of accomplices where they not only plan their crimes but also squander their gains. It has been calculated that in London in 1880 there were 4,938 public houses which were the resorts of criminals and prostitutes exclusively.'[8]

In Belgium it was estimated that alcohol was responsible for over a quarter of the number of crimes committed each year; in Germany forty-one per cent of crimes were attributed to some degree of drunkenness; in France fifty per cent; in Sweden three-quarters and in Holland four-fifths. In England ten thousand out of 29,752 people convicted at assizes and fifty thousand out of 90,903 people convicted by magistrates, were believed to have been drawn into crime by frequenting disreputable public houses. In America sixty-seven per cent of serious crimes of violence (compared with thirty-three per cent in Europe) were attributed to drunkenness.[9] And in New York out of 49,423 men and women arrested in a given period, 30,509 were found to be habitual drunkards.[10] The increase of alcoholism in the United States during recent years has, in fact, been considerable and it is now said that of seventy million Americans who drink, three million are chronic, excessive drinkers and 750,000 are alcoholics This rate of alcoholism is believed to be the highest in the world.[11]

Temperance societies, high taxes, laws against the unrestricted sale of liquor and limitations upon the number of places where it could be bought, have alike always been incapable of preventing alcoholism all over the world. Sweden, where the addiction was as extensive as anywhere in Europe, took severe measures to curb its growth. Between 1855 and 1864 taxes on the distillation of brandy were raised from two francs to the hectolitre to thirty-two francs. Local authorities bought up drink shops and encouraged the tenants to make their profit out of tea and coffee rather than spirits. Men found drunk in the streets lost their right to vote after their third offence, after their fifth offence they were sentenced to six months imprisonment and after the sixth to a year. But the results were disappointing. In 1851 it was calculated that there was one drunkard to every nineteen inhabitants; in 1865 the ratio was still very much the same—one drunkard to every twenty-two inhabitants.[12] And although an encouraging reduction was made in the number of crimes committed after the middle of the century, many other reasons apart from a decrease in drunkenness could be found to explain this.

In Sweden, as elsewhere, when spirits became expensive or difficult to obtain, men did not become more sober but more adventurous. In Scotland miners who could not afford whisky any-more, began to use laudanum; in Germany ether became almost as popular as alcohol.[13]

Drugs, in fact, before the nineteenth century was over had al-ready become almost as urgent a problem as alcohol, particularly in the United States. In the 1890's over forty-four per cent of the 1,392 convicts in San Quentin were addicted to the use of opium on their admission to the prison as compared with forty-nine per cent who were listed as alcoholics.[14] In 1928 a gangster estimated that of the American criminals he knew 'fifty per cent, at the lowest estimate, took drugs in one form or another'.[15]

By 1938 the planting of marijuana seeds had become so common in back gardens all over New York that the Government felt obliged to issue a pamphlet, *Marijuana: Its Identification*.[16] In later years the retail value of the drugs smuggled into the port of New York alone has been estimated at three hundred million dollars a year;[17] and it has also been estimated that not more than between two and five per cent of the marijuana smuggled across the Mexican border is discovered.[18] The sale of drugs to children has been a source of enormous revenue to those who control the traffic and although much of the trade is in relatively harmless marijuana cigarettes, these 'reefers' sometimes lead to the subsequent use of a more dangerous drug such as heroin. Heroin and morphine, both derivatives of opium, are depressants and, therefore, not in themselves likely to be causes of crime; but an addiction is soon formed and once addicted a man will often do almost anything to get money to pay for a 'fix'. Even if he does not need to commit a crime to pay for it, the very act of buying the drug from a pedlar makes him a criminal under the Harrison Act. There are no public clinics all of which have now been closed by order of the Commissioner of Internal Revenue. Nor are there, as there are in England, any physicians licensed to prescribe drugs to addicts. The United States Bureau of Narcotics believes that public clinics failed in their efforts and that licensed physicians would also fail and prefers a repressive policy of penal legislation.[19]

After the Second World War various synthetic drugs became available and were at least partly responsible for the large increase in addiction amongst adolescents. A report published in 1953 estimated that there were five hundred young addicts in Chicago[20] and the numbers of arrests of addicts under twenty-six were five times greater between 1947 and 1951 than they were between 1937 and 1941.[21] In 1962 it appeared that barbiturates were in the words of a Chicago narcotics official, 'replacing marijuana as the first step toward addiction'.[22]

'When you're on that stuff you just don't care,' a girl who had injected amphetamine into her veins told the police after her arrest. 'I was involved in a lot of burglaries and I couldn't have done it without a shot . . . I was even a prostitute for three months.'[23]

Benzedrine is a trade name for one form of amphetamine and in the 1940's packets of this drug, containing fifteen times the average daily dose a doctor would prescribe, were being smuggled into prisons where the convicts went on violent rampages. There were savage riots in some prisons when the use of Benzedrine inhalers, from which convicts extracted the drug, was forbidden.

According to an officer of the Narcotics Bureau there were 'at least two hundred known users' of amphetamine in Kansas City alone. 'At least twice as many,' he thought, 'we don't know about. The men range from eighteen up, with most in their early twenties. The women are mainly from fourteen to twenty-five. They come from the most expensive neighbourhoods and the poorest.' Practically all those who used the drug admitted that they had been involved in criminal acts while they were 'hopped up'.[24]

Fortunately few narcotics are a spur to criminality in themselves. Most drug takers are interested only in sexual stimulation, heightened perception or escape from dreariness or anxiety; and it seems from recent investigations such as that carried out by Dr Lawrence Kolk which revealed that three quarters of the addicts he studied had never been arrested and the majority of those who had been were charged only with being in unlawful possession of the naroctics they craved,[25] that drugs may not be so direct a cause of crime as has often been supposed. Certainly the addict, unlike the alcoholic, is not so likely to be dangerous when he has the drug as when he is deprived of it.

The statistics, though, have always been contradictory, just as the statistics about the relationship between drunkenness and crime have also been contradictory. Aschaffenburg's supposition that the habitual drunkard was less criminal than the occasional drunkard has for example been both confirmed and contradicted by American statistics some of which have suggested that the professional criminal was not so much addicted to alcohol as the occasional offender and others which have suggested that he was more so.[26] In 1895 it was estimated that only a fifth of murderers in America were even occasional drunkards,[27] but in 1918 figures were published which indicated that sixty per cent of the worst murders, at least half the sexual offences and eighty-two per cent of the minor crimes of violence were due mainly to alcohol,[28] while later researches suggested that only a minority of criminals, although a considerable one, had been excessively intemperate. 'Most men who are drunk do not commit serious crimes.'[29] An inquiry carried out in 1953, however, contradicted this by indicating that although half the men arrested for rape were sober, two thirds of those arrested for all other crimes were more or less under the influence of alcohol.[30] In any case, perhaps these investigations are not in themselves of vital significance for alcoholism and criminality may in many cases be traced to the same root cause. At least it was certain in the nineteenth century that Spain and Italy had relatively little drunkenness and yet had the highest homicide rates in Europe.

It was certain, too, that everywhere crimes were most frequent on the days and in the months when the most alcohol was drunk. In Germany one survey revealed that out of 2,178 crimes committed over a particular period, fifty-eight per cent were committed on Saturday nights as compared with one per cent on Mondays.[31]

Alcohol, the temperature and the idleness of holidays were, however, not the only causes of an increase in crime on certain days and at certain times of the year. Even the weather has been found to exercise an influence. Fog favoured the street robber in London for obvious reasons and, as an American bank robber confessed, September was a 'very bad month for robbing banks'.

'It was bad,' he wrote, 'because the nights are fairly warm and short. The bank robber must have long nights and cold ones, when people sleep under the covers and when the windows are not wide open ... There are a lot of brave men who will get out of their beds on a warm night to chase a burglar who wouldn't even turn over on a cold night. Further, explosions are not so easily detected on a cold, windy night when the elements are raging ... Every time I have tried to "knock off a jug" in the summer I have failed.'[32]

(4) The weather, too, by having an effect on human emotions was held responsible for much impulsive crime, particularly amongst women.[33] Consciousness of an approaching storm often resulted in quarrels and violence and a tendency amongst female prisoners to 'break out' in hysterical tantrums. According to Kraepelin, psychopathic personalities were peculiarly susceptible to the emotional effects of these barometric variations.[34]

(5) Race was naturally discovered to be an important factor in the causation of crime. It explained, Enrico Ferri believed, the high homicide rate in Latin countries and the high suicide rate in Teutonic countries, as Saracen blood explained the intense homicidal criminality in Corsica and Sicily. The influence of race was particularly noticed in America where different nationalities mingled in similar social and economic conditions. The incidence of murder amongst foreign-born immigrants was found for instance, to vary enormously according to the country from which the murderer came. There were, over a number of years, 5.8 murders to the 100,000 amongst immigrants born in Denmark, Sweden and Norway; 9.7 to the 100,000 amongst those born in Germany; 10.4 to the 100,000 amongst Englishmen; 12.2 amongst Austrians; 17.5 amongst Irishmen; 27.4 amongst Frenchmen and as many as 58.1 amongst Italians. All of these nationalities, with the exception of the French and the Italians, were apparently twice as liable to be murderous in the United States as in their native countries; and much more likely to be murderous than the native-born American. Obviously there were other reasons, apart from race, which were

the cause of this, just as there were other reasons, apart from race, which were responsible for the high conviction rate (two and a half times that of the white population) amongst Negroes. The immigrant came to the United States and suddenly found himself, generally as a lonely individual or as a member of a small and defenceless family, in a strange and hostile-seeming world. He was usually poor, often unable to speak English, frequently despised for his manners or customs or hated as a threat to reasonable·wages and full employment. He was generally a countryman living for the first time in a town. If he got into trouble, he probably had no money for a lawyer and, like the Negro or the Puerto Rican or the Mexican, no money for a fine. The states which received the highest number of immigrants, especially Italian and Irish immigrants, predictably had the greatest number of crimes.[35]

The work that the immigrants did was considered responsible for at least some of these crimes. It was to be expected that occupations that require little intellect or training and which are boring, ill-paid and repetitive would furnish more than their proportion of criminals. This was understandable and seemed to be borne out by the facts. In Europe, though, where the effect of occupations on crime had long been studied and where attempts to establish a closer connection had been made, the conclusions of the students of this particular aspect of criminology were often curious. In France, for example, the greatest tendency to sexual crimes was found amongst shoemakers, a fact which could apparently be referred not only to their alcoholism but 'to the effect upon the genital organs of their position when at work'. Men accustomed to the sight of blood (butchers) or to the use of dangerous weapons (soldiers) or to isolation (shepherds) or to chastity (priests) were guilty of a 'savage cruelty in their deeds often accompanied by abnormal lubricity'.[36] Female servants, lawyers, bankers, brokers and doctors were disproportionately criminal in the United States as well as in Europe. The crimes of ministers of religion were nearly always sexual.[37] So far as despair was a cause of crime, the study of the occupations of suicides was also felt to be instructive. Generally speaking, the most prone to commit suicide amongst professional men, in England and Wales at least, were doctors, solicitors, teachers, civil servants, bank clerks, insurance agents and commercial travellers. Amongst tradesmen the highest rates were amongst innkeepers and shopkeepers. Other men with an unusual disposition to suicide were farmers, garage proprietors, dock workers, cotton spinners, boiler-makers, shoemakers, tailors, electricians and bankers.[38] Attempted suicide —no longer a crime in England—was the only offence, apart from offences that are peculiar to their sex, which women were almost as likely to commit as men.

In fact everywhere women were far less criminal than men. In Austria in the nineteenth century, female criminals were only fourteen per cent of the total, in Spain less than eleven per cent, in Italy 8.2 per cent.[39] Most Protestant countries had a rather higher rate but it usually remained lower than twenty per cent. In the United States the ratio was about twelve men to one woman (four to one amongst Negroes) but in France and England the ratio was as high as from four to one, although it has since sharply fallen to between seven and eight to one.[40] In an informative study by Hermann Mannheim it was shown that there was only one woman for every seventy-nine men convicted of burglary and the ratio for shopbreaking, perhaps a more obviously male activity, was 1 : 243[41]* Apart from limitations imposed upon them by inferior strength and child bearing, women are probably inclined to be less criminal than men because they can get men to commit crimes for them rather than because they are necessarily more virtuous themselves. There are also crimes which most laws do not recognize as capable of being committed by a female offender. The female ponce, for instance, does not exist as a criminal in the United States or in England. The Lesbian's conduct is less strictly regulated than that of the male homosexual and rape is a specifically male crime although a woman can be charged with committing an indecent assault. More important, perhaps, than any of these reasons for the low incidence of female crime, is the fact that the

---

* The ratio for drunkenness, however, was 1:4, which accounted to some extent for the fact that English women appeared more criminal than they did in other European countries where drunkenness was not punishable. In America a recent study[42] has suggested that 'the numerical sex differential in crime as visualized in the past is a myth'. Among the reasons given for this view are that the crimes of women are more often committed in the home and, therefore, more easily concealed; that women are often involved in the crime of abortion but rarely prosecuted; that the male victim or partner in sexual relations will usually not prosecute the woman because he does not want to admit the relationship although larceny by prostitutes is in fact very common; and that sex violations of boys and girls by women do not leave physiological evidence such as is left in corresponding sex attacks by men on girls.

woman who might otherwise become a criminal can turn to prostitution and remain within the law.

There were and there still are, economic factors which lead a girl to become a prostitute, although well over half the girls questioned at the New York Reformatory for women at a time when these factors were more valid than they afterwards became, said they had been in reasonable employment as servants, or factory girls before they became prostitute.[43] There may be sexual factors, too, although these are rarer and, indeed, many prostitutes have or develop Lesbian instincts and most of them derive little pleasure from the often unusual sexual acts which they are asked to perform. Women, indeed, seem usually to drift idly into prostitution after an unsatisfactory or unhappy affair with a selfish man, for reasons similar to those which lead some men to drift idly into crime. They are usually very young, as the men who drift into crime are young. Indeed, the youth of most offenders has always been, and continues to be, a problem of universal concern.

It was often felt—as it is often felt now—that defective education was a likely reason for this widespread youthful delinquency. But while it was granted that education might improve a boy's mind and that it had certain obvious therapeutic qualities, it had, as Dr Goring said, very little if any effect on conduct. 'It may well be,' he thought, 'that lack of education and criminality are the results of a common factor, native incapacity.'[44] There were those, indeed, who believed that education was actually harmful. Lombroso suggested that the instruction given in the prisons of France, Germany and Sweden was directly responsible for the 'large numbers of forgeries by recidivists';[45] and he was not the only writer to point out the dangers of educating a criminal mind and thereby no doubt sharpening its native intelligence. Dante's aphorism was often quoted: *'Che dove l'argomento della mente s'aggiunge al mal voler ed alla possa nessun riparo vi puo far la gente.'* ('When intelligence is united with power and wickedness, the efforts of men are vain.')

Nor did improvements in standards of living and of housing have the effect that was at one time expected. The pattern of crime changed but the amount of crime did not. The prisons were fuller than ever and this was only partly because the agencies of law enforcement were so much more efficient. Desperate need may no longer be a cause of theft—although even in affluent societies there are far more people living on the verges of poverty than is commonly supposed—but there are other motives. Slums gradually disappear, but the housing estates and blocks of flats which take their place are often more harmful as sources of boredom and frustration than the packed and dirty but always lively slums.[46] A United Nations report published in 1960 contended that it is in the countries in which the standard of life has risen most that the increase in delinquency has been greatest.[47] Crime to an uncertain extent does follow fluctuations in economic life but it seems that 'to *become* penniless or to *lose* work is an even more significant crime risk than to *be* poor or unemployed'.[48]

It was often felt, too, and with more justification, that a religious faith sincerely held, more particularly the Christian faith, would, like education, help to keep a man from crime. But although the letter of Christianity can be taught, the spirit of it must be felt and men who merely professed themselves to be Christians were as likely as atheists, if not more likely than atheists, to become criminals. Of seven hundred criminals examined by Ferri only one said that he did not believe in God; and a contemporary examination of over twenty-eight thousand convicts in English prisons revealed only fifty-seven who said they were atheists.[49] A recent American study showed that over eighty-eight per cent of five hundred criminals examined attended church, although irregularly, and only three per cent did not attend at all.[50] The sex offender is more frequently than not 'a professed member of a religious denomination'.[51] Prisoners often pretend to be religious in the hope that they will obtain greater privileges if they do so and in the fear that they will be denied privileges if they do not;* and the views of one of Ferri's criminals who said that it was God who gave thieves 'the instinct to steal', are not uncommon.

In his researches for a recent book which fully and fairly analyses the influences which tend to make men criminals,[53] Lord Longford, himself a devout Christian, did not find much evidence to suggest that the decline in religious observance was one of these

---

* In America 'it has been hinted that the announced religious preferences of prison populations have at times varied with the religious complexion of the parole boards which control exits from prison'.[52] And it may well be, of course, that those young churchgoers who stay out of prison do not do so because they go to church but because in other respects their upbringing, as is likely in a churchgoing family, has been more satisfactory than that of delinquents. The fact that Roman Catholics have a higher crime rate than Protestants has little, if any, religious significance as there are so many other factors, not only social and economic, which tend to produce this result.

influences. He did, however, find—as few students of the problem have failed to find—that family surroundings especially in the early life of the criminal were an undoubted influence in most cases.

There seems, indeed, no surer way of keeping a boy from a life of crime than providing him with a full and happy and worthwhile childhood in a family which loves him and which he loves.*

But to provide such a happy home for every potential criminal in need of one is a Utopian dream; and, perhaps, because disunited families are apparently becoming ever more commonplace, crime will become ever more commonplace, too. The respect, loyalty and affection as well as the sense of mutual responsibility and of a common purpose which a happy family life engenders were at the root of ancient methods of law enforcement in which the family was the smallest of various interdependent units. The strength of the family in that sense has largely gone. Nothing has been found to take its place; and so the problem of the young criminal continues and, indeed, seems to deepen.

(ii)

Apart from the restlessness and vigour, impatience and frustration of youth, apart from alcohol and drugs, thwarted sexual desires, insanity, biological and psychological anomalies, poverty and squalor, the decline of religion and of moral standards, broken

---

* This is quite as true of girls and, according to Oettingen, an illegitimate girl is almost twice as likely to be a criminal as a girl who is not illegitimate.[54] The mere provision of a family background for either boys or girls is not, of course, enough. Of the twenty-three case histories of the young and repeatedly convicted criminals examined by Sir Leo Page in his *The Young Lag* only a small minority came from broken homes, most of the rest were the sons of parents who, although in some cases 'highly respectable', had made no effort to keep their children honest either by discipline or by example and encouragement. The number of large families was high. The average number of children was five. 'After all that has been written about the lamentable consequences of the broken home we are still,' says Lady Wootton, 'without information as to the frequency with which, or the ages at which, or the reasons for which, homes are broken in a "normal population." '[55] In America, where broken homes have also been interpreted as a cause of crime, it has been estimated that in the 'normal population', 'more than one out of five homes with children is a broken home'.[56] Nevertheless, an important recent study has shown that 'families rated as wholly lacking in "cohesiveness" were thirty-one times as prevalent among delinquents as among non-delinquents'.[57]

homes, illegitimacy and the birth rate, climate, diet and temperature, racial, occupational and geological factors, wars and revolutions, the probability of escape, the undue severity or careless insufficiency of punishments, the tendency of employers to dismiss offenders rather than prosecute them, bad or non-existent systems of sentencing, inadequate penal institutions and methods of reform, all of which were seen as causes of crime and all of which had had their influence for centuries, other causes were recognized as being specifically the outcome of modern civilization. Sexual crimes, for instance, were apparently increasing at a rate and in a way that could only be accounted for by the advance of civilization. In France sexual assaults on children increased by more than three times between 1826 and 1882, rapes by nearly six times. Sexual crimes in Germany increased by five times in fifty years. In England there were said to be more than eight times as many rapes between 1851 and 1855 as there had been between 1830 and 1834.[1] And whereas rape was formerly considered a crime more likely to be committed in the country than in the town, as the twentieth century progressed, it was found to be an increasingly urban crime as, indeed, were nearly all other offences with the notable exception of malicious damage to property which remained predominantly, as apparently it always had been, the crime of countrymen.[2] The most striking increase in sexual crimes was shown to be in assaults upon children, and this was nearly always an urban crime and often the crime of an educated and apparently civilized man.

It was not only the frustrations engendered by an intensifying competition for employment or status, the obvious unjustness in the distribution of wealth, the density of population and the sprawling and depressing industrial slums, which were blamed for modern civilization's failure to make men civilized, but the very laws, amenities and pleasures of the city itself. The more laws there were, the more laws there were to break.

There was comfort, of course, in the reflection that the creation of hundreds of new offences, many of them comparatively trivial, made criminal statistics look much more frightening than they were. Immense increases in crime often meant little more than immense increases in the number of careless motorists. 'Out of a hundred thousand persons arrested in Chicago in a recent year, more than one half were held for the violation of legal precepts which did not exist twenty-five years before. Of the inmates of the prisons of the Federal Government at the present time, seventy-six per cent are there for crimes which were not crimes fifteen years ago.'[3] Arrests in New York have been commonly made for offences as relatively unimportant as making an unnecessary noise, spitting in public, having a dustbin filled to within four inches of the top.[4] In London men have been prosecuted for breaking the conditions of their licences to sell vegetables by offering rhubarb, which, it was lengthily argued, was a fruit.[5] But although violations of a new law, which may have made some activity a crime when it was previously an accepted practice, are perhaps not important in themselves and almost certainly are not indicative of suddenly developed criminal instincts, they may, nevertheless, in the end have a deleterious effect on general standards of morality. A crime is only a crime when a law, prompted by expediency, religion, morals, prejudice or party feeling, makes it so. The transactions of merchants or seamen have been made the crimes of smugglers by the statutes of Governments; and when import duties have been lowered smugglers have found themselves respectable again. Before 1737 publicly to stage a play in London which lampooned the Government was a legal enterprise, after that date to do so without the Lord Chamberlain's permission was a breach of the Licensing Act. Before the Obscene Publications Act, the printing and sale in England of the whole of *Lady Chatterley's Lover* was considered illegal. Since November 1960 hundreds of thousands of copies of the book have been sold without interference. Henry Miller's *Tropic of Cancer* may be bought openly in New York but the publication of his *Sexus* and other parts of *The Rosy Crucifixion* would undoubtedly be considered a criminal act as the publication of *Lolita* would have been in the year that Vladimir Nabokov was born. Adultery has usually been considered a sin but it is only the actions of legislators that have made it a crime as well. Fornication was not a statutory offence in the American colonies until Puritan influence made it one in 1692 and as recently as twenty-five years ago it was still a crime in twenty-three states and in the District of Columbia and remains so now in some of them. Before 1938 it was illegal in England for a doctor to end the pregnancy of a woman unless her life was in danger. In that year, after a gynaecological surgeon, Aleck Bourne, operated on a girl of fourteen (who had been raped and made pregnant by some guardsmen) and then reported his operation to the police, it was established that therapeutic abortion could be justified if there

were reasonable grounds for supposing that a continued pregnancy
would permanently impair the mother's mental or physical
health. Homosexuality between consenting adults is a crime
punishable by imprisonment in many parts of the modern world
although in other parts it is accepted. There were innumerable
prosecutions in London for street betting until betting shops were
made legal by statute, and the Anatomy Act of 1832 ended the
criminal trade in corpses which Burke and Hare had found so profitable a few years before. According to Tarde, of the ten crimes
which Hebraic law punished with stoning, nine had ceased to be
offences in civilized European societies by the beginning of the
nineteenth century. Many modern criminals 'would have been the
ornament and moral aristocracy of a tribe of Red Indians'.[6]

But the power of governments to create crimes (which had always induced men to commit them as an act of protest against
authority) has made hundreds of new regulations inevitable. The
ramifications of the law, its complications, its apparently motiveless
interference with private lives have led to its widespread evasion;
and the more it is avoided the less it is respected. This is nowhere
so evident as it is in large cities where the violation of certain laws
and many moral conventions is an accepted part of everday life,
where the man that violates them can point to a thousand others
who do so too, where the anonymity and perhaps the loneliness
and frustration of existence are emphasized by the impersonality of
large business organizations and factories and by the restless competition for a place in the sun. All these things tend to condition
men to accept crime not as an evil but as a means of getting what
they want quickly and as an escape from routine and boredom.
The family, the church, the club, and other traditional forms of
social control are associated with the tired and aimless regularity of
older, pitiable or contemptible lives and so lose their hold on their
unruly members who look to more exciting means of satisfying
a need for stimulation. Drink and drugs and speed and sex are
exciting, and so is crime and in cities the opportunities for crime are
extensive and the rewards are high, the chances of escape are
greater and most of the police are overworked and some of them
may be corruptible.

In large cities, too, there is little sense of permanence. People
come and go.* But wherever they go, the advertisements insisting

* Sheldon Glueck noticed, for instance, that two-thirds of the names in the
Boston City Directory changed every year.[7]

that yesterday's luxuries are today's necessities stay with them; and with them as well is the whole pantechnicon of twentieth century entertainment arousing desires, creating hopes, displaying different and enviable lives and making them wonder and want.

The study of the influence of films and television plays which seem to portray violence for violence's sake, of sports which rely on violence and pain for their appeal to the public, of pornographic and sadistic novels, of horror comics and sensational newspapers as possible causes of crime has only recently begun, but the imitativeness of criminals and potential criminals and their susceptibility to mass hysteria have long been noticed. A frequent cause of crime is the desire to become notorious and the gratification of this desire is often only possible by the commission of some crime which will be sure to be reported at length, perhaps with photographs, in the newspapers. John Wilkes Booth was intensely concerned that his behaviour after shooting Lincoln in Ford's Theatre in Washington was not reported as he would have liked. 'I struck him boldly,' he protested, 'and not as the papers say; I walked with a firm step through thousands of his friends; was stopped but pushed on.'[8] Many murderers have appeared more concerned that their trials should be fully reported in the press than that they should be acquitted, and many other criminals have been inspired in their crimes by the reported crimes of others. Despine recorded the fact that as soon as a popular newspaper reported in 1872 that numbers of children were being abandoned in France, eight children were abandoned in Marseilles in a single day. The murderer Dufresne confessed to having become obsessed with hatred for a particular enemy and after reading an account of the trial of Verger, he said, 'I will do as Verger,' and he went out to commit his murder. At Bergamo, in Paris and in Florence women have been strangled soon after reports of other stranglings had appeared in the newspapers. And in 1857 in New York when a woman killed her husband, three other women did the same a few days later.[9] There were several murders by children after the Jack the Ripper atrocities in London. Courvoisier who cut the throat of his seventy-two-year-old employer Lord William Russell at his house in Park Lane in 1840 confessed that he had been first inspired to do so by the adventures of Jack Sheppard whose career was then the subject of many books and plays.[10] Tarde believed that the laws of imitation applied as much to crime as to other aspects of social life and quoted as examples the fashions of cutting corpses into pieces and of throwing vitriol to disfigure faces both of which began in Paris in the 1870's and soon spread to other parts of France.[11] Of the many recent murders which have been regarded as imitative are those committed by Haigh, who supposedly copied the acid-bath methods formerly employed by Georges Sarret in France, and the murder by Samuel Furnace of a rent collector whose body he burned in the hope that it would be mistaken for his own in the same way and for the same reason that Alfred Arthur Rouse had murdered a man whose remains were found in Rouse's burned-out car.

'It has often been pointed out that a crime of a sensational nature is often followed by a wave of imitations committed by people of weak intellect whose imaginations have been inflamed by the newspaper reports,' writes Peter Wildeblood who was imprisoned in 1954 for homosexual offences. 'After we were arrested and remanded on bail, Edward Montagu and I received many hundreds of letters from such people, including young boys. One boy of fifteen used to try to telephone me almost every day during the weeks when I was waiting for the trial to begin.'[12]

Measures have been taken in the past to reduce the causes of imitative crime; but there clearly was a limit to the steps which could reasonably be taken in a free society. After Courvoisier's murder of Lord William Russell, the Lord Chamberlain refused licences for the performance of plays with the name 'Jack Sheppard' in their title. There were scores of other plays, though, that might have had a similar effect on a disordered mind and if Harrison Ainsworth's book *Jack Sheppard* was to be banned, what other books might not be safe? Works of literature could not be judged, as Mr Justice Stable observed during a celebrated trial, by what was suitable reading for a young schoolgirl. In fact it seems that pornography is enjoyed more by adults than by children, that delinquent children do not read much anyway and that when they do read obscene books or comics these have little effect on their subsequent behaviour just as they have little discernible effect on the subsequent behaviour of adults.[13] 'Where juveniles are concerned,' Terence Morris wrote recently when considering the effects of books, films, television and other forms of entertainment on the suggestible offender, 'modern psychology is emphatic, and criminological research supports the view that it is personal, face-to-face relationships which are of prime importance in moulding the behaviour pattern of individuals.'[14] Often when an offender confesses that he was induced to commit his crime by, for instance, something he saw on television, this is nothing but his own rationalization of his behaviour. It may be, too, that he is thinking along the same lines as the boy whose conversation in a remand home with a fellow delinquent was recorded by Professor Cyril Burt. 'Oo's the beak tomorrer' the boy asked, wondering how he would get on in court the following day.

'Old W.'

'What d'yer s'y to 'im?'

'S'y its the pitchers. 'E always makes a speech about it and nods at yer for provin' 'is point.'[15]

Although films and television probably 'have no significant effect upon any but a tiny fraction of their audiences',[16] it cannot, however, be doubted that a few abnormal minds are seriously affected by what they see and read. In 1960 a youth committed a murder while holding-up a bank on the day that another youth was hanged at Wandsworth. He said that he was possessed by the spirit of Legs Diamond, the American gangster whose life had just been the subject of a film. But to argue from this that films about gangsters ought to be banned would not be rational. Long before the experiment of prohibition was made with such disastrous results in the United States, Luke Pike made an observation on nineteenth-century attempts to prohibit the sale of alcohol which might equally well be made in this connection. 'To prohibit or to restrict the sale of spirits, wine and beer because they have a maddening effect upon some particular persons,' he wrote, 'would be no more rational than to clothe the British Army in uniform of a different colour because scarlet has a maddening effect on bulls.'[17] To ban *Lolita,* because it could encourage a man to commit the crime of copulating with a young girl—in this case, as is usually the case in reality, a highly provocative and already sexually-experienced girl—below the age of consent, might not be irrational if the depraving tendencies of the book could be proved; and to ban *Lady Chatterley's Lover* because a man could be prompted by it to commit the crime of buggery with a female companion might also not be irrational if it could be shown that the sexual acts which Lawrence so evasively describes are, in fact, immoral, ought to be criminal or could ever be successfully prosecuted. But as it seems unlikely that either of the books can be shown to fulfil these conditions and as they are both works of literary distinction, to ban them, as Mr Gerald Gardiner said when defending the publication of Lawrence's book, would 'on a balance of probabilities' be against the public good.

It is not, of course, to be denied that totalitarian governments have achieved some success in combating crime by violently repressive measures but 'they ignore the fact that higher and more pervasive values for which mankind has fought and bled through centuries of oppression are at the same time trampled underfoot'.[18] And Ferri, who followed Mussolini from Socialism to Fascism and died in 1929, would have recognized more clearly the abiding truth of this if he had lived for ten years longer and been able to witness the sad history of penal methods in National Socialist Germany. But although Ferri laid undue emphasis on the responsibility of the state to combat excessive individualism, his insistence upon the need for systematic measures of social defence against the criminal and his demand for 'penal substitutes'— a diminution of crime by removing the conditions which help to create it—foreshadowed much of the best modern criminological thought.

This urgent need for the reformation of the whole basis of society was a theme which has made a strong appeal to sociologists and criminologists in America where the validity of theories suggesting that crime has single or isolated causes has long been questioned and where the most important attempts to discover these various causes have been continually made since the First World War ended. The abnormal personality of the criminal and the physical and social conditions in which he lives have been carefully studied and confirmed. E. H. Sutherland, for example, in the belief (comparable to Tarde's) that the behaviour of criminals was to be largely explained by the 'principle of differential association', the pressures of association with other criminals;[19] William Healy and Augusta Bronner in their influential suggestion that this behaviour developed at an earlier age from the thwarted desires of the child leading to 'major emotional disturbances';[20] and Sheldon and Eleanor Glueck in their theory that the secret lay in a process of criminal maturation[21] have all laid foundations upon which new theories and studies can be built.

Most modern theories, while not necessarily rejecting any specific cause put forward as an explanation of crime, suggest that the individual and his environment must be studied against the general culture characterizing society, and that, as Dr Howard

Jones has put it, the criminologist must take a synoptic view of a science that 'studies the social phenomenon of crime, its causes and the measures which society directs against it'.[22] 'If we would change the amount of crime in the community,' writes Professor Tannenbau, 'we must change the community.' The cause of crime in the United States, he believes, is to be found in all the pervasive conflicts that have characterized her history, such as those resulting from immigration and from the strong tradition of individualism inherited from the early pioneers, which reflect the dynamic quality of American civilization. 'Crime is a maladjustment that arises out of the conflict between a group and the community at large. The issue involved is not whether an individual is maladjusted to society, but the fact that his adjustment to a special group makes him maladjusted to the large society because the group he fits into is at war with society.'[23] Professor Taft has formulated a similar theory which supposes that failures in a 'dynamic, complex, materialistic' culture, develop 'patterns of behaviour hostile to the interests of the general community'.[24] The study of these patterns of anti-social or undesirable behaviour— or Professor Walter Reckless's 'social vulnerabilities'—are now widely accepted both in England and in America as being the true field of criminological inquiry.

Although many criminologists do not agree with them, preferring Professor Jerome Hall's view that 'Criminology is synonymous with the Sociology of Criminal Law',[25] both Professor Thorsten Sellin and Professor Hermann Mannheim endorse the belief that criminology should not be concerned with violations of laws but with violations of standards of conduct. 'It is the object of criminology to study criminal behaviour and the physical, psychological, and socio-economic factors behind it; how and why people commit crimes.'[26] The study continues at an increasing rate and upon a more extensive scale than ever before. No completely satisfactory answers have yet been found.

CHAPTER THREE

THE CRIMINAL'S PSYCHOLOGY

'I looked at the men and women walking along the sidewalk and I felt a high contempt for them all—poor fish! Working themselves to death for starvation money.'

JAMES SPENSER, 1933

'THERE can be no psychology of the criminal—only of specific criminal types.'[1] And although, as Max Grünhut has said, 'the psychological characteristics of habitual criminals are too vague to allow a statistical assessment of this most disquieting form of persistent criminality',[2] there are, nevertheless, in the confessions and recorded conversations of professional criminals, certain opinions, certain attitudes towards society, certain rationalizations which are common to most of them and which offer some chance of understanding them.

There is, in the first place, the insistence that crime is not so much a fall from grace as a way of life.

'If I were not a thief by vocation, I should become one by calculation,' said the French criminal Leblanc to a Prefect of Police. 'It is the best profession. I have computed the good and bad chances of all the others, and I am convinced by the comparisons that there is none more favourable or more independent than that of the thief. In our profession we depend on nobody. We enjoy the fruits of our experience and ability. I know well that we may end in prison; but out of the 18,000 thieves in Paris, not one tenth are in prison, so that we enjoy nine years of freedom against one of prison. Besides, where is the working man who is not sometimes without work? ... The fear of being arrested and the pretended remorse that people talk of, are things to which one soon gets accustomed, and which finish by giving a pleasurable emotion.

'And then if we are arrested we live at the expense of others who clothe us, feed us and warm us, all at the cost of those whom we have robbed.

'I will say more. During our detention in prison we think out and prepare new means of success. If I regret anything, M. Prefect, it is that I am condemned to only a year. If it had been for five I should have been sent to a central prison, where I should have met some old hands, who would have taught me some new tricks, and I should have returned to Paris clever enough to live without working.'[3]

More recently an English professional criminal has repeated this belief in the advantages of the criminal life in similar terms and spoken, too, of crime being work like any other—hard work, a skilled business.

He did not know a straight job he could do which would bring him the £2,000 to £2,500 a year he made from crime. He could 'reel off a whole lot of reasons' that had made him become a criminal, but they were only part of the answer. He came from a neighbourhood where nearly everyone he knew was dishonest 'where stealing was a necessity at some times, an adventure at others, but was always acceptable whatever the reason'. He wanted to impress other children, get a 'reputation for being a tearaway'. He had been horrified by poverty and by the 'terrifying dreariness of the lives of other people who were "straight"' including his father. He had, as well, a 'tremendous hatred of authority' and a 'desire for adventure, for living dangerously'. But in the end, he made his reasoned decision to lead a life of crime as he might have decided to become a plumber or a greengrocer. For crime was 'just business that's all'.[4]

'I work for my living,' he insisted. 'Most crime—unless its the senseless, petty thieving sort—is quite hard work, you know. Planning a job, working out all the details of the best way to do it—and then carrying it out, under a lot of nervous strain and tension—and having to run round afterwards, if its goods, fencing the stuff, getting a good price for it, delivering it to the fence and so on—all this needs a lot of thinking and concentration. It certainly is work, don't kid yourself about that.'[5]

'I'm a businessman,' Al Capone insisted. 'Hell, it is a business. I'm thirty-two years of age and I've lived a thousand . . . I can't change conditions. I just meet them without backing up.'[6]

'It's difficult to explain to a layman the pride of a professional thief,' explained another American criminal, Jack Black. 'Day after day he takes chances and is proud that he can keep his end up and pay for the things he needs.'[7]

The chances of arrest and imprisonment are risks which he accepts without question.

'If you ask a prisoner why the punishment did not deter him from the crime, you generally get no answer because he has never thought about it,' Enrico Ferri wrote, 'or else he replies, as I have often found, that if you were afraid of hurting yourself when you went to work, you would give up working.'[8]

'I don't want to do eight years, no,' an English criminal has said, 'but if I have to I have to, and that's all there is to it . . . Coal miners don't spend their time worrying about the risk they might get killed by a fall at the coal-face either.'[9]

Nor do huntsmen, an American convict reminded an English visitor, give up hunting after they have a fall. 'I have had a bad fall, and no mistake,' the convict said. 'But I count on better luck another time.'[10]

This strong and widely held belief that next time he will not get caught is often nourished by the capacity of the paranoic to falsify his memory to fit an imagined past.

'I never thought of anything like that,' a young thief told a magistrate when asked if he was afraid of being sent back to prison. 'You never do. You always think you are going to get away with it.'[11] He was unlucky last time, but next time his luck would hold.

'Even when in prison which they hated,' wrote a former American criminal of his fellow convicts, 'they did not think about being arrested again. Consequences didn't concern them much. They thought only of getting by and they were too egoistical to think that they would ever get caught again. It was only a "bum rap" that landed them in jail this time and they would know better next time, so they thought.'[12]

The professional criminal will rarely admit, as William Healy noticed, that he has made a mistake, for he is essentially vain. The honest workers are contemptible fools and could not make a living out of crime even if they wanted to; but he lives as he wants to live and if he is by chance arrested, that is an interlude in his career, certainly no cause for changing it. Even death in the electric chair may be accepted as one of the 'breaks of the game'. The honest man does not even give himself the chance of making real money and he is a fool and a slob because of it. James Spenser, an ex-convict from Dartmoor, who dared not risk another conviction in England which would probably have resulted in his being made to serve a further five to ten years of preventive detention after his sentence of penal servitude had expired, went to America in the hope that if he were to be arrested he might be mistaken for a first offender. After he had made his 'first gangland pay' he described his pleasure in looking down on those who had never earned so much so quickly.

'I took the Buick out by myself,' he wrote, 'and drove round for a while ... I looked at the men and women walking along on the sidewalk and I felt a high contempt for them all—poor fish! Working themselves to death for starvation money! "Hell," I said to myself. "They've got no guts. They just work and work and work. And when they have sweated for four months, they'll have earned less than I have in four hours ... If I have a creed at all, I think Darwin summed it up for me in his 'survival of the fittest'." '[13]

Talk of goodness, justice, mercy, humility, honesty, morality seems to many, if not most, habitual criminals nothing but hypocrisy. The rich often behave far worse than they do, but no one penalizes them. The rich are protected by unfair laws which will allow a man to cheat his creditors by pretending to be bankrupt but will imprison a thief in a stinking prison because he steals money in a less devious way; which will allow a rich financier to destroy the hopes and even the lives of small investors and working-men, but will hang a half-witted carpenter who loses his temper and kills his nagging wife.

'A landlord gets money out of people when he puts their rents up, by extortion, by playing on the fact that they've got nowhere else to live,' the professional criminal complains. 'And the law upholds him in doing it. Yet really all he's doing is stealing money from people. But if I go along and steal that money from him he screams to the law, and they come after me to try and get his money back for him. If his tenant screams to the police that his landlord's robbing him, they do nothing of course.'[14]

The violence of the criminal is also, he contends, perfectly defensible. Governments use it in the furtherance of their aims as do the police, so why should not he use it in furtherance of his?

He is not violent for violence's sake, like the sadist or the psychopath, but he will use force as a tool of his trade when necessary. He believes, in Mussolini's phrase, that occasions arise when force 'must be used surgically'. 'If I've got to whack a bloke with an iron bar to make him let go of a wages-bag he's carrying, O.K. so I'll whack him. If he let's go without any trouble, I don't. That's all.'[15] The American professional criminal will sometimes carry a gun, but to the English 'really professional criminal somebody who uses a shooter is out completely; he's the amateur pure and simple. Only kids do things like that.' But in either case the victim is not considered so much a victim as a man who gets in the way. 'I feel,' said Robert Allerton, 'if someone takes a job as night watchman he's got to be prepared to be hit if he tries to make a hero of himself. I wouldn't have touched him if he'd left us alone, but since he tried to stop us he got what he earned. Personally I think he was stupid.'[16]

Sometimes violence is used not 'surgically' but compulsively or for pleasure. Ten out of a hundred criminals, Rossi believed, display on occasions an exaggerated cruelty and, according to Ferrero, the post of executioner at Rochefort prison was always eagerly sought for by the inmates. But whatever the reason for violence, remorse for having used it is extremely rare. When the habitual criminal is a psychopath this is particularly noticeable. Despine said that nothing resembled the sleep of the just more than the slumber of murderers.[17] And Dr Santo de Santis of Rome found that the more hardened a criminal was the less likely he was to dream, and Dr Santis believed that this unemotional dream life was caused by a general anaesthesia of sensibility in the conscious life[18]—the sort of anaesthetized sensibility, perhaps, which led the forger and supposed poisoner Thomas Wainewright, who referred to his crimes as 'speculations', to reply sardonically, when asked how he could have murdered so innocent and trustful a girl as Helen Abercrombie, 'I don't know, unless it was because she had such thick legs.'[19] This sort of anaesthetized sensibility, was, of course, a common trait of the conventional American gangster. 'Why the hell should I,' asked one gangster at once impatient, puzzled and consciously cynical, when asked if he had any remorse about the murders he had committed. 'Why the hell should I? They're dead, ain't they?'[20] These are the words of what psychiatry terms a sociopathic personality, a man not legally insane who is plausible and shameless, undisturbed by the evil he has done. The Irish Dion O'Banion was a characteristic example of this type of psychopath.

'O'Banion was a complex and frightening man, whose bright blue eyes stared with a kind of frozen candour into others,' writes Kenneth Allsop in his history of Chicago's prohibition era. 'He had a round, frank Irish face, creased in a jovial grin that stayed bleakly in place even when he was pumping bullets into someone's body... The police credited him with twenty-five murders but he was never brought to trial for any of them. Like a fair number of bootleggers he disliked alcohol. He was an expert florist, tenderly dextrous in the arrangement of bouquets and wreaths. He had no apparent comprehension of morality; he divided humanity into "right guys" and "wrong guys" and the wrong ones he was always willing to kill and trample under.'[21]

'Three hundred dollars!' he once exclaimed furiously when he was told that two policemen had asked for that sum in order to let a convoy of illicit beer pass down a Chicago street. 'To them bums! Why, I can get them knocked off for half that much.'[22]

There is usually the same attitude amongst professional criminals towards the victims of robbery as towards the victims of violence. 'I just don't think about other people,' admitted Andrew Russell who at the age of twenty-one had been convicted of forty-five serious crimes. 'I just said to myself that if a man has a car he probably has plenty of money, or anyway he has the insurance money, and he can buy himself another one. Or, really, I didn't really think at all about it one way or another.'[23] 'I just never thought about any of that,' said Laurence Williams, a young burglar when asked about his theft of the savings of a man who could certainly not afford the loss of them. 'I wanted some money and I heard there was some there, so I just went after it. I never thought about the householder one way or the other. He didn't mean anything to me.'[24] The American murderer Hickman was asked before his execution whether he would rob a poor old man who had worked hard to save a little money for his retirement. 'Why, certainly,' Hickman said. 'There's nothing wrong in that. The fellow with the brains should get everything he can.'[25]

'They appear to think that by virtue of their existence in the world,' a chaplain wrote recently of the persistent offenders in the prison where he worked, 'society—to which they contribute nothing—owes them a good living, and when it is not forthcoming they take it as by right. They

have almost persuaded themselves that stealing is not so much a crime
as a legitimate redistribution of capital.'²⁶

Occasionally an attempt is made to justify the crime, although the
justification is never conscious and the suggestion that it is a justification is usually angrily denied. 'The cheap bastards are paying
girls only eight dollars a week to be on their feet all day and they
ought to be beat,' said a man who had robbed a store, and this was
not just an excuse, but was 'actually the way the thief feels about
it. He would probably pick out the bigger stores to beat even if
they paid the girls a hundred dollars a week, but it eases his conscience a little to have this justification.'²⁷

Whether the professional criminal justifies his actions or not, he
rarely attempts an excuse for the reckless way he spends his money
once he has got it. Just as the need for an adventurous, irregular
life is common to many criminals, their wild and vanity-flattering
extravagance is common to most. They have risked their liberty
and perhaps their lives to get their money, but they are prepared
to scatter it like dust on gambling, drink, clothes or women.

'I've gone into a crib, a gambling place,' says one of them, 'not
once, but many times with two or three hundred quid in my pocket
—and come out with exactly nothing. One time a girl took sixty
quid out of my pocket and I never even noticed it'd gone until somebody told me months afterwards she'd had it.'²⁸ 'The spending was
simply terrific,' said another who was the housekeeper for a gang
of six English thieves in 1947 when rationing was still, for honest
people, an inescapable feature of post-war life. 'We lived as none
of us had lived in our lives. I bought absolutely everything any
one of us wanted on the black market. We had hundreds of pounds
coming in, so what did prices matter? I used to buy eggs at twelve
shillings a dozen; legs of pork for fifty shillings; whisky at four
pounds and five pounds. As long as I got the best nobody cared
what I spent . . .'²⁹ 'I spent three hundred pounds in five days,'
said a third, 'mostly on girls and clothes.'³⁰ Others have confessed,
'we got quite a bit of money at times but it all went in a flash'; 'my
share was sixty pounds. I went back to London after that, but it
didn't last many days. Easy come, easy go.'³¹

'Crime does not pay,' Danny Ahearn told the New York Crime
Commission in 1928, 'because you never wind up with anything . . .
because if you make it you are going to throw it away anyway.
Ninety-nine per cent of them are gamblers and you wind up losing

your money ... You throw it away in cabarets, you are a habitual drunkard or you turn out to be a pipey; so it does not pay.'[32]

But so long as their luck lasts, most professional criminals do not concern themselves with the thought that crime will not pay in the end. They are scarcely ever reformed. The length of their confinement in penal establishments seems to have very little effect upon their subsequent behaviour.[33] 'There are very few cases in which a man or a woman who has turned thief ceases to be one ... When you can turn an old thief into an honest worker, you may turn an old fox into a house dog.'[34] Between eighty and ninety per cent of habitual criminals sentenced to preventive detention in England under the Prevention of Crime Act 1908 reverted to crime on their discharge.[35]

The relapse of one professional criminal who tried to reform has been well described by Albert Bourke who, on his release from prison in Australia where he had developed religious feelings, decided to lead an honest life. One day he saw a man lying drunk in the road.

'Instead of going on,' he said, 'I stopped and sat on the top rail of a fence over against him. No one was about. I thought to myself, "This is a gift if I were on 'the cross'. But I'm religious now and cannot touch him." I resolved, however, to have a close look at him. When I got close beside him I noticed a bulge in one of his trouser pockets. "That I may know what a chance I am throwing away," I said to myself, "I'll just see what he has in that pocket." I found there nine pounds ten in gold. Taking a sovereign I put the rest back in his pocket. I intended to take this pound merely as a loan, and closely examined his features that I might know him again, to return it to him when I should be in better circircumstances. When I had reached Harris Street, which was only a short distance from where he was lying, I looked back at him. Pulling the catechism and prayer-book out of my pocket, I looked at them. I cast my lamps over their pages and became sceptical. There was a sink close at hand. Throwing them both into the sink, I danced about and swore and blasphemed like a maniac. I then went back to the bug and got the eight pounds ten. I also took a little silver which he had in his trouser pocket, and his boots which were new; and, only I saw a man at a distance coming towards us, I should have taken his trousers.'[36]

Albert Bourke's sure eye for the humorous and the grotesque is common amongst habitual criminals, although this has always been more apparent in their lively conversation and in their rare and sometimes expressive drawings and paintings than in the usually flat and unrevealing 'confessions' and 'memoirs' that are written for them. They seem to see life with the eyes of a cruel caricaturist. Their drawings are often sexual and nearly always outlandish. Women are shown with enormous pendent breasts or indulging in sexual activities of improbable agility. Scenes of violence are common, as are scenes depicting authority in ludicrous distress. The background is often a prison. Their wall inscriptions, which were carefully studied in the nineteenth century, indicated the same interests, although in prison food is apparently of paramount importance and obscene writings were more common amongst women. In general their art seems to reflect their view of the world which has, perhaps, not greatly changed since Louis Desprez described it to Gautier as having 'the aspect of an immense gaol alternating with an immense brothel'.[37]

Certainly their slang, or cant as it should properly be called, still has more words to do with prisons and sex than with any other aspects of their lives, apart of course from crime itself. Of the 1,063 slang terms in common use amongst convicts in American prisons almost three-quarters of them are to do with crime, prison life and sex, homosexual terms considerably outnumbering hetero-sexual. Parts of the body and descriptions of them account for 13.34 per cent of the rest of the slang terms, idleness and vaga-bondage 5.35 per cent, drugs 3.48 per cent, alchol 3.19 per cent, gambling 1.22 per cent.[38]

Many of the words are very old, with Anglo-Saxon or Sanskrit roots (pal, bamboozle, bosh are all old gipsy words) and some of them such as fence, which is at least three hundred years old, have been accepted into the English language and permanently enriched it. Originally invented to provide a secret language un-known to authority, like the symbols and signs of tramps and gipsies and the secret words of the ghetto, criminals' slang has become universally popular and only the slang of sex perverts and drug addicts remains to any real extent occult. The use of the telephone and the consequent dangers of wire-tapping led to the invention of some new secret words in America, but generally neologisms are now more admired for their sardonic humour and picturesqueness than for their hidden meanings, however esoteric their derivations might be. French criminal cant provides many examples of this cynical humour which delights in turning the sublime into the ridiculous, in debasing beauty and virtue. To induce someone to lead a criminal life is to set him free; conscience becomes *muette* (a dumb woman), the thief is *l'ami*, to steal is *servir*. A face is a muzzle; a mouth is a beak; a bottom is a windmill; but a pickpocket becomes a fingersmith. There is much play with puns and abbreviations. *Saucisse* becomes *moi* (from *moi-s-aussi*); a prostitute is a cod and her bully or ponce is a mackerel, a *maquerau*, so a *mac; avoir ses aff* is to menstruate (*avoir ses affaires*). Many of the terms quickly become unfashionable as others replace them or they may change their meaning or pronunciation. In the early eighteenth century in London a prostitute was a bunter or a buttock, a knife was a chife, to be hanged was to be cast or nubbed or toped, a case was a house frequented by thieves usually a brothel, a trunk was a peter, a pickpocket was a file. Now a pickpocket is generally a dip (in America, a wire), a prostitute has become a brass, a peter is a safe, chife for knife is pronounced chiv, toped for hanged has become topped. Case is still sometimes used for house (or as a verb meaning to inspect a building with a view to burglary) but to go case is to have sexual intercourse. Frequently a word which seems characteristically American can be traced to an English origin. Frisk (to search a person), deck (pack of cards), gonoph (thief), mob and phoney (from 'fawney man'—*fainne* is Irish for finger-ring—a pedlar of false jewellery) have all been recorded in England before their adoption in America. Many words have two meanings, one to do with the criminal's sex life, the other with his prison life. A bird is a term of imprisonment as well as a girl; screwing means having sexual intercourse as well as burgling. There are numerous other words for sexual intercourse and almost as many for being drunk. The French criminal, it has been estimated, has eighty terms for drunkenness but not one for sobriety, and he has had in his time 150 words to choose from to mean prostitute.

Peculiarly English is the rhyming slang which turns feet into plates (plates of meat) stairs into apples and pears, hat into titfer (tit for tat). Also peculiarly English are the extinct back slang and thieves' Latin. 'Pass her a pot of beer and a bit of tobacco,' could become in a Victorian public house in London's East End, 'Sap her a top of reeb and a tib of occabot.' Thieves' Latin was even more difficult to use than back slang and consisted in reversing the position of the syllables of a word with more than one syllable and making two syllables of all monosyllabic words by adding a vowel at the beginning or end. Despite its difficulty, quick-witted criminals could apparently, by dint of much practice, talk in this way at such speed that only an initiate could understand them. The hard work involved, however, ensured that this form of cant never became popular for although he can be violently energetic by fits and starts the habitual criminal is the natural enemy of prolonged exertion. He finds it difficult, in fact, to concentrate on anything for long. He does not read much, except in prison and even then he usually prefers picture-papers to books. A prisoner, such as the one described by Dostoevsky who asked if he might remain in prison when he was due to be released so that he might finish the book that he was reading, would be hard to find in England or America. Russian prisoners at this time evidently derived much pleasure from reading Shakespeare which an English convict described as 'such a child's book'.[39] This convict's own favourite reading matter was the Boys' Own Paper, then much admired in English prisons. The books most sought after were sentimental, particularly historical romances,[40] although books about prisons and prisoners were also popular.[41] The modern convict is an avid reader. In America he reads between five and ten times more books than the average user of a public library and in England 'it is a fact', as Frank Norman has said, 'that books play a great part in the life of the geezers in nick'. But while books by such writers as Conrad and Steinbeck are often in demand, most prisoners still prefer magazines or 'Westerns, crime mysteries and war narratives'[42] of little literary merit and even, in default of pornography, sentimental love stories of no merit at all.

For the habitual criminal, it has often been noticed, can be exceptionally sentimental and emotional despite his anaesthetized sensibility. He is nearly always fond of animals, lavishing on what pets he can get hold of in prison an affection which is almost obsessive.

'Geezers in the nick are very fond of animals and if they see anyone hurting one that person has a good chance of getting a thick earhole. Most nicks are over run with cats and they are very fine cats too, the reason for them being such healthy cats is they don't seem to mind the grub even if we do but of course they are born to it.'[43]

Basil Thomson, a prison governor of long experience, could remember 'only one case of cruelty to an animal and that was immediately reported by the convicts themselves, who declined to

work with a man who had kicked a cow'.[44] Thomas Wainewright's
'sole living companion' after his transportation to Tasmania was
a cat. Wainewright 'seemed to be possessed by an ingrained
malignity of disposition which kept him constantly on the very
confines of murder, and he took a perverse pleasure in traducing
persons who had befriended him'. But for this cat he 'evinced an
extraordinary affection'.[45] Most professional criminals are also
extremely fond of children, partly at least, perhaps, because
children can be given presents and the vanity and egocentricity
of the criminal are flattered by their ready, delighted acceptance.
'How many you got left, kid?' asked Al Capone when a little news-
boy came up to him in a restaurant clutching a pile of papers one
cold winter evening. 'About fifty, I guess,' said the boy. 'Throw
them on the floor and run along home to your mother,' said Capone
and gave him a twenty dollar bill.[46] Criminals, in fact, are fond
of all living creatures which are small and defenceless, who cannot
be suspected of harbouring a wish to wrong them or cheat them.
This fear that everyone else, including a best friend or a wife, may
turn out to be a potential enemy is, Professor Tannenbaum thinks,
at the heart of the criminal's philosophy which 'may be described
as a war psychosis'. The motivating force is fear. Jealousy,
revenge, suspicion, hate are the elements from which his life is
woven. He instinctively distrusts the people about him and so sets
great store by his own loyalty to the gang and the gang's loyalty
to him. The informer is the lowest form of life—the stool-pigeon,
the rat.[47]

This loyalty, however, whatever its origins and motives is in a
sense a virtue. The criminal must go to prison, even die, as a good
mafioso or member of the Camorra must, rather than betray one
of his kind to the law. It may be true that 'most of the stuff about
honour among thieves is bunk'[48] in that the criminal will often
readily double-cross or frame a fellow criminal if it will profit himself. But it is true, too, that, within the limits of self-interest, the
average criminal makes much of his fidelity to his associates in
crime 'and a violation of its unwritten code is constructive heresy
in the craft'.[49] The criminal's devotion to this code was nicely
epitomized by the dying words of Frank Gusenberg, the only man
still alive when, after several members of Bugs Moran's gang had
been killed by machine-gun bullets in a Chicago garage in 1929,
the police arrived on the scene of what became known as the St
Valentine's Day Massacre. 'Who shot you?' a police sergeant asked

Gusenberg. With fourteen machine-gun bullets in his body, Gusenberg muttered his reply: 'Nobody shot me.'[50]

Even the professional criminal's frequently protested social conscience is often no more than the outcome of resentment and selfishness. Once he has got what he wants out of life, himself, he tends to stop talking about the plight of others. His real heroes are not do-gooders but go-getters. An English criminal has recently been quoted as expressing admiration for Albert Schweitzer, but a more representative reaction to this great man would be to wonder what was his racket. Everyone has his racket, just as everyone has his price. The criminal's heroes are those who delight in proclaiming these truths, who flaunt their success in the face of failure. The rich American gangster in his silk suit and crocodile shoes, his sharkskin tie and Brooks Brothers shirt, with his Cadillac and girl friends and expensively scented hair, his gold wrist watch and his beach house in California, is the professional criminal's real hero because in that figure he sees the incarnation of his own desires. When Tony Accardo was summonsed on a charge of disorderly conduct he delighted his fellow-criminals by driving to court in his most expensive car and by describing himself, while wearing his most expensive suit, as an unemployed labourer. He delighted others, besides criminals, for such effrontery arouses in even the more conventional citizens a reluctant admiration and envy.

Tony Accardo, the *New York Herald Tribune* reported, 'didn't care to say where he worked last. About the murder of Joe Aello? Never heard of him. Where was he during October? Not sure. In Chicago? Maybe. Why was he in custody? No idea. Ever arrested before? Oh, yes, lots of times. What for? Never found out. Would he sign the statement? No.'[51]

As well as being the heroes, men like Accardo are the aristocracy of the criminal class, a class which has gradations as carefully guarded and respected as those observed in the servants' hall of a nineteenth-century ducal palace. 'There is no more caste in the heart of India than in an American penitentiary. A bank burglar assumes an air with a house burglar, sneers at a pickpocket; a pickpocket calls a forger a "short-story writer".'[52] 'The pride of the homicide prompts him to ignore the thief; the highway robber despises the petty offender; and all together execrate the ravisher; while the forger and the embezzler congratulate themselves that they are "not as other men".'[53] 'The confidence tricksters, swindlers and forgers are in a lower social scale than the screwsmen,' says the retired safe-breaker Eddie Chapman. But they can look down upon the sexual offenders, 'ponces' and the despised informers.[54] Nathan Leopold discovered when in prison in America that to call a man a thief or robber was to compliment him, while men guilty of embezzlement or forgery were regarded with disdain. 'Rape-o' was a strong term of disparagement and men convicted of deviant sex crimes were utterly despised.[55] 'Wolves,' or the active participants in homosexual relations in prison, are, however, generally respected although the passive participants are regarded with 'good-humoured' contempt.[56] Amongst the most admired qualities that an American prison leader can possess are, so it seems, skill as a gambler, courage, good knowledge about a particular technique of crime, a large store of dirty stories, participation in some spectacular crime, riot or escape, a proved attractiveness to women, a great capacity for eating, the ability to seduce younger prisoners and to play a guitar.[57] But none of these qualities would be so much admired in an embezzler as they would be in a bank robber.

'In my racket,' said a car thief, 'we wouldn't have a sneak thief of any kind. It takes guts to steal cars and we wouldn't trust our lives with a low piker like a petty thief.'[58]

An Australian scholar and research worker, who spent three weeks at Parkhurst Prison in 1948 to study the treatment of men sentenced to preventive detention, found that when they left the 'hall' in which they had served the last few months of their terms of penal servitude, their status rose 'tremendously'. They were now the prison aristocrats and were 'treated with a mixture of sympathy and awe—sympathy because, in the average prisoner's rigid criminological conservatism, the detainee is wronged by society and is suffering a "double" and unjust punishment for his crime; and awe because of his membership of a privileged and wealthy aristocracy'.[59]

'It's the money that counts, you see,' an old criminal once said. 'That's what we're after and that's what we admire about those who've got it.'

Lombroso could 'never forget how upon the day when five ministers of the realm of Italy rose as one man to deny or to justify the thefts of Tanlongo and Co. running up to more than thirty millions, seven children were sent to weep for a month and a half in prison cells for having stolen a herring worth thirty-five centesimi'.[60] Most habitual criminals would share, perhaps, Lombroso's pity for the imprisoned children but, unlike him, their anger that the rich had once again got away with it, would be at least partly conditioned by their regret that they had not themselves been partners in Tanlongo and Co. When they succeeded in becoming partners in similar, if more actively criminal enterprises, they plead the tolerance accorded by society and the law to the unpunished but no less harmful speculations of high finance.

'What's wrong with the syndicate?' demanded Sam Giancana, Chicago's 'Number Two hood' recently. 'Two or three of us get together on some deal and everybody says it's a bad thing. But those businessmen do it all the time and nobody squawks.'[61]

This is the eternal plea of the criminal. It is not entirely specious.

'I've made my money by supplying a popular demand,' Al Capone once said indignantly. 'If I break the law my customers are as guilty as I am. When I sell liquor its bootlegging. When my patrons serve it on silver trays on Lake Shore Drive its hospitality. The country wanted booze and I've organized it. Why should I be called a public enemy ...? The funny part of the whole thing is that a man in this line of business has so much company. I mean his customers. If people didn't want beer and wouldn't drink it, a fellow would be crazy for going round trying to sell it. I've seen gambling houses, too, in my travels, and I never saw anyone point a gun at a man and make him go in. I never heard of anyone being forced to go to a place to have some fun.'[62]

In this sense, as in others, society gets the criminals it deserves. One day, some years ago the then Bishop of Exeter was on a visit to Dartmoor Prison. He asked the Governor if it were true that most men sentenced to penal servitude were mentally defective.

'No,' the Governor said. 'But think what you yourself would have been if your father, your mother or both, and most of your brothers and sisters had been thieves.'

'You think that I would have been a thief too?' The Bishop reflected a moment and then added, 'Well, perhaps you are right.'[63]

The Bishop, unlike many men who live within the law, was honest enough to admit that even he was a potential criminal. Most of us have the seeds of criminality within us and most of us who do not, in fact, become criminals have remained law-abiding without conscious effort. We have not shared the criminal's motives, prejudices, surroundings or temptations. Different circumstances, a different upbringing, a different education have helped us to stay within the law as a matter of course and habit, have helped us to consider the ethics of obedience and unselfishness, patience and charity, have helped us perhaps to enjoy vicariously pleasures and excitements and even violence which the criminal feels he must experience himself. We must remember that we are not necessarily better men, but certainly more fortunate ones. We must remember Freud's thesis that the actions of neurotic patients are exaggerations of reactions common to us all, and that the actions of the criminal are exaggerations of normal human impulses. And we must remember, too, how much we owe our lawfulness to the opinion which those we know would entertain of us if we committed a crime they did not condone and were sent to prison. For 'opinion', as Beccaria said two hundred years ago, 'that tormentor of the wise and the ignorant, has exalted the appearance of virtue above virtue itself'.[64]

Part IV

THE CRIME CULT

THE CRIME CULT

*'You cannot conceive the ridiculous rage there is of going to
Newgate, the prints that are published of the malefactors, and
the memoirs of their lives set forth with as much parade as
Marshal Turenne's.'*

HORACE WALPOLE, 1750

(i)

'Nothing contributes so much to the entertainment of the town at present
as the adventures of the famous housebreaker and gaolbreaker John
Sheppard,' a London newspaper told its readers on 7 November 1724.
''Tis thought the keepers of Newgate have got above two hundred
pounds already by the crowds of people who flock daily to see
Sheppard.'[1]

For a fortnight Jack Sheppard remained on view and crowds of
people came every day and paid four shillings each to look at him.
When he came out to be hanged, a journalist believed that there
were two hundred thousand people lining the route of the procession between Newgate and Tyburn. Sheppard, wearing a new
black suit, got up into the cart, smiling and waving in acknowledg-
ment of the cheers, and sat down next to the prison chaplain and
behind the hangman who was sitting on his coffin. The parade of
carts and carriages, marching soldiers and mounted constables
stopped at the church of St Sepulchre where it was customary for
girls to throw flowers and coloured ribbons into the condemned
man's cart. It stopped again at a wayside tavern, as was also cus-

tomary, so that Sheppard could drink his last pint of mulled sack. In his speech on the scaffold he recommended everyone to read the account of his adventures which Mr Defoe had written for him and then the rope was put about his neck and the cart drove away from under him, leaving him to kick in the air as he was slowly strangled. After he had been hanging for about a quarter of an hour, a soldier jumped on to the scaffold, slashed through the rope with his sword and passed the body to a friend in the crowd so that it could be taken away for resuscitation. Some other people in the crowd believing that it was to be taken to the surgeons for dissection, struggled for possession of it and there was a riot. There was another riot that night when a rumour spread that Sheppard's body had been stolen and a company of footguards with drawn bayonets had to be called out from the Savoy.

One of the broadsheets, describing Sheppard's adventures, which was already on sale referred to the charming, irresponsible, little thief who had great talent as a prison-breaker although scarcely any as a criminal, as a 'Prometheus, something more than a man, a supernatural'.[2]

The verdict was a common one. The criminal hero had a long history, but not until now had any period contributed so much to the romance of crime.[3] The marauding knights of the Dark Ages may have possessed some of the romantic ideals subsequently attributed to them, but the face they presented to their contemporaries was not a heroic one. Robin Hood may have robbed the rich, as all successful criminals do, but his unselfish largesse to the poor seems to have been exaggerated by ballads intent on creating a champion for the weak against the oppression of the strong. In fact, if Coke is to be believed, Robin Hood, far from being the dashing outlaw of Sherwood Forest, was a brigand who lived in Yorkshire 'in woods and deserts, by robbery, burning of houses, felony, waste and spoile, and principally by and with vagabonds, idle wanderers, night walkers and draw-latches.'[4] By the time of the Restoration, the criminal hero was more firmly established and the outlandish character of the self-styled Colonel Blood, who, amongst other exploits, stole the crown jewels from the Tower of London in 1671, caught the imagination of the country and, indeed, of Charles II who pardoned him.[5] It was not, however, until the early Hanoverian period that the cult of the criminal assumed such proportions that foreign visitors, accustomed to lesser manifestations of it in their own countries, remarked on it as if it were a peculiarly English characteristic. Even a man like Dick Turpin, a brutal butcher who stocked his shop by stealing cattle and sheep, could be cheered as he went to the gallows at York in 1739 wearing a new fustian frock coat and a pair of pumps and followed by five poor men hired as mourners at ten shillings each. Turpin at the outset of his short and vicious career had once shouted at an old woman whose money he was trying to find, 'God damn your blood, you old bitch, if you won't tell us I'll set your arse on the grate.' And he and his companion did 'actually place her on the fire'. The action was characteristic of a gang of ruffiians who beat and kicked their victims 'with great severity', once poured hot water from a kettle on an old man's head and raped a maid who was hiding in a dairy. When the gang was broken up by a member who betrayed the others for a reward of a hundred pounds and Turpin became a highwayman, he murdered a man who tried to arrest him. But all this was forgiven at his death by the spectators who 'seemed much affected by the fate of a man distinguished by the comeliness of his appearance'.[6]

The highwayman had become used to such reverence. Claude Duval, a Frenchman who came to London with an English family at the time of the Restoration and devoted the rest of his life to highway robbery and making love roughly to ladies of fashion, was not much less brutal than Turpin and once snatched a feeding-bottle from a baby's mouth because it was made of silver. 'But when justice at length overtook him, and he was cast for death, crowds of ladies visited him in the condemned hold; many more in masks were present at his execution.'[7] The highwayman McLean, so Walpole told Horace Mann in 1750, was the only topic of conversation in London in August that year and after he had been condemned to death three thousand people went to see him on a single day including Lady Caroline Petersham and Miss Ashe who wanted 'to comfort and weep over this fallen hero'.[8]

The dead bodies of men like this—and indeed of all criminals—were believed to have mystical properties. The belief is as old as recorded history. The Romans valued the blood of criminals as a cure for epilepsy and the belief in its remedial and prophylactic properties for many other complaints, including gout, survived for more than two thousand years. In Prussia women attended executions with spoons and cups and cloths to soak up the precious liquid and in 1861 at Hanau several men leapt on to the scaffold to drink the blood gushing from the neck of a decapitated corpse. At Berlin in 1864 sodden handkerchiefs were sold by the executioner for two thalers each.[9]

Nor was blood all that was prized. The French *bourreaux* made ointments from the fat of their victims,[10] and in Germany the genital organs of thieves were greatly prized.[11] In England children were taken on to the scaffold to have the hand of the corpse, damp with 'death sweat', rubbed against their skin as a cure for scrofulous diseases;[12] and a foreign visitor once saw 'a young woman, with an appearance of beauty, all pale and trembling, in the arms of the executioner, who submitted to have her bosom uncovered, in the presence of thousands of spectators, and the dead man's hand placed upon it.'[13] The fingers and thumbs of thieves, it was believed, improved the trade of shopkeepers; and a small bone in a purse kept it from being empty. People came to ask for bones from the body of the notorious Marquise de Brinvilliers, said Madame de Sévigné, as though they were asking for holy relics.[14]

Criminals, themselves, supposed that a candle placed in the hand of an executed thief would not be seen by eyes other than their own and the candle should, if possible, be made from the fat of unborn babies. Among the twenty victims of the murderer Bastian Grübl were 'five pregnant women, whom he had caused to live in debauchery with his companions. He cut them open and cut off the hands of the infants and made candles of their hands to be used in burglaries.'[15]

Even the rope that had strangled the criminal was supposed to have magical properties and after the executions at Tyburn it was regularly sold by the inch at a tavern in Fleet Street. Sometimes there was a fight on the scaffold for possession of this valuable commodity and often, as at Jack Sheppard's execution, there was a fierce struggle for the corpse between the mob and the surgeons' messengers who had a right to carry it off to the dissecting table.

No contemporary writer was more fully aware than Henry Fielding of the dangers of these unhealthy superstitions and of associating public executions in the popular mind not with shame and dishonour but with pride and glory.

'The day appointed by law for the thief's shame,' he wrote in 1751, 'is the day of glory in his own opinion. His procession to Tyburn and his last moments there are all triumphant.'[16]

Fielding's ironical *History of Jonathan Wild the Great* continues the attack on the hero-worship of the criminal, and has the same purpose as William Page's biography of Claude Duval. But while Fielding and his brother John deplored the effects of the immense output of broadsheets and sentimental ballads idealizing the criminal, and of the numerous poor imitations of John Gay's *Beggar's Opera,* few of their contemporaries supported them.

Fielding's own views are given in the preface to his great novel, *The Adventures of Joseph Andrews.* 'Great vices,' he wrote there, 'are the proper objects of our detestation, smaller faults of our pity, but affectation appears to me the only true source of the ridiculous.' In Fielding's hands social satire became a great art. Some of his work displayed the almost ferocious irony of Swift; some of it had the vivid, forceful conviction of his friend Hogarth; but Fielding's subtlety, humour and compassion gave to all his best work qualities which were unique. When Joseph Andrews is robbed and left naked none of the passengers in the coach will help him. But the postillion does and takes off his greatcoat to give him. The postillion is a 'lad', Fielding explains in a casual, almost dismissive aside, 'who hath since been transported for robbing a hen-roost'.

Fielding's concern for 'persons of inferior rank and therefore of inferior manners' had been shared by Defoe, who gave in *Moll Flanders* for instance, a touching portrait of a girl whom circumstances had contrived to ruin. But it was throughout the eighteenth and nineteenth centuries an unfashionable concern. Gothic novels by such writers as Walpole and 'Monk' Lewis, preoccupied with fantasy and evil, developed later into works of literary importance —Stevenson's *Dr Jekyll and Mr Hyde* and many of the works of Edgar Allan Poe and Sheridan Le Fanu are characteristic of these. It was not, however, until Charles Dickens concerned himself, as Bulwer Lytton had done, with 'persons of inferior rank' and those who fell into crime, that Fielding's protests were continued by a comparable artist. By the end of the nineteenth century to write about criminals and violence was a respectable literary ambition and to read about them an almost universal practice. Books by Conrad, by Dostoevsky, by Stendhal, Zola and Hugo treated of crime and violence because crime and violence, as they understood, were natural and a part of life and to try to understand these things is to try to understand ourselves. The memoirs of Lacenaire, the French poet, murderer, thief and forger which had been interrupted by the executioner, and those, supposedly written by the former criminal Eugène-François Vidocq, assumed a growing importance while the lives revealed in Henry Mayhew's *London Labour and the London Poor,* and in particular in the volume which dealt with the underworld were recognized as being the raw material with which serious novelists should work.

There were, however, at the same time hundreds of lesser writers who used this material for quite different reasons. And the popular success of 'penny dreadfuls' and newspapers which luridly described contemporary crimes, while having perhaps less effect on the morals of the susceptible than their critics maintained, no doubt contributed much to the slough of disesteem—deeper in England than in America—into which the novel of crime and violence has fallen. To indulge a taste for vicarious sadism and brutality and to satisfy a pathological interest in the depraved, the abnormal and the obscene are not the purposes of the serious writer; but so long as the public demands such indulgences and satisfactions, they will continue to be supplied by cheap and worthless books, bad films and popular newspapers.

One popular English Sunday newspaper in recent years was, for example, censured by the Press Council for publishing a confession to. murder by a man, Donald Hume, who had been found not guilty of the crime at his trial. After having been acquitted on the murder charge, Hume pleaded guilty to having dropped parcels containing bits of the victim's body into the sea for someone else and was sent to prison. On his release he confessed to the *Sunday Pictorial* that he was the murderer after all. Hume could not have committed the murder in the way he said he did—and whether he committed it at all is still a matter of debate—but his confession would certainly have been published by another newspaper if it had not been secured by the *Sunday Pictorial* for two thousand pounds. Indeed, according to a letter published in the *Spectator* in 1962, Hume was tentatively offered ten thousand pounds for a confession to be published in the *People.* The competition for such stories is always fierce and the demand for others like them is insatiable. That Hume was reported to have received numerous offers of marriage before and after his trials is not a matter for surprise. Few violent criminals escape this attention and no aggressive psychopath would want to. It is part of the crime cult and has always been so.

The trial of Hume was the subject of an excellent book by Rebecca West; his life has been told in another book by John

Williams and a film company has bought an option on the rights to film it. 'The enormous interest' taken in criminals and their trials 'by the members of the public, most of whom have never entered a court of law in their lives', is due, Lord Birkett thought, 'to the undying curiosity of men and women about other people's lives . . . They are taken out of their ordinary everyday world of convention and usage into a world that sometimes is quite fearful in its fascination . . . They find escape from the rigid bounds to which life has assigned them.'[17] This is true of divorce cases as well as of murder trials; it can even be true of a civil action such as the case of the Tichborne claimant. It is as true of Italy and France and Germany as it is of England and America. *L'affaire Peugeot*, *L'affaire Lacaze* and the trial of Marie Besnard in France, the Montesi case and the *Balletti Verdi* scandal in Italy, the murder of Rosemarie Nitribitt and the trial of Vera Bruehne in Germany have in recent years offered such fascinating stories about the rich, the famous, the grotesque and the depraved that all other news has seemed pallid and boring beside them.

But while books about these cases can have a merit which is not only literary; while Rebecca West's book about the Hume case,[18] Sybille Bedford's book about the case of Dr Bodkin Adams,[19] F. Tennyson Jesse's novel based on the tragedy of Edith Thompson[20] and Meyer Levin's novel about Leopold and Loeb[21] are only four of many distinguished works with a trial for murder as their underlying theme; and while it is true, as Lord Birkett said, that 'a healthy, as distinct from a morbid, interest in crime and punishment is of very great social value', it is impossible to escape the conclusion that much of the interest *is* 'morbid'. The space given to the trials of Heath and Christie was greater, so it has been estimated, than that given by English newspapers to any other case since the War. And it would be absurdly hypocritical to suggest that most of us—perfectly normal people as we are considered to be—did not find them fascinating. We may not have shared the emotions of the groups of people who waited (as they always do wait) outside the prison to learn that they had been hanged; but our interest in Heath and Christie was still not, in Lord Birkett's sense, healthy. It could, nevertheless, be argued that the interest in the behaviour of such men is so general that those who do not share it, or profess not to share it, are the unnatural ones: just as it could be argued that crime which, in Raymond Mortimer's phrase, 'exposes hidden lives like a spade opening up an ant-hill,' is consequently one of the most stimulating fields of study for us all. At least it is better to accept this compulsive interest in crimes, however revolting they may be, as naturally and inevitably human, rather than to find pious reasons for making money out of it as the editors of such publications as the Newgate Calendar did in the eighteenth century and as the editor of the Sunday newspaper with the largest circulation in the world still felt obliged to do in the twentieth. What is more obviously harmful is the tendency of some newspapers, particularly in America, where the laws relating to contempt of court are less exacting, to interfere in criminal proceedings in the name of the freedom of the Press and of the Press's responsibility for public enlightenment. It is frequently suggested that newspapers increase crime by teaching its technique, by making it seem attractive, exciting, profitable and common, by giving prestige to criminals and by advocating methods of dealing with them which are as stern as their readers would like them to be but which are not, in fact, repressive. How justified these criticisms are is a matter of conjecture. There can, though, be no conjecture about the harm done by newspapers during the trial in Cleveland in 1954 of Dr Sheppard for the murder of his wife, nor during the trial in New York four years later of Peter Manceri for the murder of a stranger in a park. In both cases newspapers, by satisfying a public demand for stories about the accused, made prejudicial and unwarranted presumptions of their guilt.

In the eighteenth century when the human taste for sadism and violence could be indulged less vicariously, the danger of corruption as Fielding saw it, came not so much from the detailed descriptions of atrocities, perversions and tortures in books like Smith's *History of the Most Notorious Highwaymen* and Johnson's *History of the Most Notorious Pirates* as from the tendencies of such books to make heroes out of villains. The criminal in a sense, of course, was bound to be a hero, for he was a rebel, a free man in a society in which those who were not free were exploited and oppressed. He was in revolt against the law and against morality. He was a sort of talisman of liberty and of pleasure. And people's imagination has always been more readily caught by the outsider than by the upholder of authority, by the gay and daring sinner than by the humdrum saint, although the saint may be the real upholder of liberty which the criminal does not want for others but only for himself. The Sicilian bandit, the train robber of the

American West, the Australian bush-ranger, even the Chicago gangster are all folk heroes. Gasparone and Giuliano, Jesse James and Billy the Kid, Ned Kelly and Joe Byrne, Al Capone and Jim Colosimo are all remembered with admiration while the men who tried to bring them to justice have long since been forgotten. The selfishness, brutality and greed of Dick Turpin have been replaced in the public imagination by the chivalry of Harrison Ainsworth's hero who, in the immensely successful novel, *Rookwood*, rode to York on Black Bess. The real Ned Kelly has been replaced by the tragic, legendary figure in Sidney Nolan's beautiful pictures. Rod Steiger is only the most recent of the actors who have perpetuated the fascination of Al Capone. This creation of a mythical figure out of a reality which is far less romantic and the continued idealization of that myth by books and films continues to concern those whose responsibility it is to adminster or enforce the law. The Inspectors of Constabulary in England and Wales, when reporting in June 1962 on an increase of crime the previous year, said that the effect of much objective anti-crime propaganda 'is dissipated by the glamour with which crime and criminals are exploited for the amusement of the public'.[22]

Since the appearance of Raffles there have, of course, been few criminal heroes in the traditional manner. Budd Schulberg's Terry Malloy and Willard Motley's Nick Romano are victims of conditions and it is the conditions which are the heart of the books. The criminal hero has, it seems, been replaced by the psychopath, the descriptions of whose ghoulish activities fulfil a modern need for an obscene violence which has disappeared from the streets, and by the private detective whose character and methods are now often indistinguishable from those of the hero he has succeeded.

The private detective was not always so violent. He, at least, has a respectable ancestry.

(ii)

Shortly after settling down at 221B Baker Street, Dr John H. Watson, M.D., late of the Army Medical Department, was taken out on his first case with the equivocal Sherlock Holmes who, a few days before, had satisfied his new friend's curiosity by telling him what his occupation was. 'I have a trade of my own,' he had told him. 'I suppose I am the only one in the world. I'm a consulting detective, if you can understand what that is. Here in London we have lots of Government detectives and lots of private ones. When these fellows are at fault, they come to me, and I manage to put them on the right scent.'

Watson was irritated by Holmes's conceit, but his irritation must have been mild compared with that endured by Gregson and Lestrade, the Scotland Yard detectives whom Holmes treated with such patronizing indulgence. These two, Holmes decided, were 'conventional—shockingly so', but at least the 'pick of a bad lot'.

During this first case that Holmes and Watson studied together, Lestrade was unable to discover much of significance in a room where a man had been found dead. He was shown what he had missed by Holmes who 'whipped a tape measure and a large round magnifying glass from his pocket. With these two implements he trotted noiselessly about the room sometimes stooping, occasionally kneeling and once lying flat upon his face. So engrossed was he with his occupation that he appeared to have forgotten the presence' of Lestrade, Gregson and Watson in the room 'for he chattered away to himself under his breath the whole time, keeping up a running fire of exclamations, groans, whistles and little cries.'

'There has been a murder done and the murderer was a man,' Holmes announced when he had finished. 'He was more than six feet high, was in the prime of life, had small feet for his height, wore coarse, square-toed boots and smoked a Trichinopoly cigar. He came here with his victim in a four-wheeled cab, which was drawn by a horse with three old shoes and one new one on his fore-leg. In all probability the murderer had a florid face, and the finger-nails of his right hand were remarkably long. These are only a few indications,' he added with what we may be sure was more than a hint of condescension, 'but they may assist you'.

Lestrade and Gregson, Watson noticed, 'glanced at each other with an incredulous smile'.

'If this man was murdered,' asked Lestrade, 'How was it done?'

'Poison,' said Sherlock Holmes curtly, and strode off.[1]

During the years in which Holmes was managing to put Scotland Yard 'on the right scent', the age of the private detective of fact was already passing. But for many years after the creation of the Metropolitan Police in 1829, there was no special detective force, and criminal investigation remained largely in the hands of those who had been detectives in the past. The private detective of modern fiction is not, then, so much a myth as an anachronism. But the myth of this private investigator, brilliant, wily and astute, always able to outwit the stolid, unimaginative man from Scotland Yard has been slow to die.

The most celebrated of the early fictional detectives were, admittedly, Scotland Yard men. In 1852 Charles Dickens introduced to the readers of *Bleak House* the character of Inspector Bucket, 'a stoutly-built, steady-looking, sharp-eyed man in black of about the middle age'.[2]

Bucket is a pleasant fellow who 'notices things in general, with a face as unchanging as the great mourning ring on his little finger, or the brooch, composed of not much diamond and a good deal of setting which he wears in his shirt'.[3] He is 'mildly studious in his observation of human nature, on the whole a benignant philosopher not disposed to be severe upon the follies of mankind ... To outward appearance rather languishing for want of an object. He is in the friendliest condition towards his species, and will drink with most of them. He is free with his money, affable in his manners, innocent in his conversation.'[4]

But Bucket is a clever rather than a brilliant detective and although based in large part on Inspector Charles Frederick Field, whom Dickens so greatly if patronizingly admired, he remains within his creator's pages a somewhat shadowy and lifeless figure.

This cannot be said of Sergeant Richard Cuff. In *The Moonstone*, published in 1868, Wilkie Collins described this Scotland Yard detective as

'A grizzled, elderly man, so miserably lean that he looked as if he had not got an ounce of flesh on his bones in any part of him. He was dressed all in decent black, with a white cravat round his neck. His face was as sharp as a hatchet, and the skin of it was as yellow and dry and withered as an autumn leaf. His eyes, of a steely light grey, had a very disconcerting trick, when they encountered your eyes, of looking as if they expected something more from you than you were aware of yourself. His walk was soft; his voice was melancholy; his long lanky fingers were hooked like claws.'[5]

Despite his depressing appearance, however, and although he was rarely amused, Cuff had a pleasant, dry humour. When he whistled *The Last Rose of Summer* it sounded 'the most melancholy tune going', but he had an endearing passion for rose-growing; and when he interviewed anyone his voice was dispiriting but as he tried 'his luck drearily this way and that way' and fired 'shot after shot, as it were, at random, on the chance of hitting something,' he showed a wonderful patience.[6]

To some degree his character was founded upon that of Chief Inspector Jonathan Whicher, some of whose cases were described in a series of articles in *Household Words*, where he is called 'Sergeant Witchem'.[7] Inspector Whicher had been in charge of investigations into the murder of the three-year-old Savile Kent whose body had been found with his throat cut in a privy near the house in Wiltshire where he lived. Whicher applied for a warrant for the arrest of Constance Kent, Savile's sister, but she was later discharged through lack of evidence. She afterwards confessed to the crime and although her confession has since been considered suspect, Whicher's reputation as one of the most skilful detective officers of the day was increased by it.

Before Whicher had arrived in Wiltshire, the local police, in their appalling incompetence, had destroyed most of the evidence; and the stupidity of the regrettably real Superintendent Foley was Wilkie Collins's source for the ineptitude of the fictional Superintendent Seegrave, the pompous local policeman whose activities persuaded Franklin Blake that a cleverer head was needed to solve the mystery of the missing moonstone.

But although the deductions of Sergeant Cuff, the police detective, are quick and clever, Wilkie Collins allows him to make the sort of human mistakes which, twenty years later, were not permitted by Conan Doyle to the private detective, Sherlock Holmes.

Sherlock Holmes's consciousness of his own almost invariable infallibility is, nevertheless, one of his most endearing qualities. Through Boswell's eyes we grow to love Samuel Johnson; through the devoted Dr Watson's eyes we grow to share his affection for the often infuriating Holmes.

Holmes's conceit does not allow him to admit that he had ever had a predecessor of any talent. Edgar Allan Poe's Auguste Dupin, whose adventures were related in the *Murders in the Rue Morgue*, was dismissed as 'a very inferior fellow' whose trick 'of breaking in on his friends' thoughts with an apropos remark after a quarter of an hour's silence' was 'really very showy and superficial'. Emile Gaboriau's Lecoq was, also, in his opinion unworthy of comparison with himself. The mention of his name made Holmes sniff 'sardonically. "Lecoq was a miserable bungler," he said, in an angry voice; "he had only one thing to recommend him and that was his energy. That book made me positively ill. The question was how to identify an unknown poisoner. I could have done it in twenty-four hours. Lecoq took six months or so. It might be made a text-book for detectives to teach them what to avoid." '[8]

In time, Watson grew accustomed to Holmes's conceit and 'bumptious style of conversation', but although he had found him 'certainly not a difficult man to live with' on first acquaintance, he later discovered that he had several tiresome habits. He was a heavy smoker and on occasions 'littered the carpet round his chair with cigarette ends' or filled the rooms at Baker Street with smoke from the 'reeking amber of his pipe'. He took drugs and often for days on end 'was in a mood which his friends would call taciturn and others morose. He ran out and in, smoked incessantly, played snatches on his violin, sank into reveries, devoured sandwiches at irregular hours, and hardly answered the casual questions which I put to him.'[9]

But it was difficult in the end not to like Holmes and impossible not to feel the force of his personality. And although Conan Doyle himself believed that character could only be developed in the detective story at the expense of the plot, this idiosyncratic consulting detective of Baker Street was, despite the fragmentation of his character which Desmond MacCarthy and other critics have noticed, a creation of genius. And like all such creations his example has been closely followed. Sexton Blake even lived in the same street; Nero Wolfe shared at least his vanity; no memorable private detective since his time has been refused a personality in some way eccentric. G. K. Chesterton's Father Brown, A. E. W. Mason's Hanaud, R. Austin Freeman's Dr Thorndyke all showed, before the First World War began, that the tradition of idiosyncrasy was being closely followed. The tradition was still strong after the War, for even when the detective story became a kind of intellectual puzzle some sort of extravagant characterization was still deemed essential. Agatha Christie's Hercule Poirot, the pompous little Belgian dandy with his carefully tended moustaches, his distrust of fresh air, his hatred of the cold, his galoshes, his dogmatic manner and his intentionally uncertain command of the English language is an odd and delightful figure. Albert Campion, although his tirelessly and absurdly facetious conversation makes him a less likeable person, has as unconventional a personality. He lives above a police station in Bottle Street in rooms behind a door marked 'Mr Albert Campion. The Goods Dept'. He is, according to Margery Allingham, 'a tall, thin young man with a pale inoffensive face and vague eyes behind enormous horn-rimmed spectacles' and has 'a well-bred, slightly high-pitched voice'. John Dickson Carr, who as Carter Dickson has invented the highly eccentric Sir Henry Merrivale, has another curious hero in Dr Fell who lives at 1 Adelphi Terrace. Fell is 'vast' and 'ruddy-faced' and wears eye-glasses on a black ribbon. He is jovial and talkative and carries out chemical and photographic experiments with enormous excite-ment and industry. When at rest he sits 'wheezing over his double chins, his big mop of hair rumpled and his hands folded on his cane'. Like so many of the most successful private detectives he has a habit of talking to himself.

All these figures, however, are in a sense living beyond their time. The golden age of the detective story is already over. Before the Second World War, as Julian Symons has said, detective novels were written in accordance with 'conventions as strict as those of Restoration comedy'.[10] This, of course, contributed to their popularity. One of the conventions was that, apart from providing a puzzle which could be solved without trickery and a coherent story which could be followed without undue effort, the detective story should provide a moral. Virtue must triumph over evil, the guilty one must be revealed and punished, and the reader must be comforted with the knowledge that although he has been enjoy-ing the struggle—perhaps even enjoying vicariously the pleasures of sin—the moral order will prevail in the end. Since the War few fresh detectives have been created. The stories are clever—although few original ideas are left—and often well-written; they are still enjoyed by archbishops and frequently written by men who have distinguished themselves in other fields. Michael Innes (J.I.M. Stewart), Nicholas Blake (Cecil Day Lewis), and Edmund Crispin are all skilful writers of detective stories. But none of their books can hope to command the sales or the *réclame* which, for instance, *The Murder of Roger Ackroyd* commanded in 1926.

The heroes of today are more likely to appear in thrillers of suspense than in detective stories which are gradually being re-placed by science fiction. Certainly the emergence of popular heroes from Scotland Yard is now extremely rare.

The official detective when he does appear still tends usually to bear at least some relationship to Freeman Wills Crofts's brisk, homely and efficient Inspector French, 'a stout man in tweeds, rather under middle height, with a clean-shaven, good-humoured face and dark blue eyes which, though keen, twinkled as if at some perennially fresh private joke. His air was easy-going and leisurely, and he looked the type of man who could enjoy a good dinner and a good smoke-room story to follow.'[11] The detectives of Edgar Wallace were men of the same reliable stamp. Admittedly, Inspector Elk had an apparently obsessive hatred of education and entertained a curious selection of guests in his house in Gray's Inn Road, but he was shrewd and kindly and reassuring. Detective-Superintendent Craig had no discoverable idiosyncrasies at all and although Detective-Inspector James Sepping looked more like an 'athletic young man about town' than a detective and spoke in a drawl which he had brought 'from Oxford to the Metropolitan Police', he, too, was essentially a reliable man from a conventional mould. The fact that he was more expensively educated than most detectives was then something of an original touch but upper-class detectives subsequently became well-known figures. Dorothy L. Sayers's Lord Peter Wimsey and Ngaio Marsh's Chief Detective-Inspector Roderick Alleyn are two of them.

One of the very few official detectives who has caught the public imagination since the war, John Creasey's (or so far as these stories are concerned J. J. Marric's) Gideon, has no such social pretentions. Nor has Gideon's French counterpart, Maigret. Maigret is determinedly bourgeois. Brusque yet sympathetic, he enjoys a drink and a pipeful of tobacco, he understands the world but remains aloof from its temptations. He lives simply in a flat in the Boulevard Richard-Lenoir and for twenty years spent his holidays with relations in the same village in eastern France. He is, like his counterpart from Scotland Yard, contentedly married.

In this respect at least the traditional Scotland Yard detective resembles the most famous hero of the 1920's, Captain Hugh Drummond, D.S.O., M.C., whose devotion to his wife Phyllis was unquestionable. 'Bulldog' Drummond, as he is known to posterity is, superficially, in the Richard Hannay mould; for, like John Buchan's Major Richard Hannay, late of the Lennox Highlanders, he has had a brilliant war record and, like Hannay, he is as 'tough as a sjambok'. 'I thrive on the racket,' Hannay said when asked if he had recovered from his wounds, 'and I eat and sleep like a schoolboy.'[12] There is no doubt that Drummond did too. But Drummond did more than eat and sleep like a schoolboy, and it is difficult to picture him being entrusted by the Foreign Office with the vital mission of finding 'Greenmantle'.

Drummond's behaviour towards strangers was unnerving. He would 'burble at them genially, knock them senseless with a flow of greeting on the back and then resuscitate them with a large tankard of ale'. He stood 'just six feet in his socks, and turned the scale at over fourteen stone. And of that fourteen stone not one ounce was made up of superfluous fat. He was hard muscle and bone clean through ... he was a magnificent boxer, a lightning and deadly shot with a revolver, and utterly lovable'. He had a 'complete absense of fear', 'cool resourcefulness in danger,' and a 'marvellous gift of silent movement, especially in the dark'. It was 'his face and his boxing abilities that caused him to be nicknamed Bulldog. His mouth was big, and his nose was small and he would not have won a prize at a beauty show. In fact, it was only his eyes—clear and steady with a permanent glint of lazy humour in them—that redeemed his face from positive ugliness.'[13]

Stories of the exploits of this astonishing man sold in their hundreds of thousands. The book from which these descriptions of him have been taken was reprinted by Messrs Hodder and Stoughton thirty-two times in ten years. In it Carl Peterson, the arch-criminal, the unscrupulous swine, the unspeakable devil, the damnable wholesale murderer, the ineffable swine, as Drummond variously describes him, sends a foul brute of a poisonous spider, squat and utterly loathsome to Phyllis, his adorable wife. Phyllis cowers in a corner, her eyes dilated with horror.

'She fainted and her husband went berserk ... He hurled heavy pieces of furniture about as if they were out of a doll's house ... At last he had it and with a grunt of rage he hit it with the poker between the beady staring eyes. He hit it again and again.'

'If I ever lay hands on the man who sent this brute,' he said quietly, 'I will do the same to him.' In the end he does not kill Carl Peterson with a poker but grabs him by the throat, his eyes hard and merciless, and tries to force him to swallow some particularly virulent poison which the unspeakable devil has forced an English scientist to manufacture for him. The glass tips, the poison spills on Peterson's wrist and he dies in agony. Drummond previously had narrowly avoided a similar fate and as he risked falling into the ominous liquid in a desperate effort to save his chums, he called out to them, 'Cheer oh! old lads—and all that sort of rot ... You might—er—just tell—er you know, Phyllis and all that.' 'For a moment his voice faltered: then with that wonderful cheery grin of his, he turned to face certain death.'

But he is saved in the nick of time and is soon, in Phyllis's phrase, 'off on the warpath again'. Phyllis has compensations, though. Hugh is not a poor man. He has an expensive house in Brook Street and can afford both a maid and a butler who is a good egg although he behaves sometimes like a 'blithering juggins'. And Hugh does not gamble or get drunk; he smokes occasionally, enjoys a pot of ale, never looks at another woman and seems not to doubt that Phyllis would never look at another man. (Her attendance at a dance without Hugh one night passes without recorded comment by the chronicler of their adventures.) He appears to have had a violent antipathy for Jews and Communists, but then so perhaps had she. And despite his sudden accesses of rage and brutality, he is always kind and considerate to her; he loves animals, especially dogs—'topping little beasts'; he hob-nobs with Duchesses obscuring his 'extraordinary personality' by an 'air of fatuous nonsense'; and he has, after all, the distinction of being the leader of a gang of anti-criminals more dangerous by far, so one of his enemies said, 'than all the police of England'.

He was the last great hero of his type. By the time his creator, 'Sapper,' died, a new generation of heroes had already stolen the imagination of the English-speaking world. Dashiell Hammett, the first and perhaps the greatest of the writers in the new school of violent realism, and himself once a private detective in Pinkerton's Agency, published *The Maltese Falcon* in 1929 and *The Glass Key* in 1930. His heroes like those of Raymond Chandler, whose first successful book came out a decade later, incarnated, as Cyril Connolly has said, 'the rootless individualism of modern man, at war with criminals yet distrusted by authority'.[14] Philip Marlowe, Chandler's tough, weary, cynical, hard-boiled and hard-drinking 'private eye' from Los Angeles, is the epitome of these men. He fights criminals but the man who is also fighting them by more official methods is often, like Nulty, the detective-lieutenant attached to the 77th Street Division, a 'lean-jawed sourpuss with long yellow hands [and] a smile as cunning as a broken mouse-trap'. Marlowe is sometimes out of work and frequently in a savage temper. He is often to be discovered taking a drink from the bottle in his office desk. He smokes a pipe to look thoughtful when he is not thinking and cigarettes for pleasure. He is very quick witted and has a sardonic turn of phrase. When he sees a blonde he thinks she would 'make a bishop kick a hole in a stained glass window'; a cigarette on a stomach empty but for stale whisky tastes 'like a plumber's handkerchief'; an unwanted meal like 'a discarded mail bag'. It is difficult to think of him without remembering Humphrey Bogart. And his progeny, like that of Sherlock Holmes, is legion. In the United States in 1959 there were over sixty different television programmes which had a detective for a hero and very few were police detectives; nearly all were 'private eyes', 'smarter than the cops, craftier than the crooks, too quick to be caught and domesticated by the classiest doll'.[15] These 'private eyes' were invincible and improbable. They did not bear much resemblance to Hammett's Sam Spade or Chandler's Philip Marlowe—although both these characters were portrayed—and still less to the sadistic satires created by Mickey Spillane and other writers whose heroes have mashed up the lips of their dolls in the style of James M. Cain. But although prone to neither alcoholic nor sexual excesses they were nevertheless still able to enjoy life. They seemed to like their occasional drinks, their even rarer but obviously expensive meals, and their almost invariable winning of the beautiful girl in the end.

The odd man out in this company is Erle Stanley Gardner's Perry Mason, a shadowy figure with limited sensual appetites. He is not a private detective but a lawyer. His clients expect him to behave like a private detective in the preparation of their cases, however, and he obliges them. The reader can discover almost nothing about him. Very infrequently a clue is provided as to his appearance. He has, for instance, long legs. He runs his office, the reader is assured, 'without regard for appearances or conventions', for he has 'sufficient ability to scorn' them. Apart from his disregard of the conventions of the legal profession, he does not, however, appear to be an unconventional man. He is certainly not a *jouisseur*. He smokes, he drinks a little, he notices that women have 'seductive smiles' but he is never seduced. His face often wears 'a worried frown'. Sometimes his conversation barely escapes facetiousness and he has a poor sense of humour. His relationship with his secretary, Della Street, is equivocal. She is unbelievably competent, she calls him 'chief' and seems to be in love with him. She is inclined to look 'as crisply efficient as a nurse in a freshly starched uniform'. Very occasionally when they have a meal together or go dancing they enjoy 'one of those rare periods of intimacy which come to people who have worked together'. In *The Case of the Sleepwalker's Niece* he is actually discovered kissing her in the office. He draws her towards him with 'something of solemnity in his manner'. Della Street raises her half-parted lips to his eagerly; but then, there is a knock on the door and they suddenly break away from each other. At the end of *The Case of the Drowsy Mosquito* he asks her, somewhat ambivalently to marry him, but he seems relieved when she refuses.

Perry Mason's private behaviour and attitude are not, of course, at all characteristic of the modern hero. Despite his ruthless, forensic *expertise* Mason is an anachronistic figure; it is the older Philip Marlowe, cynical, hard-drinking, tough and sensual who epitomizes the new hero in America.

In England, too, the new hero enjoys women and food and drink in a way that Hugh Drummond had never done. Dennis Wheatley's Gregory Sallust is 'no ascetic'. He likes gambling, he enjoys eating expensive meals and drinking good wine, he knows 'from past experience that he could sweep most women off their feet inside a week' and would do so more often were he not such 'a lazy devil'. He is not good-looking but in a way quite different from 'Bulldog' Drummond, for his scarred, lean face with its thin lips has a sinister, 'almost satanic look'. He is not above using a broken bottle in a fight. He bears a more than superficial resemblance to Simon Templar known as 'The Saint', whose improbable adventures are recorded by Leslie Charteris. 'The Saint' is better looking than Gregory Sallust. His tanned face is 'cut in a mould of rather reckless humour' ... He has 'a rakish curve to his jaw', a 'careless backward curl of black hair', a 'gay filibuster's mouth'. But he has Gregory Sallust's elegance and charm and sexual fascination. He likes drinking martinis and making love and driving 'huge super-charged superstreamlined' sports cars. He is tall and he looks strong. Also he wears 'his clothes with a gay and careless kind of elegance'. He fights crime because he has to fight something and he does not much care whether he himself transgresses the law in doing so.

Undoubtedly the most skilfully conceived and most significant hero in this tradition is Ian Fleming's James Bond. Bond is a Secret Service Agent, one of the very few who are licensed to kill on active service.

He has 'a dark, clean-cut face, with a three-inch scar showing whitely down the sunburned skin of the right cheek. The [blue] eyes are wide and level under straight rather long black brows. The hair is black, parted on the left, and carelessly brushed so that a thick black comma falls down over the right eyebrow. The longish straight nose runs down to a short upper lip below which is a wide and firmly drawn but cruel mouth. The line of the jaw is straight and firm.'[16]

He is an all-round athlete, an expert pistol shot, boxer and knife-thrower; he speaks French and German; he smokes heavily—he has special cigarettes with three gold bands on them—he drinks a lot and is frequently to be found in bed with young women. He was created a CMG in 1953.

His $4\frac{1}{2}$-litre battleship-grey Bentley with the supercharger by Amherst Villiers is described as his 'only personal hobby'. He drives it 'hard and well and with an almost sensual pleasure'.[17] His other interests are gambling—he loves the 'dry riffle of the cards and the constant unemphatic drama of the quiet figures round the green tables'—drinking champagne and his own special ice-cold drink of Gordon's gin, vodka and Kina Lillet and eating well-cooked food—the ordering and eating of one expensive meal takes up five of Ian Fleming's pages.[18] Breakfast is his favourite meal.

'When he was stationed in London it was always the same. It consisted of very strong coffee, from De Bry in New Oxford Street, brewed in an American Chemex, of which he drank two large cups, black and without sugar. The single egg, in the dark blue egg cup with a gold ring round the top, was boiled for three and a third minutes.[19]

These same faddy, pedantic and expensive tastes are reflected in the clothes he wears and in the way he talks to barmen and waiters. He is a snob and a perfectionist although his own taste is sometimes questionable. He lives in a 'comfortable flat' in a square in Chelsea off the King's Road and has an elderly Scots housekeeper.

He is tortured with distressing frequency and in a variety of unpleasant and often surrealistic ways. Once he is tied naked to a chair from which the cane seat has been cut out and is beaten from below by a 'three-foot-long carpet beater in twisted cane'.[20] And once he is tied to a polished metal table with a slit in it and cruelly massaged by a Korean with a naked chest and a bowler hat while a whirring circular saw slowly travels up the slit between his legs.[21]

There is something of the sadist and of the masochist in his own nature. About to climb—severely burned and with the marks of a giant squid's suckers on his skin—into a sleeping bag with a girl in Jamaica his eyes become 'fierce blue slits'. He bites her hard until she gives a little scream and wrenches his head away by the hair.[22] At the end of another adventure his 'passionate, rather cruel mouth' comes 'ruthlessly down' on the mouth of a girl who has come into his cabin 'wearing nothing but a grey fisherman's jersey that was decent by half an inch'.[23] All his girls have lovely breasts and he rarely fails to feel the 'peak hard with desire under his fingers'.

These feelings of sexual excitement do not appear to trouble the calm unemotional life of Della Street and the picture of Phyllis Drummond's 'shifting languidly' as she lies naked and moaning on a bed is inconceivable.

But then the idea of Hugh Drummond or Richard Hannay cheating at cards, as Bond does, or playing an unsportsmanlike game of golf, as Bond also does, is inconceivable, too. And this is at least part of the reason for Bond's immense popularity. Not only is he peculiarly talented as an agent and a lover, a sportsman and a connoisseur of fashionable luxuries, but he is the epitome of the bad man which every good man has inside him, wanting to get out.

Whether or not the admiration which Bond, as a man and as a professional murderer, arouses amongst his numerous devotees and whether or not the feelings of wonder and approval which far less skilful writers than Ian Fleming so easily evoke for their more violent and more callous heroes, have any real importance in the etiology of crime, there is little doubt that the truly popular hero of today has even fewer conventional virtues than the actively criminal hero of the past. That this is of sociological significance cannot be denied.

Part V

THE DETECTION OF CRIME

THE DETECTION OF CRIME

'You mentioned your name as if I should recognize it, but beyond the obvious facts that you are a bachelor, a solicitor, a Freemason, and an asthmatic, I know nothing whatever about you.'

SHERLOCK HOLMES, 1893

(i)

The Bow Street Runners survived for ten years after the Metropolitan Police Act of 1829, and, with the paid constables of the Police Offices created in 1792, continued to be the country's only detectives, available as before for individual hire, 'private speculators in the detection of crime,'[1] more concerned now with jewel robberies than with murders, which, being a less profitable field, they left to the new police. They were, though, still regarded as the only real experts in detection, an opinion which the magistrates and particularly the Chief Magistrate at Bow Street, Sir Richard Birnie, and his successor Sir Frederick Roe, both of them jealous of the new system, did much to foster. There were other reasons, too, which hindered the establishment of a special police department devoted to criminal investigation.

The prejudice against a professional police force, despite its obvious success, had been slow enough to die; the prejudice against a professional detective force died even more slowly. Government detectives smacked altogether too much of foreign methods. The French police system of the *ancien régime* had apparently survived, in its essentials, both the Revolution and Napoleon's Empire and was still continually pointed out as an instrument of tyranny and political espionage which would inevitably serve as a model for a force of British detectives under Home Office direction.

The activities of the extraordinary Eugène-François Vidocq had done much to increase this fear. Vidocq was a former army officer who had been sentenced to eight years hard labour for forging an order for the release of a prisoner in Lille gaol. He had been sent to the galleys at Brest, had escaped twice and been recaptured, but after escaping a third time he had successfully disappeared into the Paris underworld from which he had emerged in 1809 to offer his services as a police spy to the Head of the Second Division which was responsible for the central direction of those *Officiers de Paix* who were attached to the twelve *arrondissements* of Paris. As in England at this time law enforcement had become a highly localized affair, the *Officiers de Paix* losing interest in criminals once they had crossed over into another *arrondissement* for which they were not responsible.[2] Vidocq was to alter that. His offer to serve as a police spy was accepted on condition that he went back to prison in Paris and operated from there. He was so successful that when he came out of prison, he was made an agent of the Prefecture and began the process of development which was to transform the criminal investigation department of the Prefecture into the highly efficient *Sûreté*, now the *Police Judiciaire*.

He began with only four men but by the 1820's he had twenty-eight. His offices were in a dark, forbidding house, Number Six, Petite Rue Sainte-Anne, leading from the Sainte-Chapelle to the quai des Orfèvres. And from here he directed a network of spies, informers, and ex-convicts like himself, in a war against crime which was completely successful. His unrivalled knowledge of the underworld and its ways, his reliance on criminals to catch criminals, his unprecedented files of criminal records, his daring raids on criminal strongholds were all reasons for this success. In 1817 with only twelve full-time assistants he was responsible for over eight hundred arrests.[3]·

Ten years later he was not only famous, he was rich. He retired from police work and started a paper-mill which employed only ex-convicts. This venture was a failure, but the *Sûreté*, since he had left it, had also been a failure and in 1832 Henri Gisquet, the new Prefect of Police, asked him to return to his office near the quai des Orfèvres as official chief of the *Sûreté*. But Vidocq's days of triumph were now almost over. A scandal involving one of his agents who was imprisoned for complicity in a daring burglary which, it was widely believed, had been organized by Vidocq himself, led to his resignation. He opened a private inquiry agency which was suppressed by his jealous enemies at the Prefecture and he died in poverty in 1857.[4]

His enormous energy and skill in tracking down criminals amounted almost to genius, but he was throughout his life regarded with suspicion. The French Police of the Restoration, already attacked for their political bias were now, because of him, attacked again for being pervaded by criminals. The fact that a man with a criminal record was given such authority 'had a bad effect', Baron Pasquier who had approved Vidocq's original appointment, admitted. 'It contributed much on several occasions to the discrediting of the police.'[5]

In England Vidocq's reputation for instigating many of the crimes he detected was emphasized by all those who wished to prevent anything like the Paris *Sûreté* being created in London. At least, so they could comfort themselves, the new Metropolitan Police wore a uniform and this in itself seemed a safeguard against the spying activities of a secret police—that is, until the case of Constable William Popay made it clear that Peel's 'cut-throat mob' were not, after all, above such methods themselves.

Popay, an energetic and zealous constable in Walworth, wanting to obtain information about the revolutionary activities of the National Political Union which had been formed in London after the rejection of the Reform Bill by the House of Lords, represented himself as an advanced Radical and attended the meetings of a particularly violent 'class' of the Union in Camberwell. The Union attacked the House of Commons as being full of 'borough-mongers' creatures,' the House of Lords as being a 'hereditary hospital of incurable national nuisances', the King as 'the puppet of a base scoundrelocracy'[6] and above all the new police as being an 'organization of spies employed by the Government to provoke, betray and eventually enslave the working classes'. One day the enterprising Constable Popay was seen by a fellow member of the National Political Union sitting in a police office inspecting a ledger. He was immediately recognized as the fiery young artist who for months had been inciting his comrades to violence, insulting the Government and denouncing the police.

The Union petitioned the House of Commons, protesting against 'policemen disguised in clothing of various descriptions' living amongst them and 'seeking their lives'.[7] While the Union's charges were patently exaggerated, the petition was one that the House could not ignore and a Committee was appointed to inquire into the allegation of widespread espionage. The Committee found Popay's conduct reprehensible and asked for his dismissal;[8] and although they did not complain of the 'occasional employment of policemen in plain clothes' they thought that such employment should be strictly limited and solemnly deprecated 'any approach to the employment of spies'.[9]

Hopes of the early establishment of an efficient detective force had been dashed. The Bow Street Runners were disbanded in 1839 but no professional detectives took their place. Three years later, however, a particularly savage murder was committed and the murderer, Daniel Good, was not arrested for some time. The incapacity of the new police was again compared in the newspapers with the shrewdness and cunning of the old Bow Street Runners. Discerning readers, though, were less inclined to accept these unfair verdicts now and were beginning to realize that Peel's 'blue lobsters' were not so terrible after all. And when Good was arrested the Commissioners were able to persuade the Home Secretary to sanction a small detective branch, of two inspectors and six sergeants, as an experiment at Scotland Yard.

Charles Dickens interviewed these men at the offices of his new twopenny weekly *Household Words* and found them, in his almost boyish enthusiasm, far preferable to those whom he extravagantly derided as the old 'humbugs' of Bow Street. But there remained 'many great difficulties in the way of a detective system' which was still, so the Commissioners wrote in their report in 1869, 'viewed with the greatest suspicion and jealousy by the majority of Englishmen' and was 'entirely foreign to the habits and feelings of the nation'.[10] This suspicion was greatly increased eight years later when the details of a Scotland Yard scandal were revealed to a horrified country. It appeared that three senior inspectors had been accepting large sums of money from a gang of swindlers which operated fraudulent betting agencies on an immense scale. The inspectors had not only taken bribes and commissions, they were found guilty, too, of intercepting telegrams from Paris addressed to Scotland Yard and of forging telegrams purporting to come from Scotland Yard and intended for police authorities in Holland.[11] The disclosures came 'as a thunderclap to the community', the Attorney General said dramatically, 'and spread over England the greatest possible alarm'.[12]

But they had, like the murder committed by Daniel Good, an ultimately beneficial effect on the development of Scotland Yard, the whole organization of which was completely and immediately overhauled on lines recommended by Howard Vincent, a young barrister who had made a special study of the Paris police. A separate detective force, with Vincent himself at its head, as Director of Criminal Investigations, was formed in 1878. The first years of the Criminal Investigation Department were unhappy ones. The uniformed policemen resented the higher pay and superior status given to the detectives who, some of them suspected, might be used to spy on them as the *contrôle générale* did in Paris. The experiment of appointing gentlemen of good education as detectives without preliminary training as policemen, was a complete failure. And the accusations that the police were sinister *agents provocateurs*, as they had been at the time of Popay, were repeated in 1880 when a police officer's wife admitted in court that she had pretended to a chemist, named Titley, that she wanted him to help her procure an abortion. Apart from accusations of underhand methods and inefficiency, the police had also to cope with an increasing crime rate in the 1880's, complicated by the dynamite war waged by the Fenians, by riots of unemployed labourers in the West End, and by the alarming activities of growing numbers of East End anarchists. But all these troubles, serious as they were, seemed insignificant in the summer of 1888 when London became the scene of a series of murders which aroused an unreasoning fear comparable only to that excited by the Ratcliffe Highway murders of 1811.

The series began on 6 August 1888 when a thirty-five-year-old woman, Martha Turner, was found on a stairway in Whitechapel with her throat deeply slit by a long-bladed knife. Soon the police were being subjected to attacks of such deep virulence that the Commissioner, General Sir Charles Warren, a military formalist, who decided that the only means of dealing with the problem was to track the murderer down with bloodhounds, was forced to resign.

Martha Turner's murder on 6 August was followed on 31 August by that of another woman Anna Nicholls, aged forty-two. Eight days later a third woman, Annie Chapman, aged forty-eight, was found dead in a backyard in Hanbury Street. All three of these women were prostitutes, all three were drunkards and the throats of all three had been savagely cut. The bodies of Anna Nicholls and Annie Chapman had, in addition, been systematically mutilated.

On 26 September 1888, the Central News Agency received a letter written in red ink.

'Dear Boss,' it read, 'I keep on hearing the police have caught me, but they won't find me just yet. I have laughed when they look so clever and talk about being on the right track. That joke about leather apron gave me real fits. I am down on whores and I shan't quit ripping them till I do get buckled. Grand work this last job was. I gave the lady no time to squeal. How can they catch me now. I love my work and want to start again. You will soon hear of me with my funny little games. I saved some of the proper red stuff in a ginger beer bottle over the last job to write with but it went thick like glue and I can't use it. Red ink is fit enough I hope, *ha, ha*. The next job I do I shall clip the lady's ears off and send to the police officers just for jolly wouldn't you. Keep this letter back till I do a bit more work, then give it out straight. My knife's so nice and sharp I want to get to work right away if I get a chance. Good luck.

Yours truly, Jack the Ripper.

They say I'm a doctor *ha ha*.[13]

The letter was photographed and printed on a poster which was circulated in thousands all over London. But Jack the Ripper remained at large and on 30 September the bodies of two more prostitutes were found. One was Elizabeth Stride, aged forty-five, the other Catherine Eddowes, aged forty-three. The throats of both had been cut, both bodies had been mutilated and attempts had been made to cut off their ears. All five murders had been committed between eleven at night and four in the morning in an area of about one square mile; and although all the victims were middle-aged and drunken prostitutes from the East End, fear of meeting a death like theirs spread fast throughout London and thousands of respectable people locked and bolted their doors as soon as it was dusk. What were the police doing? the newspapers demanded, and the answers did not comfort them.

On 9 November in a room in Spitalfields the body of Mary Kelly was found. She was younger than the other victims and had been mutilated with an even greater brutality. Her throat had been cut, her breasts cut off, her heart and liver cut out and laid upon a nearby table. The outcry against the police who could permit such a monster to roam the streets of the greatest city in the world reached a new pitch. The murderer, it was even suggested, was a policeman.

Chief Inspector Alberline, who was in charge of the investigations, believed on the contrary that he was a Polish barber who went to live in Jersey City; Sir Melville MacNaghten, later an Assistant Commissioner of the Metropolitan Police, said that he was a man who 'committed suicide on or about the 10 November 1889'; Sir Basil Thomson, one of Sir Melville's successors as Assistant Commissioner, said that the C.I.D. believed the murders to be 'the work of an insane Russian doctor'. Certainly a Russian barber, who had a knowledge of surgery, was working in Walworth at the time of the murders and had assisted a doctor at a Camberwell clinic. He was suspected of having murdered a girl in Paris before he came to London and after his return to Russia he was arrested in St Petersburg for the murder of a woman in 1891. He died in an asylum and was named by the Russian Secret Police as the man 'wanted for the murder of five women in the East Quarter of London in 1888'.[14]

Whether or not this man was Jack the Ripper, it was certain that Scotland Yard had been unable to bring the murders home to him or to anyone else. There had been detectives in the Metropolitan Police since 1842, newspapers protested, but not one of them in more than forty years had proved worthy of his hire. It was a sweeping charge, but an understandable one. For many years after the Bow Street Runners had ceased to exist as a detective force, individual Runners, who had gone into business as private detectives, were consulted by victims of crime who preferred to pay their fees rather than to call in the official detectives at Scotland Yard.

The clients of Henry Goddard, for instance, very rarely considered the possibility of asking the new police to help them. Goddard was a Bow Street Runner until August 1839 when the Runners were disbanded and thereafter he became a private detective, obtaining most of his work through the agency of John and Daniel Forrester who were employed as quasi-official detectives by the Corporation of the City of London. Goddard was so successful that he became the first Chief Constable of the County of Northampton in 1840. He resigned nine years later and, returning to London, he was given an appointment in the department of the Gentleman Usher of the Black Rod at the House of Lords which allowed him enough spare time to resume his private detective work. He was still practising in that capacity as late as 1864 when he acted for the Gresham Life Assurance Society in tracking down their Secretary who had absconded with some of the Society's funds. Although the man caused a notice of his death to be published in *The Times* and had gone abroad under an assumed name, Goddard was able to trace him to Scott's Hotel in Melbourne, Australia.[15]

Goddard travelled extensively in the service of his clients and in 1853 he went to America in an effort to trace John Todd, a distiller who was supposed to have fled there from Newcastle-on-Tyne with ten thousand pounds belonging to his creditors. Goddard sailed from Liverpool and in eleven days arrived in New York where he stayed at Collins Hotel.

'I engaged the service of Gill Hayes, the renowned American police-officer, for his assistance in going with me to make enquiries of bankers and ship-owners,' Goddard wrote in his memoirs. 'But from these we could not obtain any information. We then visited and made enquiries at all the hotels and boarding houses, looking over their books; not that we expected to see the name of Todd, but as it is the custom for all travellers to write their names in these books we thought it probable, as we were in possession of his signature, that we might trace some letters in an assumed name.'

But as they had no luck, Goddard then decided that Todd had probably made his way West as so many fugitives did. So he packed his things, and sailed up the Hudson to Albany to make inquiries there. Believing that local land agents would know 'all newcomers for miles around' he went to see them all from Albany to Buffalo, from Buffalo to Detroit, from Detroit to Chicago, from Chicago to Milwaukee and from Milwaukee to Janesville. And at Janesville, after having asked thousands of questions and skilfully followed his long and devious trail, he found his man.[16]

The Bow Street Runner was helped in his work by an intimate knowledge of the underworld, on the edge of which he often lived and into which he was sometimes accepted as a go-between. The Scotland Yard detective had no such advantage. He had not yet developed his later ability to acquire a knowledge of it from observation rather than participation, and his use of 'coppers' narks' was limited by the wary eye of a suspicious public ready at any moment to accuse him of methods 'entirely foreign to the habits and feelings of the nation'. Cases in which detectives could feel justified in resorting 'to artifice', Sir William Harcourt, the Home Secretary said in the 1840's 'must be rare indeed. As a rule, the police ought not to set traps for people.'[17] This was then an almost universally held opinion.

Towards the end of the nineteenth century, however, the prejudice against the 'prying snoopers' of Scotland Yard began slowly to die. The widely publicized investigations that led to the arrests of James Neill Cream and Milson and Fowler, the Muswell Hill murderers, demonstrated that the official detectives could be quite as shrewd as the hundreds of private ones whose fictional exploits provided so much material for the cheap books and magazines which poured from the presses of Victorian London. And in the early years of the new century the trials of Robert Wood and Crippen encouraged the belief of an increasingly admiring public that although Scotland Yard might make mistakes, its organization, experience and wealth of records made it unlikely that the detection of crime could be placed in more capable hands. In 1928 this belief in the growing prowess of Scotland Yard was deepened by the arrest of two men for a murder which had shocked the country. The investigations which led to their arrest are characteristic of modern police detection at its most thorough and painstaking.

At about six o'clock in the morning of 27 September in the previous year, Police Constable George William Gutteridge was found lying dead by the side of a road at How Green near the Essex village of Stapleford Abbots. He had been killed by two shots fired at his head at close range and while he was lying on the ground, two more shots had been fired at him, one at each eye. He was holding a pencil in his hand, his notebook was near by and his whistle was hanging loose from his breast pocket on its chain. Two bullets were found, one in his clothing, the other imbedded in the earth by the roadside, and these were the only clues. There were signs that a car had stopped suddenly and driven into a bank, but the marks were not clear.

The Chief Constable of Essex decided to ask for the help of Scotland Yard, and a Chief Inspector, James Berrett, and a detective sergeant, came out from London immediately and set to work with the help of the Essex detectives. They began a long series of interviews which were soon to number more than a thousand.

Misleading information came to them from scores of local people anxious to help or to appear to help, to seem important to themselves and others, or merely to cause trouble. The activities of an unpopular and eccentric man, who in earlier times would have been denounced as a wizard, were carefully investigated because local suspicion about him was so strong, although it seemed unlikely that he knew anything about the murder and, in fact, did not. A local criminal, also suspected by the villagers, was watched and questioned. Tramps were questioned, gunsmiths and garage owners, friends and neighbours of the dead constable were interviewed; but little was discovered which seemed revealing and what seemed revealing turned out to be the fruits of gossip, malice or resentment. The Criminal Record Office were asked for the names of criminals at liberty whose past records and whose known methods suggested that they might have been responsible for the crime. Their whereabouts on the night of the murder were carefully checked and one of them was discovered to be missing from his lodgings and to have left behind him some cuttings from newspaper reports about the crime. His description was circulated in the *Police Gazette* and his photograph was published in the newspapers. He came to Scotland Yard and cleared himself of suspicion.

There were, as is usual in any murder case, false confessions. A man gave himself up at Basingstoke and a detective drove sixty miles in a thick fog to talk to him as his story seemed superficially credible, only to discover that he was an epileptic who had confessed to another murder a few months before. There were, as is also usual in any murder case, false clues. A revolver was found by a boy beside the Thames at Hammersmith on the day after the murder and the following day a tin of cartridges was found on a plot of waste ground nearby. After careful examination by a gun expert, the revolver and the cartridges were found to have no connection with each other. There were, however, some fingerprints on the cartridge tin and these were then sent to the Finger-Print Bureau to be compared with the twenty thousand prints of known car thieves and housebreakers. Once again the inquiries were unrewarding.

But if, so the police believed and still believe, every line of inquiry was pursued assiduously, however unpromising it seemed, sooner or later some helpful clue would be uncovered. And two helpful clues were uncovered now.

At the post-mortem examination it was noticed that there were marks of black powder on the constable's face, indicating that the cartridge used by his murderer must have been of a pattern long since obsolete; and under one of the seats of a Morris Cowley found abandoned in a passage-way in Brixton was discovered a cartridge case. The car was one which had been stolen on the night of the murder from a doctor's garage in Billericay a few miles from the scene of the murder.

On the running board of the car were marks which a Home Office analyst discovered to be bloodstains, and on the near side wheels were particles of earth and dried grass which were found to correspond with the soil and grass in the bank at How Green. Photographs of the car and things missing from it—including the doctor's attaché case—were circulated in the *Police Gazette* and in the newspapers. At Stapleford Abbots and Billericay the inquiries intensified until the police had called at every shop, railway station and garage in the neighbourhood and had interviewed hundreds more people. Over five hundred houses were visited along routes which the car might have driven between Billericay, where—according to a neighbour of the doctor who had heard it started up—it was stolen at half past two in the morning, and Brixton, where it was found at six o'clock. And so the police were eventually able to trace out the circuitous route which the car had followed in the driver's anxiety to avoid the main road back to London. It appeared from the evidence of the fifteen people who claimed to have heard it and from the mileage, recorded on the speedometer and checked with the doctor's records, that the car had been driven at high speed. It seemed logical, then, to suppose that a man who could drive so fast along twisting country lanes, not all of which were signposted, must know the district well; and there was at least one man with a criminal record known to carry a gun, who did know the district and who could drive a car, being, in fact, as he later described himself, 'a motor engineer'.

His name was Frederick Guy Browne. But although he had very recently come out of Dartmoor, having served a sentence of four years' penal servitude for fraud, he could not be found. He had wanted to serve every day of his term, so he told his wife and friends, because he did not want to have to report to the police when he was released. Before long, though, the police called on him.

On 13 November he had stolen a car in Tooting and had taken it up to Sheffield to sell it. While driving it in a reckless way through the middle of the town, he was reported to the police by a van driver who had had to drive into a wall to avoid a collison. He gave a false name and address and presented somebody else's driving licence. But diligent inquiries by the Sheffield police, helped by an informer who had been in Dartmoor with Browne, led to his arrest at his Battersea garage in January 1928. 'What I can see of it,' Browne said morosely to the detective who arrested him, 'I shall have to get a machine gun for you bastards next time.'

Browne was charged with the theft of the car in Tooting and held in custody while the police collected evidence on which he could be charged instead with the murder of Police Constable Gutteridge. There seemed no doubt that he had committed the murder, for found in his car and in his office were not only the several revolvers he delighted in possessing, but a number of surgical implements which had belonged to the Billericay doctor. He vehemently denied the murder, however, insisting that he was at home in London with his wife all night on 26 and 27 September. He kept loaded revolvers, he said, 'to frighten anyone in case they interfered with' him. He had been robbed while taking cars to the country in the past and he did not want to be caught again. The medical tweezers, lint bandages, freezing fluid and high volatile spirit 'were kept in the garage for cases of emergency and accidents' and some of them were 'bought at Sheffield at a chemist's near the Infirmary—opposite in fact'. He had heard about the murder but that was all. 'I do not take the newspapers in,' he said, 'because I do not read them. I have not the patience . . . I have had no connection with the murder of P.C. Gutteridge, and personally am not interested in it, because it does not interest me.'

Having obtained this curious statement from Browne, Chief Inspector Berrett left for the north to talk to the informer who had helped the Sheffield police in their search for the dangerous driver the previous November. This man said that after the murder Browne had often been seen with a man called 'Pat', and he agreed to come to Scotland Yard to try to identify 'Pat' from photographs in the Criminal Record Office. He was able to do so. 'Pat' was found to be an ex-convict, William Henry Kennedy with a long series of convictions for crimes ranging from 'loitering' and indecent exposure to 'frequenting' and housebreaking. Kennedy told a story quite different from Browne's.

He well remembered 26 September, he admitted. Browne, for

whom he worked as a book-keeper and general clerk, had asked him to go with him to Billericay to steal a car. They had stolen the Morris Cowley and Browne drove it through 'country lanes at great pace' until they reached 'a kind of main road on the way to Ongar'.

'When we got some distance up this road,' Kennedy said, 'we saw someone who stood on the bank and flashed his lamp as a signal to stop. He did so quite willingly, and when the person came up we saw it was a policeman ... The policeman came up close to the car and stood near Browne and asked him where he was going and where he had come from ... The policeman flashed his light in both our faces and was at this time standing close to the running board on the off side. He then asked me if I knew the number of the car, and Browne said, "You'll see it on the front of the car." The policeman said, "Yes, I know the number, but do you?" I said, "Yes, I can give you the number," and said, "TW6120". He said, "Very well, I'll take particulars," put his torch back in his pocket and pulled out his notebook, and was in the act of writing when I heard a report quickly followed by another one. I saw the policeman stagger back and fall over by the bank at the hedge. I said to Browne, "What have you done?" and then saw he had a large Webley revolver in his hand. He said, "Get out quick." I immediately got out and went round to the policeman, who was lying on his back, and Browne came over and said, "I'll finish the—," and I said, "for God's sake, don't shoot anymore, the man's dying," as he was groaning.

The policeman's eyes were open and Browne, addressing him, said, "What are you looking at me like that for?" and stooping down, shot him at close range through both eyes ... He gave me the revolver and told me to load it while he drove on. I loaded it and in my excitement I dropped an empty shell in the car.'

Kennedy's long statement, so his counsel later pleaded, 'had been pumped out of him by four hours of interrogation, of promises, hopes and threats,' when he 'was in such a state of mental helplessness that he did not know what he was doing or signing'. It was an allegation which the police have frequently had to face since, and have sometimes had difficulty in refuting satisfactorily. But on this occasion, there was no doubt that it had been entirely voluntary—Kennedy's wife who had come to Scotland Yard from Liverpool with him had urged him to tell the truth—and he had been given ample opportunity to eat and to rest before he said anything. The magistrate at the police court admitted the statement in evidence and later, at his trial at the Central Criminal Court, Kennedy, declining to go into the witness box, said that it represented his complete defence.

It was unfortunate for Browne that, although the statement was not evidence against him at his trial, it had been published in the newspapers after the police court proceedings. Presumably the members of the jury had read it and were unable to put it out of their minds as the judge frequently asked them to do. The freedom of newspapers to print evidence given in magistrates' and coroners' courts seems to point to at least one unsatisfactory feature in the English system of criminal legal procedure. Notwithstanding Browne's undoubted guilt of a savage crime, it was argued at the time that the law had not been fair to him. It was also argued that it was unfair that the law should have allowed the police to keep both him and Kennedy in custody so long while evidence to convict them was being collected.[18]

But these feelings were not widespread. Most people felt proud of detectives who could investigate a case with such thoroughness, intelligence and patience. They read with admiration that they had been able to prove that the cartridge case found in the car could only have been fired in Browne's revolver and in no other revolver, that the unused cartridges found in Browne's possession included obsolete ones containing black powder and cordite, that the two bullets found at How Green had been fired by charges of black powder and cordite, and that the marks on the constable's face had been made by either black powder or cordite.

The police could not, of course, have proved any of these things without the help of experts in a science that was relatively new. Today forensic science is as integral a part of police work as the use of the traditional and still indispensable 'copper's nark'; but for centuries the possible uses of science in crime detection remained unknown or disregarded.

(ii)

In the autumn of 1786 a young woman, her throat savagely cut, was found dead in a cottage in Kirkcudbright. On the path which led to the cottage there was a trail of foot-prints and beside the prints there were spots of blood. Neither the murder nor the clues which the murderer had left behind him were remarkable; but the thoroughness with which the murder was investigated was, by eighteenth-century standards, astonishing. Impressions of the foot-prints were taken with the greatest care and the wound in the girl's throat was examined minutely. It was possible then to establish that the murderer was left-handed and that the soles of his boots were heavily studded and had been recently mended.

One of the men who attended the girl's funeral was a left-handed man named Richardson. His shoes were inspected and were found to correspond with the impressions of the prints which had been taken. Richardson's cottage was carefully searched and hidden in an attic was a pair of stockings caked with dried blood and mud. The mud was compared with the soil around the girl's cottage and found to be exactly like it and quite different from the soil around Richardson's.[1]

The evidence given at Richardson's trial would be common-place in a murder trial today; but in 1786 the search for a motive was not only the principal but often the only problem to which attention was given in criminal investigations. The routine search for clues, which might lead to the discovery of the criminal or which might secure his conviction, was unknown. In 1788 Dr Samuel Farr's *Elements of Medical Jurisprudence* was published in Scotland and by 1807 there was a chair of Medical Jurisprudence at Edinburgh University. It was not, however, until after Alfred Swaine Taylor's *Elements of Medical Jurisprudence* had been published in London in 1836 that forensic science began to be recognized in England as a serious and important field for study;[2] and it was to be many years before this study revealed much of lasting value. The full significance of finger-prints was not appreciated until the turn of the century; nor until then was it possible to differentiate between different sorts of blood.

In fact, it was impossible to be certain before 1850 whether a stain had been made by blood at all; and until 1895, when Bordet, a French biochemist, discovered an infallible method, it was not possible to differentiate between human and animal blood, although certain French scientists had made the doubtful claim some years before that sulphuric acid mixed with different types of blood gave indications of their nature. Modern methods of determining the different groups of blood and of establishing from which part of the body stains originated, would undoubtedly have strengthened the defence of Steinie Morrison who was convicted on a charge of murder in 1911. In the case of William Shaw who was executed in 1721 for the murder of his daughter Catherine in an Edinburgh tenement, it might well have established his innocence.

Catherine Shaw was continually quarrelling with her father over a man she wanted to marry and he disliked. In October 1721 neighbours heard the sounds of a particularly violent quarrel, the slamming of a door and later a woman's groans. They went up, knocked on the door and when there was no reply they sent for the police who smashed it in. Catherine Shaw was found in a pool of blood with a knife by her side. She could not speak but nodded her head when asked if her father was responsible. When William Shaw was found he was pale and nervous and there were bloodstains on his clothes and hands. He admitted the quarrel but said that when he had left the house his daughter was alive and he had not touched her. The blood on his clothes and hands, he insisted, was his own. He had been bled a day or two previously and when the bandages had been removed the scars had opened up. No one believed him. He was convicted and executed.

Some time later the new tenant of the Shaws' rooms found a piece of paper concealed in an opening beside the chimney. It was a note from Catherine Shaw saying that she had killed herself in desperation because her father would not let her marry the man she loved. Shaw's body was taken down from the chains in which it had been hung, and buried.[3]

Steinie Morrison was also not believed when he claimed that the blood on his shirt had fallen from his own nose and had not come from Leon Beron whose body had been found dead on Clapham Common with a mark roughly in the shape of an S cut in each cheek. Tests in a forensic laboratory might have revealed minute hairs and epithelial cells in the blood to substantiate Morrison's claim.

The first forensic science laboratories were, however, not established in England until many years after Morrison had been convicted. It was felt that their expense would not be justified when independent consultants were always available, that the police would become lazy when they could rely on them and would get into the habit of handing everything over to the scientists who worked in them, even that they would be used for the fabrication of evidence. For the fabrication of evidence by the police was not, after all, unknown. In one debate on science laboratories, the behaviour of the police in a case in 1879 was resurrected. In February of that year an old clergyman of seventy-seven was shot and seriously wounded as he came downstairs, sword in hand, to investigate the sounds of what he took to be burglars in his dining-room. The police suspected two Irish poachers, Murphy and Brannagan, and interviewed them. They searched their clothes but found nothing incriminating on them. Murphy's fiancée, however, afraid that the police might not be satisfied, went through the pockets of his coat and finding some rabbit fur and blood on the lining, she hid the coat in her cottage. When the police came back, as she had expected they would, and asked to see Murphy's clothes again, she gave them the jacket of his brother-in-law who could have had nothing to do with the crime. Soon afterwards the two Irishmen were arrested and, although at the preliminary inquiry no mention had been made of these discoveries, at their trial two fragments of newspaper were produced and a button attached to a bit of torn cloth. One fragment of newspaper, the police alleged, had been found at the rectory and the piece it matched had been found in Murphy's coat. The button had also been found at the rectory and the piece of cloth to which it was attached exactly fitted a hole in Brannagan's trousers. A tailor said that the button could not have been torn off in the way the police suggested and neither the rector nor his daughter could identify the prisoners who were, nevertheless, both sentenced to penal servitude for life. Years later another man confessed that he and a friend of his had committed the crime. The police were prosecuted, but it was found that there was insufficient evidence of deliberate conspiracy.[4]

By the beginning of the 1930's, after several murders by poison had been widely reported in the Press, the prejudice against forensic science laboratories was largely overcome. Some police forces, and in particular Nottingham, had followed the example of several Continental forces and established small laboratories of their own. And in 1934 Lord Trenchard, who had been appointed Commissioner of the Metropolitan Police three years before, established a police laboratory at Hendon. Soon afterwards other similar laboratories were established and were immediately considered indispensable to modern methods of criminal investigation.

By then precision instruments had made it possible for experts trained in their uses to help the police in a variety of ways. Cartridges and bullets could be examined for the marks which would serve to identify them as having been fired from specific guns; tools could be examined to discover whether or not they had caused the marks and scratches found on the surfaces of doors or safes or window frames; documents could be examined to detect the work of the forger or to identify the particular typewriter which had been used to write them. The numbers and letters erased not only from documents but from metal and leather could be recreated. Bloodstains and fresh blood (also semen and saliva for forty per cent of men secrete their blood group in their body fluids) could be studied to reveal clues to identify which remained hidden throughout the lives of William Shaw and Steinie Morrison.

The uses to which a scientific knowledge of blood can now be put in criminal investigations is well illustrated by the deductions which the forensic pathologist, F. E. Camps, was able to make when he was called recently to a hotel in London where the body of a naked girl had been discovered in one of the bedrooms on the fourth floor. The girl had been beaten about the head and there was a handkerchief in her mouth.

The first thing that Dr Camps noticed when examining the body was that the condition known as hypostasis—the cooling and congealing of the blood on the underside of a corpse—was noticeable on the girl's chest, abdomen and on the front of her legs although she was lying on her back. From this Dr Camps knew that she had been turned over after death. The hotel manager denied that he had touched the body but when pressed he admitted that it was he who had pushed the girl over on to her back. He could not, however, give a description of the man who had booked the room as it was the sort of hotel to which couples go just to make love and this couple—one of thirty-seven sleeping in the hotel that night —had not booked in till after midnight.

On the walls of the room were splashes of blood. The tear-like shape of some of these splashes indicated that the blood had hit the wall from the left and of others that the blood had come from the right. Dr Camps believed that the murderer might, therefore, have been injured himself and a subsequent examination of the stains in the laboratory proved that he was right. The ones pointing from left to right were Group A, the others were Group B. The girl's blood was Group A; so the blood group of the murderer was determined. There were minute dried particles of this blood under the girl's finger-nails so presumably the man had been scratched. The colour of his hair was also determined when a rubber contraceptive with a flaxen pubic hair sticking to it was found under the bed. As the hair of the head is always lighter in colour than the pubic hair, the man's hair, it was then known, must have been very fair indeed.

By the measurement of temperature and the state which rigor mortis had reached it was possible to discover the approximate time of the murder. Blood cools after death and the body stiffens. The rigor begins with the head and travels down to the feet and then diminishes again. The muscles of the girl's jaw and arms were set when examined at eleven o'clock but her abdomen and legs were still flaccid, so the time of death could be fixed at between six and seven that morning.

The evidence of a taxi driver who had taken a fair-haired young man with a scratched face from Sussex Gardens to Paddington at that time led immediately to the arrest of the murderer who committed suicide before he could be brought to trial.[5]

The significance of finger-prints is, like the varying properties of blood, a recent discovery. The use of finger-prints as a means of identifying criminals seems to have been first suggested in the nineteenth century by Sir William Herschel, a commissioner in Bengal, who had formed a large collection of prints which he used in connection with legal documents and as a protection against personation. Although the use of prints as a system of identification had long been known, and their permanent character had been scientifically propounded in 1823, Herschel's suggestion did not cause much interest until Sir Francis Galton, the British anthropologist and cousin of Charles Darwin, made it his business to convince his countrymen that individual finger-prints were unique and therefore of extreme importance in the field of personal identification. At the same time Juan Vucetich in the Argentine and Henry Faulds and Sir Edward Henry in England studied the practical problems of classification, and Henry devised a new system of classification, still in use at Scotland Yard, by which quick identifications could be made.

Meanwhile, however, a new method of criminal identification was gaining favour. It was invented by Alphonse Bertillon, the French anthropometrist, who had introduced it into the Criminal Record Office in Paris of which he was head. Based on the discovery that the measurements of certain parts of the human body remain constant throughout adult life, the system greatly impressed a committee which was appointed in 1894 to report on the best means of identifying habitual criminals. But although a Registry of Anthropometric Measurements came into being, it had been recognized by 1899 that the measurements taken were frequently so imprecise as to be useless. Accordingly attention turned once more to finger-prints.

A single print secured a conviction for burglary in 1902; and in 1903 the City of Bradford established the first provincial finger-print bureau. It was not, however, until 1904 that the demands for an accurate and certain system of criminal identification gained much general support. It became clear in that year that in 1896 a fearful misjustice had been done. On the evidence of at least ten different women Adolf Beck, a forty-four-year-old Norwegian who had lived a somewhat unsettled life in South Africa, South America and London, was convicted of a series of frauds and sentenced to penal servitude for seven years. He had, so one of these women said—and the evidence of the others was almost identical —accosted her in the street, asked if he had the honour of addressing Lady Everton, was told that he had not, but remained in conversation with her for some minutes. He called to see her the next day, mentioned that he was a cousin of Lord Salisbury's and asked her to go on a Mediterranean cruise with him. She would need new clothes, he said, and he gave her a list of the things she would want. She would also need new jewellery, although some of her pieces might do if they were re-set. He would take them to the jewellers himself and would send them back in their new settings by the one-armed porter at his hotel.

After his conviction, an anonymous letter, suggesting that Beck's methods bore a strong resemblance to those of a man calling himself John Smith who had been convicted at the Old Bailey eighteen years before, came into the hands of the police who decided that Beck and Smith must be the same man. Beck was given the convict number worn previously by Smith and the problem seemed satisfactorily solved. Three years later, however, Beck's solicitor found that the man who had been sentenced as John Smith was really Wilhelm Meyer and that he had been in London throughout Beck's trial. Meyer was a circumcised Jew and the prison records confirmed that Smith had been circumcised, although Beck was not. All that happened, though, was that Beck was given a fresh number and remained in prison until 1901 when he was released on ticket of leave.

Two years later women were being defrauded again in exactly the same way as before. Beck was once more arrested and once more convicted. But while awaiting sentence, another fraud which could not possibly be blamed on Beck, who was in prison, was committed by Wilhelm Meyer. Apart from a shape and height common to them both, the two men did not look much alike. One had a fresh complexion, the other's complexion was dark; one had brown eyes, the other blue.[6] It is certain that their finger-prints would have been different.

The year after Beck received his free pardon and compensation of four thousand pounds—about five hundred pounds for each year he had had to spend in prison—a newly established Finger-print Department at Scotland Yard had its first success when the finger-prints of Stratton, a violent criminal, were found on an empty cash box in a house in Deptford where an old oilman had been battered to death. Thereafter finger-prints were recognized as being a highly important aspect of criminal investigation. Although the judge in the Stratton case warned the jury not to convict on the evidence of a finger-print alone, it was soon accepted that a well-marked print was an infallible means of identification. The criminologist, Balthazard, showed that to discover even twelve points of resemblance between the finger-prints of two men, 16,777,216 prints must be examined; to find seventeen points of resemblance, over 17,000,000,000 prints would have to be compared.[7] On only one occasion, apparently, has it seemed possible that two criminals had identical finger-prints. Those of a male criminal were found to be exactly the same as those of a woman convicted of importuning some years before. Eventually it was discovered that both sets of prints were those of the same person whose sex had changed.[8]

As the records at Scotland Yard grew, criminals took to wearing gloves; but in several cases, even so, the prints came through and were identified. A sweaty or oily hand in a thin glove will leave an identifiable mark, as can a naked finger on cloth, and an area of a square millimetre photomicrographed may show sufficient pores for accurate recognition. The ridges cannot be permanently removed by sandpaper but will reappear exactly as before, and criminals knowing this have undergone extensive surgical operations to make the skin smooth and themselves scarcely recognizable.

In spite of the undoubted success of Scotland Yard's Finger-print Department, which has now more than one and a half million prints on its files, it was a long time before there was any comparable department in the United States. Many police authorities and prisons only had photographs as means of identification in

1900 and many more were still using and instituting systems based entirely on Bertillon's. In 1904 St Louis was the first American city to discard measurements in favour of finger-prints after two Negroes in the Federal Penitentiary at Leavenworth were found not only to look alike but to have virtually identical measurements.[9] But few other cities immediately followed St Louis's example. In 1905 a finger-print department was set up in the Department of Justice but it was later transferred to Leavenworth where the prisoners were put in charge of the files and, of course, tampered with them. By 1924 over a million finger-print records and Bertillon files had piled up without any efficient method of making quick use of them.

But slowly reports of the successful operations of foreign finger-print departments had their influence on American police departments. Many years before, the police in London, Americans were told, had arrested a burglar within an hour and a half of a constable finding a severed finger on top of a spike on a warehouse door.[10] And a Deputy Chief of New York's Homicide Bureau has written of the scepticism of the Chief Inspector of Detectives being removed when a set of finger-prints, belonging to an English thief, was sent to Scotland Yard without any clue as to whose they were and a message identifying them was received by return of post.[11]

It was not until 1930, however, that there was a permanent Division of Identification and Information within the Federal Bureau of Investigation. And even then the well-founded suspicion that finger-prints could be successfully forged made courts wary of accepting evidence based on this method of identification alone. It is, of course, also necessary to have them on record and 'it is not easy,' as Professor Reiss has said, 'to run in the streets after every suspicious man and beg him to be kind enough to let his finger-prints be examined'.[12]

The identification of the victims of murder by the police often presents problems to which finger-prints can provide no answer but which modern advances in medical science have helped to solve. Perhaps the most remarkable of identifications in recent years was that of the remains of a corpse found on Potters Bar golf course in 1948.

Two small boys, looking for golf balls in a pond near the fairway, pulled out a nasty and evil-smelling lump which they buried under some leaves. A few days later some other boys were playing by the pond when they discovered a human hand and forearm. They ran to tell some nearby golfers who fetched the police. It was impossible to tell much from the hand, for decomposition was far advanced, but it had obviously been roughly sawn off and the neat, well-shaped finger nails, which appeared to have been manicured, suggested that it was the hand of a woman. When the pond was dragged, however, and the mud excavated, other parts of the body were discovered and amongst them was a man's pelvis.

All the decomposed fragments of the body were taken to the laboratory and from them an extraordinary amount of information about this man was elicited. Adipocere had set in so it could be assumed that the dismembered pieces of his corpse must have been in the pond for at least six months. The skull indicated that he had been battered to death and the sutures in the region of the temple, which rarely close before the age of forty-five, suggested that he had been about forty. He had been about 5ft 2in in height. In the upper jaw the teeth sockets had almost disappeared so it was estimated that he had lost his upper teeth ten years before. There were no teeth in the lower jaw but the sockets were well-defined and there were signs of a root abscess not long before his death. The septum—the bone which separates the nostrils—was deformed, and the sinuses gave indications that the man had been suffering from some sort of chronic trouble there—possibly catarrh. An examination of the collar bone, shoulder blades and decomposed muscle tissue showed that he had been left-handed. The tissue of the knees was extremely well-preserved so he probably spent an unusual amount of time on his knees. The joints of his big toes were very stiff.

Amongst the forty-eight people who had been reported missing to Scotland Yard from June to November of the previous year there was one, Albert Welch, whose description exactly fitted the portrait which the experts had been able to draw. He was a railway signal linesman who had to kneel down a good deal in the course of his work. Casts of glycerine-gelatine and formaline made in a pair of boots found in his garden shed, showed that he had stiff toe joints. Fellow workers testified that he had complained of tooth ache shortly before his disappearance and that he had suffered from chronic catarrh. He was 5ft 2in in height and he was left-handed.[13]

The identification of the remains of Albert Welch, remarkable as it may appear and impossible as it may have seemed when the decomposed lumps were pulled out of the pond, owed more to infinite care than to any other faculty or skill of which the expert can now make use. Increases in scientific knowledge constantly extend the powers of the criminal investigator but it is care which reveals the so easily disregarded evidence which this knowledge can evaluate.

The confused medical evidence given in 1875 during the trial of Henry Wainwright, whose long dead and dismembered mistress was found in parcels wrapped up in oil cloth in a building in Southwark, was characteristic of a period when medical witnesses not only contradicted each other and themselves but seem often to have taken not even the most elementary trouble to study the matters on which they would be questioned. The work of such men as Lacassagne and Edmond Locard in France, of Hans Gross in Austria, of Sir Bernard Spilsbury in England and Calvin H. Goddard in America ensured that for the future the importance of science and technology in criminal investigation would be finally recognized and that an infinite capacity for taking pains was certainly one indispensable attribute of the criminal investigator of genius.

In finding the facts, in assembling and interpreting them, in making deductions from them, the criminal investigator may now rely on a wide variety of experts whose accuracy he may generally leave unquestioned. It may be accepted as rare, for instance, that a coat sent to a forensic science laboratory will not be examined with such care that any clue it might contain as to the identity and habits of its owner will be extracted from it. Even the dust it contains can be revealing and often indicates the occupation of its owner.

In the summer of 1937, a Brighton detective when buying a new suit was asked by the tailor for advice about some clothes which had been left in his shop some time before by two customers who had also bought suits from him and said they would pick up their old ones later. The detective, concerned about several recent cases of safe-breaking in the district, took the old suits to the police laboratory where a vacuum cleaner extracted particles of asbestos, alum, iron filings and wood pulp. The ballast from the safes which had been broken contained four different sorts of sawdust—mahogany, oak, elm and pine. These were also found in the dust sucked out of the suits and soon afterwards the two safe-breakers were arrested.[11]

The tracing by a xylogist of the wood used in the construction of the ladder which had been used to gain access to Charles Lindbergh's nursery in 1932 displayed an astonishing patience and ingenuity; and the subsequent trial of Bruno Hauptmann, whose attic contained wood from which the ladder had been made, did much to make Americans aware of the immense importance of forensic science which had until then been widely considered a European fad.

In 1921, at the trial of Sacco and Vanzetti, the District Attorney had refused an offer from Dr George Burgess McGrath, the distinguished Medical Examiner in Boston, to prove conclusively that the hairs in a cap found at the shoe factory where the murder had been comitted came from one of the prisoners' heads. The District Attorney believed that the jury would reject the evidence with scorn and that the prosecution would become a national laughing-stock. And it was not until it was revealed, at the trial which followed the St Valentine's Day Massacre of 1929, that the Chicago Police Department had no laboratory in which to examine the assassins' bullets, that two philanthropic jurors decided to remedy the omission and finance a project which eventually developed into the model North Western University's Crime Detection Laboratory.[15] By the 1930's, however, forensic science was beginning to gain a new respectability in America.

At Hauptmann's trial the evidence of handwriting experts was admitted without undue complaint. Albert S. Osborn who gave evidence for the prosecution had already decided before Hauptmann was arrested that the ransom notes were written by a German who had spent some time in America. When specimens of Hauptmann's writings were obtained, Osborn said that the evidence of identity was 'overwhelming'. Osborn had already distinguished himself in 1900 at the trial of Albert T. Patrick, a lawyer, whose rich client, William M. Rice, was murdered by chloroform poisoning in an apartment on Madison Avenue. Patrick had presented for payment several cheques signed apparently by Rice but in reality, so Osborn contended, signed by the lawyer. To prove his point Osborn had the signatures photographed and enlarged and placed under a glass metrically ruled in squares. It was then seen that the signatures were identical which would not have been the case if they had been genuine.

Photographic and mechanical aids to the detection of forgery have now made the handwriting expert a rare figure in the courts and the days are fortunately past in which an acknowledged expert like Bertillon could continue to insist that the handwriting on a document was that of Dreyfus even after Esterhazy had confessed that it was his, and in which the English expert, Charles Chabot, could testify that the writing on a libellous postcard was undoubtedly that of the Lord Mayor of London, only to be contradicted by a witness who admitted that he had written the card himself. In any event, now that the ultra-violet ray can be used in addition to the microscope, the emphasis in the detection of forgeries has been removed from the writing or painting of the forger to the materials which he has used. Hans Gross told the story of the alleged discovery in 1820 of the manuscript of various fourteenth-century poems written in the Bohemian Slav language by a previously unknown poet whose work was good enough to impress Goethe. For many years the poems were accepted as genuine until the examination of the manuscript by an analytical chemist revealed that the ink contained Prussian blue which had not been discovered until the beginning of the eighteenth century.[16] The forger, van Meegeren, careful not to make a similar mistake, took the trouble to use only materials which he believed would have been available to Vermeer and ground his earth and stone by hand so that under the microscope the particles would be seen as not having been mechanically produced.

Evidence obtained by spectrographic analysis, for example, in an English court as early as 1818, but now comparator microscopes, quartz spectrographs for determining the inorganic properties of material, spectrophotometers for colorimetric analysis and X-ray diffraction units for the identification of samples without destroying any part of them, are all in common use.

Evidence obtained by spectrographic analysis, for example secured the recent conviction of a motorist who knocked down and killed a bicyclist. The motorist whom the police suspected of having committed the crime had thoroughly washed the car. No blood, fibres or human hairs were found on it, but there was a dent on the mudguard and expert examination revealed that on this dent was the imprint of a tweed fabric. On the bicycle there was the only other clue—a tiny speck of greyish paint. By spectrographic analysis this speck was found to be made up of five layers of paint and to correspond exactly with the paint on the car. A dummy weighing the same as the dead man was dressed in his coat and a car was driven into it at speed. A replica of the dent on the suspect's car, with an identically patterned imprint, was thus obtained.[17]

The reconstruction of a crime to get evidence of this sort is not uncommon in England and America but the reconstruction in the presence of the criminal is a more specifically Continental method. In its purpose it is a survival of the old practice of taking a suspected murderer into the presence of the corpse and making him take hold of its hand and profess his innocence. Even in the absence of supernatural signs from the body, the murderer often broke down and confessed.

A classic example of the effectiveness of reconstruction is provided by the arrest of Pierre Voirbo by the detective Gustave Macé in France, where films of reconstructed crimes have sometimes been shown to juries. Voirbo was suspected of having murdered his erstwhile friend Père Désiré Bodasse parts of whose body, eventually identified by a stocking on a leg discovered in a well, were found in various parts of Paris in 1869. Bodasse had previously been supposed to be still alive as, although no one had seen him for some time, there was always a candle burning in his room at night. Macé searched the room and found that it was covered in dust and full of empty candle boxes. It had a tiled floor which was noticeably uneven. The counterfoils of some Italian stock were found in the room, and the certificates themselves were later found in Voirbo's cellar. Voirbo was arrested but the *juge d'instruction* could get nothing from him. He had had nothing to do with Bodasse's death, he insisted, and had been given the certificates.

Macé took Voirbo up to Bodasse's room, threw a jugful of water on to the tiled floor and watched Voirbo's agitated face as the water settled in the hollows. Macé told the *gendarmes* with him to take up the tiles which the water had covered and underneath them were bloodstains. Voirbo confessed that it was there that he had cut up his victim's body.[18]

In the United States efforts to discover guilt and innocence by more scientific methods than the unnerving effects of reconstruction have received wider favour. Physiological disturbances due to emotional causes may not be apparent to the observer but a lie detector may be able to register them accurately. Alternations in the rhythm of breathing, changes in the pulse rate and in the electrical resistance of the skin due to sweating can all be registered by this machine which, it is claimed, when skilfully used is infallible. Evidence of innocence obtained by these machines is not, however, accepted in many American courts as it is not accepted in any English court. And there is no doubt that psychopaths often do not know whether they are speaking the truth or not. Truth drugs such as sodium amytal, can be used to make discoveries about the unconscious mind but under their influence men do not always speak the truth and they are more likely to be of use to the psychotherapist than to the criminal investigator. In any event, the constitutional right of a man, not to 'be compelled in any criminal case to be a witness against himself', afforded by the Fifth Amendment to the United States Constitution, is always carefully safeguarded in American courts; and while the proof of innocence by perfected scientific means might be acceptable to the American conscience, in certain circumstances, it is doubtful that the proof of guilt would be accepted at all. Certainly scientific methods of detection, when considered to be a threat to the freedom of the individual, have always been viewed with suspicion by a people who, while admiring their ingenuity, are apprehensive about their use in a democratic society. It is not only prejudice which has led to the distrust which still exists in Britain, as well as in America, of evidence unearthed by the techniques of forensic science.

Part VI

THE GREAT MELTING POT

THE NEW WORLD

'Nothing less will content me, than whole America.'
EDMUND BURKE, 1775

'AMERICA is God's Crucible, the great Melting-Pot where all the races of Europe are melting and reforming . . . God is making the American.'[1] The process is still continuing.

Men went to America because they were persecuted, because they were adventurous or rebellious, because they were ambitious or because they were hungry; and the New World took them in. They came from all over Europe and from Asia and they went into the melting pot with the children of men from Africa who had been taken there against their will and with the children of deliquescent aboriginal tribes. Most of them settled down to become the hundred per cent Americans of Theodore Roosevelt's ideal, but there were many who did not.

The immigrant arrived physically exhausted sometimes, unsure of himself often and conscious nearly always of the jealousies, resentments, disdain and disregard that seemed to surround him. There were problems of language to overcome and problems created by the traditions, customs and experiences of his past. He came from the countryside, perhaps, and he went to live in a town slum, partly to be near others who spoke his language and made him feel less alone, but mainly because he could not afford to live anywhere else. Soon he married and his children grew up and grew away from him, Americans to their parents but foreigners still to the world outside; and so new problems and new conflicts were created.

In the industrial cities foreign quarters developed. There were Jewish quarters, Sicilian quarters, Irish and Negro quarters, each with its own shops, churches, cafés and ways of life, and each a rival of its neighbour. Most of the immigrants, whatever their nationality, were exploited by employers quick to take advantage of the regular flow of cheap foreign labour; they were intimidated by the fear of unemployment and lock-outs, by the fists and guns of strike breakers; they were suspicious of the police because they had more often than not come from countries where the police were considered the natural enemies of the people; and they were, above all, suspicious of their foreign neighbours. 'Every Irish kid was raised to kill a Swede,' was more than the traditional cry of the trouble-maker.

In 1891, in New Orleans, a mob shouting, 'Kill the Dagoes,' dragged out eleven prisoners from the gaol and shot them all to death. In 1919 when the simmering anger and resentment of the Negroes, who had come to Chicago from the South to find work and had been forced to keep inside the poorest part of the city, exploded into riots, nearly forty people were killed and a thousand were left without homes. In 1923, when Nails Morton died, thousands of Jews attended his funeral to pay tribute to a man who had protected his race from their enemies. Speakers at the service ignored the fact that he had been a violent bootlegger who, two years before, had with another Jew shot two policemen in a café. And in 1925 when two other policemen were killed, their Sicilian murderers became heroes in the Italian community after the prosecution at their trial had made some adverse comments about Sicilian morality. The racial antagonism of the gang wars was not superficial.

There were, of course, other reasons apart from racial susceptibilities that turned gangsters into heroes. America, for all its faults and for all the disappointments that the immigrants felt when hope was transformed into reality, was a country nearer to freedom than those most of them had left. It might be impossible for a Negro to become President of a big corporation and at least extremely difficult, if not also impossible, for a poor Italian to get into Harvard; but it was a country that presented opportunities for them both to become rich. And riches in such a society are greatly to be admired. The gangster with his pearl grey hat and silk tie, his spats and diamond belt buckle was a living demonstration of one way of acquiring them.

'When I was twelve years old we moved into a neighbourhood where there lived a mob of gangsters and big crooks,' a young criminal confessed. 'They were all swell dressers and had big cars and carried gats. Us kids saw these swell guys and mingled with them in a cigar store on the corner. Jack Gurney was the one in the mob that I had a fancy to. He used to take my sis out and that way I saw him often. He was in the stick-up racket before he was in the beer racket and was a swell dresser and had lots of dough. He was a nervey guy and went in for big stuff. He was a mysterious fellow and would disappear for several days but always come back. He was looked up to as the leader of his mob and anybody would be glad to be in his place ... he was what a fellow would call a big hit to me. I liked to be near him and felt stuck up over the other guys because he came to my home to see sis.'[2]

Boys like this, who saw in the gangster exciting qualities which their parents lacked, formed gangs of their own; and these gangs filled the emotional gap that had opened up between the immigrant parent and the Americanized child. The criminal activities of the gang became normal activities and the boy who did not join in them was the nonconformist. So gradually whole communities—and they were usually foreign communities—developed in which crime was an accepted activity, a development which gave rise to the Chicago ecological school of criminology. 'The general point of view of the parents in these communities seems to be that thievery from the railroad is not wrong because it is a big corporation,' wrote Frederic M. Thrasher in his classic study of gang life. 'Whole neighbourhoods sometimes engage in stealing from the tracks'.[3] Once this sort of venial theft is accepted as normal, other more serious crimes begin to be accepted too. 'The boys from sixteen to twenty used to hang around the corners and wait for some old drunkard whom they would beat and take from him whatever valuables he may have,' a young man is quoted as having said in Clifford Shaw's and Henry McKay's *Social Factors in Juvenile Delinquency.* 'People would stand by and stare and even laugh as the boys would rob the drunkard. This would happen during the day when everybody could see it and the older people only was amused by it.'[4] 'There wasn't a day that somebody didn't get pinched. You don't think anything about an arrest in that neighbourhood.'[5]

And so the slum remained the breeding ground of crime and the boys' street gang the school of adult crime, not only because of the physical conditions of poverty, not only because violence and cunning were the easiest and perhaps the only means for the slum child to acquire the sort of success he had been taught to admire, but also because in slums the criminal was not the outsider that he is elsewhere. It was the honest man who was more likely to feel alone.

Diffuse as the reasons are, the white American criminal always tended to be the son of parents who were themselves born in Europe and he was more likely to be of Italian, Irish or Jewish than of any other blood. The nationality of the prisoners per one hundred thousand of the population of each national group accepted into the Colorado State Prison in the ten years before 1938 displays a tendency which was general throughout the United States;

> Irish 47.1
> Italian 45.7
> German 38
> Mexican 36.6
> Polish 32.1
> Russian 30
> English 28.2
> Scandinavian 17.5[6]

Many of the causes which inclined the child of the immigrant to crime operate with even greater force upon the Negro who has a longer tradition of poverty and disdainful treatment.

According to a report issued by the Federal Bureau of Investigation in 1956, Negroes account for thirty per cent of all arrests and for sixty per cent of all arrests for crimes involving violence or the threat of it, although they constitute only ten per cent of the population. Negroes, of course, are an underprivileged part of that population and a white policeman may arrest a black man more readily than one of his own race; but he may also, on the other hand, often overlook a crime which he considers 'typically Negro' and which would involve a white man in arrest. He may also be insufficiently diligent, so Negro organizations complain, in arresting Negroes for committing crimes against other Negroes and these, in fact, constitute the majority of Negro crimes. It may then be possible that the Negro crime rate may be even higher than these figures suggest.

There is even a 'conspiracy of concealment', which operates

to keep the official figures low, for Negro leaders and organizations exert pressure on politicians and officials to play the problem down and with the important Negro vote in mind many politicians agree to do so.[7]

During the Second World War, heroin could be bought on almost any street corner in Harlem and marijuana was offered for sale in the lavatories of most restaurants, the brothels were always full and white girls of thirteen and fourteen were brought up from the Times Square area to appear in *exhibitions* and pornographic films. Ten years later, according to Harold Danforth, a former detective in the District Attorney's office, Harlem remained 'despite its decent people who vigorously fight these conditions, a cancer on the face of the City of New York ... Few politicians like to attack the problem because of the major vote factor; they don't like to be accused of being anti-Negro.'[8]

The large number of foreign voters in modern American cities has, in fact, had a profound influence upon politics and, because of the methods adopted in the manipulation of these groups to secure control of the machinery of Government, has also had an indirect influence upon crime. The groups have been manipulated not so much by the men who offer themselves for election, as by the party managers who work behind the scenes to win support and campaign funds from the most powerful and influential members of the district. As these members in many districts had frequently gained their power and influence through crime, the politicians and the criminals became associated in the mind of the American, who was inclined to think the one as much a racketeer as the other. The American, with his passion for the idea of freedom has never wanted a stronger government than patriotism demanded and has allowed a system to develop which he knows to be ruled by self-interest but which he views with a kind of cynical detachment, sometimes even with amused indulgence. It has, indeed, been suggested that the consequences of the system were inevitable. 'Evil and unhealthy as the relationship between crime and politics is, it is still to be taken,' Professor Tannenbaum believes, 'as a typical, that is a natural and inevitable, aspect of the kind of community' his fellow Americans have.[9]

The relationship has led to numerous scandals involving municipal governments. In 1868 Tammany Hall, the New York political machine, at that time controlled by William Marcy Tweed who had been alderman, congressman and senator, nominated the corrupt District Attorney, Oakey Hall, as Mayor of New York. Two years later the 'Tweed Ring' had robbed the city of nearly two hundred million dollars. In 1871 Tweed was convicted of grand larceny, but the power of Tammany Hall was not broken and by the turn of the century it was actively co-operating with the leading criminals in New York. Nor did the fall of Oakey Hall lead to any permanent improvement in the morals of the City's mayors. James J. Walker, Mayor in the 1920's, was shown to have accepted large sums of money from corporations anxious to obtain city contracts; and William O'Dwyer, while frequently issuing statements deploring the sinister influence of Tammany Hall, continued to give city appointments to men with criminal connections. His successor Vincent Impelliteri has been accused of doing the same thing.

Corrupt mayors were not confined to New York. William Hale Thompson, the calculatingly anti-British Mayor of Chicago who said that he would 'punch King George in the snoot' if he ever had the effrontery to come to his city, proved himself a faithful friend to the bootleggers. And Alberto Alonzo Ames, Mayor of Minneapolis, was actively associated with commercialized vice there and allowed the police force to co-operate with the criminals.

Nor has the corruption been confined to municipal governments. Under the administration of President Harding graft was widespread in many departments of the Government. In more recent years the activities of the 'five per centers' during the Truman administration and of the Russian-born Boston millionaire, Bernard Goldfine, which resulted in the fall of President Eisenhower's chief of staff, Sherman Adams, and the 1962 Billie Sol Estes scandal, show that the corruption condemned sixty years before by Lincoln Steffens[10] has not yet disappeared from public life.

Perhaps the most unfortunate of the consequences of this association of politics and crime has been its effect on the judiciary. Judges as well as district attorneys hold elective offices and have frequently found themselves, after their election, obliged to favour those who helped to place them in their positions of profit and power. At the funeral in 1926 of the unfrocked priest turned gangster, Anthony D'Andrea, who had gained control of many of Chicago's brothels as well as of the Unione Siciliana and had stood as a candidate for an aldermanship in 1916 in order to break the Irish hold on his ward, there were no less than twenty-one

judges as honorary pall bearers. And amongst the eight thousand
people in the funeral *cortège*, which stretched for two and a half
miles, were many other equally important city officials.[11] Many of
these later attended the funeral of the Irish gangster, Dion
O'Banion whose solid silver coffin, costing ten thousand dollars,
was followed to its grave by twenty-six lorry loads of flowers worth
fifty thousand dollars under the eyes of more than twenty thousand
people.[12]

Nor did the power of gangsters to influence the verdicts
of judges end with Prohibition. When Samuel Seabury, a retired
Judge of the New York Court of Appeals, was summoned by the
Appellate Division to investigate the city's lower courts, he suggested in his report, published in 1932, that there had been no perceptible improvement since 1875, the year in which a similar
inquiry had been held. The sure way to a judgeship was still undeniably through politics. A magistrate who said that he had
learned that the Mayor of New York had 'decided to appoint a
Hebrew from the Bronx', was asked this question:

'Now, Judge Silberman, what I am anxious to have you state, if you will
and if you know, is just why you, Jesse Silberman, were selected to be
magistrate up there rather than some other Hebrew up there in the
Bronx who was a member of the bar in good standing.'

'I have stated the reasons,' Judge Silberman replied. 'I was active
in the Party.'[13]

Clearly a judge elected for this reason, particularly in a large
cosmopolitan city like New York, might find it difficult to forget
a forthcoming election when a case involving political, religious or
racial interests came before him.

But the Seabury Report revealed graver scandals than the
questionable verdicts of some judges. It appeared that for years
lawyers, members of the District Attorney's staff and of the vice
squad had been combining to block the course of justice by accepting bribes from prisoners who could afford to pay for their release
and even from innocent people who had been framed by the police.
When it was decided to prosecute, a bargain was usually struck
with the accused who agreed to plead guilty to a lesser crime than
the one he had committed, so that the prosecutor could claim a
conviction without interfering unduly with the criminal's career.

In cases where the prosecution demanded the full penalty for
the crime, the demand was often based upon a confession by the

prisoner extracted dishonestly or illegally by the police, and this often resulted in an unjust acquittal.

'I have tried 130 murder cases,' a criminal lawyer wrote in 1928, 'and I have won 126 of them. Many of these cases were based as far as the prosecution was concerned on confessions extorted from the defendant by the "third degree" ... If it had not been for the dishonest methods used by the police towards these defendants, I could not have won ten of the 130 cases ... The jury saw that their methods had been unfair and acquitted defendants who might have been convicted except for the police.'[14]

The sympathy of juries was not the only reason for the large number of acquittals in American courts. Various jealously guarded constitutional safeguards for the protection of individual liberty can be used, and still are used, by the criminal to escape justice. The Fifth Amendment to the United States Constitution, so frequently invoked in Senate Committees, provides that no person 'shall be compelled in any criminal case to be a witness against himself'. The Fourth Amendment guarantees the Common Law 'right of the people to be secure in their persons, houses, papers and effects against unreasonable searches and seizures'. Warrants must give details of the place to be searched and the things to be seized and must only be issued upon 'probable cause, supported by oath or affirmation'.

It has always been the duty of American courts to insist on the rights of the defendant, even when he is strongly suspected of crime, so that public confidence in the fairness of the law should be retained and increased. This has, of course, led—in England, where American Common Law and attitudes to justice had their origins, as well as in the United States—to what Roscoe Pound of Harvard has called the 'sporting theory of justice'.

'So far from being a fundamental fact of jurisprudence,' this theory, Pound said, was peculiar to Anglo-American law and had been strongly curbed in modern English practice.

'With us, it is not merely in full acceptance, it has been developed, and its collateral possibilities have been cultivated, to the furtherest extent. The effect of our exaggerated contentious procedure is not only to irritate parties, witnesses and jurors, in particular cases, but to give the whole community a false notion of the purpose and end of the law. Hence comes, in large measure, the modern American race to beat the law.'[15]

The chief qualification of the American lawyer, according to Sheldon Glueck, 'is an ability to keep constantly alert to discover open or rusty joints in the armour of justice'.[16]

Caryl Chessman's long fight to prevent the State of California carrying out a sentence of death demonstrated to the world how technicalities, originally introduced as defences against tyranny, may be used for quite different purposes by men who know of their existence. But Chessman is only the most celebrated of those who have taken advantage of these technicalities to delay punishment. A man indicted in July 1904 for a murder committed in the previous March was tried in January 1905. The trial took three weeks, after which the usual motion for a new trial was made by a bill of twenty-six exceptions. A year later the Supreme Court denied the motion for a new trial. The prisoner was accordingly sentenced to be electrocuted; the sentence was immediately followed by petitions for a writ of error and a pardon. He was eventually executed two years and five months after his arrest.[17] Sacco and Vanzetti were executed six years after their conviction; and the life of the Negro, Paul Crump, was spared in July 1962, nine years after he had been condemned to death for murder.

Meticulous regard for the technicalities of procedure can also be used to avoid sentence altogether. *The Journal of Criminal Law and Criminology* cites the case of a burglar, who was proved to have broken into a particular house, being acquitted because the indictment named six persons who were said to be living in the house when, in fact, only five of them did live there.[18]

This concern for accuracy and strict order was not unfortunately reflected in the conduct of most courts. Lawyers touting for business, and bail bondsmen who charged as much as twenty per cent interest on the sums lent to those who could not afford their own bail, were regular features, during the first twenty or thirty years of the present century, of most municipal courts which are often sordid enough even today. An observer quoted in the *Cleveland Crime Survey* described a typical court in a large city in the middle West.

'Though I sat within fifteen feet of the bench and witness chair and strained my ears, I could seldom catch a word of what was going on ... The prosecutor had no papers whatever. He lolled against the bench. For each case he was handed a copy of the affidavit and that is all he ever looked at. He took a glance at the paper to ascertain the nature of the case. He then mumbled something to the judge . . . Other times he called the police officer or other chief prosecution witness and mumbled some question . . . In a few cases the attorney for the defence took part in the interrogation. Generally, however, he seemed to simply wander and stand around, mysteriously going in and out, sometimes approaching the bench, sometimes going to the benches and talking to somebody, and every once in a while would go up and whisper something in the judge's ear . . . While this mumbling and whispering were going on in the immediate vicinity of the bench, the main aisle leading from the door into the courtroom and to the bench was the scene of constant comings and goings. It was never quiet a second . . . Not only was it impossible to hear what was going on in the trial, it was generally impossible to see what was going on.'[19]

Apart from the lack of dignity in the municipal and some federal and state courts, apart from the excessive technicalities of procedure and the sometimes corrupt and often inefficient or prejudiced judges who dealt out punishment without regard to the character of the offender and apart, too, from a general unwillingness to make use of extra-legal sciences, there were other obstacles —legacies from colonial times when the insistence on local rights was even stronger than it is today—that placed heavy shackles on justice. Not only were the rules for the interstate rendition or extradition of criminals technical and involved, but the crossing of a state line, involving an automatic change of jurisdiction, might enable a man to commit an offence without the fear of the heavy punishment to which he would have been liable in the state that he had left. In 1931, for example, the maximum punishment for perjury was five years' imprisonment in Connecticut, twenty years in New York, life imprisonment in Maine, and ten years together with a fine of from five hundred to two thousand dollars and forty lashes in Delaware. In West Virginia bigamy was punished sixteen times as severely as incest, whereas in Wyoming and Colorado punishment for incest was ten times as severe as that for bigamy.[20]

Today fornication is a crime punishable by three years' imprisonment in Arizona but in most other states is not an offence at all unless 'open and notorious'; ages of consent range from twelve in Alabama to twenty-one in Tennessee; adultery can be punished by five years' imprisonment in Connecticut and by a fifty dollar fine in Kentucky although elsewhere it is only a sin; in one state it is against the law to ride a jackass more than six miles an hour and in another a child may not pass from the seventh to the eighth grade until he can recite *The Star-Spangled Banner.*

'Under the Sullivan Law,' an English criminal discovered in New York in the late 1920's, 'you can be jailed even for trying to buy a gun, so naturally no decent citizen dare attempt it. But every crook just takes the ferry across to New Jersey where the Sullivan Law doesn't operate, and there he can choose his special automatic or his favourite revolver in any gunsmiths and buy it just as though he were buying a cigarette-case and with no more questions asked.'[21]

The impunity enjoyed by many of this man's friends and enemies was, of course, emphasized by the difficulty of obtaining juries who were not either intimidated or corrupted and, indeed, of obtaining witnesses.

When the German bootlegger, Arthur Flegenheimer, known to posterity as Dutch Schultz, had avoided arrest for his more serious crimes, he was, like so many others of his kind, eventually brought to court in Syracuse for income-tax evasion. Immediately he paid ten thousand dollars to a public relations man to 'create a good press and feeling among the local citizens'. Advance agents were sent into the town with wads of dollar bills in their pockets to go into bars and announce that the drinks were on Mr Flegenheimer. Children's parties were given and large sums were given to local charities. The jury at his trial, although the prosecution's case seemed satisfactorily proved, could not agree. Before his new trial at Malone, Dutch Schultz made even more strenuous and expensive efforts, going so far as to hire the local dance hall for a party to which the whole town was invited. 'Everybody's drinking on me tonight, gents,' Schultz said each time he entered the bar. 'Come and get it.'[22] This time he was acquitted.

The reluctance of intimidated witnesses to testify in court was an even greater obstacle to the enforcement of the law. Most of the witnesses questioned by the Attorney-General John Bennett during his investigations under what he called the 'antiquated Donnelly Act' impressed him as being 'men solely desirous of saving their businesses which, in several instances, represented the culmination of a lifetime of industrious work. Some of them lied, most of them were reluctant but quite a few frankly admitted that while they discountenanced violence, they felt that the law afforded them no escape from their difficulties.'[23]

Quite often, indeed, they were right. Nor are the dangers yet past. In the elections of 1946, a Republican Party worker, Joseph R. Scottoriggio was murdered by four men who kicked him to death in front of thirty witnesses. Only one of the thirty said that he could recognize any of the murderers and he soon found that he just didn't 'know anything. Not a damn thing.' A detective in the District Attorney's office had seen his mother warn him by drawing a finger across her throat, the Mafia sign of silence.[24]

It is a sign which in America still has a terrible and far-reaching significance.

CHAPTER TWO

GANGS AND SYNDICATES

*'The funny part of the whole thing is that a man in this line
of business has so much company.'*

AL CAPONE, 1926

'WASHINGTON—Salvatore Moretti, an extremely contemptuous
New Jersey gambler and racketeer, testifying:
Counsel Rudolph Halley: "Do you know what the Mafia is?"
Salvatore Moretti: "What?"
Halley: "The Mafia? M-a-f-i-a?"
Moretti: "I am sorry, I don't know what you are talking about."
Halley: "You never heard that word before in your life?"
Moretti: "No, sir. I did not."[1]

The Senate Crime Investigating Committee decided in 1950, however, that Moretti knew very well, as all racketeers must know, that
the Mafia

'Is a secret conspiracy against law and order which will ruthlessly
eliminate anyone who stands in the way of its success in any criminal
enterprise in which it is interested. It will destroy anyone who betrays
its secrets. It will use any means available—political influence, bribery,
intimidation, etc.,—to defeat any attempt on the part of law enforcement
to touch its top figures or to interfere with its operations.'[2]

The Mafia came to America before the end of the nineteenth century. Originating in Sicily hundreds of years before, its traditions
of loyalty and secrecy, like those of the Camorra, the Spanish
secret society which was already operating in Naples in 1568, are

implicitly observed and rigidly enforced. To break the *Omerta*—the unwritten code of honour of the Mafia—is an unpardonable act punished by death.

For almost a hundred years the power of the Mafiosi has been growing in America. As early as 1890 a grand jury in New Orleans found that no Italian was prepared to say anything regarding the murder of a police officer who had given offence to the Mafia. The hold that the society and the more loosely organized Unione Siciliana were able to maintain over the poor immigrants in New York and other large cities, soon extended to whole communities whether Italian or not. By the beginning of the twentieth century, the Mafia had become entangled with so much which could be intimidated or corrupted in American society that its entwining grasp on the life of the nation has never been completely broken. By bribing the police, by frightening its rivals and opponents, by coming to terms with politicians and lawyers, it has, in its time, been profitably involved in every more or less disreputable business and traffic in America. In 1909 the Mafia and its allies in crime had so well secured police protection for illegal gambling that any gambling house which paid the necessary bribes was allowed to operate without interference. If public opinion required it, the police would apologize to Mont Tennes, who organized the entire racket and the hundreds of bookmakers that were permitted to share in its immense profits, and then make a token raid on a building where they would 'leave expensive paraphernalia untouched while tearing up some playing cards'.[3]

The co-operation of the police with criminals was never so evident as it was in the 1920's when the passionate disgust of the 'Old America' with the new civilization of the cities and with the Catholic immigrant[4] forced upon the nation the Eighteenth Amendment to the American Constitution, known as the Volstead Act, which made it, for all practical purposes, illegal to manufacture, sell or import alcohol in the United States. Immediately alcohol became America's biggest industry. Few of those who drank it before 17 January 1920 were prepared to stop drinking it just because it had become illegal to do so. Indeed, what the Anti-Saloon League triumphantly heralded as a new 'era of clear thinking and clean living' became, as a skilful and entertaining historian of the period has observed, perhaps 'the most alcoholic period in American history'.[5] In a single year of prohibition over 1,000,000,000 gallons of liquor and wine were drunk, making profits, so it was assessed, of $4,000,000,000 dollars for the professional bootleggers.[6] In New York the number of speakeasies was double that of the legal saloons which had existed before Prohibition; and in Chicago liquor could be had everywhere— in speakeasies; in bars which should have been padlocked but stayed open, flouting the law; in restaurants and drug stores where it was served in coffee cups and milk-shake glasses; in private houses where citizens studied the liquor recipes published in magazines and newspapers and made 'coffin varnish', 'panther piss,' 'tarantula juice' or 'bust-head' from the ingredients they had bought in one or other of the numerous shops specializing in 'do-it-yourself kits for the home moon-shiner'.[7]

But it was much more than the most alcoholic period in American history; it was also the most violent. Over seven thousand people were killed in fights between rival gangs in Chicago alone during the fourteen years of Prohibition; and it has been estimated that the fights in New York cost a thousand lives. Nor was it only the gangsters who died. Of nearly half a million gallons of so-called whisky and gin seized and analysed in New York in 1927, ninety-eight per cent contained poisons. In the following year sixty people died of wood alcohol poisoning in that one city alone. How many innocent people were accidentally shot by gangsters and by federal agents and state police officers it is impossible to say. The accuracy of a report issued by the National Commission on Law Observance and Enforcement which gave some figures was questioned by a Senator who said that the deaths of more than fifty citizens had been concealed by Government agents. It was at least certain that in some areas, particularly along the Mexican and Canadian borders, Government agents were so reckless with their guns that people dared not go out at night.[8]

The violence, however, was only the most obvious of the immediate results of Prohibition. Another result was less evident and more persistent. The bootlegger could not have survived without the co-operation of the public who drank the goods he supplied. 'All right, I break the Prohibition Law,' Al Capone, the most famous of all the bootleggers, conceded. 'But so do my customers. Somebody had to throw liquor on that thirst. Why not me?' Capone welcomed the law because it increased his annual income by at least $40,000,000. His thousands of customers welcomed Capone because he helped them to break a law which they resented as an unnecessary interference with their pleasures.

Two years after Prohibition had begun, the President of Columbia University warned his countrymen, 'that disregard of law and contempt for law have greatly increased and are still increasing in this country'. The only shame, as the Wickersham Committee reported, was getting caught. The only shame, indeed, for a young man was not getting drunk, and numerous speakeasies opened up near schools and colleges to ensure that the youth of the country had no excuse for staying sober.

It was not only the co-operation of the public which was necessary to the bootleggers' success. Prohibition agents, customs officers, policemen and politicians, judges, mayors, district attorneys and even congressmen, all accepted bribes and commissions from gangsters whose protectors and servants they eventually became. Many prohibition agents, in fact, were actually appointed through the influence of the gangsters whose activities they were expected to repress; and many police chiefs were appointed by mayors who remained in office only by consent of the criminals who were the real rulers of the city. 'I own the police,' Johnny Torrio once said, and the boast was not an idle one.

Torrio, a quiet, polite, apparently respectable man who did not smoke or drink or swear, came to Chicago in 1910. Four years before, the Chicago *Tribune* had told its readers, 'a reign of terror' was upon the city. There had been a burglary every three hours, a hold-up every six hours, and a murder every day. For the Italian Black Hand extortionist, Big Jim Colosimo, it had been a city of limitless opportunities. Between 1910 and 1920, with the help of a wife who had been a madame in a brothel, Colosimo extended his dominion over its underworld until he was making $500,000 a year and was able freely to indulge his passion for diamonds. But in the tenth year of his success, Colosimo was murdered. His assassin, so the Chicago police believed, was the head of the Unione Siciliana, who had been lavishly paid for this service by the small, quiet Sicilian, Torrio.

By then Torrio, originally Colosimo's bodyguard, had become almost as important in the Chicago underworld as Colosimo himself. But he was a man of more exceptional talents than his former employer, 'the nearest thing to a master mind,' in fact, so the historian of Chicago's underworld thinks, that his country has ever produced.[9] Before 1920 he was mainly concerned with vice, but thereafter he could turn his attention to liquor; and he taught his fellow criminals to understand that they could make far more out of this new racket in association than by competing for its spoils. It was the beginning of the Syndicate.

To develop his business, Torrio enlisted the help of an Italian from New York, Alphonse Capone. Capone was not a Sicilian, and so could never become a *capo mafioso* as Torrio was; but he was soon accepted by the *mafiosi* as a leader of indispensable abilities and was able to gain virtual control of the Unione Siciliana by means of a nominee whom he had managed to get elected President. Within a few years Capone had not only assumed the leadership of Torrio's gang and its associates, but by violence, bribes and alliances he had become undisputably the most powerful man in Chicago's underworld. Other gangs of Italians and Sicilians, such as those controlled by the Aiello and Genna families, were forced into submissive alliance or were dismembered. The power of rival Jewish and Irish gangs, notably that controlled originally by Dion O'Banion, was gradually destroyed.

O'Banion was shot in his flower shop while preparing a wreath for one of the lavish funerals which followed the death of every important Chicago gangster; his successor, the Polish Hymie Weiss, was shot in the street; six men who remained with George Bugs Moran, Weiss's successor, were shot in a garage on St Valentine's Day 1929. To achieve and maintain his power and simultaneously to make an immense fortune, required, of course, more than bullets. In April 1924, for instance, Capone used some of the seven hundred odd men who were then working for him to intimidate the voters in the suburb of Cicero. 'Automobiles filled with gunmen paraded the streets slugging and kidnapping election workers,' according to the *Illinois Crime Survey*. 'Polling places were raided by armed thugs and ballots taken at the point of the gun from the hands of voters waiting to drop them in the box.'[10] Capone's nominee was elected mayor and thereafter Cicero was ruled not from City Hall but from the Hawthorne Inn where Capone had his headquarters. Once when the mayor did not do something Capone had ordered him to do, the gangster went to his office, knocked him down the steps and, while a policeman looked on unconcernedly, kicked him as he lay in the street.

The police were not merely owned by Capone and Torrio, they were gangsters themselves. In 1923, well over half of them in Chicago were officially estimated as being engaged in the liquor business, 'not in connivance, but actually'.[11] Bootleggers' lorries on their way to make deliveries were seen out of warehouses by patrolmen who later entered speakeasies to have a drink or to give warning of a possible raid. Sometimes a saloon keeper was served with an injunction and later fined; but a few days later—as he would have done in eighteenth-century London—he opened up elsewhere under another name.

In 1930, the Chicago Crime Commission, founded by a group of private citizens who were determined to reveal the corruption in the life of their city, decided to inaugurate a campaign 'to keep the light of publicity shining on Chicago's most prominent, well-known and notorious gangsters to the end that they may be under constant observation by the enforcing authorities.' The repercussions of this campaign went far and deep. The publicity given to every questionable act and every reprehensible avoidance of action on the part of those whose duty it was to administer the law, resulted in a new drive against crime. Even Al Capone, named Public Enemy Number One by the Commission, was affected by the clamour. He was already, in fact, slipping from power. He had been arrested in Philadelphia in 1929 on his way back from Atlantic City, where the New York gangster Frank Costello had assembled a conference to extend his own interest and to settle the unprofitable and dangerous rivalry of which the St Valentine's Day massacre had been a recent symptom. Capone was charged with 'being a suspicious character and carrying a deadly weapon'. He was convicted and sentenced to a year's imprisonment. When he was released in March 1930 he had to face a growing opposition not only from the Chicago Crime Commission and a newly formed Citizens' Committee backed and financed by several rich businessmen, but also from criminal rivals the most important of whom was Roger the Terrible Touhy, son of a Chicago policeman and, so it was afterwards alleged, ally of the Mayor of Chicago who had pledged to drive Capone out of town in his election speeches and had made the police force available to Touhy for this purpose. Certainly after the new Mayor was elected, gang murders increased at a fast rate and most of those who died were Capone's men. By the end of 1932, so Touhy said many years later, Capone's gang was ready to surrender. Its leader, who had never filed a tax return, had already been defeated by the combined efforts of the United States Treasury and the Department of Justice, and was in prison, where he was to remain for eight years, eventually falling victim to a brain disease caused by the syphilis he had contracted in his youth.[12]

But although his power had so suddenly waned, Capone was never to be forgotten. He was, and remains, a legendary figure. He was a calculating murderer, a vicious man subject to fits of ungovernable rage; but he loved his family and was generous to his friends. He was tough but he was sentimental. He was not a fluent conversationalist, but he spoke pleasantly in a soft voice with occasional flashes of wit. He lived in a magnificently flamboyant way, expensively dressed with diamonds flashing on his tie and on his fingers, with girls in his hotel suite, a bigger bodyguard than the President's and an armoured car that weighed seven tons. He loved the limelight and his enormous fan mail; his donations to charities were lavish; he was a megalomaniac; he was a popular hero. It is not only Americans who can admire a man like this.

The son of a Neapolitan barber brought up in the slums of Brooklyn, Capone fought his way to prominence, if not respectability, in a society which believes so wholeheartedly in unrestricted free enterprise and in success that it can admire the rich and successful more readily than it can condemn any methods by which riches and success are attained. Even without the particular qualities that made Capone 'a good guy', as Nelson Algren has called him, he would have been admired for the ruthless opportunism that earned him his hundreds of millions of dollars.

Dutch Schultz, a rich opportunist as well, was a far less appealing character and he, too, even now, has his admirers. Schultz's career in New York between his first and last conviction in 1917 until he was shot in New Jersey in 1935 at the age of thirty-three is a typical and revealing one.

His father was a German Jew who deserted his family and left his son to drift into juvenile crime. Before he was twenty Dutch had made money out of selling beer, operating speakeasies and slot machines, managing labour unions, restaurants, taxis and boxing matches. He made a considerable fortune from the 'numbers racket' by which punters placed bets on the figures that would appear in the financial pages of the next day's newspapers. By 1930 he occupied a position in New York similar to Capone's in Chicago. Legs Diamond tried to replace him and was killed in October 1931; Vincent Mad Dog Coll also tried and was shot in a telephone booth by machine-gunners.

Like Capone, Schultz was helped and protected by politicians whose elections to office he brought about by bribes, threats, and violence. He helped to return William Copeland Dodge as District

Attorney and James T. Hines, the white-haired Tammany Hall politician whose sons were at Harvard and Yale. But the more prosperous he became and the more protection he bought, the less secure Schultz felt. He became increasingly paranoic and aggressive. He surrounded himself with guards whom he did not trust and women he suspected of cheating him. Once he shot in the back a member of his gang who, he believed, had stolen twenty-one thousand dollars from him. As the blood from the dead man soaked into the hotel carpet, Schultz pointed to another of his men, and said, 'Smash his nose'. The corpse was removed and the bleeding nose was left to drip on to the stain. When the doctor came he was told that the boys had had a fight over a game of cards.

As well as being brutal, Schultz was a pathological miser. 'You can insult Arthur's girl,' one of his advisers once said, 'even steal her from him; spit in his face, push him around and he'd laugh it off. But don't steal even a dollar that belongs to him. You're dead if you do.'

'Personally I think only queers wear silk shirts,' said Schultz himself whose shabby, ill-fitting suits contrasted oddly with the smart, slick clothes of other gangsters. 'A guy's a sucker to spend fifteen or twenty dollars on a shirt. Hell, you can get a good one for two bucks.'

But Schultz's parsimony was one of the few traits he did not share with his fellow gangsters. Like many of them he was so superstitious that during a trial at which he was acquitted he accepted a rosary in the morning and a *mezuzah* in the evening with the comment that he needed all the luck he could get; like many of them he was so anxious to be taken for a respectable businessman that he did all he could to gain admittance to the houses of the rich and well-born and was constantly asking to be introduced to 'guys like book writers and singers'; and like most of them he was devoted to his mother. He spoke of her just before dying. 'Mother is the best best,' he said, 'and don't let Satan draw you too fast.'[13]

Although by the middle of the 1930's, gangsters like Schultz were dying out, as Prohibition itself had died, a new generation was already in existence. Frank Costello, Albert Anastasio, and Charles Lucky Luciano, all of them born in Italy or Sicily and all of them engaged in criminal activities throughout the era of Prohibition, were only three of the more important of those who inaugurated a new style of gangster, no less unscrupulous than the old, but more cautious and circumspect, anxious to make crime an industry, and more than ever careful to integrate it with politics and legitimate businesses.

On lines suggested by the Sicilian Johnny Torrio, Capone's former employer, a Crime Syndicate had been formed before Schultz's death. A board of directors, each with equal powers, had been formed to negotiate between rival gangs, to settle their disputes, and to bring them together into a criminal organization with a soundly based policy for progressive crime. Each gang leader retained control of his area and no criminal activity was to be permitted there without his permission; but the Syndicate's directors acting together had the ultimate authority.

The Syndicate was, at first, limited to the gangs of the East Coast. Costello, whose main interest was gambling; Luciano, who specialized in prostitution and more particularly in drugs; Joseph Doto or Joe Adonis, a specialist in political and labour rackets; Bugsy Siegel and Meyer Lansky, specialists in enforcement; and Louis Lepke Buchalter, the labour union racketeer, were its first principal members. But soon the idea spread to other areas until the organization of a national Crime Syndicate became a very real possibility.

In order to make murder, when it was considered necessary, less easily punishable by the authorities and less likely to lead to reprisals within the underworld, Murder Incorporated, a 'Combination' founded in Brooklyn, was used by members of the Syndicate as an execution squad and was responsible for at least sixty-three murders in nine years. Murder Incorporated, whose chief executioners were Albert Anastasio and Abe Kid Twist Reles, indulged in other criminal activities besides professional murder; but it was to plan a murder on its behalf that the Syndicate, so it is believed, approached Murder Incorporated in 1935.

A few months before, Thomas Dewey, a young and highly talented lawyer from Michigan, who had already become famous as a fearless prosecutor of criminals while serving as chief assistant to the District Attorney of New York's southern district, had been appointed a special prosecutor of organized crime. Dewey had had an immediate success and the Syndicate was concerned that his investigations would soon take him to its leaders. But although a murder plan was prepared, the Syndicate eventually decided that it would be dangerous to execute it and that, in any event, as Dewey's authority was limited to the southern district the worst that could happen was that the Syndicate would have to withdraw from Manhattan Island. The now violently aggressive Dutch Schultz, who had not been invited to join the Syndicate because he was considered to be too reckless, dissented from this view. After leaving the Syndicate meeting, which he had attended only as an observer, he boasted that he would kill Dewey himself. Some days later it was he that was dead, killed, it is supposed, on the Syndicate's orders.

The following year Murder Incorporated was approached again this time by Lepke Buchalter who gave instructions for the murder of a former van driver who was interfering with his profitable rackets in the garment industry. The police learned of this approach, which led to Buchalter's execution, from Abe Kid Twist Reles who in an extraordinary confession made while he was being held on a murder charge in 1940, implicated his associates in Murder Incorporated.

Reles disclosed enough to reveal the existence of what the Assistant District Attorney, Burton Turkis, called 'a government-within-government in which the killings and rackets worked hand in hand in a national combine of crime'. But before he could be brought into court to testify, Reles fell out of a sixth floor window in what was officially but dubiously attributed to an accident.[14]

Whether or not a 'national combine of crime' did or does, in fact, exist, as Burton Turkis thinks, is still an unsettled question; but it is generally believed that Turkis is right. The Senate Crime Investigating Committee which was appointed in 1950 under the chairmanship of Senator Estes Kefauver who had, in his own words, 'for some years been troubled by the unpleasant realization that there was a tie-up between crime and politics,' decided that, although there was no incontrovertible proof, a national crime syndicate was in all probability operating in America.

The Syndicate is, in Kefauver's own opinion, 'a loosely organized but cohesive coalition of autonomous crime "locals" which work together for mutual profit. Its activities are controlled by a foul and cynical partnership of mobsters, venal politicians, and conscienceless business and professional men—including accountants and lawyers—who travel under the false mark of "respectability".'[15] There was in 1950 no evidence to show that there was a single leader of the Syndicate although Frank Costello, whose appearances in the televised hearings of the Committee were far from successful, was, in the view of Virgil Peterson, operating director of the Chicago Crime Commission, the 'most influential underworld leader in America'.[16] Nor did very much evidence come to light as to the real power of the Mafia, but that it exercised a baleful influence over the local gangs seemed undeniable. It seemed also undeniable that it dominated the narcotics traffic which was largely directed by the Sicilian Lucky Luciano who had been deported to Italy in 1946 as an undesirable alien.

In 1957, the existence of a national crime syndicate of some sort, backed by the Mafia, seemed likelier than ever. One Sunday afternoon that winter the curiosity of a sergeant of the New York State Police was aroused by the great number of expensive cars, from as far away as Arizona, California and Florida, which drove up outside the Apalachin house of Joseph Barbara, a beer distributor and owner of a soft drink business who had been known to the police for many years as a racketeer. Inside the house were about sixty guests. Half of them had been born in Sicily or Italy, the rest had Italian blood, nearly all of them had been arrested and convicted before. Asked what they were all doing there, two of them said that their cars had broken down, one that he had come to sell Barbara some fish. Barbara, himself, said that he had not exactly been expecting his guests and the fact that he had two hundred pounds of steak in his kitchen was just a coincidence. The rest agreed that they had just dropped in as they were passing to ask how Barbara was. He had a weak heart, they said.

This, at least, was true; and Barbara has since died. But the rest of the story seemed absurdly far-fetched. The Justice Department brought all the racketeers before grand juries and later in a District Court in Manhattan, some of them were found guilty of conspiracy. The prosecution's case, however, was no more than a supposition and the United States Court of Appeals quashed the convictions. 'In America,' said one of the three judges, 'we still respect the dignity of the individual, and even an unsavory character is not to be imprisoned except on definite proof of specific crime.'[17]

These brave words reflect the price that a true democracy must inevitably pay for setting so high a store on individual freedom. By the time that the Senate Rackets Committee had reached some conclusions in 1960, the men who had been caught visiting Joseph Barbara in Apalachin were in business again and the efforts of criminals to gain control of the American economy by infiltrating the unions and legitimate businesses—infiltrations which Kefauver

believed had 'progressed to an alarming extent' ten years before
—were still being made.

The activities of the Senate Rackets Committee, like the
activities of earlier committees, were, however, severely hampered
by those constitutional safeguards against interference with personal freedom by the courts that have always been jealously
preserved.

The following exchange between Alfred Toplitz, a former
Democratic leader of the 1st Assembly District, Manhattan, and
a counsel of the New York Crime Commission in 1952 is characteristic of exchanges in many previous and subsequent hearings.

Q.   Have you held any government position?
A.   Yes.
Q.   Were you a prohibition agent with the U.S Treasury Dept. back
     in the early twenties?
A.   Yes.
Q.   Did you lose that job because of your connection with the theft
     of 4,900 cases of liquor?
A.   I didn't lose—not on that account, I can't answer that. I wasn't
     on trial for that.
Q.   During the period you were serving as a prohibition agent did
     you come to know a man named Frank Costello?
A.   I knew him before that.
Q.   And you knew him during that period?
A.   That's right.
Q.   What is the next public position you held?
A.   Chief Clerk of the Board of Elections.
Q.   You became chief clerk on 17 March 1948 and you continued
     until the end of December 1950?
A.   Yes, I think so.
Q.   What business were you in at the time you left the prohibition ser-
     vice until the time you became chief clerk of the Board of
     Elections?
A.   (By Counsel) Well, the witness will refuse to answer on the grounds
     that his answer may tend to degrade or incriminate him.
Q.   Do you know a man named Joe Adonis?
A.   Casually.
Q.   How long have you known him?
A.   I have seen him around at different cafés. I was never intimate
     with him. I knew him casually.

Q. Did you know a man named—referred to generally as Trigger Mike Coppola?

A. No. Know him when I see him. But I wouldn't say I knew him.

Q. Didn't you testify in private hearings, Mr Toplitz that you had known Trigger Mike for fifteen—twenty years?

A. I seen him around for fifteen or twenty years, but I never knew him as what I would—I'd say just casually, Mr Mathews.

Q. Do you know Frank Erickson?

A. Yes.

Q. How long have you known him?

A. I should say for fifteen years. Not intimately; just know him being around him . . .

When questioned about other gangsters Toplitz said that he knew them 'just casually', although he later admitted that he called them all, including Costello and Erickson, by their Christian names.

Q. All these underworld people you've been questioned about, you call them by their first names and they call you by yours.

A. Well, I never had much—I don't always have conversation with them. I greet them. I never socialized.

Q. Mr Toplitz, what was your source of income and support prior to the time you became Chief Clerk of the Board of Elections?

A. (By Counsel) The witness will refuse to answer on the grounds that his answer may tend to degrade or incriminate him.

Q. Mr Toplitz, you lived rather expensively during the years before you became chief clerk and since you've become chief clerk, have you not?

A. The same objection.

Q. Are you a man of substantial means?

A. The same objection.

Q. Do you pay as much as sixty-five dollars a pair on occasion for shoes?

A. The same objection.

Q. Or $153?

A. The same objection.[18]

The evidence of Sidney Moses, the Democratic district leader of another Assembly District was quite as revealing. Moses was a Member of the State Assembly and had once been a Deputy Commissioner of Borough Works and Secretary of Tammany Hall.

Q. Do you know Frank Costello?
A. I met him a couple of times.
Q. You have had dinner with Costello?
A. I had dinner once with him. I met him at the Copacabana with Mr Toplitz.
Q. He attended an intimate family ceremony?
A. A *Bar Mitzvah*, that's correct. A confirmation, my son's confirmation.
Q. Frank Costello was at the confirmation?
A. I didn't invite him there. I don't know how he got there.

Moses admitted to knowing other gangsters besides Costello and to having curiously ill-defined business associations with them. He was also obliged to admit that he had used Democratic Party funds for non-political purposes. A man with a long police record was shown to be a manager of a restaurant owned by his father. Another man for whom Moses had found a job as a city official spent his time as one of the managers of the Flamingo Lounge.

Q. You were asked by the Commission to supply a financial questionnaire of your own income and expenses over a period?
A. That's right.
Q. You declined to do that?
A. That's correct.
Q. And you still decline to do it?
A. Of course.[19]

The pervasive influence and far-reaching power of the new gangsters extended even to the appointment of Supreme Court Judges. The telephone conversation of one of these, Thomas A. Aurelio, with Frank Costello was tapped and published:

Aurelio: 'Good morning, Francesco. How are you? And thanks for everything.
Costello: Congratulations. It went over perfect. When I tell you everything is in the bag, you can rest assured.
Aurelio: It was perfect. Arthur Klein did the nominating; first me, then Gavagan, then Peck. It was fine.
Costello: That's fine ... Well we will have to get together, you, your Mrs and myself; and have dinner some night real soon.
Aurelio: That would be fine, but right now I want to assure you of my loyalty for all you have done. It's undying.'[20]

The influence of the Sicilian, Thomas Lucchese, (his real name is Gaetano and he is also known as Brown) who apparently took over much of Costello's importance when Costello was imprisoned for contempt of Senate in 1952, seems to have been no less extensive than that of his predecessor. Lucchese, who lived in a luxurious house at Lido Beach on Long Island, led a life of apparent respectability. He had a charming family, a son who was a graduate of West Point, a daughter at Vassar. His neighbours, to whom he was always courteous and kind, said that he entertained congressmen, Supreme Court Justices and New York County judges. He was a generous host but he himself had simple tastes and drank little. He knew both the Mayor of New York and the City's former Police Commissioner.

He owed his success, indeed, largely to the help of such men. One of his first allies was James Hines, the Tammany Hall politician who had been so invaluable a friend to Dutch Schultz, and he contributed to the mayoral campaign fund of William O'Dwyer.[21]

Lucchese's early criminal career after his arrival from Sicily in 1911 is very obscure. He was arrested once in 1921 for stealing a car and again some time later in connection with a murder investigation. It has been suggested that he has had connections at various times with bootlegging, narcotics, night-clubs, real estate and dress manufacturing. But it seems that, by some arrangement with Lepke Buchalter involving narcotics, which the Mafia have always largely controlled, he was already deeply involved in the garment racket in the early 1930's.

The garment industry in New York was one of the earliest to feel the pressure of organized crime. In 1932 the 107th Street Mob began a campaign to take over a large share of the profits of the industry by extorting money by threats of violence from the transport owners. Soon gangsters like Johnny DioGuardi, who was arrested many times for assault and extortion and became himself a regional director of the United Automobile Workers, were obtaining important positions for themselves in the unions and, in particular, in the International Ladies' Garment Workers Union. Employers found themselves being obliged either to pay gangsters to keep unions from organizing their labour, or, if their labour was already organized, to pay the union as the only means of avoiding strikes or the implementation of various provisions in the union's rules.

An even more profitable field for extortion than the garment area was the water-front and here the Syndicate still apparently operates despite the reforms brought about by the Waterfront Commission. It was estimated in 1953 that two per cent of the $7,000,000,000 value of the cargo in foreign trade—that is to say $140 million a year—found its way into the hands of the Syndicate. At this time all the piers in Brooklyn were said to be controlled by Thomas Toddo Marino, a rich and quiet Sicilian with a long criminal record, who settled all disputes with Vincent Mangano and Joseph Profaci, two other important *mafiosi*.

'Take the matter of thieving,' said John W. McGrath, a former President of the National Association of Stevedores in an interview a few years ago. 'That's up to the insurance companies and the steamship lines. If I went to my longshoremen inquiring about cargo thefts, what would happen? The hiring boss would look at me and say "What the hell business is that of yours? You didn't lose anything did you? It wasn't your stuff stolen?" And that's as far as I'd get with that ... I want to stay in business. I can't afford to stick my neck out.'[22]

Pilferage, however, although it accounted for the loss of four million dollars worth of goods a year, according to an estimate published in the New York *Journal of Commerce* in 1956, still constituted only a small part of crime on the water-front. Apart from the narcotics traffic, the main profits were derived from the exploitation of labour which the union leaders were sometimes powerless to prevent and in some cases actively encouraged.

Budd Schulberg's Johnny Friendly, the President in *On the Waterfront*, of Longshoremen's Local 447, whose boys saw to it that work was only given to those prepared to see him grow rich by graft and by taking a share of the longshoremen's money, was not a caricature. Union leaders like this were not uncommon in the 1950's; and the corruption was as widespread in the higher ranks of the unions as in the lower. The New York State Crime Commission hearings in 1952 disclosed that several important union officials, including Joseph P. Ryan the life President of the International Longshoremen's Association, had accepted payments for various services. The shipping owners and contracting stevedores also paid money to gangsters to ensure that there was no individual pilfering, that organized pilfering was restricted to outgoing cargoes which could not be inspected until their arrival, and that brave and honest longshoremen did not air their grievances or encourage others to strike. So long as there were no regular labour gangs, and men assembled at 'shape-ups' to be picked for work by a union man who, often enough, expected to be paid for his favours, labour on the water-front could be tightly controlled by gangsters who lent money at enormous rates of interest to the temporarily unemployed. And although the 'shape-up' has now been replaced by organized hiring centres there is still a labour surplus which gangsters can exploit.

An agent from the District Attorney's office, whom Thomas Dewey sent to work on the docks in his efforts to break the water-front gangs, found that the 'loan sharks' actually paid out the wages to the men having deducted both their debts and a 'kickback' based on the number of hours the man had worked. When, representing himself as a stevedore from another port, the agent asked for work he was told a union book would cost him a hundred dollars. He bought one, however, for twenty-five dollars having given the official of the International Longshoremen's Association an admittance card to a brothel. After the agent had completed his investigations and the local gang leader had been arrested, two hundred longshoremen were taken in for questioning but they refused to testify against him. 'Who the hell wants to be a hero, mister?' one of them said. 'Talk and you're dead.'[23]

'I finally collected together nine witnesses,' the agent wrote when describing his subsequent investigations into an assault committed on the water-front by a white man who attacked three Negroes with a hatchet. 'But as the days slipped by my nine witnesses began to disappear. It was like trying to control drops of mercury. A man would disappear and after I had spent three or four frantic days prowling around Harlem to find him, I would return downtown only to find another had vanished.'[24]

It was not only fear that kept the gangs in control of the water-front. Most longshoremen, Ed Reid thinks, did not want a change in conditions any more than the ship owners did. Both had 'been brought up in the tradition of the water-front jungle which glorifies the law of the survival of the fittest. The ship owners want a constant, controlled pool of labour and the longshoremen live for the day of the "big killing".' And, after all, they worship the gangsters as the only heroes they know, and many of them are criminals themselves.[25]

There was, too, a long tradition of violence in labour relations which was not limited to the water-front. Industrial disputes had frequently in the past been settled by force. In mining villages before the First World War pit owners employed guards to shoot miners on strike. Machine-guns were sometimes loaded into freight cars which took them through the villages, usually little more than a single street beside the railway track.

'The nine guards would fire a couple of rifle shots from the cars to incite the strikers to return the fire, and then the machine-guns would be brought into action and the train would move the length of a village at a snail's pace, spitting bullets at the rate of 250 a minute, perforating the tents and shacks and mowing down and maiming and killing men and women and defenceless children.'[26]

In 1915 nineteen strikers were killed and wounded by sheriffs' deputies paid by the American Agricultural Company. And after the war companies specializing in strike breaking were formed and offered employers their services. Messrs. Berghof Brothers and Wadell, one of these firms of 'labour adjusters', claimed that they were able to provide ten thousand men for strike breaking within seventy-two hours. A gangster, Peter De Vito, was said to have been paid over fifty thousand dollars in five weeks in 1929 for breaking various strikes in Brooklyn, including those of the Oil Company of New York and of the American Can Company.[27] It is understandable that the reply of organized labour was violent and that the unions developed rackets of their own.

The labour racketeer remains a real menace in American industrial relations; and it has always been difficult to break his power. In 1943, for instance, Joe Fay who began his career as the business agent of a local of the Union of Operating Engineers and rose to be its International Vice-President despite the suspicion that he had been involved in the murder of a rival construction union official, was indicted on a charge of extorting $420,000 and of conspiring to extort $703,000 from contractors whom he had threatened with strikes. He was sent to prison but a few years later the *New York Journal-American* revealed that politicians, labour leaders and builders were regularly visiting him in his cell as he was 'still the boss of the construction industry'.[28] Over a third of the delegates discovered at Joseph Barbara's Apalachin house in 1962 were involved in various labour rackets, sixteen of them in the garment industry.

A labour leader who in 1963 was still in control of the powerful International Brotherhood of Teamsters is James Hoffa. His predecessor as President of this union, which has a membership of well over a million and a half, was Dave Beck who built his house at Seattle with union funds and then sold it to the union for $163,000. Despite convictions for income-tax evasion and grand larceny, Beck enjoyed a pension of $50,000 a year from the Union and boasted in 1959 that he was a millionaire. His successor Hoffa was elected President in 1957 with a salary of $50,000 plus $15,000 a year for remaining President of a Detroit local, together with an unlimited expense account. These payments, according to evidence given to a Senate Committee under the chairmanship of Senator John McClellan, are not the only ones that Hoffa has received. Indeed, the evidence collected by the Committee's investigators, led by Robert F. Kennedy, showed that Hoffa, in the words of an interim report, ran a 'hoodlum empire'. Hoffa's power, the Committee's report added, was 'extraordinary . . . That this power is now lodged in the hands of a man such as Hoffa [is] tragic for the Teamsters Union and dangerous for the country at large.'

It appeared from the evidence of terrified witnesses—one of whom said that his life had been made 'a living hell' since his first appearance—that Hoffa's Union accepted bribes for calling off strikes and that some of this money may have found its way into Hoffa's own pocket; that a construction firm in which Hoffa was interested used $235,000 in Teamster funds as working capital; that the Union had business-like connections with gangsters and was largely staffed by hoodlums; that when imprisoned some of these officials continued to receive their salaries; that at least one strike in which taxis were burned and blown up was only ended when the taxi owners were paid $15,000 for forcing their drivers to join the Union; that some Union officers carried guns, the holsters being charged to 'office supplies'; that one of these officers had threatened to etch the word 'rat' in acid on a recalcitrant driver's forehead; and that an employer who balked at the Teamsters' demands was threatened with death, had fire-bombs thrown into his lorries and marijuana planted in his employees' cars.

The activities of Frank Kierdorf, one of the Union's business agents in Michigan, are characteristic. Kierdorf, a man with a long criminal record who had once tried to run over an employer in his car, approached a businessman in 1956 and gave him a union recognition form which he asked him to sign. The businessman said that his men had not been in any union before but that he had no objection to their joining one and so he would ask them to vote on it. Kierdorf said there would be no vote. A week later a Teamster picket line stopped all deliveries by road to the factory. The employer began to use the railway and suggested that the whole question should be taken up with the state mediator. Again Kierdorf said no; and then he began to use violence. One day four men jumped out of his Cadillac and beat one of the factory's drivers over the head with an iron pipe. The driver had to have twenty stitches in his head. The employer gave in. Kierdorf then said all the office staff must join the union too. The employer was permitted to avoid this, however, by paying two thousand dollars and a monthly cheque of seventy-five dollars.

In August 1958 Kierdorf was burned to death after having tried to burn out a dry-cleaning shop in a suburb of Flint, assisted, so the police believed, by other Teamster officials.

Hoffa, who had been helped in his career in New York by Johnny DioGuardi, one of the most experienced extortionists in the garment industry, and in Chicago by a former Capone gangster, Joseph Glimco, was a contemptuous witness at the Committee hearings. He did not use the Fifth Amendment, as one of his Philadelphia officials did when accused of misappropriating four hundred thousand dollars of the funds of his local, but he displayed what one Senator called 'the best forgettery of anyone I have ever known'. In a single session of the Committee he replied that he could not remember to over a hundred questions. But although he was roundly condemned by the Committee, and a new law—debarring anyone convicted of a major crime from holding union office for five years after conviction—was passed in an effort to break the grip of criminals on his Union, Hoffa's personal grip was seen to be as firm as ever at the Teamsters' convention at Miami in 1961. Here, despite charges that union funds had been squandered on an expensive house and swimming pool for the mistress of an official; that $2,000,000,000 had been lent to a criminal lawyer for real estate speculations; that calls for democracy within the union had been crushed by force; that elections had been rigged; and, above all, that their President was not nearly so concerned about the welfare of his members as he so frequently protested, Hoffa was confirmed in office with an increase of twenty-five thousand dollars a year in his salary, a salary which he was still enjoying in January 1963 when, for the fourth time in five years, he walked free from a federal trial.[20]

Even at seventy-five thousand dollars and expenses, Hoffa's income may not have been so large as that of other officials in his Union. The Chicago Crime Commission, for instance, estimated the income of the President of one Teamster Local, at $840,000, much of it from kickbacks and extortion payments.

The Teamsters, however, were not the only Union who worked in this way in Chicago. Other unions, also condemned by the McClellan Committee, used no less violent methods and the gangsters, seeing the possibility of large profits, moved in to exploit them.

Throughout the 1950's restaurants in Chicago were bombed and burned out and in 1958 the biggest of them all, owned by a man who had given evidence to the McClellan Committee, was ruined by a fire that caused $1,000,000, worth of damage. After another witness had testified that a professional picket, put round his restaurant by a Local of the Hotel and Restaurant Employees' and Bartenders' International Union, had slashed the car tyres of his employees and menacingly shouted out the licence numbers of his customers' cars. Tony Accardo (the former Capone gunman and an immensely rich inheritor of some of his powers) and Abraham Teitelbaum (a lawyer who had passed legal fees received from a worried restaurant owner over to the Union) were questioned by the Committee and evaded replying by invoking the Fifth Amendment.

Unions dominated by gangsters were, though, only one of Chicago's problems. The rackets unearthed by the McClellan Committee were proliferous. A characteristic one was that operated by a Chicago firm of gramophone record distributors, owned by a gangster who was an acquaintance of Accardo, which had been forcing jukebox owners to buy its records and pay protection money for each jukebox they owned. One owner had been persuaded to hire an ex-convict, Rocco Pranno, as a well-paid business adviser after Pranno had taken him for a ride to the river in his car with cement weights tied to his legs.[30]

But Chicago was not, even so, the most lawless big city in the United States. According to the *Uniform Crime Reports,* issued by the Federal Bureau of Investigation it was, in fact, apart from Buffalo, the least lawless of all. The city with the highest rate of serious crimes that year was Los Angeles with a rate of fifty-one serious crimes for each thousand citizens. Other lawless cities were

Atlanta (44.7 for each thousand citizens), St Louis (43.8), Denver and Seattle (39.3), Newark (37.4), Houston (35.3), Dallas (35.2), San Francisco (34.8), New Orleans (29.2), Detroit (28) and Indianapolis (28). Cleveland, Minneapolis, Boston and Pittsburg all had rates under 25. New York (17.7), Philadelphia (16.9), Cincinatti (16.0), Kansas City (13.3) and Chicago (12.9) had rates under 20. But only Buffalo (8.5), of the twenty-two cities mentioned, had a rate under ten.*

The high crime rate among Negroes everywhere—and of Mexicans and Puerto Ricans in some states—makes it necessary, of course, to qualify any assumptions which might be made about the lawlessness of white populations in areas where Negroes are numerous, badly housed or socially ostracized; just as assumptions must also be qualified in the light of the activities—both in the reporting and preventing of crime—of the police. And some police forces were little better equipped to deal with criminal acts let alone to discover, report or prevent them, than they had been fifty years before.

* In 1962 Washington seemed to be the city in which crime was increasing faster than anywhere else. It recorded more assault and battery cases than any other large city; only one other city had a higher rate of theft and only two others had a higher rate of murder. A third of those convicted of robbery were under twenty, and a majority of all convicted criminals were Negroes. Almost fifty-five per cent of the population are coloured.

CHAPTER THREE

COPS AND G-MEN

'It is a matter of common knowledge that for many years there has been a fixed scale of prices for advancement.'
CHIEF JUSTICE JOHN P. McGOORTY, 1931

THE influence of English precedents and of English prejudices about police persisted well on into the nineteenth century in America. In colonial times, and for many years afterwards, the idea that the law could best be enforced by members of local communities taking it in turns, as in England, to act as constables and watchmen was rarely questioned. And it was not until 1844 that New York City established the first publicly paid police force in the United States.[1] By then the rapid growth of other cities had made efficient professional forces essential and New York's example was soon followed; but many towns continued to rely on amateur watchmen for night-time duty, and uniforms were not general till after the Civil War.[2]

The same arguments that had been used to delay the creation of professional policemen in England had been used in the United States and had resulted in the same limitation of their power. The American policeman, like the English policeman, was granted few rights beyond those possessed by any citizen. He could be prosecuted for wrongful arrest and was legally obliged to warn prisoners taken into custody that anything they said might be used in evidence at their trials. As in England too, local jealousies and rivalries were strong and contributed to that traditional reluctance to entertain the thought of a force with anything resembling national control.

It was at least partly due to this lack of a complete and effective system of law enforcement that lynching began in the nineteenth century to assume the proportions of a national crime, particularly in the West and the South where the problems of existence in the extending territories of the frontier were already beginning to leave their imprints both for good and for evil on the social system of America. In the West the settlers and pioneers in search of land or wealth, the restless looking for adventure and the unruly retreating from justice, all advanced ever deeper into territories where the only law was their own. In 1849 when men rushed into California to fill their pockets with the gold that had been discovered there, a committee of vigilantes was established in San Francisco with the boast that as the law could not clean up the town, the people would do it.

In the South, gamblers and white men who advocated the abolition of slavery suffered most frequently at the hands of the lynching mob before the Civil War; but after it, racial antagonism and the distrust of the outsider were at the root of most lynchings. The formation in Tennessee in 1866 of the Ku Klux Klan which, although originally a secret society whose members were mainly concerned with amusing themselves, soon developed into an organization devoted to racial and religious persecution, gave to lynching a new and dangerous significance.

Before the end of the nineteenth century almost three quarters of the lynchings were taking place in the Southern states and they were mostly of Negroes—usually of Negroes accused of rape, the injured woman being sometimes required to put the match to the kindling. Between 1889 and 1899 there were, on average, 187.5 lynchings a year, nearly all of them carried out with impunity and hardly any of them resulting in even the formal arrest of the ring-leaders. After 1900, however, the crime of lynching began to decline.[3] In the years between 1899 and 1909 the numbers of lynchings dropped by half. By 1924 the average was down to 46.2 a year, by 1934 to seventeen and by 1944 to 3.9; and in the years that followed, although it was still difficult to obtain the conviction of a lyncher in a Southern courtroom, it was clear that this was a crime which could no longer expect much public sympathy. In 1954 in Mississippi two men were acquitted of lynching a fourteen-year-old Negro who was supposed to have made offensive remarks and whistled at the wife of one of them; and in 1959, again in Mississippi, no indictment was made when a gang of hooded men dragged out a Negro from a gaol where he was being held on a charge of raping a white woman, and shot him to death. The Federal Bureau of Investigation prepared a report on the case but as no federal kidnapping law had been violated, the guilty men had to be left to Mississippi law and Mississippi took no action against them. In the same year, however, when four white men were accused of raping a Negro girl in Florida, the white jury obeyed the judge's direction to consider the charge 'without regard to race, color or creed' and found them all guilty.[4] This regard for equality of justice under the law is one which other Southern States are now beginning to adopt.

The rapid decline in lynching during the 1920's and 1930's owed more, indeed, to the development of the human conscience than to any increasing respect that the Americans felt in these years for their police forces which were still usually, and with justification, regarded as corrupt and nearly always as corruptible.

The limitations upon the power of the police, for instance, imposed by an inbred devotion to personal liberty, were disregarded without care or repentance. The use of arrests as a method of initiating criminal prosecutions had become so extensive that in some years nearly half the number of people arrested were subsequently released without being charged.[5] To avoid the necessity of complying with the law in this respect suspects or unwilling witnesses were sometimes moved about between 'half a dozen different police stations' so that lawyers and bailsmen could not find them.[6]

'To obtain confessions or admissions,' the National Commission on Law Observance and Enforcement reported in 1931, 'the officers (usually detectives) proceed "to work" the prisoner. "Work" is the term used to signify any form of what is commonly called the third degree, and may consist in nothing more than a severe cross-examination. Perhaps in most cases it is nothing more than that, but the prisoner knows that he is wholly at the mercy of his inquisitor and that the severe cross-examination may at any moment shift to a severe beating. This knowledge itself undoubtedly induces speedy confessions in many instances and makes unnecessary a resort to force. If the prisoner refuses to answer, he may be returned to his cell with notice that he will stay till ready to "come clean". The cell may be specially chosen for the purpose—cold, dark, without bed or chair. The sweat box is a small cell completely dark and arranged to be heated till the prisoner, unable to endure the temperature, will promise to answer as described. Or refusal to answer may be overcome by whipping, beating with rubber hose, clubs, or fists, or by kicking or by threats or promises.

Powerful lights turned full on the prisoner's face, or switched on and off, have been found effective. The electric chair is another device to extort confessions. The most commonly used method is persistent questioning, continuing hour after hour, sometimes by relays of officers. It has been known since 1500, at least, that deprivation of sleep is the most effective torture and certain to produce any confession desired.'[7]

The resort to force and illegal arrest was often justified—and is still justified—by the police on the grounds that it is the quickest and frequently the only means of uncovering evidence. Scientific methods of crime detection on the European model were almost unknown and few police departments had any of the elaborate technical devices which were already considered essential in Europe. Some had no equipment for photographing criminals let alone forensic laboratories or systematic methods of keeping records. In Boston there were 'no records similar to the dossiers customarily found in European departments. Scanty notes recording the names of witnesses, addresses, and court appearances' were 'all that appeared in the special officer's notebook'.[8] And these officers were 'likely to rely more upon chance, or upon the traditional trial and error methods of detectives, the use of stool pigeons and the "third degree" than upon the skilful technique of investigation which continental police administrators have appropriately called *police scientifique*'.[9]

The personnel of the police was as strongly criticized as the haphazard methods employed. Salaries as in England were low, and the more profitable positions were usually won through political connections or even bought. 'It is a matter of common knowledge,' said Chief Justice John P. McGoorty in 1931, 'that for many years there has been a fixed scale of prices for advancement.'[10] Investigations into the murder by gangsters of the newspaperman Jake Lingle in Chicago in 1930 revealed that 'hundreds of patrolmen' had been asked 'if they wanted to buy sergeancies'. 'Captaincies,' it was reported, cost five thousand dollars and up, depending on where the captain wanted to be assigned.'[11]

Chiefs of Police were often appointed by mayors who were virtually controlled by gangsters. At one time San Francisco was 'so completely dominated by the gangsters that three prominent gamblers who were in control of the politics of the city and who quarrelled about the appointment of the police chief settled their quarrel by shaking dice to determine who would name the chief for the first two years, who for the second two years and who for the third.'[12]

In such conditions it was not surprising that chiefs of police were birds of passage and that Chicago had thirty-one in the sixty-three years between 1870 and 1933.[13] Nor is it surprising that not one of the 257 gang murders in Chicago between 1923 and 1929 resulted in a conviction nor that in ninety per cent of the cases the murders remained unsolved.[14] Few chiefs of police, anywhere, had any particular qualifications for the appointment. 'I know that my man is going to be a good chief,' the Mayor of Indianapolis once said, 'because he has been my tailor for twenty years.'[15]

The men they controlled had few qualifications either. In some forces, many of them had already found some other career unsatisfactory or been dismissed and drifted into the police for want of a better-paid job. In one force more than half the men were over thirty when they were appointed, one man was seventy-four and another seventy-eight.[16] In Boston in 1928 a fifth of the whole force had formerly been cab drivers, chauffeurs or truck drivers, many of the others had been unskilled labourers and all of them received the barest minimum of training to make them into policemen who, it was admitted, required 'physical courage, tact, disciplined temper, good judgment, alertness of observation and specialized knowledge of law and procedure'.[17] Yet, despite these admitted requirements, in the simple tests which police candidates were required to take, the physical examination was considered the only one of any real importance. And in Chicago the importance attached to what was loosely described as 'experience', assumed 'a peculiar, if not sinister, appearance'.[18] There were, in fact, police officers with criminal records in several cities other than Chicago.

Training in some smaller towns was not merely inadequate but virtually did not exist. The police chief in one small town told a Crime Commission in New York in 1927:

'I say to [the recruit] that now he is a policeman, and I hope that he will be a credit to the force. I tell him that he doesn't need anybody to tell him how to enforce the law, that all he needs to do is to go out on the streets and keep his eyes open. I say, "You know the Ten Commandments, don't you? Well, if you know the Ten Commandments and you go out on your beat and see somebody violating one of those Commandments, you can be sure he is violating some law." [19]

Unqualified and untrained the men slipped easily into crime. A commission of inquiry which made its report in 1932 found that rackets amongst the police were common, as common as they had been before the First World War when the celebrated Charlie Becker, a police lieutenant in charge of the New York Vice Squad, was the chief collector of protection money from the City's brothels and gambling houses.

In the 'Doctor's Racket', the 1932 commission reported, an accomplice went into a surgery supposedly for treatment while the doctor was out. He put money down on the table and undressed. When the nurse protested police officers came in and arrested her on a charge of prostitution. In the 'Landlady Racket' the accomplice booked a room for himself and a woman who claimed to be his wife. When the couple were in bed, the landlady was arrested for keeping a house of prostitution. Prosecutions were, of course, rarely brought but the profits made from bribes, blackmail and fees shared with corrupt lawyers were immense. Five police officers, whose bank accounts were analysed by the Commission, 'in a few years accumulated more than five hundred thousand dollars.' [20]

The Commission related the history of a woman arrested by two policemen and arraigned on a charge of prostitution: 'She was then taken to the office of a "Fixer" who told her that he was a "big man in the Grand Street Boys" and that for six hundred dollars he could fix everything in such a way that it would make no difference if she were guilty or innocent. The "Fixer" further stated to her that the said sum of six hundred dollars which she had paid to him would include his own services, the services of an attorney and the necessary bribe for the arresting officer.' An attorney was retained but as he did not get his share of the six hundred dollars the woman was persuaded to give him an additional two hundred although he did not attend the court on her behalf. Eventually she paid out $1,200. All the same she was convicted. [21]

Real or imagined infractions of the gambling laws were an even more profitable field for the collection of bribes and blackmail than vice. In 1929 in New York, 4,328 people were arrested for bookmaking, and of these all but 161 were discharged. [22]

Not all police forces, of course, were as pervaded by corruption as these reports imply. But few of them were entirely honest and nearly all of them operated from station houses which corroborated the poor opinion the public had of their protectors. A typical station house in the 1930's was described by a writer who emphasized its squalor and muddle:

'The desk dominates the whole and the entire work of the station centres round it. Prisoners stand in front or at one side of it while the facts required in booking an arrest are entered by the desk officer; patrolmen and citizens gather there . . .

At times great confusion results from such concentration of the station's work. It is not uncommon to find standing side by side a person reporting the loss of property, a mother enquiring about a lost child, a policeman waiting for instruction, and one or more prisoners. Citizens upon crossing the threshold are frequently confronted with unpleasant scenes: a violent or abusive woman under arrest for drunkenness, an unspeakably filthy vagabond, or a prisoner struggling to resist arrest.'[23]

The confusion in the Station house was reflected in the muddle occasioned by the complete lack of any sort of centralization in the police department as a whole. Instead of a single responsible police authority in each state, there were state police and county police and city police, and the lack of co-operation between them was often as great as the lack of co-operation between the police authorities in the English parishes in the eighteenth century.

The result of all this, as the *Encyclopaedia of the Social Sciences* put it, was 'the most complete decentralization of police authority known to the civilized world, accompanied by an extraordinary degree of duplication and conflicting jurisdiction'.

An attempt to remedy some of these defects in American law enforcement had been made in 1907 when the Attorney-General, Charles Joseph Bonaparte, proposed the establishment of an investigating agency with federal powers under the general direction of the Department of Justice. It was essential, Bonaparte insisted, that the Government should have more satisfactory means of enforcing federal law and of preventing criminals escaping justice by moving across state boundaries and from one jurisdiction into another. The proposal met with the same storm of protest that had greeted proposals for a detective force in England.

'I believe that it would be a great blow to freedom and to free institutions,' Congressman Waldo of New York told the House, 'if there should arise in this country any such great central secret-service bureau as there is in Russia.' And Congressman Smith of Iowa, remembering perhaps that the Attorney-General was a grand-nephew of Napoleon I, said that no system of spying on the people, such as prevailed in France under the Empire, 'should be allowed to grow up'. Newspapers, as also in England, reported the views of Congress approvingly. There was 'no desire for a general detective service or national police organization', a Chicago newspaper thought. On the contrary there was 'a bitter abhorrence of such a scheme'. It was 'considered absolutely contradictory to the democratic principles of government'.[24]

The existing practice of the Department of Justice of hiring Secret Service agents from the Treasury Department for police work was bad enough, but this new proposal, it was considered, would make matters a great deal worse by bringing the formation of a secret police so much nearer. To warn the Attorney-General that such an extension of federal power would not be tolerated, Congress passed a law prohibiting the employment of Secret Service detectives by other Government departments including the Department of Justice.*

But Bonaparte was not deterred. Soon after Congress adjourned, a Bureau of Investigation was quietly established in his Department in July 1908. The reaction of Congressmen and newspapers when this became known was predictable.

'If Anglo-Saxon civilization stands for anything,' said Congressman Sherley of Kentucky in a passionate speech which won wide praise, 'it is for a government where the humblest citizen is safeguarded against the secret activities of the executive of the Government . . . Not in vain did our forefathers read the history of the Magna Carta and the Bill of Rights.'[25]

The Attorney General, strongly backed by the President, Theodore Roosevelt, refused to give way. And it was, in fact, ultimately difficult for Congress to find adequate and acceptable reasons for abolishing the new force of federal detectives when some steps to combat the rising wave of crime in the United States

---

* The Secret Service agents had been organized by the Treasury Department after the Civil War to deal with a sudden increase in the crime of counterfeiting; but they had for years been employed by President Theodore Roosevelt in his campaign against political and business corruption, particularly against industrial combines, the 'trusts', which were ignoring the Sherman Anti-trust Act and against the dishonest Government officials who were embezzling the vast reserves of land in the West of which they were the appointed guardians.

were so obviously required. Detectives, President Roosevelt insisted, were the country's defenders against the criminal and it was the 'duty of every true American to help the country's defenders' in time of crisis. If Congress persisted in its obstructive campaign, it would be unable to deny the charge that it was encouraging crime. In the face of the President's determined defence of the Attorney-General's action and his telling suggestions that they were befriending and shielding criminals, Congressmen felt bound to give way. Instead of calling for the abolition of the new detective force, they called now, in Congressman Sherley's phrase, for its hedging about 'with all the safeguards essential to the preservation of the people's liberties'.[26] The Attorney-General promised to keep a close eye on the Bureau's activities and, although a long debate followed on the manner in which he should supervise and control it, the Sixtieth Congress came to an end with no clear limitations drawn and a Bureau of Investigation firmly in existence.

At first, however, there seemed little work of importance that the new Bureau could satisfactorily do. Most police work was still done, as it continues still to be done, by local forces. National problems, such as smuggling, counterfeiting, tax evasion and mail robberies, remained the concern of the special police forces maintained by the Treasury and Post Office Departments. The first Chief of the Bureau, Stanley W. Finch, admitted that he would only be concerned with what little was left over and this was troublesome but relatively unimportant work in connection with laws passed by Congress which forbade the shipment between state and state of contraceptives, prize-fight films and obscene books and which made illegal the transportation of liquor into states which prohibited its consumption. It was not, in fact, until the White Slave Traffic Act, introduced by Representative James Robert Mann of Illinois, became law that the Bureau was given an opportunity to carry out its first large-scale operation. The Mann Act was the result of a public outcry against commercialized vice which had reached its culmination when the U.S. Attorney in Chicago seized documents disclosing that a vice syndicate had been operating in the United States for ten years and had imported no less than twenty thousand women and girls into the country.[27] The Act was intended to put a stop to this traffic and to prevent the widespread shipment of women across state boundaries, mainly from country districts to brothels in the towns. The Bureau set to work to enforce the federal law with embarrassing energy.

Circular letters were sent to postmasters, chiefs of police and other officials in the towns in every state, asking whether or not there were 'any houses of prostitution in their towns'. Wherever there were, agents of the Bureau went to the town, hired a local lawyer, and called at the police station to ask for the help of a city detective. The three men would then visit the various brothels, houses of assignation and suspected rooming-houses and investigate all the residents and employees. In cases where no breach of the Mann Act was involved, the Bureau's agent, who had been provided with a copy of all relevant State laws, urged the local police to make arrests for any violation of them.

While the success of the Bureau in controlling and limiting commercialized vice was not doubted, it drew upon itself much criticism for its interpretation of the Mann Act as a measure directed not only against commercial vice but against private immorality. The Government man (soon to be known simply and universally as the G-man) began arresting ordinary citizens who crossed state borders with prostitutes even if no question of profit was involved. The heavyweight champion, Jack Johnson, was put in prison for persuading a girl, whom he subsequently married, to leave her brothel and go away with him into another state; and the son of a well-known Democrat was later arrested on a similar charge.

Ill-considered arrests under the Mann Act were not the only cause of criticism of the FBI by a people as jealous of their personal freedom as the English and far more resentful of Government interference in local affairs. The enthusiasm with which the FBI enforced the draft laws in the First World War, and arrested men who avoided military service, was another reason for the distrust with which the G-men were regarded during their early years. Raids were made all over the country on towns where numbers of draft-evaders were believed to be hiding; people were constantly being stopped in the street, in hotels, in railway stations and bars and asked to show their draft registration cards. Buses and lorries sometimes had to be commandeered to transport the enormous numbers of men arrested to the police stations and on occasions even the drivers of these buses and lorries were taken in as well, for they could not produce their registration cards either. Thousands of men who were not draft dodgers at all were kept locked up, some for more than twenty-four hours.

'In the midst of all the excitement, and labouring under instructions to proceed with utmost rapidity, the raiders resorted to rough-and-ready actions, such as the wholesale arrest of everyone in a crowded barber shop when the barbers' gowns and the lather on the patrons' faces made it difficult to estimate ages quickly. Action under similar pressure brought to the police stations carload after carload of grey-haired men ... Some who were dragged into the Bureau's net were physically unfit, crippled or hobbling on canes, like the seventy-five-year-old man detained in a public square along with others held by the raiders for questioning ... The work was made all the more difficult by the inadequacy of the night lighting in the streets of the raided cities; the inability of some of the young and the old to control their fright when arrested, to answer questions clearly, without suspicious hesitation and stammering.'[28]

The protests against 'Prussianism', 'terrorism', the activities of 'press-gangs' came from all over America. 'In the West,' said Senator Thomas of Colorado voicing a general opinion, 'we have another name for that sort of procedure, although we use it against animals and not men. We call it a round-up, and even then the mavericks are all cut out.' President Wilson asked for a full report. The Attorney-General said the raids were 'contrary to law' and the G-men had acted 'out of an excess of zeal for the public good'.[29]

When the war ended the FBI was widely resented, and widely despised, and in December 1918 when it became known that for some time it had been engaged in investigating the political opinions of hundreds of respected American citizens its reputation fell to new depths. It appeared that the Bureau had not limited itself to the compilation of a list of pro-Germans (including William Randolph Hearst, William Jennings Bryan, President Wilson's first Secretary of State, and Judge John F. Hylan, a future Mayor of New York) but had devoted its attention to various political groups which it believed had traitorous intentions. Some of these groups, such as the Industrial Workers of the World did endorse views which were justifiably considered dangerous but the evidence given by FBI experts before an investigating committee called for by the Senate, was little short of ludicrous. And it seemed clear enough, before the committee's hearings were over, that if the threat to national security existed on so large a scale as these experts insisted, the Bureau of Investigation was incapable of meeting it. Its incapacity, indeed, appeared less than ever in doubt when despite several arrests and the outlay of immense sums it was unable to discover those responsible either for a bomb explosion in the Federal Government building at Chicago, in which four people were killed, or for the despatch of numerous bombs through the mail and by personal delivery to Government officials and private citizens. Members of the I.W.W. and radicals in general were naturally blamed for these outrages but proof of their responsibility was never obtained.

It was obvious that some new specialist organization was urgently required. And in August 1919 a new anti-radical Division of the Bureau, later to be known as the General Intelligence Division, was created. Put in charge of it was a twenty-four-year-old lawyer of exceptional talents, J. Edgar Hoover, a 'slender bundle of high-charged electric wire' as a journalist extravagantly described him.

Five years later this young man was called to the office of President Calvin Coolidge's new Attorney-General, Harlan Fiske Stone. Coolidge had entrusted Stone, a big, honest, gruff man, with the task of restoring public confidence in the Department of Justice which had not escaped the recent charges of corruption levelled at the whole Harding administration during the time of the Teapot Dome oil-field scandal. In particular, Stone was to re-organize the Bureau of Investigation, the Chief of which, William J. Burns, had been closely connected with the suspicious activities of the previous Attorney-General, Harry Daugherty, whose resignation Coolidge had felt compelled to demand. Burns also resigned a few weeks after Stone had taken office and made it possible for the new Attorney-General to appoint in his place a man he could trust to carry out Coolidge's intentions.

'Sit down,' Stone said brusquely as Hoover came into his office. 'Young man, I want you to be acting director of the Bureau of Investigation.'

'I'll take the job, Mr Stone,' Hoover replied, 'on certain conditions.'
'What are they?'
'The Bureau must be divorced from politics and not be a catch-all for political hacks. Second, promotions will be made on proved ability and the Bureau will be responsible only to the Attorney-General.'

'I wouldn't give it to you under any other conditions,' Stone said abruptly. 'That's all. Good-day.'[30]

Eight years later Stone felt able to write to Hoover to say, 'I often look back to the days when I first made your acquaintance in the Department of Justice and it is always a comfort to me to be able to see how completely you have confirmed my judgment when I decided to place you at the head of the Bureau of Investigation. The Government can now take pride in the Bureau instead of feeling obliged to apologize for it.'[31]

Hoover's triumph was the more remarkable because he had begun his great work of reformation at a time when the Government had not only felt obliged to apologize for the Bureau but to fight demands for its complete disbandment. Even those who advocated its survival did so, often enough, because they wanted it to remain—as many Englishmen hoped Peel's Metropolitan Police would turn out to be—a means of satisfying claims on patronage. The abolition of such appointments, the dismissal of incompetent agents and those with political ties, and the bringing of all investigations, which would be limited to violations of federal laws, under the guidance of the Attorney-General, were the ideals which Hoover immediately set himself and which eventually he carried largely into effect. He was able to rely on Stone's whole-hearted support. Once when an angry and influential Senator complained to Stone that young Hoover had transferred an agent because he had been too active in politics, Hoover was called to the Attorney-General's office to explain his conduct. When Hoover had done so, Stone said that he did not think the Bureau was on 'entirely sound grounds'. Hoover began to think he ought to resign. Then Stone said, 'I'm surprised you didn't fire the fellow at once.'[32]

Hoover's new appointments were men trained as lawyers, like himself, or as accountants, and they were expected to conform to uniform operating procedures and to observe a strict code of conduct. They were carefully selected and highly trained not only in investigating techniques, in law and administration but in the use of pistols, machine-guns and rifles, and in ju-jutsu. To help them in their work a forensic science laboratory was established in 1932 and a training academy in 1935. The United States had long lagged behind Europe in the training of detectives and in the development of scientific methods of detecting crime, but with Hoover's inspired and ruthless leadership the FBI began to overcome the disabilities imposed by a late start.

Throughout the 1930's the national reputation of the FBI grew. Admittedly during the first half of the decade its reputation was that of a relentless organization of tough, fast-shooting, brave but not over-intelligent commandos, fighting the gangsters with their own weapons, rather than that of an efficient and disciplined force. But the exigencies of the time demanded such men, although their methods seem on occasions to have been unnecessarily violent and peculiarly adventitious. The arrests of Alvin Karpis and John Dillinger are characteristic of their style.

Karpis was, in Hoover's own characteristically flamboyant phrases, head of the 'shrewdest, most cold-blooded gang in America', 'Public Rat Number one.'[33] His capture had been effected by Hoover himself who, angered by a Senator's question during a 1936 hearing of the Senate Appropriations Committee, had decided to demonstrate that he was not merely an administrator. Why wasn't G-man Hoover out risking his own neck when most of his men were, the Senator had wanted to know. So Hoover 'boiling mad' flew down to New Orleans to lead the raid on Karpis's headquarters personally.

Hoover and his men rushed into the building, guns in hand and dragged Karpis out into a waiting car. Hoover has described the scene:

' "Put the cuffs on him, boys," I said.

Then it developed that not one of us had a pair of handcuffs. They were in the other cars. A crowd was gathering and we had to move fast, so the two agents bound the hands of the hoodlum with their neckties.

"To the Post Office Building," I instructed the driver.

The car with the four of us turned into Canal Street. After it had gone a few blocks, I asked the Oklahoma agent who was driving:

"You know how to get there in a hurry, don't you?"

"No, sir," he replied. "I was never in New Orleans before in my life."

"Mr Hoover," broke in Karpis who hadn't said a word up to then, "if you mean the new Post Office, I know where that is, because I was just goin' to rob it." '[34]

The arrest of John Dillinger was even more haphazard. Dillinger, a wild bank robber, the son of strict Quaker parents from Indianapolis, had been wounded in a skirmish with the FBI and had gone into hiding in Mooresville. Later he had been traced to Little Bohemia, Wisconsin, and the shooting lodge in which he was living there was surrounded by G-men armed with rifles and machine-guns. When a car left the lodge, the G-men opened fire but Dillinger was not in it. Dillinger's gang returned the fire and one of them, Baby Face Nelson, killed a G-man and wounded two others. The gang escaped in another car, leaving their girl friends behind.

Rewards were now offered for information leading to Dillinger's capture by several states and by Congress, and these tempted a woman friend of Dillinger, a brothel keeper known as Anna Sage, to betray him. She told an FBI agent that she would go with Dillinger to either the Marbro or the Biograph Cinema in Chicago on 22 July. G-men surrounded both cinemas and were instructed not to 'unnecessarily endanger' their own lives. 'If Dillinger offers any resistance,' they were told, 'each man will be for himself. It will be up to each of you to do whatever you think necessary to protect yourself in taking Dillinger.'[35] Dillinger chose to see Clark Gable at the Biograph rather than the film at the Marbro and, in spite of some recent plastic surgery by which he had tried to disguise his face, he was immediately recognized. The G-men waited for him to come out. One of them, remembering Dillinger's previous escapades, was frankly terrified.

'My throat was parched,' he confessed afterwards, 'My knees wouldn't stay still . . . I stood with my cigar shaking in my mouth . . . I had one gun stuck between my trousers and shirt on the left side and another gun in the same fashion on the right. Later, after leaving this scene, I tried to button up my coat and found both buttons gone. Apparently I had grabbed for my gun without thinking and I am frank to say I do not know how it came into my hand.'[36]

Dillinger was not given much chance to think either. He seemed to sense that he was in danger as he came out of the cinema and, glancing over his shoulder, he darted sideways apparently reaching for his gun. Three agents opened fire simultaneously and Dillinger fell, mortally wounded, on the pavement.

The FBI fights with more care and subtlety now, because those whom they are fighting are more careful and subtle too. The painstaking inquiries which led to the remarkable achievements of the FBI as an intelligence and counter-espionage agency during the Second World War and its subsequent part in the discovery of evidence, which resulted in the conviction of the spies Klaus Fuchs, Harry Gold, David Greenglass and the Rosenbergs, have secured the inviolability of a reputation which the recent revelations of Jack Levine, a former agent, about the questionable methods employed by the vain and power-conscious J. Edgar Hoover, have done little to damage. It remains a complex, highly efficient, although highly secretive organization controlled by a central headquarters in Washington with over fifty field divisions spread all over the country. It has over six thousand special agents and more than eight thousand other employees.

But even these numbers, added to the two hundred thousand policemen of the United States, are not enough to check the increase of professional crime, organized by those whom Hoover has called the 'barons of the underworld' who annually rob the nation of well over twenty thousand million dollars.

The threat is so real and so urgent because these 'barons' can now adopt in society positions of quasi-respectability. They can become something more than millionaires, and their position is strengthened by the growth of what Professor Sutherland defined as 'white collar crimes'—crimes committed by people of 'respectability and high social status' in the course of their occupations.[37]

Thousands of 'white collar crimes' are committed every year by lawyers, bankers, advertising agents—in fact by professional men, businessmen and employers of all sorts. They are not only harmful in themselves but lead to the acceptance and condonation of other crimes more obviously and conventionally reprehensible.

Britain, of course, has her 'white-collar criminals' too. Indeed, making fraudulent claims or denials to the income-tax inspector or the customs officer is a national pastime; and there is obviously no lack of purchasers for the immense quantities of insurance stamps and lorry-loads of cigarettes that are stolen every year. But in America, so Americans repeatedly tell themselves, 'virtually the whole of society is involved in the habit of fraud'.

In 1959 'by conservative estimate,' Frank Gibney has written, '$5,000,000,000 changed hands under innumerable desks, counters or expensive restaurant tables in kick-backs, pay-offs or bribes. The country's employers lost more than $500,000,000 to embezzling employees . . . More of the public's money evaporated through retail chiselling. $500,000,000 went down the drain in home-repair frauds alone. Officials of the Securities and Exchange Commission do not even attempt to measure the high cost of stocks worth slightly more than the paper they are printed on, aside from putting it in the "hundreds of millions" . . . The aggregate of rubber checks bounced a third higher than last year and about a hundred per cent higher than in 1952. The yearly loss to banks and individuals is now figured at well over a half-billion.'[38]

The corruption pervades every part of the national life. 'It is a nice question,' Professor Taft has said, 'whether Americans are more money-minded or sports-minded. Commercialization of sports includes both interests.'[39] Annual expenditure on gambling, much of it on sporting events and most of it illegal outside Nevada —the law is so strictly drawn in some other states that even the giving of a prize at home can be a crime—has been estimated as being $20,000,000,000.[40] College football players, even Olympic sportsmen, have accepted bribes, as well as jockeys and boxing champions, to lose matches or races and so make more money for the organized criminal gangs whose principal source of income is gambling.[41]

Occasionally a police investigation or a Senate Committee exposes a particular scandal or a specific racket, a few arrests are made and a few convictions are obtained but gradually the protests die down and the racketeers return.

The police investigations into the call-girl racket in 1952 revealed, for instance, the activities of prostitutes who were earning, in the words of one of them, 'a hundred dollars a toss and more'. The arrest of Minot Frazier Jelke III, the plump heir to a fortune, who had been acting as procurer and pimp, for a time alarmed some of his clients who, according to the Prosecutor, were 'well known all over the country'. But soon afterwards the call-girls were back in business again. 'Everything is the same,' admitted one who did not allow her clients to indulge in normal sexual intercourse, as it made her hips too fat, but charged fifty dollars for other services. 'Everything is the same. Nothing has changed.'[42] It is a familiar admission.

But although Americans seem to be, as one of their most distinguished sociologists has put it, 'the most criminal people on earth,'[43] or, as others have suggested, the most acquisitive,[44] the tide of corruption, strong as it still may be, seems to be ebbing while in the new affluent societies of Europe it appears to be rising fast. And Americans have their compensations and rewards. A more rigid society than the American could have been made to produce less professional crime, as Hitler showed in Germany and Stalin in Russia, but it would also have produced less of those special virtues and achievements which are specifically and recognizably American. America may have paid a high price for her freedom, but its benefits are now shared by the world.

Part VII

PRESENT PROBLEMS

CHAPTER ONE

CAPITAL PUNISHMENT

'For my part, I am fairly sure that I have made the choice. And, having chosen, I think that I must speak out, that I must say that I will never again be one of those, whoever they be, who compromise with murder.'

ALBERT CAMUS, 1958

(i)

'Is it not absurd,' wrote Cesare Beccaria in 1764, 'that the laws which detest and punish homicide, in order to prevent murder, publicly commit murder themselves.'

It was not, however, for more than a century after the appearance of *Dei Delitti e delle Pene* that the entire abolition of the death penalty became a matter of serious dispute in most European countries. Even then the voices of many influential criminologists and sociologists were raised in its defence.

Cesare Lombroso, writing in the 1890's, believed that capital punishment should be retained for the 'born criminal', incapable of reform. 'The fact that there exist such beings as born criminals,' he thought, 'organically fitted for evil, atavistic reproductions, not simply of savage men but of the fiercest animals, far from making me more compassionate towards them, as has been maintained, steels me against all pity.'[1]*

Raffaele Garofalo, the practical Neapolitan lawyer went further

---

* This 'social hygiene' theory, predictably, found much favour in Nazi Germany, where Lombroso was much misquoted, and where sterilization laws were applied on an immense scale even to the congenitally blind and to alcoholics.

373

than this. Capital punishment was, in his view, the one which the criminal really dreads and its continuation was, therefore, justified if only because social interests were more important than individual rights, and, 'metaphorically speaking, the individual represents but a cell of the human body'.[2]

Already, though, these views amongst criminologists and sociologists were becoming rarer. Enrico Ferri, the young professor who was Lombroso's friend, wrote in a book first published in 1881 that to be effective the death penalty would have to be applied 'resolutely in all cases' if 'the only positive utility which it possessed, namely artificial selection' were to be drawn from it.

'In Italy, for example, it would be necessary to execute at least one thousand people every year ... otherwise the death penalty must be considered as an unserviceable and neglected means of terror, merely to be printed in the codes and in that case it would be acting more seriously to abolish it.

So regarded it is too much like those motionless scarecrows which farmers set up in their fields, dotted about with the foolish notion that the birds will be frightened away from the corn. They may cause a little alarm at first sight; but by and by the birds, seeing that the scarecrow never moves and cannot hurt them, lose their fear, and even perch on the top of it. So it is with criminals when they see that the death penalty is never or very rarely applied; and one cannot doubt that criminals judge of the law, not by its formulation in the codes, but by its practical and daily application.'[3]

But although Ferri advocated the abolition of the death penalty, he did so on the grounds that no country would 'have the courage' to apply it with unwavering determination to the great number of 'born criminals, guilty of the most serious crimes of violence' which was the only way of making it effective as a deterrent. That it would be effective as a deterrent if these ruthless measures were adopted, he did not deny. His friend Lombroso, as indeed Lombroso's demolishing critic Tarde, could give examples of the superficial success of savagely repressive measures; and there are many more recent examples which might be adduced in support of Ferri's theory. But the evil consequences of this sort of repression are impossible to calculate; and the statistics which Ferri cited elsewhere in his work seemed to suggest that the death penalty, even when vigorously applied, did not, in fact, have a very good record as a deterrent. Ferri noticed, for instance, that at Ferrara, over a number of years, a succession of lawyers had been executed for forgery and that the executions followed each other at very short intervals.[4]

He noticed, too, what had often been noticed before, that the numbers of men condemned to death who had previously been present at executions was extraordinarily high and that murders were often committed in towns where, on the same day, executions had been carried out. Tuscany, where there had been no death penalty for a century was 'one of the provinces with the lowest number of serious crimes'; and in France, in spite of the increase of general crime and of population, charges of murder, parricide and homicide dropped from 560 in 1826 to 530 in 1888 though the number of executions diminished in the same period from 197 to nine.[5]

During the next century statistics, more scientifically compiled than these, presented overwhelming evidence in support of the abolitionists' demands. And, one after the other, the countries of Europe decided to listen to the voice of reason and humanity and to follow the example of those countries which had already abolished the death penalty. Belgium, Holland, Luxembourg, Portugal, Rumania and Italy had dispensed with capital punishment by the end of the nineteenth century and experts from some of these countries were asked to give guidance to a Select Committee on Capital Punishment appointed in England in 1929. 'The lesson has been learnt,' said the Belgian Minister of Justice, 'that the best means of inculcating respect for human life is to refrain from taking life in the name of the law.'[6] 'It is definitely established,' the Government of the Netherlands categorically informed a subsequent Royal Commission, 'that the abolition of the death penalty in the ordinary penal code' (most countries retain it for use against traitors and in time of war) 'has not resulted in an increase or worsening of crime.'[7]

Nor was any permanent increase noticed by Norway which abolished capital punishment in 1905, nor by Sweden which abolished it in 1921. Denmark dispensed with it in 1930, Switzerland in 1942, Italy (the Fascists having re-introduced it for certain crimes in 1931) in 1948, Finland in 1949, West Germany (after Hitler had restored a uniformed headsman with a ritualistic axe) in 1949, Austria in 1950. 'The general view,' said Ivar Strahl, Professor of Criminal Law in the University of Upsala, 'is that the abolition of the death sentence has not entailed any increase in the number of crimes.'[8] In Italy the homicide rate fell from an annual average of 10.6 per 100,000 of the population in 1880 to 3.5 in 1920. It rose sharply, as was to be expected in the post-war chaos, in 1946 but afterwards fell again, and continued to fall after the death penalty was abolished. The same is true of West Germany.[9] The Council of Europe's publication, *The Death Penalty in European Countries* (1962) concludes that the information collected from all the countries concerned, although incomplete, 'does make it possible to say that the abolition of capital punishment was not reflected in any European country by an increase in the number of crimes formerly punishable by death.'

The experiences of foreign countries did not, however, until recently, have any great effect on the actions of British Governments or, apparently, on public opinion. The arguments that these experiences were not applicable to Britain had always found ready acceptance. There were differences in the definition of crimes, in the practice of the courts, in the methods of compiling criminal statistics; there were differences in moral standards and in social and economic conditions. All these factors led to a rejection of the advice given by the 1929-1930 Committee, after 'prolonged examination of the situation in foreign countries', that 'capital punishment may be abolished in this country without endangering life or property or impairing the security of society'.[10] Even when the statistics from foreign sources compared the effects of the abolition of capital punishment in neighbouring countries whose ethnic and economic conditions are very similar—such as Australia and New Zealand—or in neighbouring states of the same country where different methods of punishment apply—such as in the United States of America—even then, the British attitude was one of scepticism, despite the fact that these statistics had been most revealing. For instance, in Queensland—now, with New Zealand, one of the very few parts of the British Commonwealth to be without the death penalty—there was a slight rise in the homicide rate after the abolition of capital punishment in 1922, but so there also was in neighbouring New South Wales where it was not abolished until 1955. And in subsequent years the Queensland rate dropped, whereas the New South Wales rate did not. In the United States, Massachusetts, which retains the threat of the death penalty, shares an almost identical homicide rate with Rhode Island, a similar and neighbouring New England state, which abolished it in 1852.[11] Washington was without the death penalty between 1913 and 1919 and the murder rate increased slightly. It continued to increase, however, after capital punishment was reinstated.[12] A recent analysis of the FBI *Uniform Crime Reports* shows, in fact, that 'homicide rates are generally higher in states with capital punishment than in those which have abolished it'.[13]

The Royal Commission, which was appointed in 1949, after considering a wealth of similar evidence could not but agree with one of its witnesses, Dr Thorsten Sellin the distinguished Professor of Sociology at the University of Pennsylvania and President of the International Society of Criminology, that 'both death-penalty states and abolition states show rates which suggest that these rates are conditioned by other factors than the death penalty'.[14] There was, in fact, the Royal Commission concluded, 'no clear evidence, in any of the figures' which they examined, that the abolition of capital punishment 'led to an increase in the homicide rate or that its re-introduction led to a fall'.[15]

But still, those who protested against the abolition of the death penalty in Britain continued to object, it did not follow that what happened in one country would necessarily happen in another. The now traditional arguments in favour of retention were repeated— there was no satisfactory alternative, it was the ultimate deterrent and its abolition would lead not only to an increase in murder but to professional criminals carrying firearms and even to lynch law, that with the crime rate as it was this was no time for experiment, that public opinion demanded its continuance, that all the sympathy was being given to the murderer and none to the poor victim.

There were other arguments, too, which were not often put forward by those who wanted to retain capital punishment nor always given their due importance by those who wished to abolish it.

When Sir James Stephen, the influential Victorian judge, propounded the view in 1883 that 'the proper attitude of mind towards criminals is not long-suffering charity but open enmity',[16] he was expressing an opinion which, admitted or not, is still widespread. Stephen had no doubt that hanging was morally justified and that a tenderness prevailed upon the subject of punishment which seemed to him 'misplaced and exaggerated'.[17] It is a view which many modern judges, with some notable exceptions particularly amongst those who are Liberals or Roman Catholics, continue to share. They would not presumably go so far as to agree with Stephen that 'it is morally right to hate the criminal' or even, perhaps, with the former Lord Chief Justice, Lord Goddard, that 'it is praiseworthy that the country should be willing to avenge crime', but they do see themselves 'as repositories of the public conscience, and . . . as instruments of public retribution'.[18]

'The ultimate justification of any punishment,' as a Lord of Appeal, Lord Denning, has said, 'is not that it is a deterrent but that it is the emphatic denunciation by a community of a crime'; and Lord Denning believed that there were some crimes which 'in the present state of public opinion', demanded the 'most emphatic denunciation of all: namely the death penalty'.[19] Until recently the leaders of the Anglican Church allied themselves with this denunciatory view. In 1956 the then Archbishop of York gave it as his opinion in the House of Lords that 'retribution was a moral necessity within our penal code'; and the Archbishop of Canterbury said that the death penalty was not 'always un-Christian and wrong'.[20]

These were moral attitudes which found wide acceptance then and still, indeed, find acceptance now. Many Christians are gradually, it seems, coming to the view that while some sort of denunciation is a necessary element of punishment there are other equally important elements which the infliction of the death penalty would destroy. But there are many others, Christians and non-Christians alike, who support the death penalty for reasons which can be made to appear both utilitarian and moral but which may well be neither.

Psychologists have seen the criminal as the 'convenient scapegoat to whom man can transfer the feeling of his own tendency to sinfulness; and, by the punishment of the criminal, man deludes himself into a feeling of righteous indignation, thus bolstering up his own self-respect'.[21] In some primitive societies criminals were put in wicker-work cages built in the form of an idol and then burned; and in ancient Britain and in Gaul they were sacrificed as offerings to appease the anger of the gods. Afraid, insecure, with a sense of guilt seeking satisfaction in vicarious suffering, men destroyed criminals so that they would not suffer themselves or become polluted or contaminated by contact with them. And in time the satisfactions which such punishments of the hated criminal gave to the people's social conscience were advocated as necessary to the development of group solidarity. Punishment inflicted in fear and hate in accordance with this natural law of retaliation, became punishments inflicted in vengeance and explained as a social necessity.

For centuries our 'predecessors cut off nose and ears, quartered, boiled in water and oil and poured melted lead down the throat; but they succeeded only in multiplying crimes and making them more horrible, for the frequency and ferocity of punishments hardened men. In the time of Robespierre even children played at guillotining'.[22] The guillotine and the hangman's noose are still in use and the emotional attitudes adopted towards them are still deep within us. The firm belief of Lord Goddard and his supporters that the death penalty should be retained is no less emotional than the firm belief of Victor Gollancz that it is 'absolutely wrong' and should, therefore, be abolished even if that were to lead to an increase in the murder rate. But the difference is that Victor Gollancz is frankly emotional whereas those who support Lord Goddard profess to believe in the death penalty not because it is emotionally satisfying but because it has the utilitarian value of being uniquely deterrent. Retentionists have not often had the courage to admit, as Lord Goddard has, that they see virtue in a desire for vengeance; but many of them have been satisfied, no doubt, that they have been revenged and at the same time fulfilled what Beccaria believed was the true purpose of punishment —'to prevent the criminal from doing further injury to society, and to prevent others from committing the like offence'.[23] It is for this reason that the leaders of the movement for abolition followed the good example of the Howard League for Penal Reform and of Roy Calvert, the Quaker author of *Capital Punishment in the Twentieth Century* and secretary of the National Council for the Abolition of the Death Penalty, in presenting their case dispassionately, in arguing not that the death penalty was 'absolutely wrong' which was a matter of opinion but that it was absolutely unnecessary which was, they had good grounds for believing, a matter of fact, and that there were alternatives to it which would give society the protection it had the right to demand.

Most criminals who were executed, they continually pointed out, were mentally abnormal, and elsewhere in Europe, particularly in Scandinavia, there were institutions where such people could be kept and treated and possibly even cured although it was appreciated that castration as performed upon willing patients (who were sexual offenders) at Herstedvester in Denmark, in Sweden and at the Van der Hoevan clinic at Utrecht would probably not yet be condoned by public opinion. Life-long imprisonment might for some murderers be a more cruel punishment than death and in 1930, when Sir Alexander Paterson advocated retention of capital punishment, prison conditions might certainly have made it so. But Sir Alexander, apparently, changed his views before he died and agreed that the improved prison system which he had sought, now offered a suitable alternative to the death penalty.[24] And murderers themselves, after all, are not in the habit of refusing reprieves and very few of them would have to be detained so long that they would be without hope of seeing the outside world again.

The question of how long the convicted murderer should be detained remains, of course, an extremely important one. In England a man sentenced to life imprisonment has his case reviewed regularly by the Home Secretary and may be released after two or three years and rarely serves more than fifteen years—the average period served by a man whose release is justified by some mitigating circumstances is nine years, while in America the average length of a life sentence is about ten years, although it is not unusual to find men serving a 'double life' sentence, or 'life plus ninety-nine years'. If capital punishment were to be abolished there would presumably be demands in England for a minimum term and suggestions have already been made that the periodical review of a murderer's sentence should be undertaken by a committee and, indeed, that the sentence itself should be imposed by a panel after guilt has been established in court.[25] But although society's reprobation of the 'heinous crime of murder' must be clearly marked, there is no reason, as the Home Office has discovered, why most murderers cannot safely be released long before the expiration of fourteen years, which is at present the maximum fixed sentence that can be passed for any single offence.

In all European countries it has been found that released murderers have very rarely been any further danger to society. A recent report issued in America indicates that paroled robbers are a far greater danger to life than paroled murderers are.[26] In the nineteenth century Eastern Siberia was 'full of liberated assassins', according to Prince Kropotkin, but there was 'hardly another country where you could travel and stay with greater security'.[27] In Britain, between 1930 and 1949, 183 murderers were reprieved and subsequently released; the large majority of them became good citizens and none of them was guilty of another murder.[28]

Between 1956 and 1960, seventy-six people were released from life imprisonment and none of these committed another murder either.[29] Even if every murderer were to be sent to prison for life, the population of Britain's always overcrowded prisons would only increase by the slightest fraction and the argument of Sir Ronald Howe, a former Deputy Commissioner at Scotland Yard, that it is a waste of money to keep people 'we don't think are very much good',[30] might well be applied to thousands of people who are not even criminals, let alone murderers. Murderers, in fact, are generally good prisoners. Of ninety-one reprieved murderers serving sentences in 1952, all except twelve were in the 'Star' class.[31] 'Taking murderers as a class,' said a prison governor, 'there are a considerable number who are first offenders and who are not people of criminal tendencies. The murder is in many cases their first offence against the law. Previous to that they were law-abiding citizens and their general tenor of life is still to be law-abiding.'[32] Another experienced Governor said that he had 'known many murderers whose sentences were commuted', and, with one exception, they 'were always a good influence in prison and qualified themselves for positions of trust'.[33] The exception was Steinie Morrison and there is good reason to believe, as Julian Symons[34] and James Edward Holroyd[35] have argued, that he did not commit the murder for which he was sentenced.

'In all countries,' says Sir Ernest Gowers (who, when he accepted the appointment of chairman of the Royal Commission in 1949, was 'disposed to regard abolitionists as people whose hearts were bigger than their heads' but in the end became convinced that they were right,)[36] 'in all countries,' he says, 'it would appear that murderers are better behaved than most prisoners.'[37] Cases of murder in the United States 'committed by persons pardoned from the death penalty are rare if not almost unknown'.[38] And in six European countries (Belgium, Denmark, Holland, Norway, Sweden and Switzerland) whose statistics were examined by the Royal Commission in 1949 'released murderers who commit further crimes of violence are rare, and those who become useful citizens are common'.[39]

Nor was it likely, the abolitionists insisted, that the end of capital punishment would lead to professional criminals carrying firearms. The countries in Europe where armed robbery was most prevalent were those which still retained the death penalty. Across the French border, in Belgium, for instance, as Reginald Paget pointed out in a House of Commons debate, the criminal is rarely armed and Belgium's last civil execution was in 1863. In the United States, the carrying of firearms was most prevalent in those states where capital punishment was most frequently inflicted; and, according to one experienced prison warder, who after twenty years in his profession had 'never seen a single criminal who would have refrained from using a gun because of any idea that he might get the death sentence', the criminal's fear of the gallows was 'a fairy story built up by well-meaning people to deter others'.[40] The reluctance of the professional English burglar to carry a gun, despite what he told the police about the deterrent effect of the hangman's rope, was conditioned by his knowledge that burglary without a gun usually earned him a shorter prison sentence than burglary with one.[41] The English robber is also, apparently, no more likely to carry a gun when he is liable to capital punishment if he uses it than when he is not. The death penalty was in abeyance for eighteen months in 1956-1957 when its future was being debated in the Houses of Parliament. But this had no appreciable effect on the habits of the robber, anyway in London where thirty-five per cent of robberies in England take place.[42] In any event, murder by shooting in England is not common and usually occurs in the course of a quarrel.[43]

The argument that with crime as it was this was no time for innovations in the law was effectively answered by the retentionists themselves who used it first in one way and then in another and, as Gerald Gardiner has pointed out, they once contradicted themselves publicly on the same day and in the same place. The occasion was a debate in the House of Lords when one judicial member said that it was no time to alter the law in view of the 'great increase in crime' and another member said that it was no time to alter the law as things 'were going so well'.[44] In any case, it is difficult to argue convincingly that England's low murder rate is due to capital punishment when Holland, where there has been no civil execution since 1860, has a murder rate even lower and when America, where most states retain the death penalty, has a murder rate more than ten times as high.

The charge that all the sympathy, which was the victim's due, was being lavished on the murderer was one the abolitionists had been answering for more than a century. The truth is that the various promising, but so far unrealized, schemes for giving practical expression to this sympathy—by making it possible, for instance, for the murderer not only to earn his own keep and his family's, as he does in Sweden, but to make restitution to the victim's family with or without the help of the state—have always been supported and often been initiated by abolitionists.

The argument that public opinion required the retention of the death penalty was a more difficult one to answer. A much-discussed poll conducted in 1948 by the *Daily Telegraph,* a newspaper with a large majority of Conservative readers, showed sixty-nine per cent in favour of capital punishment and only fifteen per cent against it. But as the Attorney-General observed in the House of Commons, 'The poll made it quite clear that the anxiety of the public in regard to this matter is based almost entirely on reasons which were unanimously rejected in the House as being invalid and irrelevant.' A subsequent poll, conducted in 1955 by the *Daily Mirror,* which has a large majority of Labour readers, suggested that now the population was two to one against the death penalty. But as only thirty-seven thousand replies were received to the paper's questions and as it enjoys a greater circulation than any other daily newspaper in the world, the only valid inference was that 'no great proportion' of its 'numerous readers were feeling a lively interest in the subject at that time.[45] It was, nevertheless, encouraging that of those who troubled to answer the *Daily Mirror's* question, half of them were against hanging. This proportion was still not perhaps by then, a true reflection of the attitude of the country as a whole but was almost certainly a reflection of opinion in the House of Commons, although the House of Lords remained with few exceptions obdurately against abolition.

The slight change in the climate of opinion was probably not, though, so much due to the education of the public by the reasoned arguments of the abolitionists as to the massive publicity given to various murder trials by the national Press. A human illustration which appeals to the emotions is more effective in matters of this kind than an abstract argument which appeals to the mind. Already the abstract arguments and counter-arguments were becoming well-worn and overstated. There were men who still refused to understand that the doctrine of an 'eye for an eye' was not only a primitive and solely retributive one but that, even when it was laid down by the ancient tribes for which it was designed, it was intended as a restraint upon vengeance and that, in any event, it had been later condemned in the New Testament as its misinterpretations have since been condemned by Jewish scholars. Those who believed that punishment should be primarily retributive might wonder whether it was right for man to take human life but they would be comforted to be reminded that few religions had propounded this theory because few religions did not lay emphasis on the belief in a life after death. They might even believe with the then Lord Chancellor that the chance of hanging an innocent man—one of the abolitionists' most reiterated fears—was 'not a possibility which anyone (could) consider likely'.[46] But they could not presumably fail after 1953 to wonder whether or not the possibility, however unlikely it had seemed, had in fact been realized just as they could not presumably fail to feel some emotion, other than hate or disgust, for those who had been hanged.

Innocent people had, of course, been condemned to death for centuries. Chief Baron Kelly went so far as to suggest in evidence before the Royal Commission on Capital Punishment in 1864 that in the course of some forty years no less than twenty-two people, who were afterwards proved to have been innocent, had been sentenced to death.[47] In the past, bias on the part of judges and juries and wholly inconclusive evidence were usually responsible. They were certainly responsible for the hanging of Elizabeth Fenning, a small, young, pretty and intelligent maidservant who was wrongly convicted of attempting to poison her master and his wife and son with arsenic in 1815. They were also largely responsible for the conviction and hanging in 1829 of Daniel Leary for the supposed poisoning of the man with whom he lodged, Benjamin Russell, who probably died of heart-failure. Mistaken identity and an unfair trial were responsible for the hanging of the poor and acutely shy Edmond Pine in Ireland in 1835.[48] These, of course, are all early nineteenth century cases, but in 1879 Charles Peace confessed to the murder of a policeman for which John Habron had been sentenced to death three years before; in 1909 Oscar Slater was condemned to death for the murder of an old lady in Glasgow and wrongfully imprisoned for nineteen years; in 1913 Steven Tonka, a Hungarian, was hanged for the murder of a man who, it was afterwards discovered, had committed suicide; in 1923 two Dutchmen, Tuennisen and Klundert, were convicted of murder and proved innocent six years later. In Sweden in 1932 a man found guilty of murdering his wife was acquitted fifteen years later after a retrial. The German Federal Ministry of Justice has recently reported to the Council of Europe that between 1853 and 1953 there were twenty-seven death sentences which are 'now established or presumed' miscarriages of justice.[49]* And even today, when an English murder trial is always characterized by great care, mistakes are still possible. A case which was tried as recently as 1947 provided the abolitionists with a useful illustration.

On a Sunday morning of October of the year before, a middle-aged prostitute, Olive Balchin, was found battered to death on a bomb site in Manchester. She was fully dressed and by her side lay a blood-stained hammer of curious shape. She had been seen the night before by a publican in Deansgate who said that she had been arguing in the street at about midnight with a man 'thirty to thirty-five years of age, 5ft 7in tall, of proportionate build, full round face, clean-shaven, dark hair, dressed in a blue suit, of clean and tidy appearance'. A somewhat similar description was given to the police by a shopkeeper who had sold a leather-dresser's hammer to a man who had called at his shop on Saturday evening at about a quarter to six and said he wanted a hammer 'for general purposes'. But although the man the publican had seen arguing in the street and the man to whom the shopkeeper sold the hammer were both apparently about the same age, height and build and although both had either 'dark' or 'black' hair and were of 'clean appearance', one was described as having a 'full round face', the other as having 'a very pale face, thin features'.

A week after the murder, Graham Rowland, a man known to have been a former friend of Olive Balchin's, was arrested. He did not seem to fit either of the two descriptions given to the police but he had two previous convictions for crimes of violence. He had, also, what he admitted was an 'uncontrollable temper' and had recently quarrelled with the dead woman whom he believed might have given him the venereal disease from which he was suffering.

'If I had been sure it was her, I would have strangled her,' he told the police. 'Has she V.D.? If she gave it to me she deserved all she got.'

After making this damaging statement he then lied about his movements on Saturday night. At identification parades he was picked out by both the publican and the shopkeeper despite their earlier conflicting descriptions. It seemed an easy case for the Crown to prove; and, to the jury's satisfaction, it was proved. The

* The most recent example is of a German pilot released from prison in February 1963 after serving ten years of a twenty-two years sentence for a murder he had not committed.

defence pointed out, without effect, that no traces of blood were found on Rowland's only suit after the most careful scientific examination and that the landlord of a lodging house in Ardwick swore that Rowland had slept the night of the murder in his house. After Rowland had been sentenced to death, a man in Liverpool, David John Ware, confessed to the murder. His confession was clearer, more detailed and more convincing than most confessions given in such circumstances and the parts of it which could be checked were all shown to be true. Ware's confession—subsequently withdrawn—was examined by Mr J. C. Jolly K.C., appointed by the Home Secretary after Rowland's appeal had been dismissed by the Court of Criminal Appeal, but despite its apparent authenticity, it was supposed to be invented. Leslie Hale and Sydney Silverman are not the only men who have good grounds for believing that it was not. In August 1951, four years after Rowland had been hanged, Ware was charged with attempted murder and found guilty but insane.

'I have killed a woman,' he told the police at Bristol, 'I don't know what's the matter with me. I keep on having an urge to hit women on the head.'[50]

The trials of Rowland and Ware were little noticed at the time, but within the next few years, five murder trials—three of them in 1953—caught the imagination of the public and did more than any abstract arguments could, to bring the whole issue of capital punishment into national debate.

The first was of Derek Bentley, a nineteen-year-old mentally retarded epileptic who was found guilty as an accomplice of the murder of a policeman by his sixteen-year-old friend Christopher Craig. It was Craig who fired the gun but as he was under eighteen he could not be hanged. Bentley, who shouted, 'Let him have it, Chris!' before the shot was fired, was hanged on 28 January 1953, the jury having recommended him to mercy and two hundred Members of Parliament having placed a Motion upon the Order Paper disagreeing with the Home Secretary's opinion that there were 'not sufficient grounds on which to advise the exercise of Her Majesty's mercy'.[51]

The following month Miles Giffard, the schizophrenic whose confession is printed on page 215 was hanged for the murder of his parents. After the trial one of the jurors wrote to the Home Secretary to say that she thought Giffard was insane and had consequently disagreed with the verdict. She was of French origin and did not understand English law, and owing to a misunderstanding her disagreement with the other jurors was not made known to the judge.[52]

In the spring of the same year John Reginald Halliday Christie, a former War Reserve Constable, was arrested for the murder of his wife. He readily confessed to it and to the murders of five other women whose bodies and skeletons the police had found at various times at his seedy North Kensington house, 10 Rillington Place. The horror which this ghoulish and supposedly respectable man aroused in a fascinated public was increased when it became known that one of the murders to which he had confessed was that of Mrs Evans whose husband, Timothy John Evans, had been hanged three and a half years before.

Evans, an undersized and mentally retarded long distance van-driver, had been charged in December 1949 with the murder of his wife and child. He had confessed to the murders, apparently to protect Christie who had tried to help Mrs Evans commit abortion, but later in Brixton prison he said, 'Christie done it'. He continued to say so at his trial, at which Christie was a witness for the prosecution, but the jury did not believe him. Evans was tried for the murder of his baby girl, the prosecution having decided not to proceed on the charge of murdering his wife, but most of the evidence against him was intended to show that he had killed his wife as well. He was hanged at Pentonville on 9 March 1950.

When Christie confessed to the murder of Mrs Evans, he said:

'She lay on the quilt. I got on my knees but found I was not capable of having intercourse with her owing to my having fibrositis and enteritis . . . I turned the gas tap and as near as I can make out I held it close to her face. When she became unconscious I turned the tap off. I was going to try again to have intercourse with her but I found it was impossible. I couldn't bend over. I think that's when I strangled her. I think it was a stocking I found in her room.'

After Christie had been found guilty and sentenced to death, public opinion demanded an inquiry and the Home Secretary appointed Mr John Scott Henderson, Q.C. to conduct one. Mr Henderson's finding that there was 'no doubt that Evans was responsible for both murders', resulted in outcries of protest both in Parliament and outside it. Articles and books were subsequently written which did much to show that Mr Henderson was almost certainly wrong and the latest of these books, *10 Rillington Place,* a passionate

indictment by Ludovic Kennedy, raised important questions which
have never been answered.

The case of Evans and Christie was still being discussed when,
some months later, Mrs Stylou Christophi, a Cypriot of peasant
stock, was hanged for the murder of her daughter-in-law of whom
she was violently jealous. She had knocked her unconscious with the
ash plate from her kitchen stove and then strangled her with a
scarf and tried to burn the body. Like Derek Bentley and Timothy
Evans she was mentally retarded and medical evidence of schizophrenia was given at the trial. Both the prison doctor and the
public generally believed her to be mad.[53]

The next year—in 1955—an attractive model from South
Kensington, Ruth Ellis, was hanged for shooting her former lover,
David Blakeley, as he got out of his car one day in London. Mrs
Ellis, who had been twice married and had two children, was
at this time living with another man. Blakeley, with whom she
had remained friendly, had told her that he wanted to end their unsatisfactory relationship. She had waited for him in the street, she
admitted, intending to kill him. She wanted to plead guilty and
refused to appeal. It was suggested at her trial that she was
'hysterically and emotionally immature'. A fortnight previously she
had had a miscarriage.[54]

Although these six cases were the ones that were most widely
reported and are most generally remembered, between 1949 and
1956 a hundred other murderers were hanged. The brief reports
of their crimes make pitiful reading:

'Margaret Allen, forty-three, killed in a quarrel an elderly woman friend.
The judge described the act as "senseless, unjustified and purposeless".
Defence: Insanity. Allen was the twentieth child of a family of twenty-
two. At twenty-nine she went to a hospital, afterwards said that she had
had an operation which changed her sex, and had worn men's clothes
ever since. After her execution Chaplain Walker, of Strangeways,
resigned from the prison service ... Rex Harvey Jones, twenty-two,
Rhondda Valley miner, strangled his girl friend of twenty on a Welsh
mountain side after intimacy. He said he had drunk seven pints of beer.
He called the police and led them to the body. He had an exemplary character. The judge told the jury, "You have to steel your hearts against
good character and steel your hearts in order to see that justice is done."
The jury made a "strong recommendation to mercy". Jones was
hanged ... Piotr Maksimowski, thirty-three, a refuse collector in a

settlement camp in Buckinghamshire, had lived for five months with a woman when she confessed that she was married, with two children. They made a suicide pact; he cut her wrists, then cut his own wrists, and went to the police station "dishevelled and obviously distraught and with his shoes on the wrong feet". Victim had no injury except wrists cut, which could only have been inflicted with her consent. He refused legal aid. Hanged 29th March 1950 . . . Albert Price, thirty-two, painter, murdered his wife with an axe and suffocated their two children in their sleep because his mind broke down when after years of financial trouble, they received notice of eviction and had nowhere to go. He then tried to commit suicide but lacked courage. The jury made a "strong recommendation to mercy". Price was hanged . . . Dennis Albert Reginald Moore, twenty-three, a Norwich labourer strangled his fiancée, twenty-one days before they were to have been married, then called the police. Next to the victim's body lay a note written in lipstick; "I love her—good-bye all." The girl's father agreed that they were a "devoted couple". Two psychiatrists for the defence testified that Moore was immature, unstable, and liable to outbursts of explosive rage, during which he did not know what he was doing. Hanged . . . Donald Neil Simm, thirty-two, a machinist of Slough, became jealous of his wife's friendship with another man, and after some drinking shot both of them as they were returning from a dance. Simm was a heavy drinker, had had a nervous breakdown, and had spent two months at a hospital for nervous and mental diseases. Hanged . . .'

These pathetic stories, taken from *Hanged by the Neck* by Arthur Koestler and C. H. Rolph, are not exceptional ones. Murders are not usually committed by professional criminals. Out of the 106 murderers who were hanged between 1949 and 1956, only thirteen of them had killed strangers in order to escape the consequences of some other crime. Twenty-two of them had killed members of their family and twenty-three their lovers or girl-friends. Very few had any previous criminal record; no less than forty-nine, however, had some definite record of insanity, epilepsy or psychoneurotic anxiety states, and others, who may also well have had such a record, refused to offer any defence at their trials. An analysis by Sir John Macdonell, Master of the Supreme Court, of murders committed between 1886 and 1905 gave a similar picture. Ninety per cent of the murderers were men and nearly two thirds of their victims were their wives, mistresses or girl-friends. 'I hesitate to draw any conclusions from imperfect data,' Sir John wrote, 'but I am inclined to think that this crime is not generally the crime of the so-called criminal classes, but it is in most cases, rather an incident in miserable lives.'[55]

Hanging does not deter in cases like these. Only the most frantic abolitionists, of course, suggested that the death penalty was no deterrent at all. All punishments are deterrent in some degree and capital punishment may well be the most powerful—that is not to say necessarily powerful—deterrent of all for some people, but these are not the sort of people who are likely to commit murder.

Sir Alexander Paterson, whose views were much quoted by the retentionists, told the Select Committee of 1930, that 'with professional criminals the dread of the gallows is a strong deterrent. They have tasted prison and lost their fear of it. They may have misused their lives but they are loath to lose them'.[56] Many experienced police officers still endorse this view. It is presumptuous to suggest that they are wrong and impossible to prove it. But the fact persists and recurs that professional criminals are rarely murderers whether threatened with death or not. Statistics suggest that in the last century the numbers of various crimes which were then capital ones, decreased by over ten per cent in the first three years after the death penalty for them was abolished, compared with the three years preceding abolition.[57] If this was the effect of abolition on crimes which are usually premeditated, abolition of the death penalty for a crime which is usually less premeditated than any other might well be expected to have a similar effect.

Just as it was only the most obdurate of abolitionists who suggested that the death penalty was not a deterrent at all, so it was only the most obdurate opponents of abolition who refused to agree that there was something wrong with a criminal law which allowed Derek Clide Adams, for example, a thirty-one-year-old patient of an institution for mental defectives, who had murdered a woman in a fit of jealousy,[58] to suffer the same penalty as John George Haigh the 'acid-bath murderer' who had calmly confessed to the murders of six people for gain.

There was, also, clearly something wrong with a law which found a burglar who shot a policeman guilty of the same crime as a woman who 'gassed her son, a hopeless imbecile, who had to be attended like a baby. She had been told that she must enter a hospital immediately to undergo an operation. She at first said she could not have the operation because there was no one to look after her son, but it was made clear to her that she could not live more than six months unless the operation was performed'.[59]

To evade hanging poor, desperate people such as this, verdicts of insanity or of manslaughter were given, or it was left to the Home Secretary to use the Royal Prerogative of Mercy to confine executions to the worst cases, or sometimes, if more rarely, the accused was acquitted of a crime which he had obviously committed. A witness told the Royal Commission of 1864, in fact, that criminals preferred to be indicted on a capital charge because there was more chance of getting off.[60] And certainly in 1952-1954, apart from verdicts of insanity and manslaughter, the proportion of acquittals to convictions in murder trials was one to four.[61]* During the first fifty years of this century there were 7,454 murders known to the police in England and Wales. Suspects who committed suicide numbered 1,674, and verdicts of insanity were given in 1,273 cases. Only 1,210 murderers were sentenced to death and of these no more than 632 were executed.[62]†

But while the low proportion of executions to murders was comforting—the chance of a murderer being hanged was twelve to one against—the dangers of men worthy of mercy being hanged was always present so long as the law remained so rigid and so long as the final decision rested as an unfair burden in the hands of the Home Secretary whose views were often different from those of the jury. Home Secretaries, when in office, have usually been in favour of retaining the death penalty—presumably because public opinion has appeared to be—and although their personal feelings should not be involved—and no doubt rarely were consciously involved—the fact remains that out of seventy-five murderers recommended to mercy in 1940-1949 twenty-four were hanged and the percentages for other decades are similar.

By the time the Royal Commission was appointed in 1949—despite various recommendations made by the Royal Commission of 1864-1866 and the Select Committee of 1929-1930—relaxation of the rigidity of the law had not progressed beyond the abolition of

---

* There is, however, no evidence to suggest that juries are now more ready to convict even when the death penalty is not involved. There was an exceptional number of acquittals in 1960 in trials for non-capital murder.[63]

† In Scotland during the same period there were less murders and more reprieves. The annual average number of murders known to the police was 2·52 per million in Scotland compared with 3·89 in England and Wales. There were no executions in Scotland between 1928 and 1945.

the death penalty for pregnant women and children under eighteen and the removal of infanticide from the category of murder.

The Royal Commission was appointed after two clauses (one suspending capital kinds of murder) had been inserted, one after the other, in the Criminal Justice Bill 1948 and had both been rejected by the House of Lords.* The Government in its dilemma over a dispute between the two Houses of Parliament, in which the Lords were supposed to have public opinion on their side, fell back on the traditional British expedient of a Royal Commission to 'do at leisure what they had failed to do in a hurry'.[64] The Royal Commission was not asked to give advice about the abolition of the death penalty but to study the possibilities of its limitation.

The members began their enquiry 'with the determination to make every effort to see whether we could succeed where so many have failed, and discover some effective method of classifying murders so as to confine the death penalty to the more heinous'.† But they had to 'conclude with regret that the object of their search was chimerical and must be abandoned'.[67] The members of the Commission decided, then, that the court—for this purpose meaning judge or jury or both together—should decide the question on the facts of each case. They believed that the judge could not be expected to bear the responsibility alone, but that the judge and jury together or the jury by themselves should be able to exercise discretionary powers. In America it had been found that a jury could exercise these powers responsibly and in Western European countries, where the judge and jury sat together, the results had also been rewarding. The proposal that the experiment should

---

* Most of the bishops and apparently all but one of the judges of the King's Bench Division were in favour at this time of retaining capital punishment. The Lord Chief Justice, Lord Goddard, played a prominent part in the debate. In his 'humble opinion' there were 'many, many cases where the murderer should be destroyed'. Lord Goddard's successor, Lord Parker, said in 1960 that 'it is only the so-called intellectual section of the population who are against capital punishment'. But he also said at this time, when commenting upon the many recent reprieves in Canada, that 'either the verdict of the court should be strongly supported or the death sentence should be abolished'.[65] For this reason and others, and not least because the present law is, as Lord Parker says, 'ridiculous', many other judges are coming to the view that the death penalty must go.

† In America, where there are degrees of murder, the difference turns upon premeditation. As Mr Justice Cardozo has said, however, 'the presence of a sudden impulse is said to mark the dividing line, but how can an impulse be anything but sudden when the time for its formation is measured by the lapse of seconds. Yet the decisions are to the effect that seconds may be enough'.[66]

be tried in England found little support, however, and the Lord Chief Justice, Lord Goddard, went so far as to say that he would resign if it were adopted.

But the reformers refused to allow all the conclusions of the Royal Commission to be forgotten. There was a growing feeling in the House of Commons that the law must be altered. Although the abolitionists drew most of their support from the Labour benches, there were now increasing numbers of Conservative Members, encouraged by the unequivocal stand of men like Christopher Hollis and Nigel Nicolson, who were prepared to speak and vote as their consciences told them to and not as many of their electors would have liked them to. And they were no doubt justified in thinking, as Nigel Nicolson put it, that public opinion was moving closer to their position.*

In February 1956, after Sydney Silverman, with the backing of other Members of Parliament of all parties, introduced his Death Penalty (Abolition) Bill, the House of Commons resolved on a free vote, 'that the death penalty no longer accords with the needs or the true interests of a civilized society'. The Bill was eventually passed by the Commons; but it was rejected by the Lords without on this occasion any help from the bishops but with a good deal of help from what the *Spectator* called 'hitherto unknown rustics who thought, perhaps, that abolition was in some way a threat to blood sports'. The following year, however, an important change was made in the law by an Act which created a distinction between

---

* Public opinion does not appear, however, to have moved as fast in the last few years as most Members had then hoped. A Gallup Poll made in March 1960 showed that seventy-eight per cent of those questioned still favoured the death penalty, although fifty per cent of them thought that regard should be had to extenuating circumstances; and another Poll made in April 1961 showed seventy per cent still favouring it. A Poll carried out four years before by the French Institute of Public Opinion suggested that French public opinion was the same as British: seventy-eight per cent of those questioned were in favour of capital punishment. It appears that in America the proportion of those in favour is lower than this. A National Poll in 1958 showed that only forty-two per cent of those questioned favoured the death penalty. Public opinion in those countries which do not have capital punishment does not seem to be in favour of restoring it. Only fifteen per cent of those questioned by the Norwegian Gallup Institute in 1960, for instance, were in favour of restoration. West Germany is an exception. There is a strong movement to re-introduce capital punishment there. Of those questioned in a poll in 1958, eighty per cent were in favour of re-introduction.[68]

capital and non-capital murder and introduced the defence of 'diminished responsibility'.

This Act retained the death penalty for:

(a) any murder done in the course or furtherance of theft;

(b) any murder by shooting or by causing an explosion;

(c) any murder done in the course or for the purpose of resisting or avoiding or preventing a lawful arrest, or of effecting or assisting an escape or rescue from legal custody;

(d) any murder of a police officer acting in the execution of his duty or of a person assisting a police officer so acting;

(e) in the case of a person who was a prisoner at the time when he did or was a party to murder, any murder of a prison officer acting in the execution of his duty or of a person assisting a prison officer so acting.'[69]

Under a later Section of the Act a murderer previously convicted of another murder done on a different occasion (both murders having been committed in Britain) was also liable to the death penalty;[70] but for all other types of murder the penalty was to be life imprisonment. And provision was made for people charged with murder to be convicted only of manslaughter by a Section which provided that 'when a person kills or is party to a killing of another, he shall not be convicted of murder if he was suffering from such abnormality of mind (whether arising from a condition of arrested or retarded development of mind or any inherent causes or induced by disease or injury) as substantially impaired his mental responsibility for his acts and omissions in doing or being a party to the killing'.[71]

The Act had little, if any, appreciable effect on the number of murders committed. The slight increase after the Act was a continuation of a trend noticed many years before. There were, on average, 130 murders a year known to the police in England and Wales in the ten years between 1931 and 1940, 150 a year between 1941 and 1950, 137 between 1951 and 1955, 150 in 1956, 174 (including twenty-three verdicts of manslaughter under Section two of the Act) in 1957, 153 (including twenty-eight manslaughter verdicts under Section two) in 1958 and 161 (including twenty manslaughter verdicts) in 1959.[72] But the gradual increase was very small indeed compared with the general increase in recorded crime and in population.

After the Act there was, however, one curious alteration in

the types of murder committed. As was to be hoped there was a slight decrease in the number of murders by shooting;[73] but while robbery continued to play a relatively small part in murder compared with jealousy, anger, despair and insanity, 'the number of murders for robbery or financial gain rose from six a year to twelve a year after the Homicide Act, in spite of the fact that murder in the course or furtherance of theft is capital murder.'[74] And so, as some abolitionists had predicted, the professional criminal was apparently no more and perhaps even less deterred by the death penalty after the Act than he had been before it.

But convictions of capital murder were now generally limited to those who killed in pursuit of criminal activities. And for this reason, if for no other, the Act cannot be discounted as an entire failure. Twenty-one murderers were hanged between the beginning of 1954 and the suspension of the death penalty in 1956, but only six in 1958, four in 1959 and three in 1960.* Of the four men executed in 1959, one (Gunther Fritz Podola) was a habitual criminal who had shot a policeman, two were burglars who had killed the people they were robbing and only one was of the type that characterised the large majority of men executed before the Act came into operation when there were about thirteen executions a year. But this one executed man, Bernard Hugh Walden, a crippled lecturer at Rotherham Technical College who shot a girl with whom he was infatuated and her boy-friend, raised the whole debate again. Walden was said to be suffering from 'chronic paranoic development'. He had been convicted of a homosexual offence in 1949 and thought of himself as a 'victim singled out by fate'. 'I am not as other men,' he said. 'I am a cripple and must be armed to put me on fair terms with others . . . I have an absolute right to kill.'[77] The jury recommended him to mercy, but he was hanged at Leeds in August 1959.

* This trend has been noticeable in other European countries, too. In France there were sixteen executions in 1951 but since 1952 there have never been more than four civil guillotinings in any one year. There were thirteen executions in Greece in 1954, nine in 1960. Between 1950 and 1956 there were no more than about five executions a year in Spain. In Turkey, however, there were seven in 1959, twenty in 1960 and six in the first six months of 1961.[75] South Africa, it is worth while noting, which has a population of about fifteen million has carried out an average of sixty-eight executions a year in the past decade. About four of those executed each year are white men and about six a year are non-white men executed for rape.[76]

In the following year James Harris and Francis Forsyth were hanged for the murder of a man they, and two other youths with them, intended to rob on a public footpath; and once again the emotions of the country were roused. Forsyth was only eighteen and it was admitted that he had no intention to kill but had kicked his victim with his pointed 'winkle-picker' shoes to 'keep him quiet', while Harris rifled his pockets.[78] They had both been drinking.

It was felt that, although the law was not as cruelly illogical as it had been in 1956, there must be something wrong with an Act which permitted the death penalty to be inflicted on youths such as these and on the illiterate James Hanratty who had been diagnosed as mentally defective in 1952 and was hanged ten years later, but which would allow men like Christie to escape; which allowed a man who calculatingly poisoned for money to be sent to prison, and a man who was discovered while breaking into a shop, and in panic knocked down and accidentally killed the shopkeeper, to be hanged. Indeed by now there were many people in the country who agreed with the Bishop of Woolwich's later observation that the 1957 Homicide Act was 'one of the most unsatisfactory pieces of legislation ever passed in this country'; and many more who felt with him that hanging would 'go altogether at the next big push'.[79]

In the autumn of 1961 a significant step was taken by the Church of England, when the Lower House of the Convocation of Canterbury recorded a large majority vote for the end of capital punishment.* At the same time a Conservative Party conference demon-

---

* In January 1962 the Upper House of the Convocation of Canterbury also voted for the abolition of capital punishment. They did so without a single dissentient voice. The new Archbishop himself spoke for abolition. Dr Fisher had not done so, believing that the death penalty should be 'retained for certain offences'. William Temple (one of the greatest of their predecessors) was a convinced abolitionist and once wrote that unless capital punishment could be proved to be 'uniquely deterrent', which he did not think it was, the case against it seemed to be 'overwhelming'.[80] But few of his bishops then agreed with him. The recent change in the Church of England's attitude is symptomatic of a growing feeling in most other churches that the death penalty should go. The Roman Catholic Church has not yet taken an official position, but although the right of the state to take life is not denied, many Catholics believe that it should not exercise it. The Society of Friends has long been an influential leader of the movement for abolition both in England and America. And practically all other leading Churches in the United States, except apparently the Lutheran Church, have followed the Quakers' example.

strated a similar change of heart. 'The time is bound to come,' C. H. Rolph, a former Chief Inspector of the City of London Police and one of the abolitionists' most intelligent, well-informed and influential propagandists, felt able to write in the *New Statesman* at the end of that year, 'when those still in favour of hanging will be reduced at last to two groups, neither of them further reducible: those who will always spurn facts and have fenced themselves round with inherited slogans and those who shun the subject as too distasteful for their attention.'[81]

It is often suggested that when so many thousands of good and honest people are killed every year in accidents in their homes and on the roads—about thirty-seven thousand Americans die as a result of road crashes each year now—and when thousands more are dying of hunger and when, indeed, the lives of us all are threatened by nuclear war, to spend time and effort worrying about the fate of a few murderers is a misapplication of energy. To quote as a refutation of this suggestion John Donne's view that any man's death diminishes us, for we are involved in mankind, is, perhaps, as commonplace as the suggestion itself. But Donne's plea for human awareness is of lasting significance; and to reject the threat of intentionally inflicted death when that threat has been shown to offer little if any protection either to ourselves or to those whom it is our duty to protect, may be to take at least one step nearer salvation.

(ii)

In the United States, as in England, the debate has long continued and remains unresolved.

The early colonists did not fully adopt England's savage penal code. In the New England colonies, for instance, only twelve offences were made punishable by death and the number soon lessened. Capital punishment was restricted to the crime of murder alone by Ohio as early as 1788 and in 1794 this example was followed by Pennsylvania. By 1812 the federal law recognized only three capital crimes—treason, murder and rape—out of a former seventeen.

Apart from restricting the death penalty to murderers, Pennsylvania also made an early attempt to redefine the crime itself by dividing it into categories. Many other states subsequently adopted the same method of differentiating between the vicious killer and the irresponsible or passionate one. But it has never been entirely successful. Premeditation has had to be the usual means of determining between first and second-degree murders; but it has been held that an instant of time is enough to admit of premeditation. In any case, juries have usually decided the matter for themselves without undue regard to premeditation, finding a man guilty of first-degree murder if they think he should be executed and of second-degree if they think he should be spared.

Despite the liberal example of the American legislators of the eighteenth century, however, those states which have abolished the death penalty altogether are still in the minority. There are only seven of them (Michigan, Wisconsin, Maine, Minnesota, Alaska, Hawaii and Delaware); two others (Rhode Island and North Dakota) retain it for murder committed in prison by a man serving a life sentence; and one (Massachusetts) has not employed it since 1947. The rest still can and occasionally do employ it, although in all of them, except the District of Columbia, the alternative penalty of life imprisonment is now permitted. Nine states restored capital punishment after having been without it for periods ranging from two to twenty-eight years, often following the 'commission of a particularly brutal murder',[1] as in the case of Missouri which abolished it in 1917 and restored it in 1919 when two policemen were killed in a gun fight. Unlike England, where since 1861 only four offences—high treason, murder, piracy with violence[2] and the destruction of public arsenals and dock-yards[3]—have carried the death penalty, the United States now have as many as thirty capital offences under various state laws. Apart from the various offences which have been re-instituted as capital crimes under federal law (bank robbery, kidnapping, espionage and selling narcotics to a minor) these include, for instance, helping a person commit suicide in Arkansas and burning a railway bridge in Georgia. In practice, however, the death penalty is rarely inflicted on anyone other than a murderer except Negroes convicted of rape in the Southern States. Of the men executed in 1958-1959 all were guilty of murder except fifteen negroes and one white man executed for rape in the South and a Negro executed for armed robbery in Texas. In fact the death penalty is now comparatively rarely inflicted at all except in the South. In the 1930's there were, on average, 167 executions a year; but during the 1950's the average dropped to seventy-two. By 1959 the number was down to forty-nine all of them men, for women are now virtually exempt[1]—and in 1961 the number fell still further to forty-two.

This slow decline of capital punishment seems to have satisfied public opinion, but the decline is not fast enough to satisfy the abolitionists; and, led by the American League to Abolish Capital Punishment and local committees in the different states, they are trying to hasten it.

Their arguments differ little from those used in Britain. They have, of course, a different list of mistaken or dubious verdicts to illustrate the dangers of an irrevocable sentence; and the list is equally disturbing. The Governor of Sing Sing gave a long list of mistaken verdicts to the British Select Committee of 1929-1930.[5] And there are many more recent examples, some of them the result of verdicts brought in on the evidence of confessions extorted by the police. Barbara Graham executed in California in 1955 may not have been guilty; Wilbur Coffin executed in Quebec was also probably innocent; James Fulton Foster condemned to death in Georgia in 1958 was released when a policeman confessed to his crime; in Massachussets a Puerto Rican bus boy was also recently released after serving three years of a life sentence when the real murderer confessed.

In the United States special care has advisedly been taken to refute the claim that the death penalty is a deterrent and, in particular, the repeated claim of law-enforcement authorities that its retention is essential in order to help policemen in the exercise of their dangerous duties and to stop criminals killing them.

This claim was recently expressed by the Commissioner of Police in Chicago.[6] But the fact that over three hundred Chicago policemen have been murdered this century seems to point, not so much to the deterrent value of the death penalty, but to the need of some revision in the Illinois State law.

An important study made by Dr Thorsten Sellin, of the University of Pennsylvania, bears out this view. Professor Sellin made his study after the President of the Chief Constables Association of Canada had objected to the abolition of capital punishment in that country because it would 'adversely affect the personal safety of police officers'. The number of policemen murdered, he added, without quoting the evidence for his assertion, was greater in those countries which had no death penalty.[7]

But after a detailed investigation of the murders of policemen in over 250 northern United States cities (excluding Chicago whose record was so bad that to include it would have given an inaccurate impression of the general picture). Dr Sellin concluded that, although the differences were small, the abolition states appeared to have fewer killings of policemen than the death-penalty states. 'If this is the argument upon which the police rest their opposition to the abolition of capital punishment,' he wrote, 'it must be concluded that it lacks any factual basis.'[8]

Allowance must, of course, be made for the fact that in general 'death penalty states', whether as cause or effect, have a supposedly higher proportion of criminals than 'abolition states' and that, in any event, the differences between Dr Sellin's ratios were minimal. His figures, nevertheless, could not be contradicted by the retentionists; and the abolitionists may well, therefore, regret that no figures can be adduced in support of their theory that even if the claim for the deterrent force of the death penalty could be proved, it would not outweigh what Mr Justice Frankfurter of the Supreme Court of the United States has called 'the social loss due to the inherent sensationalism of a trial for life'.

The degrading effects of this sensationalism, fostered, they believe, by a Press as anxious to exploit it as the English Press but less hampered by English laws of contempt of court, has long been an urgent theme of American sociologists. 'I am strongly against capital punishment,' said Mr Justice Frankfurter expressing their view, 'for reasons that are not related to concern for the murderer or the risk of convicting the innocent . . . When life is at hazard in a trial, it sensationalizes the whole thing almost unwittingly; the effect on juries, the Bar, the public, the judiciary, I regard as very bad.'[9]

This is true of English murder trials too. During the long, tense trial of James Hanratty in 1962 'the proceedings were made even more ghoulish', the *Observer* reported, 'by the behaviour of some Press men who were still apparently bartering over the price at which the stories of the Hanratty family and Valerie Storie [the girl Hanratty had raped and shot] could be bought. The general approval of the verdict by the local populace [the trial was held at Bedford Assizes] made the proceedings like Newgate in modern dress'.

It should be said, though, that Sir Charles Oman was probably right when he said during the House of Commons debate in 1929 that 'the public and the newspapers revel quite as much in a big financial swindle or a high-class divorce case ... If a criminal cuts up his victim into fifty pieces, that is what the newspapers and their readers revel in, not in the fact that this person is going to the gallows in the end'.[10] But of course, most of us would 'revel in' a report of the hanging, too, if that could be printed.

Apart from the general and incalculable affect on the public as a whole, the death penalty, it has been suggested with good cause, has a specifically evil effect 'on mentally or emotionally disturbed people' who are actually incited to crimes of violence by executions.*[11] The confessions and behaviour of numerous criminals and murderers give emphasis to this opinion. Imitative murders are frequent enough, but even more common are murders by psychopaths who take little trouble to avoid arrest not only because, like Heath and Haigh, they have a 'lack of judgment and foresight almost beyond belief' but also because they are anxious to attain the notoriety of some recently executed hero of theirs. When the murderer Rhodes was arrested in 1925, the police found in his pocket newspaper cuttings about an executed murderer whom Rhodes referred to as 'a hero'.[12] Marjeram, who stabbed a girl to death in 1930, told the police as soon as he arrived at the station, 'I want to read the account of the murder and all that has been said in the newspapers about me—there must be a lot about me as a job like this has not been done for a long time.' He had never met the girl before and made no attempt at a sexual assault. He appeared to enjoy his trial and sat laughing while the jury were considering the verdict. A few days before the murder, he had been serving a sentence for theft in a prison where there had been an execution of a murderer who was also, in Marjeram's opinion 'a hero'.[14] In 1961 the murderer Terry was hanged for committing a murder on the day of Forsyth's execution.

'Mike O'Brien was one big hero in the place,' wrote a former American gangster recalling the time he had spent in prison when he was young. 'He had done a lot of time and was in for big stuff and, besides, everybody had read about his brother, Smiling Jack O'Brien being hung for picking off a copper. He was certainly looked up to for that. I admired him. I used to watch him all the time in the yard and in the mess. I couldn't help it. Something about him caught my eye every time I

---

* Dr Thorsten Sellin told the Royal Commission of the case of a man who had committed murder with a view to being executed as he wanted to die and had a conscientious objection to suicide.[13]

got close to him. That wasn't only true in my case, but for everybody it was true, especially the young crooks.'[15]

'Everybody had read about his brother being hung'; and practically everybody in Chicago in 1924 read about the trial of Nathan Leopold and Richard Loeb for the murder of a fourteen-year-old boy whom they had killed simply for the thrill of committing the 'perfect murder'. Certainly the two girls of eighteen who helped their boy friends kill an old woman in Chicago during the trial knew all about it. 'Leopold and Loeb are the same age as us,' they said when they were arrested.[16]

But the immense publicity given to this trial had another effect. It served as a means of bringing the whole issue of capital punishment to the conscience of America. For Clarence Darrow, the brilliant advocate, who defended Leopold and Loeb, was a vehement abolitionist. 'Hanging men,' he had said twenty years before, 'does not prevent murder. It makes murderers.' Now in a speech of passionate eloquence, which made the tears stream down the judge's face, he pleaded for the lives of the two 'mentally diseased' boys who were, he insisted, not responsible for their admitted act. 'I am pleading for the future,' he told the court. 'I am pleading for a time when hatred and cruelty will not control the hearts of men, when we can learn by reason and judgment and understanding and faith that all life is worth saving, and that mercy is the highest attribute of men.'

His plea was not in vain. His young and clever clients were sentenced to imprisonment for 'life plus ninety-nine years'. Loeb died in prison, hacked to death by an insane fellow homosexual; but Leopold demonstrated that the murderer, however foul and savage and motiveless the murder, is not necessarily irredeemable. He was a good prisoner, running rehabilitation courses for other convicts until he became seriously ill in 1945 after having volunteered to take part in malarial experiments. He was released in 1949 and went to work in a leper colony.

The two Italian radicals, Nicolo Sacco and Bartolomeo Vanzetti, who were waiting in vain for a new trial at the time of the Leopold-Loeb murder, were given no such opportunity. Convicted of murder in 1921, they were not electrocuted until six years later. The evidence at their trial had been more concerned with politics and patriotism than with the murder and armed robbery at a shoe-factory with which Sacco and Vanzetti stood nominally charged;

and the judge was criticized in a subsequent report for his political bias. But seven motions for a new trial were dismissed and then on 27 August 1927, in the face of protests from such disparate sympathizers as Shaw, Wells, Dreyfus, Einstein and Mussolini, as well as from the abolitionists, the two men were executed.

Sacco and Vanzetti waited for six years to be electrocuted; but Caryl Chessman waited for twelve years after his death sentence for kidnapping in 1948 before he was gassed at San Quentin in 1960. And by the time he died he had become a kind of folk-hero throughout the world as Sacco and Vanzetti had been. Popular songs and poems had been written about him, Hollywood was preparing to make a film about him, autobiographical books by him had been translated into more than a dozen foreign languages, petitions, protests, demands, appeals, came into the office of California's Governor, Edmund G. Brown, at the average rate of a thousand a day. He was a 'symbolic cause for the opponents of capital punishment'. A leading French abolitionist went to Sacramento especially to plead for his life; the Brazilian Supreme Court Justice Nelson Hungria thought that Caryl Chessman was 'the most eloquent assurance of the need to wipe out, once and for all, the death penalty, that ugly stain on civilization'.[17]

Chessman had also become more than that. He had become a means of attacking the whole structure of American law and, indeed, of American life. In Europe and South America, newspapers were full of editorial condemnation, much of which ignored the facts that American courts had repeatedly spared Chessman, not to lengthen his 'terrible agony', but in accordance with the traditional ideas of American justice, and that it was Chessman himself who with great skill and some cynicism had made use of every possible legal manoeuvre erected by American law for the protection of the accused. He was an extremely resourceful, determined and talented man, but unlike Sacco and Vanzetti, he was ill cast in the role of martyr.

He was born in Los Angeles, the son of a disillusioned and often out of work father. His mother was crippled in a car accident when he was nine. He was small and frequently ill and he was unpopular at school; but he developed at an early age a talent for argument together with a gross conceit which never left him. 'His ego is so apparent,' a detective once said of him, 'that it almost reaches out and grabs you by the throat.'

After several spells in prison he was arrested in 1948 and convicted and sentenced in Los Angeles County Superior Court on a total of seventeen counts. He had been, rather uncertainly, identified as the 'Red Light Bandit', a gunman who drove a car, flashing a light like that of a police car, into lovers' lanes in the outskirts of Los Angeles and then robbed the men at pistol-point. Twice he had, the prosecution said, forced women to perform what the indictments called 'an unnatural sex act' (which was, in fact, fellatio) and once he tried to rape a girl of seventeen who was later confined in a state hospital as a schizophrenic although this illness, according to a psychiatrist, 'would have developed regardless of any alleged attempted rape'.[18] He was sentenced to death under a Californian statute, known as 'the little Lindbergh law', which makes it a capital offence to kidnap for the purposes of robbery with bodily harm.

Eight times a date was set for his execution over the ensuing twelve years and eight times he was reprieved. The eighth reprieve, granted ten hours before he was due to die, came not as a consequence of any legal manoeuvre but in response to a telegram from an assistant Secretary of State warning that the Government of Uruguay were afraid that, if Chessman were executed, there would be hostile demonstrations against President Eisenhower during his forthcoming visit there. Hundreds of other telegrams had been received that week but it was this one which helped the Californian Governor to make up his mind. He had long been an opponent of capital punishment and although he had no doubt that Chessman was both guilty and unrepentant and that he should not be singled out for clemency—'the evidence of his guilt is overwhelming', he had once said, 'his attitude has been one of steadfast arrogance and contempt'—Brown believed that he now had an opportunity to remove the death penalty from Californian law. The state legislature did not agree with him and, at a special session called to consider his proposal that capital punishment having proved 'a gross failure' should be abolished, he was charged with 'ducking his responsibility' and of trying to make the legislature 'a court of last resort for Chessman'. The proposal came to nothing and the Governor found himself in an even worse position than before. He was criticized by Californians for having 'given way to Washington' (a scarcely forgivable action by a loyal Californian) and by retentionists everywhere for having renounced California's moral right to put Chessman to death. 'If he is executed tomorrow,' a London newspaper had said the day before Chessman was reprieved for the last time, 'it will be a day when it will be rather unpleasant to be an American.'[19] The Governor had unwittingly given such commentators new grounds for attack.

On 2 May watched by no less than sixty witnesses, including two women reporters sitting in the front row, Chessman, who had with what now seems some possible justification protested his innocence to the end, inhaled hydrocyanic gas in San Quentin's green octagonal gas chamber and just over six minutes later he was dead. It appears that yet another stay of execution was granted just before he died, but that it came just a few minutes too late.[20] This is not unlikely. Certainly, three years before, Burton Abbot was dying in the same gas chamber when the Governor of San Quentin received a telephone call granting a stay of execution for him.[21]

'Now that the state has had its vengeance,' Chessman wrote in a statement he had prepared for publication after his death, 'I should like to ask the world to consider what has been gained.' For once he was not speaking only for himself.[22]

In America, as in every other country in the western world where capital punishment is still practised, the abolitionists are hopeful now that their campaign will soon be won. 'The gallows is a piece of medieval furniture completely out of place in a civilized modern society. When it has gone the way of the rack and the block those who now firmly believe in it will soon be wondering why it was retained so long.'[23]

Lord Altrincham is probably right. But it is as well to remember for how many years such hopes have been held.

'On the whole, we may perhaps be well satisfied that capital punishment—"the shameful practice", as it has been epigrammatically styled, "of hiring for a guinea an assassin to accomplish a sentence which the judge would not have the courage to carry out himself"—is threatened with extinction in civilized countries.'[24]

Havelock Ellis wrote these words in 1890.

CHAPTER TWO

CORPORAL PUNISHMENT

'A practice than which nothing tends more to harden and degrade.'

REPORT OF THE COMMITTEE ON
JUVENILE DELINQUENTS (1817)

'I will strive in my mind to judge those Members of Parliament who now advocate the revival of corporal punishment charitably,' Sir Robert Rawlinson said in the nineteenth century when opposing one of those recurrent demands to extend the uses of flogging, 'by considering that they have never seen it as I have feebly attempted to describe it: the degraded man lashed to the triangles, the white clean skin of an Englishman exposed to the cool morning air, to be scored, cut up and scarred into a pulpy, blood-smeared lump of living human flesh.'[1]

Englishmen can still be judicially flogged. The instruments used are the 'cat-o'-nine-tails' (the tails being lashes of whipcord, each about an eighth of an inch thick and thirty-three inches long) and the birch (a bundle of twigs forty inches long and nine ounces in weight for boys under sixteen and forty-eight inches long and twelve ounces in weight for those over sixteen). The birch twigs have to be soaked in water before they are used as they are brittle and would break; but, even so, they do break and usually a new bundle has to be used after every fourth stroke. The 'cat' has to be changed as well after every few strokes as the wet tails flick blood over the spectators.[2]

That flogging is a brutal punishment no one could deny; that to use it is to sanction brutality seems, therefore, unarguable; that

406

its more extensive use is still advocated by many intelligent people, who may or may not be driven by sadism or other unadmitted or unrealized sexual impulses, is a fact; that we are all cruel or violent in some degree, that a taste for violence is a deeply rooted human experience and that all societies rationalize and condone it are also facts; but that flogging is or ever has been a useful deterrent seems most unlikely. Violent criminals, themselves, predictably do not look at it as a deterrent at all, although some of them say it has done them good. 'I particularly remember one who was most vehement in his protestations,' Hugh J. Klare has written. ' "It did me good," he exclaimed, and when I asked him whether he had subsequently contained his violent behaviour, he scornfully denied it. And to his way of thinking it may have done him good —by confirming his opinion of authority, and of himself.'[3]

'I should think the product I am today ought to prove thrashings are no good,' an English criminal has recently said. 'What you feel is anger, resentment, and most of all, a determination somehow to get your own back. But being deterred? The idea never gets a look in . . . The "cat" was another occupational risk that's all. I've never had it myself, but I did plenty of things that I would have got it for if I'd been caught. I've met quite a few men who've had it, and up to now I've not met one on whom it had the effect it was supposed to, of putting him off. It only increased their viciousness and bitterness, so far as I can judge. And in certain cases it's increased their standing in the criminal world, they're quite proud of it and look on themselves like heroes . . . If they brought back public executions for sheep stealing, I'd probably go in for stealing sheep. There's something of the challenge in this, you know.'[4]

Albert Bourke, who received fifty lashes for continual violence while in prison, endorsed this view, 'the fifty lashes took no more effect on me,' he said, 'than a shower of rain could take on a bullock.' A prison doctor giving evidence to an investigating committee in 1837 said, 'I never knew a convict benefitted by flagellation. I have always found him afterwards to be a more desperate character than before; and after the lash had been inflicted he was generally amongst those who had it repeated.'[5]

Lord Goddard, making use of the ill-conceived argument which is used by those who would retain hanging, suggests that 'for years past we have thought too much of the criminal and not enough of the victim'. The same protest was made in the House of Lords in 1832 when vigorous objections were made to a Bill which proposed abolishing capital punishment for small larcenies. Lord Goddard does not recommend the hanging of thieves but does strongly advocate the efficacy of 'a good larruping' for young criminals; and his successor as Lord Chief Justice said in 1960 that he would like corporal punishment extended 'in certain circumstances' and that 'the great majority' of the 'persons concerned with the administration of the criminal law' whom he had consulted, agreed with him.[6] A more general agreement with these views might be assured if it could be shown that 'a good larruping' —Lord Goddard's choice of term seems more suited to the no doubt usually innocuous beatings at Marlborough which he remembers than to the floggings in the prison punishment shed which he has presumably not seen—if it could be shown that flogging, was, in fact, likely to achieve anything except a satisfying vengeance. To accuse a man of thinking more of the criminal than of his victim too often means nothing more than to regret that the pleasures and satisfactions of revenge have been denied. Only by thinking of the criminal can the numbers of victims be reduced; and only by imposing useful punishments—including the liability to make compensation to the victim or the victim's family—can society be honourably satisfied. Flogging is not a satisfactory punishment, not so much because it is violent—all punishments are violent to some extent—but because it is morally damaging and ineffective.

In February 1863 a Member of Parliament was attacked in the street by two men one of whom grabbed him tightly by the throat while the other robbed him of his money. It was the last of a series of attacks made in this way in the streets of London and resulted in the Security from Violence Act which authorized the flogging of men convicted of robbing with violence and of men who attempted to garrotte their victim with intent to commit an indictable offence. Flogging had long been favoured as a punishment in England. The Anglo-Saxons whipped their prisoners with knotted cords and it was 'not an uncommon practice for mistresses to whip or have their servants whipped to death'.[7] After the Whipping Act of 1530 had authorized the public whipping of naked vagrants, flogging seems to have become more common than ever. Throughout the sixteenth and seventeenth centuries, men and women were sentenced to be whipped at Quarter Sessions for an immense variety of offences. Not only rogues and vagabonds, but the mothers of illegitimate children, Scottish pedlars, beggars, drunkards, fortune tellers, sex offenders and even lunatics were all flogged for their crimes or misfortunes.* Children were frequently flogged by their parents at the time of executions 'to impress upon their minds the awful lessons of the gallows'.[8] Not until 1791 did a statute forbid the whipping of female vagrants, not until 1812 was the number of strokes limited to three hundred and public flogging of women continued till 1817 and later than that in Scotland.

By the middle of the nineteenth century, however, it had been accepted that the repeated floggings of previous centuries could no longer be permitted in a civilized country. In 1843 the Commissioners on the Criminal Law reported that in their opinion flogging tended to render the offender 'callous and greatly to obstruct his return to any honest course of life'.[9] And thirty years later it was, in fact, restricted to the offences covered by the Security from Violence Act.†

The belief that flogging offenders deterred and corrected them was, however, still strong. 'I would have the back' of the ruffians 'scarified often and deep', wrote Charles Dickens whose views, more ready to reflect public opinion than to change it, had much altered since the middle of the century.[10] And in 1874 there was a clamour for the extension of corporal punishment to men found guilty of 'brutal assaults'. Judges, chairmen of Quarter Sessions and magistrates were invited by the Home Secretary to give their opinions on the subject. The majority of them 'were in favour of that extension which public outcry demanded'.[11] Many of them referred to the ending of garrotting since the 1863 Act had made that offence punishable by flogging. In fact, the members of the gang that had been guilty of most of these offences in 1862 and 1863—there were 'very few persons concerned', according to the police[12] and nearly all of them had been in a 'model' prison[13]—had been arrested and been given further heavy prison sentences before

* The reason given for flogging lunatics—it was a reason also sometimes given for flogging criminals—was that the attack on the body would drive the devils out of it. And occasionally the pain and shock did have a beneficial effect on the madman's raving. A less often admitted reason for flogging lunatics was that it was the means whereby the keeper could relieve his feelings of exasperation, fear or dislike.

† In the United States flogging as a penal measure is now only retained by Maryland where it was last applied in 1948 and Delaware where the most recent flogging took place in 1952.

the Act came into operation. Garrotting, as Herbert Asquith told the House of Commons in 1900, 'was put down without resort to the lash.'[14]

Conversely when there was a sudden outbreak of robbery with violence in Liverpool in the 1880's and 1890's, after seventy-two floggings had been inflicted for this offence in ten years, there were twenty more offences in 1893 than there had been in 1883.[15] In 1938 a Committee on Corporal Punishment issued a report, which included an analysis prepared by the Howard League, of the after-prison records of 440 men convicted of robbery with violence between 1921 and 1930. Of the 142 who had been flogged for their offences, well over half committed other serious crimes after their release. Of the 298 who had not been flogged less than forty-four per cent committed serious crimes again. The Committee were prepared to admit that a man 'might take good care to avoid doing anything which might earn him a second flogging' but the only result of this was that he committed other crimes for which corporal punishment was not imposed. The Committee recommended, therefore, that the use of corporal punishment as a court penalty should be entirely abandoned. Ten years later it was. By the Criminal Justice Act of 1948 the punishment of flogging was limited to the offences of gross violence to prison officers, mutiny and incitement to mutiny committed by prisoners. Its effect on the incidence of robbery with violence was noticeable. In the three years before the Act, there had been on average 874 such offences; in the three years after the Act the average fell to 768.

Punishment can never be effective when it is administered by someone who is not respected or when it expresses the hatred or anger of the disciplinarian or when to be punished is to become a hero. It may achieve some immediate effect but it cannot lead to lasting remorse or a changed attitude. A recent and exhaustive study by Sheldon and Eleanor Glueck revealed that parents of young American delinquents are 'more apt than parents of nondelinquents to employ physical punishment'.[16] Dr Norval Morris's study of 270 confirmed recidivists published the following year,[17] showed that the three of these who had been flogged were all convicted of further crimes of violence and of the eight who had been birched, six were known to have committed more violent crimes afterwards.

Public opinion, nevertheless, apparently still favours flogging. In October 1961, after a clear and forceful speech by the Home

Secretary, the Conservative conference at Brighton decisively rejected a motion calling for corporal punishment for violent crimes. But a year before as many as seventy-eight per cent of those questioned in a Gallup Poll wanted a return to birching or flogging or both—descriptions of those who made up this percentage showed that the feeling was very much the same in all classes, the 'workers' slightly preponderating—and another Poll taken in April 1961 indicated that seventy-three per cent of the population still wanted corporal punishment back.

In recent years robbery has greatly increased in England, but the offenders are 'primarily thieves who occasionally, though rather rarely, use force to achieve their objects . . . Recourse to firearms is very rare indeed'.[18] If it seems true that men are no more likely to rob with violence when they cannot be flogged than when they can, it also seems true that the continued use of flogging or the threat of flogging has not proved an answer to the problems of prison discipline. 197 assaults were made on prison officers in 1960, and 213 the year before.[19] In America assaults are more common and, although the admitted use of the whip has all but disappeared from the official records of prisons and reformatories, only 'corporal punishments of the humiliating type' are disapproved of in the American Prison Association's *Manual of Correctional Standards* (1954) which reports that 'in several men's institutions where women are confined, women as well as men are flogged with a heavy leather strap as punishment for both minor and major infractions of the rules. The punishment is usually inflicted by a male employee'.[20] It is in prisons such as these that discipline is most difficult to maintain.

It is, perhaps, possible that it is still necessary 'to hold in reserve, as an ultimate sanction, the power to impose corporal punishment for serious offences against discipline in prisons'.[21] But this is not the experience of practically every other civilized country. In 1951 the International Penal and Penitentiary Foundation decided to undertake a study of modern methods of penal treatment. In their subsequent report, based on the replies to a questionnaire received from twenty-five countries, corporal punishment in prisons was said 'to have gone out of use in all countries'.[22] It was necessary to draw attention, in a footnote, to the fact that this observation did not apply to Great Britain and Northern Ireland. Nor does it apply to all institutions in the United States.[23]

CHAPTER THREE

PRISONS

*'After a while you forget why you are there all you know is
that you are there and thats all. Maybe one day they will
find some thing for all these wasted men to do. What people do
not seem to realize is that by sending a man to the nick for a
few years they are punishing him for doing wrong: Yes! but
they are also doing thereselves a great wrong, for as sure as
Hells a mouse trap, when that man gets out he will rob someone else.'*

FRANK NORMAN, 1958

BEFORE the Second World War there were usually about ten thousand prisoners in England and Wales; during the first half of 1961
there were over 28,500[1] of whom more than seven thousand were
sleeping three in a cell. 'What these figures mean in terms of overcrowding can be gauged from the fact that on at least one occasion
at a local prison men had to sleep on the floor of the chapel on the
night of reception; there was nowhere else to put them.'[2]

'What can you do with 1,700 men,' asked Mr R. D. Fairn, the
chief director of the Prison Commission in 1962 when complaining
about the overcrowding at Wandsworth, 'except count them, clean
them, feed them and lock them up?'[3]

Despite painstaking efforts to classify prisoners and separate the
corrupt from the corruptible, overcrowded prisons inevitably mean
that the ideal is impossible.

'The older men are always going at you. They make out that the game
pays. They want to fix up where to meet you on the outside.' 'To listen

to the chaps here drives me half out of my mind. They talk of thieving, thieving, thieving and nothing else.' 'Older men here mix with the younger chaps and keep telling you things. There are chaps here who pretend that they are in for getting thousands of pounds and that they have got it all salted away for when they come out. They try and persuade you that the job pays. I know it doesn't really but it frightens me having all these men here around you worse than what you are. Some of the chaps tell me that in the end you have to do whatever these older men want.'[4]

These comments by young criminals may be tendentious but the situation they describe exists.

The present prison building programme in Britain is more ambitious than any that has been attempted for more than a hundred years. Speaking in London in 1962, Mr R. A. Butler, then Home Secretary, said that of the various proposed establishments described in a recent White Paper,[5] twelve had already been opened and eleven more would be opened before the middle of 1963.[6] But even so, the problems of dealing with a prison population, which had already by the middle of 1962 risen to over thirty thousand, would not be solved. It will be years before the Victorian fortress prisons can be dispensed with, and the new prisons will contain some of the worst defects of the old.

Mr A. W. Peterson, the new Chairman of the Prison Commission, referring to the work of the Development Group which had been 'studying the whole question of prison design', said in a speech in 1959 that the prison of the future would have smaller cell blocks with adequate association rooms and less obtrusive security precautions. Each block would house about seventy-five to eighty prisoners and contain a dormitory for eight or ten men 'for whom dormitory accommodation is preferable'.[7] As separate lavatories will only be provided for the men who sleep in dormitories, the majority of men, therefore, will continue to go through the regular morning procedure of 'slopping out'.

A man who spent several months in Wormwood Scrubs has described, in a restrained and moving book, what this process means, how the men queue up each morning in front of the 'recesses' on their landings, chamber-pots in hand, waiting their turn to empty them. 'The general effect, with three landings in view,' he thought, 'was rather like some curious Neapolitan slum.'[8]

'I staggered out of the peter doppy from sleep,' another ex-convict wrote of his days in Wandsworth. 'There was about fifty men already there with their pots queuing up to empty them. The stink was enough to turn my guts over. Eventually it was my turn, the sink into which the slops were emptied was blocked and there were lumps of shit and pieces of paper floting in it . . . I blindly through the contence of my pot into the sink on top of the rest, and rushed away without looking, back to my peter. I did that same thing every morning and afternoon for two years.'[9]

At Wormwood Scrubs, too, the lavatories were frequently blocked. 'There were two sit-down lavatories in the shop and two stand-up ones shared by eighty prisoners . . . Fortunately most of the prisoners were chronically constipated because of the food.'[10] 'The sanitary arrangements are the most sickening part of the Scrubs,' a demonstrator against atomic weapons said in 1960, 'You can smell it all over the halls.' He was lucky with food, he added, being a vegetarian but normally it is cooked in such gigantic quantities that all the food value is destroyed'.[11] In Brixton, another demonstrator said, the food is 'appalling'. In 1962 at Stafford where, apparently, prisoners are told to scrub floors with nail-brushes and where one lavatory serves a hundred men, the best food came from sacks labelled: 'Grade III Pigmeal.'[12]

The Prison Commissioners' Report for 1960 gives an average menu and shows how immensely prison food has improved since the war. 'Soup as a course and a varied sweet dish are now served with dinner; potatoes are peeled and cooked in a variety of ways.'[13] Cold ham and tomato and a cup of tea might well be given for supper instead of the bread, margarine and cocoa (without sugar) served in the 1930's. But by the time the food reaches the prisoner it often enough still resembles the meals which Frank Norman remembers having eaten when he was imprisoned:

'Soup, mince meat, potatoes and cabbage, (I have never seen such cabbage as you get in the nick) for sweet their was a sort of suit pudding, which is known as duff. It was like trying to eat a piece of rubber . . . It states on the rule card, (there is one in every peter) that the food will be varied, appetizing, and of newtritious value, the words should be, you will eat what you get and like it, or go without.'[14]

Most prisoners soon get used to the food and they soon get used to 'slopping out'. They become accustomed, too, to the overcrowding. They learn to accept the enforced and unnatural celibacy. Occasionally a man is tempted by 'queers' who, at times like Christmas when 'disaplin' is 'pretty laxt' and there aren't 'maney screws about', will 'make up their faces with white tooth pouder and put red dye on their lips by wetting the covers of books', but 'this is a very dodgy business indeed as if you get captured at it you can lose half a streatch remishion and no messing about. So it isn't worth the trouble, although quite a lot of that sort of thing goes on'.[15] It is, though, as Peter Wildeblood has said, more likely to be 'of the emotional kind'.[16] What the prisoner cannot accept is that his punishment is being inflicted, as an American convict once put it, 'by those who are not themselves free of guilt . . . We can really work up a hate for the man whose authority somehow rests on the assumption of moral superiority and is a part of a whole conspiracy to humiliate and degrade us.'[17] 'When you go in, you notice straight away,' an intelligent English prisoner told the *Observer,* 'that there is an attempt to humiliate you: the officers want to make it quite clear that they are in authority. They establish this ritual about calling them "sir".'[18] In Brixton when the officers bring letters in the morning they open the cell door and 'throw the letters on the ground' so that the prisoners have to bend down and pick them up.[19]

Everyone connected with the prison is seen by the embittered convict as to some extent a part of this conspiracy to humiliate. To one habitual criminal a psychologist was 'a dirty-minded old woman out for kicks'; a Church Army captain, 'a preaching humbug'; a chaplain, 'a glorified Entertainments Officer' whose efforts were only successful with homosexuals and sex offenders as Church service gave them an opportunity to 'sit next to some other poof they fancy'; a prison visitor, 'an amiable sort of old boy' who only gave up his time for 'some sort of self-satisfaction, a feeling he was doing good in the world' but who, 'underneath all his good', had 'a really dirty mind'; a psychiatrist, 'a smooth-talking clever doctor' who had 'conned the Prison Commissioners' into giving him a job.[20]

But the real victim, the almost universal victim, of the prisoner's resentment is the prison officer.

'What the comishoners don't seem to realize is that if you don't treat a man like a hueman being he won't act like one . . . Although there are people like the Howard Leag for prison reform and Welfare Officers and all sorts of other nossey bastards the people who run the nicks are the screws and most of them are no good, make no mistake about that! So don't get the idea that nicks are good places for reforming people, all they are any good for is locking people up in and that's all. So why do they keep on all the time about how good they are. The fact is the nicks stink the screws are ignorant inhueman sadistic and a percentage of them are bent.'[21]

The Commissioners, of course, understand far more about this than they are given credit for. In their 1960 Report they write that 'in a year in which the number of receptions of convicted prisoners has reached the highest figure for forty-five years, and the population of already overcrowded prisons had continued to increase, the first concern of the prison service has been to preserve good order and discipline and to provide for the basic needs of inmates. In such conditions, individualized treatment is bound to suffer; continuity of staff cannot be maintained'.[22] And by no means all prison officers are as bad as habitual criminals like to suggest. Violence in large prisons is not uncommon. A man who makes a nuisance of himself may well get beaten up. But 'if you're an ideal prisoner you don't come across violence'. And there are some dedicated men, and particularly dedicated women— 'specially some of the younger ones they're getting in now'—in the prison service. The bad officers, though, have a disproportionate effect on the atmosphere.[23]

The difficulties of finding suitable men to work long and irregular hours, in bad conditions for little money and with poor prospects of promotion are almost insuperable. Practically all prisons are understaffed, few have sufficient social workers, most of them do not have staff psychologists, the older ones include many bad prison officers; and while in 1960 the numbers of prisoners increased by hundreds, the increase in established men officers was only eleven. The number of established women officers fell by sixteen although the numbers of women prisoners had also grown.[24] The prison Commissioners' Report for 1961 showed that this trend was continuing. There were more women prisoners than ever but a decrease of women officers. There was a slight increase in established men officers but the increase was fractional compared with the increase in prisoners.

Discontented officers guarding discontented men had had, and continues to have, a serious effect on discipline. There were 322 escapes from prisons in 1960, compared with 205 two years before;[25] a 'loose canvas restraint jacket' had to be brought into use to control violent prisoners over a hundred times;[26] and five prisoners were birched—all for 'gross personal violence to an officer', aggravated in two cases by incitement to mutiny.[27] The number of lesser assaults on officers, the Commissioners admitted, was 'regrettably high'.[28] There were less escapes from closed prisons in 1961 but this was due to those who attempted to escape being removed to a special wing at Durham Prison rather than to any general improvement in prison discipline.

The newcomer to prison life, as D. L. Howard has said, soon joins in the general insulting banter about the 'screws' and soon picks up the language of resentment, expressing his 'personal inadequacy in hatred of all custodial staff' to ease the 'pains of emotional deprivation and social rejection'.[29]

In these circumstances it is inevitable that 'the purposes of the training and treatment of convicted prisoners', as laid down by Rule Six of the *Prison Rules,* should not be realized. The ideal of establishing in them 'the will to lead a good and useful life on discharge' and fitting them to do so, has become a chimera. Vocational training is given but even in Borstals to only thirty per cent of the inmates. Evening classes are held and, although there is no evidence to prove that they help a prisoner to live a better life when he comes out, they do improve the atmosphere of prison life; but 'it is not easy to teach or learn while sitting in a little huddle in the centre of a long, tall, grim building, with wire netting overhead, and iron staircases leading up to the galleries of cells'.[30]

Work in prison is still largely devoted to boring activities connected with the running of the prison or to jobs like picking flock mattresses and obsolete telephone equipment to pieces and sewing mail-bags together. And in many prisons this work occupies only about two hours a day. So long as prisons exist there can be little hope of reforming the prisoner until he is allowed to work properly —and is paid a reasonable wage for doing so.

As it is the cost of maintaining him is about £460 a year excluding the cost of new buildings and building maintenance;* and in America, where the problems are very similar and where the

---

* According to the Prison Commissioners Report for 1961 the cost of maintaining each inmate is £695 a year at Borstals and £720 a year at Detention Centres. A Borstal for 174 boys opened in 1963 in Staffordshire cost £570,000.

number of inmates in State and federal penal institutions has now risen to well over two hundred thousand, it is even more. At Alcatraz, the crumbling, obsolescent maximum security prison in San Francisco Bay, still in use in 1963, the cost of maintaining each prisoner is over $125 a week.

Less than thirty of the country's state and federal institutions have been built since the War and many of even the most recent ones are designed like monkey-cages with hundreds of steel-barred cells in great concrete halls. Sanitation is on the whole much better than it is in an English prison—although in some of the municipal and county gaols where an additional eighty-five thousand to ninety thousand persons are incarcerated, half of them awaiting trial, it is still appalling—but the emphasis on maximum security has made it extremely difficult to carry out the process of rehabilitation which the American Correctional Association has stressed as being the real purpose of imprisonment. 'No other single factor has so retarded the development and success of rehabilitative programs as has the lag in correctional architecture.'[31]

Most prisons, as in England, are little more than places of detention and in some of them there are as many as four thousand men, a high proportion of them serving very long sentences or sentences subject to detainers which make them liable to be tried on other charges in different jurisdictions when they are released. Conditions, of course, have on the whole improved immensely. 'The American penal system tends to be anarchic, complicated, naively monolithic and lay-determined,' Professor Louis B. Schwartz wrote in 1962. 'But it is, at the same time, experimental, creative and progressively more merciful. With the passing of the frontier and the receding into history of Puritan theocracy, the forces which produced the current penal system are yielding to new influences.'[32] Men are still marched about but not in lock step; they are given adequate food in dining rooms and, although often they have to sit at narrow tables all facing in one direction, eating in silence while guards armed with machine-guns watch them from behind screens, in some prisons there are separate tables where they can sit in small groups as in a restaurant; they have good libraries and good schools; usually they have a visiting room instead of a bullet-proof corridor divided by a steel partition; they have less uncomfortable uniforms with minor differences to show the results of a grading system, opportunities to watch films and television and play games. Most prisons still have irons, handcuffs or chains for use on recalcitrant inmates but only in a very few of them are they regularly employed. With all these changes the atmosphere of prison life has, however, not greatly altered. 'Men marching but not going any place new,' as Professor Taft has described them. 'Men listless or rebellious or cowed. Men looking forward to a future of crime, or to a struggle to get a job and social recognition. Men who "can take it" but who get less than nothing out of it. Such a picture is not fair to a few prisons and some reformatories.'[33]

It is not fair, for example, to a prison such as San Quentin where modern techniques are faithfully and earnestly employed. San Quentin contains twice as many prisoners as it was designed to hold; but they sleep in clean cells where they have wireless headphones and proper sanitation. The fearful jute mill described by James Spenser in 1928 is modernized and employs seven hundred men, and there are clothing and furniture factories as well as a printing works, a naval renovation plant and opportunities for outside work and for trade apprenticeship. Many prisoners go to school every day; many more go to night school. An alert and intelligent English visitor in 1962 noticed 'very little sign of listlessness or inattention'.[34] Great stress is laid upon Group Counselling which was first tried out in its modern form in San Quentin under the auspices of the liberal Warden Clinton Duffy and the progressive California Department of Corrections. In Group Counselling, now also being developed in English prisons, small groups of men, including a member of the staff, discuss their family problems, their fears and prejudices, their worries, their likes and dislikes, loves and hates. Whether or not this form of group therapy does much to reform criminals permanently may be doubted, but it certainly lessens tensions and makes discipline much easier to maintain.

Prisons like San Quentin and some other institutions like Chino and the open prison at Seagoville should not, however, be taken as representative of the American system as a whole. In California men are recruited for the prison service on merit and the standard of entry is high; but elsewhere the evil of politics is still evident and still operating in the selection of candidates. In 1947 it was estimated that three quarters of the country's thirteen thousand prison guards had been 'selected unscientifically, although over two fifths of the states provided for civil service appointments'.[35] The numbers of unsuitable guards are less now but there are still very many, particularly in women's prisons where homosexuality and dope addiction are still common and where female guards have been known to recruit prostitutes and shop-lifters for crime syndicates.[36] Riots have been less frequent since the epidemic of 1952 but the riot at Montana State Prison in 1959 was not the only serious one that year.

At the Montana prison, where mismanagement by political appointees had already led to a riot in 1957 and a sit-down strike in 1958, convicts, led by a homosexual burglar and his nineteen-year-old friend who had clubbed a man to death three years before, attacked members of the prison staff and held them as hostages. Armed with knives and meat axes, and almost delirious from the effects of kitchen-made 'pruno' alcohol and narcotics stolen from the dispensary, the convicts threatened to burn their hostages in naptha taken from the laundry unless the use of buckets as lavatories came to an end, unless young prisoners were no longer locked up with older men and a hated state parole commissioner was dismissed. The riot was only ended when National Guardsmen led an attack on the barricaded block with bazookas, machine-guns and rifles. 'Things are going to get a lot tougher around here,' the Warden was quoted as saying when the trouble was temporarily over.[37]

But toughness has been found to be no remedy. Keeping men occupied at useful and profitable work is at least a more promising one. But in America, as in England and for similar reasons, the problems of prison labour have not been satisfactorily solved. And enforced idleness in overcrowded conditions increases the problems of discipline.

'The three most common major disciplinary problems' in American prisons are apparently 'gambling, sex and fighting. The fighting frequently results from the gambling and sex problems. Inability to pay a gambling debt . . . may lead to fighting, as may also the "eternal triangle" in a homosexual relationship'.[38] The gambling problem has been overcome in Nevada's State Prison in Carson City by allowing convicts to bet openly under supervision rather than trying vainly to prevent them from gambling in secret. But the homosexual problem, which seems to be far more widespread than it is in English prisons, cannot be overcome so simply. It surely cannot be overcome by the curious method adopted in one large penitentiary in the West where those discovered in homosexual activities were forced to wear women's clothes.[39] The abnormality of life without women permeates the whole atmosphere of prison life. 'It is expressed not only in pathological sex conduct but indirectly in other emotional storms.'[40] No solution to the problem, so the International Penal and Penitentiary Foundation reports, has ever been found. 'As a matter of fact, the only countries that have tried to find a direct solution are the South American states and the Soviet Union. Two methods have been put into practice; 1. to allow the prisoner to have marital intercourse at more or less frequent intervals (Argentine): 2. to organize colonies in which a prisoner may live with his family (Brazil, U.S.S.R.).'[41] The practice recently adopted by Mexico and some other Latin American and Scandinavian prisons of allowing women to sleep overnight with their men has not been generally followed elsewhere and would not, apparently, be welcomed by the prisoners in San Quentin because, so they have said in their Group Counsel meetings, 'Every guy would know what they were here for.'[42] And to extend to the San Quentin inmate the right of the prisoner in Sweden of going out of prison on leave or the privilege of the Columbian prisoner of visiting his wife in a certified rooming-house or, if not married, of visiting a prostitute, would lead to many objections, not only on the grounds of security. In some Southern States, however, men leave the prison on furlough although the practice does not appear to be officially admitted.

The problem is aggravated in America by there being no adequate classification system (in 1951 only about a third of the state penal systems had any classification committee or centre at all and the position is only slowly improving)[43] and by there being few alternative types of institution in all but the most populous states, almost half of which do not have separate prisons for women.

But it is doubtful that even the most modern penal system with ideal methods of diagnosis, prediction and classification, of worthwhile employment and education, with well-equipped buildings and an intelligent staff prepared and able to employ psychological techniques to fit the prisoner for a better and more useful life outside, would succeed in its aims without a more fully awakened public conscience. The state of prisons today, both in America and in Britain is 'far more serious than that which Howard described nearly two hundred years ago. Disease, wholesale brutality and squalor such as would create a public scandal are,' as Terence Morris, one of England's most talented young sociologists, has said, 'absent, but in their place is the dismal reckoning that after 150 years of experimentation with penal techniques we are still as far away as ever from success. The public is not seriously concerned . . .'[44]

The public is not concerned and believes, perhaps, that more than enough money is being spent already. The idea that prisons should primarily be places of detention and punishment is still widespread. Sir Alexander Paterson's celebrated aphorism that men are sent to prison *as* a punishment and not *for* punishment has become a principle of penological thinking, but it is still not generally accepted. Whenever a proposition is made to establish a new prison, there is always strong local opposition—soon, as it happens, overcome by the unexpectedly good behaviour of the prisoners—although an open prison offers 'a far better chance of preparing a prisoner to lead an honest life on release than can be attempted behind high walls and prison bars'.[45] The establishment of England's first psychiatric prison at Grendon Underwood where abnormal prisoners can receive treatment for their illnesses and delusions, was also severely criticized, although similar institutions on the Continent and in California at the Medical Facility at Vacaville have shown promising results.

The suggestion that this type of treatment will be given to all criminals in the future and that prisons as we know them will, therefore, become anachronisms is probably unrealistic, although it seems that far more offenders are, in fact, mentally ill and not simply criminal than is generally recognized. Certainly there can be no doubt that the modern prison and the modern Borstal do not have much better records as reformatory agencies than those which preceded them. According to the Report of the Central After Care Association for 1960, sixty per cent of the men discharged from corrective training and from long-term sentences of preventive detention since 1954 had been reconvicted by the end of 1960.* And in 1961 well over half of the men who were sentenced to imprisonment had been in prison at least once before. Over fifty-eight per cent of young men discharged from Borstals in 1954 and over fifty-nine per cent of young men discharged from prisons, have

---

* In 1962 the Howard League for Penal Reform submitted to the Home Secretary's Advisory Committee on the Treatment of Offenders a well-argued recommendation that as preventive detention had proved itself yet another penological failure, it should be completely abolished. Undoubtedly, as the Home Office Report, *Persistent Offenders* (1963), shows, liability to preventive detention does not act as a deterrent.

been reconvicted. Six out of ten offenders discharged from Borstals in 1955 had been found guilty of a further offence within three years of their discharge.[46] And as it cannot be shown that the other forty per cent have not returned to crime but only that they have not been caught, nor that, even if they have remained honest, they would not have done so without Borstal training, these figures may be even more disturbing than they appear. Now that every effort is made to prevent young offenders being sent to prison and now that Borstals are, therefore, being increasingly filled with boys whose future is pessimistically predicted—a process which will be accelerated by the Criminal Justice Act of 1961 which envisages the abolition of short-term imprisonment for young offenders—the Borstals' success rates seem likely to drop lower than ever. The prospects in America are even more depressing. 67.6 per cent of the total number of men committed to federal prisons during 1959 had been in prison before;[47] and it has been admitted by the Secretary of the American Correctional Association that there is 'a habitual roving criminal group in the United States,' numbering three million, 'which our penal system is doing nothing to reduce'.[48]

Clearly as long as the characteristic penal institution in both countries continues to remind 'the observer at one and the same time of a pre-1914 doss-house, a military transit camp and a public cleansing station',[49] and so long as psychological techniques are hindered on the one hand by prejudiced cynics and on the other by wild enthusiasts, there are few grounds for hope.

Some men who break the law must be confined for long periods; a few, perhaps, for the whole of their lives. For many, as Hugh J. Klare has suggested, 'treatment in a closed institution, given at the right moment, and lasting for the right time may be the only chance' which they will get 'of growing out of anti-social attitudes'.[50] But for most of them there can be no satisfactory future until penal reform is recognized as an urgent and necessarily expensive problem which concerns us all.

CHAPTER FOUR

POLICE

'The Cozzpots are not all idiots.'

Robert Allerton, 1961

'Was there ever a moment when you deliberately said, "I am going to stay on this side of the fence. I am going to be a criminal"?'
'Yes, definitely. Especially when I was assaulted by the police. After I had assaulted a policeman I was badly beaten in the police station.'
'By the policeman you had assaulted or by his mates?'
'By his mates. By his father-in law, actually.'
'When you say assaulted, what did it actually consist of?'
'Well I got a thrashing with the fists and boots. Everything went in —truncheons . . . they didn't mark me on the face. It was on the fatty side of the body—on the calf and such-like.'
'How many of them were at it?'
'Two or three. In the police cells. They come in and start arguing with you, and before you know where you are, you're getting belted.'
'Did you complain about this to anybody?'
'Well, who can you complain to? They're all policemen there.'[1]

The professional criminal talks and writes of policemen as though to be beaten up by them is an occupational hazard and to escape conviction by bribing them—'putting in the bung'—is an everyday occurrence. Allegations of such brutality and such corruption, of improper methods of questioning, of statements and confessions obtained by threat and force have been made against the police ever since professional police forces existed. They were made with some flimsy support during the Browne and Kennedy case in the

424

spring of 1928; and they were repeated with more justification in the summer of the same year after a Miss Savidge, who had been charged with an offence in Hyde Park, was interrogated at Scotland Yard. This time the issues were felt to be of such public importance that a Royal Commission on Police Powers and Procedure was appointed. In many countries a suspected person or one who is believed to have relevant information can be brought before an examining magistrate and can be punished for refusing to answer his questions. In France the *juge d'instruction* and in Scotland the procurator-fiscal are given this power of examining suspects by law; but in England and the United States, interrogations of this sort are left to the police who are constantly attacked for over-stepping the narrow limits of their power, which does not extend to any form of compulsion and theoretically leaves them open to an action for wrongful arrest or false imprisonment if they abuse their authority. The practice of the police with regard to interro-gations and taking statements had not been the subject of a public enquiry before 1928 and while the members of the Commission reported that the methods of the police left little room for com-plaint and that 'third degree' as understood in the United States did not exist in England, they emphasized the need for control and limits on police powers of questioning.

These powers had been rather loosely defined in 1906 after two policemen had been rebuked by judges on the Midland Circuit, one for not cautioning a suspect before asking him questions, the other for doing so. The Judges of the High Court were asked to make some ruling on the matter and eventually decided that neither a prisoner in custody nor any person whom a police officer had 'made up his mind to charge' should be questioned without a cau-tion. Prisoners wanting to make a statement should also be cautioned, and so should suspects when formally charged. The words should be: 'Do you wish to say anything in answer to the charge? You are not obliged to say anything unless you wish to do so, but whatever you say will be taken down in writing and may be given in evidence.'

These Judges' Rules, elaborated by the Royal Commission, have not always been strictly observed. Nor, so the Royal Com-mission discovered, did the police always observe the regulations about search warrants. It had 'long been the practice of the police to search' the house of a man who had been arrested or for whose arrest a warrant had been issued. The Commission were satisfied that the practice was 'necessary and proper in the interests of justice', but their suggestion that the position should be regularized by a Statute was not adopted and has not been adopted since. It is still accepted by courts, police and criminals alike that there should be a difference between what is right in law and what is done in practice.

Although police procedure regarding searches received the approval of the Commission and allegations of police corruption were said to be much exaggerated, there were other aspects of police behaviour which were matters of concern. Further safeguards were recommended, for instance, with regard to the statements made by prisoners and to the holding of identification parades, two matters which remain of concern today, although it it is not likely that many suspects would share the experiences of Major R. O. Sheppard who, having been wrongfully accused by a prostitute in Piccadilly of having stolen her handbag, was lined up on an identification parade with what men could be found in the streets outside the police station at one o'clock in the morning. 'None of the others looked in the least like an army officer,' Major Sheppard complained with understandable indignation, 'and four of them were wearing chokers.'[2]

The Royal Commission of 1929 was followed by another which published its somewhat complacent report in 1962. This pointed out 'the substantial case for creating a national police service',[3] but only in a Memorandum of Dissent by Dr A. L. Goodhart was it recommended that the present system of large numbers of partially autonomous local forces should be ended. And suggestions which had regularly appeared in the Press the previous winter that 'relations between the police and the public have never been worse',[4] were denied. The Commission, indeed, referred to the Government Social Survey which indicated that 'relations between the police and the public are good. There is no reason to suppose that they have ever in recent times been otherwise. Most people have great respect for the police.'[5]

This is true although a vociferous minority both in Britain and America have no respect for them at all and do their best to provoke them, and although a larger minority are continually criticizing them for using methods without which their work would be impossible. They are, as Colin MacInnes one of the most understanding of writers has observed, 'doing the dangerous and difficult job society demands without any understanding by society of what their moral and professional problems are'. In 1959 there were 1,700 complaints against the police in the London area, two hundred of which were regarded as proved. But this, as the Report says, is 'very small in relation to the number of policemen'—about one complaint for every twenty thousand hours of police duty—and many of them were made by angry drivers. A majority of the Commission did not think there was any justification for changing the present system of investigating these complaints at police head-quarters, although it may well be thought that an independent enquiry—outside the scope of the new Chief Inspector of Con-stabulary—is, in fact, often justified. For the fact that 'most people have great respect for the police' does not necessarily mean that the police do not take bribes, use violence unnecessarily, employ unfair means of getting evidence or give false evidence in court, all of which, of course, they sometimes do. Nor does it necessarily mean that if 'most people' believed these abuses to be widespread they would no longer entertain this 'great respect' for the police whose methods, after all, very rarely concern them.

It may be, indeed, that 'most people' are not so much con-cerned with how the police behave in dealing with offenders and obtaining their conviction as with how many they arrest in the first place. Their record in this respect does not seem, on the sur-face, to be very good. Perhaps Donald McLachlan was right, when calling in the *Sunday Telegraph* for 'the Trenchard of the sixties' and lamenting the fact that only one per cent of police recruits have passes at advanced level of the General Certificate of Education, to say that 'the police seem to be outwitted and outpaced'. 'Thirty years ago,' he continued, 'preventable crime in London was rising in just the same way, and the police were being outwitted and out-paced. But after Lord Trenchard had used the new broom as Com-missioner of Metropolitan Police for three years, crime had fallen by more than twenty per cent from 23,740 cases in June 1933, to 18,400 in June 1935. By reorganizing Scotland Yard, cleaning out corruption, tightening up discipline and modernising the methods of fighting crime, he put London's policemen ahead of crime.'[6]

If they were ahead of crime then, they cannot be said to be ahead of it now. Scotland Yard was said by *The Sunday Times* at the beginning of 1962 to believe that it was 'beginning to beat the crime wave. Though it has a long way to go, especially in the face of the recent series of successful payroll and mailbag raids, police chiefs say that measures in 1961 have reduced the rate of increase in crime'. But although the Flying Squad had a record year in the amount of property recovered, there were few other indications that Scotland Yard's reported optimism was justified. According to expert evidence given to a Royal Commission on the Police in 1962, 'the average annual value of property stolen or obtained by fraud in the country is probably of the order of twenty million pounds, of which less than a quarter is recovered'. And according to figures collected by the Institute of Criminology at Cambridge 'seventy per cent of the perpetrators of some kinds of robbery escape altogether'.[8] Before the War about half of the crimes committed all over the country were eventually cleared up, but in the last twenty-five years the detection rate has dropped by about five per cent. Forty-five per cent were cleared up in 1961 compared with forty-four per cent the year before. Improved rates of pay have helped to increase the numbers of police and so one reason for the decline in efficiency is being slowly removed. But although new courses on police training are being established for promising constables there are still too few training facilities for the C.I.D. And all the time, the modern criminal is becoming more expert and cunning.

'He can discover where police boundaries lie and when wireless frequencies change. He can live in an area policed by one force and operate in another's territory. Aided by motorways and fast transport he can make a "getaway" that will take him through six separate police districts within the hour. In the use of explosives and electronic devices he is becoming efficient—as in evolving new kinds of fraud.'[9]

It seems then that, although the country's traditional prejudice is against a more powerful centralized police, there are good reasons for Dr Goodhart's recommendations, given in his Memorandum of Dissent to the Royal Commission Report, and for Sir Ronald Howe's repeated suggestions that there should be a national C.I.D.

Before the existing British Police are deprived of their traditional title of being the 'most wonderful in the world', it should be remembered, though, that the carelessness and stupidity of the public are responsible for a large proportion of preventable crime, that America's loss to the 'barons of the underworld' alone is estimated as being $22,000,000,000, and that in that country in an average year (1956) only 13.2 per cent of serious offences known to the police ended in conviction,[10] that the Italian,

Enrico Ferri, wrote in the nineteenth century that 'seventy per cent of discovered crimes go unpunished'[11] and that at the beginning of the twentieth century there was only one conviction for house-breaking in London to every twelve known crimes of this sort,[12] that a man sitting down to protest against the hydrogen bomb in Trafalgar Square was likely to have been more gently treated than a man protesting against the O.A.S. in Paris, that while we read with dismay in the *Guardian* of four Birmingham policemen pleading guilty at Warwick Assizes to charges of breaking and entering we can learn from *Time* that a few months before more than ten times as many policemen in Denver, Colorado—where salaries start off at $393 a month and 'almost any able-bodied young man who is not a certifiable moron can join the force'—had been implicated in crimes that over ten years had brought them in more than $250,000.[13]

It may no longer be true, as it was when the Wickersham Report was published, that 'the great majority of police are not suited either by temperament, training or education for their position'.[14] It may also no longer be true that the American cop is as wild with his gun as he was in Chicago in 1926 and 1927 when eighty-nine people were shot, 'not all by any means gangsters'.[15] But it is true that the corruption in American police forces in recent years has not been limited to Denver. In March 1960 many of Chicago's 11,200 policemen were found to be part-time burglars; and in 1949 'a gambling syndicate had a finger in Brooklyn, a finger that did not get burned because cops were paid over twelve million dollars a year in graft to keep the heat off.'[16] Harry Gross, a bookmaker in New York, who admitted to paying a million dollars a year in police protection, named numerous policemen whom he had bribed and eighteen of them were tried and convicted of perjury or contempt of court and forty-one were dismissed as was the Police Commissioner. Four years later a new Commissioner chose Stephen Patrick Kennedy, the son of an Irish immigrant, to be his chief inspector. Eighteen months later the terse, efficient Kennedy was Commissioner himself. 'Apply the law and apply it vigorously,' Kennedy told his men. 'It's not your job to become confused with the vagaries of the why-oh-why school. The policeman has a job to do, and if he does it honestly and intelligently, he gains respect. That's a damned sight more important than being liked.'[17]

Kennedy's policemen were not greatly liked and nor are

Michael Murphy's, but they are much more respected than their predecessors and most of their contemporaries. There are over twenty-three thousand of them, almost as many men as would make two army divisions. They have helicopters, boats, emergency trucks, mounted troops, narcotic squads (to keep track of twenty-three thousand known drug addicts), bomb-disposal units and now, following the example of the St Louis police, a squad in the Tactical Patrol Force whose members, disguised as women, act as decoys to trap robbers and sex criminals. They have a crime laboratory which is the biggest in the world after the FBI's and finger-print files with more than 3,700,000 cards. They also have a confidential squad that spies on the rest of the department. And regrettably they need it. In March 1959 three of Kennedy's men were arrested for blackmailing a bookmaker; two others for blackmailing a sailor they saw take a girl into a hotel; four others were found to have permitted gambling to go on unchecked in their district in Harlem; one was arrested for a homosexual offence; and yet another for raping and murdering an elderly woman.[18]

But New York's Police Department is one of the best in America, and if corruption exists in it, there are few other departments that have proportionately less of it, and few other departments that are not still involved in some way with gambling or 'shake-down' rackets. If it still appears unnecessarily violent, Kennedy and Murphy would excuse its violence by protesting that it was at war, and being at war it must use the weapons of war. If its men sometimes appear to be stupid, so do hundreds of America's other 177,000 policemen, for it is not a profession that has ever attracted many young men of talent. The usual qualifications, even now 'concern little more than age, weight, height, residence, and citizenship, together with some sort of character investigation, and perhaps certain mental standards'.[19] And the quality of those applying for admission has, apparently, in the last few years 'seriously degenerated'.[20]

'The cozzpots are not all idiots,' an English criminal has guardedly admitted. None of them should be. To be a good policeman requires far more qualities than he is as yet expected to possess or is trained to acquire and until the implications of this are accepted it is hardly likely that there will be less professional criminals.

CHAPTER FIVE

THE YOUNG OFFENDER

'Juvenile delinquency, particularly in the United States, has come to be considered one of the most urgent social problems of the day, and the epidemic of arrogance and crime seems to be spreading so fast that it obliterates the best efforts society can make to control it—or even to understand it.'

VIRGINIA HELD, 1959

ONE warm evening in August 1957 eighteen members of a gang, called the Egyptian Dragons, went into a park in upper Manhattan armed with knives, sticks, lead pipes, belts and a machete. The youngest was thirteen, the oldest nineteen, most of them were under fifteen. They were looking for some boys who belonged to a rival gang. They did not find them; but they did come across a fifteen-year-old cripple. They attacked him instead and killed him.

Eleven of the boys were sent to a reformatory; the other seven were brought to trial the following year. Three of them were acquitted after New York City's longest murder trial, two were found guilty of manslaughter, two of second degree murder. All the four found guilty came from broken homes; two of them were Negroes, one was born in Puerto Rico, one in the Dominican Republic. The Puerto Rican said that he had been drunk; one of the Negroes said that he used his machete just 'to show the others' that he was 'doing something'.[1]

Both the crime and those who committed it were symptomatic of a growing problem which was disturbing the world.

Nowhere was the problem more keenly felt than in New York.

An investigation carried out by the New York *Times* in 1958 revealed the extent of this problem and its dangers. Many gang members were illiterate with little interest outside the gang except comic books, cowboy and gangster films and dancing with their girl friends who slept with them and carried their weapons for them; many of them smoked marijuana and drank themselves into the mood for fighting with cheap wine; some of them, particularly the gang leaders, were alert and intelligent; but practically all of them were bored and frustrated or, as they put it themselves, 'shook-up'. Courage in a fight and loyalty to the gang were the only virtues universally admired. The gang's territory, or 'turf', even if it were only, as it often was, a few crumbling blocks, had to be fanatically defended at all costs. These territories were mainly concentrated in the poorest parts of the city where the Negroes and the Puerto Ricans live, where the population was always moving and changing, where hundreds of families were living on poor relief and hundreds more were broken. Three quarters of the city's juvenile delinquency was attributable to no more than twenty thousand such families, that is to say seventy-five per cent of the young criminals came from one per cent of the total number of families in the city.[2]

Was juvenile delinquency really such a big problem, it was often asked. Or was it made to seem so?

Undoubtedly the precocity of criminals has long been noticed. At the end of the eighteenth century, of the three thousand convicts under twenty years of age in London prisons, nearly half were under seventeen; many were only nine or ten and some were six. Boys of eleven and even nine were visited by their mistresses, girls of the same age who worked as prostitutes and brought part of their takings into the prisons with them.[3] Of a hundred criminals examined by Rossi and Lombroso, thirty-five had begun to drink alcohol 'between the ages of two and ten; six had become addicted to the practice of masturbation before the age of six, and thirteen had had sexual intercourse before the age of fourteen'.[4] In England at that time less than a quarter of the convicts in borough and county prisons were over forty, and in convict prisons where most recidivists served their longer sentences only a third of the prisoners were over thirty-five. The most criminal age, both in England and on the continent, was well under thirty. Carefully prepared French statistics, which illustrated in more detail the general experience of other European countries, indicated that it

was, in fact, between twenty and twenty-five; although for women
the peaks of criminality were reached between thirty and thirty-five
and for the less serious offences, between twelve and fourteen.
While the numbers of boys under twenty-one who are now in
prison is very small, this is due to reforms in the penal system of
Europe and not to any decrease in youthful crime. In fact, in England, the number of boys sentenced by the courts to imprisonment,
because other forms of training are considered unsuitable, is increasing fast.[5] Increasing at an even faster rate are the numbers
of boys found guilty by the courts. In 1907 less than a third of
offenders were under the age of twenty-one; in 1946 the proportion was more than a half;[6] by 1960 it had risen to about sixty
per cent and this trend continues. The number of boys under
sixteen found guilty has more than trebled in thirty years.[7] In
1938 the most criminal age for male offenders was only thirteen
and the most criminal age for female offenders was nineteen.*
This table[8] shows the numbers of those found guilty in 1938 for
every hundred thousand of the population:

Age	Males	Females
8	220	9
9	451	27
10	703	37
11	931	62
12	1111	66
13	1315	73
14	1141	84
15	1145	97
16	1110	91
17	867	99
18	740	106
19	766	108
20	665	94
21–24	559	77
25–29	431	62

* The Committee on Children and Young Persons recommended in 1960 that
children should not be held to be criminally responsible until they were at least
twelve. In 1963 the government proposed raising the age from eight to ten,
almost no other European country is the age fixed below thirteen. In Austria,
Germany, Norway and Czechoslovakia it is fixed at fourteen, and in Denmark
and Sweden at fifteen.

Age	Males	Females
30–39	307	61
40–49	182	50
50–59	101	30
60 and over	51	10

Twenty years later the proportions have not greatly altered, the most criminal age remaining roughly the same for boys and dropping to about fourteen for girls; and in 1961 there were over fifteen per cent more offenders between fourteen and seventeen than there had been the previous year and over nine per cent more offenders under fourteen. But if it is true that the young are becoming progressively more criminal, most criminals seem always to have been young and the young seem always to have been violent. Certainly it is not difficult to find examples of their wanton violence at any period. In the nineteenth century, for instance, a man was found dead in the streets of Milan with eighty-two wounds in his body. His murderers were five youths aged between fifteen and nineteen who had all taken part in the murder which had been committed because they wanted to get enough money for a visit to a brothel. In the same period, when there were two thousand boys under twenty-one in the prisons of Paris and 'each of the Parisian gangs of young assassins included a girl who had scarcely reached nubility', two youths had killed a woman who had befriended them and bitten off her fingers to get at the rings.[9] But, at least, in the past it had been possible, or so it was maintained, to discover some reasonable motive for violence. Now the motive was often as unreasonable as that of the fourteen-year-old boy who confessed to the police in 1957 that he had killed another boy by stabbing him in the back to 'get the feeling of knife going through bone'. Another young murderer complained, 'I did not get the thrill I expected.'[10] Violence committed not for gain but for 'kicks' had not, of course, been unknown before; but after due allowance had been made for the increased attention paid to neurotic behaviour in every form, for the sudden activities of police forces which gave publicity to a situation which had existed largely unknown for years, for the growth of population, for the misinterpretation of juvenile crime statistics, and for the attitudes of mind which condemn acts committed in a new suburb that would have been tolerated in a slum, the fact of a real increase in such violence and in juvenile crime generally—particularly in America—seemed unquestionable.

By 1962 youths under eighteen were responsible, according to the *Uniform Crime Reports*, for a very high proportion of the numbers of burglaries and rapes in America, although the exact proportion is impossible to estimate owing to the fact that a youthful offender is more likely to lay himself open to arrest.[11] There can, however, be little possibility of misinterpreting the figure published by a Committee of the United States Senate in 1955 which showed that 1,250,000 children between ten and sixteen get into trouble with the police every year.[12] In Washington most of the 150 assaults made upon the police in 1959 were by boys under eighteen. Baltimore, Detroit, San Francisco, Los Angeles and Philadelphia, as well as New York, had to take emergency measures against juvenile crime.[13] All over the country research teams were at work endeavouring to discover the root of the problem; and organizations such as the New York City Youth Board sent out special workers to try and understand the delinquents by talking to them and their families.

The whole structure of American society was found—as in the case of adult crime—to be responsible both in its virtues and in its failings. The restless youth and vigour of America, the constant talk of 'roots' but the simultaneous wandering and migrations, the growing tightness and isolation of groups divided by religion and race, income and education, the need to belong and to conform, the weakening bonds of family life and the conflict between parents and their children, the easy discipline in many American schools and the new depressingly uniform and cloistral suburbs, were all blamed by American sociologists for the rebelliousness of the country's youth. Even the reliance on psychiatric therapy was held by some to be dangerous because it had an 'undesirable effect on the offender himself, by helping him to take his offence too lightly'. And it was not only the offender who failed to 'appear unduly upset' and to be without a sense of guilt but other members of the family also showed little concern. 'Although the parents sometimes vocalized their shock and grief their behaviour did not indicate it.'[14]

Most of these factors applied also in Europe and had led to similar results; but a peculiarly American aggravation was the disastrous lack of adequate penal measures. There is nothing in America, even now, to compare with the British Borstal system.

Probation services are under-staffed and thousands of youths are thrown into jails because there are no other places for them to be held or trained. And when they come out they have learned little which hinders them from returning to gang life, to the dream-like world where the Valiant Crowns and the Royal Knights, the Demons, the Chaplains and the Imperials still wait with hunting knives and Molotov cocktails, torn off car aerials and home-made zip guns to defend their territory against all invaders.

The gang fights, or 'rumbles', that so frequently break out are nearly always superficially the result of 'turf' invasions or racial rivalries, like the 'rumble' in September 1959 when two Puerto Ricans, known as 'Cape Man' and 'Umbrella Man', led their gang into battle against the young white 'gringos' of the Clinton district and killed two of them as they ran away from their playground. But racial intolerance is no more than a superficial explanation. The attitudes of mind that lead to the 'rumble' are not so easily accounted for. They are far more diffuse and complicated; they are born perhaps in the bitterness of poverty and squalor, and bred in homes which are not homes at all; they are symptoms of lone-liness and anger and resentment; they are the outcome of that same idleness and boredom that led nine London youths to go out in the summer of 1958 with coshes and iron bars to beat up the West Indian 'Spades' of Notting Hill because they had black faces; they induce the Roman Catholic Monsignor Joseph A. McCaffrey, at one extreme to attack the kindness and gentleness of over-sympathetic judges and social workers and to demand 'more jails' and 'force to meet force', and Norman Mailer, at the other extreme, to plead for sympathy for the juvenile delinquent whose knife 'is very meaningful to him' being his 'sword—his manhood'. They result in drunkenness and vice as well as in violence. They are at least partly responsible for the sharply rising rate of venereal diseases—syphilis among children between fifteen and nineteen increased 78.3 per cent in New York in 1959[15]—and they affect girls as well as boys. According to Arthur J. Rogers of New York's Youth Board girls 'will do anything to please members of the gangs'. 'They are promiscuous, truant and violent,' he told a Senate Sub-committee on Juvenile Delinquency. Whereas they used mainly to be guilty of sex offences, they are now, although still carelessly promiscuous, more and more involved in stealing and crimes of violence. They are often pregnant and 'use alcohol and narcotics excessively'.

They search, in fact, like their boy friends, for the lasting satisfactions of pleasure which, without the discipline of hard work, the comfort of achievement or the capacity for happiness, it is impossible for them to obtain. Driven to drink and drugs and new sexual experiences by the insipidity of so many other easily obtainable and too familiar diversions, they feel driven in turn to protest by means of crime and violence against the boredom and frustrations of a confusing life that offers so much and seems to give so little, that provides few challenges but great apparent injustice, that is unsatisfying and above all not exciting.

And it is, perhaps, in the need for excitement that the first germs of a criminal life can be traced.

'When we were shoplifting we always made a game of it,' an American thief said when remembering the days of his boyhood. 'For example, we might gamble on who could steal the most caps in a day, or who could steal caps from the largest number of stores in a day, or who could steal in the presence of a detective and then get away. We were always daring each other that way and thinking up new schemes. This was the best part of the game. I would go into a store to steal a cap, by trying one on, and when the clerk was not watching walk out of the store, leaving the old cap. With the new cap on my head I would go into another store, do the same thing as in the other store, getting a new hat and leave the one I had taken from the other place. I might do this all day and have one hat at night. It was the fun I wanted, not the hat. I kept this up for months and then began to sell the things to a man on the West side. It was at this time that I began to steal for gain.'[16]

English youths, too, frequently speak of this need for excitement, this determination to gain acceptance or friendship by showing a lack of fear:

'I got in with a lot of other chaps. I met them at cafes and dances. There were four of us who went together. I didn't do it for money but for excitement' ...[17] 'It was partly the drink, I suppose, but partly for the excitement and adventure; anyway I said I would go with him[18] ...' 'It wasn't really to steal that I did it. Of course, when I got in I looked about for something to take. The other boy had done it before and he told me it was very exciting, and when he was caught they didn't do anything to him. I hoped, of course, we wouldn't be caught if we were careful. I didn't go in just to pinch something. It was for devilment, more.'[19]

'That was the kick of my whole life,' another young American thief admitted when telling the story of how at the age of eight some bigger boys in the street persuaded him to climb through a small window. 'I was scared but made up my mind to go through anyway. I was too thrilled to say no . . . I felt like a big-shot after that night and the big guys said I could go with them every night they went robbin' Almost every night we went robbin' '[20]

Apart from the gratification of a craving for excitement, the boy found satisfaction in the knowledge that he belonged to a gang, that he had found acceptance by boys so much bigger and more naughty than he was. He had admired them before, now he was one of them. A deep sense of loyalty to the gang soon developed. It was for him, as for so many other delinquent children, a substitute for a family where he felt he was not wanted and a substitute for a school where he was not a success. The activities of the gang are eventually accepted by the young member as normal, almost as inevitable, whatever they are. Criminal and non-criminal activities seem scarcely distinguishable anymore—'We would gather wood together, go swimming, or rob the Jews on Twelfth Street.'[21]

It is being together that is important. Of six thousand thefts studied in the *Illinois Crime Survey* in 1929 over ninety per cent were committed by two or more boys acting together.[22] Another study revealed that out of 5,480 young offenders found guilty of a variety of crimes only 18.2 per cent had acted alone.[23] In England more than seventy per cent of young criminals act in gangs.[24] It was not so much that an accomplice was necessary as that crime, in Lombroso's words, is 'a sort of pleasure expedition which is not so enjoyable unless carried out in company'.[25]

When the expedition ends in the juvenile court, the pleasure is over and the boy feels suddenly alone. He may be treated as a first offender but he is likely in fact to have committed many previous offences for which he has not been punished. 'Criminal conduct as a whole,' Sheldon Glueck decided after his elaborate investigations into the careers of hundreds of juvenile delinquents, 'is the gradual development of a related series of anti-social acts . . . By the time delinquents and criminals fall into the hands of the police courts and punitive and correctional agencies they are in many respects the finished products of failure and neglect on the part of our most cherished social institutions.'[26]

Glueck found that the great majority of them were in desperate need of pity and understanding. Having examined the case histories of a thousand juvenile offenders tried in Boston juvenile courts and over five hundred young adult male criminals tried in the criminal courts of Massachusetts, he discovered that almost a third of the boys and a seventh of the young men had a parent or a brother or sister who was mentally diseased or defective; that a large proportion of the parents, many of whom had been born abroad, had had no formal education and between a third and a half of them were actually illiterate; that the children themselves were not only poorly educated and in a majority of cases subnormally intelligent, as compared with control groups of honest schoolchildren in three different cities in Massachusetts, but also in poor health (over a quarter of the young criminals had syphilis); that bad housing was so general that only 2.8 per cent 'resided in regions that could fairly be called favourable; that is localities in which there was an absence of street gangs and centers of vice and crime together with opportunity for wholesome recreation'; and that hardly any of either the children or the young men had been successful in their jobs or were free from some sort of emotional instability.

In almost every case the homes from which they came were, if not broken by desertion, separation or divorce, 'abnormal or deleterious'. In many of them, drunken, criminal and sexually promiscuous parents or relatives had made criminality 'almost a tribal condition'.[27]

The same patterns in juvenile delinquency can be traced in England where in 1962 the joint chairman of the West London Juvenile Court said that its 'really important' cause was the 'horrible irresponsibility' of parents.[28]

'One of the most significant facts facing those responsible for the training and after-care of these boys,' said Mr Frank C. Foster, director of the Borstal division of the Central After-Care Association recently, 'is that we are trying to present as acceptable to them standards that must seem to them completely unreal, if not farcical, when compared with their manner of life in their natural habitat. We are trying in a brief period to reshape a pattern of conduct that is the product of years of sordid experience.'[29]

There can be no doubt that the evidence in support of this view is overwhelming and that at least one reason why juvenile delinquency is not a serious problem in the Jewish community is the strength of the family in most Jewish lives; nor can it be doubted that it is as dangerously shortsighted of a parent to be unnecessarily strict as to be lazily or selfishly indulgent. But although all recent social studies have shown that an abnormal family life is a more or less important cause of juvenile delinquency—stressing, perhaps, the decline in the authority of the father, the absence of a working mother or, as John Bowlby has done, early maternal deprivation or, sometimes, the high wages earned by their children —there is far less agreement about other causes. Lady Wotton has recently emphasized the contradictions in these studies. 'On the whole,' she has written, 'it seems that offenders come from relatively large families. Not infrequently (according to some investigators very frequently) other members of the delinquents' (variously defined) families have been in trouble with the law. Offenders are unlikely to be regular churchgoers, but the evidence as to whether club membership discourages delinquency remains wildly contradictory . . . Most of them come from the lower social classes, but again evidence as to the extent to which they can be described as exceptionally poor is conflicting . . . Their health is probably no worse than that of other people, but many of them have earned poor reputations at school, though these may well be prejudiced by their teachers' knowledge of their delinquencies.'[30]

Contradictory, too, is the evidence in these studies concerning the effects of wartime misery and dislocation, of violence in films and on television, of the decline in the influence of the Christian churches, of the stresses and intensified desires and resentments created by an affluent society which sees poverty as more of a disgrace than a misfortune, of the attitudes of mind created by a welfare state whose benefits fall on just and unjust alike. What is clear is that it is an almost universal problem, although according to the Council of Europe's study of juvenile delinquency published in 1960 some countries, notably Denmark and Belgium, were much less affected by it than others. But the French had their *blousons noirs*, the Germans their *Halbstarken* ('the half-strong') the Swedes their *Skinnknutte* (the 'leather-jackets') the Japanese their *taiyozoku* (the 'children of the sun') the Russians their *stilyagi* (the 'style boys'). What is also clear is that it is not a new problem. A committee was appointed to study 'juvenile delinquents'—the cumbersome term was even then in use—in 1817. Juvenile crime was a serious problem in the 1860's as it is in the

1960's. The outlandish clothes of the English Teddy Boy of the 1950's were no more provocative than the zoot suits worn by young men in wartime America. 'It is hard to see why public opinion is shocked by the fact that a large proportion of crimes are committed by the young,' Winifred Elkin has written. It is an indication that people find it easier to accept the demands of society as they grow older.' And, after all, about eighty per cent of first offenders in England, most of them young, do not get into trouble again; and even these eighty per cent are a small minority of a generation which may be different from others but has not yet been convincingly shown—despite the statistics which are sometimes interpreted to support such a theory—to be appreciably more criminal.

But the concern which is felt about the increasing criminality of this minority, and the much larger minority in the United States, is justified. Drifting, shiftless, destructive and aggressive, with what the Prison Commissioners' Report for 1961 described as a common characteristic of 'negativeness', the young offenders—the persistent adult offenders of the future—are still one of the most urgent problems to be faced by the affluent societies in which they live.

CHAPTER SIX

THE SEXUAL OFFENDER

*'A person who carnally knows in any manner any animal
or bird; or carnally knows any male or female person by the
anus or by or with the mouth; or voluntarily submits to such
carnal knowledge; or attempts sexual intercourse with a dead
body is guilty of sodomy and is punishable with imprisonment
for not more than twenty years.'*

NEW YORK PENAL LAW, SECTION 690, 1950

'We used to go to dives where there was all the prostitutes hanging
about. Charlie had two girls; they gave him all their money, and he
gave me some. I saw blokes were making a lot of easy money, thieving
and poncing. After I'd been going for some months—I was eighteen
then—I found a girl who took a liking to me and started to live with
me. She used to walk alongside the Strand, soliciting . . . This girl, this
prostitute—they don't call it "prostitute", they'd say "I'm soliciting"—
this girl used to take fellows in a taxi. There's drivers in the West that
do it, they take 10s. a time. The driver stops the taxi in a side street and
goes for a walk, it only takes about five minutes. Some of the blokes give
a lot of money; the Yanks, they got no idea of English money; when
they're new they think a fiver's the same as a pound note. They don't
get the real thing. This girl I was with, she was on the game for sixteen
months, she had the real thing only three times. These girls, they know
how to move their legs so a fellow doesn't know; they got a way of fix-
ing things so a fellow thinks he's having it natural when he isn't.

'Well, I was with this girl all the time. Sometimes she'd make twenty
pounds a night and she'd give it to me. If you're a ponce the girl is like
a wife. They want you more or less to be like a husband to them. She

442

gives you the money and if you're kind you buy her clothes and things and protect her . . . The girl went over West and I used to watch. If a policeman comes you walk up and say, "I've been waiting here for hours," and he can't do a thing.'[1]

In August 1954 a Departmental Committee was appointed, under the chairmanship of Mr John Wolfenden, to consider the law, practice and procedure relating to prostitution and to make recommendations. It decided that the sort of public solicitation for immoral purposes which this ponce described should be ended by the provision of a progressive increase of penalties for street offences. The existing repeated fines of two pounds, which had been the penalty since 1840, were described as a 'farce'. The prostitute had come to accept the fine as a sort of tax on her activities, a licence to continue practising her profession.

The Government agreed with the view of the Committee and a Street Offences Bill, providing for an increase in the maximum fine to twenty-five pounds and three months' imprisonment, became law. Opposition to the Bill was raised on the grounds that prostitution would thereby be made more covert and, therefore, more professionally organized. 'If we want to drive women off the streets,' asked one Labour Member, 'where would we prefer them to go?' He warned of an increase in 'part-time pimping' by taxi-drivers and hotel employees as 'there is in New York'.

Of course, this was, in fact, one result of the new law. The hundreds of prostitutes who used to be seen every night walking slowly up and down London's streets disappeared from public view, but most of them remained in business. The Wolfenden Committee, however, had not supposed it possible to abolish prostitution, just as it had not believed it right that it should be legalized. The law, in its opinion, should not be 'concerned with private morals or with ethical sanctions'.

Prostitution continued, as it had always continued, but Mr Butler, the Home Secretary, had done the best that he could. It is beyond the reach of the law to find an ideal solution. In Italy, after a law sponsored by the Socialist Angelina Merlin banned state-supervised brothels in 1958, the syphilis rate increased until in 1960 there were twice as many people infected as there had been in 1957; and the number of prostitutes, according to *Il Tempo* also showed a 'marked increase'. In Holland, after women were forbidden to solicit in the street, they took to sitting under red-shaded lamps at open windows in the De Walletjes district of Amsterdam. In Soho and Montmartre, as in Galveston and Phoenix, the occasional changes which the law makes in a prostitute's life from time to time are only superficial.

Prostitution was only one of the problems which the Wolfenden Committee was required to consider. It was asked also to report on any changes it considered desirable in the law relating to homosexuality. It did so in a report which an American criminologist has justly described as 'modern in spirit and thinking, clear and brilliant in exposition, a monumental example of the sociological and scientific approach.'[2] It suggested that homosexuality, defined as 'a sexual propensity for persons of one's own sex', being essentially a medical, psychiatric, psychological and social problem, was not properly within the province of the criminal law, and should, therefore, no longer be a criminal offence provided that the homosexual behaviour was 'between consenting adults in private'.[3] This recommendation received general approval. It was supported by the Archbishop of Canterbury and by the Roman Catholic, Lord Pakenham (now the Earl of Longford) whose views on penological questions are rightly respected. It was supported, also, by doctors and psychiatrists. But it was not supported by the Government whose spokesman declared that public opinion did not agree with the Committee.

Public opinion, it was suggested, supported the minority opinion of one of the Committee's members, who said that the criminal law carries with it a 'moral' sanction and to remove this sanction would be regarded as condoning practices which were the cause of much 'public concern and disgust'.[4] Whether or not this concern and disgust arose from the tendencies of men, so often noticed by psychologists, to condemn most strongly what they most dislike or fear in themselves, it was certainly true that these feelings existed. It was also true that there existed widespread misconceptions about the nature and effects of homosexuality. It was probably true that the number of homosexuals was greater than was commonly supposed, but there was no evidence to suggest that the number was increasing. The number of exclusive homosexuals was perhaps between four per cent and five per cent of the total population of male adults, although the Committee believed that the proportion of men who had had some sort of homosexual experience during their lives was probably greater than the thirty-seven per cent estimated by the Kinsey Report in America.

Psychoanalysts agree that homosexual tendencies exist in every-one; and it cannot be doubted that many homosexuals are also heterosexual nor that homosexuality can exist in a personality otherwise perfectly intact. It was with these considerations in mind, as well as in the knowledge that some homosexuals benefit from treatment, that in many cases homosexuality may be a transitional phase in the adolescent or immature, and that it is not so much a 'disease' as a condition of varying gradations, that the Wolfenden Committee, having decided that it was not a function of the law to cover all the fields of sexual behaviour, made its recommend-ations.*

The acceptance of these recommendations would have brought English criminal law into line with that of many European coun-tries. For the time being, however, homosexual behaviour by con-senting adults, as well as buggery whether committed upon a con-senting man or a consenting women, remain crimes in Englad, al-though Sapphic practices do not unless the Lesbian has been guilty of indecent assault under the Offences against the Person Act.

The position in America is complicated not only by the vary-ing laws in different states but by laws which do not differentiate between types of homosexual conduct, such as anal or oral, passive or active, and which allow heterosexual conduct involving fellatio or cunnilingus to be covered by the same legal restrictions that are imposed upon homosexuality.[5] Some states, for instance, draw the sharp distinction between male and female homosexuality which has been drawn in England and most European countries (excluding Austria, Greece, Finland and Switzerland which have specific statutes against Lesbianism); but other states make no such distinction, while the law in a few is too vague to allow any clear interpretation at all. So far as male homosexuality is con-cerned, in New York in 1950 homosexual conduct between con-senting male adults and between boys from sixteen to twenty-one was reduced to a misdemeanour and in the Criminal Code of

* A recent American study (Irving Bieber's *Homosexuality*) suggests that more men can be reoriented by psychoanalytic treatment from complete homosexu-ality to complete heterosexuality than the Wolfenden Committee supposed. It also suggests that homosexuality is not a constitutional disorder genetically determined but that it is 'acquired and discovered as a circumventive adaption for coping with fears of heterosexuality,' the fears usually being caused by an unaffectionate father and an excessively affectionate mother who has awakened a premature eroticism which is denied fulfilment and which has made other women appear dangerous.

Illinois, revised in 1961, this conduct is no longer a crime. But in most of the rest of the United States it can still be punished severely, even by life imprisonment.[6] In some courts a person convicted of sodomy, and certain other sexual crimes, could be sentenced to an indeterminate term after psychiatric examination under the so-called 'sexual psychopath' laws. These laws are necessarily imperfect, and the imperfection is emphasized by the difficulties in detecting a psychopath, let alone defining one, and by the doubtful prospects of curing him. But at least they are steps in a promising direction.

Most American states, however, still reflect in their laws the Puritan morality of colonial times when capital punishment existed for adultery—and was occasionally put into effect—and when fornication was vigorously punished, the punishments sometimes resulting, it has been suggested, in homosexuality but hardly ever in subsequent celibacy. Nevertheless laws against fornication and adultery remain and one State even has a statute forbidding masturbation.[7] These laws, are, of course, openly ignored and because they are ignored the law itself falls into disrepute. Rape, in some states, is still a capital offence but J. Edgar Hoover's index of rape continues to rise irregularly and in consequence an 'inordinate fear of the fortunately rare but dangerous type of criminal, miscalled the sexual psychopath has been created'.[8]* In fact, the number of cases of rape—14,561 in 1958—includes very few which result in convictions for 'forcible rape', the great majority of them being 'statutory rapes' or sexual intercourse with a female below the age of consent, an age which in many states is well above that fixed by most countries in Europe.[9]

According to the Kinsey Reports, which indicated how widely laws regulating morals are disregarded, nearly three quarters of American men had 'experienced sexual intercourse' before they were twenty and only a very small proportion were virgins when they were married;[10] nearly half the female population had also 'experienced sexual intercourse' before marriage and about a

---

* 'The proportion of mental defectives is notably high among sexual delinquents,' Professor Leon Radzinowicz has recently written, 'and about a third of these mental defectives have been found guilty of offences solely against children.'[13] But the violent sex fiend is more often a creature of imagination than a real public menace. Only an estimated five per cent of convicted sex offenders in America have committed crimes of violence; and, so far as murder is concerned, there is far more danger of being killed by a relative than by an unknown sex maniac.[14]

quarter had committed adultery after marriage and before the age of forty.[11]

Investigations in other countries might well reveal a comparable acceptance of what *Esprit*, in a special issue devoted in 1961 to *La Sexualité*, called the 'new religion' of sex. Industrialization, more effective methods of contraception, the decline of religious sanctions, an increase in biological knowledge and in the knowledge that conceptions of morality vary from time to time and from place to place, and a reduced fear of venereal disease can all be seen as causes of this 'sexual revolution', a revolution which Norman Mailer thinks will be the only 'meaningful and natural' one for the twentieth century.[12] It can certainly be welcomed in so far as it lessens the widespread evils of sexual frustration and narrow intolerance but its effect on crime cannot be ignored.

By the time actual or potential delinquents have reached the age of fifteen they are likely to have had a wide variety of sexual experiences. The boy has come to accept the fact that after a dance or a visit to the cinema or the café he will 'go case'; and the girl has come to expect him to do so. In addition to feelings of insecurity and attitudes of sluggish inappetence engendered in the girl, and the callousness engendered in the boy, there are more tangible consequences of this casual, repetitive copulation. While illegitimate births may not be increasing fast, it seems certain that criminal abortions are. There are now, in fact, probably as many as three hundred a day in England. In France it has been estimated that there are as many as there are births; and in the United States there are, it is suggested, almost two million a year.[15] Venereal disease, despite the efficacy of penicillin and prophylactics, also continues to increase in all three of these countries. Indeed, of 106 nations reporting to the World Health Organization in 1962, seventy-six had a rising rate of syphilis. In America at least four thousand people died of the disease in the year ending 30 June 1962, and as many as nine million are believed to have or to have had it. It is spread mainly by young girls and male prostitutes.[16] But disease and abortion, uncared-for and unwanted children, family quarrels and occasional resultant violence are only some of the consequences of sexual delinquency.

Apart from sexual impulses which may lead directly to murder, rape, homosexuality and other specifically criminal acts such as bestiality, indecent exposure, incest and various punishable forms of heterosexual intercourse, the desire for sexual excitement leads to the establishment of vice rackets and vice centres which in turn generate more crime whether of a sexual nature or not. Prostitution is in itself rarely now considered a crime, and in England is not a crime, but the prostitute is a social outsider, as the criminal is, and they are natural friends. She may now be mainly used in the Western World as a means of satisfying 'the craving for variety, for perverse gratification, for mysterious and provocative surroundings, for intercourse free from entangling cares and civilized pretence'.[17]

But she remains at the centre of a criminal problem which is, apparently, growing year by year both in England and in America and which neither repressive measures nor the sexual freedom of the 'new religion' has been able to solve.

Part VIII

PROGRESS AND PALINDROME

CHAPTER ONE

PROGRESS AND PALINDROME

'It is better to prevent crimes than to punish them.'

CESARE BECCARIA, 1764

AN essential aspect of the new theory and practice of penology, which has been developing throughout the twentieth century, has been epitomized by the Webbs: 'The most practical and the most hopeful of "prison reforms" is to keep people out of prison altogether.'[1]

Although the origins of the idea of probation have been traced to some Warwickshire magistrates, who in 1820 began to sentence young offenders to one day's imprisonment on condition that they were 'more carefully watched and supervised by their parents in future', and to Matthew Davenport Hill, the Recorder of Birmingham, who in 1840 instituted a register of supervisors,[2] the criminal courts of Boston, Massachusetts, were the first to employ, in 1878, the regular services of a probation officer. By 1915 the system was apparently so successful that only twelve per cent of those released on probation were subsequently committed to institutions as compared with 44.3 per cent of the former inmates of reformatories.[3]

Other states had less success, for not enough care was taken in making probation orders and there was little agreement as to what type of offender was suitable for this sort of treatment. Some states imposed no limitations; others decided that it was suitable only for misdemeanants; Iowa did not allow persons suffering from venereal disease to be placed on probation; North Carolina, on the other hand, only allowed it in the case of those suffering from venereal disease and those convicted of second-degree prostitution.

In England before 1907 it was confined to first offenders; but now any offender can be put on probation, for not less than one or more than three years, except those convicted of murder, high treason, and offences under the Piracy and Dockyards Prevention Acts.[4] It is widely used, particularly for first offenders and the young. About four out of every ten offenders under seventeen and one out of six adults convicted in the courts are put on probation. Twenty-eight thousand offenders were dealt with in this way in 1956, thirty-three thousand in 1959, and now the service is in danger of breaking down for there are far from enough probation officers. Many of them are dealing with more than twice as many probationers as they can reasonably look after; some of them are inexperienced and incompetent; some are lazy. The best and most conscientious are not only overworked (with often as many as a hundred cases to look after) but underpaid as well, and the increases they have recently received are not likely to improve the position very much. Ideally probation is 'a form of social service preventing further crime by a readjustment of the culprit under the encouraging supervision of a social worker guided by the courts of justice'.[5] But too often it does not succeed because the courts have been insufficiently discriminating in those that have been given the opportunities of probation and in the conditions imposed. Confirmed criminals tend to feel that a man put on probation has not so much been given a second chance as let off altogether, even when one of the conditions of the order requires him to live in a 'probation hostel'; and, as Edwin Chadwick said 130 years ago, 'it should be borne in mind that the escape of one delinquent must do more mischief than the conviction of perhaps half a dozen guilty men can effect good, in the way of example ... The depredator who has escaped punishment due to his offence is constantly present; an encouraging example of success to all of his class.'[6]

The recidivist with two or more previous convictions rarely proves a good subject for probation. About half the adults and rather more than half the juveniles of this sort revert to crime within three years.[7] 'None of these probation officers have got even one step along the road with me,'[8] one habitual criminal said recently, and it is true of many others like him.

Probation, nevertheless, as a report published in 1958 by the Department of Criminal Science at Cambridge decided, 'emerges unquestionably as a generally effective measure of treatment whatever the sex and age of an offender happened to be'.[9] Unless the service is greatly improved and extended this may soon no longer be true.

America faces a similar problem. The number of cases which the majority of probation officers have to handle—sometimes as many as three hundred at once—is as excessive as it is in England; and most states 'lack adequate control over the qualities of personnel'.[10] There are over three hundred federal probation officers and the numbers are increasing but 'the case load of ninety-four remains far too high'.[11] At the same time the conditions imposed are often either too lax or much too severe. Parolees in some jurisdictions are, for instance, regularly required not to visit any place where liquor is sold or drunk, not to go to dances, to save a proportion of their earnings while supporting their dependants, to attend church, to be at home by ten o'clock every night, not to borrow money, not to write to friends in prison and to observe many other rules which make life both tedious and dangerously frustrating.[12] All penologists in America, though, 'seem to look upon probation as one of the most promising methods of protecting society against crime'.[13] Clearly in both countries there is hope for the system and a need for its encouragement; just as in America, with well-trained parole agents and a feasible system of supervision, there is hope for parole.

Now that pardons (which in the middle of the nineteenth century accounted for over forty per cent of the releases from American prisons) are little used anymore, over half the men released come out on parole. At first the system had little success. The men released on parole were often chosen as arbitrarily as those formerly pardoned at Ohio State Prison where 'whenever the convicts exceeded the number of 120, the Governor of the State was forced to grant pardons in order to create room in the prison for the newcomers'.[14] Politics played a leading role in the operations of many parole boards and secured the release of hundreds of men who returned immediately to crime. As late as 1938, eighteen states attempted to keep in touch with parolees by correspondence alone—written reports were required but no one checked the accuracy of the replies—and fourteen states had no parole officers.[15] Even now a parolee faces exploitation when he comes out of prison; but at least, as a convict in San Quentin said years ago, 'A man startin' out on parole, with prison officers backing him up and seein' that he gets a square deal has it all over th' guy what does his time and goes out without knowin' where he's goin' t' sleep the first night. I been watching the game a whole lot lately. There's more men comin' back here after doin' their time an' being discharged with five dollars, an not knowin' what they'll do when they get out than there is men what have been paroled.'[16]

Statistics go some way towards bearing out this contention, but whether paroled or not, the man released from prison is likely to share the same experience in the outside world.

'I've been let out before and it's always the same thing,' a parolee has been quoted as saying. 'I knew first of all that people would know I was a convict. Maybe my cheap suit and shoes and new hat wouldn't give it away but I still knew inside of me that everybody on the train and in the street would know ... Personally I'm finished with telling about my record. It's better to deny it and eat for a few days than to admit it and starve. Anyway I landed a job and it's like it always was, talk behind your back all the time and you worried sick about whether the auditor will find a penny missing and they land you for it. Of course there's the cops too. Every time someone spits in the subway you get dragged in, and you can't get away from the feeling that you're branded like a steer on a ranch.'[17]

The feelings of bitterness, suspicion and inferiority which this man feels are common to most ex-prisoners and to expect such men immediately to adapt themselves to society, merely because they have behaved well in prison or because the term of their sentence has expired, seems wholly unreasonable.

In 1832 Archbishop Whateley suggested that no one whose conduct had compelled society to lock him up should be again let loose till he had given 'some indication of amended character'. And it was to make it more likely that he would find it possible to live in society after his release that Sir Walter Crofton instituted in Ireland a period of comparative freedom for a man nearing the end of his sentence by allowing him to work away from the prison during the day provided he returned to his quarters at night. But Whateley's idea of sentencing a man to imprisonment for an indeterminate period has not received much official favour either in England or America, nor have there been many opportunities to put the old Irish system into modern practice, although some prisons now let out privileged men for day-time work.

Most states in America—though not the federal system—have laws which provide maximum and minimum sentences for various offences, but these are not indeterminate laws in the true sense and have often resulted in judges imposing sentences which make the two limits virtually the same—sentences which prescribe, for example, a minimum limit of twenty-four and a half years and a maximum limit of twenty-five years.[18] These, correctly speaking, are indefinite sentences such as those used in England when a boy is ordered to undergo Borstal training for a period which is left to the court's discretion. And the effect has been, and continues to be, that many prisoners are kept confined far too long while others are released too soon.

Prisoners themselves, of course, do not on the whole like the idea of an indeterminate sentence which they regard as vague and unsettling and capable of being used tyrannously against them. Many of them, and certainly most professional criminals, prefer to feel that they have paid the price of their crimes by a known number of years' loss of freedom. For somewhat similar reasons prison officials tend to agree with them. But Dr Karl Menninger, supporting the views of Sheldon Glueck and many distinguished American criminologists, believes that, if fully indeterminate sentences were to be imposed, behavioural science could be used to 'arrive at some diagnostic grasp of the offender's personality', and to decide 'the most suitable techniques in education, industrial training and psychotherapy' to rehabilitate him. If perceptible changes occurred, the process could 'be expedited by finding a suitable spot in society and industry for him, and getting him into civil status (with parole control) as quickly as possible'. If the prisoner could not be changed by genuine efforts to rehabilitate him, provision would have to be made for his continued confinement.[19]

Putting this theory into practice would, of course, raise immense difficulties and it is, perhaps, to be doubted that therapeutic techniques, let alone the techniques of accurately diagnosing the prisoner's emotional state or of predicting his future behaviour, have yet reached the stage when even the initial difficulties of the programme could be overcome. But a great deal more could surely be done, both in England and America, to suit punishments to criminals rather than to crimes. Far too many arbitrary sentences are still being given particularly in the lower courts.[20]* The law cannot, perhaps, be expected to distinguish between crime as an explosive event in an unhappy life, as a pattern of behaviour expressive of constant frustration and as a chosen profession. But attempts to discover the influences which lead to criminal conduct in any particular case must continually be made before there can be any hope of success in recalling the criminal from crime. Britain's first remand centre at Ashford, where two thousand young offenders were examined and reported upon in the first nine months after its opening in July 1961, is one practical answer to the problem of finding suitable and useful punishments for different sorts of offender. As Derrick Sington has said, however, it is 'a bleak, Dickensian straddle of buildings, made more forbidding by a towering barbed-wire fence' where too many boys are studied for too short a time.[21] As with nearly all the rest of the prison system lack of public concern is reflected in shortages of personnel, of training facilities and, of course, of money. For the time being boys who come from appallingly deleterious families are still placed on probation, providing the overworked probation officer with yet more impossible cases; boys from good homes and with good jobs are still sent to Borstals to mix with hardened offenders who will do their best to ensure that they remain criminals; pyromaniacs are still sent to prison and so are homosexuals, a process which a former Governor of Wormwood Scrubs has described as being like trying to cure a dipsomaniac 'by locking him up in a brewery'.[22] In America, where juvenile courts are chancery rather than criminal courts, tribunals have been set up with extensive powers to decide the treatment to be given to adolescents. But these tribunals exist in only a few states and where they do exist their constitution and arbitrary decisions are open to many objections.

Years before the First World War the French jurist Professor Raymond Saleilles insisted that 'punishment must be adapted to the nature of the criminal to whom it is applied . . . As in medicine it has been maintained that there are no diseases but only patients, so one is tempted to say that, strictly speaking, there are no crimes but only criminals.'[23] Even if ideal 'individualization of punishment' is as yet impracticable, it is at least possible to make greater efforts to stop the man, whose no doubt profitless term of punish-

* The eccentric behaviour of a judge in a Philadelphia courtroom who doubled the sentence on a defendant because, being a namesake of his, he had disgraced an honourable name, is presumably, however, not common.

ment has been completed, from drifting back into crime. Whether he leaves prison with the ten dollars that he may expect in America or the small allowance that will keep him going in England until he can draw money from the National Assistance Board, his plight may well be pitiable. Discharged Prisoners' Aid Societies do their best to help the English prisoner but they are often thought of as just another part of the system which the ex-prisoner is trying to forget. 'The general opinion of all prisoners is that these organizations are not worth a carrot,' writes Robert Allerton.[21] The picture he gives of 'pompous do-gooders', smug and self-important, doling out shillings as if they were coming out of their own pockets is, of course, a caricature now, although there was a time not long ago when it was close to the truth. And there is still sometimes in these societies an undeniable lack of human sympathy, tolerance and understanding which smaller organizations such as the New Bridge endeavour to supply. Even these organizations, unselfish and unreproachful as most of their members are, find difficulty in overcoming the resentment and suspicion which the prisoner's loss of self-esteem has engendered in him, and they cannot overcome the natural reluctance of many employers to give jobs to ex-convicts, nor can they make it un-necessary for the discharged prisoner to hand in forms to do with his insurance and income-tax, that will disclose his past.

Little enough *can* be done for the confirmed recidivist who does not want to reform, the old lag who is quite content, if not deter-mined, to remain an old lag. But for the homeless and friendless ex-convict who seems genuinely to wish to do so, little enough *is* done. Hundreds of men like this, most of them inadequate rather than vicious, come out of prison every year and sooner or later commit some new crime as a matter of course. Some are patho-logically inappetent and unemployable, permanent social cripples; others are more obviously mentally ill and perhaps irreclaimable; but there are many more who can be helped towards a normal and happy life. Mr Merfyn Turner, the former school teacher and youth leader from North Wales, has recently begun the experiment of getting a few of them together to live in a home that 'smells of cooking instead of carbolic' and to work at honest jobs, 'not through any exalted idea of "going straight" but because this is what the others are doing.' Of the first two hundred men who lived at Turner's Norman House at Islington only one went back to prison while he was staying there, and most of the rest (by no means all, of course) manage to stay out of trouble when they have left and are facing once more the challenges of loneliness and temptation. But Norman House is backed largely by London Parochial Charities and similar houses established elsewhere are helped by the Margery Fry Memorial Fund. The Golborne Rehabilitation Centre, although a National Registered charity, does not receive help from any organization at all. There is no Government support for these homes and the national mood does not, apparently, demand it. Other hopeful experiments—a building firm in Sussex and a scrap metal business in London run for the most part with ex-prisoner labour—have been initiated by former criminals who know how long it takes the discharged prisoner to settle down and to erase the prison complex from the mind. These too, however, despite their proved success in keeping men from crime, have received little official encouragement.

'It must not be forgotten,' Ferri wrote before the First World War, 'that the aiding of malefactors ought not to be exaggerated when there are millions of honest work-men more unfortunate than these liberated prisoners.'[25] This is still not to be forgotten even now, but it is important to remember that help, in money or in time, given to the discharged prisoner can be justified not only as an act of charity and sympathy but as one of expediency. Philanthropists are not necessarily sentimental. Nor are reformers.

For more than half a century the criminal law has been in the process of reform. In England the Probation of Offenders Act, 1907 was followed by the Criminal Appeal Act, 1907; by the Children Act, 1908, which provided for the establishment of juvenile courts and closed the prisons to children under sixteen except in very special cases; by the Prevention of Crimes Act, 1908 which set up the Borstal system as an alternative to imprisonment for boys between sixteen and twenty-one; by the Criminal Justice Administration Act, 1914 which made courts allow time for the payment of fines and so vastly reduced the numbers of men imprisoned in default. After the War a series of Royal Commissions, Select and Departmental Committees recommended further reforms many of which passed into law. By an Act of 1922, infanticide, committed by a mother after the stress of childbirth, was distinguished from murder; by an Act of 1931 pregnant women could no longer be sentenced to death; the Poor Prisoners' Defence Act, 1930 extended the categories of people to whom free legal aid could be granted; the Children and Young

Persons Act, 1933 gave a new recognition and a new scope to
Approved Schools which now number well over a hundred. In
1948 the Criminal Justice Act carried further the process of
gradual liberalization which many previous laws had observed and
many subsequent laws—including the Magistrates' Courts Act,
1952 the First Offenders Act, 1958 and the Criminal Justice
Act, 1961—have extended. A similar process has taken place,
and is taking place, in the United States.

Remembering the appalling injustices of the past it is impossible
not to feel grateful for all this. There may be comfort, too, in the
knowledge that when crimes appear to be increasing this is due
to factors other than a more criminal population no longer intimidated by the severity of punishment. Robbery with violence, for
example, showed a marked increase in 1958 but this was largely
attributable to a change in the classification of crimes of that
sort; suicides have also increased but this is due to an increase
in the average person's expectation of life, for suicide is usually
committed by the elderly.[26] The preparation of statistics, in any
event, involves many possibilities of error and of misinterpretation,
particularly in the United States where there are not only as strong
reasons as there are in England for juggling with local figures but
many different jurisdictions with contradictory definitions of crimes
and far from uniform attitudes towards them. Certainly it cannot
be doubted that some newspapers tend to invent crime waves when
published statistics provide no evidence that they exist and popular
imagination does the same. Nor can it be doubted that if statistics
had been prepared in the past on as elaborate a scale as they are
prepared today, any possible comparisons between our world and
that of our ancestors would be in favour of ours.

That English people are now convicted of well over a million
crimes every year sounds horrifying; but more than half of them
are for comparatively trivial non-indictable offences like parking
a car in a street where parking is forbidden or failing to buy a dog
licence, and well over eighty per cent of all offences reported in
the United States are traffic violations. New laws constantly necessary in a highly civilized, industrial country may make us all liable
to criminal behaviour of some sort; just as fashions in what is considered to be permissible or at least not punishable behaviour may
create new crimes. Numerous new offences have been invented by
Statutes dealing with production and trade; and incest, to take
only one example of an offence against the person, was not a

crime, except during the Commonwealth, until made so in 1908.

All these reasons make it necessary to qualify any general assertions that crime is increasing at a rate which threatens the future of civilized society and that, therefore, the principle of decreeing 'gentle punishments for the benefit of the people' as propounded by Canute and ignored by the criminal law for a thousand years, has been proved a wrong principle. It is a fact that forty thousand persons were convicted of indictable offences in 1895 compared with 153,000 in 1959; but it cannot necessarily be deduced from this that England and Wales were less criminal places then than they are today. Indeed it is likely that they are less criminal now. In 1959 4,500 people were convicted of stealing bicycles and 21,675 cars were stolen or illegally 'borrowed'; in 1895 there were no cars or bicycles left about waiting to be stolen.[27] Between 1857 and 1866 there were, according to the only figures available, an average of 114 murders committed every year; in 1937, when more murders were likely to be reported or discovered and the population had doubled, there were still 114.[28] In 1961 there were 132 murders (three less than the year before) but it is impossible to believe, on the basis of what few figures have come down to us, that in 1461 there were not, proportionately, at least fifty times as many. 'Crime has failed to keep pace with increase of population,' Luke Pike wrote in 1873. 'The apparent number of criminals can be made to appear formidable only by including in it persons guilty of offences which previous generations would not have considered crimes.'[29] In our own day Professor Leon Radzinowicz has warned that 'there is a tendency to exaggerate the incidence and gravity of crime. It is to be regretted that those who voice public uneasiness about the increase in crime, and who try to mobilize it, not to say exploit it, in order to bring about certain changes in our penal legislation and practice, so frequently indulge in colourful descriptions of a state of lawlessness which bears no relation to the actual incidence and distribution of offences.'[30]

But it is, of course, as dangerous to feel satisfied as to be unjustifiably alarmed. The influences which turn men to crime may be different and less compelling than those of the past, but thousands of men become criminals just the same.

There were eight per cent more serious crimes in England and Wales in 1961 than in 1960 and eight per cent more in London in 1962 than in 1961. There are now well over two and a half million serious crimes known to the police every year in America including between ten and twelve thousand murders, and in 1962 there were more than ever before. Perhaps there are as many again that are not known to the police, so that it may well be that only one in every four crimes is ever traced to the culprit and those who enjoy the highest chances of impunity are the ones who have reached the top of their profession. This is certainly not to say, though, that the new penology has failed. 'The great thing,' Ferri was surely right in thinking, 'is to be convinced that, for social defence against crime, as for the moral elevation of the masses of men, the least measure of progress with reforms which prevent crime is a hundred times more useful and profitable than the publication of an entire penal code.'[31]

It is, of course, inept to make extravagant claims for modern reformative techniques and psychological treatment. Crime will always be with us. But at least these techniques and this treatment offer the best chance—indeed, perhaps, the only remaining chance —of combating it in a civilized society.

It is as true as it was when Beccaria wrote his great book that the solution lies not in making punishments more severe, but in making them more certain and in relating them to each individual criminal, so that if he is reformable he may be reformed.

To devise ways of achieving these objects, to learn from the lessons of history that cruel punishments do not reduce the amount of crime but even tend to extend it and that to punish criminals with any severity at all without attempting either to understand them or to change the soil which continues to produce them is as dangerous as it is short-sighted, to understand that punishment for its own sake is evil and that there are germs of evil in the best of us and seeds of good in the worst, to recognize that there are no cheap or quick solutions to the problem of crime which has deep and intractable roots running beneath the whole surface of life, to encourage studies which may lead to an explanation of criminal conduct and of all irrational behaviour, these should be the endeavours, the aspirations and hopes of the future.

BIBLIOGRAPHY AND REFERENCES

ONLY those books about crime, criminals and the law which are referred to or have been quoted directly or indirectly in the text are listed in the bibliography. The full titles of general historical works are given in the list of source references. The names of publishers are given only to those books which are believed to be still in print. The dates are not always of the first editions but of the ones I have used.

The bibliography is divided into sections which roughly follow the scheme of the book. But many of the books listed in each section are not, of course, limited to the subjects indicated.

REFERENCES

THE AGE OF CHIVALRY (*Pages 3-19*)

1 *Tacitus: Germania* (Ed. J. F. Stout), 23
2 Attenborough, 9-13
3 Laws of Ethelbert (Attenborough, 5)
4 Laws of Alfred (*Ibid*, 75)
5 Laws of Alfred (*Ibid*, 83)
6 Laws of Alfred (*Ibid*, 73, 81)
7 Laws of Ine (*Ibid*, 39)
8 Laws of Alfred (*Ibid*, 69)
9 Ives, 6; Laws of Ine (Attenborough, 27-29)
10 Laws of Ethelstan (*Ibid*, 151)
11 J. Johnson, *Ecclesiastical Laws* (1720)
12 *Saxon Chronicle* quoted by Ives, 8
13 Stephen, i, 17
14 Pike, i, 204
15 Pike, i, 53-54; Laws of Ethelstan (Attenborough, 145, 171-173)
16 Stephen, i, 27
17 Walter Besant, *Mediæval London* (1906), ii, 148
18 Pike, i, 389-392
19 Attenborough, 135
20 Pike, i, 111
21 *Ibid*, i, 195-196
22 Jeudwine, 155-156
23 *Ibid*, 140
24 Pike, i, 226
25 Pike, i, 243-244
26 *Ibid*, 247
27 *Ibid*, 271-272
28 *Ibid*, 250
29 *Ibid*, 247-248
30 *Ibid*, 250
31 G. G. Coulton, *Medieval Panorama* (Cambridge University Press, 1947), 321
32 Jeudwine, 151
33 Kenneth H. Vickers, *England in the Later Middle Ages* (1904), 13; Pike, i, 198-202
34 Attenborough, 145
35 Coulton, 65
36 Blackstone, *Commentaries* (1765-1769)
37 13 Edw. I; Pike, i, 220
38 Attenborough, 31
39 13 Edw. I (Statuta Civitatis, London); Lee, 30-32
40 34 Edw. III, c. 1
41 Lee, 57
42 Vickers, 13
43 Jeudwine, 152
44 Pike, i, 288
45 Jeudwine, 188
46 Holdsworth, i, 615
47 T. J. Mazzingli, *Sanctuaries* (1887)
48 Pike, i, 293-294
49 *Ibid*, i, 253-255
50 *Ibid*, i, 414
51 Vickers, 185
52 *Ibid*, 250; Coulton, 82
53 Vickers, 258
54 G. M. Trevelyan, *History of England* (1943), 241

THE AGE OF LEARNING (*Pages 20–41*)

1 Trevelyan, 273
2 J. D. Mackie, *The Earlier Tudors* (O.U.P. 1952), 196
3 Coulton, 380
4 Pike, ii, 53-54
5 Trevelyan, 322
6 Evelyn Waugh, *Edmund Campion* (1935)
7 A. L. Rowse, *The England of Elizabeth* (Macmillan, 1950) 385
8 *Ibid*, 374
9 22 Hen. VIII c. 9
10 Stephen, i, 246
11 Andrews, 106
12 1 Edw. VI c.3
13 14 Eliz. c.5
14 18 Eliz. c.3
15 39 Eliz. c.5
16 Rowse, 289
17 *Ibid*, 382
18 Andrews, 84
19 *Ibid*, 161
20 W. C. Sydney, *England and the English in the 18th Century* (1892) ii, 290
21 Pike, ii, 82-84
22 Griffiths, *Newgate*, 98
23 Blackstone, *Commentaries* (1765-1769)
24 *The Newgate Calendar*, quoted by Pringle, *Thief-Takers*, 132
25 Prior, *Life of Burke*, quoted by Sydney, ii, 304
26 Pike, ii, 162-153
27 *Daily Courant* 1 June 1731, quoted by Peter Quennell, *Hogarth's Progress* (Collins, 1955), 85
28 Andrews, 217
29 H. C. Lea, *History of the Inquisition in the Middle Ages*, quoted by Coulton, 118
30 Pike, ii, 133
31 Richard Lewinsohn, *A History of Sexual Customs*, (Trans. Longmans, 1958), 130
32 *Ibid*, 128-135
33 Pike, ii, 236-237
34 Sydney, i, 281
35 Pike, ii, 289-290
36 Sydney, i, 285, 290
37 Pike, ii, 186
38 *Ibid*
39 *Ibid*
40 Pike, ii, 188-189
41 *Ibid*, ii, 180-181
42 *Ibid*, ii, 231-232
43 Lombroso, *Crime: Causes and Remedies*, (Trans. 1911)
44 Kershaw, 7
45 Schmidt, 59
46 *Ibid*, 22-25
47 *Ibid*, 110
48 *Ibid*, 112-113
49 Andrews, 87-88
50 *Ibid*, 91
51 Griffiths, 158
52 Pike, ii, 284-285
53 Andrews, 141
54 Pike, ii, 280
55 *Ibid*, ii, 211-212
56 Sir Frank MacKinnon, *Grand Larceny*, (1937), 39
57 11 Hen. VII c.21
58 Pike, ii, 206
59 Sydney, ii, 276
60 *The Epistle from Jack Sheppard to the late Lord Chancellor of England* (1725)
61 *Newgate Calendar*, (Ed. Sir Norman Birkett, The Folio Society, 1951), 17-23

62 26 Geo. II, c.19
63 19 Geo. II, c. 34

64 Pringle, *Thief-Takers*, 72
65 Lee, 283

THE AGE OF ELEGANCE (*Pages 42-50*)

1 Cadogan, 25
2 *Ibid*, 32
3 Henry Fielding, *Enquiry* (1751)
4 Cadogan, 20
5 *Order Book*, Westminster Sessions (1721) quoted by M. Dorothy George, *London Life in the 18th Century* (L.S.E. 1951), 31
6 *Order Book*, Middlesex Sessions (1725) quoted by George, 32
7 George, 24
8 *Ibid*, 42
9 John Fielding, *Account of Police* (1758)
10 *The Weekly Journal* 9 June 1716, quoted by Sydney, i, 177

11 César de Saussure, *A Foreign View of England* (Trans. 1902), 112
12 *Annual Register*, 1760, quoted by Sydney, ii, 213
13 *Annual Register*, 1763, quoted by Sydney, ii, 213
14 Jonathan Swift, *Journal to Stella* (1784)
15 Sydney, i, 213
16 25 Geo. II, c.37
17 4 Geo. I, c.11
18 Frederick J. Lyons, *Jonathan Wild* (1936) *passim*
19 Henry Field, *Enquiry* (1751)
20 *Ibid*
21 Quoted by Sydney, i, 72
22 *Ibid*, ii, 283
23 *Ibid*, ii, 284

THE LAW REFORMERS (i) (*Pages 53-68*)

1 Beccaria, xxxvi
2 *Ibid*, quoted by Elio Monachesi in *Pioneers in Criminology*, (Ed. Mannheim), 45
3 Montesquieu, *L'Esprit des Lois* (1748)
4 Radzinowicz, *History of English Criminal Law*, i, 285, 288-297
5 Colquhoun, *Treatise on the Police* (1795), 5
6 *Parliamentary Debates* (1810) xv
7 Blackstone, *Commentaries* (1765-1769)

8 Sir Thomas Fowell Buxton, *Parliamentary Debates* (1819), xxxix
9 9 Geo. I, c.22 (Waltham Black Act, 1722)
10 *Ibid*
11 *Ibid*
12 *Ibid*
13 43 Geo. III, c.119
14 33 Geo. II, c. 30
15 9 Anne, c.16
16 9 Geo. II, c.29
17 26 Geo. II, c.6
18 Andrews, 3
19 A. W. Hamilton, *Quarter Ses-*

sions from *Queen Elizabeth to Queen Anne* (1878), 71, quoted by Radzinowicz, i, 140

20 J. C. Jeaffreson, *Middlesex County Records* (1886-1892), quoted by Radzinowicz, i, 141

21 A. Marks, *Tyburn Tree: History and Annals* (n.d.), quoted by Radzinowicz, i, 142

22 Townsend's evidence before the Committee of 1816, quoted by Cadogan, 83

23 Reith, *Police Idea*, 92

24 Radzinowicz, i, 148

25 Sir Archibald Macdonald, *Parliamentary Debates* (1785) quoted by Reith, 92

26 Radzinowicz, i, 468

27 William Eden, *Principles of Penal Law* (1771), 25

28 Reith, 131; Phillipson, *passim; Memoirs of the Life of Sir Samuel Romilly* (1840), *passim*

29 *Memoirs of the Life of Sir Samuel Romilly*, i, 278

30 *Calendar of Home Office Papers* (1760-1765), i, quoted by Radzinowicz, i, 119

31 Romilly, *Observations on the Criminal Law* (1810)

32 *The Gentleman's Magazine*, quoted by Pringle, *Thief-Takers*, 12

33 10 & 11 Will. III, c.23; 12 Anne, c.7; 24 Geo. II, c.45

34 *Parliamentary Debates* (1810) quoted by Reith, 135, 136, 144

35 *Parliamentary Debates* (1811), xix

36 Koestler & Rolph, 31

37 18 Geo. II, c.27

38 3 Geo. III, c.34

39 Hinde, 110

40 Radzinowicz, i, 513

41 *Ibid*, i, 558-559

42 39 Eliz. I, c. 17

43 Horace Twiss, *The Public and Private Life of Lord Chancellor Eldon* (1844), ii, 324, quoted by Radzinowicz, i, 524 (n.q.)

44 52 Geo. III, c. 16

45 57 Geo. III, c.126; 54 Geo. III, c.42

46 Radzinowicz, i, 541

47 *Parliamentary Debates* (1819), xxxix

48 *Report from the Select Committee on Criminal Laws* (1819), 9

49 7 & 8 Geo. IV, c.29

50 4 Geo. IV, c.54

51 7 & 8 Geo. IV, c.28

52 7 & 8 Geo. IV, c.29

53 4 Geo. IV, c.48

54 7 & 8 Geo. IV, c.29; 7 & 8 Geo. IV, c.30; 9 Geo. IV, c.31; 11 Geo. IV & 1 Will. IV, c.66

55 *The Morning Herald* 30 Jan. 1837, quoted by Radzinowicz, i, 598

56 7 & 8 Geo. IV, c.29

57 J. S. Taylor, 47

58 *Parliamentary Debates*, quoted by Reith, 224

59 Tuttle, 9

60 Gardiner, 28

61 Koestler & Rolph, 32

62 Radzinowicz, i, 219-220

63 Andrews, 142; Jeremy Bentham, *Principles of Penal Law*

64 Pike, ii, 453

65 Gardiner, 29
66 *Parliamentary Debates*, quoted

by Radzinowicz, i, 692
67 *Ibid*, i, 604

THE LAW REFORMERS (ii) (*Pages 68-85*)

1 *Newgate Calendar* (Ed. Sir Norman Birkett), 169
2 *Ibid*, 172
3 J. Laurence, *A History of Capital Punishment* (n.d.), 45
4 *The Crocker Papers* (Ed. L. J. Jennings, 1885), iii, 15, quoted by Radzinowicz, i, 203
5 *Newgate Calendar*, 174
6 Griffiths, *Newgate*, 177
7 C. M. Atkinson, *Jeremy Bentham* (1905), 549
8 James Boswell, *The Life of Samuel Johnson* (Everyman's Edition, 1920), ii, 447
9 Griffiths, *Newgate*, 424
10 *Ibid*, 427
11 *Ibid*, 428
12 Philip Collins, 240
13 Cadogan, 146
14 *Report of the Royal Commission* (1864-1866), 632, quoted by Gardiner, 29
15 Capital Punishment Amendment Act
16 Griffiths, *Newgate*, 422
17 Kershaw, 74-75
18 Gillin, 335; Barnes & Teeters, 307
19 Griffiths, *Newgate*, 441
20 *Ibid*, 440-441
21 *Ibid*, 528
22 Duff, 52-53
23 *Home Office Memorandum of Evidence to Royal Commission 1864-1866*, quoted by Koestler and Rolph, 11
24 Duff, 21
25 *Ibid*, 53
26 Gowers, 12
27 *Ibid*, 17
28 Duff, 32
29 James Berry, *My Experience as an Executioner*, quoted by Duff, 122
30 *Ibid*, quoted by Duff, 121
31 Gowers, 12
32 *Ibid*, 16-17
33 Albert Pierrepoint's evidence before the Royal Commission (1949-1953), quoted by Koestler and Rolph, 15
34 Koestler and Rolph, 12
35 Koestler, *Reflections on Hanging* (1956)
36 *Lancet*, 20 August 1955, quoted by Koestler and Rolph, 67
37 Gowers, 19
38 *Ibid*
39 II Samuel 12, 31
40 Schmidt, 60
41 *Ibid*, 56
42 The Bamberg MS, quoted in Schmidt, 95-96
43 Kershaw, 35
44 Macaulay's *History of England*, quoted by Radzinowicz, i, 188 (n.86), 189 (n.89)
45 Kershaw, 34
46 *Ibid*, 65
47 *Ibid*, 30-31
48 *Ibid*, 41
49 *Ibid*, 20
50 Andrews, 119
51 *Ibid*, 128

52 *Ibid*
53 Kershaw, I
54 *Ibid*, 81
55 *Ibid*, 89
56 *The Death Penalty in European Countries* (Council of Europe, 1962)
57 Kershaw, 98
58 *The Death Penalty in European Countries*
59 Gillin, 355
60 Lewis E. Lawes, *Life and Death in Sing Sing*, quoted by Joyce, 154
61 Duff, 98-99
62 Joyce, 151
63 Gillin, 355

64 Kershaw, 104
65 *Ibid*, 107
66 Koestler and Rolph, 20
67 Gowers, 20
68 Radzinowicz, i, 187 (n.83)
69 Schmidt, 42
70 Gowers, 23
71 Duff, 21
72 *Ibid*, 206
73 Gowers, 20
74 Martin, 161
75 Duff, 11
76 Koestler and Rolph, 29
77 Duff, 66-67
78 Schmidt, 39
79 Radzinowicz, i, 184

THE POLICE REFORMERS (i) (*Pages 86–125*)

1 De Saussure, 129
2 22 Geo. II, c.24; 7 & 8 Geo. IV, c.31
3 1 Eliz. I, c.2
4 1 Car. II, c.1
5 29 Car. II, c.7
6 29 Car. II, c.7
7 13 Geo. III, c. 80
8 3 Car. I, c.1; 29 Car. II, c.7
9 *An address to the Public from the Society for the Suppression of Vice* (1805), quoted by Radzinowicz, iii, 168
10 9 & 10 Will. III, c.32
11 Sheila Birkenhead, *Peace in Piccadilly* (Hamish Hamilton, 1958), 71
12 Daniel Defoe, *The Poor Man's Plea in relation to all the Proclamations* (1698) quoted by Radzinowicz, ii, 15
13 Hesketh Pearson, *The Smith of Smiths* (Hamish Hamilton, 1934), Penguin Books Edi-

tion (1948), 66
14 *Ibid*, 69
15 Radzinowicz, iii, 205
16 1 Geo. I, c.5
17 10 Geo. II
18 8 Geo. II, c. 16
19 12 Geo. II, c.16
20 Henry Fielding, *Amelia* (Everyman's Library Edition, 1930), 6
21 *The Discoveries of John Poulter, alias Baxter* (1761), 14
22 4 Will. III, c.8
23 Radzinowicz, ii, 84
24 10 & 11 Will. III, c.23
25 Radzinowicz, ii, 113
26 *Ibid*, ii, 115
27 1 Edw. VI, c.3
28 Radzinowicz, ii, 139
29 *Ibid*, ii, 145
30 *A Treatise on the Police and Crimes of the Metropolis* (1829)
31 Radzinowicz, ii, 148
32 Lyons, *Jonathan Wild, passim;*

An Answer to a . . . libel, entitled a Discovery of the Conduct of Receivers and Thief-Takers, (1718)

33 4 Geo. I, c.11

34 De Saussure, 132

35 Pringle, *Thief-Takers, passim*

36 *Ibid*, 134-139

37 *Gentleman's Magazine* (1746), quoted by Pringle, *Hue and Cry*, 68

38 Pringle, *Hue and Cry*, 64

39 *Report from the Committee on the State of the Police* (1816)

40 Pringle, *Hue and Cry*, 76

41 Henry Fielding, *Journal of a Voyage to Lisbon* (1755)

42 Pringle, *Hue and Cry*, 88-89

43 *General Advertiser* 5 Feb. 1750, quoted by Pringle, *Hue and Cry*, 88

44 Radzinowicz, iii, 52

45 Pringle, *Hue and Cry*, 193

46 Lee, 224-225

47 Pringle, *Hue and Cry*, 129

48 Radzinowicz, iii, 60

49 *Ibid*, ii, 70

50 *Ibid*, ii, 68

51 *Report from the Committee on the State of the Police* (1816)

52 Fitzgerald, *passim*

53 *Report on the Police of the Metropolis*, (1828)

54 *Ibid*

55 Letter from the Home Office to a magistrate at Great Marlborough Street, 20 Jan. 1818, quoted by Radzinowicz, ii, 280

56 Burn, i, 811

57 Evidence of John Harriott, Magistrate of Thames Police Office before the Committee on the State of the Police, (1816)

58 Radzinowicz, ii, 307

59 Allen, 29

60 Radzinowicz, ii, 287

61 *Ibid*, ii, 296

62 *Report from the Committee on the State of the Police* (1816)

63 *The Morning Herald* 30 Oct. 1802, quoted by Lee, 185

64 Radzinowicz, ii, 279

65 *Report from the Committee on the State of the Police* (1817)

66 *A List of Houses of Resort for Thieves of Every Description* (1815)

67 *First Report from the Committee on the State of the Police* (1817)

68 *A List of Houses of Resort for Thieves of Every Description* (1815)

69 *Ibid*

70 *Report from the Committee on the State of the Police* (1816)

71 *The Whole Four Trials of the Thief-Takers and their Confederates . . . Convicted at Hick's Hall and the Old Bailey* (1816), quoted by Radzinowicz, ii, 335-337

72 John Fielding, *A Brief Description of London* (1776), xxii

73 *Strong Admonitions to the Several Citizens of London and Westminster wherein are Suggested Means of Security* (1812)

74 58 Geo. III, c.70

75 42 & 43 Vict. c. 22

76 Christopher Hibbert, *King Mob* (Longmans, 1958), 131

77 Nathaniel Wraxall, *Historical Memoirs of My Own Time* (1815)

78 Hibbert, 61, 65

79 *Ibid*, 92

80 *Ibid*, 54
81 Jonas Hanway, *The Citizen's Monitor* (1780) xxi, quoted by Reith, *Police Idea*, 85
82 Reith, *Police Idea*, 85-87
83 Radzinowicz, iii, 102
84 *Ibid*, iii, 92
85 Reith, *Police Idea*, 90-91
86 *Ibid*, 95
87 *Ibid*, 97
88 32 Geo. III, c.53
89 39 & 40 Geo. III, c.87
90 Radzinowicz, iii, 132
91 Sir Robert Peel, quoted by Radzinowicz, ii, 181
92 *Second Report on the State of the Police* (1817)
93 *Report on the Police of the Metropolis* (1828)
94 *Report from the Committee on the State of the Police* (1816)
95 Radzinowicz, ii, 96
96 Colquhoun, *Treatise on the Police*, preface
97 *Ibid*
98 *The Monthly Magazine* 1 Sept. 1806, quoted by Radzinowicz, iii, 237
99 Colquhoun, *Treatise on the Police*
100 *Observations on a Late Publication entitled 'A Treatise on the Police of the Metropolis'* (1800), quoted by Reith, 120
101 Colquhoun, *Treatise on the Commerce and Police Force of the River Thames,* (1800)
102 Created by 39 Geo. III, c.49
103 39 & 40 Geo. III, c.87
104 Thomas de Quincey, *Confessions of an English Opium Eater* (1901), 290
105 *Account of the Dreadful Murder of Mr. Marr and Family*
(n.d.), quoted by Radzinowics, iii, 315
106 A. Knapp and W. Baldwin, *Newgate Calendar* (1826), iv, 52
107 Radzinowicz, iii, 316-320
108 *Ibid*, iii, 320-321
109 *Ibid*, iii, 327
110 *Ibid*, iii, 325
111 *Ibid*, iii, 328 (n.11)
112 *Strong Admonitions to the Several Citizens of London and Westminster* (1812)
113 J. W. Ward, *Letters to Ivy* (1905), 146 quoted by Radzinowicz, iii, 347
114 Reith, *Police Idea* 162-163
115 *Annual Register* (1816), quoted by Reith, 164
116 Leiutenant Joliffe, quoted in *Three Accounts of Peterloo* (Ed. F. A. Burton), 50
117 Horace Twiss, *The Public and Private Life of Lord Chancellor Eldon* (1844), quoted by Reith, 201
118 George Pellew, *Henry Addington, First Viscount Sidmouth*, quoted by Reith, *Police Idea*, 203
119 Reith, *Police Idea*, 188
120 Griffiths, *Newgate*, 445-448; John Stanhope, *The Cato Street Conspiracy* (Jonathan Cape, 1962)
121 Reith, *Police Idea*, 215
122 *Ibid*, 224
123 Irish Statutes, 26 Geo. III, c.24
124 *Parliamentary Debates* (1828), xcvi
125 10 Geo. IV, c.44
126 Reith, *A New Study of Police History*, 129

THE POLICE REFORMERS (ii) (*Pages 125-130*)

1 Reith, *A New Study of Police History*, 131
2 Lee, 243
3 Reith, *A New Study*, 143
4 Lee, 240
5 Reith, *A New Study*, 145
6 Radzinowicz, ii, 256
7 Reith, *A New Study*, 155
8 Lee, 245
9 Reith, *A New Study*, 151
10 Lee, 243
11 Reith, *A New Study*, 162-167; Lee, 256-260
12 *First Report of the Constabu-lary Commissioners*, 13, quoted by Lee, 272
13 2 & 3 Vict. c.93
14 Authorized by 5 & 6 Vict., c.109
15 Lee, 286-287
16 *Ibid*, 290 and 283
17 7 & 8 Geo. IV, c.18
18 Lee, 290
19 19 & 20 Vict., c.69
20 Lee, 336-337
21 Humphry House, quoted by Philip Collins, 196
22 Radzinowicz, iii, 431

THE PRISON REFORMERS (i) (*Pages 131-139*)

1 D. L. Howard, *John Howard;* Dixon, *John Howard, passim*
2 John Howard, *State of the Prisons*, 1
3 Lee, 292
4 John Howard, *passim*
5 Griffiths, *Newgate*, 266
6 24 Geo. III, c.54; Hinde, 13
7 William Smith, *The State of Gaols*, quoted by Hinde, 14
8 Griffiths, *Newgate*, 144
9 Hibbert, 170
10 Griffiths, *Newgate*, 273
11 Ives, 17; Grünhut, 28
12 Lind, *Health of our Seamen*, quoted by Griffiths, 272
13 Buxton, *Inquiry* (1818)
14 Griffiths, *Newgate*, 364
15 D. L. Howard, *English Prisons*, 8
16 Hinde, 18
17 Henry B. Wheatley, *Hogarth's London* (1909), 391
18 Quoted by Peter Quennell, *Hogarth's Progress* (Collins, 1955), 76
19 John Ireland and John Nichols *Hogarth's Works* (1883), iii, 249
20 Guy, *John Howard's Winter Journey*, quoted by Hinde, 31
21 John Howard, *passim*
22 D. L. Howard, *English Prisons*, 16

THE PRISON REFORMERS (ii) (*Pages 139-150*)

1 4 Geo. I, c.11
2 Blackstone, *Commentaries* (1765-1769)
3 39 Eliz. I, c.4
4 18 Car. II, c.3
5 Quoted by Grünhut, 73

6 Phillipson, *passim*
7 Quoted by Cadogan, 159
8 David Collins, *An Account of the English Colony in New South Wales* (1798), *passim*
9 Cadogan, 163
10 *Ibid*
11 Laing, *History of New South Wales*, quoted by D. L. Howard, 27
12 Quoted by Cadogan, 169-170
13 Quoted by D. L. Howard, *English Prisons*, 29
14 Ives, 157
15 Quoted by Cadogan, 172
16 Charles Darwin, *The Voyage of the Beagle* (1836)
17 Quoted by Ferri, *Criminal Sociology*, 249
18 Hinde, 72-73
19 Quoted by Hinde, 75
20 Charles White, *Convict Life* (1889), 499

21 Cadogan, 188-192
22 Hinde, 84
23 John Vincent Barry, 'Alexander Maconochie' in *Pioneers in Criminology* (Ed. Mannheim, 1960), 73
24 Alexander Maconochie, *Crime and Punishment* (1846), quoted by Barry, 75
25 *Ibid*, quoted by Barry, 74
26 *Ibid*, quoted by Barry, 76
27 *Ibid*, quoted by Barry, 81
28 Clay, 247
29 John Vincent Barry, *Alexander Maconochie of Norfolk Island* (O.U.P. 1958) *passim*
30 W. P. Ullathorpe, *Memoirs of Bishop Willson* (1887); Martin Cash, *Adventures* (1870), 135-141
31 Marcus Clarke, *Stories of Australia in the Early Days* (1897), 195

THE PRISON REFORMERS (iii) (*Pages 150-168*)

1 Quoted by Reith, *Police Idea*, 91
2 *Report of the Society for the Improvement of Prison Discipline*, quoted by Cadogan, 100
3 Griffiths, *Newgate*, 407
4 Cadogan, 109
5 *First Report of the Inspectors of Prisons* (1836), quoted by Griffiths, 402-416
6 Griffiths, *Newgate*, 407-411
7 J. Whitney, *Elizabeth Fry* (1937), quoted by D. L. Howard, 36
8 Quoted by Hinde, 64
9 C. C. Western, *Remarks upon Prison Discipline* (1825), quoted by Hinde, 68
10 Griffiths, *Millbank*, quoted by D. L. Howard, 43
11 Quoted by Grünhut, 43
12 Quoted by D. L. Howard in *English Prisons*, 61
13 Drähms, 335-336
14 Grünhut, 46
15 Lewis, 112
16 Dickens, *American Notes*, 69
17 *Ibid*
18 Quoted by Gillin, 392
19 Crawford, 17
20 5 & 5 Will. IV, c.38
21 Philip Collins, 7
22 Dixon, *John Howard* (1848)

23 Dickens, 75
24 Mayhew and Binney, *The Criminal Prisons of London* (1862), quoted by D. L. Howard, 67
25 *Penal Reform in England* (Ed. Radzinowicz), 166
26 Crew, 88
27 *Ibid*
28 *Ibid*, 89
29 Dostoevsky, *Buried Alive in Siberia* (Trans, 1881), quoted by Grünhut, 209
30 Quoted by Hinde, 73
31 Quoted by Hinde, 76
32 4 Geo. IV, c.64
33 5 & 6 Will. IV, c.38
34 16 & 17 Vict., c.99
35 Quoted by D. L. Howard, *English Prisons*, 91
36 *Report of Royal Commission* (1854), quoted by Ives, 193
37 28 & 29 Vict., c.126
38 40 & 41 Vict., c.21
39 Philip Collins, 19
40 40 & 41 Vict., c.21 sec. 17 (4)
41 D. L. Howard, *English Prisons*, 103
42 *Report of Royal Commission* (1879), 627

43 *Ibid*, 355; Philip Collins, 21
44 *Report of Royal Commission* (1879), 680
45 Hinde, 214
46 *Ibid*, 135
47 Quoted by D. L. Howard, *English Prisons*, 107
48 61 & 62 Vict., c.41
49 Cicely M. Craven 'The Trend of Criminal Legislation' in *Penal Reform in England* (Ed. Radzinowicz), 20
50 Quoted by S. K. Ruck, *Paterson on Prisons* (Frederick Muller, 1951)
51 *Ibid*
52 1 & 2 Vict., c.82
53 20 & 21 Vict., c.48
54 29 & 30 Vict., c.117
55 56 & 57 Vict., c.48
56 62 & 63 Vict., c.12
57 Quoted by Hinde, 108
58 8 Edw. VII, c.59
59 Quoted by D. L. Howard, *English Prisons*, 120
60 Grünhut, 119
61 Page, *Young Lag*, 260
62 *Ibid*

THE PRISON REFORMERS (iv) (*Pages 168–181*)

1 Lewis, 221-222; Gillin, 489
2 Leavit, *The Man in the Cage* (1912)
3 Lowrie, 224
4 Gillin, 498
5 *The Illinois Crime Survey*, 716-717
6 Tannenbaum, *Crime and the Community*, 80-81
7 *Ibid*, 333
8 *Ibid*, 80-81
9 Philip Klein, *Prison Methods* in *New York State* (1920), 201
10 Tannenbaum, *Crime and the Community*, 330; Martin, 135
11 *Parliamentary Papers* (1837), xxxii, quoted by Hinde, 116
12 Quoted by Lombroso, *Crime: Its Causes and Remedies*, 334-335
13 Gillin, 560

14 Tannenbaum, *Crime and the Community*, 349
15 Gillin, 559
16 *Ibid*, 558
17 Grünhut, 129
18 *The Prison System in Illinois*, quoted by Tannenbaum, 293
19 Quoted by Grünhut, 129-130
20 Donal E. J. MacNamara, 'Prison Labor and Employment' in *Crime in America* (Ed. Bloch), 62
21 Hobhouse and Brockway, 109
22 Glueck, *Crime and Justice*, 170
23 Spenser, 279
24 *Ibid*, 272
25 Fishman, 51-52
26 *New York Evening Post*, 25 Jan. 1934, quoted by Tannenbaum, 445
27 Gillin, 563
28 *Ibid*, 536

29 Tannenbaum, *Wall Shadows*, 73
30 Shaw, *Jackroller*, 58
31 Grünhut, 89
32 *Ibid*, 91
33 Lombroso, *Crime: Its Causes and Remedies*, 396
34 Gillin, 635
35 Gluecks, *500 Criminal Careers*
36 Quoted by Sheldon Glueck, *Crime and Justice*, 52
37 Tannenbaum, *Crime and the Community*, 314
38 Gillin, 597
39 *Proceedings of the National Congress of Social Works* (1918), 117
40 Tannenbaum, 69
41 Gillin, 598
42 Danforth, 2-21
43 Hassler, 154-156
44 Glueck, *Crime and Justice*, 54
45 Hassler, *passim*

L'UOMO DELINQUENTE (i) (*Pages 185-196*)

1 Lombroso, Introduction to Ferrero, xii
2 Marvin E. Wolfgang, 'Cesare Lombroso' in *Pioneers in Criminology* (Ed. Mannheim), 170
3 Ferrero, xiv-xv
4 F. J. Gall, *Les Fonctions du Cerveau*, quoted by Ellis, 31
5 *Della fossetta cerebellare mediana in un criminale* (1872), quoted by Wolfgang, 187
6 Stanley, 174
7 *Ibid*, 202-203
8 Spenser, 35
9 Lombroso; Ferrero; Ellis; Drähms, *passim*
10 Stanley, 65

11 Quoted by Ellis, 88
12 Ferrero, 264-265
13 Lombroso, *Crime: Its Causes and Remedies*, 437
14 Joly, 92-93
15 Stanley, 91
16 Tarde, *Criminalité Comparée*, 52
17 Ferri, *Criminal Sociology*, 23-24; Thorsten Sellin, 'Enrico Ferri' jn *Pioneers in Criminology* (Ed. Mannheim), 284-286
18 Garafalo, *Criminology* (Trans. 1914)
19 Schlapp, *The New Criminology* (1928)
20 *Ibid*, 28-29

21 von Hentig, *The Criminal and His Victim*, 8
22 Wolfgang, in *Pioneers in Criminology* (Ed. Mannheim), 224
23 Saleilles, 134
24 Quoted by Clarence Ray Jeffery, 'The Historical Development of Criminology' in *Pioneers in Criminology* (Ed. Mannheim), 370
25 Ferri, 386

L'UOMO DELINQUENTE (ii) (*Pages 197–224*)

1 Edwin D. Driver, 'Charles Buckman Goring' in *Pioneers in Criminology*, 339
2 *The Physical Bases of Crime* (1914), quoted by Gillin, 94
3 Goring, 263
4 *Ibid*, 180
5 Thomson, 85
6 Aschaffenburg, *Crime and its Repression*, 177
7 Quoted by Ellis, 156
8 Goddard, *Feeblemindedness*, 7
9 Murchison, 'American White Criminal Intelligence' in *Journal of Criminal Law and Criminology*, quoted by Gillin, 119
10 Gillin, 41
11 Herbert A. Bloch, *Crime in America*, 239
12 *A Report on the Mental Deficiency Survey*, quoted by Gillin, 108
13 *Report of the Board of Managers of Elmira Reformatory*, 1922 (1923); *Annual Report of the Commissioners of Correction* (1921), 71
14 Gillin, 591
15 *Statistical Review of State Prisons and Correctional Schools* (Illionis, 1940), quoted by von Hentig, *Criminal and his Victim*, 178
16 Kahn, *Sing Sing Criminals*, 83
17 Grünhut, 163
18 East and de Hubert, 7; Barnes and Teeters, 7; Jones, 58
19 Ferrero, 287
20 William Healy, quoted by Gillin, 126
21 Healy, *The Individual Delinquent* (1915)
22 *American Journal of Sociology* (July, 1916), quoted by Gillin, 99
23 Healy and Bronner, *New Light on Delinquency* (1936)
24 Gillin, 128
25 Schlapp, 242–243
26 Oswald Cockayne, *Leechdoms, Wort Cunning and Starcraft* (1864), ii, 335
27 W. A. F. Browne, *What Asylums Were* (1837), 101
28 Exodus, 21
29 Koestler, 71: Ives, 257; Ellis, 368; Ives, 258
30 Ives, 257
31 Schmidt, 121
32 Sir Edward Coke, *Institutes*, quoted by Mullins, 21
33 Ives, 252
34 Schlapp, 299–301
35 Sheldon Glueck, *Crime and Justice*, 181
36 Harold Scott, 108
37 Peter Scott, 'Henry Mauds-

ley', in *Pioneers in Criminology* (Ed. Mannheim), 158-159

38 *Report of the Royal Commission on Capital Punishment*, quoted by Howard Jones, 175

39 Weihofen, 158

40 Winifred Overholser, 'Isaac Ray' in *Pioneers in Criminology* (Ed. Mannheim), 121

41 *Time*, 26 May 1961

42 Rolph, *Personal Identity*, 141

43 Page, *Young Lag*, 97

44 *Ibid*, 170-171

45 *Ibid*, 159

46 Bernard Glueck, 157

47 Ferrero, 272-274

48 Rupert Furneaux, *Famous Criminal Cases*, vi (Odhams, 1960)

49 Page, *Young Lag*, 58

50 *Ibid*, 50

51 *Ibid*, 52

52 *Ibid*

53 *Ibid*, 42

54 Gardiner, 246

55 Stephen, ii, 185

56 Friedreich's *Blätter für gericht*, xxxviii, quoted by Ellis, 8-11

57 *Encounter*, Sept. 1960

58 *Report of Royal Commission* (1953), 462

59 *The Trial of N. G. C. Heath* (Ed. M. Critchley; Notable British Trials Series, 1951)

60 *The Trial of J. G. Haigh* (Ed. P. T. Butler, Lord Dunboyne; Notable British Trials Series, 1953)

61 Thomson, 179

62 *The Times*, 7 March 1953

63 Quoted by Rolph, *Personal Identity*, 144-149

64 *Observer*, 18 March 1962

65 *Time*, 23 May 1960

66 Quoted by Gillin, 106

67 Quoted by Peter Scott in *Pioneers in Criminology* (Ed. Mannheim), 147

68 *Ibid*, 152

69 *Time*, 23 May 1960

70 *Guardian*, 9 March 1962

71 *Encounter*, May 1962

72 Rhodes, *Genius and Criminal*, 111

73 *Judge Barker Case Studies*, Series I, Case 9, quoted by Gillin, 123

74 Bernard Glueck, 258

75 Ferrero, 37

76 *Ibid*

77 *Ibid*, 38

78 Wilhelm, Stekel, *Peculiarities of Behaviour*, i, 259, quoted by Schlapp, 217

79 Schlapp, 252

80 *Ibid*, 216-217

81 Ferrero, 137

82 Ferri, *Criminal Sociology*, 145

83 Henry H. Goddard, *The Kallikaks* (1912)

84 Howard Jones, 35, 40

85 Richard Dugdale, *The Jukes* (1877)

86 J. Lange, *Verbrachen als schiksal* (1929), quoted by Grünhut, 143

CAUSES AND CURES (i) (*Pages 225-237*)

1 Lacassagne, quoted by Ellis, 24.

2 Lombroso, *Crime: Its Causes and Remedies*, 22

3 Ferri, *Crime in its Relation to Temperature*, quoted by Lombroso, 8

4 Ferri, *Criminal Sociology*, 79

5 Lombroso, *Crime: Its Causes and Remedies*, 83

6 Wootton, 53

7 *Ibid*, 56

8 Lombroso, *Crime: Its Causes and Remedies*, 95

9 Bonger, 639-643

10 Lombroso, *Crime: Its Causes and Remedies*, 92-93

11 Taft, 286

12 Lombroso, *Crime: Its Causes and Remedies*, 270

13 Aschaffenburg, 88

14 *San Quentin Prison Report 1891* (1892), quoted by Drähms, 121

15 Spenser, 125

16 von Hentig, *The Criminal and his Victim*, 164

17 Reid, *Shame of New York*, 146

18 Taft, 306-307

19 *Ibid*, 311

20 *Drug Addiction Amongst Young Persons in Chicago* (1953), quoted by Taft, 310

21 Taft, 310

22 *Newsweek*, 13 Aug. 1962

23 *Time*, 2 Feb. 1959

24 *Ibid*

25 von Hentig, *The Criminal and his Victim*, 162

26 Bosco, *Omicidio negli stati uniti*, quoted by Lombroso, 93

27 *Ibid*

28 Howard, 'Alcohol and Crime' in *American Journal of Sociology* (1918), quoted by Gillin, 234

29 Taft, 241; Barnes and Teeters, 91

30 Lloyd M. Shupe, 'Alcohol and Crime' in *Journal of Criminal Law, Criminology and Police Science* (Jan.-Feb. 1954)

31 *Jahrbuch der Westphalischen Gefrangnisse* (1871), quoted by Lombroso, 91

32 Callahan, 71-72

33 Dexter, *Weather Influences* (1904), quoted by Gillin, 85

34 Kraepelin, *Clinical Psychiatry*, quoted by von Hentig, 361

35 *Compendium of the 10th Census of the U.S.* (1880) quoted by Lombroso, *Crime: Its Causes and Remedies*, 57

36 Lombroso, *Crime: Its Causes and Remedies*, 196-205

37 von Hentig, *Criminal and his Victim*, 325, 342

38 Statistics for 1921-23, quoted by von Hentig, *Criminal and his Victim*, 303

39 Lombroso, *Crime: Its Causes and Remedies*, 182

40 Ellis, 261-262; Gillin, 58; Howard Jones, 127

41 Mannheim, *Social Aspects of Crime* (1940)

42 Otto Pollak, *The Criminality of Women* (1949)

43 Kneeland, *Commercialized Prostitution in New York* (1917), quoted by Gillin, 270

44 Quoted by Gillin, 221

45 Lombroso, *Crime: Its Causes and Remedies*, 114

46 Fyvel, 13-15

47 *Report on the Second U.N. Congress on the Prevention of Crime and the Treatment of*

Offenders (1960), para 72 (iii), quoted by Howard Jones, 68

48 Grünhut, 145
49 Drähms, 78
50 Taft, 275
51 Walter Bromberg, *Crime and the Mind* (Lippincott, 1948), 85

52 Taft, 275
53 Pakenham, *Causes of Crime* (1958)
54 Quoted by Lombroso, *Crime: Its Causes and Remedies*, 147
55 Wootton, 315
56 Taft, 191
57 Gluecks, *Delinquency Unravelled* (1950), 107-133

CAUSES AND CURES (ii) (*Pages 237–245*)

1 Lombroso, *Crime: Its Causes and Remedies*, 255
2 Gillin, 280; von Hentig; *Criminal and his Victim*, 237
3 *The Annals of the American Academy of Political and Social Science* (1931), quoted by Tannenbaum, *Crime and the Community*, 31
4 von Hentig, *Criminal and his Victim*, 234
5 Claud Mullins, *15 Years' Hard Labour* (Gollancz, 1948), quoted by Page, *Young Lag*, 278
6 Tarde, *Criminalité Comparée*, 27
7 Glueck, *Crime and Justice*, 9
8 Quoted by Ellis, 166
9 Lombroso, *Crime: Its Causes and Remedies*, 211
10 *Trial of Jack Sheppard* (Ed. Horace Bleackley: Notable British Trials Series, 1933), 64-126
11 Tarde, 231
12 Peter Wildeblood, *Against the Law* (Weidenfeld and Nicolson, 1955)
13 Kinsey, Pomeroy and Martin, *Sexual Behaviour in the Human Male* (1953); Howard Jones, 70-72
14 *Times Literary Supplement*, 23 June 1961
15 Cyril Burt, *The Young Delinquent*, quoted by Mullins, *Crime and Psychology*, 147
16 *Times Literary Supplement*, 23 June, 1961
17 Pike, ii, 586
18 Glueck, *Crime and Justice*, 24
19 Sutherland and Cressey, *Principles of Criminology* (1955)
20 Healy and Bronner, *New Light on Delinquency* (1936)
21 Gluecks, *500 Criminal Careers* (1930) *Physique and Delinquency* (1956)
22 Howard Jones, 1, 10
23 Tannenbaum, *Crime and the Community*, 8, 25, 26
24 Taft, 341
25 Quoted by Clarence Ray Jeffery, 'The Historical Development of Criminology', in *Pioneers in Criminology* (Ed. Mannheim), 369
26 Mannheim, *Group Problems in Crime and Punishment*, 261

THE CRIMINAL'S PSYCHOLOGY (*Pages 246–261*)

1 von Hentig, *Criminal and his Victim*, 102
2 Grünhut, 391
3 Ellis, 243-244; Bonger, 585
4 Parker and Allerton, 106
5 *Ibid*, 88-89
6 Quoted by Allsop, 349-350
7 Black, 240
8 Ferri, 101
9 Parker and Allerton, 88
10 Anderson, 8
11 Page, *Young Lag*, 135
12 Shaw, 106-107
13 Spenser, 30
14 Parker and Allerton, 98
15 *Ibid*, 93
16 *Ibid*, 97
17 Despine, *Psychologie Naturelle* (1868)
18 Ellis, 151
19 *Ibid*, 144
20 Spenser, 292
21 Allsop, 68
22 *Ibid*, 72
23 Page, *Young Lag*, 205
24 *Ibid*, 254
25 Joseph Catton, *Behind the Scenes of Murder* (1940)
26 *Report of the Prison Commissioners* (1949), quoted by Hinde, 229
27 Sutherland, 175-176
28 Parker and Allerton, 85
29 Page, *Young Lag*, 226
30 *Ibid*, 262
31 *Ibid*, 95, 161
32 *Report of the New York Crime Commission* (1928), 447
33 Norval Morris, 369
34 Basil Thomson, quoted by Ferri, *Criminal Sociology*, 35
35 Norval Morris, 79
36 Quoted by Ellis, 177-178
37 Quoted by Ellis, 168
38 Clemmer, 89
39 Ellis, 219
40 *Ibid*
41 Thomson, 115
42 *Report of the Prison Commissioners* (1961), 19
43 Norman, 165
44 Thomson, 122
45 Ellis, 17
46 Allsop, 88
47 Tannenbaum, *Crime and the Community*, 174
48 Spenser, 121
49 Drähms, 71
50 Allsop, 135
51 New York *Herald-Tribune*, 14 Nov. 1930, quoted by Tannenbaum, *Crime and the Community*, 174
52 Tannenbaum, *Crime and the Community*, 174
53 Drähms, 72
54 *Sunday Telegraph*, 1 April 1962
55 Leopold, *Life plus 99 Years* (1958)
56 Nelson, *Prison Days and Nights* (1932)
57 Donald Clemmer, 'Leadership Phenomena in a Prison Community' in *Journal of Criminal Law and Criminology* (1938), quoted by Taft, 588
58 Shaw and McKay, 247
59 Norval Morris, 71
60 Lombroso, 419
61 *Time*, 20 April 1959
62 Allsop, 351
63 Thomson, 51
64 Beccaria, 36

THE CRIME CULT (i) (*Pages 265–273*)

1 Quoted by Sydney, ii, 279
2 Daniel Defoe, *The History of the Remarkable Life of John Sheppard* (1724)
3 Lecky, *History of England in the 18th Century* (1904), ii, 112
4 Quoted by Radzinowicz, i, 50 (n.2)
5 Maurice Petherick, *Restoration Rogues* (Hollis and Carter, 1951), 13-39
6 *Newgate Calendar*, 125
7 Griffiths, *Newgate*, 110
8 Quoted by Radzinowicz, i, 168
9 Ellis, 351
10 Kershaw, 116
11 Schmidt, 94
12 Cadogan, 140
13 Quoted by Radzinowicz, i, 190
14 Ellis, 350
15 Schmidt, 176
16 Henry Fielding, *Enquiry* (1751)
17 *Times Literary Supplement*, 23 June, 1961
18 Rebecca West, *Train of Powder* (Macmillan, 1955)
19 Sybille Bedford, *The Best We Can Do* (Collins, 1958)
20 F. Tennyson Jesse, *A Pin to See the Peepshow* (1934)
21 Meyer Levin, *Compulsion* (Simon & Schuster, 1956)
22 *Guardian*, 29 June 1962

THE CRIME CULT (ii) (*Pages 273–285*)

1 Conan Doyle, *A Study in Scarlet* (1887) Edition of 1904, 53
2 Dickens, *Bleak House* (1853), 217
3 *Ibid*, 219
4 *Ibid*, 504
5 Wilkie Collins, *The Moonstone* (Folio Society, 1951), 87
6 *Ibid*, 112
7 Kenneth Robinson, *Wilkie Collins* (Bodley Head, 1951), 220
8 Conan Doyle, *A Study in Scarlet*, 31
9 Conan Doyle, 'The Second Stain' in *The Return of Sherlock Holmes* (1905)
10 Julian Symons, *The Detective Story in Britain* (Longmans for the British Council and the N.B.L., 1962)
11 Freeman Wills Croft, *Inspector French's Greatest Case* (1925)
12 John Buchan, *Greenmantle* (1916)
13 'Sapper', *The Final Count* (1925)
14 *The Sunday Times*, 25 March 1962
15 *Time*, 26 Oct. 1959
16 Ian Fleming, *From Russia with Love* (Cape, 1957)
17 Ian Fleming, *Casiono Royale* (Cape, 1953)
18 Ian Fleming, *Moonraker* (Cape 1955)
19 *From Russia with Love* (Cape, 1957)

20 *Casino Royale* (Cape, 1953)
21 *Goldfinger* (Cape, 1959)

22 *Dr. No* (Cape, 1958)
23 *Goldfinger* (Cape, 1959)

THE DETECTION OF CRIME (i) (*Pages 289–302*)

1 *Report of the Parliamentary Committee* (1837)
2 Stead, *The Police of Paris*, 94
3 *Ibid*, 96
4 Stead, *Vidocq* (1953), *passim*
5 Quoted by Stead, *The Police of Paris*, 96
6 Lee, 253
7 *Ibid*, 255
8 Reith, *A New Study*, 185
9 Lee, 256
10 Quoted by Moylan, 184-185
11 Lee, 368-369
12 Moylan, 185

13 Original in Scotland Yard Library
14 Donald McCormick, *The Identity of Jack the Ripper* (1959)
15 Goddard, 234-253
16 *Ibid*, 204-218
17 Quoted by Moylan, 188
18 W. Teignmouth Shore, *The Trial of Browne and Kennedy* (Notable British Trials Series); Sir Traver Humphreys, *A Book of Trials* (William Heinemann, 1953); Moylan, 358-276

THE DETECTION OF CRIME (ii) (*Pages 302–316*)

1 Rhodes, *Clues and Crimes* (1933), 112-116
2 Cuthbert, 13
3 Rhodes, 135-136
4 *Ibid*, 125-127
5 Cuthbert, 29-32
6 Rolph, *Personal Identity*, 76-92
7 Rhodes, 85
8 Scott, *Scotland Yard*, 136
9 Whitehead, 129-130
10 Rhodes, 101

11 *Ibid*, 78-79
12 Quoted by Raymond B. Fosdick, *European Police Systems* (1915), 336
13 Cuthbert, 38-42
14 *Ibid*, 66-67
15 Whitehead, 139
16 Gross, *Criminal Investigation* (Trans. 1907)
17 Cuthbert, 83-84
18 Rhodes, 60-67

THE NEW WORLD (*Pages 319–330*)

1 Israel Zangwill, *The Melting-Pot*
2 Quoted by Tannenbaum, *Crime and the Community*, 249-250

3 Thrasher, 155
4 Shaw and McKay, 'Social Factors in Juvenile Delinquency', *Reports of National Commission on Law Obser-*

vance and Enforcement, No. 13, Vol. ii.
5 Ibid, 120
6 von Hentig, The Criminal and his Victim, 284
7 Time, 21 April 1958
8 Danforth, 218
9 Tannenbaum, Crime and the Community, 128
10 Lincoln Steffens, The Shame of the Cities (1904)
11 Tannenbaum, Crime and the Community, 98-99
12 Allsop, 84
13 Seabury Report (1932), 137-138
14 Sheldon Glueck, Crime and Justice, 75
15 Quoted by Gillin, 760
16 Sheldon Glueck, Crime and Justice, 80
17 Gillin, 178
18 Quoted by Gillin, 754
19 Cleveland Crime Survey (1922), 97-98
20 Lekkerkerker, Reformatories for Women in the United States (1931), quoted by Tannenbaum, 48
21 Spenser, 23
22 Danforth, 66
23 Sheldon Glueck, Crime and Justice, 23
24 Danforth, 301

GANGS AND SYNDICATES (Pages 331–352)

1 Estes Kefauver, Crime in America (Gollancz, 1952), Four Square Books Edition, 28-29
2 Ibid
3 Illinois Crime Survey (John Landesco, Organised Crime in Chicago), 876-880
4 Sinclair, passim
5 Allsop, 25
6 Ibid, 33
7 Ibid, 32-34
8 Herbert Asbury, The Great Illusion (1950); Sinclair; Allsop, passim
9 Herbert Asbury, The Underworld of Chicago (1942)
10 Illinois Crime Survey (Landesco), 1011
11 Quoted by Allsop, 17
12 Fred D. Pasley, Al Capone (1930); W. R. Burnett, Little Caesar (1929)
13 Reid, The Shame of New York, 59-66
14 Turkis and Feder, Murder, Inc. (1952); Barnes & Teeters, 24-29
15 Kefauver, 17
16 Ibid, 18
17 Time, 1 June 1959, 28 Dec. 1959, 12 Dec. 1960
18 Quoted by Reid, 102-108
19 Ibid, 106-119
20 New York Times, 29 Aug. 1943
21 Reid, 84
22 Ibid, 151
23 Danforth, 151
24 Ibid, 237
25 Reid, 146
26 Harry W. Laidler, Boycotts and the Labor Struggle (1915), 299
27 Tannenbaum, Crime and the Community, 39
28 Danforth, 270

29 *Time*, 14 July 1958, 18 Aug.
1958, 1 Sept. 1958, 15 Sept.
1958, 5 Jan. 1959, 22 Jan.
1959, 22 June 1959, 27 July
1959, 31 Aug. 1959, 28 Sept.
1959, 14 July 1961, 4 Jan. 1963
30 *Ibid*, 26 May 1958, 21 July
1958, 2 March 1959

COPS AND G-MEN (*Pages 353–370*)

1 Taft, 394
2 Gillin, 720
3 Raper, 37
4 *Time*, 22 June 1959
5 Ernest Jerome Hopkins, *Our Lawless Police* (1931)
6 A. L. Beeley, *The Bail System in Chicago* (1927), 24
7 *Reports of the National Commission on Law Observance and Enforcement* (Report 11, 1931), 47-48
8 Leonard V. Harrison, *Police Administration in Boston* (1934), 159
9 Sheldon Glueck, *Crime and Justice*, 35
10 Tannenbaum, *Crime and the Community*, 240
11 *New York Times*, 29 June 1930, quoted by Tannenbaum
12 August Vollmer, David E. Monroe and Earle W. Garrett, 'Police Conditions in the United States' in *Report on Police* (1931), 45
13 Tannenbaum, *Crime and the Community*, 153
14 *Chicago Police Problems* (1931), 3
15 *Reports of the National Commission on Law Observance and Enforcement* (Report 11, 1931), 22
16 Vollmer, Monroe and Garrett, 62

17 Harrison, 28
18 *Chicago Police Problems* (1931), 47
19 *Report of the New York Crime Commission* (1927), 143
20 *Seabury Report*, 83
21 *Ibid*, 26-28
22 Tannenbaum, *Crime and the Community*, 142
23 Harrison, 110-111
24 Lowenthal, 4
25 *Ibid*, 8
26 *Ibid*, 11
27 Whitehead, 73-74
28 Lowenthal, 26
29 *Ibid*, 35
30 Whitehead, 73-74
31 *Ibid*, 77
32 *Ibid*, 19-27
33 Hoover, *Persons in Hiding*, 41, 71
34 Frederick L. Collins, *The FBI in Peace and War* (1943), 287
35 Whitehead, 106
36 Purvis, 278
37 E. H. Sutherland, *White Collar Crime* (1949)
38 Frank Gibney, *The Operators* (Gollancz, 1960), 6-7
39 Taft, 55
40 *Ibid*, 247; Barnes & Teeters, 29-30
41 David D. Allen, *The Nature of Gambling* (Coward-McCann 1952)

42 Quoted by Reid, *The Shame of New York*, 237

43 Gillin, 701

44 Barnes and Teeters, 12-15

CAPITAL PUNISHMENT (i) (*Pages 373–397*)

1 Lombroso, *Crime: Its Causes and Remedies*, 427

2 Garofalo, *Criminology*, 224

3 Ferri, *Criminal Sociology*, 242-243

4 *Ibid*, 106

5 *Ibid*, 242

6 *Report of the Select Committee on Capital Punishment* (1929-1930), quoted by Koestler, 171

7 Koestler, 171

8 *Ibid*, 172

9 *Ibid*, 175

10 *Report of the Select Committee on Capital Punishment* (1929-1930), 453

11 Gardiner, 140

12 Taft, 373

13 Lyle W. Shannon, 'The Spatial Distribution of Criminal Offences by States' in *Journal of Criminal Law, Criminology and Police Science*, quoted by Taft, 372

14 *Report of the Royal Commission on Capital Punishment* (1949-1953), quoted by Gowers, 101

15 *Ibid*, 102

16 Stephen, ii, 179

17 *Ibid*, ii, 93

18 Rose, *The Struggle for Penal Reform* (1961)

19 *Report of the Royal Commission on Capital Punishment* (1949-1953), quoted in *Times Literary Supplement*, 23 June, 1961

20 Quoted by Tuttle, 118

21 White, *Insanity and the Criminal Law*, 13

22 Lombroso, *Crime: Its Causes and Remedies*, 383

23 Beccaria, 43

24 Tuttle, 67

25 *Sunday Times*, 25 Feb. 1962

26 Gardiner, 55; Joyce, 212

27 Kropotkin, *In Russian and French Prisons* (Trans, 1900)

28 Gardiner, 59

29 *Hansard*, 9 March 1961, quoted by Koestler and Rolph, 72

30 *Guardian*, 9 March 1962

31 Gowers, 122

32 *Report of Royal Commission* (1949-1953), quoted by Koestler and Rolph, 71

33 Thomson, 174

34 Julian Symons, *A Reasonable Doubt*, Cresset Pass (1960)

35 James Edward Holroyd, *The Gaslight Murders* (Allen and Unwin, 1960)

36 Gowers, 8

37 *Ibid*, 122

38 *Report of Royal Commission* (1949-1953), quoted by Koestler and Rolph, 73

39 *Ibid*

40 Quoted by Weihofen, 150

41 Gardiner, 44

42 F. C. McClintock and Evelyn Gibson, *Robbery in London* (English Studies in Criminal Science, 1961), xiv

43 *Murder* (Home Office Research Unit Report, 1961), 20-21
44 Gardiner, 17
45 Gowers, 69
46 Sir David Maxwell Fyfe, 14 April 1948, quoted by Hale, 9
47 Duff, 51
48 Hale, 17-49
49 *The Death Penalty in European Countries* (Council of Europe, 1962)
50 Hale, 69-89
51 Koestler and Rolph, 121
52 *Ibid*, 122
53 Gardiner, 70; Koestler and Rolph, 125
54 Koestler and Rolph, 127; Gardiner, 70
55 Quoted by Koestler and Rolph, 69-70
56 *Report of the Select Committee* (1929-1930), quoted by Gowers, 45
57 Gardiner, 36
58 Koestler and Rolph, 125-126
59 *Report of Royal Commission* (1949-1953), quoted by Gowers, 30
60 *Report of Royal Commission* (1864-1866), quoted by Gardiner, 37

61 *Criminal Statistics: England and Wales* (1955)
62 Gowers, 91
63 *Murder* (Home Office Research Unit Report, 1961)
64 Gowers, 53
65 Quoted in *Observer*, 25 Feb. 1962
66 Quoted by Glueck, *Crime and Justice*, 102
67 *Report of Royal Commission* (1949-1953), quoted by Gowers, 38-39
68 Joyce, 83; *The Death Penalty in European Countries*, 53-54; Barnes & Teeters, 321
69 Homicide Act (1957) Sec. 5
70 *Ibid*, Sec. 6
71 *Ibid*, Sec. 2
72 *Murder* (Home Office Research Unit Report, 1961), 4
73 *Ibid*, 21
74 *Ibid*, 41
75 *The Death Penalty in European Countries*
76 *Observer*, 29 July 1962
77 Morris and Blom-Cooper, 20
78 *Ibid*, 23
79 *Daily Telegraph*, 9 Oct. 1961
80 William Temple, 'The Death Penalty', in *Spectator*, 1935, quoted by Tuttle, 49
81 *New Statesman*, 8 Dec. 1961

CAPITAL PUNISHMENT (ii) (*Pages 397-405*)

1 The Massachusetts Commission Investigating Capital Punishment, quoted by Mrs Herbert B. Ehrmann in 'Capital Punishment Today—Why?' in *Crime in America* (Ed. Bloch), 81
2 Piracy Act (1837) Sec. 2

3 Dockyards Protection Act (1772) Sec. 1
4 *Crime in America*, 80-82; *Time*, 21 March 1960
5 Gowers, 69
6 *Capital Punishment*, B.B.C. Documentary, *24 Oct. 1961*
7 Joyce, 165

8 Quoted by Koestler and Rolph, 64
9 Quoted by Gowers, 59-60
10 Quoted by Tuttle, 35
11 The Legislative Research Analyst, quoted by Ehrmann in *Crime in America* (Ed. Bloch), 83
12 Calvert, 115
13 Gowers, 85
14 Gardiner, 50-52
15 Shaw, 108-109
16 Gillin, 363
17 *Time*, 21 March 1960
18 Joyce, 43
19 *Daily Herald*, 18 Feb. 1960
20 Joyce, 35-36; Milton Machlin and William Woodfield, *Ninth Life* (Sidgwick and Jackson, 1962)
21 *Ibid*, 147
22 Caryl Chessman, *Cell 2455 Death Row* (Prentice-Hall, 1954); *Time*, 29 Feb. 1960, 21 March 1960; Joyce, 19-51
23 Lord Altrincham, 'Goodbye to the Gallows', *Guardian*, 18 Jan. 1962
24 Ellis, 298

CORPORAL PUNISHMENT (*Pages 406-411*)

1 Quoted by Ellis, 340
2 Rolph, *Commonsense about Crime and Punishment*, 119
3 Klare, 98
4 Parker and Allerton, 34, 101-102
5 Quoted by Ives, 155
6 Quoted by Rolph, *Commonsense about Crime and Punishment*, 130
7 Andrews, 209
8 *Ibid*, 210-224
9 Quoted by Rolph, *Commonsense about Crime and Punishment*, 122
10 Philip Collins, 255
11 Pike, ii, 574
12 *Ibid*, ii, 575
13 Ives, 204
14 Rolph, *Commonsense about Crime and Punishment*, 123
15 *Ibid*, 125
16 Gluecks, *Unravelling Juvenile Delinquency* (1960)
17 Morris, *The Habitual Criminal* (1951)
18 McClintock and Gibson, xiv
19 *Report for the Prison Commissioners for 1960* (1961), 15
20 Quoted by Taft, 559
21 *Cadogan Committee Report* (1938)
22 *Modern Methods of Penal Treatment* (International Penal and Penitentiary Foundation, n.d.), 117
23 Barnes and Teeters, 457

PRISONS (*Pages 412-423*)

1 *Report of the Prison Commissioners for 1960* (1961), 1
2 *Ibid*, 15
3 *Guardian*, 30 April 1962

4 Page, *Young Lag*, 37, 142, 215

5 *Penal Practice in a Changing Society* (H.M.S.O., 1959)

6 *The Times*, 3 May 1962

7 *Howard Journal*, quoted by Rolph, 139

8 Wildeblood, 104

9 Norman, 20

10 Wildeblood, 119

11 *Observer*, 14 Jan. 1962

12 *Ibid; Inside Sick (Prison Reform Council*, 1963)

13 *Report of the Prison Commissioners* (1961), 68

14 Norman, 26

15 *Ibid*, 32, 87

16 Wildeblood, 109

17 Hassler, 97, 103

18 *Observer*, 14 Jan. 1962

19 *Ibid*

20 Parker and Allerton, 124-140

21 Norman, 84

22 *Report of the Prison Commissioners* (1961), 5

23 *Observer*, 14 Jan. 1962

24 *Report of the Prison Commissioners* (1961), 9, 53

25 *Ibid*, 15, 144

26 *Ibid*, 145

27 *Ibid*, 143, 144

28 *Ibid*, 15

29 D. L. Howard, *English Prisons*, 134

30 Michael Wall, *Guardian*, 22 May 1962

31 *Handbook of Correctional Institutional Design and Construction* (Federal Prison Industries, 1949), 2; *Manual of Correctional Standards* (American Prison Association, 1954)

32 *The Annals of the American Academy of Political and Social Sciences*, 'Crime and the American Penal System', Jan. 1962, 1

33 Taft, 485

34 Lord Altrincham, *Guardian*, 5 April 1962

35 Taft, 500

36 Barnes & Teeters, 411

37 *Time*, 27 April 1959

38 Vernon Fox, 'Problems of Prison Discipline' in *Crime in America* (Ed. Bloch,) 53

39 Barnes & Teeters, 98

40 Sheldon Glueck, *Crime and Justice*, 60

41 *Modern Methods of Penal Treatment*, 136

42 Quoted by Rolph, *Commonsense about Crime and Punishment*, 169

43 Taft, 516

44 Terence Morris, 'In the Nick' in *Twentieth Century* (Winter 1962), 39

45 Rolph, 140

46 *Report of the Prison Commissioners* (1961); Morris, 'In the Nick', 22-23; Alan Little, 'The Borstal Boys' in *Twentieth Century* (Winter 1962), 39

47 *Federal Prisons, 1959*, 26

48 Quoted by Barnes and Teeters, 586

49 Morris, 'In the Nick', 31

50 Klare, 9

POLICE (Pages 424–430)

1 'My Side of the Fence' in *Twentieth Century* (Winter, 1962), 73
2 Rolph, *Personal Identity*, 37
3 *Report of the Royal Commission on the Police* (H.M.S.O., 1962,) 480
4 *Topic*, 3 Jan. 1962
5 *Guardian*, 1 June 1962
6 Donald McLachlan, *Sunday Telegraph*, 7 Jan. 1962
7 *Sunday Times*, 7 Jan. 1962
8 McClintock and Gibson, xiii
9 *Guardian*, 27 Oct. 1961
10 Uniform Crime Reports (1957)
11 Ferri, 223

12 *Report of the Metropolitan Police* (1900), quoted by Ives, 245
13 *Time*, 3 Nov. 1961
14 Vollmer, Monroe and Garrett; 58
15 *Illinois Crime Survey* (1929), 606
16 Reid, *Shame of New York*, 26
17 *Time*, 7 July 1958
18 *Ibid*, 16 March 1959
19 Taft, 400
20 John Duffy 'Proposed Experiment in Police Selection', in *Crime in America* (Ed Bloch), 163.

THE YOUNG OFFENDER (Pages 431–441)

1 *Time*, 28 April 1958
2 *New York Times*, March 1958; *Time*, 7 April 1958
3 *Report of the State of the Police* (1818)
4 Lombroso, *Crime: Its Causes and Remedies*
5 *Report of the Prison Commissioners* (1961), 4-7
6 *Penal Reform* (Ed. Radzinowicz), 8-9
7 *Ibid*
8 *Ibid*
9 Lombroso, 178
10 Melitta Schmideberg, 'The Child Murderer,' in *Crime in America* (Ed. Bloch), 209
11 *Uniform Crime Reports* (FBI), quoted by Taft, 113; Barnes & Teeters, 65
12 Taft, 629

13 Fyvel, 263-264
14 Schmideberg, in *Crime in America* (Ed. Bloch), 209
15 *Time*, 29 Feb. 1960
16 Shaw and McKay, quoted by Tannenbaum, *Crime and the Community*, 251
17 Page, *Young Lag*, 86
18 *Ibid*, 193
19 *Ibid*, 74
20 Shaw and McKay, quoted by Tannenbaum in *Crime and the Community*, 252-253
21 Thrasher, 36
22 *Illinois Crime Survey* (1929), 663
23 Shaw and McKay, 195
24 Grünhut, 346
25 Lombroso, 225
26 Sheldon Glueck, *Crime and Justice*, 200

27 Gluecks, *1,000 Juvenile Delinquents; 500 Criminal Careers, passim*
28 Quoted on ITV, 2 May 1962
29 *Guardian*, 5 Oct. 1961
30 Wootton, 134-135
31 *The English Penal System* (1957)

THE SEXUAL OFFENDER (*Pages 442-448*)

1 Fyvel, 40-41
2 Canio Louis Zarrilli, 'A Critical Analysis of the Report on Homosexuality and Prostitution', in *Crime in America*, 276-277
3 Wolfenden Report, 115
4 *Ibid*, 119
5 Zarrilli, 270
6 *Crime and the American Penal System (Annals of the American Academy of Political and Social Sciences*, Jan. 1962)
7 Barnes & Teeters, 101; Taft, 316
8 Taft, 4
9 Barnes & Teeters, 99
10 Kinsey, Pomeroy and Martin, *Sexual Behavior in the Human Male*
11 Kinsey, Pomeroy, Martin and Gebhard, *Sexual Behavior in the Human Female*
12 Quoted in *Encounter*, Nov. 1962
13 *Journal of the Institute of Comparative Law*, University of Paris, 1906, quoted by Joyce; 65
14 Barnes and Teeters, 102-103
15 *Ibid*, 46; *Times Literary Supplement*, 1 March 1963; John Hewetson, 'Birth Control, Sexual Morality and Abortion' in *Twentieth Century* (Winter 1962/3)
16 *Time*, 21 Sept. 1962
17 Kingsley Davis, 'The Sociology of Prostitution', in *American Sociological Review*, quoted by Taft, 323

PROGRESS AND PALINDROME (*Pages 451-461*)

1 Webb, *English Prisons*, 248
2 *The Results of Probation* (Ed. Radzinowicz), xi
3 Tannenbaum in *Crime and the Community*, 432
4 11 & 12 Geo. VI. c. 58 (Sec. 3 (1))
5 *The Results of Probation*, xi
6 *London Review* (1829) quoted by Radzinowicz in introduction to McClintock and Gibson, xiii
7 *The Results of Probation*, 7
8 Parker and Allerton, 134
9 *The Results of Probation*, 4
10 Taft, 464; Barnes and Teeters, 560
11 Taft, 465; Barnes and Teeters, 576
12 *Survey of Release Procedure*, iv, 212
13 Taft, 466

14 Lewis, 38

15 Tannenbaum, *Crime and the Community*, 444

16 Lowrie, *My Life in Prison* (1912), quoted by Gillin, 684

17 Linder, 471-473

18 Sheldon Glueck, *Crime and Justice*, 223

19 Karl Menninger in a speech to the Criminal Law Section of the American Bar Association

20 Roger Hood and Peter McNeal, *Sentencing in Magistrates' Courts* (Stevens, 1962)

21 *Guardian*, 16 May 1962

22 R. D. Grew, *Prison Governor* (Herbet Jenkins, 1958)

23 Salielles, *The Individualization of Punishment*, 9-10

24 Parker and Allerton, 130

25 Ferri, 217

26 *Depression and Suicide* (Mental Health Research Fund) 7

27 Giles, 151

28 *Penal Reform in England* (Ed. Radzinowicz), 4

29 Pike, ii, 480

30 Quoted by W. F. Deedes, 'Crime and the Conservatives', in *Daily Telegraph*, 5 Oct. 1961

31 Ferri, 135

BIBLIOGRAPHY

HISTORY OF PENAL METHODS AND CRIMINAL LAW

ANDREWS, William, *Bygone Punishments* (1899)

ATTENBOROUGH, F. L., (Ed.) *The Laws of the Earliest English Kings* (1922)

BARNES, Harry Elmer, *The Story of Punishment* (1930)

BLACKSTONE, Sir William, *Commentaries on the Laws of England* (1765-1769)

CADOGAN, Edward, *The Roots of Evil* (1937)

CHITTY, J, *Criminal Law* (1826)

COKE, Sir Edward, *Institutes of the Laws of England* (1797)

GILES, F. T., *The Criminal Law* (Penguin Books, 1961)

GRUNHUT, Max, *Penal Reform A Comparative Study* (O.U.P., 1948)

ELKIN Winifred A., *The English Penal System* (Pelican Books, 1957)

HOLDSWORTH, Sir William, *A History of English Law* (1923-1938)

IVES, George, *A History of Penal Methods* (1914)

JEUDWINE, J. W., *Tort, Crime and Police in Mediaeval Britain* (1917)

MAZZINGLI, T. J., *Sanctuaries* (1887)

PHILLIPSON, Coleman, *Three Criminal Law Reformers: Beccaria, Bentham, Romilly* (1923)

PIKE, Luke Owen, *A History of Crime in England* (1873-1876)

POLLOCK, Frederick and MAITLAND, F. W., *History of English Law* (1893)

RADZINOWICZ, Leon, *A History of English Criminal Law* (London: Stevens; New York: Macmillan, 1948-1956)

(Ed.) *Penal Reform in England* (Macmillan, 1946)

ROBERTSON, A. J., *The Laws of the Kings of England* (1925)

ROSE, Gordon, *The Struggle for Penal Reform* (Stevens; Quadrangle, 1961)

STEPHEN, Sir James Fitzjames, *A History of the Criminal Law of England* (1883)

TAYLOR, J. Sydney, *A Comparative View of the Punishments Annexed to Crime in the United States of America and in England* (1831)

WILSON, Margaret, *The Crime of Punishment* (1931)

CRIMINOLOGY AND PENAL PHILOSOPHY

ANDERSON, Sir Robert, *Criminals and Crime* (1907)

ASCHAFFENBURG, Gustav, *Crime and Its Repression* (Trans. 1913)

BARNES, Harry Elmer and TEETERS, Negley K., *New Horizons in Criminology* (Prentice-Hall, 1959)

BECCARIA, Cesare, *An Essay on Crimes and Punishments* (Trans. 1769)

BONGER, W. A., *An Introduction to Criminology* (Trans. 1936) *Criminality and Economic Conditions* (Trans. 1916)

BOWRING, John, *The Works of Jeremy Bentham* (1843)

CALDWELL, Robert G., *Criminology* (Ronald Press, 1956)

DE QUIRÓS, C. Bernaldo, *Modern Theories of Criminality* (Trans. 1911)

FERRI, Enrico, *Criminal Sociology* (Trans. 1895)

FIELDING, Henry, *An Enquiry into the Causes of the Late Increase of Robbers* (1751)

GAROFALO, Raffaele, *Criminology* (trans. 1914)

GILLIN, John Lewis, *Criminology and Penology* (1927)

HALL, Jerome, *General Principles of Criminal Law* (Bobbs-Merrill, 1947) *Theft, Law and Society* (1935)

HENTIG, Hans von, *The Criminal and His Victim: Studies in the Sociobiology of Crime* (Yale University Press, 1948) *Punishment: Its Origin, Purpose and Psychology* (1937)

HURWITZ, Stephen, *Criminology* (Allen and Unwin, 1952)

JONES, Howard, *Crime and the Penal System* (University Tutorial Press, 1962)

JOLY, Henri, *Le Crime* (1888)

LAURENT, Emile, *Le Criminel* (1908)

LOMBROSO, Cesare, *Crime: Its Causes and Remedies* (Trans. 1911)

MANNHEIM, Hermann, *Group Problems in Crime and Punishment* (London: Routledge; New York: Humanities Press, 1955)

Social Aspects of Crime in England between the Wars (1940)

(Ed. *Pioneers in Criminology* (Stevens; Quadrangle, 1960)

MORRIS, Terence, *The Criminal Area* (London: Routledge; New York: Humanities Press, 1958)

MUELLER, Gerhard O. W. (Ed.) *Essays in Criminal Science* (London: Sweet & Maxwell; New York: Rothman, 1961)

MULLINS, Claud, *Why Crime?* (London: Methuen; Philadelphia: Saunders, 1945)

PAGE, Sir Leo, *Crime and the Community* (Faber, n.d.)

PAKENHAM, Frank, Lord LONGFORD, *Causes of Crime* (Weidenfeld and Nicolson, 1948)

The Idea of Punishment (Chapman, 1961)

PARMELEE, Maurice, *Criminology* (1922)

RADZINOWICZ, Leon, *A History of English Criminal Law* (1948-1956)

In Search of Criminology (London: Heinemann; Cambridge, Massachusetts: Harvard University Press, 1962)

RECKLESS, Walter, *The Crime Problem* (Appleton-Century-Crofts, 1950)

SALEILLES, Raymond, *The Individualization of Punishment* (Trans. 1911)

SUTHERLAND, E. H., with CRESSEY, Donald, *Principles of Criminology* (Lippincott, 1954)

TAFT, Donald R., *Criminology* (Macmillan, N.Y., 1956)

TANNENBAUM, Frank, *Crime and the Community* (Columbia University Press, 1951)

TARDE, Gabriel, *La Criminalité Comparée* (1886)

Penal Philosophy (Trans. 1912)

VOLD, George B., *Theoretical Criminology* (O.U.P., 1958)

WOOD, A. E., and WAITE, J. B., *Crime and Its Treatment* (1941)

CAPITAL PUNISHMENT

CALVERT, Roy, *Capital Punishment in the 20th Century* (1936)

CAMUS, Albert, *Réflexions sur la peine capitale* (Calman-Lévy, 1957)

496   BIBLIOGRAPHY

CHRISTOPH, James B., *Capital Punishment and British Politics* (London: Allen & Unwin; Chicago: University of Chicago Press, 1962)

The Death Penalty in European Countries (Council of Europe, 1962)

DUFF, Charles, *A Handbook on Hanging* (1928)

DUFFY, Clinton and HIRSHBERG, Al, *88 Men and 2 Women* (London: Gollancz; New York: Doubleday, 1962)

ELLIOTT, Robert G., *Agent of Death* (1940)

GARDINER, Gerald, *Capital Punishment as a Deterrent: And the Alternative* (Gollancz, 1956)

GOWERS, Sir Ernest, *A Life for a Life* (Chatto and Windus, 1956)

HALE, Leslie, *Hanged in Error* (Penguin Books, 1961)

Hanging, Not Punishment Enough (1701)

HOLMES, Paul, *The Sheppard Murder Case* (New York: McKay, 1961; London: Cassell, 1962)

JOYCE, James Avery, *The Right to Life: A World View of Capital Punishment*. The American title was *Capital Punishment: A World View* (New York: Nelson, 1962)

KENNEDY, Ludovic, *10 Rillington Place* (Gollancz, 1961)

KERSHAW, Alister, *A History of the Guillotine* (London: Calder, 1958; New York: Taplinger, 1959)

KOESTLER, Arthur and ROLPH, C. H., *Hanged by the Neck* (Penguin Books, 1961)

KOESTLER, Arthur, *Reflections on Hanging* (Gollancz, 1956; Macmillan, N.Y., 1957)

MADAN, Martin, *Thoughts on Executive Justice* (1785)

MORRIS, Terence and BLOM-COOPER, Louis, *Murder in Microcosm* (Observer, 1961)

MONTAGU, Basil, *The Punishment of Death* (1812)

Murder (H.M.S.O., 1961)

OAKES, C. C., *Sir Samuel Romilly* (1935)

OLLYFFE, George, *An Essay Humbly Offer'd for an Act of Parliament to Prevent Capital Crimes* (1731)

Report of the Royal Commission on Capital Punishment (H.M.S.O., 1953)

ROMILLY, Sir Samuel, *Observations on the Criminal Law of England* (1810)

SCHMIDT, Hans, (Ed. Albrecht Keller), *A Hangman's Diary: The Journal of Master Franz Schmidt* (1928)

TUTTLE, Elizabeth Orman, *The Crusade Against Capital Punishment in Great Britain* (Stevens; Quadrangle, 1961)
WOLFGANG, Martin E., *Patterns in Criminal Homicide* (University of Pennsylvania Press, 1958)

POLICE

ALLEN, L. B., *Brief Considerations on the Present State of the Police of the Metropolis* (1821)
ARMITAGE, Gilbert, *History of the Bow Street Runners* (n.d.)
BURN, R., *The Justice of the Peace and the Parish Officer* (1831)
Chicago Police Problems (1931)
COATMAN, John, *Police* (O.U.P., 1959)
COLQUHOUN, Patrick, *A Treatise on the Commerce and Police Force of the River Thames* (1800)
A Treatise on the Police of the Metropolis (1795)
DEUTSCH, Albert, *The Trouble with Cops* (Crown, 1954)
The Discoveries of John Poulter alias Baxter (1761)
FIELDING, Sir John, *An Account of the Origin and Effects of a Police* (1758)
Plan for Preventing Robberies within Twenty Miles of London (1755)
FITZGERALD, F., *Chronicles of Bow Street Police Office* (1888)
FOSDICK, Raymond B., *American Police Systems* (1920)
European Police Systems (1915)
HANWAY, Jonas, *The Defects of the Police* (1775)
HARRISON, Leonard V., *Police Administration in Boston* (1934)
HOPKINS, Ernest Jerome, *Our Lawless Police* (1931)
HOWE, Sir Ronald, *The Pursuit of Crime* (Arthur Barker, 1962)
LEE, W. L. Melville, *A History of Police in England* (1901)
MEEK, Victor, *Cops and Robbers* (Duckworth, 1962)
MOYLAN, Sir John, *Scotland Yard and the Metropolitan Police* (1934)
PRINGLE, Patrick, *Hue and Cry* (Museum Press, 1955; William Morrow & Co., 1956)
The Thief-Takers (Museum Press, 1958)
REITH, Charles, *A New Study of Police History* (Oliver and Boyd, 1956)
The Police Idea (1938)

Report of the Royal Commission on Police Powers and Procedure (1930)

Report of the Royal Commission on the Police (H.M.S.O., 1962)

Report on Police (Washington, 1931)

Reports on the Police of the Metropolis (1816, 1817, 1818 and 1828)

ROLPH, C. H., (Ed.) *The Police and the Public* (Heinemann, 1962)

SCOTT, Sir Harold, *Scotland Yard* (London: Deutsch, 1954; New York: Random House, 1955)

STEAD, P. J., *The Police of Paris* (Staples Press, 1951)
     Vidocq (London: Staples Press, 1953; New York: Roy, 1954)

A Treatise on the Police and Crimes of the Metropolis (1829)

VAUX, J. H., *Memoirs* (1827)

PRISONS

BAKER, Peter, *Time Out of Life* (Heinemann, 1961)

BARRY, John Vincent, *Alexander Maconochie* (O.U.P., 1958)

BEHAN, Brendan, *Borstal Boy* (London: Hutchinson; New York: Knopf, 1958)

BRYAN, Helen, *Inside* (Houghton, 1953)

CLAY, W. L., *The Prison Chaplain* (1861)

CLAYTON, Gerold Fancourt, *The Wall is Strong* (John Long, 1958)

COLLINS, Philip, *Dickens and Crime* (London: Macmillan; New York: St. Martins, 1962)

COX, William B., BIXBY, F. Lowell and ROOT, William T. (Eds.) *Handbook of American Prisons and Reformatories* (1933)

CRAWFORD, William, *Penitentiaries in the United States* (1834)

CREW, Albert, *London Prisons of Today and Yesterday* (1933)

DE BEAUMONT, G. and DE TOCQUEVILLE, A., *On the Penitentiary System in the United States and its Application in France* (Trans. 1833)

DICKENS, Charles, *American Notes* (1855)

DIXON, W. Hepworth, *John Howard and the Prison World of Europe* (1848)

DOSTOEVSKY, Feodor, *Buried Alive in Siberia* (Trans. 1881)

Du Cane, Edmund F., *The Punishment and Prevention of Crime* (1885)

Duffy, Clinton D., *San Quentin*. American title *San Quentin Story* (New York: Doubleday, 1950)

Fishman, J. F., *Sex in Prison* (1934)

Fox, Lionel, *English Prison and Borstal Systems* (London: Routledge, 1952)

Garrett, P. M. and MacCormick, A. H., *Handbook of American Prisons and Reformatories* (1929)

Grew, B. D. *Prison Governor* (Herbert Jenkins, 1958)

Griffiths, Arthur, *Memorials of Millbank* (1884)
The Chronicles of Newgate (1884)

Handbook of Correctional Institution Design and Construction (Federal Prison Industries Inc., 1949)

Hassler, Alfred, *Diary of a Self-Made Convict* (Chicago: Regnery, 1954; London: Gollancz, 1955)

Hinde, R. S. E., *The British Penal System* (1773-1950) (Duckworth, 1951)

Hobhouse, Stephen and Brockway, A. Fenner, *English Prisons To-day* (1922)

Howard, D. L., *John Howard: Prison Reformer* (Christopher Johnson, 1958)
The English Prisons (Methuen, 1960)

Howard, John, *The State of Prisons* (1780)

Klare, Hugh. J., *Anatomy of Prison* (Hutchinson, 1960)

Klein, Philip, *Prison Methods in New York State* (1920)

Kropotkin, Prince Peter Alexeivich, *In Russian and French Prisons* (Trans. 1887)

Lawes, Lewis E., *Life and Death in Sing Sing* (1928)

Lewis, O. F., *The Development of American Prisons and Prison Customs* (1922)

Martin, John Bartlow, *Break Down the Walls* (New York: Ballantine, 1954; London: Gollancz, 1955)

McKelvey, Blake, *American Prisons* (1936)

A Manual of Correctional Standards (American Prison Association, 1954)

Merrow Smith, L. W. and Harris, James, *Prison Screw* (Herbert Jenkins, 1962)

Modern Methods of Penal Treatment (International Penal and Penitentiary Foundation, n.d.)

Nelson, Victor, *Prison Days and Nights* (1932)

O'HARE, Kate, *In Prison* (1923)

OSBORNE, Thomas Mott, *Within Prison Walls* (1914)

Penal Practice in a Changing Society (1959)

Reports of the Commissioners of Prisons (H.M.S.O.)

Reports of the Federal Bureau of Prisons

Reports of the Committee of the Society for the Improvement of Prison Discipline

The Prison Service Journal

Prison World (*American Journal of Corrections*)

The Prison and the Prisoner: A Symposium (Boston, 1917)

RUCK, S. K., (Ed.) *Paterson on Prisons* (Frederick Muller, 1951)

RUGGLES-BRISE, Evelyn, *The English Prison System* (1921)

SELLIN, Thorsten, *Pioneering in Penology* (1944)

SMITH, Ann D., *Women in Prison* (Stevens; Quadrangle, 1962)

SMITH, M. Hamblin, *Prisons and a Changing Civilization* (1934)

Statistical Review of State Prisons and Correctional Schools in Illinois (1940)

TANNENBAUM, Frank, *Wall Shadows* (1922)

VILLETTE, J., *Annals of Newgate* (1776)

WEBB, Sydney and Beatrice, *English Prisons under Local Government* (1922)

WILDEBLOOD, Peter, *Against the Law* (Weidenfeld and Nicolson, 1955)

WINES, Frederick H., *Punishment and Reformation* (1910)

THE CRIMINAL

BOWLBY, John, *Forty-four Juvenile Thieves* (1946)

DRAHMS, August, *The Criminal* (1900)

ELLIS, Havelock, *The Criminal* (1901)

FERRERO, Gina Lombroso, *Criminal Man According to the Classification of Cesare Lombroso* (1911)

FINK, Arthur E., *Causes of Crime* (1938)

GLUECK, Sheldon and Eleanor T., *500 Delinquent Women* (1934)

     500 Criminal Careers (1930)

     Physique and Delinquency (Harper, 1956)

GORING, Charles, *The English Convict* (1913)

HEALY, William, *The Individual Delinquent* (1915)

HEALY, William and BRONNER, Augusta, *Delinquents and Criminals* (1926)

New Light on Delinquency (1936)

HOOTON, E. A., *The American Criminal: An Anthropological Study* (1939)

LOMBROSO, Cesare, *L'Uomo Delinquente* (1876)

The Female Offender (Trans. 1895)

MORRIS, Norval, *The Habitual Criminal* (London: Longmans; Cambridge, Massachusetts: Harvard University Press, 1951)

POLLACK, Otto, *The Criminality of Women* (University of Pennsylvania Press, 1950)

Physical Bases of Crime: A Symposium (Easton, 1914)

REIWALD, Paul, *Society and its Criminals* (International Universities Press, 1955)

Report of the Departmental Committee on Persistent Offenders (1932)

SHELDON, William H., *Varieties of Delinquent Youth* (Harper, 1949)

WOOTON, Barbara (with SEAL, Vera G. and CHAMBERS, Rosalind), *Social Science and Social Pathology* (London: Allen & Unwin; New York: Macmillan, 1959)

RESPONSIBILITY AND MENTAL DISEASE

DUGDALE, R. L., *The Jukes: A Study in Crime, Pauperism, Disease and Heredity* (1877)

EAST, Sir W. Norwood (Ed.), *The Roots of Crime* (Butterworth, 1954)

EAST, Sir W. Norwood and HUBERT, W. H. de B., *Report on the Psychological Treatment of Crime* (1939)

Society and the Criminal (H.M.S.O., 1951)

GLUECK, Bernard, *Studies in Forensic Psychiatry* (1916)

GLUECK, Sheldon, *Mental Disorder and the Criminal Law* (1925)

GODDARD, H. H., *Feeblemindedness* (1914)

GUTTMACHER, Manfred S. and WEIHOFEN, Henry, *Psychiatry and the Law* (Norton, 1952)

HENDERSON, D. K. and GILLESPIE, R. D., *A Textbook of Psychiatry* (1946)

KAHN, Eugen, *Psychopathic Personalities* (1931)

MULLINS, Claud, *Crime and Psychology* (1943)

MAUDSLEY, Henry, *Responsibility in Mental Disease* (1874)

PLAYFAIR, Giles and Derrick SINGTON, *The Offenders* (Secker and Warburg; Simon and Schuster, 1957)

RHODES, Henry T. F., *Genius and Criminal* (1932)

ROLPH, C. H., *Personal Identity* (Michael Joseph, 1957)

SCHLAPP, Max G. and SMITH, Edward H., *The New Criminology* (1928)

WEIHOFEN, Henry, *The Urge to Punish* (New York: Farrar, Straus, 1956; London: Gollancz, 1957)

WHITE, William A., *Insanity and the Criminal Law* (1923)

THE CRIMINAL'S PSYCHOLOGY

AHERN, Danny, *How to Commit a Murder* (1930)

BLACK, Jack, *You Can't Win* (1926)

CALLAHAN, Jack, *Man's Grim Justice* (1928)

CATTON, Joseph, *Behind the Scenes of Murder* (1940)

CLEMMER, Donald, *The Prison Community* (1940)

DAVITT, Michael, *Leaves from a Prison Diary* (1885)

KAHN, Samuel, *Sing Sing Criminals* (1936)

LAWES, Lewis E., *Meet the Murderers* (1940)

LEOPOLD, Nathan F., *Life Plus 99 Years* (Doubleday: Gollancz, 1958)

LOMBROSO, Cesare, *Palimsesti del Carcere* (1888)

NELSON, Victor, *Prison Days and Nights* (1932)

NORMAN, Frank, *Bang to Rights* (Secker and Warburg, 1958)

PAGE, Sir Leo, *The Young Lag* (Faber, 1950)

PARKER, Tony and ALLERTON, Robert, *The Courage of his Convictions* (London: Hutchinson; New York: Norton, 1962)

PARTRIDGE, Eric, *A Dictionary of the Underworld, British and American* (Routledge; Macmillan, N.Y., 1960)

PHELAN, Jim, *Lifer* (1938)

SHAW, Clifford R., *Brothers in Crime* (1938)

   The Jackroller (1930)

   Natural History of a Delinquent Career (1931)

SPENSER, James, *Limey* (1933)

SMITH, M. Hamblin, *The Psychology of the Criminal* (1933)
STANLEY, Leo, *Men at Their Worst* (1940)
THOMSON, Basil, *The Criminal* (1928)
WARREN, Paul, *Next Time is for Life* (Dell, 1953)

THE DETECTION OF CRIME AND FORENSIC SCIENCE

COLLINS, Frederick L., *The FBI in Peace and War* (1940)
CUTHBERT, C. R. M., *Science and the Detection of Crime* (London: Hutchinson; New York: Philosophical Library, 1958)
FITZGERALD, Maurice, *Criminal Investigation* (Greenberg, 1953)
GODDARD, Henry, (Ed. Patrick Pringle) *The Memoirs of a Bow Street Runner* (London: Museum Press; New York: Morrow, 1956)
GROSS, Hans, *Criminal Investigation* (Trans. 1907)
HOOVER, J. Edgar, *Persons in Hiding* (1938)
LOCARD, Edmond, *L'Enquête Criminelle* (1920)
LOWENTHAL, Max, *The Federal Bureau of Investigation* (William Sloane, 1950)
PURVIS, Melvin, *American Agent* (1936)
RHODES, Henry T. F., *Clues and Crime* (1933)
    Alphonse B. Bertillon (Abelard-Schuman, 1956)
SIMPSON, C. Keith, *Modern Trends in Forensic Medicine* (Butterworth, 1952)
SODERMAN, H. and O'CONNELL, J. J., *Modern Criminal Investigation* (Funk and Wagnalls, 1952)
TAYLOR, A. S., *Elements of Medical Jurisprudence* (1836)
TURNER, R. F., *Forensic Science and Laboratory Techniques* (Springfield, Ill.: Charles C. Thomas, 1949)
WALLER, George, *Kidnap* (New York: Dial; London: Hamish Hamilton, 1961)
WHITEHEAD, Don, *The FBI Story* (Random House, 1956)

ORGANIZED CRIME IN THE UNITED STATES

ALLSOP, Kenneth, *The Bootleggers* (London: Hutchinson; New York: Doubleday, 1961)

Annual Reports of the Police Department (New York)

ASBURY, Herbert, *The Gangs of New York* (1928)
    The Underworld of Chicago (1942)
    The Great Illusion (Doubleday, 1950)

BURNETT, W. R., *Little Caesar* (1929)

Criminal Justice in Cleveland (1922)

DANFORTH, Harold R. and James D. HORAN, *The D.A.'s Man* (New York: Crown, 1957; London: Gollancz, 1958)

GIBNEY, Frank, *The Operators* (New York: Harper; London: Gollancz, 1960)

JOHNSON, Malcolm, *Crime on the Labor Front* (McGraw-Hill, 1950)

KEFAUVER, Estes, *Crime in America* (Doubleday, 1951; Gollancz, 1952)

The Kefauver Committee Report (Didier, 1951)

KENNEDY, Robert F., *The Enemy Within* (Harper, 1960)

LAIDLER, Harry S., *Boycotts and the Labor Struggle* (1913)

MOONEY, Martin, *Crime Incorporated* (1938)

NESS, Eliot and FRALEY, Oscar, *The Untouchables* (Messner, 1957)

PASLEY, Fred D., *Al Capone* (1930)

PETERSON, Virgil W., *Barbarians in our Midst* (Little, Brown, 1952)

RAPER, A. F., *The Tragedy of Lynching* (1933)

REID, Ed., *The Shame of New York* (Random House, 1953; Gollancz, 1954)
    The Mafia (Random House, 1952)

Reports of the Chicago Crime Commission

Report of the New York Crime Commission (1928)

Report of the Senate Select Committee on Improper Activities (1958)

Reports of the National Commission on Law Observance and Enforcement

ROOT, Jonathan, *The Life and Bad Times of Charlie Becker* (Secker and Warburg, 1962)

SINCLAIR, Andrew, *Prohibition* (Boston: Little, Brown; London: Faber, 1962)

SMITH, Alson, *Syndicate City* (Regnery, 1954)

SONDERN, Frederick, *Brotherhood of Evil: The Mafia* (Farar, Straus and Cudahy; Gollancz, 1959)

STEFFENS, Lincoln, *Shame of the Cities* (1904)

SUTHERLAND, E. H., *White-Collar Crime* (Dryden Press, 1949)
The Illinois Crime Survey (1929)
THOMPSON, Craig and RAYMOND, Allen, *Gang Rule in New York* (1940)
THRASHER, Frederic M., *The Gang: A Study of 1313 Gangs in Chicago* (1927)
TURKIS, Burton B. and FEDER, Sid, *Murder, Inc.* (Farrar, Straus & Cudahy, 1951)
TYLER, Gus (Ed.), *Organized Crime in America* (London: Cresset; Ann Arbor: University of Michigan Press, 1962)

JUVENILE DELINQUENCY

BAGOT, J. H., *Juvenile Delinquency* (1941)
BLOCH, Herbert A. and FLYNN, Frank T., *Delinquency: The Juvenile Offender in America To-day* (Random House, 1956)
BURT, Sir Cyril, *The Young Delinquent* (1925)
COHEN, Albert K., *Delinquent Boys* (The Free Press, 1955)
FYVEL, T. R., *The Insecure Offenders* (Chatto and Windus, 1961) American title *Trouble-makers* (New York: Schocken, 1962)
GITTINS, John, *Approved School Boys* (H.M.S.O., 1952)
GLUECK, Sheldon and Eleanor T., *Juvenile Delinquents Grown Up* (1940)
    Unravelling Juvenile Delinquency (The Commonwealth Fund, 1950)
    1000 Juvenile Delinquents (1934)
Juvenile Delinquency in Post-War Europe (The Council of Europe)
MANNHEIM, Hermann and WILKINS, Leslie T., *Prediction Methods in Relation to Borstal Training* (H.M.S.O., 1955)
MORRISON, W. D., *Juvenile Offenders* (1896)
PUFFER, J. A., *The Boy and His Gang* (1912)
Report of the Committee for Investigating the Causes of the Alarming Increase of Juvenile Delinquency (1816)
ROSE, A. G., *Five Hundred Borstal Boys* (Blackwell, 1954)
RUBIN, Sol, *Crime and Juvenile Delinquency* (London: Stevens; Dobbs Ferry, N.Y.: Oceana, 1961)

SALISBURY, Harrison, *The Shook-Up Generation* (New York: Harper, 1958; London: Michael Joseph, 1959)

SELLIN, Thorsten, *The Criminality of Youth* (1940)

SHAW, Clifford R., and McKAY, Henry D., *Juvenile Delinquency in Urban Areas* (1942)

SHULMAN, Harry Manuel, *Juvenile Delinquency in American Society* (Harpers, 1961)

STEINER, Lee R., *Understanding Juvenile Delinquency* (Chilton Co., 1960)

TAPPAN, Paul W., *Juvenile Delinquency* (McGraw-Hill, 1949)

WHYTE, William F., *Street Corner Society* (1943)

THE SEXUAL OFFENDER

BIEBER, Irving, *Homosexuality* (Basic Books, 1962)

DRUMMOND, Isabel, *The Sex Paradox* (Putnam's, 1953)

GLOVER, Edward, *The Psychopathology of Prostitution* (1945)

GUTTMACHER, Manfred S., *Sex Offences* (Norton, 1951)

HAUSER, Richard, *The Homosexual Society* (Bodley Head, 1962)

KARPMAN, Benjamin, *The Sexual Offender and His Offenses* (Julian Press, 1954)

KINSEY, A. C., with POMEROY, W. B. and MARTIN, C. E., *Sexual Behavior in the Human Male* (Saunders, 1948)

KINSEY, A. C., with POMEROY, W. B., MARTIN, C. E. and GEBHARD, Paul H., *Sexual Behavior in the Human Female* (Saunders, 1953)

LEWINSOHN, Richard, *A History of Sexual Customs* (London: Longmans, 1958; New York: Harper, 1959)

MURTAGH, John M., and HARRIS, Sara, *Cast the First Stone* (McGraw-Hill, 1957)

REES, J. Tudor and USILL, Harley V., (Eds.) *They Stand Apart* (Heinemann, 1955)

REINHARDT, James M. *Sex Perversions and Sex Crimes* (Thomas, 1957)

Report of the Committee on Homosexual Offences and Prostitution (Wolfenden Report) (H.M.S.O., 1957)

ROLPH, C. H., (Ed.) *Women of the Streets* (Secker and Warburg, 1955)

WEST, Donald J., *The Other Man* (Whiteside & William Morrow, 1955)

PROBATION AND THE DISCHARGED PRISONER

RADZINOWICZ, Leon, (Ed.) *The Results of Probation* (London: Macmillan; New York: St. Martins, 1958)
ST JOHN, John, *Probation: The Second Chance* (Vista Books, 1961)
TURNER, Merfyn, *Safe Lodging* (Hutchinson, 1961)

GENERAL

Annals of the American Academy of Political and Social Sciences
The American Journal of Sociology
BEDFORD, Sybille, *The Faces of Justice* (London: Collins; New York: Simon & Schuster, 1961)
BLOCH, Herbert A., (Ed.) *Crime in America* (Philosophical Library, Inc., 1961)
The British Journal of Criminology
Criminal Statistics in England and Wales (H.M.S.O.)
Federal Probation
GLUECK, Sheldon, *Crime and Justice* (1936)
The Howard Journal
The Journal of Criminal Law, Criminology and Police Science
MAYHEW, Henry, *London's Underworld* (Ed. Peter Quennell) (William Kimber, 1950)
McCLINTOCK, F. H., and GIBSON, Evelyn, *Robbery in London* (English Studies in Criminal Science) (London: Macmillan; New York: St. Martins, 1961)
Notable British Trials Series (Hodge)
ROLPH, C. H., *Commonsense about Crime and Punishment* (Gollancz, 1961)
SCOTT, Sir Harold, (Ed.) *The Concise Encyclopaedia of Crime and Criminals* (London : Deutsch; New York: Hawthorn, 1961)
Uniform Crime Reports (FBI)

INDEX

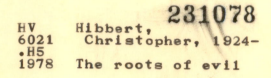

231078

HV	Hibbert,
6021	Christopher, 1924-
.H5	
1978	The roots of evil

DATE			
APR 1 1 1981	FEB 0 4 1992		
	APR 2 8 1993		
JUN 3 0 1981	JUN 0 8 1994		
MAR 2 1982			
MAR 2 3 1982			
APR 1 3 1982			
APR 2 7 1982			
OCT 5 1982			
OCT 2 6 1982			
MAR 2 5 1987			
OCT 4 1988			